ARCHITECTURE EXAM REVIEW

VOLUME II: NONSTRUCTURAL TOPICS

SIXTH EDITION

D1543797

David Kent Ballast, A.I.A.

PROFESSIONAL PUBLICATIONS, INC.
Belmont, CA

How to Locate Errata and Other Updates for This Book

At Professional Publications, we do our best to bring you error-free books. But when errors do occur, we want to make sure that you know about them so they cause as little confusion as possible.

A current list of known errata and other updates for this book is available on the PPI website at **www.ppi2pass.com/errata**. We update the errata page as often as necessary, so check in regularly. You will also find instructions for submitting suspected errata. We are grateful to every reader who takes the time to help us improve the quality of our books by pointing out an error.

ARCHITECTURE EXAM REVIEW, VOLUME II: NONSTRUCTURAL TOPICS
Sixth Edition

Current printing of this edition: 1

Printing History

edition number	printing number	update
5	1	Minor revisions.Copyright updated.
5	2	Minor corrections.
6	1	New edition. Revised and reorganized to reflect current exam.

Printed in the United States of America

Professional Publications, Inc.
1250 Fifth Avenue, Belmont, CA 94002
(650) 593-9119
www.ppi2pass.com

ISBN 1-59126-028-0

Library of Congress catalog card number 2005900139

TABLE OF CONTENTS

LIST OF FIGURES

LIST OF TABLES

PREFACE AND ACKNOWLEDGMENTS

The Architect Registration Examination (ARE) continues to change. Version 3.0 is part of an evolutionary process that began in February 2004 after the National Council of Architecture Registration Boards (NCARB) conducted an intensive practice analysis study. In this version of the ARE, NCARB has eliminated the site section and block diagram vignettes from the graphic divisions and reduced the number of questions in the multiple-choice divisions. In addition, some content areas, such as practice and project management, have been strengthened, and a few new content areas have been introduced, most notably in sustainability and "green architecture." Questions have also been added to cover new material technologies, and questions that pertain to site design have been introduced into several other divisions. Further exam changes are expected until the goals of the practice analysis are fully achieved.

In response to the Version 3.0 changes, I have reorganized and greatly expanded *Architecture Exam Review, Volume II: Nonstructural Topics*. Comparing this new edition with the previous one you will notice several changes. First, I have reorganized the book by grouping chapters into sections that represent the nonstructural portions of the multiple-choice divisions of the exam. Second, I have added new chapters on energy efficiency and alternative energy sources, sustainable design, and practice and project management. Third, I have enhanced some chapters with supplemental information on new material technologies, pre-design, and construction documents and services. Finally, the two chapters on site planning and building design have been moved from this book to a new, expanded edition, *Architecture Exam Review, Volume III: Graphic Divisions*.

As always, it is impossible to precisely match the organization and content of a review book with the actual exam because of the overlap of subject matter found in the various divisions. For example, while you are most likely to find a question on construction documents in the Construction Documents and Services division, you might also find one in

the Pre-Design division. Questions on building codes are scattered throughout all divisions. Because of this, I suggest you use the major sections of this book (Sections 1–4) to begin your study on any one exam division. Then, review the chapters on building regulations (Section 5). Finally, make liberal use of the index to focus on any particular subject in which you feel your skills are weak. For example, sustainability has a chapter of its own in the Mechanical and Electrical section (Section 2), but you will find useful information on sustainability and "green architecture" in several other chapters as well. You may also want to scan the Table of Contents headings to see where major topics are covered.

As anyone who has taken the ARE can tell you, any one version of the exam is not the same as the last. Although the field of knowledge tested is the same, questions differ as they are drawn randomly from a large pool of questions and as new questions are written. For example, one section of the test may have a lot of history-related questions while the next may have just a few. Because of this and the fact that the ARE covers such a vast body of knowledge, no one study guide can possibly provide all the information that may be included in any one version of the exam. As you use this book to review, if you feel you are weak in any one area, use the Recommended Reading list at the back of the book for suggestions on additional study material.

Be aware that the test writers have reintroduced questions pertaining to site design into the other divisions, and questions in the Pre-Design division may cover material about the other divisions. In spite of this crossing of division lines, most past candidates believe you should take the Pre-Design division last so you are familiar with the types of questions you may see. For help with structural topics, use the companion volume, *Architecture Exam Review, Volume I: Structural Topics*.

You will find that this book and the related volumes are valuable parts of your exam preparation. Although there is no substitute for a good formal education and the broad-based experience provided by your internship with a practicing architect, this review guide will help direct your study efforts to increase your chances of passing the ARE.

A final word of advice: Even though you may have a good grasp of the information and knowledge in a particular subject area, be prepared to address questions on the material in a variety of forms and from different points of view. For example, you may have studied and know definitions, but can you apply that knowledge when a question includes a definition-type word as part of a more complex situation-type of question? For practice, be sure to try the sample questions at the end of each chapter. You may also want to study with the companion volume, *Architecture Exam Review, Solved Problems: Multiple-Choice Divisions*, for problem-solving practice.

Many people have helped in the production of this book. I would like to thank all the fine people at Professional Publications, including Heather Kinser (project editor), Kate Hayes (typesetter), and Amy Schwertman (illustrator). Thanks also to technical reviewer Gary E. Demele, AIA, who kept me on the right track and provided valuable input.

INTRODUCTION

ABOUT THIS BOOK

Architecture Exam Review, Volume II: Nonstructural Topics gives a thorough review of the nonstructural subjects most likely to appear on the multiple-choice divisions of the Architect Registration Examination (ARE). The sample questions in this book will prepare candidates for what to expect from this completely computer-based exam. Sample questions are given for each subject so that candidates can test their knowledge of the material, and answers are provided and thoroughly explained.

This book is organized into sections that generally follow the exam divisions, and the chapters are arranged by subject to help candidates organize their study efforts. To see how the chapters correspond to the exam divisions, reference the following list.

Multiple Choice Divisions:

- Pre-Design (Chs. 2–4)

- General Structures (Chs. 13–16)

- Lateral Forces (Chs. 1, 2, 8, 13, 14)

- Mechanical and Electrical Systems (Chs. 5–11)

- Building Design/Materials and Methods (Chs. 12–22)

- Construction Documents and Services (Chs. 23–28)

Graphic Divisions:

- Site Planning (Chs. 2, 4)

- Building Planning (Chs. 3, 29, 30)

- Building Technology (Chs. 5–11)

For more information, see the companion volumes titled *Architecture Exam Review, Volume I: Structural Topics* (specifically, for more on General Structures and Lateral Forces); *Architecture Exam Review, Volume II: Graphic Divisions*; and *Architecture Exam Review, Solved Problems: Multiple-Choice Divisions*.

THE ARCHITECT REGISTRATION EXAMINATION

The ARE is a uniform test administered to candidates who wish to become licensed architects after they have served their required internships. It is given in all fifty states, nine Canadian provinces, and five other jurisdictions including the District of Columbia, Guam, the North Mariana Islands, Puerto Rico, and the Virgin Islands.

The ARE has been developed to protect the health, safety, and welfare of the public by testing a candidate's entry-level competence to practice architecture. Its content relates as closely as possible to situations encountered in practice. It tests for the kinds of knowledge, skills, and abilities required of an entry-level architect, with particular emphasis on those services that affect public health, safety, and welfare. In order to accomplish these objectives, the exam tests for (1) knowledge in specific subject areas, (2) the ability to make decisions, (3) the ability to consolidate and use information to solve a problem, and (4) the ability to coordinate the activities of others on the building team. It also includes some practice and project management questions.

The ARE is developed jointly by the National Council of Architectural Registration Boards (NCARB) and the Committee of Canadian Architectural Councils (CCAC), with the assistance of the Chauncey Group International and Prometric. The Chauncey Group serves as NCARB's test development and operations consultant, and Prometric operates and maintains the test centers that administer the ARE.

Although the responsibility of professional licensing rests with each individual state, member boards of each state subscribe to the exam prepared by the National Council of Architectural Registration Boards (NCARB). One of the primary reasons for a uniform test is to facilitate reciprocity—that is, to enable an architect to more easily gain a license to practice in states other than the one in which he or she was originally licensed.

The ARE is administered and graded entirely by computer. The exam is offered six days a week at a network of test centers across North America. Candidates can take the exam sessions in any order on any day and can stagger the sessions to fit their schedules. The results are scored by computer and are processed within two to four weeks for the multiple-choice divisions and within four to six weeks for the graphic divisions. Results are then forwarded to individual state boards of architecture, which process them and send them to individual candidates. If a candidate fails a division, he or she must wait six months to retake that division.

To apply for registration a candidate should obtain the requirements for registration from the board in the state, province, or territory where the candidate wants to be registered first. The exact requirements vary from one jurisdiction to another, so contact the local board.

Candidates may schedule any division of the ARE at any time and in any order. Divisions can be taken individually, to give time for adequate preparation and disperse exam costs, or taken together in any combination.

At the NCARB website, www.ncarb.com, candidates can download the *ARE Guidelines*, which includes descriptions of each division and of how to apply, pay for, and take the ARE, along with other useful information. The site provides current information about the exam, education requirements, training, examination procedures, and NCARB reciprocity services. It includes sample scenarios of the computer-based examination process and examples of costs associated with taking the computer-based exam. Information is also available from Professional Publications at www.ppi2pass.com.

EXAMINATION FORMAT

The ARE is organized into nine divisions that test various areas of architectural knowledge and problem-solving ability.

Multiple Choice Divisions:

- Pre-Design
- General Structures
- Lateral Forces
- Mechanical and Electrical Systems
- Building Design/Materials and Methods
- Construction Documents and Services

Graphic Divisions:

- Site Planning
- Building Planning
- Building Technology

The time allotted for each section varies, but most candidates do not need the entire time to complete the multiple-choice divisions. The graphic divisions are scheduled for a fixed length of time and include breaks.

For the multiple-choice divisions, the candidate is presented with a question and multiple-choice answers. The candidate clicks on the desired choice. A fixed number of questions is displayed within a maximum time limit.

The graphic divisions are also presented on a computer screen as individual vignettes, each designed to test a particular area of knowledge and skill. The graphic divisions consist of a total of 13 vignettes: five for Site Planning, two for Building Planning, and six for Building Technology. Along the side of the screen are toolbars for sketching and drawing the solution. The software is similar to CAD but is a proprietary CAD program developed by NCARB and does not resemble any commercial CAD software.

For the graphic portions of the exam, the computer uses a complex method of grading based on categories of Acceptable, Unacceptable, and Indeterminate responses. Along with point values for design criteria, the computer uses the responses and grading categories to score the solutions.

TAKING THE MULTIPLE-CHOICE DIVISIONS

Types of Questions Asked

The ARE multiple-choice divisions use several types of questions and variations of each of these types. The form of the answer response in all cases is multiple choice with four possible answers.

The first type of multiple-choice question is based on either written, graphic, or photographic information. In its simplest form it will ask the examinee to select the correct answer from one of four possible choices. However, some problems will require calculations to determine the correct solution.

The second multiple-choice question type lists four or five items or statements, and the four possible answer choices will be combinations of those statements. The examinee may be asked to correctly rank the various statements in some order, or may be asked which of the statements is correct or incorrect.

A third type of multiple-choice question presents a written situation that could be encountered in actual practice. Drawings, diagrams, photographs, forms, tables, or other data may also be provided. The question asks the examinee to select the best answer from four options, which could be words, phrases, or statements, given the context of the presented situation.

Keep in mind that multiple-choice questions often require the examinee to do more than simply select an answer based on memory. For example, it might be necessary to combine several facts, review data given in the test information package, perform a calculation, or review a drawing.

Tips for the Multiple-Choice Problems

Even with the new computer format, taking the ARE can be an arduous and anxiety-filled process, especially for candidates who choose to take several or all of the divisions at once.

Following are some tips that many candidates find helpful when preparing for the multiple-choice divisions of the ARE.

- Make a notation of the most doubtful answers. If there is time at the end of the test, go back and recheck these answers. Remember, the first response is usually the best.

- Many times, one or two choices can be easily eliminated. This may result in a guess, but at least the chances are better between two choices than among four. Also, unanswered questions are counted wrong, so guess if necessary.

- Some questions may appear too simple. Although a few very easy and obvious questions are included, it's more likely that the simplicity should serve as a red flag that it might be best to reevaluate the solution for exceptions to a rule or special circumstances that would make the obvious, easy response incorrect.

- Watch out for absolute words in a question, such as "always," "never," or "completely." These often indicate some little exception that can turn what reads like a true statement into a false statement or vice versa.

- Be on the alert for words like "seldom," "usually," "best," or "most reasonable." These indicate that some judgment will be involved in answering the question, so look for two or more options that may be very similar.

- Occasionally there may be a defective question. This does not happen very often, but if it does, make the best choice possible under the circumstances.

Flawed questions are usually discovered. Either they are not counted in the test or any one of the correct answers is credited instead.

Study Guidelines

An examinee's method of studying for the ARE should be based on both the content and form of the exam and on school and work experience. Because the exam covers such a broad range of subject matter, it cannot possibly include every detail of practice. Rather, it tends to focus on what is considered entry-level knowledge and knowledge that is important for the protection of the public's health, safety, and welfare. This is not to say that other types of questions are not asked, but this awareness should help direct the focus of any review schedule.

An examinee's recent work experience should also help determine what areas to study the most. A candidate who has been involved with construction documents for several years will probably require less work in that area than in others with which he or she has not had recent experience.

This review manual was prepared to help candidates focus on those topics that will most likely be included in the exam in one form or another. Some subjects may seem familiar or may be easy to recall from memory. Others may seem completely foreign; these are the ones to give particular attention to when using this book. It may be wise to study additional sources on these subjects, take review seminars, or get special help from someone who knows the topic.

The following steps provide a useful structure for organizing an exam study program.

step 1: Start early. It is not advisable to review for a test like this by starting two weeks before the date. This is especially true for candidates taking all portions of the exam for the first time.

step 2: Go through the review manuals quickly to get a feeling for the scope of the subject matter. Although this book and the companion volume on the structural portions of the exam have been prepared based on the content covered by the exam, it may be best to review the detailed list of tasks and considerations given in the NCARB study guides.

step 3: Based on this review and a realistic appraisal of personal strong and weak areas, set priorities for study and determine which topics need more study time.

step 4: Divide review subjects into manageable units, and organize them into a sequence of study. It is generally best to start with less familiar subjects. Based on the exam date and plans for beginning study, assign a time limit to each study unit. Again, a candidate's knowledge of a subject should determine the time devoted to it. For example, a candidate may want to devote an entire week to earthquake design if it is an unfamiliar subject, and only one day to timber design if it is a familiar subject. In setting up a schedule, be realistic about other life commitments as well as personal ability to concentrate on studying for a given amount of time.

step 5: Begin studying, and stick with the schedule. This, of course, is the most difficult part of the process and the one that requires the most self-discipline. The job should be easier for candidates who started early and are following a realistic schedule, allowing time for recreation and other personal commitments.

step 6: Stop studying a day or two before the exam to relax. By this time, no amount of cramming will help.

Here are some additional tips.

- Know concepts first, and then learn the details. For example, it is much better to understand the basic ideas and theories of waterproofing than it is to attempt to memorize dozens of waterproofing products and details. Once the concept is clear, the details and application are much easier to learn and to apply during the exam.

- Do not overstudy any one portion of the exam (for candidates planning to take more than one session at a time). It is generally better to review the concepts than to become an overnight expert in one area. For example, the exam may ask general questions about plate girders, but it will not ask for a complete, detailed design of a plate girder.

- Solve as many practice problems as possible, including those in this book, the ones provided with NCARB's practice program, and any others that are available.

- Visit website forums to discuss the exam with others who have taken it and are preparing to take it. Although the exam questions change daily, it is a good idea to get a feeling for the types of questions asked, the general emphasis, and areas that previous candidates found particularly troublesome.

- A day or two before the first test session, stop studying in order to relax as much as possible. Get plenty of sleep the night before the test and every night between test days for staggered test sessions. Allow plenty of time to get to the exam site, to avoid transportation problems such as getting lost or stuck in traffic jams. Try to relax as much as possible during study periods and during the exam itself. Worrying too much is counterproductive. Candidates who have worked diligently in school, have obtained a wide range of experience during internship, and have started exam review early will be in the best possible position to pass the ARE.

Test Materials

It is neither necessary nor permissible to bring any reference materials or scratch paper to the test site. Scratch paper is provided by the proctor and must be returned when leaving the exam room. However, *do bring* a scientific, nonprogrammable, noncommunicating, nonprinting calculator to the multiple-choice exams. For the graphic divisions a calculator is built into the software.

HOW SI UNITS ARE USED IN THIS BOOK

This edition of *Architecture Exam Review, Volume II: Non-structural Topics* includes equivalent measurements, using the Système Internationale (SI), in the text and illustrations. However, the use of SI units for construction and book publishing in the United States is problematic. This is because the building construction industry in the United States (with the exception of federal construction) has generally not adopted the metric system, as it is commonly called. Equivalent measurements of customary U.S. units (also called English or inch-pound units) are usually given as a *soft* conversion, where customary U.S. measurements are simply converted into SI units using standard conversion factors. This always results in a number with excessive significant digits. When construction is done using SI units, the building is designed and drawn according to *hard* conversions, where planning dimensions and building products are based on a metric module from the beginning. For example, studs are spaced 400 mm on center to accommodate panel products that are manufactured in standard 1200 mm widths.

During the present time of transition to the Système Internationale in the United States, code-writing bodies, federal laws (such as the ADA), product manufacturers, trade associations, and other construction-related industries typically still use the customary U.S. system and make soft conversions to develop SI equivalents. In the case of some product manufacturers, they produce the same product using both measuring systems. Although there are industry standards for developing SI equivalents, there is no perfect consistency for rounding off when conversions are made. For example, the International Building Code shows a 152 mm equivalent when a 6 in dimension is required. The Americans with Disabilities Act Guidelines (ADAAG) gives a 150 mm equivalent for the same customary U.S. dimension.

To further complicate matters, each book publisher may employ a slightly different house style in handling SI equivalents when customary U.S. units are used as the primary measuring system. The confusion is likely to continue until

the United States construction industry adopts the SI system completely, precluding the need for dual dimensioning in publishing.

For the purposes of this book, the following conventions have been adopted.

When dimensions are for informational use, the SI equivalent rounded to the nearest millimeter is used.

When dimensions are given and they relate to planning or design guidelines, the SI equivalent is rounded to the nearest 5 mm for numbers over a few inches and to the nearest 10 mm for numbers over a few feet. When the dimension exceeds several feet, the number is rounded to the nearest 100 mm. For example, if you need a space about 10 ft wide for a given activity, the modular, rounded SI equivalent will be given as 3000 mm. More exact conversions are not required.

When an item is only manufactured to a customary U.S. measurement, the nearest SI equivalent rounded to the nearest millimeter is given, unless the dimension is very small (as for metal gages), in which case a more precise decimal equivalent will be given. Some materials, such as glass, are often manufactured to SI sizes. So, for example, a nominal $1/2$ in thick piece of glass will have an SI equivalent of 13 mm but can be ordered as 12 mm.

When there is a hard conversion in the industry and an SI equivalent item is manufactured, the hard conversion is given. For example, a 24 × 24 ceiling tile would have the hard conversion of 600 × 600 (instead of 610) because these are manufactured and available in the United States.

When an SI conversion is used by a code agency, such as the International Building Code (IBC), or published in another regulation, such as the ADA Accessibility Guidelines, the SI equivalents used by the issuing agency are printed in this book. For example, the same 10 ft dimension given previously as 3000 mm for a planning guideline would have a building code SI equivalent of 3048 mm because this is what the IBC requires. The ADA Accessibility Guidelines generally follow the rounding rule, to take SI dimensions to the nearest 10 mm. For example, a 10 ft requirement for accessibility will be shown as 3050 mm. The code requirements for readers outside the United States may be slightly different.

Throughout the book, the customary U.S. measurements are given first with the SI equivalent shown in parentheses. When the measurement is millimeters, no suffix is shown. For example, a dimension will be indicated as 4 ft 8 in (1422). When the SI equivalent is some other unit, such as volume or area, the suffix is indicated. For example, 250 ft² (23 m²).

This book uses different abbreviations for pounds of force and pounds of mass in customary U.S. units. The abbreviation used for pounds of force (pounds-force) is lbf, and the abbreviation used for pounds of mass (pounds-mass) is lbm.

MATHEMATICS

Successful completion of the ARE does not require any complex mathematics. Calculations are usually simple and straightforward, requiring the four basic math functions with a few additional bits of knowledge. The following sections should provide sufficient refresher information for the structural and nonstructural portions of the exam.

SI AND IMPERIAL UNITS

Since 1985 the ARE has been given in both imperial units and SI (metric) units for both U.S. and Canadian candidates. The units the United States has been using are also known by various other names including English, U.S. customary, U.S. standard, and inch-pound. SI stands for *Système International d'Unités*. The United States has been slow to convert to SI units, but change is beginning. For example, since 1994 all design work for federal construction projects has been done only in metric units. In addition, the increasing number of projects in foreign countries by U.S. architectural firms requires that more and more work be done in SI units.

Recognizing this change, NCARB is phasing out the use of imperial measurements on the ARE. Full implementation of the SI (metric system) is planned for the future.

In this book, imperial units are given first in most cases with the SI equivalent in parentheses. In the text, the SI numbers are followed by the units, such as mm for millimeters or kg for kilograms. However, to avoid clutter, only the SI numbers are given on the illustrations (in parentheses immediately after the imperial units); units such as millimeters are not included. Following standard conventions, all distance measurements in illustrations are in millimeters unless specifically indicated as meters. In some cases, examples, sample questions, and solutions are in imperial units only.

ARCHITECT'S AND ENGINEER'S DIMENSIONING SYSTEM

Architects usually work with units of feet, inches, and fractions of an inch or in SI units (metric), whereas engineers and landscape architects work with decimals of a foot and with feet and inches. Engineering dimensions are typically found on site drawings, with both elevations and distances being shown in decimal format. Examinees should be able to convert from one to the other.

Calculators are available that allow the user to add, subtract, multiply, and divide in feet and inches format, but even without this type of calculator, the conversion is fairly simple. Remember that the basic unit of measurement is the foot; only the fractions of a foot are different.

To convert from an architectural to an engineering dimension, first divide the fraction of an inch (if any) as it appears to convert to a fraction of an inch. Then combine this with the number of inches. Finally, divide the inches with the decimal equivalent of the fraction by 12 to obtain the decimal part of a foot.

Example 1.1

Convert 4 ft 5⁵/₈ in to decimal format.

First, convert ⁵/₈ in.

$$\frac{5}{8} \text{ in} = 0.625 \text{ in}$$

Combined with the number of inches, the fractional part of a foot (5⁵/₈ in) is 5.625 in.

Dividing by 12,

$$\frac{5.625 \text{ in}}{12 \dfrac{\text{in}}{\text{ft}}} = 0.469 \text{ ft}$$

VOLUME II: NONSTRUCTURAL TOPICS

The number of feet stays the same, so the equivalent decimal dimension is 4.469 ft.

Example 1.2

Convert 15.875 ft to feet and inches format.

First, convert the decimal to inches.

$$(0.875 \text{ ft})(12 \text{ in}) = 10.50 \text{ in}$$

Then, convert the decimal of an inch to a fraction. This can be done to any fractional unit of an inch by multiplying the decimal by the desired unit. For instance, to convert to eighths of an inch, multiply by 8, or

$$(0.50 \text{ in})(8) = 4/8 \text{ in or } 1/2 \text{ in}$$

The complete conversion is then the sum of the parts, or 15 ft $10^1/_2$ in.

TRIGONOMETRY

Trigonometric functions occur frequently in various types of architectural applications. Some of the most common functions, such as the sine, cosine, and tangent, relate to the right triangle. See Fig. 1.1. A useful mnemonic device is to remember the old Indian chief SOH-CAH-TOA. In other words, the sine of an angle, S, is equal to the side opposite the angle, O, divided by the hypotenuse, H. The cosine of an angle, C, is equal to the side adjacent to the angle, A, divided by the hypotenuse, H. Finally, the tangent of an angle, T, is equal to the side opposite the angle, O, divided by the side adjacent, A.

Knowing any two sides of a right triangle, the other side can be found with the Pythagorean theorem, which states that the sum of the squares of the two sides equals the square of the hypotenuse.

$$A^2 + O^2 = H^2 \qquad 1.1$$

LOGARITHMS

In the past, logarithms were used to multiply and divide very large numbers. This was because multiplication could be accomplished by simply adding the logarithms of two numbers and converting the resulting logarithm back to a whole number. Logarithms are no longer used for this purpose, but they are used with acoustical calculations, so examinees should be familiar with the concept.

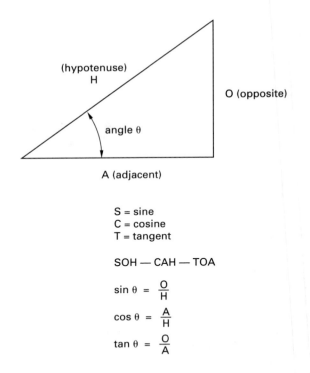

Figure 1.1 Functions of a Right Triangle

A logarithm of a number, x, is simply a number that, when used as the exponent of another number (known as the *base*), will yield the original number, x. There are two commonly used bases for logarithms: the common and the natural. *Natural logs* are not used in architectural work, but the base of the common log is 10. For example, the *common log* of 100 is 2. This means that if the base of 10 is raised to the second power (2), then the resulting number will be 100. Other even-numbered logs are

$$\log 1 = 0$$
$$\log 10 = 1$$
$$\log 100 = 2$$
$$\log 1000 = 3$$
$$\log 0.1 = -1$$
$$\log 0.01 = -2$$
$$\log 0.001 = -3$$

For numbers that fall between these even powers, the log is zero or a whole number, known as the *characteristic*, and a decimal, known as the mantissa. For example, the log of 78 is 1.89209. Because 78 is between 10 and 100, you would expect the log to be between 1 and 2. Logarithms of numbers can be found in log tables, but any good calculator also has log functions available at the touch of a button.

PROFESSIONAL PUBLICATIONS

In performing acoustical calculations, logarithms must be manipulated. The following formulas are useful to remember.

$$\log xy = \log x + \log y \qquad 1.2$$

$$\log \frac{x}{y} = \log x - \log y \qquad 1.3$$

$$\log x^n = n \log x \qquad 1.4$$

$$\log 1 = 0 \qquad 1.5$$

SECTION 1: PRE-DESIGN

PRE-DESIGN—
ENVIRONMENTAL ANALYSIS
AND PROJECT PLANNING

Nomenclature

d	vertical distance between contours	ft (m)
G	slope of land	%
L	horizontal distance between points of a slope	ft (m)

Competent architectural design depends on a thorough understanding of the environmental factors affecting the selection of a building site and its development. These factors include the larger context of the surrounding community and urban setting as well as the smaller scale influences of the immediate site. This chapter reviews the effects of the larger environmental issues on the planning of a building project. Ch. 4 focuses on site analysis prior to starting design work.

Included here is a review of the historical patterns of urban development, planning concepts, the effect of development patterns on social behavior, land analysis, transportation influences, climatic and ecological considerations, legal constraints, and economic influences and how all of these affect the development of a building site.

INFLUENCES ON URBAN DEVELOPMENT

Contemporary city and community planning has antecedents in the historical development of the city and in the theories of many designers and planners who felt that rational development of the land and cities could improve living conditions. Many development concepts and city forms have been tried; some have failed but portions of others have been successfully employed in urban planning.

An architect must have knowledge of the history and theory of city planning in order to understand the relationships between an individual building project and the larger context of the community and city in which it is located. The larger environment affects how the site is developed and how the building is designed, and the building, in turn, affects the community of which it is a part.

Historical Influences

The first human settlements began as collections of people engaged in agricultural pursuits rather than leading a nomadic life. As surplus food became available and ceremony, religion, and leadership began to develop, the embryonic form of the city was apparent. Living quarters surrounded the archetypes of the granary (the place where food was stored), the temple (where ceremonial rites and social interaction took place), and the palace (where the administration of the village was conducted). For security, villages were often walled in or otherwise situated for protection from other village populations or nomadic tribes seeking to take the food they could not produce.

All these basic components of the city were present in the Greek cities, but in a more highly developed form. The activities of the palace, which included trade and exchange of goods as well as religious ceremony, had developed to a point where separate places were required for these activities. The temple became the center for religious activity, while the agora became the marketplace. The agora was not just a location for the trading of goods but was also a place for meeting people, exchanging news, and conducting other business. The walled Greek cities also had special facilities, such as theaters and stadiums, for other activities.

The form of the medieval city was similar to that of earlier villages; it started at the crossroads of two main streets and was irregular in layout. Medieval cities were organized around the church and the market because these represented the two most important aspects of life. The structures were near the center of the city, and surrounding them was an informal ring of streets loosely connected, with intersecting streets running from the church to the gates of the city wall. See Fig. 2.1.

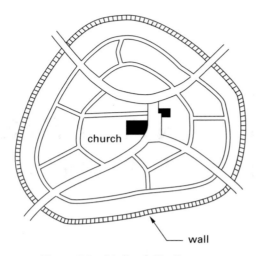

Figure 2.1   Medieval City Form

With the invention of gunpowder, the usual medieval fortification of the high wall was no longer sufficient to protect the city. The star-shaped city developed with regularly spaced bastions at points around the wall so that the entire enclosure and all approaches to the city could be defended before the enemy could get close enough for their cannons to be effective. Streets radiated out from the center, thus allowing the defense to be controlled from one point and making it possible to easily move troops and materials. See Fig. 2.2.

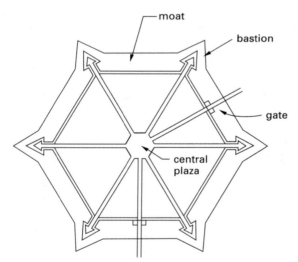

Figure 2.2   Star-Shaped City Form

During the Renaissance, city planning took on greater importance. Although military and defense considerations were still important, planners paid more attention to the aesthetics of urban design. City plans combined symmetrical order with radial layout of streets focused on points of interest. The primary organization of the radial boulevards

was overlaid on a grid of secondary streets or over an existing road system.

Christopher Wren's plan for the rebuilding of London after the great fire of 1666 and Haussmann's plan for Paris reflect the Renaissance approach. In the unrealized London plan, Wren proposed main avenues linking major religious and commercial facilities. These were to be superimposed on a gridiron plan for other streets.

In Paris, George-Eugène Haussmann advocated straight, arterial boulevards connecting principal historic buildings, monuments, and open squares. These were designed to create vistas and work in conjunction with the major buildings that were part of the plan. During the period from 1853 to 1869, a large part of Paris was demolished to implement Haussmann's plan. Although the purpose of the plan was to minimize riots, facilitate defense of the city, and clear out slums, the plan also improved transportation and beautified the city.

In contrast to the use of straight boulevards promoted by Haussmann, the Austrian architect and town planner Camillo Sitte advocated just the opposite. In his book *City Planning According to Artistic Principles*, published in 1889, Sitte proposed that cities be laid out on the principles of medieval towns, with curving and irregular streets. He felt this street configuration would provide a variety of views and be much more interesting than the standard grid or radial city layouts of the time. From a practical standpoint, Sitte proposed using T-intersections to reduce the possible number of intersection traffic conflicts. He also suggested creating civic spaces around a pinwheel arrangement of streets, which became known as a *turbine square*.

The Industrial Revolution of the eighteenth and nineteenth centuries in England brought about a fundamental change in the design of cities. The factory system required that the work force be close to the factory and the source of power and transportation. As production expanded, so did the population of the factory towns. The emphasis was on turning out the goods, and the cities soon became overcrowded, filthy, and devoid of open space and recreational activities. Although the Industrial Revolution began in England, it rapidly spread to northwestern Europe and the northeastern United States, carrying with it the resulting ills of its environment.

The response to the living conditions brought about by the Industrial Revolution spawned a reform movement. The first concern of many of the reformers was to alleviate the unspeakable housing conditions that existed, to reduce crowding, and to improve the water supply and sewage systems. Later, the reformers and planners realized that there was also a need for open space and recreation. All these concerns sparked interest in city planning where factories, housing, and other features of urban life could coexist.

One of the most well-known examples of the reform movement is the *Garden City* concept published by Ebenezer Howard in 1898. Howard attempted to combine the best of city and country living in his town-country idea. He proposed that a 6000 ac (2428 ha) tract of land be privately owned by the residents. At the center of his idealized city, there would be civic buildings in a park. These would include a town hall, a concert hall, a theater, a library, and other municipal buildings. See Fig. 2.3. Surrounding this core would be housing and shops with industrial facilities in the outermost ring. The urban part of the town would support 30,000 people on 1000 ac (405 ha) of land. The remaining 5000 ac (2023 ha) would be reserved for a greenbelt and agricultural use and house 2000 people.

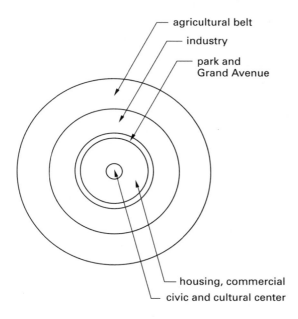

Figure 2.3 Diagram of Ebenezer Howard's Garden City Concept

A hectare (ha) is 10 000 m². One acre contains 4046.87 m².

Two cities were built in England using Howard's ideas: Letchworth in 1903 and Welwyn Garden City in 1920. Although they followed the Garden City concept, they did not become independent cities but instead were satellite towns.

Another city plan developed as a reaction to the conditions of the Industrial Revolution was the *Cité Industrielle* by Tony Garnier in 1917. This city was to have been built in France and included separate zones for residential, public, industrial, and agricultural use, linked by separated vehicular and pedestrian circulation paths. The buildings would be placed on long, narrow lots with ample open space between them.

Garnier's plan was one of the first to emphasize the idea of zoning, an idea that would later become vital for city planning.

In the United States, early attempts at city planning reflected the diversity of ideas and styles brought from the Old World. Towns laid out in the colonies were a reaction to the Renaissance ideals and reflected the agrarian lifestyles of the settlers. They were planned around a central commons, which was the focus of community life. Houses were free-standing structures set back from the front street, and the lots included backyards as well. This was one of the influences that helped set a precedent for single-family detached housing, prevalent even today.

Philadelphia was typical of many of the early towns. Begun in 1682, it was based on a *gridiron street system* with regularly planned public open spaces and uniform spacing and setback of buildings. Its use of the grid system became the model for later planning in America and for the new towns established as the West was settled.

Savannah, Georgia, was similarly designed in 1733. It was based on a ward of 40 house lots bounded by major streets in a grid system and contained an interior square, two sides of which were reserved for public use.

The grid system was encouraged by the Ordinance of 1785, which established the rectangular survey system of the United States. This system divided the country into a grid of 24 mi squares, each subdivided into 16 townships, each 6 mi on a side. These were further subdivided into 36 1 mi² sections.

One early American city that broke with the grid system was Washington, DC. Its layout represented a significant step in city planning because of the scale of the project and because Washington was America's capital city. Pierre Charles L'Enfant was the designer. Unlike the simple grid systems of Philadelphia and Savannah, L'Enfant's design was based on the Renaissance and Baroque planning concepts of diagonal and radial streets superimposed on a rectangular grid.

The Washington plan centered on the capitol, the mall, and the executive mansion. Each of these and other, smaller circles and squares were connected with broad avenues, creating a coherent transportation system based on vistas terminating in either a building or monument. Modifications were made to the original L'Enfant plan over the years, but the basic layout of Washington remains true to L'Enfant's vision.

In landscape and park design, Frederick Law Olmsted was one of the preeminent leaders. He was one of the first landscape architects to preserve the natural features of an area while adding naturalistic elements. With architect Calvert

Vaux, Olmsted designed New York's Central Park in the 1850s, which inspired similar designs for metropolitan parks across the country and in Canada. Later, Olmsted designed Prospect Park in Brooklyn, Riverside Park in New York, Audubon Park in New Orleans, the Metropolitan Parks System in Boston, and the grounds of the U.S. Capitol in Washington, DC.

One of the most profound changes in American urban design began with the *Columbian Exposition* in Chicago in 1893. Designed by architects Daniel Burnham and John Root and by landscape architect Frederick Law Olmsted, the Exposition grouped classical buildings symmetrically around formal courts of honor, reflecting pools, and large promenades. It started the *City Beautiful* movement in the United States and revived interest in urban planning. Some of the typical results of emulating the layout of the Columbian Exposition included civic centers organized around formal parks, a proliferation of classical public buildings, and broad, tree-lined parkways and streets.

In the 1920s and 1930s, architects such as Frank Lloyd Wright and Le Corbusier envisioned cities with vast open spaces. Wright proposed in his plan for Broadacre City that every home should be situated on at least an acre of land. Le Corbusier saw the city consisting of office and housing towers surrounded by large green spaces. Most city planners agree that both schemes would have resulted in very dull cities and a type of urban sprawl probably worse than what exists today.

A fairly recent notion of town planning is the new town concept. It is an extension of the idea that entirely new communities can be built away from the crowding and ugliness of existing cities. The idea started in Great Britain in the 1940s and soon spread to the United States and elsewhere. New towns were supposed to be autonomous centers including housing, shopping, and business, surrounded by a greenbelt. Originally, the population was to be limited to about 30,000, but this was later increased to 70,000 to 250,000 people.

Several new towns were built in England. However, they never became truly independent cities because they lacked significant employment centers; they still depended on nearby cities for jobs. In the United States, Columbia, Maryland, and Reston, Virginia, began as new towns but suffered from the same problems as their British counterparts. They never became truly separate cities; instead, they depended on the jobs of nearby Washington, DC, and other areas.

These new towns and previous visions of utopia have all suffered from the same problems: they are usually static in their conception, and they lack the vitality and interest of a city that has evolved over time.

A more recent planning concept is new urbanism. *New urbanism* is a planning philosophy that attempts to counter the many undesirable aspects of city development, including suburban sprawl, reliance on the automobile, environmental deterioration, housing segregation, loss of farmland, and single-use development. The movement was begun in the late 1980s with the construction of Seaside, Florida, by Andres Duany and Elizabeth Plater-Zyberk. Other planners and architects who developed the principles of new urbanism include Peter Calthorpe and Peter Katz.

New urbanism planning concepts work at the building, neighborhood, district, and regional levels in new developments as well as urban and suburban infill projects. One of the primary urban design features is the development of neighborhoods intended for mixed use: housing within walking distance of shops, offices, and other services, and a variety of residential types, from apartments above shops to single-family houses. At the regional level, new urbanism promotes the connection of neighborhoods and towns to regional patterns of pedestrian, bicycle, and public transit systems while reducing dependence on the automobile and establishing connections to open space and natural systems. At the street and building level, new urbanism encourages individual buildings to be integrated with their surroundings, to support the street as a place for pedestrians, and to provide users with a clear sense of location and time. The preservation or reuse of historic structures is also supported.

There are many other precepts of the new urbanism movement, including regional planning, a mix of residential types (including affordable housing), safe streets, sustainable design principles, and the integration of civic, institutional, and educational facilities into neighborhoods. Some of the small-scale design features that may be found in new urbanism designs include village squares, backyard garages, front porches, and picket fences.

Development Patterns

The form of urban development can be viewed at two scales: the larger scale of the city or metropolitan region and the smaller scale of the community and neighborhood. In the twentieth century, the pattern of development at the city scale has generally been determined by geographic features and the layout of transportation, most notably the highway. In some cases where effective city and regional planning has been undertaken, land use plans have also determined, to a certain degree, the form of development.

Cities begun near a major geographic feature such as the junction of two rivers or a large body of water tended to develop along the water and ultimately away from it. When begun in less confining circumstances, cities have grown more or less equally in all directions, usually in a uniform grid pattern.

With the proliferation of the automobile, cities have expanded in a number of typical patterns. These are shown diagrammatically in Fig. 2.4. Each of these patterns affects the planning of the smaller-scale communities and neighborhoods and ultimately can have an effect on the design of individual building projects.

The simplest pattern is the *expanding grid*. In this pattern a city is formed at the junction of two roads and laid out in the prevalent pattern exemplified in the initial plan of Philadelphia. Growth simply follows the grid pattern until some natural feature, limiting population, or economics stops it. The strict grid pattern is usually characteristic of smaller cities. Larger United States metropolitan areas follow other patterns but are almost always infilled with some type of grid.

The *star pattern* revolves around the urban core, and development follows radiating spokes of main highways or mass transit routes. Higher density development tends to form around the spokes, with lower density development between.

The *field pattern* has no central focus or apparent overall organization scheme. Development takes place in an amorphous network of highways and natural features. Los Angeles is a typical example of this type of pattern.

With the *satellite pattern*, there is a central urban core with other major cores surrounding it. The central core is linked

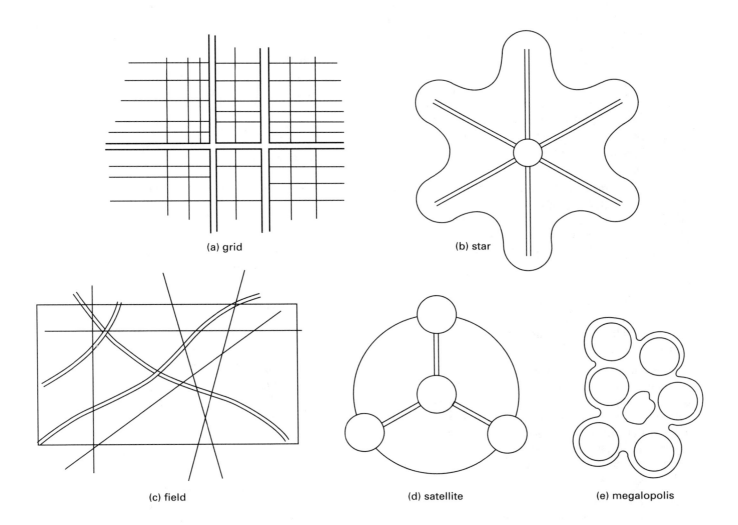

(a) grid

(b) star

(c) field

(d) satellite

(e) megalopolis

Figure 2.4 Patterns of Urban Development

to the others with major highways, and often the outer cores are connected with a road system called a *beltway*. It is then possible to travel from center to center or around the city without having to go through the core. The outer cores often begin as major shopping areas, peripheral business centers, or transportation centers. Houston is an example of this type of pattern. Often, a satellite pattern starts out as a star pattern.

Finally, the ultimate in urban development is the *megalopolis*. Here, two or more major urban centers near each other grow together as the space between is developed. Many sections of the northeastern United States and southern California can be considered megalopolises.

Although large-scale urban development can affect the way people view the city and how individual parcels of land are developed, it is within the smaller community and neighborhood scale that architects must plan sites and design buildings. One idea that is useful in linking the urban scale with the community scale is the concept of imageability proposed by Kevin Lynch.

Imageability is the quality of a physical environment that gives it a high probability of evoking a strong image in the mind of a given observer. For example, the hills of San Francisco are part of the image of that city in the minds of most people who visit it or live there. Everyone maintains a mental image of the environment; it is vital to orientation, way-finding, and general well being.

In *The Image of the City*, Kevin Lynch identified five basic elements of the urban image: paths, edges, districts, nodes, and landmarks. These are created by buildings, natural features, roads, and other components of the city. Site planning and building design should respond to existing image elements and enhance them if possible.

A *path* is a way of circulation along which people customarily, occasionally, or potentially move. A path may be a street, pedestrian walkway, railroad, transit line, or river. Since circulation is an important part of any physical environment, paths are usually at the center of a person's image.

Edges are linear elements other than paths that form boundaries between two districts or that break continuity. An edge may be a shoreline, a line of buildings against a park, a wall, or a similar feature. Sometimes an element is a path if used for circulation and an edge if seen from afar. For example, a highway can be perceived as an edge of one neighborhood and a path when one is traveling on it. Edges may be either solid or penetrable.

Districts are two-dimensional areas that people perceive as having some common, identifying character and that they can enter. A district can be perceived from the inside if one is in it or can be identified as an element of the city if one is outside. Back Bay in Boston or Georgetown in Washington, DC, are examples of districts.

Nodes are strategic centers of interest that people can enter. They may be the intersection of paths, places where modes of transportation change, plazas, public squares, or centers of districts.

Landmarks are similar to nodes in that they are point references, but people cannot enter them—they are viewed from the exterior. A tower, monument, building, or natural feature can be a landmark.

Many of the large-scale elements of imageability are interwoven with the smaller community and neighborhood. However, there are additional patterns of development that are also intimately related to an individual site. One is the pattern of the street. Initially, community and neighborhood development followed the layout of the street, usually a grid. Blocks between the streets were subdivided into lots, and each lot was developed as a separate entity. Although this development method persists today, other approaches have emerged.

One of these approaches is the superblock, which is an outgrowth of the new town concept. This is shown diagrammatically in Fig. 2.5. One of the first trials of this development scheme was in the new town of Radburn, New Jersey, by Henry Wright. Here, the attempt was made to plan a large piece of land that limited the intrusion of the automobile. The superblock was surrounded by a continuous street, and vehicular access was provided with cul-de-sacs.

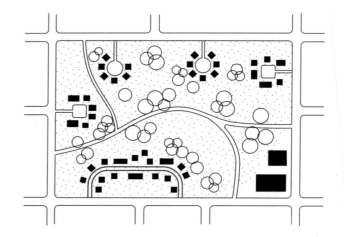

Figure 2.5 Superblock Concept

The superblock concept minimizes the impact of the car on housing and allows the development of pedestrian circulation and park space within the block. This concept was used in the planning of Chandigar, India, by Le Corbusier, and of Brasilia by Costa and Niemeyer. In theory, the separation of the automobile on the side of the house that faces the street from the pedestrian and living area on the other side seems to be an admirable goal. However, because much of contemporary life revolves around the automobile, this separation can be counterproductive to neighborhood social interaction. As a result, the driveways and parking spaces of superblocks are often used more than the quiet park spaces.

A variation and extension of the superblock idea is the *planned unit development*, or PUD. With this approach, each large parcel of land can have a mix of uses: residential, commercial, recreational, and open space designed with variable lot sizes and densities. Industrial developments can also be planned as PUDs. PUDs must conform to certain standards as promulgated by the local planning agency and must be approved by the planning agency, but within the restrictions the planner has wide latitude in determining how the site is developed.

The standards for PUDs include such things as the uses permitted, total floor area ratio (ratio of developed floor space to land area), amount of open space required, parking spaces required, living space ratio (open space less parking space), maximum heights, and setbacks at the perimeter.

Planned unit developments offer many advantages. They make more efficient use of land by grouping compatible uses without the sometimes unnecessary requirements of setback regulations in zoning ordinances. This grouping allows the extra land to be given over to open space or common use areas. They also provide a variety of housing options, from single-family detached to row houses to high-rise apartments and condominiums. PUDs also recapture some of the diversity and variety of urban living that many people find desirable.

The Effects of Development Patterns on Social Behavior

The physical environment affects human behavior. This is true at any scale, from the plan of a city to the arrangement of furniture in a room. A great deal of research has been conducted in the field of environmental psychology; some of the results remain inconclusive, while other theories have been shown to provide a reliable basis for making design decisions. Be familiar with the following principles.

Density is one characteristic of human settlements that has received a great deal of attention. It refers to the number of people per unit of area. For example, a city might be referred to as having a density of 50 people per acre. Density refers only to a ratio, not to the total number of people or how they are distributed. The 50 people could be evenly distributed over the acre or they could all be housed in a few high-rise buildings in one part of the land parcel.

For a long time, high density was equated with undesirable living conditions. However, research has shown that there is much more involved when talking about density. The first consideration is that density should not be confused with crowding. Four people sharing a bedroom would be crowding, but if each of the same four people had adequate personal space while still occupying the same overall living space (the same density) they probably would not be crowded.

The perception of crowding also depends on cultural influences and circumstances. Some cultures find living in closer proximity to one another normal and desirable, whereas people from other cultures would find the same density crowded. In a similar way, being densely packed in a restaurant for a few hours would not seem crowded to most people, but trying to relax on a park bench at the same density would be uncomfortable. Regardless of the interpretation of density, however, there are limits to the density under which people can comfortably live, work, and play. Studies have shown that excessive density can cause poor physical and mental health and spawn a variety of antisocial behaviors.

Different cultures and socioeconomic groups respond to and use physical environments differently. The entire range of a particular group's pattern of living, working, playing, and socializing may flourish under one kind of environment and suffer under another. Taking cultural and social differences into account when designing housing and other facilities is critical to a successful project.

Regardless of the specific culture of a group, all people need and want social interaction with their family, friends, neighbors, and other groups to which they belong. A building, neighborhood, or city can promote or hinder such interaction. Providing spaces to gather, to watch other people, to cross paths, and to meet informally is a way the architect can encourage this vital part of human life. Spaces, buildings, rooms, and even furniture can be considered *sociopetal* if they tend to bring people together. A group of chairs facing each other, circular gathering spaces, and radial street plans are examples of sociopetal environments. *Sociofugal* refers to conditions that do just the opposite; they tend to discourage interaction or social contact.

In addition to interaction, people need a place they can call their own, whether it is their house, a seat at a conference table, or one end of a park bench. This is the concept of *territoriality* and is a fundamental part of animal behavior (humans included). When someone personalizes a desk at the office with family pictures, plants, individual coffee mugs, and the like, he or she is staking a claim to a personal territory, small and temporary as it may be. In a more permanent living environment, such as a house or apartment, territorial boundaries are provided by walls, fences, and property lines. Often, boundaries are more subtle. A street, a row of trees, or something very small such as a change in level may serve to define a person's or group's territory.

Closely related to territoriality is the concept of *personal spaces* that surround each individual. This idea, proposed by Edward T. Hall, states that there are four basic distances that can be used to study human behavior and serve as a guide for designing environments. The actual dimensions of the four distances vary with the circumstances and with cultural and social differences, but they always exist. The architect should be aware of personal distance needs and design accordingly, as forcing people closer together than the situation suggests can have a negative effect on them.

The closest is *intimate distance*. This ranges from physical contact to a distance of about 6 in to 18 in (150 to 460). People only allow other people to come within this distance under special conditions. If forced this close together, as on a crowded bus, people have defense mechanisms, such as avoiding eye contact, to minimize the effect of the physical contact.

The next distance is the *personal distance*, from about 1½ ft to 2½ ft (460 to 760) for some cultures, or more for others. If given the choice, people will maintain this distance between themselves and other people.

Social distance is the next invisible sphere, ranging from about 4 ft to 12 ft (1200 to 3660). This is the distance at which most impersonal business, work, and other interaction takes place between strangers or in more formal situations.

Public distance is the farthest, ranging from about 12 ft (3660) outward. The greatest amount of formality can be achieved at this distance. In addition, this distance allows people to escape if they sense physical danger from another person.

Another principle concerning the effects of development patterns on social behavior is *diversity*. The human animal needs a diverse and stimulating environment. In a monotonous urban setting, community, or building, people tend to become depressed, become irritated, or suffer some other type of negative influence. Over a long period of time, living in a dull, nonstimulating environment can even affect personality development.

Environment can also have an effect on criminal behavior. Oscar Newman developed concepts of what he called defensible space, and published them in the book *Defensible Space* and later in an expanded volume called *Creating Defensible Space*. The concepts of defensible space have spawned the newer term "crime prevention through environmental design" (CPTED).

Newman's original concept of *defensible space* described a range of design elements that used the basic concepts of surveillance, territoriality, and real and symbolic barriers to reduce crime. For example, instead of having the entry to an apartment building open directly to the public area of a street, a low wall could be built to indicate a separation of public and semipublic space. A large window could also be placed next to the front door so residents and passersby could observe activity both inside and outside the door.

Newman's research showed that relatively simple changes in design could reduce criminal behavior. CPTED takes the idea further and includes additional methods to reduce crime, such as electronic surveillance, alarms, and human resources.

COMMUNITY INFLUENCES ON DESIGN

Catchment Areas

Nearly all land development is dependent on or affected by some surrounding base of population within a geographical region. The term used to describe this is the *catchment area*. For example, the developer of a grocery store bases the decision to build on the number of people within a certain distance from the proposed store location. The population within this catchment area is the primary market for the services of the store. In a similar way, a school district is the catchment area for a particular school building.

The boundaries of catchment areas may be determined by physical features such as a highway or river, by artificial political boundaries such as a city line or school district limit, or by nebulous demarcations such as the division between two ethnic neighborhoods. Often, when site location studies are being made, a developer knows that a certain number of people must reside within a specified distance from the proposed site to make the project economically feasible. By using population information from census data or other types of surveys, a determination can be quickly made to see if the catchment area will support the land development.

The size and boundaries of a catchment area are dependent on several factors. A residential catchment area, for example, may increase in size with an increase in the population of the surroundings, either through a geographical expansion or with the construction of new housing. Conversely, the expansion of an employment center may create the demand for more workers and increase the employment catchment area. Boundaries are often determined by the availability of transportation. A convenience store that depends on neighborhood customers will have closer boundaries than will a shopping center accessible by major highways.

In many cases, the composition of a catchment area must be known in some detail in order to make development decisions. Simple gross population numbers are not enough. The developer of a high-end retail store needs to know how many people or families with an average income over a particular amount reside within a certain distance from the store site. A school district would have to know how many children of a particular age reside within an area. This kind of information is usually available from census data and local planning agencies.

Accessibility to Transportation

Transportation of all types is critical to the selection and development of a building site. This is true at all scales, from accessibility by major freeways to the individual road system and pedestrian paths around a small site. Something as simple as a one-way street that makes turning into a site from one direction difficult or impossible may be enough to render the property undesirable for some uses.

The following considerations should be examined when analyzing a site for development.

- Is there an adequate highway system to bring the catchment area population to the site?

- Are there adequate traffic counts for businesses that depend on drive-by trade?

- Would the development create additional traffic that would overload the existing road system or require new roads to be built or expanded?

- Is there adequate truck access for servicing the site?

- Does the surrounding transportation network create an undesirable environment for the development? For example, a small site bounded by two freeways may be too noisy for an apartment building.

- Is there safe and convenient pedestrian access to the site if required?

- Are there public transportation lines nearby? How can people get from the mass transit stops to the site?

- Are rail lines available for industrial projects?

Neighborhoods

Any development project is an intimate part of the area in which it is located. Architects must be sensitive to the existing fabric of a neighborhood that may influence how a project is designed as well as to the impact the project may have on the surroundings. A *neighborhood* can be defined as a relatively small area in which a number of people live who share similar needs and desires in housing, social activities, and other aspects of day-to-day living.

The original concept of the neighborhood as a part of city planning was developed by Clarence Perry in 1929. Although his ideas had physical design implications, they were primarily proposed as a way of bringing people together to discuss common problems and to become involved in the planning process. He felt that the ideal way to do this was to base the neighborhood on an area within walking distance of an elementary school, which would serve as the community center of neighborhood activity. Additionally, Perry proposed that the district be surrounded by major streets rather than intersected by them.

The neighborhood has become the basic planning unit for contemporary American urban design. This is in part due to the need for a manageable size on which to base city planning, as well as to the increased importance placed on citizen participation in the planning process, an idea suggested by Clarence Perry. The neighborhood is the scale most people can readily understand and identify with, the part of a city that people come in contact with on a daily basis and that influences their life the most.

Site development must be sensitive to the existing neighborhood. This can include such criteria as respecting pedestrian paths, maintaining the size and scale of the surrounding buildings, using similar or compatible materials, not creating uses that conflict with the surroundings, respecting views and access to important structures in the area, and trying to fit within the general context of the district.

Public Facilities

Public facilities include such places as schools, shops, fire stations, churches, post offices, and recreational centers. Their availability, location, and relative importance in a neighborhood can affect how a site is developed. For example, if a church is the center of social activity in a neighborhood, the designer should maintain easy access to it, surrounding development should be subordinate to or compatible with it, and the designer should give consideration to maintaining views or enhancing the church's prominence in the community. In another case, the path from a school to a recreation center may have special importance. The neighborhood may want the link maintained and improved by any new building along the way.

LAND ANALYSIS

Topography

A study of a site's topography is an important part of environmental analysis because existing land conditions affect how development can take place, what modifications need to be made, and what costs might be involved. Topography describes the surface features of land. Commonly used in land planning and architectural site development, a topographic map shows the slope and contour of the land as well as other natural and artificial features.

A topographic map is developed from a topographic survey by a land surveyor. In addition to information on the contours of a site, a survey will include such data as property boundaries, existing buildings, utility poles, roads and other manufactured features, and trees and other natural features like rock outcroppings and heavy vegetation. Figure 2.6 shows a simplified example of a topographic map.

The *contour lines* on a map are a graphic way to show the elevations of the land in a plan view and are used to make a slope analysis to determine the suitability of the land for

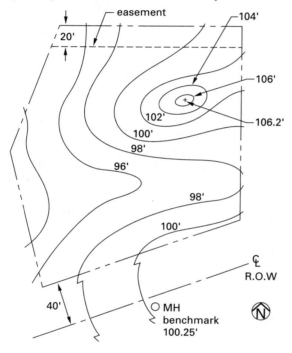

Figure 2.6 Topographic Map

various uses. Each contour line represents a continuous line of equal elevation above some reference benchmark. The *contour interval* is the vertical distance between adjacent contour lines. The contour interval on a map will vary depending on the steepness of the slope, the scale of the map, and the amount of detail required. Many large-scale maps of individual building sites use 1, 2, or 5 ft (0.5 m or 1 m) contour intervals, and small-scale maps of large regions may use 20 ft or 40 ft (5 m or 10 m) contours. The relationship between a contour map and a section through the contours is illustrated in Fig. 2.7.

Knowing the contour interval and the horizontal distance between any two contour lines, the slope of the land at that

point can be determined. The slope is represented in percent, each percent being 1 ft (1 m) of vertical rise for every 100 ft (100 m) of horizontal distance. Thus, a slope of 6½% would rise (or drop) 6½ ft (6½ m) within 100 ft (100 m).

The slope is found using the formula

$$G = \left(\frac{d}{L}\right) \times 100\% \qquad 2.1$$

Example 2.1

Find the slope between points A and B in Fig. 2.7 if the horizontal distance between them is 80 ft.

Because the contour interval is 5 ft, the vertical distance between the two points is 15 ft. The slope is

$$G = \left(\frac{15 \text{ ft}}{80 \text{ ft}}\right) \times 100\%$$
$$= 19\%$$

For slope analysis, the existing contours can be divided into general categories according to their potential for various types of uses. Slopes from 0% to 4% are usable for all types of intense activity and are easy to build on. Slopes from 4% to 10% are suitable for informal movement and outdoor activity and can also be built on without much difficulty. Slopes over 10% are difficult to climb or use for outdoor activity and are more difficult and expensive to build on. Depending on the condition of the soil, very steep slopes, over 25%, are subject to erosion and become more expensive to build on. Table 2.1 gives some recommended minimum and maximum slopes for various uses.

Table 2.1

Recommended Grade Slopes for Various Uses

	slopes (%)		
	min.	preferred	max.
ground areas for drainage	2.0	4.0	
grass areas for recreation	2.0		3.0
paved parking areas	1.5	2.5	5.0
roads	0.5		10.0
sanitary sewers			
(depends on size)	0.5–1.5		
approach walks to buildings	1.0		5.0
landscaped slopes	2.0		50.0
ramps	5.0		8.33

Respecting the natural contours and slope of the land is important not only from an ecological and aesthetic standpoint but also from an economic standpoint. Moving large

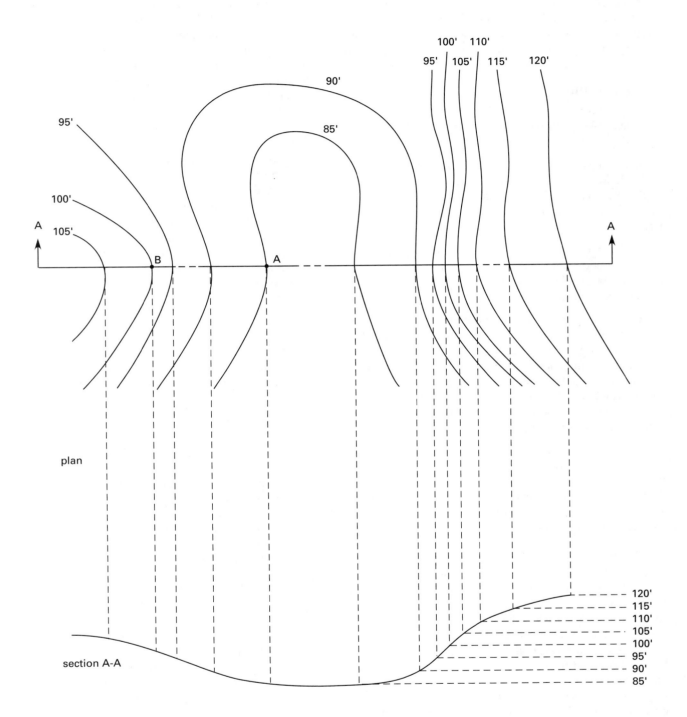

Figure 2.7   Representation of Land Slope with Contour Lines

quantities of earth costs money, and importing or exporting soil to a site is not desirable. Ideally, the amount of earth cut away in grading operations should equal the amount required to fill in other portions of the site. Topography and the use of contours is described in more detail in Ch. 4.

Natural Features

Every site has natural features that may be either desirable or undesirable. A complete site analysis will include a study of these features.

A view analysis may be required to determine the most desirable ways to orient buildings, outdoor areas, and approaches to the buildings. Undesirable views can be minimized or blocked with landscaping or other manufactured features.

Significant natural features such as rock outcroppings, cliffs, caves, and bogs should be identified to determine whether they must be avoided or can be used as positive design features in the site design.

Subsurface conditions of groundwater and rock must be known also. Sites with high water tables (about 6 ft to 8 ft [1800 to 2400] below grade) can cause problems with excavations, foundations, utility placement, and landscaping. The water table is the level underground in which the soil is saturated with water. Generally, the water follows the slope of the grade above, but it may vary slightly. Boring logs will reveal whether groundwater is present and how deep it is.

Sites with a preponderance of rocks near the surface can be very expensive and difficult (sometimes impossible) to develop. Blasting is usually required, which can increase the site development costs significantly (and may not be allowed by city code restrictions).

Drainage

Every site has some type of natural drainage pattern that must be taken into account during design. In some cases the drainage may be relatively minor, consisting only of the runoff from the site itself and a small amount from adjacent sites. This type of drainage can easily be diverted around roads, parking lots, and buildings with curbs, culverts, and minor changes in the contours of the land. In other cases, major drainage paths such as gullies, dry gulches, or rivers may traverse the site. These will have a significant influence on potential site development because they must, in most cases, be maintained. Buildings need to be built away from them or must bridge them so that water flow is not restricted and potential damage is avoided. If modification to the contours is required, the changes must be done in such a way that the contours of the adjacent properties are not disturbed.

The development of a site may be so extensive that excessive runoff is created due to roof areas, roads, and parking lots. All of these increase the *runoff coefficient*, the fraction of total precipitation that is not absorbed into the ground. If the runoff is greater than the capacity of the natural or artificial drainage from the site, holding ponds must be constructed to temporarily collect site runoff and release it at a controlled rate.

Soil

Soil is the pulverized upper layer of the earth, formed by the erosion of rocks and plant remains and modified by living plants and organisms. Generally, the visible upper layer is topsoil, a mixture of mineral and organic material. The thickness of topsoil may range from just a few inches to a foot or more. Below this is a layer of mostly mineral material, which is above a layer of the fractured and weathered parent material of the soil above. Below all of these layers is solid *bedrock*.

Soil is classified according to grain size and as either organic or inorganic. The grain size classification is

Gravel: particles over 2 mm in diameter

Sands: particles from 0.05 mm to 2 mm in diameter; the finest grains just visible to the eye

Silt: particles from 0.002 mm to 0.05 mm in diameter; the grains are invisible but can be felt as smooth

Clay: particles under 0.002 mm in diameter; smooth and floury when dry, plastic and sticky when wet

All soils are a combination of the preceding types, and any site analysis must include a subsurface investigation to determine the types of soil present as well as the water content. Some soils are unsuitable for certain uses, and layers of different soil types may create planes of potential slippage or slides and make the land useless for development.

Gravels and sands are excellent for construction loads and drainage and for sewage drain fields, but they are unsuitable for landscaping.

Silt is stable when dry or damp but unstable when wet. It swells and heaves when frozen and compresses under load. Generally, building foundations and road bases must extend below it or must be elastic enough to avoid damage. Some nonplastic silts are usable for lighter loads.

Clay expands when wet and is subject to slippage. It is poor for foundations unless it can be kept dry. It is also poor for landscaping and unsuitable for sewage drain fields or other types of drainage.

Peat and other organic materials are excellent for landscaping but unsuitable for building foundations or road bases. Usually, these soils must be removed from the site and replaced with sands and gravels for foundations and roads. Refer to Ch. 12 for more information on soil.

TRANSPORTATION AND UTILITY INFLUENCES

This section reviews some general guidelines for analyzing the transportation and utilities servicing a site. Review Ch. 4 for more detailed design criteria.

Roads

Roads provide a primary means of access to a site. Their availability and capacity may be prime determinants in whether and how a parcel of land can be developed. There are four basic categories of roads: local, collector, arterial, and expressway.

Local streets have the lowest capacity and provide direct access to building sites. They may be in the form of continuous grid or curvilinear systems or may be cul-de-sacs or loops.

Collector streets connect local streets and arterial streets. They, of course, have a higher capacity than local streets but are usually not intended for through traffic. Intersections of collector and local roads may be controlled by stop signs, whereas intersections with arterial streets will be controlled with stop lights.

Arterial streets are intended as major, continuous circulation routes that carry large amounts of traffic on two or three lanes. They usually connect expressways. Parking on the street is typically not allowed, and direct access from arterial streets to building sites should be avoided.

Expressways are limited access roads designed to move large volumes of traffic between, through, and around population centers. Intersections are made by various types of ramp systems, and pedestrian access is not allowed. Expressways have a major influence on the land due to the space they require and their noise and visual impact.

Site analysis must take into account the existing configuration of the street system and fit into the hierarchy of roads. Entrances and exits from the site must be planned to minimize congestion and dangerous intersections. Figure 2.8 illustrates some general guidelines for road layout.

Roads must be laid out both in the horizontal direction and the vertical direction, called *horizontal alignment* and *vertical alignment*, respectively. The straight sections of roads are called *tangents*, and the curved portions are arcs of a circle so that a vehicle can be steered easily and safely. Simple curves with a uniform radius between tangents are preferred. There should generally be a minimum of 100 ft (30 m) between curves in opposite directions and 200 ft

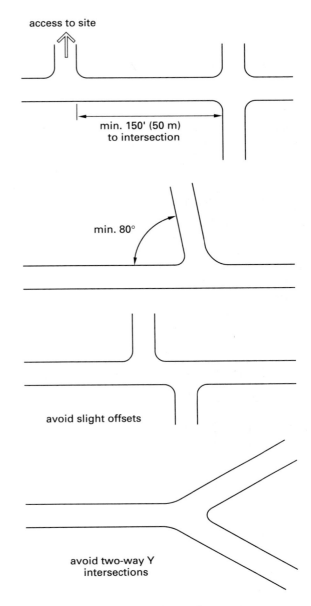

access to site

min. 150' (50 m) to intersection

min. 80°

avoid slight offsets

avoid two-way Y intersections

Figure 2.8   Guides for Road Layout at Intersections

(60 m) between curves in the same direction. Multiple-radius curves should be avoided.

Vertical alignment must be designed to provide a smooth transition between grade changes and to avoid overly steep grades. Depending on weather conditions and design speeds, streets should not have more than a 10% grade.

Public Transit

The availability and location of public transit lines can influence site design. A site analysis should include a determination of the types of public access available (whether bus, subway, rail line, or taxi stop) and the location relative to the site. Building entrances and major site features should be located conveniently to the public transit. In large cities, site development may have to include provisions for public access to subway and rail lines.

Service Access

Service to a site includes provisions for truck loading, moving vans, and daily delivery services. Ideally, service access should be separate from automobile and pedestrian access to a site and a building. Space for large-truck turning and loading dock berths needs to be provided. Local zoning ordinances usually specify the number and size of loading berths, but generally they should be 10 ft to 12 ft (3050 to 3660) wide, at least 40 ft (12 200) long, and have a 14 ft (4270) vertical clearance. A minimum turning radius of 60 ft (18 300) should be provided unless some other maneuvering method is possible.

Utility Availability

Site analysis must determine the availability, location, and capacity of existing utilities. The development potential of a site is dependent on the availability of the necessary utilities of water, sanitary sewers, storm sewers, telephone service, gas service, electric service, and other public utilities. Utility lines that have to be extended from a considerable distance add greatly to the cost of development.

Generally, utility lines follow the street layout and right-of-way. Sanitary sewers, storm sewers, and water mains are located under the road, whereas electric and communication lines are adjacent to the roads. Gas lines may either be under the road or next to it within the right-of-way. Utilities can also be located in easements, portions of privately owned land that public utility companies can use for the installation and maintenance of their lines.

When new services must be installed, sanitary and storm sewer location takes precedence because sewers must use the flow of gravity and therefore depend on the natural slope of the land. Collection systems drain to municipal disposal systems or to private, on-site treatment facilities.

Municipal Services

Depending on the location of the site, municipal services may include police protection, fire protection, trash removal, and street cleaning. The development site plan must provide access for these services, many of which require large land areas. For example, local fire protection officials may require an unobstructed strip of land around buildings to allow for fire fighting, in addition to suitable access roads from the street to the building. In some climates, adequate provisions must be made for snow removal or snow stacking.

CLIMATIC INFLUENCES

For any given site there are two aspects to climatic analysis: the macroclimate and the microclimate. The *macroclimate* refers to the overall climate of the region and is reflected in the weather data available from the National Weather Service. From this information a region can be classified as cool, temperate, hot-arid, or hot-humid. The *microclimate* refers to the site-specific modification of the macroclimate by such features as land slope, trees and other vegetation, bodies of water, and buildings.

The microclimate of a site can have a significant influence on its development; undesirable climatic effects can be minimized by careful planning, and desirable effects can be used to enhance the comfort of the inhabitants.

Wind Patterns

Both prevailing wind patterns and microclimate wind effects must be studied during site analysis. Buildings can then be located to take advantage of breezes or to avoid cold winds. Wind on the top of a hill, for example, can be about 20% higher than wind on flat ground. The *leeward* side of a hill (the side away from the wind direction) experiences less wind than the *windward* side. Near large bodies of water, warm air rises over the warmer land during the day and causes a breeze from the water. At night the pattern may be reversed; cold air flows down a hill and settles in low-lying regions, causing pockets that remain colder than higher elevations during the first part of the day. On a large scale, this results in an inversion where warmer air holds colder air below, trapping pollution.

Wind patterns can be modified by buildings and trees. For a line of trees 50 ft to 150 ft (15 m to 46 m) deep, wind velocity can be reduced from 30% to 60% to a distance 10 times the height of the tree line, depending on the density of the trees, and about half that to a distance of 20 times the tree height. For a single row of trees the effect is different. Refer to Ch. 7. Buildings can affect similar types of wind modification.

In general, in temperate climates the best microclimates for wind are on south- or southeast-facing slopes, in the middle of the slope or toward the top of a hill rather than at the very top or bottom of the slope.

Solar Orientation

The amount of solar radiation received on the ground surface depends on the angle of the sun's rays to the surface. At the macroclimate scale, this is why summer is warmer than winter; the sun is higher in the sky. (Also, there are longer days.) It also accounts for the fact that lower latitudes are warmer than higher latitudes. On a microclimate scale, south-facing slopes tend to be warmer, especially in the winter, than other slope orientations or flat surfaces. Ski runs, for example, are usually located on north-facing mountains to avoid the direct radiation of the sun.

The amount of radiation absorbed or reflected is affected by the surface material. The fraction of the radiant energy received on a surface that is reflected is called the albedo and ranges from 0.0 to 1.0. Zero albedo is a flat black surface that absorbs all the energy and reflects none, whereas an albedo of 1.0 corresponds to a mirror, reflecting all the energy striking it. Natural materials such as grass and vegetation have low albedos; snow and pavement have high albedos.

Closely related to albedo is *conductivity*, which is the time rate of flow of heat through a material. Highly conductive materials let heat pass through them quickly, whereas materials of low conductivity retard the passage of heat. Natural materials generally have low conductivity, and metal, concrete, and masonry have relatively high conductivities.

Combined, albedo and conductivity affect the microclimate. Ground surfaces with low albedo and high conductivity tend to moderate and stabilize the microclimate because excess heat is quickly absorbed, stored, and released when the temperature drops. Surfaces with grass and other vegetation are cooler in hot weather for this reason. On the other hand, surfaces with high albedo and low conductivity, such as pavements or concentrations of buildings, are much hotter than what the macroclimate would normally produce.

SUSTAINABLE DESIGN

Sustainable building design (also known as *"green" building design*) is an increasingly important part of architectural design. Sustainable design addresses a wide range of concerns, including the environmental impact of a building, the wise use of materials, energy conservation, the use of alternative energy sources, adaptive reuse, indoor air quality, recycling, reuse, and other strategies to achieve a balance between the consumption of environmental resources and the renewal of those resources. Sustainable design considers the full life cycle of a building and of the materials that comprise the building. Accordingly, it considers the impact that raw material extraction will have through all the stages of fabrication, installation, operation, maintenance, and disposal.

This section discusses sustainable design as it affects site evaluation, site selection, and the development of project concepts. Subsequent chapters cover alternative energy systems, new material technologies, building systems, hazardous material mitigation, indoor air quality, energy conservation, and adaptive reuse.

General Ecological Considerations

Ecology is the study of living organisms in relation to their environment. Applied to site development, the word takes on a slightly broader meaning. The need to understand the impact of construction on the surrounding natural environment is a key factor in the ecology of site development. This concern has been codified with the requirement that federal agencies file environmental impact statements (EISs). This requirement was started as one of the provisions of the National Environmental Policy Act of 1969 and is enforced by the Environmental Protection Agency (EPA). It requires a formal process to predict how a development will affect the environment, including the air, water, land, and wildlife. Many states have similar laws that require EISs for state-sponsored development. Another factor in the ecology of site development is the need to be cognizant of the impact of smaller-scale building on the surroundings, whether the environment is rural or in the heart of a city.

One concern that should be investigated during site analysis for semirural or rural development is the impact on natural landforms, water runoff, wildlife, and existing vegetation. The development should disturb the natural contours of the land as little as possible. Existing drainage patterns must be left intact, and additional runoff caused by roofs and paving should not exceed the capacity of the existing drainage paths. The development should also avoid significantly disturbing existing ecological systems of plants and wildlife.

For urban sites, slightly different concerns should be studied. The relationship of the building and its users to the surrounding environment remains a factor, but the impact of this relationship is more on artificial systems than on natural ecosystems. The development should minimize the production of noise, pollution, or other detrimental emissions. Building placement should avoid undesirable wind conditions, either on the site itself or around nearby buildings. The effect of a building blocking sunlight from adjacent buildings and outdoor spaces should be studied and minimized when possible. Similarly, the development should avoid any possible annoying reflection or glare on neighboring buildings. Finally, the impact of development on the utility and transportation systems must be thoroughly understood. Specific guidelines for achieving these goals are given in the following sections and in Ch. 8.

Site Analysis

In addition to the previously discussed influences of community, land, transportation, and climate on site selection and building design, a number of sustainability issues should be considered when analyzing a site. These include the following.

- Determine what sites or portions of a site should *not* be built on. These include wetlands or sites within 100 ft (30 m) of wetlands, elevations lower than 5 ft (1.5 m) above a 100-year floodplain, habitats for endangered species, potential historic sites (i.e., burial grounds), and prime farmland. *Wetlands* are areas that are inundated or saturated by surface water or groundwater at a frequency and duration sufficient to support a prevalence of vegetation typically adapted for life in saturated soil conditions. They are sometimes referred to as *jurisdictional wetlands*.

- Determine the historical and cultural qualities of the surrounding area. Areas with significant historical or cultural importance may suggest that new development reflect the massing, architectural style, and landscape design of surrounding development to integrate with the community and preserve the area's cultural heritage.

- Analyze what types of development might surround the site in the future. Such development could affect the location of the building, connection with transportation or other infrastructure, solar access, local microclimate, view corridors, and shared facilities such as parking or service access.

- Analyze existing air quality. This should be done by a qualified laboratory or service and includes an assessment of the existing air quality as well as an estimation of the effects of the proposed development on air quality in the area.

- Have the soil and groundwater tested for contamination. Contaminated soil or water could make the proposed project infeasible or affect building location and mitigation methods.

- Determine the presence of endangered species. These may include plants, insects, and animals.

Site and Building Concepts Using Sustainability

The early stages of project planning and site analysis offer many ways to help create a sustainable project. The following sustainability guidelines may affect project concepts.

Building Location

- Give preference to urban sites or other sites with existing infrastructure, to minimize disruption of undeveloped land and maximize efficient use of transportation and utility services.

- Encourage mixed-use development of residential, commercial, retail, and entertainment facilities, to give people the option of living near the buildings where they work and do much of their shopping and relaxation.

- Locate buildings near public transportation.

- Locate buildings in such a way as to minimize tree and vegetation clearing, take advantage of solar access, and minimize the detrimental effects of wind.

- Minimize solar shadows on adjacent properties with setbacks or low building heights.

- Locate buildings in such a way as to maximize desirable airflow patterns.

- Locate buildings in such a way as to use gravity sewer systems.

Building Size, Shape, and Design

- Minimize the building footprint by using multiple floors, when possible.

- Design the building dimensions to optimize material use and reduce waste.

- Consider using garden roofs or highly reflective roof coverings to reduce the heat island effect.

- Plan buildings to include bicycle storage and shower/changing facilities.

Site Disturbance

- Plan buildings and parking on previously disturbed areas.

- Position buildings along landscape contours and shallow slopes, to minimize earthwork and site clearing.

- Plan utility corridors along new road or walk construction or along previously disturbed areas on the site.

- Limit site disturbance to 40 ft (12 m) beyond the building perimeter, 5 ft (1.5 m) beyond primary roadway curbs and walks, and 25 ft (7.6 m) beyond constructed areas with permeable surfaces.

Site Development

- Minimize the site development area by providing all or some parking under the building.

- Develop a site plan to minimize road length, parking, and service areas. Consolidate pedestrian, automobile, and service paths whenever possible. Double load parking lots to share access lanes and minimize paving.

- Do not develop more than the minimum parking required by the local zoning ordinance.

- Reduce heat islands by providing shade or using high-albedo materials with a minimum reflectance of 0.3.

- Use open-grid paving or other pervious paving to reduce storm water runoff.

- Plan pedestrian surfaces using permeable materials such as loose aggregate, permeable concrete, wooden decks, or spaced paving stones.

- Use mechanical or natural treatment systems for storm water, such as constructed wetlands, vegetated filter strips, infiltration basins, or bioswales. A *bioswale* is a shallow grass-lined ditch or channel designed to detain storm runoff and remove sediments and other contaminates while allowing the water to seep into the ground.

- Design vegetative buffer areas around parking lots to mitigate runoff of water containing pollutants such as oil and sediments.

- Minimize site lighting, and prevent light from spilling onto adjacent properties or into the sky.

- If allowed by local and state regulations, consider using collected rainwater for supplemental irrigation. However, the annual rainfall must be enough to make this feasible. Also, areas with poor air quality may yield water not suitable for its intended purpose. Roofing materials must be carefully selected, and the costs of collection, storage, and filtration must be evaluated. Refer to Ch. 8 for more information on rainwater collection.

  If rainwater cannot be collected, an infiltration basin may be used. An *infiltration basin* is a closed depression in the earth from which water can escape only into the soil. Do not confuse this with a *catch basin*, which is an area that temporarily contains excessive runoff until it can flow at a controlled rate into the storm sewer system.

- Use native plant materials, and minimize the use of high-maintenance lawns. Good landscaping practices can improve the aesthetics of a site, reduce water runoff, and minimize erosion while minimizing the need for irrigation and providing habitats for animal and insect species.

LEGAL AND ECONOMIC INFLUENCES

In the United States, legal regulations and economic conditions have a great influence on how land is developed. For example, most commercial, for-profit land owners attempt to maximize their return on investment while working within the legal constraints of zoning ordinances and other types of building regulations. This practice may dictate the best economic uses of the property, how much square footage must be built, and even the overall architectural form of the structure. An architect must have an understanding of these influences and how they affect site development and building design.

Zoning

The most common form of legal constraint on land development is zoning. Although human settlements have been informally separated into areas of different uses for centuries, it was not until the first part of the twentieth century that zoning took on legal status. It was originally an attempt to improve the problems of the rapidly expanding cities: crowding, factories being built too close to housing, and tall buildings blocking light and air.

The first zoning ordinance was passed in 1916 in New York City and was the first attempt by a municipal government to control the use and location of buildings throughout a city. Zoning began as a way of regulating land use, but today it has grown into one means of implementing planning policy.

Zoning is the division of a city or other governmental unit into districts, and the regulation of the use of land and the location and bulk of buildings on property within those districts. Its legal basis is largely founded on the right of the state to protect the health, safety, and welfare of the public. Municipalities receive the power to zone through the states with enabling legislation.

Zoning primarily regulates the following things.

- the uses allowed on a parcel of land depending on the zoning district

- the area of the land that may be covered with buildings

- the bulk of the structures

- the distances the buildings must be set back from the property lines

- parking and loading space requirements

Other requirements, such as regulation of signs and bonuses for providing plazas and open space, may also be included. Although zoning is primarily used in cities, special types of zoning are sometimes used. These types may include rural zoning to separate agricultural uses from forestry or recreational use, flood plain zoning, airport zoning, and historic area zoning.

Uses are established with the zoning districts and are based on residential, commercial, and industrial occupancies with subdivisions within each of these. Residential zones may include, for example, single-family, low-density multifamily, and high-density multifamily dwellings. For each zoning district, a list of permissible uses is specified, with single-family zones being the most restrictive. Each zone may be used for the purposes listed for that zone and for any use listed in a more restrictive zone. For instance, a single-family house could be constructed within a dense business zone but probably would not be because of economic and aesthetic reasons.

The amount of land that can be covered is determined by the interrelationship of two zoning restrictions: floor area ratio and setbacks. *Floor area ratio* is the ratio of the gross floor area within a structure to the area of the lot on which the structure is situated. For example, if the floor area ratio is 1.0 and a lot is 75,000 ft^2 in area, the maximum permissible gross floor space is 75,000 ft^2. Within the constraints of setbacks and bulk planes, this 75,000 ft^2 of floor space may be configured in any number of ways.

Figure 2.9(a) shows a structure occupying only 50% of the ground area. If the floor area ratio (sometimes referred to as FAR) is 1.0, then a two-story building can be constructed.

Figures 2.9(b) and 2.9(c) illustrate two instances where the same floor area ratio can result in two different building forms. In Fig. 2.9(b), the building occupies only 25% ground area. If the FAR is 3.0, then a 12-story building can be erected. In Fig. 2.9(c), the building occupies 50% of the land, so only six stories can be built. In both cases, the building area is three times the land area.

Floor area ratios must always be developed in relation to setbacks. A *setback* is the minimum distance a building must be placed from a property line. Setback distances usually vary depending on which property line is involved. The distance from the property line facing the street or the primary front of the property is known as the *front setback*, usually the greatest setback distance. The distance from the back of the lot is the *rear setback*, and the distance from the side property line is known as the *side setback*. In the example of Fig. 2.9(a), for instance, setbacks might preclude covering 50% of the site, so in order to get the maximum floor area ratio, the building would have to be more than two stories.

In addition to affecting the use of floor area ratios, setbacks also have the effect of regulating the bulk of a building and how much space results between structures. Another common zoning tool is the bulk plane restriction. This sets up an imaginary inclined plane beginning at the lot line or the center of the street and sloping at a prescribed angle toward and over the lot. The building cannot extend into

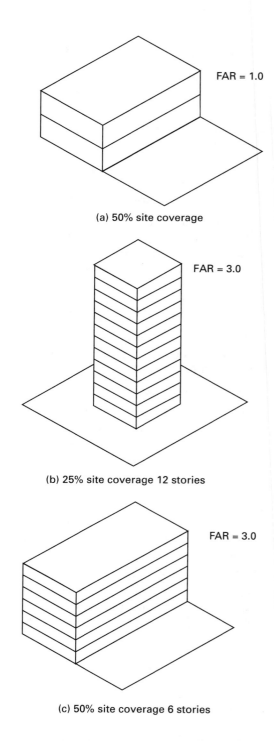

(a) 50% site coverage

(b) 25% site coverage 12 stories

(c) 50% site coverage 6 stories

Figure 2.9 Examples of Floor Area Ratios

this plane. The purpose is to ensure adequate light and air to neighboring properties and to the open space and streets around the land.

Sometimes, zoning ordinances will also place maximum limits on the number of stories of a building or the height in feet above grade level.

There are many instances when zoning restrictions create an undue hardship on a property owner or a zoning ordinance does not completely cover unusual conditions. For these cases, the property owner can apply for a *variance*, which is a deviation from the zoning regulations. Municipalities have a procedure by which owners can describe their situation and apply for a variance. A public hearing is a part of the process to allow nearby property owners or anyone interested to object to the application if they wish.

If a new zoning ordinance is being applied to existing development, there may be properties that contain nonconforming uses. These are allowed to remain unless the owner stops using the property in its original fashion or the property is demolished or destroyed by fire. Then, any new use must conform to the zoning requirements.

A zoning board (or planning commission) may also grant a conditional use permit, which allows a nonconforming use or other use in the zoning ordinance if the property owner meets certain restrictions. This is often done if the exception is in the public interest. For example, a zoning board may allow a temporary street fair in a location where it would normally be prohibited, or it might allow a church to violate a setback provision with the condition that other open space be provided for the community.

Refer to Ch. 4 for more information on zoning.

Easements and Rights-of-Way

An *easement* is the right of one party to use a portion of the land of another party in a particular way. It is a legal instrument and is normally recorded. There are many types of easements, one of the most common being a *utility easement*. This allows a utility company to install and maintain lines above or below the ground within the boundaries of the easement. Although the land belongs to the property owner, no permanent structures can be erected within the easement without permission from the party holding the easement.

Another type of easement is the *access easement*. If one parcel of land is not served by a public road and another parcel separates the first parcel from the street, an access easement may be granted, which allows the public and the owner of the inaccessible land the right to cross.

Other types of easements include *support easements* for the construction of common party walls between properties, *joint use easements* that allow two or more property owners to share a common feature such as a driveway, *scenic easements* that protect views and development in scenic areas, and *conservation easements* that limit land use in large areas.

Scenic and conservation easements are often used by public agencies to control land use without the need to purchase large tracts of property.

A *right-of-way* is the legal right of one party or the public to traverse land belonging to another. In its most common form, a right-of-way refers to the public land used for streets and sidewalks. The boundary of a right-of-way usually corresponds to the property line of adjacent property owners. In most cases, the street occupies only a portion of the right-of-way; the remainder is used for sidewalks, landscaping, and utilities. An access easement, as previously described, creates a private or public right-of-way.

Deed Restrictions

Deeds to property can contain provisions that restrict the use of the property by the buyer. These are called *restrictive covenants* and are legal and enforceable if they are reasonable and in the public interest. It is quite common for the developer of a large tract of land that is being subdivided to include restrictive covenants in the deeds. They may include such limitations as setbacks, minimum square footage of houses, the types of materials that can and cannot be used on the exterior, and similar provisions.

Because the covenants are in the deed, they are known to the potential buyer before purchase so the buyer can decide not to purchase if the covenants are not acceptable. Restrictive covenants are often used in residential subdivisions to maintain a desired uniformity of appearance, site development, and quality of construction. Most deed restrictions, however, are generally established for a certain period of years such as 10, 15, 20, or 30 years.

Land Values

As part of the overall economic analysis of a site for potential development (or adaptive reuse of an existing building), the cost of the property is vital in making a decision concerning site selection. In addition to land acquisition costs, there are costs of site improvements, building construction, appraisal, financing, professional fees, permits, and maintenance of the completed structure. If all of these cannot be paid off in a reasonable amount of time and yield a profit to the owner or developer, the site is probably a poor economic choice.

Land values are generally based on location, potential profit-making use, and local market conditions, which includes demand for the land. Location includes such things as a potential surrounding market area, population density in the region, special features of the site (such as being waterfront property), and proximity to transportation and utilities, which are especially important to residential and industrial development. Land values are based on the concept of "highest and best use," which means that the property is to be used and developed in such a way as to yield the highest return on investment. Property that is not used to this capacity is said to be underdeveloped.

There are three basic ways land is valued. A fairly common technique is the *market approach*. The surrounding neighborhood or region is investigated to find properties that have recently sold or are on the market that are similar to the property being valued. Except for adjustments to reflect the unique nature of the property, the property is assumed to have the same value as that of the similar properties. For example, if three nearby house lots in a subdivision recently sold for around $40,000 and they were all about the same size, then a fourth lot of similar size would also be valued at about $40,000. Quite often, the value is based on a unit quantity that can more easily be applied to another property that is not exactly the same. Land is commonly assigned a value per square foot or per acre, and buildings are often valued at a cost per square foot. The assumed value of another property can then be determined simply by multiplying the current market value per square foot times the area of the property being evaluated.

The second method is the *income approach*. Here, the basis is the potential the property has to yield a profit (income). The potential income is estimated (allowing for vacancies and credit losses), and then various expenses such as taxes, insurance, and maintenance are deducted. Because potential income is usually figured on a yearly basis, this amount must be capitalized to estimate the current, total value of the property.

The third method is the *cost approach*. With this method, the value of the land is estimated at its highest and best use. Then, the cost to replace the building or add improvements is calculated. The estimated accrued depreciation is figured and subtracted from the replacement cost or cost of the improvements. This adjusted amount is then added to the land value to give the total value of the property.

Tax Structure

The taxes to which a developer is subject can influence whether a project is undertaken and how the site is developed. Although the subject is very complicated, taxes become an ongoing operating cost of a development and can be estimated fairly easily if one knows the tax rate and what it is based on. Many tax rates are based on a mill levy on the assessed valuation of a piece of property. A mill is one-thousandth of a dollar, or one-tenth of a cent. The assessed valuation is a percentage of the actual value of the property, and the percentage is set by the taxing authority.

Example 2.2

The assessed valuation of developed property is based on 19% of actual value, and the mill levy is 0.04931. If a developed piece of property is estimated to have an actual valuation of $150,000, what will the yearly tax be?

The assessed value is

$$(0.19)(\$150,000) = \$28,500$$

The yearly tax will be

$$(0.04931)(\$28,500) = \$1405$$

Taxing authorities may offer various types of tax incentives to developers as a way of implementing public policy. For instance, tax credits may be given for renovating historic structures as a way of encouraging historic preservation. New business may be encouraged to move to a city by reduction or elimination of taxes for a certain time period. In any case, tax incentives may turn an otherwise uneconomical project into a viable one.

Life-Cycle Cost Analysis

A *life-cycle cost analysis* (LCC) is used to evaluate the economic performance of a material or building system over the service life of the material or system. The LCC includes all the costs associated with purchasing, installing, maintaining, and disposing of an item from the time the item is installed in a building through the duration of the LCC study period. All costs during the study period are discounted to convert future costs to their equivalent present values and account for the time value of money.

Not to be confused with the LCC is the *life-cycle assessment analysis* (LCA). The LCA of a material evaluates the environmental impacts from initial raw material extraction to final recycling, reuse, or disposal. It includes raw material extraction, material processing, the manufacture of intermediate materials, fabrication, installation in the building, operation, maintenance, and final disposal or reuse.

Refer to Ch. 8 for a detailed discussion of both life-cycle cost analysis and life-cycle assessment.

Public Works Financing

There are several methods by which government agencies can finance public works projects. These include general sales and property taxes, special sales taxes, general obligation bonds, revenue bonds (or rate-supported bonds), public enterprise revenue bonds, tax-increment financing, development impact fees, subdivision exactions, and special district assessments. These methods have different requirements and are used for different purposes.

General Sales Taxes and Property Taxes

A *general tax* is any tax imposed for general governmental purposes. Property taxes are an *ad valorem tax*, that is, a tax based on the value of property being taxed. The money collected by a municipality or other jurisdiction is placed in a general fund and used as required by that jurisdiction. Although general taxes may be used to fund public works, they are typically used to provide ongoing operation and maintenance of existing facilities and normal capital improvements, such as replacing curbs and gutters or remodeling schools. Major projects are typically funded with other methods as described in the following sections.

Depending on the local or state jurisdiction, general taxes or increases to general taxes may be limited or may require a vote of the general population. However, an increase in property taxes usually occurs when the value of property is increased by the local jurisdiction's tax assessment office, even if the rate of taxation is unchanged.

Special Sales Taxes

A *special tax* is any tax imposed for a specific purpose or by a single-purpose authority. Special sales taxes require a majority vote of the people in the district. An example this type of tax is one to fund a major transportation project.

General Obligation Bonds

General obligation bonds are issued by a city or state and backed by general tax revenue and the issuer's credit. They are used to finance the acquisition or construction of specific public capital facilities and to purchase real property. The jurisdiction issuing the bond is authorized to levy a property tax at the rate necessary to repay the principal and interest of the bonds, usually over a period of 10 to 30 years. Each general obligation bond measure requires approval of the voters. Examples of projects funded with general obligation bonds include schools, museums, and libraries. Because all taxpayers in the jurisdiction issuing the bonds must contribute a property tax to pay off the bonds, a voter majority is required.

Revenue Bonds or Rate-Supported Bonds

Revenue bonds (often called *rate-supported bonds*) are similar to general obligation bonds in that a local government issues them to pay for a facility or improvement. However, these bonds are backed by the revenue, or rates, from customers using the services that the bond funding paid for. In most cases rates increase to pay for retirement of the bonds. City water and sewer facilities often use this method of financing.

Public Enterprise Revenue Bonds

Public enterprise revenue bonds are issued by cities or counties to finance facilities for revenue-producing public enterprises. The bonds are paid off from revenues generated by the facility through the charges they impose. Airports, parking garages, and hospitals are examples of facilities that may use this method of financing.

Tax-Increment Financing

A city can use *tax-increment financing* to pay for improvements based on increased taxes due to the increased value of property. A city creates a special district and makes public improvements within that district that will generate private development. The assessed value of the property within the district is determined, and taxes based on that value are frozen for a defined period of time set forth in the development plan. Bonds are issued at the beginning of the redevelopment. Each taxing jurisdiction continues to receive its share of the taxes based on the original assessed valuation. At the end of the development period, the assessed valuation increases due to the new development, and the increased taxes (the tax increment) go into a special fund created to retire bonds issued to originate the development. Tax-increment financing is used for purchasing land, planning, and public works improvements to encourage private development. It does not require a vote by the people in the district.

Development Impact Fees

Development impact fees are costs charged to developers for off-site infrastructure improvements made necessary by new development. These fees are a way to make developers, rather than existing residents, responsible for the costs necessitated by the development. Impact fees may be made in addition to other exactions, such as hookup fees for utility service, and can be used for projects such as street improvements or construction of wastewater treatment plants. Because there is often the question of how the fee is calculated and who really benefits from the new public facilities, impact fees can be controversial.

Subdivision Exactions

Subdivision exactions are similar to development fees in that they put a burden on the developer, but in this case the exaction is not used to fund construction. Rather, subdivision exactions are requirements that developers either dedicate some land for public use or contribute cash for the purchase of land and facilities made necessary by local governments.

Special District Assessments

There are several variations of *special district assessments* (often called *business improvement districts* (BIDs) or *benefit assessments*). These fees are used to fund public space improvements, like parks or streetscapes, to enhance an area's appeal and, indirectly, its property values. A special district is established to include the properties that will benefit from the proposed improvements. If a majority of the property owners in the area agree to the arrangement, then all owners within the district's boundaries are required to contribute. Taxes are assessed on those property owners in the district who would benefit from the improvements. This type of funding is usually, but not always, used to improve or maintain existing facilities. It is not intended to encourage private development.

EVALUATING EXISTING STRUCTURES

In many cases, the architect is working on a project not to construct a new building on a piece of land, but to renovate or re-use an existing structure. In these situations, the architect must evaluate the existing structure to see if it is appropriate for the intended use. The evaluation process involves surveying the structure, documenting the survey, researching applicable regulations, and evaluating the information. This process usually involves existing buildings with no historic value, but may include historic structures, which require additional work on the part of the design professional.

The amount of work and detail included in the survey and documentation will vary depending on the basic information needed to test the project's feasibility. It may be that a quick, cursory survey of the structure's size and condition is enough to confirm that the project is not feasible within the budget and that no further survey work should be done. If the initial survey suggests that the project may work, a more extensive survey and evaluation may be undertaken. Once the evaluation shows that the structure is workable for the proposed use, yet another, more detailed survey may be scheduled, and documentation may be created to provide the basis for detailed design work and construction documents.

Surveying Existing Buildings

An existing building survey must include several components. In most cases, the survey requires laborious field measurements and site-survey techniques, unless accurate as-built drawings are available. An existing building survey should include the following.

- Site features, including parking, service access, pedestrian access, adjacent properties, microclimate, and amenities like views and water features.

- Size and configuration of the structure, including overall size and shape, height, location of columns and bearing walls, beams, and other major structural components. Also, the location of partitions, toilets, mechanical rooms, and other service areas.

- Structure, including the type, load capacity, and condition. The condition of the foundation and primary structural frame are most important because these support everything else, and correcting or reinforcing them is expensive. A structural engineering

consultant is usually needed for this portion of the survey.

- Roof, including the type, condition, and expected remaining life. Are there any signs of water damage or leaking?

- Exterior envelope, including the type and condition. Are the windows in good condition? What type of existing insulation does it have and what R-value does it provide?

- Mechanical system, including the type of heating and cooling, the capacity of the central plant, and the condition of the distribution system. A mechanical engineering consultant is usually needed for this portion of the survey.

- Plumbing, including the capacity of service to the building, sewer capacity, condition of pipes and fixtures, and number of fixtures. A mechanical engineering consultant is usually needed for this portion of the survey.

- Electrical, including the capacity of service to the building, condition of primary and secondary service, condition of wiring and devices, and condition of lighting and other electrical components. An electrical engineering consultant is usually needed for this portion of the survey.

- Fire protection, including the condition of the system, pipe sizing, and spacing of heads. A mechanical engineering or fire-protection consultant may be needed for this portion of the survey.

- Major equipment, if applicable. This component depends on the building type and may include such items as refrigeration equipment, commercial food service equipment, laboratory equipment, and the like.

- Finishes, including the condition and expected life of major surface finishes.

- Condition of the structure for accessibility. Also, the condition of the egress system and fire-rated elements.

Finally, if the building is a designated historic structure or has historic value, additional issues need to be investigated. These are discussed in the next section of this chapter.

Although not part of the actual building survey, the architect must ask the client about cost and time constraints. This is a vital part of the evaluation process that will take place later. In some cases, the client may not have a budget and may want the architect to develop an estimate of the costs involved in adapting an existing building to a new use.

Documenting Building Surveys

The building survey is typically documented in several ways. These include manually drafted drawings, CAD drawings, notes, formal reports, photographs, and videos. If architectural drawings and specifications of the structure exist, the architect should obtain these and verify them against the actual structure. The architect should also obtain any existing site surveys, soils investigations, or other documentation.

Drawings, whether manually drafted or CAD generated, should include the building structure and exterior walls as well as the location of interior partitions, doors, equipment, woodwork, plumbing fixtures, and other pertinent items. The accuracy of the survey and the drawings depends on the structure's size and complexity, the time and equipment devoted to field measurements, and the requirements of the new use of the building. Normally, measurement accuracy to within $1/4$ in is more than adequate, and $1/2$ in accuracy may even be sufficient.

The documentation should also include elevations of floors and other major features. Drawings of some elevations may also be required. The locations of mechanical and electrical equipment to remain should also be noted as required. Elements that are to be removed should be highlighted.

Finally, the project should be documented with photographs, videos, or both.

Methods of Field Measuring and Recording

Traditionally, collecting information on the size and configuration of an existing building has required the architect to visit the site and make sketches and measurements using a tape measure and traditional surveying equipment. Drawings are then produced from the measurements taken on site. This method is labor intensive and susceptible to human error as well as errors introduced by measurement tools. However, hand measuring can be a useful, low-cost method to use when measuring buildings of moderate size and complexity. Hand measuring is also well suited for recording small details that cannot be seen by instruments using other techniques.

The use of simple tape measures has recently been augmented by more precise instruments. Low-cost, line-of-sight sonic devices can be used by one person and give reasonable accuracy for many uses. However, their range is limited and they cannot precisely differentiate between closely spaced elements.

A more accurate procedure is *electromagnetic distance measurement* (EDM). This process uses a laser-based instrument with an onboard computer to measure the distance, horizontal angle, and vertical angle of the instrument's laser beam to a reflective prism target. These instruments are accurate to $\pm 1/64$ in at 1600 ft (± 0.5 at 500 m). As with hand measuring, this method requires a knowledgeable operator to select the points to be measured. Two people are usually required to operate this instrument.

A similar technique is *reflectorless electromagnetic distance measurement* (REDM). The device used in this process does not require the use of a prism reflector, but instead relies on the return signal bounced from the object being measured. The accuracy is less precise: $\pm 1/8$ in at 100 ft (± 3 at 30 m). The accuracy of REDM is affected by the obliqueness of the laser beam on the targeted point, the distance from the instrument to the targeted point, and the reflective quality and texture of the targeted point.

Several image-based techniques, other than standard photography, are available to assist in the accurate surveying of existing structures. These include rectified photography, orthophotography, photogrammetry, and laser scanning.

Rectified Photography

Rectified photography uses large-format, film-based view cameras (the type typically used for high-quality architectural photography) to photograph façades. The camera's focal plane is set parallel to the façade and gives a flat image with no perspective distortion. Dimensions can be scaled off of the image, but to improve accuracy the building plane should be relatively flat. In addition to providing the ability to scale building elements not readily accessible to hand measuring, the photograph provides an accurate image of the building, as any photograph would.

Orthophotography

Orthophotography is similar to rectified photography except that it relies on digital photography and correction of optical distortion through computer software.

Photogrammetry

Photogrammetry is the surveying of objects or spaces through the use of photography and associated software. Common techniques for the application of this method are stereophotogrammetry and convergent photogrammetry.

Stereophotogrammetry uses two overlapping photographs in a computer program to produce a digital stereo image. The image can then be used to extract information to make a three-dimensional drawing. In addition to producing accurate three-dimensional drawings, this technique also produces a photographic record. It does require specialized equipment and computer software, as well as trained technicians to do the work.

Convergent photogrammetry uses multiple, oblique photographic images of an object taken at different angles. Measurements and three-dimensional models are derived by using software that traces the multiple overlapping photographs taken from the different angles. This field measuring technique requires that reference points be established by standard surveying techniques or by measuring distances between the reference points to establish a correctly scaled coordinate system that the software can use. Although relatively inexpensive, convergent photogrammetry is slower than laser scanning. It has an accuracy of about ±0.05%.

Laser Scanning

Laser scanning uses medium-range pulsing laser beams, which are systematically sweep over an object or space to obtain three-dimensional coordinates of points on the surface of the object or space being scanned. The resulting image is a "point cloud" forming a 3-D image. From this image, plans, elevations, sections, and three-dimensional models are developed by computer software. The laser scans from one or more points, depending on the exact system being used. For multiple room interiors, the images can be stitched together to give an overall image of an entire building. Unlike photogrammetry, no surveyed reference points are required; all the information can be gathered from a single point rather than from multiple photographs. Laser scanning has an accuracy ranging from ±0.05% to ±0.01% or better.

Researching Applicable Regulations

Just as with new construction, the architect must obtain all the relevant regulations and codes that apply to the project. This includes zoning restrictions, easements, deed restrictions, covenants, historic preservation rules, energy conservation codes, and local agency regulations, as well as which building codes apply. The architect should determine from existing drawings or from the local building official the construction type of the building and its designated occupancy.

Evaluating Existing Structures

Evaluating the adequacy of an existing structure for a new use involves answering the following basic questions.

- Does the site work for the new use or can it be adapted for the new use within the constraints of time and budget?

- Is the size and configuration of the existing structure adaptable for the new use within the constraints of time and budget?

- Is the appearance and character of the structure consistent with the client's design goals and desired image?

- How much work and cost are required to repair, renovate, modify, and add to the structure for the new use? Will seismic renovation be required? The

analysis should first include the foundation and primary structural elements, as these are the most expensive to modify and are always required for any other work. Additions or modifications to the secondary structural elements are less costly and easier to accomplish.

- How much work and cost are required to repair, renovate, modify, and add to the mechanical, plumbing, electrical, and life safety systems to make the building work for the new use? If the building is not fully sprinklered, is the cost to add sprinklers justified based on code requirement trade-offs and possible lower insurance rates?

- Does the new occupancy work within the constraints of the existing building's construction type and area? If the maximum allowable area for the new occupancy is exceeded, the building may need to be separated into compartments with firewalls. This may prove to be economically unfeasible. Refer to Ch. 7 for a discussion of maximum allowable area and height based on occupancy and building type.

- What additional work is required to bring the structure in compliance with current applicable codes and regulations?

- How much of the existing structure must be modified to conform to code requirements? Can this be done within the constraints of time and budget?

- If a budget is not already established, how much will the minimum required amount of renovation cost? How much will the desired amount of work cost? How long might the project take to complete?

If extensive work and cost are required, a detailed cost analysis should be performed to see if the project is economically feasible. Even an expensive and extensive remodeling may be less costly than new construction, or the cost may be justified if the return on investment meets the client's needs. In addition, during this cost analysis the client's true needs must be separated from their wish list of features.

EVALUATING HISTORIC STRUCTURES

Planning the reuse of a historic structure presents unique opportunities and challenges. Depending on its age, a historic building may use structural systems and construction materials that are difficult to evaluate based on modern needs and building codes. The Historic Preservation Service of the National Park Service has developed a wealth of information and regulations pertaining to national historic landmarks as well as historic preservation in general. Much of this information can be found on their website.

Defining the Scope of the Problem

The first determination the architect must make is whether the structure is a designated historic landmark or simply an old building that the client would like to reuse while maintaining its historic character. If the structure is a national historic landmark or has similar landmark status on the state or local level, specific requirements will influence the kind of rehabilitation work allowed. In addition, if the owner wants to receive federal tax credits, the rehabilitation must qualify as a Certified Rehabilitation. In this case, the Secretary of the Interior's Standards for Rehabilitation (described in the next section) must be met. Requirements for national historic properties can be found by contacting the National Park Service. If the property is designated as a state or local historic landmark, the state historic preservation officer should be contacted.

Regardless of whether or not the project falls under the scope of federal, state, or local regulations, the architect, with the client, should determine which of four treatment approaches will be undertaken. If the building is a designated landmark, the state preservation officer and National Park Service should also be consulted. The four treatments, listed in hierarchical order from most historically accurate to least, include preservation, rehabilitation, restoration, and reconstruction.

Preservation attempts to retain all historic fabric through conservation, maintenance, and repair. It reflects the building's continuum over time and the respectful changes and alterations that are made.

Rehabilitation emphasizes the retention and repair of historic materials, but gives more latitude to replacement because it assumes the property is more deteriorated prior to work. Both preservation and rehabilitation focus attention on the preservation of those materials, features, finishes, spaces, and spatial relationships that give a property its historic character.

Restoration focuses on the retention of materials from the most significant time in a property's history, while permitting the removal of materials from other periods.

Reconstruction is the least historically accurate and allows the opportunity to re-create a non-surviving site, landscape, building, structure, or object in all new materials.

Specific standards and guidelines for each of these four treatments are outlined in detail and are available from the Historic Preservation Service office or at the National Park Service website.

Defining Regulatory Requirements

As codified in 36 CFR 67 for use in the Federal Historic Preservation Tax Incentives program, the Historic Preservation Service of the National Park Service has established ten general standards to guide historic preservation. These are often referred to as the Secretary of the Interior's Standards for Rehabilitation. They are to be applied to specific *rehabilitation* projects in a reasonable manner, taking into consideration economic and technical feasibility. When federal investment tax credits are involved, these standards take precedence over local requirements.

1. A property shall be used for its historic purpose or be placed in a new use that requires minimal change to the defining characteristics of the building and its site and environment.

2. The historic character of a property shall be retained and preserved. The removal of historic materials or alteration of features and spaces that characterize a property shall be avoided.

3. Each property shall be recognized as a physical record of its time, place, and use. Changes that create a false sense of historical development, such as adding conjectural features or architectural elements from other buildings, shall not be undertaken.

4. Most properties change over time; those changes that have acquired historic significance in their own right shall be retained and preserved.

5. Distinctive features, finishes, and construction techniques or examples of craftsmanship that characterize a property shall be preserved.

6. Deteriorated historic features shall be repaired rather than replaced. Where the severity of deterioration requires replacement of a distinctive feature, the new feature shall match the old in design, color, texture, and other visual qualities and, where possible, materials. Replacement of missing features shall be substantiated by documentary, physical, or pictorial evidence.

7. Chemical or physical treatments, such as sandblasting, that cause damage to historic materials shall not be used. The surface cleaning of structures, if appropriate, shall be undertaken using the gentlest means possible.

8. Significant archeological resources affected by a project shall be protected and preserved. If such resources must be disturbed, mitigation measures shall be undertaken.

9. New additions, exterior alterations, or related new construction shall not destroy historic materials that characterize the property. The new work shall be differentiated from the old and shall be compatible with the massing, size, scale, and architectural features to

protect the historic integrity of the property and its environment.

10. New additions and adjacent or related new construction shall be undertaken in such a manner that if removed in the future, the essential form and integrity of the historic property and its environment would be unimpaired.

These guidelines are widely used at the federal level, as well as by states and local historic district and planning commissions. However, the architect must research any other specific regulations that may apply.

Surveying the Historic Structure

In addition to the survey components listed in the previous section, additional work is required. The structural survey must include an assessment of settlement, deflection of beams, and structural members damaged in previous renovations or for mechanical and electrical services. The physical survey should determine if original or historic elements have been removed or altered, and if so, what their original appearance was.

The architect should identify the aspects of the building that define its historic character and set them in a list of priorities. These characteristics include the overall form of the building, its materials, spaces, and workmanship, and other notable features that distinguish it from other buildings. A physical survey of the original appearance of the structure and its current condition may call for the services of a restoration specialist to perform tests and conduct other investigations.

ARCHITECTURAL PRACTICE AND SERVICES DURING PRE-DESIGN

One of the first, and most important, decisions the architect must make during pre-design is whether or not to accept a project offered by a potential client. The factors that are involved in this decision include the current workload of the architect's office, the match between the project and the types of work the architect's office is qualified to do or prefers to do, the potential feasibility of the project, the owner's budget for both the project and for fees, and the reliability and reputation of the client.

In many cases, the amount of work the client requests exceeds the budget for either construction or professional fees, or both. In this case, the architect must either decline to accept the job, accept a lower profit margin, or negotiate with the owner to reduce the scope of the project or the scope of the architect's services. If the owner is unknown to the architect, the architect should investigate the client, including the client's ability to fund the project, their past experience with building projects, and their experience with working with design professionals.

If the architect decides to accept the job, the architect must first negotiate an agreement with the owner that determines the scope of the work, the fees required, and other aspects of the contract. Refer to Ch. 25 for more information on owner-architect agreements. This agreement may also involve developing a preliminary design and construction schedule to help determine the project's feasibility, as well as the anticipated fees required by the architect.

If another architect or design professional is, or may be, involved with the project, the architect must determine if there is any formal or informal agreement between the owner and the other design professional. The architect cannot accept work from the owner unless the other architect or design professional has severed their relationship with the owner.

Coordination with Regulatory Agencies

If the building project requires approval from planning agencies or other governmental bodies before detailed design can begin, the architect is often the professional responsible for guiding the owner's project through the approval process. The work involved may include developing preliminary site plans and land-use proposals, sketching preliminary building designs, and meeting with governmental agencies and neighborhood groups. This work, of course, requires additional fees beyond the normal fee for building design, so the architect must estimate the time and costs required for the work.

If the building presents unusual design challenges and requires zoning variances or unusual building techniques or materials, the architect will have to work with building officials or zoning regulators early in the pre-design phase to obtain advice and approval of any deviation from zoning requirements, or to use alternate means and methods of construction as allowed by building codes.

Consultant Coordination

The architect should involve the consultants in the project as early as possible. Their advice and expertise is vital to determining the scope of the building project (especially if it involves the renovation of an existing building), developing broad conceptual approaches to designing the building, and understanding the concerns of the client and other design professionals working on the project.

One of the most important tasks for the architect during pre-design is the assembly and coordination of the various consultants on the project. These may include structural, mechanical, and electrical engineers at a minimum. Additional consultants may include soils engineers, civil engineers, fire protection engineers, historic preservation specialists, security consultants, interior designers, and audio-visual consultants. The expected services of each consultant must be determined with the advice of the consultant and the approval of the client. The involvement of the client is mandatory if the owner contracts directly with the consultant for services.

The contractual arrangement between the consultant and the architect or owner must also be determined. If the owner contracts directly with the consultant, the architect avoids any problems with contract provisions and payment, but may lose some ability to direct the consultant. If the architect writes an agreement directly with the consultant and is responsible for paying the consultant, the architect has more control but may encounter problems with paying the consultant's fees if there is delayed payment from the client.

Once the consultants are retained, the architect should inform the appropriate consultants about the applicable code requirements. The architect is also responsible for informing the consultants of any design decisions that may have code implications. Although the architect is responsible for ensuring that the drawings and specifications conform to the applicable codes, AIA document C141, the Architect-Consultant Agreement, states that the consultant is responsible for code compliance regarding their area of work in the same way the architect is responsible to the owner under the AIA B141, Owner-Architect Agreement. By signing their drawings, the engineering consultants become responsible for compliance with applicable codes and regulations.

The AIA C141 document also states that each consultant is responsible for the accurate production of the consultant's own drawings and specifications. Further, the consultant is responsible for checking their own various documents for consistency. However, the architect is the prime consultant and is liable to the owner for the consultant's work.

Refer to Ch. 28 for more information on project and practice management, which is also tested in the Pre-Design division. Also refer to Chs. 29 and 30 for information on building regulations.

DEFINITIONS

Following are some of the many definitions that may appear in questions in the Pre-Design division.

Abatement: a reduction in the price of a property due to the discovery of some problem that tends to decrease the property's value

Accessory building: a building whose function is secondary to that of the main structure

Amenities: desirable features of a building or near a building that have the effect of increasing the property's value

Amortization: the payment of a loan over the life of the loan using equal payments at equal intervals. Each payment provides for a portion to be applied to the principal and the remainder to be applied to the interest.

Anchor tenant: a major tenant in shopping mall, such as a department store, that in theory serves to attract shoppers to the mall to the benefit of other, smaller stores. See also *Satellite tenant*.

Appraisal: an estimation of a property's value made by a qualified appraiser

Aquifer: a natural, underground reservoir from which wells draw water

Assessed value: the value given to a piece of property by a local jurisdiction, to be used to assess taxes on the property. The assessed value is a percentage of the actual value, that is, the value that the property would command on the open market.

Bedroom community: a region or small town that contains mainly housing and offers few employment opportunities

Blighted area: an area of a city that has been determined to contain buildings and infrastructure that are in a state of decay and in need of improvement

Boilerplate: a standard portion (generally a paragraph or more) of a written document, such as a contract or architectural specification, that appears in all similar documents

Buffer zone: a piece of land used to separate two incompatible uses

Capital expenditure: an amount of money used to make physical improvements to a property to enhance the property's value over an extended period of time

Cash flow: the amount of money that is net income from a property after expenses are paid

CC&Rs: abbreviation for "covenants, conditions, and restrictions," which are all the rules that apply to a property owner in a subdivision, condominium, or cooperative housing facility

Cluster housing: a particular type of housing development in which the houses or apartments are placed close to each other and have access to nearby common open spaces

Common area: a portion of a building or development that is available for the use of all the tenants or unit owners. Typically, common areas are owned by the property owners in the development or homeowners' association, and property owners subsequently pay the maintenance fees.

Conditional use permit (CUP): a permit given by a city or other zoning jurisdiction for a proposed use that would otherwise not be allowed in a particular zoning district. The conditional use permit provides the zoning jurisdiction with the means to impose special conditions on the proposed development, to ensure that the development will not adversely affect the surrounding neighborhood or the public safety and welfare.

Condominium: a development in which residents own their own living units but share common areas, which are maintained by the condominium corporation

Conveyance: the act of transferring an interest in a property to another person, or the document written to formalize such a transfer

Cooperative (or Co-op): a type of land ownership where the residents of individual units own an interest in the corporation that owns the entire property. Unlike the residents of a condominium, the residents of a cooperative do not own their own units directly.

Cul-de-sac: a dead-end street that has only one way in and often features a large circular turn-around space at the end

Dedication: the donation of a parcel of land by a developer for public use, such as for a park or school

Demising wall: see *Party wall*

Despoil: to remove items of value from a site

Development rights: the legal ability of a developer to develop a parcel of land

Downzoning: a change in zoning resulting in a decrease of allowable density

Easement: a portion of land of one ownership that another owner or a governmental agency has the right to use for a specific purpose

Eminent domain: the right of a governmental jurisdiction to take ownership of private property for the public good while paying fair market value compensation to the owner

Encroachment: an intrusion onto one property by the improvement to an adjoining property

Equity: the amount of money an owner of a property keeps after selling the property and paying off any mortgages; that is, the difference between the fair market value of a property and the amount of debt on the property

Fair market value (or Market value): the value of a piece of property that a buyer would pay a seller in a free transaction for the property

Fixture: an item that is attached to a building and is typically included in the sale of the building

Ground lease: a long-term lease of a property that allows the tenant to use and improve the land, but that reverts to the owner at the end of the lease

Height zoning: restrictions on the heights of buildings and structures established by local laws

Improvement ratio: the ratio of the value of improvements on a property to the value of the property alone

Inverse condemnation: a remedy by a court for a private land owner whose land has been taken away by a governmental body. See also *Eminent domain*.

Landlocked: descriptive of a parcel of land that does not border any public road

Land sale leaseback: a legal arrangement in which the owner of a property sells the property to someone else but then immediately leases it from the purchaser

Lien waiver: a document that gives up a person's right to claim a lien against property

Market value: see *Fair market value*

Mechanic's and materialman's lien: a claim placed against a property's deed by someone who provided work or materials to improve the property but was not paid for the work. Typically just called a *Lien*.

Minimum property standards: minimum standards for residential building required by the Federal Housing Administration for construction or for underwriting a mortgage

Net leasable area: the area of a building that is available for rent, which does not include common areas, structure, stairs, and the like

Occupancy permit: a document, issued by a city's building department, giving permission for a building to be occupied. More commonly called the *Certificate of occupancy*. The occupancy permit is part of the building permit process, and its cost is included in the building permit fee paid by the contractor.

Pad site: a separate location for development of retail space near (but not in) a shopping center

Party wall: the shared wall between two leased spaces or between two residential units. Often called a *Demising wall*.

Pro-forma: a financial projection for a development project meant to determine if the project is feasible, given estimates on potential income and the cost of developing the project

Restriction: a limit on how the owner of a property or building can use or improve the property. Often called a *Restrictive covenant*, it is usually contained in the deed to the property.

Riparian: related to a body of water

Riparian rights: the rights of a landowner to use or control all or a portion of the water in a body of water bordering his or her property

Satellite tenant: a minor or smaller tenant in a shopping center. See also *Anchor tenant*.

Special use permit: an exemption from zoning regulations given to a jurisdiction

Spot zoning: the application of specific zoning regulations to specific properties when nearby land is under different zoning

Underimproved land: property that is not producing the maximum income it is capable of producing given its size, zoning, and so on

Usury: the illegal practice of charging exorbitant interest rates on a loan

Variance: permission granted by a local jurisdiction to deviate from the literal provisions of a zoning ordinance where strict adherence would cause undue hardship because of conditions or circumstances unique to an individual property

Wetlands: land that has development restrictions placed on it because it is commonly flooded and may be environmentally sensitive

Zero lot line: part of a zoning regulation's setback requirements that allows a building to be constructed up to the property line with no setback

Zoning by law: the set of zoning regulations established by a local jurisdiction that regulates certain building practices within the jurisdiction

SAMPLE QUESTIONS

1. A portion of a recreation area is shown. Which location would be best for the site of a restaurant and visitor's center?

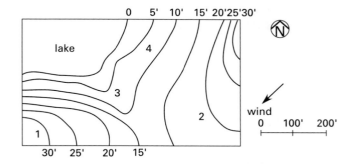

A. location 1
B. location 2
C. location 3
D. location 4

2. The owner of the lot shown wants to develop a building with the maximum allowable gross square footage.

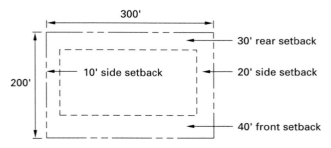

If the FAR is 2.0 and the owner builds to the setback lines, how high will the building be?

A. two stories
B. three stories
C. four stories
D. five stories

3. Much contemporary city planning in the United States is a result of

I.   the Columbian Exposition of 1893
II.   the Ordinance of 1785
III. L'Enfant's plan of Washington
IV.   Garnier's Cité Industrielle
V.   the Industrial Revolution

A. I, III, and V
B. I, II, and IV
C. I, II, IV, and V
D. all of the above

4. Which of the following would probably not be considered an element of a city's image?

    A. a group of houses

    B. a freeway

    C. a neighborhood bar

    D. an area with a high concentration of hospitals

5. Social contact and interaction in a picnic pavilion would be promoted most by

    A. making the dimensions of the pavilion small enough so that the anticipated number of users would cross into each other's "personal distance"

    B. designing benches around the support columns so people would have a place to sit and talk

    C. organizing the cooking and serving area distinct from the dining area and entrance

    D. providing a variety of informal spaces of different sizes, locations, and uses

6. If the contour interval on the map shown is 2 ft, what is the slope between points A and B?

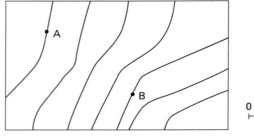

    A. 27%

    B. 53%

    C. 67%

    D. not enough information is given to answer

7. A speculative office building probably would not be built if the developer discovered that

    A. all of the catchment area was not served by arterial streets

    B. the site consisted of mostly sandy soil with a 6 ft top layer of expansive clay

    C. the vacancy rate of office space in the city was three times the national average

    D. the neighborhood community objected to the sight of parking lots

8. Which of the following causes the most foundation problems?

    A. extensive underground rock formations just below the surface

    B. a 5 ft water table

    C. expansive clay and organic soil

    D. all of the above

9. In planning a new building, an architect would have to look at regulations other than the zoning ordinance to find a requirement for which of the following?

I. the width of loading berths

II. the required size of utility easements

III. minimum lot size

IV. parking area size

V. permissible roof coverings

    A. I and IV

    B. I, II, and IV

    C. II, III, and V

    D. III, IV, and V

10. Which of the automobile entrances to the site shown is most desirable?

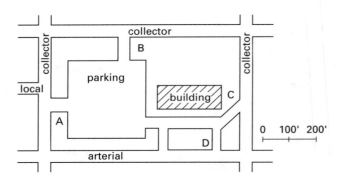

    A. entrance A

    B. entrance B

    C. entrance C

    D. entrance D

PRE-DESIGN—
BUILDING PROGRAMMING

Architectural programming is a process that seeks to analyze and define an architectural problem along with the requirements that must be met in its physical solution. It is a process of analysis, whereas design is a process of synthesis once the problem is clearly defined. The process can apply to an individual space or room, a building, or an entire complex of structures.

As building problems have become more complex and construction costs higher, determining the precise needs of the client has become more important than ever before. Programming helps the client understand the real problem and provides a sound basis for making design decisions. Sometimes it is provided by the architect as part of the entire range of design services, and other times it is performed as a separate service.

Thorough programming includes a wide range of information. In addition to stating the goals and objectives of the client, a program report contains a site analysis, aesthetic considerations, space needs, adjacency requirements, organizing concepts, outdoor space needs, codes, budgeting demands, and scheduling limitations. Refer to Chs. 2 and 4 for a review of site analysis, including soil and climatic investigation.

FUNCTIONAL REQUIREMENTS

Of all programming information, the amount of space and the relationships between spaces are two of the primary factors in determining building size and configuration. In addition to the primary function of a building in housing a specific use, there are always support spaces required that add to the overall size. These include such areas as mechanical rooms, toilet rooms, storage, and circulation space.

Determining Space and Volume Needs

Space needs are determined in a number of ways. Often, when programming is begun, the client will have a list of the required square footage for the new facility in addition to special height requirements. These may be based on the client's experience or on corporate space standards, or they may simply be a list of what currently exists. For example, space standards of a corporation may dictate that a senior manager have a 225 ft² (21 m²) office while a junior manager be allotted 150 ft² (14 m²).

These types of requirements may provide a valid basis for developing space needs, or they may be arbitrary and subject to review during programming. Where areas are not defined by one of these methods, space for a particular use is determined in one of three ways: by the number of people that must be accommodated, by an object or piece of equipment, or by a specific activity that has its own, clearly specified space needs.

People engaged in a particular activity most commonly define the space required. For example, a student sitting in a classroom needs about 15 ft² to 20 ft² (1.4 m² to 1.9 m²). This includes space for actually sitting in a chair in addition to the space required for circulating within the classroom and space for the teacher's desk and shelving. An office worker needs from 100 ft² to 250 ft² (9.3 m² to 23 m²), depending on whether the employee is housed in a private office or in part of an open office plan. This space requirement also includes room to circulate around the desk and may include space for visitors' chairs, personal files, and the like.

Through experience and detailed analysis, general guidelines for space requirements for various types of uses have been developed and are commonly used. A representative sample of these is shown in Table 3.1. Occasionally, space needs can be based on something other than the number of people but something that is directly related to the occupancy. For instance, preliminary planning of a hospital may be based on an area per bed, or library space can be estimated based on the number of books.

Table 3.1

Some Common Space Planning Guidelines

offices	100–250 ft²	net area per person	9.3–23 m²
restaurant dining	15–18 ft²	net area per seat	1.4–1.7 m²
restaurant kitchens	3.6–5 ft²	net area per seat	0.3–0.5 m²
hotel (1.5 persons/room)	550–600 ft²	gross area per room	51–56 m²
library reading room	20–35 ft²	net area per person	1.8–3.3 m²
book stacks	0.08 ft²	net area per bound volume	0.007 m²
theaters with fixed seats	7.5 ft²	net area per person	0.7 m²
assembly areas; movable seats	15 ft²	net area per person	1.4 m²
theater lobbies	30%	of seating area	
classrooms	15–20 ft²	net area per student	1.4–1.8 m²
stores	30–50 ft²	net area per person	2.8–4.6 m²

Whichever way the planning is done, the number of people that must be accommodated is determined and is multiplied by the area per person. However, this only includes the space needed for the specific activity, not the space required to connect several rooms or spaces or for support areas such as mechanical rooms. These must be added to the basic area requirements.

The second way space needs are determined is by the size of an object or piece of equipment. The size of a printing press, for example, partially determines the area of a press room. Automobile sizes determine the space needs for parking garages.

The third way space needs are defined is through a built-in set of rules or customs related to the activity itself. Sports facilities are examples of this method. A basketball court must be a certain size regardless of the number of spectators present, although the seating capacity would add to the total space required. A courtroom is an example of an activity where the procedures and customs of a process (the trial) dictate an arrangement of human activity and spacing of individual areas in the courtroom that only partially depend on the number of people.

Determining Total Building Area

The areas determined with one of the methods described previously result in the net area of a facility. As mentioned, these areas do not include general circulation space between rooms, mechanical rooms, stairways, elevator and mechanical shafts, electrical and telephone equipment rooms, wall and structural thicknesses, and other spaces not directly housing the primary activities of the building. Sometimes the net area is referred to as the *net assignable area* and the secondary spaces are referred to as the *unassigned areas*.

The sum of the net area and these ancillary areas gives the *gross building area*. The ratio of the two figures is called the *net-to-gross ratio* and is often referred to as the *efficiency* of the building. Efficiency depends on the type of occupancy and how well it is planned. A hospital that contains many small rooms and a great number of large corridors will have a much lower efficiency ratio than a factory where the majority of space is devoted to production areas and very little space is allowed for corridors and other secondary spaces.

Generally, net-to-gross ratios range from 60% to 80%, with some uses more or less efficient than these numbers. A list of some common efficiency ratios is shown in Table 3.2. In some cases, the client may dictate the net-to-gross ratio that must be met by the architect's design. This is usually the case where the efficiency is related to the amount of floor space that can be leased, such as in a retail mall or a speculative office building. Increasing the efficiency of a building is usually done by careful layout of the building's circulation plan. A corridor that serves rooms on both sides, for example, is much more efficient than one that only serves rooms on one side.

Table 3.2

Some Common Efficiency Ratios

offices	0.75-0.85
retail stores	0.75-0.90
restaurants	0.65-0.70
public libraries	0.75-0.80
museums	0.83-0.90
theaters	0.60-0.75
hospitals	0.50-0.65

Once the net area is determined and the appropriate efficiency ratio is established (or estimated), the gross area of the building is calculated by dividing the net area by the net-to-gross (efficiency) ratio.

Example 3.1

The net assignable area of a small office building has been programmed as 65,000 ft². If the efficiency ratio is estimated to be 73%, what gross area should be planned for?

$$\text{gross area} = \frac{65,000 \text{ ft}^2}{0.73}$$
$$= 89,000 \text{ ft}^2$$

The design portion of the ARE sometimes requires the examinee to provide various unassignable spaces within the context of the problem. The areas are not given. The examinee is expected to make a reasonable allowance for mechanical rooms, toilet rooms, elevators, and the like, if they are not specifically listed in the program. Table 3.3 lists some typical space requirements for projects of the size and type normally found in the design portion of the exam.

Determining Space Relationships

Spaces must not only be the correct size for the activity they support, but they also must be located near other spaces with which they share some functional relationship. Programming identifies these relationships and assigns a hierarchy of importance to them. The relationships are usually recorded in a matrix format or graphically as adjacency diagrams. See Fig. 3.1.

There are three basic types of adjacency needs: people, products, and information. Each type implies a different kind of physical design response. Two or more spaces may need to be physically adjacent or located very close to one another when people need face-to-face contact or when people move from one area to another as part of the building's use. For example, the entry to a theater, the lobby, and the theater space have a particular functional requirement for being arranged the way they are. Because of the normal flow of people, they must be located adjacent to one another. With other relationships, two spaces may simply need to have access to each other, but this can be accomplished with a corridor or through another intervening space rather than with direct adjacency.

Products, equipment, or other objects may move between spaces and require another type of adjacency. The spaces themselves may not have to be close to one another, but the movement of objects must be facilitated. Dumb waiters, pneumatic tubes, assembly lines, and other types of conveying systems can connect spaces of this type.

Finally, there may only be a requirement that people in different spaces exchange information. The adjacency may then be entirely electronic or be established through paper-moving systems. Although this is frequently the situation, personal, informal, human contact may be advantageous for other reasons.

Table 3.3

Space Requirements for Estimating Non-Assignable Areas

mechanical rooms, total	5–9% of gross building area
heating, boiler rooms	3–5% of gross building area
heating, forced air	4–8% of gross building area
fan rooms	3–7% of gross building area
vertical duct space	3–4 ft² per 1000 ft² of floor space available (0.35 m² per 100 m²)
toilets	50 ft² (4.6 m²) per water closet
water closets	1 per 15 people up to 55; 1 per 40 people over 55
urinals	Substitute one for each water closet, but total water closets cannot be reduced less than ²⁄₃ of the number required
lavatories	1 per 15 people for offices and public buildings up to 60 people
	1 per 100 people for public assembly use
hydraulic elevator, 2000 lbm (1000 kg)	7 ft 4 in wide by 6 ft 0 in deep (2235 by 1830)
elevator lobby space	6 ft 0 in deep (1830)
main corridors	5–7 ft (1500-2100)
exit corridors	4 ft 0 in; 44 in minimum by code (1220; 1118)
monumental stairs	5–8 ft (1500–2400)
exit stairs	4 ft 0 in, 44 in minimum by code (1220; 1118)

The programmer analyzes various types of adjacency requirements and verifies them with the client. Since it is seldom possible to accommodate every desirable relationship, the ones that are mandatory need to be identified separately from the ones that are highly desirable or simply useful.

DESIGN CONSIDERATIONS

During programming, general concepts are developed as a response to the goals and needs of the client. These programmatic concepts are statements about functional solutions to the client's performance requirements. They differ from later design concepts because no attempt at actual physical solutions is made during programming; programmatic concepts guide the later development of design concepts. For example, a programmatic concept might be that

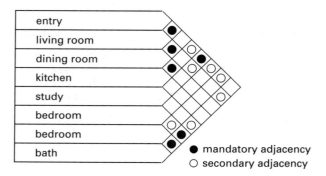

(a) adjacency matrix

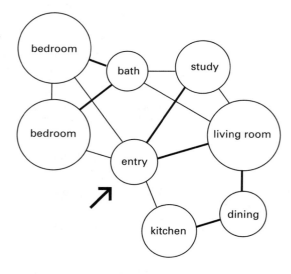

(b) adjacency diagram

Figure 3.1 Methods of Recording Space Relationships

a facility should be easily expandable by 20% every three years. Exactly how that would happen for a building would be developed as a design concept. It might take the form of a linear building that could be extended by a simple addition to one wing. Some of the more common design considerations that must be addressed during programming are outlined in the following sections.

Organization Concepts

The functional needs of a particular type of building most often influence how the physical environment is organized. At other times, the client's goal, the site, the desired symbolism, or additional factors suggest the organization pattern. There are six fundamental organization concepts: linear, axial, grid, central, radial, and clustered. These are shown diagrammatically in Fig. 3.2.

Linear organizations consist of a series of spaces or buildings that are placed in a single line. The spaces can be identical or of different sizes and shapes, but they always relate to a unifying line, usually a path of circulation. A linear organization is very adaptable; it can be straight, bent, or curved to meet the requirements of the client, the site, solar orientation, or construction. It is easily expandable and can be built in a modular configuration if desired.

Axial plans are variations of the linear system with two or more major linear segments about which spaces or buildings are placed. There may be additional, secondary paths growing out of the primary axes, and the major linear segments may be at right angles to each other or at some other angle.

Grid systems consist of two sets of regularly spaced parallel lines, which create one pattern that is very strong and one that is quite flexible. Within a grid, portions can be subtracted, added, or modified. The size of the grid can be changed to create different sizes of spaces or to define special areas. However, a grid can become monotonous and confusing if not used properly. Because a grid system is usually defined by circulation paths, it is more appropriate for very large buildings and building complexes where a great deal of circulation is required.

A *central organization* is based on one space or point about which secondary elements are placed. It is usually a very formal method of organizing spaces or buildings and inherently places the primary emphasis on the central space. Central organizations are often used in conjunction with axial or linear plans.

When more than one linear organization extends from a centralized point, it becomes a *radial organization*. Radial plans have a central focus and also have the ability to extend outward to connect with other spaces, or to expand. These types of organizing plans can be circular or assume other shapes as well.

Clustered organizations are loose compositions of spaces or buildings related around a path, axis, or central space, or they are simply grouped together. The general image is one of informality. Clusters are very adaptable to requirements for different sizes of spaces and they are easy to add onto without disrupting the overall composition.

Circulation Patterns

Circulation patterns are primary ways of organizing spaces, buildings, and groups of buildings. They are vital to the efficient organization of a structure and provide people with their strongest orientation within an environment. Paths of circulation provide the means to move people, cars, products, and services.

Circulation is directly related to the organizational pattern of a building, but it does not necessarily have to mimic it. For example, a major circulation path can cut diagonally

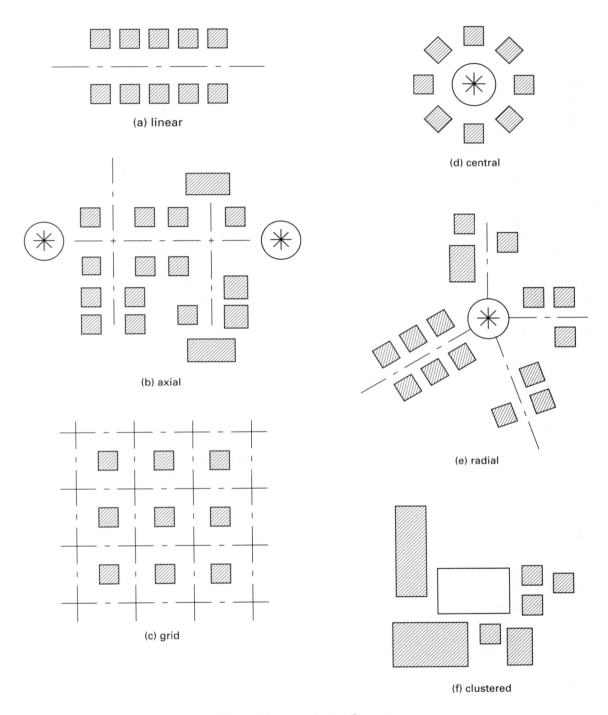

Figure 3.2 Organization Concepts

across a grid pattern. Normally there is a hierarchy of paths. Major routes connect major spaces or become spaces themselves and have secondary paths branching from them. Different sizes and types of circulation are important for accommodating varying capacities and for providing an orientation device for people using them.

Circulation for different functions may need to be separated as well. In a government building, one set of halls for the public may be separated from the internal set of corridors for the workers. A jail may have a secure passage for moving prisoners that is completely separate from other areas of public movement.

Establishing and maintaining a simple, efficient, and coherent circulation scheme is critical to successfully completing the design portion of the ARE. One of the common mistakes is to let the arranging of spaces according to the adjacency requirements take over a design and to connect the spaces with a circulation path as an afterthought. This creates a maze of awkward corridors that decreases the efficiency ratio and produces dead-end corridors and other exiting problems.

All circulation paths are linear by their very nature, but there are some common variations, many of which are similar to the organizational patterns described in the previous section. Because circulation is an important aspect of successful completion of the design portion of the examination, it is important to have a good mental picture of the various circulation concepts and the advantages and disadvantages of each. Five basic patterns are shown in Fig. 3.3, along with a hypothetical structural grid on top of them to illustrate how some patterns are better suited than others to integration of structure, adjacencies, and circulation system. Also remember that mechanical services can easily follow a logical circulation system.

The linear, *dumbbell layout* is the simplest and one of the most flexible circulation patterns. Spaces are laid out along a straight path that connects two major elements at the ends. These are usually the entrance to the building at one end and an exit at the other, although the primary entrance can occur anywhere along the path. Spaces are laid out along the spine as required. Various sizes of spaces can be easily accommodated by simply extending their length perpendicular to the path, and if outdoor spaces are required they are simply located as needed. The double-loaded corridor makes the building very efficient.

Site constraints may restrict the length of the spine, but the concept can still be used by bending the path at a right angle. With this layout, it is very easy to establish a regular, one-way structural grid perpendicular to the direction of the path. Simply extending the length of a bay can accommodate larger spaces as the program requires.

Conversely, eliminating a line or two of structure gives the location for a very large space and a long-span structural system. A two-way structural grid can also be used with this layout.

Making a complete loop results in a *doughnut configuration*. This is also very efficient because it provides a double-loaded corridor and automatically makes a continuous exitway. Building entries, exits, and stairways can be placed wherever needed. Spaces that do not need exterior exposure can be placed in the middle. Various sizes of spaces are easily accommodated on the perimeter because they can be expanded outward, just as with the dumbbell layout. A simple structural grid can be coordinated with the space layout as required. A doughnut pattern is good for square or nearly square sites and for buildings that must be compact.

A grid system is often used for very large buildings where access must be provided to many internal spaces. For the small buildings that are usually found on the ARE examination, a grid system is seldom appropriate because it results in a very inefficient layout, with single spaces being surrounded by corridors.

A radial layout is oriented on one major space with paths extending from this central area. The radial configuration generally requires a large site and is more appropriate for large buildings or building complexes. Establishing a simple structural system is more difficult with this pattern unless the circulation paths extend from the central space at 90° angles. Each corridor must also have an exit at the end if it is longer than 20 ft (6100).

Finally, a *field pattern* consists of a network of paths with no strong direction. There are major paths with secondary routes extending from or connecting the primary routes. Orientation within a field pattern is difficult, as is integrating a logical structural system.

Service Spaces

In addition to the primary programmed spaces (the net assignable), secondary spaces such as toilet and mechanical rooms must also be planned from the start. They should not be tacked on after the majority of the design work is done.

Depending on the type of mechanical system, mechanical rooms should be centrally located to minimize lengths of duct runs and piping. This is especially true with all-air systems. Mechanical rooms usually need easy access to the outside for servicing as well as provisions for fresh-air intakes.

Toilet rooms should be located to satisfy adjacency requirements as stated in the program or in an area that has easy access to the entire floor. Men's and women's toilet rooms should be back to back to share a common plumbing wall and should be near other plumbing in the building, if possible.

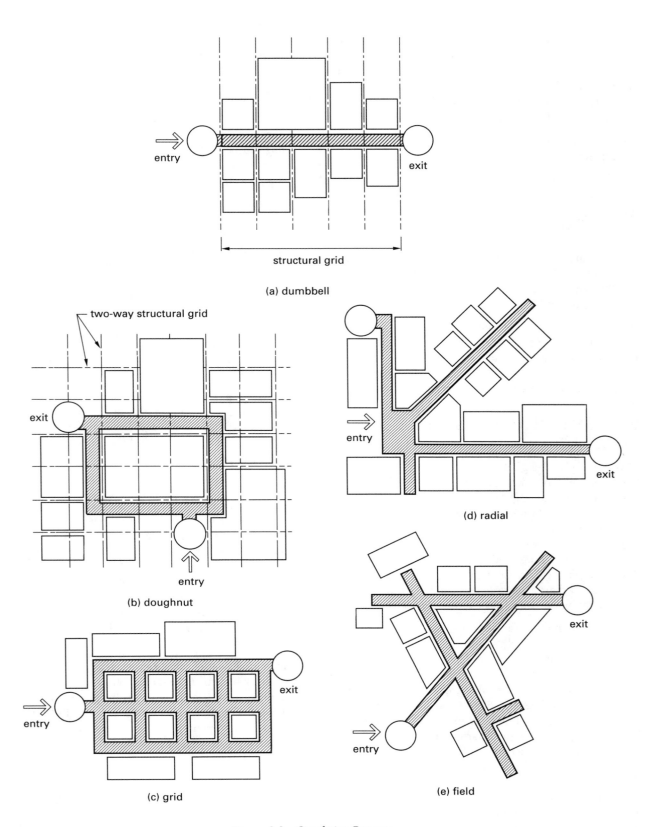

Figure 3.3 Circulation Patterns

Service access must also be given careful consideration. This includes service drives for trucks, the service entrance to the building, and access to mechanical rooms, storage rooms, and other functional areas as required by the program. The ARE design problem usually has a requirement for some type of service access that must be kept separate from the primary entrance and circulation paths.

Flexibility

Flexibility is a design consideration that involves a variety of concepts. *Expansibility* is the capacity for a building to be enlarged or added onto easily as needs change or growth occurs. *Convertibility* allows an existing building or space to be changed according to a new use. For example, a school gymnasium may be converted into classroom space in a second phase of construction. *Versatility* means the ability to use the same space for a variety of uses in order to make maximum use of limited space.

If a program calls for flexibility, the designer must know or determine what type of organizational and structural system is required. Expansibility may suggest one type of organizational and structural system, while convertibility may require a completely different approach.

PSYCHOLOGICAL AND SOCIAL INFLUENCES

Developing physical guidelines that respond to the psychological needs of people is one of the most difficult tasks in programming. Although there has been a great deal of research in the field of environmental psychology, predicting human behavior and designing spaces and buildings that enhance people's lives is an inexact process. However, the architect must attempt to develop a realistic model of the people who will be using the designed environment and the nature of their activities. This model can then serve as the foundation on which to base many design decisions.

During programming, a clear distinction must be made between the architect's client and the actual users. They are not always the same. For example, a public housing agency may be the client for a subsidized housing complex, but the actual users will be people who probably have an entirely different set of values and lifestyles than those helping to develop the program. Environmental psychology is a very complex subject, but a good starting point is to get familiar with the following concepts.

Proxemics

Proxemics is a term created by Edward T. Hall to describe the interrelated observations and theories of humans' use of space as a specialized elaboration of culture. It deals with the issues of spacing between people, territoriality,

organization of space, and positioning of people in space, all relative to the culture of which they are a part. Some of these issues are discussed in the following sections.

Behavior Settings

A behavior setting is a useful concept for studying the effects of the environment on human activity. A *behavior setting* can be thought of as a particular place, with definable boundaries and objects within the place, in which a standing pattern of behavior occurs at a particular time.

For example, a weekly board of directors meeting in a conference room can be considered a behavior setting. The activity of the meeting follows certain procedures (call to order, reading of minutes, discussions, and so forth), it occurs in the same place (the conference room), and the room is arranged to assist the activity (chairs are arranged around a table, audio-visual facilities are present, lighting is adequate).

The concept of a behavior setting is useful for the architect because it connects the strictly behavioral aspects of human activity with the effects of the physical environment on people. Although a behavior setting is a complex system of activities, human goals, administrative requirements, physical objects, and cultural needs, it provides the architect with a definable unit of design. By knowing the people involved and the activities taking place, programmatic concepts can be developed that support the setting.

Territoriality

As mentioned in Ch. 2, *territoriality* is a fundamental aspect of human behavior. It refers to the need to lay claim to the spaces we occupy and the things we own. Although partially based on the biological imperative for protection, territoriality in humans is more related to the needs for self-identity and freedom of choice. In addition to marking out objects and larger spaces in the environment, people also protect their own personal space (also discussed in Ch. 2), that imaginary bubble of distance that varies with different circumstances.

Territoriality applies to groups as well as to individuals. A study club, school class, or street gang can claim a physical territory as their own, which helps give both the group and the individuals in the group an identity. Environments should allow people to claim territory and make choices about where to be and what activities to engage in.

Personalization

One of the ways territoriality manifests itself is with the *personalization* of space. Whether it happens in one's home, at the office desk, or in a waiting lounge, people need to arrange the environment to reflect their presence and uniqueness. The most successful designs allow this to take place without major adverse effects on other people or on the environment as a whole. At home, people decorate their spaces the way they want. At the office, people bring in personal objects, family photographs, and pictures to make the space their own. In an airport lounge, people place coats and suitcases around them, not only to stake out a temporary territory but also to make the waiting time more personal and a little more comfortable.

Another way people personalize space is to modify the environment. If people using a given space find that it does not meet their needs, they can modify behavior to adapt to the environment, change their relationship to the environment (leave), or try to change the environment. The simple act of moving a chair to make viewing a screen easier is an example of modifying and personalizing a space. If the chair is attached, the design is not as adaptable to the varying needs of the people using the design.

Group Interaction

To a certain extent, the environment can either facilitate or hinder human interaction. In most behavior settings, groups are predisposed to act in a particular way. If the setting is not conducive to the activities, the people will try to modify the environment or modify their behavior to make the activity work. In extreme cases, if the setting is totally at odds with the activity taking place there, stress, anger, and other adverse reactions can occur.

Seating arrangement is one of the most common ways of facilitating group interaction. Studies have shown that people will seat themselves at a table according to the nature of their relationships with others around them. For intimate conversation, two people will sit across the corner of a table or next to each other on a sofa. For more formal situations or when people are competing, they will sit across from one another. Where social contact is not desired, two people will take chairs at opposite corners of a table.

Round tables tend to foster more cooperation and equality among those seated around them. Rectangular tables tend to make cooperation more difficult and establish the person sitting at the end in a more superior position. Strangers do not like to share the same sofa or park bench. Knowing the people and activities expected to be in a place can assist the architect in making decisions. For example, individual study carrels in a library will be more efficient than large tables because the tables will seldom be fully occupied by strangers.

In places where informal group interaction takes place, studies have shown that more than 97% of groups comprise two to four people. Designing to accommodate these sizes of groups makes more sense than anticipating groups of more people, although a plan that allows for the possibility of very large groups while preferring small groups would be the best combination. In most cases, providing a variety of spaces for interaction is the best approach.

Status

The physical environment holds a great deal of symbolism that indicates status for some human beings. Some people like colonial houses because such designs symbolize to the occupants the idea of "home." Others prefer banks of classical design with large lobbies, because that is what they think a bank should look like.

The environment can thus communicate status. In the United States, for example, someone with a corner office has more status than someone with only one exterior wall. Office size is also equated with status in many cultures. A house in an affluent neighborhood provides a higher status than one in other neighborhoods. Status can also operate at the scale of an entire building or complex. The client may want the building to symbolize some quality of the organization and to give him or her physical and psychological status in the community.

The architectural programmer should investigate the requirements or implications of status. Sometimes clients may clearly state what status-related goals they want to achieve. Other times, the programmer must raise the issue, explore it with the client, and document the response as a programmatic concept.

BUDGETING AND SCHEDULING

Establishing a budget and setting up a time frame for design and construction are two of the most important parts of programming because they influence many of the design decisions to follow and can determine whether a project is even feasible. During later stages of design, an initial budget and schedule are simply refined as more information becomes available.

Budgets may be set in several ways. For speculative or for-profit projects, the owner or developer works out a pro forma statement listing the expected income of the project and the expected costs to build it. An estimated selling price of the developed project or rent per square foot is calculated and balanced against all the various costs, one of which is the construction price. In order to make the project economically feasible, there will be a limit on the building costs. This becomes the budget within which the architect must work.

Budgets are often established through public funding or legislation. In these cases, the construction budget is often fixed without the architect's involvement, and the project must be designed and built for the fixed amount. Unfortunately, when public officials estimate the cost to build a project, they sometimes neglect to include all aspects of development, such as professional fees, furnishings, and other line items.

Budgets may also be set by the architect at the request of the owner and based on the proposed project. This is the most realistic and accurate way to establish a preliminary budget because it is based on a particular building type of a particular size on a particular site (or sites if several are being reviewed for selection).

There are four basic variables in developing any construction budget: quantity, quality, the budget itself, and time. There is always a balance among these four elements, and changing one or more affects the others. For instance, if an owner needs a certain amount of square footage built (quantity), needs the project built at a certain time, and has a fixed budget amount, then the quality of construction will have to be adjusted to meet the other constraints. In some cases, value engineering can be performed during which individual systems and materials are reviewed to see if the same function can be accomplished in a less expensive way. If time, quality, and the budget are fixed, then the amount of space constructed (quantity) must be adjusted.

Cost Influences

There are many variables that affect project cost. The first thing to remember is that construction cost is only one part of the total project development budget. Other factors include such things as site acquisition, site development, fees, and financing. Table 3.4 lists most of the items commonly found in a project budget and a typical range of percentage values based on construction cost. Of course, not all of these are a part of every development, but they illustrate the things that must be considered.

Building cost is the money required to construct the building, including structure, exterior cladding, finishes, and electrical and mechanical systems. *Site development* costs are usually a separate item. They include such things as parking, drives, fences, landscaping, exterior lighting, and sprinkler systems. If the development is large and affects the surrounding area, a developer may be required to upgrade roads, extend utility lines, and do other major off-site work as a condition of getting approval from public agencies.

Movable equipment and furnishings include furniture, accessories, window coverings, and major equipment necessary to put the facility into operation. These are often listed as separate line items because the funding for them may come out of a separate budget and because they may be supplied under separate contracts.

Professional services are architectural and engineering fees as well as costs for such things as topographic surveys, soil tests, special consultants, appraisals and legal fees, and the

Table 3.4
Project Budget Line Items

	line item		example
A	site acquisition		$1,100,000
B	building costs	ft² times cost per ft²	(assume) $6,800,000
C	site development	10% to 20% of B	(15%) $1,020,000
D	total construction cost	B + C	$7,820,000
E	movable equipment	5% to 10% of B	(5%) $340,000
F	furnishings		$200,000
G	total construction and furnishings	D + E + F	$8,360,000
H	professional services	5% to 10% of D	(7%) $547,400
I	inspection and testing		$15,000
J	escalation estimate	2% to 10% of G per year	(10%) $836,000
K	contingency	5% to 10% of G	(8%) $668,800
L	financing costs		$250,000
M	moving expenses		(assume) $90,000
N	Total Project Budget	G + H through M	$11,867,200

like. Inspection and testing involve money required for special on-site, full-time inspection (if required), and testing of such things as concrete, steel, window walls, and roofing.

Because construction takes a great deal of time, a factor for inflation should be included. Generally, the present budget estimate is escalated to a time in the future at the expected midpoint of construction. Although it is always difficult to predict the future, using past cost indexes and inflation rates and applying an estimate to the expected condition of the construction, the architect can usually make an educated guess.

A contingency should also be added to account for unforeseen changes by the client and other conditions that add to the cost. For an early project budget, the percentage of the contingency should be higher than contingencies applied to later budgets, because there are more unknowns. Normally, from 5% to 10% should be included.

Financing includes not only the long-term interest paid on permanent financing but also the immediate costs of loan origination fees, construction loan interest, and other administrative costs. On long-term loans, the cost of financing can easily exceed all of the original building and development costs. In many cases, long-term interest, called debt service, is not included in the project budget because it is an ongoing cost to the owner, as are maintenance costs.

Finally, many clients include moving costs in the development budget. For large companies and other types of clients, the money required to physically relocate, including changing stationery, installing telephones, and the like, can be a substantial amount.

Methods of Budgeting

The costs described in the previous section and shown in Table 3.4 represent a type of budget done during programming or even prior to programming to test the feasibility of a project. The numbers are preliminary, often based on sketchy information. For example, the building cost may simply be an estimated cost per square foot multiplied by the required number of gross square feet needed. The square footage cost may be derived from similar buildings in the area, from experience, or from commercially available cost books.

Budgeting, however, is an ongoing activity for the architect. At each stage of the design process, there should be a revised budget reflecting the decisions made to that time. As shown in the example, pre-design budgets are usually based only on area, but other units can also be used. For example, many companies have rules of thumb for estimating based on items such as cost per hospital bed, cost per student, cost per hotel room, and similar functional units.

After the pre-programming budget, the architect usually begins to concentrate on the building and site development costs. At this stage an average cost per square foot may still be used, or the building may be divided into several functional parts and different square footage prices may be assigned to each part. A school, for example, may be classified into classroom space, laboratory space, shop space, office space, and gymnasium space, each having a different cost per square foot. This type of division can be developed concurrently with the programming of the space requirements.

During schematic design, when more is known about the space requirements and general configuration of the building and site, budgeting is based on major subsystems. Historical cost information on each type of subsystem can be applied to the design. At this point it is easier to see where the money is being used in the building. Design decisions can then be based on studies of alternative systems. A typical subsystem budget is shown in Table 3.5.

Table 3.5

System Cost Budget of Office Buildings

subsystem	average cost	
	($/ft^2)	(% of total)
foundations	3.96	5.2
floors on grade	3.08	4.0
superstructure	16.51	21.7
roofing	0.18	0.2
exterior walls	9.63	12.6
partitions	5.19	6.8
wall finishes	3.70	4.8
floor finishes	3.78	5.0
ceiling finishes	2.79	3.7
conveying systems	6.45	8.5
specialties	0.70	0.9
fixed equipment	2.74	3.6
HVAC	9.21	12.1
plumbing	3.61	4.6
electrical	4.68	6.1
	76.21	100.0

Values for low-, average-, and high-quality construction for different building types can be obtained from cost databases and published estimating manuals and applied to the structure being budgeted. The dollar amounts included in system cost budgets usually include markup for contractor's overhead and profit and other construction administrative costs.

During the later stages of schematic design and early stages of construction documents, more detailed estimates are made. The procedure most often used is the parameter method, which involves an expanded itemization of construction quantities and assignment of unit costs to these quantities. For example, instead of using one number for floor finishes, the cost is broken down into carpeting, vinyl tile, wood strip flooring, unfinished concrete, and so forth. Using an estimated cost per square foot, the cost of each type of flooring can be estimated based on the area.

With this type of budgeting, it is possible to evaluate the cost implications of each building component and to make decisions concerning both quantity and quality in order to meet the original budget estimate. If floor finishes are over budget, the architect and the client can review the parameter estimate and decide, for example, that some wood flooring must be replaced with less expensive carpeting. Similar decisions can be made concerning any of the parameters in the budget.

Another way to compare and evaluate alternative construction components is with *matrix costing*. With this technique, a matrix is drawn showing, along one side, the various alternatives and, along the other side, the individual elements that combine to produce the total cost of the alternatives. For example, in evaluating alternatives for workstations, all of the factors that would comprise the final cost could be compared. These factors might include the cost of custom-built versus pre-manufactured workstations, task lighting that could be planned with custom-built units versus higher-wattage ambient lighting, and so on.

Parameter line items are based on commonly used units that relate to the construction element under study. For instance, a gypsum board partition would have an assigned cost per square foot of complete partition of a particular construction type rather than separate costs for metal studs, gypsum board, screws, and finishing. There would be different costs for single-layer gypsum board partitions, 1-hour rated walls, 2-hour rated walls, and other partition types.

Two additional components of construction cost include the contractor's overhead and profit. Overhead can be further divided into general overhead and project overhead. *General overhead* is the cost to run a contracting business that involves such things as office rent, secretarial help, heat, and other recurring costs. *Project overhead* is the money it takes to complete a job, not including labor, materials, or equipment. Temporary offices, project telephones, sanitary facilities, trash removal, insurance, permits, and temporary utilities are examples of project overhead. The total overhead costs, including both general and project expenses, can range from about 10% to 20% of the total costs for labor, materials, and equipment.

Profit is the last item a contractor adds onto an estimate and is listed as a percentage of the total of labor, materials, equipment, and overhead. This is one of the most highly variable parts of a budget. Profit depends on the type of project, its size, the amount of risk involved, how much money the contractor wants to make, the general market conditions, and, of course, whether or not the job is being bid.

During extremely difficult economic conditions, a contractor may cut the profit margin to almost nothing simply to get the job and keep his or her workforce employed. If the contract is being negotiated with only one contractor, the profit percentage will be much higher. In most cases, however, profit will range from 5% to 20% of the total cost of the job. Overall, overhead and profit can total about 15% to 40% of construction cost.

Cost Information

One of the most difficult aspects of developing project budgets is obtaining current, reliable prices for the kinds of construction units being used. There is no shortage of commercially produced cost books that are published yearly. These books list costs in different ways; some are very detailed, giving the cost for labor and materials for individual construction items, while others list parameter costs and subsystem costs. The detailed price listings are of little use to architects because they are too specific and make comparison of alternate systems difficult.

There are also computerized cost estimating services that only require the architect to provide general information about the project, location, size, major materials, and so forth. The computer service then applies its current price database to the information and produces a cost budget. Many architects also work closely with general contractors to develop a realistic budget.

Remember, however, that commercially available cost information is the average of many past construction projects from around the country. Local variations and particular conditions may affect the value of their use on a specific project.

Two conditions that must be accounted for in developing any project budget are geographical location and inflation. These variables can be adjusted by using cost indexes that are published in a variety of sources, including the major architectural and construction trade magazines. Using a base year as index 1000, for example, for selected cities around the country, new indexes are developed each year that reflect the increase in costs (both material and labor) that year.

The indexes can be used to apply costs from one part of the country to another and to escalate past costs to the expected midpoint of construction of the project being budgeted.

Example 3.2

The cost index in your city is 1257 and the cost index for another city in which you are designing a building is 1308. If the expected construction cost is $1,250,000 based on prices for your city, what will be the expected cost in the other region?

Divide the higher index by the lower index.

$$\frac{1308}{1257} = 1.041$$

Multiply this by the base cost.

$$(\$1,250,000)(1.041) = \$1,300,716$$

Scheduling

There are two major parts of a project schedule: design time and construction time. The architect, of course, has control over the scheduling of design and the production of contract documents but has practically no control over construction. However, the design professional must be able to estimate the entire project schedule so that the best course of action can be taken in order to meet the client's goals. For example, if the client must move by a certain date and normal design and construction sequences make this impossible, the architect may recommend a fast-track schedule or some other approach to meet the deadline.

The design process normally consists of several clearly defined phases, each of which must be substantially finished and approved by the client before the next one can begin. These are generally accepted in the profession and are referred to in the American Institute of Architects' Owner-Architect Agreement as well as in other documents.

Following programming, the first phase is *schematic design*. During this phase, the general layout of the project is developed along with preliminary alternate studies for materials and building systems. Once the direction of the project documented in schematic design drawings is reviewed and approved by the client, the *design development phase* starts. Here, the decisions made during the previous phase are refined and developed in more detail. Preliminary or outline specifications are written, and a more detailed cost budget is made.

Construction documents are produced next. These include the final working drawings as well as the full project manual and any bidding and contract documents required. These are used for the *bidding* or *negotiation phase*, which includes obtaining bids from several contractors and analyzing them or negotiating a contract with one contractor.

The time required for these phases is highly variable and depends on the following factors.

- The size and complexity of the project. Obviously, a 500,000 ft² (46 450 m²) hospital will take much longer to design than a 30,000 ft² (2787 m²) office building.

- The number of people working on the project. Although adding more people to the job can shorten the schedule, there is a point of diminishing returns. Having too many people simply creates a management and coordination problem, and for some phases only a few people are required, even for very large jobs.

- The abilities and design methodology of the project team. Younger, less-experienced designers will usually require more time to do the same amount of work than would a more senior staff.

- The type of client and the decision-making and approval processes of the client. Large corporations or public agencies are likely to have a multilayered decision-making and approval process. The time required for getting the necessary information or approval on one phase may take weeks or even months, whereas a small, single-authority client might make the same decision in a matter of days.

The construction schedule may be established by the contractor or construction manager, but it must often be estimated by the architect during the programming phase so that the client has some idea of the total time required from project conception to move-in. When the architect does this, it should be made very clear to the client that it is only an estimate and the architect can in no way guarantee an early (or any) estimate of the construction schedule.

Many variables can affect construction time, but most can be controlled in one way or another. Others, like weather, are independent of anyone's control. Beyond the obvious variables of size and complexity, the following is a partial list of some of the more common variables.

- the management ability of the contractor to organize his or her own forces as well as those of the subcontractors

- material delivery times

- the quality and completeness of the architect's drawings and specification

- the weather

- labor availability and labor disputes

- new construction or remodeling (remodeling generally takes more time and coordination for equal areas than it does for new buildings)

- site conditions (construction sites or those with subsurface problems usually take more time to build on)

- the architect (some professionals are more diligent than others in performing their duties during construction)

- lender approvals

- agency and governmental approvals

Several methods are used to schedule both design and construction. The most common and easiest is the *bar chart* or *Gantt chart*. See Fig. 3.4. The various activities of the schedule are listed along the vertical axis. Each activity is given a starting and finishing date, and overlaps are indicated by drawing the bars for each activity such that they overlap. Bar charts are simple to make and understand and are suitable for small to midsized projects. However, they cannot show all the sequences and dependencies of one activity on another.

Another scheduling tool often used is the *critical path method* (CPM) and the CPM chart. The CPM chart graphically depicts all the tasks required to complete a project, the sequence in which they must occur, their duration, the earliest or latest possible starting time, and the earliest or latest possible finishing time. It also defines the sequence of tasks that are critical or that must be started and finished exactly on time if the total schedule is to be met.

A CPM chart for a simple design project is shown in Fig. 3.5. Each arrow in the chart represents an activity with a beginning and end point (represented by the numbered circles). No activity can begin until all activities leading into a circle have been completed. The dashed lines indicate dependency relationships but not activities themselves, and thus they have no duration. They are called dummies and are used to give each activity a unique beginning and ending number and to allow establishment of dependency relationships without tying in nondependent activities.

The heavier line in the illustration shows the critical path, or the sequence of events that must happen as scheduled if the deadline is to be met. The numbers under the activities give the duration of the activity in days. Delaying the starting time of any of these activities or increasing their duration

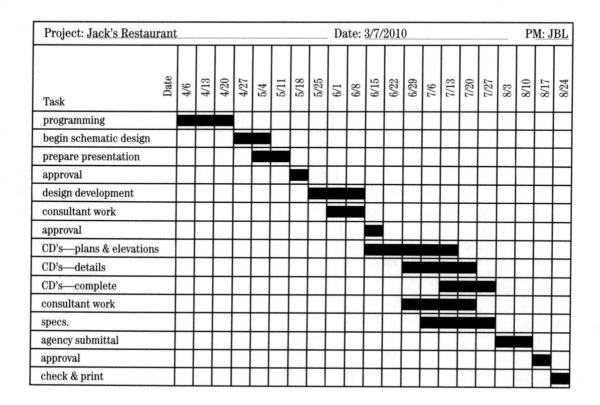

Figure 3.4 Gantt Chart

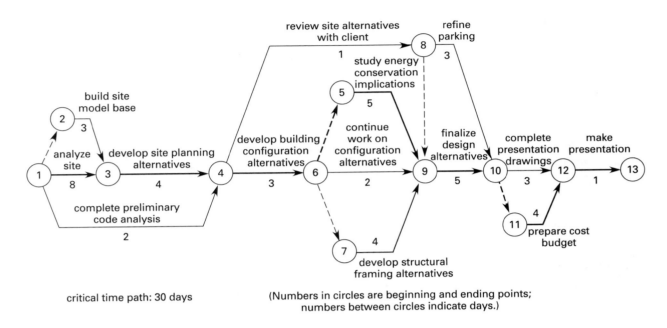

Figure 3.5 CPM Schedule

will delay the whole project. The noncritical activities can begin or finish earlier or later (within limits) without affecting the final completion date. This variable time is called the float of each activity.

Scheduling is crucial to any project because it can have a great influence on cost. Generally, the longer a project takes the more it costs. This is due to the effect of inflation on materials and labor as well as the additional construction interest and the lost revenue a client can suffer if the job is not completed in a timely manner. For example, delayed completion of a retail store or office building delays the beginning of rental income. In other cases, quick completion of a project is required to avoid building during bad winter weather, when it costs more to build, or to meet some other fixed date set by the client's needs.

Besides efficient scheduling, construction time can be compressed with *fast-track scheduling*. This method overlaps the design and construction phases of a project. Ordering of long-lead materials and equipment can occur, and work on the site and foundations can begin before all the details of the building are completely worked out. With fast-track scheduling, separate contracts are established so that each major system can be bid and awarded by itself to avoid delaying other construction.

Although the fast-track method requires close coordination between the architect, contractor, subcontractors, owner, and others, it makes it possible to construct a high-quality

building in 10% to 30% less time than with a conventional construction contract.

Refer to Ch. 28 for additional information on developing and monitoring schedules.

CODES AND REGULATIONS

A complete program for a building project will include the various legal restrictions that apply to a project. Two of the most common are zoning ordinances and building codes. Zoning is discussed in Chs. 2 and 4. Building code requirements, including provisions for making buildings accessible to the physically disabled, are reviewed in Chs. 29 and 30. In addition to zoning regulations, other land development regulations may apply. Such regulations as deed restrictions and easements are also discussed in Ch. 2.

Other regulatory agency requirements that may be in force, in addition to zoning ordinances and building codes, include special rules of the local fire department, fire zones set by the local municipality, and rules of government agencies like the Federal Housing Authority (FHA) and the Environmental Protection Agency (EPA). Additional regulations may include local health and hospital department requirements that spell out needs for restaurants and hospitals. Local and state energy conservation regulations may also be in force.

THE PROGRAMMING PROCESS

Programming is an attempt to define the problem and establish all the guidelines and needs on which the design process can be based. It is a time of analysis of all aspects of the problem and a distillation of the problem's complexity into a few clear problem statements.

One popular programming method uses a five-step process in relationship to four major considerations. It is described in *Problem Seeking* by William Peña (John Wiley & Sons, 2001). The process involves establishing goals, collecting and analyzing facts, uncovering and testing concepts, determining needs, and stating the problem. All of these steps include the considerations of form, function, economy, and time.

Establishing Goals

Goals indicate what the client wants to achieve and why. They are important to identify because they establish the direction of programmatic concepts that ultimately suggest the physical means of achieving the goals. It is not enough to simply list the types of spaces and required areas the client needs; the client is trying to reach some objective with those spaces and areas. For example, a goal for a school administration might be to increase the daily informal interaction between students and teachers.

Collecting Facts

Facts describe the existing conditions and requirements of the problem. Facts include such things as the number of people to be accommodated, the site conditions, space adjacency needs, user characteristics, equipment to be housed, expected growth rate, money available for construction, building code requirements, and climate information. There is always a large number of facts; part of the programmer's task is not only to collect facts but also to organize them so that they are useful.

Uncovering Concepts

The programming process should develop abstract ideas that are functional solutions to the client's problems without defining the physical means that should be used to achieve them. These are programmatic concepts as discussed earlier in this chapter. They are the basis for later design concepts. To use the previous example, a programmatic concept concerning increasing the daily interaction between students and teachers might be to provide common spaces for mixed flow in circulation patterns. One possible design concept in response to this could be to provide a central court through which all circulation paths pass. Programmatic concepts are listed in the following section of this chapter.

Determining Needs

This step of the programming process balances the desires of the client against the available budget or establishes a budget based on the defined goals and needs. It is during this step that wants have to be separated from needs. Most clients want more than they can afford, so clear statements of true needs at this early stage of the process can help avoid problems later. At this stage, one or more of the four elements of cost (quantity, quality, budget, and time) may have to be adjusted to balance needs against available resources.

Stating the Problem

The previous four steps are a prelude to succinctly summarizing the essence of the problem in just a few statements. The problem statements are the bridge between programming and the design process. They are statements the client and programmer agree describe the most important aspects of the problem and serve as the basis for design and as design criteria by which the solution can be evaluated. There should be a minimum of four problem statements, one for each of the major considerations of form, function, economy, and time.

Four Major Considerations During Programming

The four major considerations of any design problem are form, function, economy, and time. *Form* relates to the site, the physical and psychological environment of the building, and the quality of construction. *Function* relates to the people and activities of the space or building and their relationships. *Economy* concerns money: the initial cost of the facility, operating costs, and life-cycle costs. Finally, *time* describes the ideas of past, present, and future as they affect the other three considerations. For example, the required schedule for construction is often a time consideration, as is the need for expansibility in the future.

Programmatic Concepts

As mentioned in the previous section, the architect must develop abstract ideas about how to view and solve the client's performance problems before attempting to solve them with three-dimensional design ideas. These abstract ideas are called *programmatic concepts*. Later in the design process, the architect develops *design concepts*, which are physical solutions to the client's problems and which reflect approaches to satisfying programmatic concepts. For example, expansibility is a programmatic concept. Two corresponding design concepts that might be used to respond to this are (1) provide space on the site to build a future addition to the building or (2) build a structure larger than first needed, to allow for expansion.

The book *Problem Seeking* identifies 24 programmatic concepts that tend to recur in all types of buildings, although they generally do not all occur in the same building. These include the following.

Priority establishes the order of importance of things such as size, position, or social values. For example, an entrance and reception area may have higher priority than individual offices, to reflect the goal of enhancing a company's image.

Hierarchy relates to the idea of the exercise of authority and is expressed in physical symbols of authority. For example, to reflect the hierarchy of a traditional law firm, senior members may be given larger offices than junior members.

Character is a response to the desired image the client wants to project. This may later be expressed in design concepts using building size, shape, materials, organization, and other physical responses to project character.

Density—low, medium, or high—may relate to how a parcel of land or an individual building or space is used to respond to goals such as efficient use of land, compact use of office space, or the desired amount of interaction in a school.

Service groupings include mechanical services, such as mechanical systems, as well as other functions that support the use of the building. Distribution of supplies, storage, information, and vending areas are examples of these types of services. For example, a goal of decentralizing access to information could be accomplished by the physical design concepts of using satellite libraries throughout a facility, or by developing an electronic database accessible to all workers through computer terminals.

Activity grouping states whether activities should be integrated (or bundled together) or separated and compartmentalized. For example, compartmentalizing dining areas would respond to a goal to create an intimate dining atmosphere in a restaurant.

People grouping states the degree of massing of people derived from their physical, social, and emotional characteristics. For example, the goal of establishing work teams in a factory might suggest a concept of keeping small groups together in the same physical space.

Home base is related to the concept of territoriality and is a place where a person can maintain his or her individuality.

Relationships include the affinities of people and activities. This is one of the most common programming concepts established in any design problem because it most directly affects the organization of spaces and rooms.

Communications as a concept is a response to the goal of promoting the effective exchange of information or ideas.

This concept states who communicates with whom and how they do it.

Neighbors is a concept that refers to how the project will promote or prevent sociality and how it will relate to its neighboring facilities. For example, a building may share a common entry court with another building to foster interaction and community with other buildings.

Accessibility relates to the idea of entry to a building and to making the facility accessible to the disabled. It answers the question of how people can find the entrance and whether or not there should be multiple entrances.

Separated flow relates to segregating the flow of people, automobiles, service access, and other activities of a building. For example, people may need to be separated from automobile traffic, or public visitors to a courthouse may need to be separated from prisoners.

Mixed flow is a concept that is a response to the goal of promoting interaction among people. Conversely, mixed flow may not be a desired programmatic concept in controlled facilities.

Sequential flow is often required for both people and objects where a specific series of events or processes is required. For example, a show at an art museum may need to direct people from a starting point to an ending point. In a factory, material must progress from one station to another in a definite sequence.

Orientation refers to providing a point of reference within a building, campus, or other group of buildings to help keep people from feeling lost within a larger context. Common examples of physical design concepts used to provide orientation include a tower among a group of buildings, or a central atrium or lobby within a large building.

Flexibility includes three different components. The first, expansibility, refers to how a building can accommodate growth with expansion. The second, convertibility, refers to how a building can allow for changes in function through the conversion of spaces. The third, versatility, provides for several different activities with multifunctional spaces.

Tolerance allows for extra space for a dynamic activity (one likely to change) instead of fitting the space precisely for a static activity. For example, an indoor swimming pool area can be sized to accommodate just the pool and circulation around it. Providing for tolerance would give extra room to accommodate future bleachers or extra seating areas.

Safety focuses attention on life safety and the conceptual ways to achieve it. Building codes and other safety precautions are closely tied with this concept.

Security controls refers to ways that both people and property can be protected based on the value of the potential loss—minimum, medium, or maximum.

Energy conservation can be achieved in several ways: by keeping the heated area to a minimum, by keeping heat flow to a minimum, by using materials produced using low amounts of energy, by using recycled materials, and by using recyclable materials.

Environmental controls explores what kinds of controls are necessary to meet human comfort needs. It includes air temperature, light, sound, and humidity. This concept includes mechanical systems as well as natural means for climate control.

Phasing determines if the project must be completed in stages to meet time and cost schedules. It also states whether the project can be based on linear scheduling or must provide for concurrent scheduling to meet urgent occupancy requirements.

Cost control explores ways to establish a realistic preview of costs and a balanced budget to meet the client's available funds.

SAMPLE QUESTIONS

1. The statement "develop a multilevel system of pedestrian circulation" is an example of a

    A. need
    B. programming concept
    C. goal
    D. design concept

2. The developer of a retail shopping complex has estimated through an economic analysis that he can afford to build up to 85,000 ft² of gross building area. A central, enclosed pedestrian mall is planned to take up about 6% of the area, and the efficiency ratio is estimated to be 75%. About how much net rentable area will be available?

    A. 60,000 ft²
    B. 63,700 ft²
    C. 67,600 ft²
    D. 106,500 ft²

3. A published cost index indicates construction in city A to be 1440 and construction in city B to be 1517. The same index suggests that inflation will increase by 5% by the midpoint of construction, and the project is now budgeted to cost $1,500,000 in city A. How much should be budgeted for city B?

    A. $1,495,000
    B. $1,650,000
    C. $1,659,000
    D. $1,715,000

4. Contractor's overhead and profit typically amount to what percentage of the construction cost?

    A. 5% to 20%
    B. 10% to 20%
    C. 15% to 30%
    D. 15% to 40%

Questions 5 through 7 are based on the following programming situation.

A small medical clinic is being planned for a suburban location on an open, level site. It is to include services of general practice, obstetrics/family planning, testing and laboratories, and dental offices, along with medical offices and an administration area comprising about 70,000 net square feet of space. Access to the building is primarily by automobile.

The group developing the project wants the facility to be a comfortable, friendly place that minimizes the anxiety of a visit to the doctor and that makes it as easy as possible to get around. It expects the venture to be successful and each department to grow as the catchment area grows.

5. In order to meet the goals of the client, which of the following design responses would NOT be appropriate?

    A. Base the size of waiting rooms on a behavior setting where establishing territory should be encouraged.
    B. Group waiting areas and the reception area together to encourage social interaction.
    C. Develop a different color scheme for each of the separate services.
    D. Arrange individual chair seating against walls and other objects so it faces room entries.

6. Which of the following organizational concepts would probably be most appropriate for this facility?

    A. grid
    B. axial
    C. central
    D. radial

7. Which of the following aspects of flexibility related to expected growth of the facility is most important in developing the structural framing concept?

A. convertibility

B. versatility

C. expansibility

D. all of the above

8. Some clients discover shortly after hiring the architect for programming and design services that they must move out of their existing facility sooner than expected. The new schedule requires that construction and move-in be completed in 18 months instead of the original 21 months. What recommendation from the architect is the most feasible?

A. Consider fast-track construction.

B. Use CPM scheduling and use a negotiated contract rather than bidding.

C. Assign more staff to programming and design and work overtime to get construction started earlier.

D. Suggest that the client streamline its decision-making process and hire a construction manager.

9. Over which element of project cost does the architect typically have LEAST control?

A. escalation budget

B. percentage of site work relative to building costs

C. professional fees and consultant services

D. financing costs

10. A school district is planning a new elementary school to replace an outdated facility. A preliminary budget made during programming has shown that the available funds set aside for the school have been exceeded by 8%. What should the architect do?

I. Suggest that additional funds from other school building projects be used.

II. Review the design from a value engineering standpoint for approval by the client to see if costs can be reduced without sacrificing quality.

III. Discuss with the client the possibility of reducing the required area.

IV. Modify the statement of need concerning the desired level of finish and construction quality on noncritical portions of the facility after consultation with the client.

V. Propose that building be postponed for a school term until more money can be allocated.

A. V then IV

B. III then IV

C. II then III

D. IV then I

PRE-DESIGN AND SITE PLANNING— SITE ANALYSIS AND DESIGN

This chapter discusses the influences of a specific site on the placement and design of a building and the considerations for site development. Other pertinent topics that apply to site design are reviewed in Chs. 2 and 8.

TOPOGRAPHY

Topography affects decisions on where to place major site features such as buildings, parking areas, and drives as well as how much soil has to be moved to maintain desired slopes and drainage patterns. Topography is shown with contour lines on the topographic map, as discussed in Ch. 2. Figure 4.1 shows the common conditions contour lines represent. The examinee should be able to immediately recognize these and translate the spacing of the contour lines and the contour interval to a percentage slope using formula 2.1.

Remember that when contour lines represent a ridge they "point" in the direction of the downslope, and when they represent a valley, they "point" in the direction of the upslope. Equally spaced contour lines represent a uniform slope. As shown in Fig. 4.1, concave slopes have more closely spaced contour lines near the top of the slope, whereas convex slopes have more closely spaced contour lines at the bottom of the slope.

Any site requires some modification of the land, but the changes should be kept to a minimum. There are several reasons for this.

- Earth moving costs money.

- Excavating and building on steep slopes is more expensive than on gentle slopes.

- Excessive modification of the land affects drainage patterns that must be resolved with contour changes, drainage ditches, culverts, or other sitework.

- Large changes in elevations can require retaining walls, which add cost to the project.

- Removing or hauling in soil is expensive.

- Large amounts of cutting may damage existing tree roots.

When modifications are made to the contours as part of site design, the amount of material cut away should balance the amount of soil required for fill, to avoid the expense and problems related to removing or hauling in soil. Generally, it is better to orient the length of a building parallel to the direction of the contours rather than perpendicular to them in order to minimize excavation costs.

Both existing contour lines and new contour lines are shown on the same plan; the existing lines are shown dashed and the new ones solid. See Fig. 4.2. At the property lines, the contour lines must match up with the existing contours at adjacent properties or retaining walls must be built. Avoid modification of contour lines within the drip line of trees.

CLIMATE

Solar orientation influences three aspects of site planning: the orientation of the building to control solar heat gain or heat loss, the location of outdoor spaces and activities, and the location of building entries. Prior to design, locate the path of the sun so that you know its angle at various times of the day during the seasons. In the northern hemisphere, the sun's angle is lowest on December 22 and highest on June 21. In the northern latitudes, its angle is smaller all year long than in the southern latitudes.

During the winter, the sun rises and sets south of an east-west line through the site, and depending upon the site location, during the summer it rises and sets north of the same line. On the vernal equinox (March 21) and the

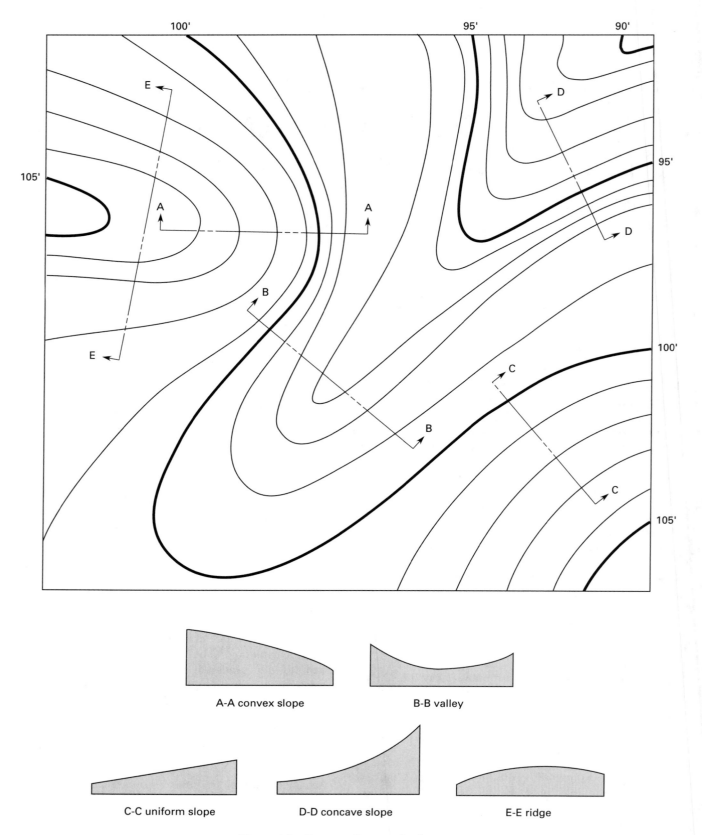

Figure 4.1 Common Contour Conditions

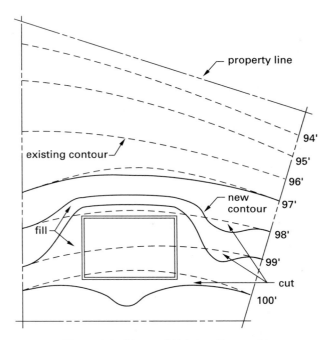

Figure 4.2 New and Existing Contour Lines

receive about twice the energy as the north and south combined.

For most northern hemisphere locations, the best overall orientation for a building is to have its principal façade facing south or slightly east or west of south. An orientation from 5° to 25°, depending on the climatic region, east of south is considered ideal to balance the desired heat gains in the winter months and to minimize the excessive heat gains on the east and west façades during the summer. See Fig. 7.1. Overhangs can be used to control the sun in the summer but let it strike the building and glass areas in the winter for passive solar heating. See Fig. 4.3. Deciduous trees can also be used to shield low buildings from the sun in the summer, while allowing sunlight through in the winter.

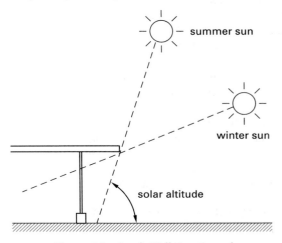

Figure 4.3 South Wall Sun Control

autumnal equinox (September 21), it rises and sets due east and west. Some representative values for solar altitude (angle above the horizon) and azimuth (angle north or south from an east-west line) are shown in Table 4.1 for various latitudes and cities.

The orientation of a building—that is, the direction its length faces, has a profound effect on energy gains and losses and on the comfort of the users. For example, for a 40° latitude, a southern exposure in the winter receives about three times the solar energy as the east and west sides, while in the summer the east and west façades of a building

On east and west façades, however, vertical sun baffles are more effective than overhangs because the sun is at a lower angle during the morning and afternoon hours in the summer. Louvers can also be used to shield a building and its

Table 4.1

Solar Angles for Representative Latitudes and Cities
(all angles are approximate to the nearest degree)

| latitude | nearest city | solar altitude/noon (degrees) | | | azimuth at sunrise/sunset[*] |
		Dec. 22	Mar./Sept. 21	June 21	
30	Houston	37	60	84	27
34	Los Angeles/Atlanta	32	56	79	28
40	Denver	26	50	73	30
42	Chicago/Boston	24	48	71	32
48	Seattle	18	42	66	34

[*] Azimuths in this table are degrees from an east-west line. They are the same for sunrise and sunset. For sunrise on December 21, the azimuth is south of east, and for sunset it is the same angle but south of west.

interior from the sun. Either exterior or interior louvers and shades are effective, but exterior louvers are more efficient since they block the sunlight before it enters the space.

In addition to building position, solar orientation can also influence outdoor activities. In hot, humid climates, it is better to locate patios, outdoor restaurants, and the like where they receive shade from the building or trees. In more temperate climates, the same spaces are best located where they have the advantage of the warming effects of solar radiation in the winter, spring, and fall. In cold climates, building entries are best placed on the south where direct sun can melt ice and snow in the winter.

The effects of wind on building location are reviewed in Ch. 2. In addition, the orientation of a building and locations of windows, plazas, and other elements can either take advantage of cooling breezes in hot, humid climates during the summer or shield the building and occupants from cold winds in the winter. In most temperate climates prevailing wind patterns often change with the seasons, so a wind analysis is required to determine the direction of summer and winter winds. Shielding a building as much as possible from winter winds can reduce the heat loss through the walls, and providing for natural ventilation can help cool the building during the summer. Wind breaks can be formed with vegetation, buildings, or other manufactured site elements such as screens and fences.

Design Strategies for Climatic Regions

The United States and Canada can be divided into four general climatic regions: cool, temperate, hot-humid, and hot-arid. The approximate extent of each of these regions is shown in Fig. 4.4. Many of the general physical design strategies used by architects to respond to climate depend on the region in which the building is located. Some of these include the following.

Cool Climates

- Use compact forms with the smallest surface area possible relative to the volume.

- Use large, south-facing windows with small windows on the east and west and with minimal or no windows on the north.

- Use interior materials with a high thermal mass.

- Include summer shading for glazed areas.

- Use dark or medium-dark colors for the building exterior.

Temperate Climates

- Plan rectangular buildings with the long direction oriented generally along the east-west axis and facing slightly to the east. See Fig. 7.1 for suggested building orientations for various climatic regions.

- Provide shade in the summer, and allow the sun to fall on glazing and the building in the winter.

- Use south-facing openings to capture winter sunlight.

- Plan for the cooling effects of wind in the summer; block the wind in the winter.

- Use medium colors for the building exterior.

Hot-Humid Climates

- Provide shade for all openings.

- Maximize natural ventilation with large openings, high ceilings, and cross ventilation.

- Construct buildings using light materials; minimize thermal mass.

- Use light colors for the building exterior.

Hot-Arid Climates

- Use compact forms with the smallest surface area possible relative to the volume.

- Minimize opening sizes.

- Provide shade for openings.

- Maximize thermal mass.

- Use light colors for the building exterior.

Alternative Energy Systems

During the early stages of design many alternative energy systems and methods can affect the overall project concept. Such systems can affect the location, massing, shape, orientation, and primary material choice of the building as well as the configuration of other site elements like parking and landscaping. Refer to Chs. 7 and 8 for more information on both passive and active energy conservation techniques as well as sustainability principles.

Following are several brief summaries of the design strategies that can affect a project concept and overall building configuration in the early stages of project planning.

Passive Solar Heating

- If passive solar heating is used, orient the long axis of the building in the east-west direction so the southern collection surfaces face directly south or within approximately 15° of true south. Passive

Figure 4.4 Climatic Regions of the U.S.

solar heating methods should be integrated with daylighting design. Both of these design strategies will result in a building that is long and relatively narrow.

- If thermal mass is used it may be featured as a design element.

- Use deciduous trees to let sunlight fall on windows during the winter months and shade the glass during the summer. Either deciduous or evergreen trees can be used on the east and west façades to block the low angle of morning and afternoon sun. However, even bare deciduous trees can block about 20% of winter solar heat gain.

Natural Cooling

- Be aware of the following natural cooling methods. *Passive solar cooling* utilizes the concepts of shading, natural ventilation, radiative cooling, evaporative cooling, and ground coupling. *Radiative cooling* uses thermal mass to store heat during the day and release heat to the outside at night. *Ground coupling* uses the stable coolness of the earth to cool a building, typically by using a ground-source heat pump.

- Use trees and other landscaping to shade windows and other surfaces, unless direct solar radiation is needed for daylighting or passive or active solar heating. If a site has existing landscaping, locate the building such that it takes advantage of shade.

- To avoid excessive heat gain, use fixed shading devices. These are typically horizontal elements when used on the south side of a building and vertical elements when used on the east and west sides. A building can also be designed wider at the upper stories than at ground level to make it self-shading.

- Minimize glazed areas on the east and west façades.

- Use water elements and wind for an evaporative cooling effect.

- Use light-colored or reflective materials to minimize radiant heat gains.

- Limit the use of paving, to avoid heat buildup around the structure. This can be done by using a pervious paving material that supports vehicles but allows grass or other vegetation to grow through it. If extensive paving must be used, select a color that has a high reflectance. Trees can also be used to shade the paving during hot summer months.

- Use natural ventilation strategies to locate the building on the site such that it takes advantage of prevailing winds. The overall form of the building should be either narrow or spread out so breezes can filter through the building. Courtyards may also be used.

Active Solar

- Be aware that active solar collectors on a building can make a significant adverse visual statement unless they are placed on sloped roofs or are concealed with parapets.

- Position solar collectors so they do not reflect sunlight at other buildings or at occupied areas around the building.

- If solar collectors are used, locate them such that they avoid shade from buildings and trees. If collectors are mounted on the building, this factor can dictate the building's location. If collectors are mounted away from the building, an additional area on the site must be designated for the accompanying site disturbance.

Photovoltaics

- Be aware that if photovoltaics (PV) are deemed to be feasible for a building project, large surfaces may be required for mounting. These can take the form of large, flat roofs or buildings designed with sloped surfaces to optimize the PV panel's exposure to the sun. New technologies are integrating PV technology with other building materials such as glass or roofing shingles. These are known as *façade-integrated photovoltaics*. Refer to Ch. 7 for more information on photovoltaics.

DRAINAGE

Any development of a site interrupts the existing drainage pattern and creates additional water flow by replacing naturally porous ground with roof area and paving. The architect must provide for any existing drainage patterns through the site and account for additional storm water that does not seep into the ground, which is called *runoff*. The site design must also create positive drainage away from the buildings, parking areas, and walks to avoid flooding, erosion, and standing water.

The two basic types of drainage are aboveground and underground. *Aboveground* drainage involves sheet flow, gutters built into roadways and parking areas, ground swales as part of the landscaping, and channels. *Underground* drainage utilizes perforated drains and enclosed storm sewers that carry the runoff from the site to a municipal storm sewer system or to a natural drainage outlet such as a river. In a given project, combinations of several methods of drainage may be used.

Sheet flow is simply the drainage of water across a sloping surface, whether it is paved, grass, or landscaped. In most cases, sheet flow is directed to gutters or channels, which are then emptied into a natural water course or storm sewer. Gutters are often used because they can be built along with the roadway or parking area and naturally follow the same slope as the paved surface. They can easily be drained into sewers, which also typically follow the path of roads.

Areas for surface drainage require minimum slopes to provide for positive drainage. Some of these are listed in Table 2.1. Although the table indicates that a slope as little as one-half of 1% may be sufficient for some drainage, this is only applicable for very smooth surfaces that have been carefully constructed. Most paved surfaces should have at least a 1% to $1^1/_2$% slope to account for paving roughness and variations in installation tolerances.

Underground systems use piping with a minimum slope of 0.3%. The storm drains collect water from roof downspouts, drain inlets, catch basins, and drain tiles surrounding the building foundation. A drain inlet simply allows storm water to run directly into the storm sewer. A catch basin has a sump built into it so that debris will settle instead of flowing down the sewer. Periodically, the sump must be cleaned out. Large storm sewer systems require manholes for service access and are located wherever the sewer changes direction, or a maximum of 500 ft (152 m) apart. Storm sewers are completely separate from sanitary sewers.

The capacity of a drainage system is based on the size of the area to be drained, the runoff coefficient (that fraction of water not absorbed), and the amount of water to be drained during the most severe storm anticipated in the design. Frequently, the system is planned for 25-year storms; other times a 10-year storm is used. These periods are simply the average frequency at which storms of a particular magnitude are likely to occur. If the site development creates a runoff in excess of the capacity of the existing municipal storm sewer or natural drainage course, a holding pond may be needed on the site. This collects the site runoff and releases it into the sewer system at a controlled rate without letting the excess water flood other areas.

Refer to Ch. 8 for more information on drainage as it relates to sustainability.

UTILITIES

Determine the locations of existing utilities prior to beginning design. These may include, but are not limited to, sanitary sewer lines, storm sewers, water lines, gas, electricity, steam, telephone, and cable television. If possible, the building should be located to minimize the length of utility lines between the structure and the main line.

Sanitary sewers and storm sewers usually take precedence in planning because they depend on gravity flow. The invert, or lowest, elevations of the existing public sewer line should be established, since the effluent must flow from the lowest point where the sewer line leaves the building to the main sewer. This portion of the horizontal piping of the sanitary sewer system outside the building is known as the *building sewer*. The actual connection of the building sewer to the main line must occur above the invert of the main line at any given point in order not to interfere with the free flow.

The minimum slope of the building sewer is 0.5% to 2.0% depending on the size of the pipe; a greater slope is required for smaller pipes. In some cases, the run of the building sewer will have to be longer than the shortest distance between the building and the main line simply to intercept the main line at a point low enough to allow for proper slope. See Fig. 4.5.

Other utilities, such as water and electricity, do not depend on gravity, so there is a little more flexibility in locating the building relative to these services. However, the total distance should still be minimized. In the case of electrical service, the location of the main electric lines may dictate the location of transformers and service entry to the building.

CIRCULATION

There are three major types of site circulation: automobile, pedestrian, and service. Both the site design and building design portions of the examination include all three.

Automobile Circulation

Planning for automobile circulation includes locating the entry drives to the site and providing on-site roads to reach the parking areas and the building drop-off point. The entire automobile circulation system should provide direct, easy

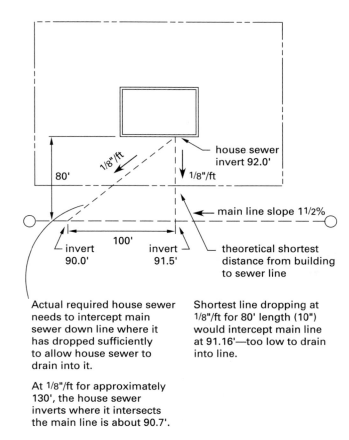

Actual required house sewer needs to intercept main sewer down line where it has dropped sufficiently to allow house sewer to drain into it.

At 1/8"/ft for approximately 130', the house sewer inverts where it intersects the main line is about 90.7'.

Shortest line dropping at 1/8"/ft for 80' length (10") would intercept main line at 91.16'—too low to drain into line.

Figure 4.5 Sewer Layout Based on Slope Required

access to the parking areas and building without excessive drives, turnarounds, dead ends, or conflicts with service areas and pedestrian circulation.

The size of the site, its relationship to existing public roads, and the expected traffic will help determine whether you should use a one-way loop system with two entry drives or a two-way system with one entry drive. In either case, you should lay out the roads so a driver can go directly to the parking area, drop-off point, or loading area. Forcing traffic through the parking area to get to the loading or the drop-off area should be avoided.

Figure 4.6 gives some design guidelines for on-site roads. Entry drives to the site should be as far away as possible from street intersections and other intersecting roads in order to avoid conflicts with vehicles waiting to turn and to avoid confusion about where to turn. Roads should be of sufficient width to make driving easy and to allow two vehicles to pass. Curves should be gradual, following the natural topography, and there should be no blind curves.

Unless the slope is very gentle, roads should not be laid out perpendicular to the slope but should be across it slightly to minimize the grade. Limit roads to a maximum slope of

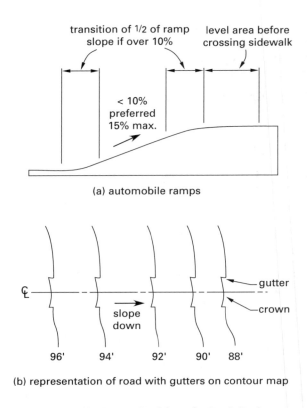

(a) automobile ramps

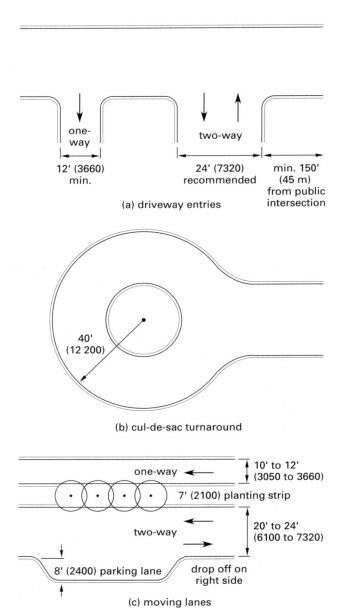

(a) driveway entries

(b) cul-de-sac turnaround

(c) moving lanes

Figure 4.6   Design Guidelines for On-Site Roads

(b) representation of road with gutters on contour map

Figure 4.7   Design Guidelines for Road Grades

15% for short distances, although 10% or less is preferable. If a road does slope more than 10%, there should be transition slopes of one-half of the maximum slope between the road and level areas. Ramps crossing sidewalks must have a level area between the ramp and the sidewalk.

Roads should have a gradual slope, a minimum of $1/4$ in/ft (20 mm/m), for drainage from the center of the roadway, called the *crown*, to the sides. If the road has a gutter, it should be 6 in (150) high. Sometimes the representation of roads and gutters on a topographic map or site plan is confusing. Figure 4.7 shows a simple road sloping down, with a uniform pitch from the crown, and with gutters on either side. As shown in Fig. 4.1, the contours of the road point toward the direction of the slope, and the pointed contours representing the gutters point in the direction of the "valley" (in this case the gutter).

Pedestrian Circulation

Like roadways, pedestrian circulation should provide convenient, direct access from the various points on the site to the building entrances. If connections with adjacent buildings, public sidewalks, public transportation stops, and other off-site points are required, the circulation system must take these into account as well. Sidewalks should provide for the most direct paths from one point to another since people will generally take the shortest route possible. Pedestrian circulation paths should not cross roads, parking lots, or other areas of potential conflict. There should be collector walks next to parking areas so people can travel from their cars directly to a separate walk.

When these walks are next to parking where cars can overhang the walk, they should be a minimum of 6 ft (1800) wide. Required amenities such as seating, trash containers, and lighting should be provided. Walks should slope a minimum of $1/4$ in (6) perpendicular to the direction of the paving for drainage. Figure 4.8 summarizes some of the design guidelines for exterior walks.

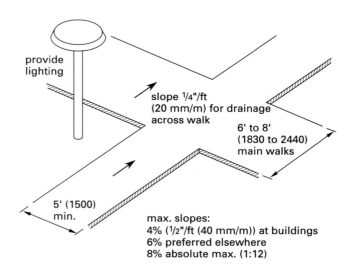

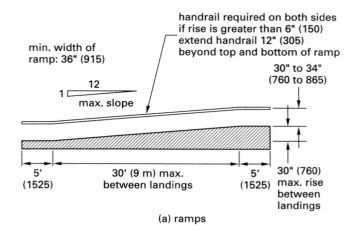

(a) ramps

Figure 4.8 Design Guidelines for Exterior Walks

Changes in elevation are accomplished with ramps and stairs. There must be provisions for making the site accessible to the physically disabled. Requirements for curb cutouts and ramps are shown in Fig. 4.9, and general guidelines for exterior stairs are shown in Fig. 4.10. When a ramp and adjacent stairway serve the same areas, the bottom and top of the ramp and stairway should be adjacent to each other if possible. As with walks, stairways and ramps should be illuminated.

Service Circulation

Service and automobile circulation should be kept separate. This is usually stated as a specific program requirement on the ARE, but if not it should be done anyway. Service access is typically related to some space in the building program. Service trucks may use the same entry and drives as automobiles use (unless specifically stated otherwise), but the loading area should be separate. The examination does not require planning for large trucks. However, sufficient turn-around space or backing areas should be provided to allow for maneuvering. Figure 4.11 shows some common guidelines for service drives for moderate-sized trucks.

PARKING

Plan parking so it is efficient, convenient to the building, and separate from pedestrian circulation. The size of the site, topography, location of entry drives to the property, and relationship to the service drive and building drop-off area will determine the location of the parking area. The number of cars to be parked is determined by requirements of the zoning ordinance or by the building program.

The basic planning unit for parking is the size of a car stall. The standard size is 9 ft 0 in (2740) wide and 19 ft 0 in

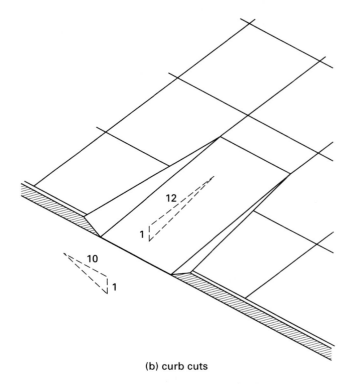

(b) curb cuts

Figure 4.9 Access Requirements for the Physically Disabled

(5800) long for standard-size cars and 7 ft 6 in (2290) wide and 15 ft 0 in (4570) long for compact cars. Individual zoning ordinances may have slightly different requirements, so always verify particular codes; but these dimensions are good ones to use for most planning. Since a large percentage of cars today are compacts, most zoning ordinances now allow sizing of a certain percentage of required parking spaces for compact cars. However, for the purposes of the

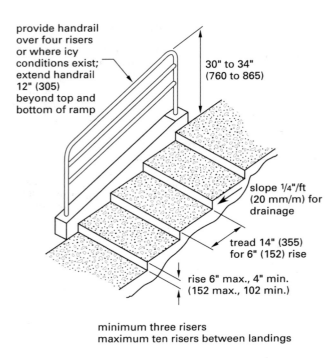

provide handrail
over four risers
or where icy
conditions exist;
extend handrail
12" (305)
beyond top and
bottom of ramp

30" to 34"
(760 to 865)

slope ¼"/ft
(20 mm/m) for
drainage

tread 14" (355)
for 6" (152) rise

rise 6" max., 4" min.
(152 max., 102 min.)

minimum three risers
maximum ten risers between landings

Figure 4.10 Design Guidelines for Exterior Stairs

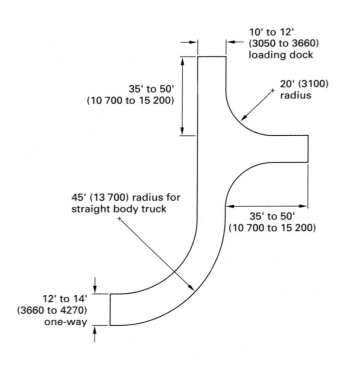

10' to 12'
(3050 to 3660)
loading dock

20' (3100)
radius

35' to 50'
(10 700 to 15 200)

45' (13 700) radius for
straight body truck

35' to 50'
(10 700 to 15 200)

12' to 14'
(3660 to 4270)
one-way

Figure 4.11 Design Guidelines for Service Drives

ARE, it is best to use the standard-size dimension unless otherwise stated in the problem.

Layouts for two types of parking are shown in Fig. 4.12. 90° parking is the most efficient in terms of land use, but angled parking is easier to use, forces a one-way circulation pattern, and requires less total width, for either a single- or double-loaded layout. Most parking lots should allow for continuous through circulation. Dead-end parking areas require a back-up space and are only appropriate for parking a few cars. The most efficient layouts are those that use

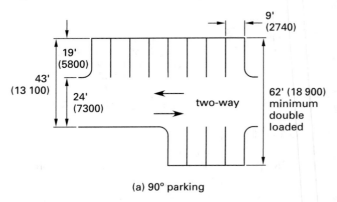

9'
(2740)

19'
(5800)

43'
(13 100)

24'
(7300)

two-way

62' (18 900)
minimum
double
loaded

(a) 90° parking

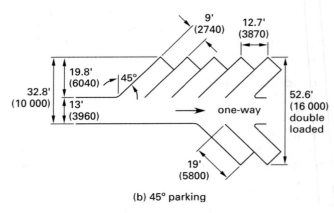

9'
(2740)

12.7'
(3870)

19.8'
(6040)

45°

32.8'
(10 000)

13'
(3960)

one-way

52.6'
(16 000)
double
loaded

19'
(5800)

(b) 45° parking

Figure 4.12 Parking Layouts

double-loaded configurations or that utilize a drive as the back-up space.

Unless otherwise required by the program, examinees must include at least one parking space for the physically disabled. Design guidelines for such a space are shown in Fig. 4.13. This space should be located close to the building entrance and should be identified with the international symbol for accessibility. If a van-accessible space is required, as it is with the Americans with Disabilities Act, the access aisle must be 96 in (2440) wide and level with the accessible route.

Establish drainage in parking areas as part of the site design. The minimum slope should be 1½% with a maximum

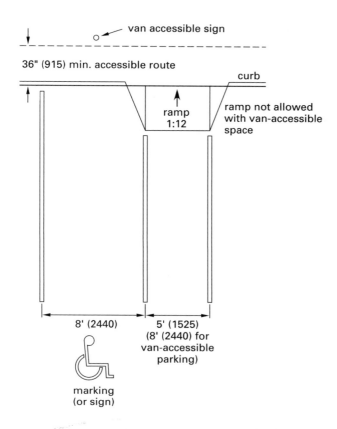

Figure 4.13 Parking for the Physically Disabled

slope of 5%, but for convenience in calculating, use 2% or 3% when figuring parking slopes. Water should drain toward the edges of the parking area where it can run off into the landscaping or be collected and diverted to storm sewers or other natural water courses. Figure 4.14 shows three basic drainage patterns, depending on the orientation of the length of the lot to the contour lines. If curbs are used, there must be some way for the water to drain out, either with curb cutouts or drains to a storm sewer.

One useful rule of thumb is that the change in elevation from one side of a double-loaded parking area to the other (62 ft [18 900]) for a minimum 1½% slope is about 1 ft (300). With an absolute maximum of a 5% slope, the maximum change in elevation for 62 ft is about 3 ft (900). This is a useful way to quickly check new contour lines when designing a parking area.

LANDSCAPING

Landscaping is a vital part of site development. In addition to its purely aesthetic qualities, landscaping can improve energy conservation, moderate noise, frame desirable views, block undesirable views, create privacy, fashion outdoor

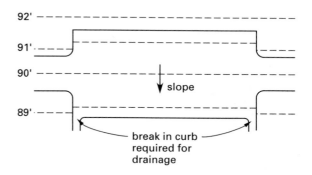

(a) drainage perpendicular to length of lot

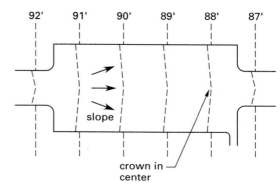

(b) drainage parallel to length

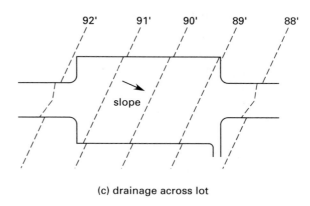

(c) drainage across lot

Figure 4.14 Drainage Patterns in Parking Lots

spaces, provide shade, retard erosion, and visually connect a building to its site. It is required in some communities.

The use of landscaping to moderate the microclimate is discussed in Ch. 2 and covers the use of deciduous trees to block sunlight in the summer while allowing it to enter a building in the winter. Trees can also moderate the wind and thereby reduce heat loss from wall surfaces. Slowing the normal wind patterns can also make outdoor spaces more pleasant to use. If trees are employed as a windbreak, evergreens should be used so they will remain effective in the winter.

Grass, shrubs, and groundcover lower the albedo of the site. *Albedo* is that portion of the radiant energy that is reflected as it falls on a surface. Combined with the low conductivity of plant materials, a well-landscaped site can reduce the daytime temperature around the building significantly and in some cases can raise the nighttime temperature slightly.

Plants are like any other design material in that they have form, size, color, texture, and other qualities that can serve the purposes of the designer and create the kind of image desired. Unlike other materials, however, plants grow.

The mature size and height of the tree or shrub must be known so adequate spacing between plants and between plants and buildings can be provided. Generally, planting strips with trees in parking areas and between other paved areas should be at least 7 ft (2130) wide, whereas landscaping strips for grass or groundcovers between paved areas should be at least 4 ft (1220) wide.

Because most trees and shrubs take so long to grow, existing healthy landscaping, especially large trees, should be saved whenever possible. The contours of the land cannot be changed around existing trees out to their drip line, so careful planning is necessary. Trees and other landscaping also need protection during construction.

PROPERTY DESCRIPTIONS

The boundaries of a site can be described in one of several ways. One of the most common is based on the United States survey system that was begun in 1784. This system laid out the majority of the United States except for those lands surveyed prior to the establishment of the control system and land based on some other system or land grant.

The system starts with a set of east-west lines called parallels that follow the lines of latitude of the earth, and with a set of north-south lines called *meridians*. There are several meridians and parallels that serve as the basis for the grid layout. These are called the *principal meridians* and *base lines*, respectively. Other meridians are called *guide meridians*, and other parallels are called *standard parallels*. They are referred to as being east or west, north or south of the base lines and principal meridians. See Fig. 4.15.

The parallels and meridians are 24 mi apart, and the squares they form are called *checks*. Since the meridian lines converge because of the shape of the earth, the south line of

the first and each successive guide meridian is adjusted to be 24 mi from the principal meridian and adjacent guide meridians.

Each of the 24 mi squares is divided into 16 townships, each 6 mi on a side. The townships are referred to by a number referenced to a principal meridian and base line. The row of townships running east and west is referred to as a *township* (the same term but a different meaning), and the row of townships running north and south is referred to as a *range*.

The townships are numbered sequentially beginning at a base line. Those north of the base line are *north townships* and those south are *south townships*. Ranges are also numbered sequentially beginning at a principal meridian, either east or west. Therefore, a typical description of a township (the 6 mi² parcel of land) might be "township 13 north, range 7 east of the 6th principal meridian." This would typically be abbreviated to T.13N, R.7E, 6th PM.

Each township is then further divided into 36 sections, each section being a one-mile square. These are numbered sequentially starting in the northeast section, moving west, dropping down, then moving east, and so on, from sections 1 to 36 as shown in Fig. 4.15.

Sections are commonly further divided into quarter sections, and those quarter sections into four more parcels. A complete description of such a portion of a section might read: "The SE ¼ of the NW ¼, Section 12, T.13N, R.7E of the 6th PM, located in the County of Merrick, State of Nebraska."

Because so much urbanization has occurred in the past 100 years and subdivision of land has become common, property is often described by its particular lot number within a subdivision, the subdivision having been carefully surveyed and recorded with the city or county in which it is located. Figure 4.16 shows one such property.

In addition to the lot and subdivisions reference, a typical property description will include the bearings of the property lines and their lengths, along with any permanent corner markers set by the original subdivision surveyor. The property line bearings are referred to by the number of degrees, minutes, and seconds the line is located either east or west of a north-south line.

Another method that is sometimes used is the *metes and bounds description*. With this approach, the description is a lengthy narrative starting at one point of the property and describing the length and direction of each line around the property boundary until the point of beginning is reached.

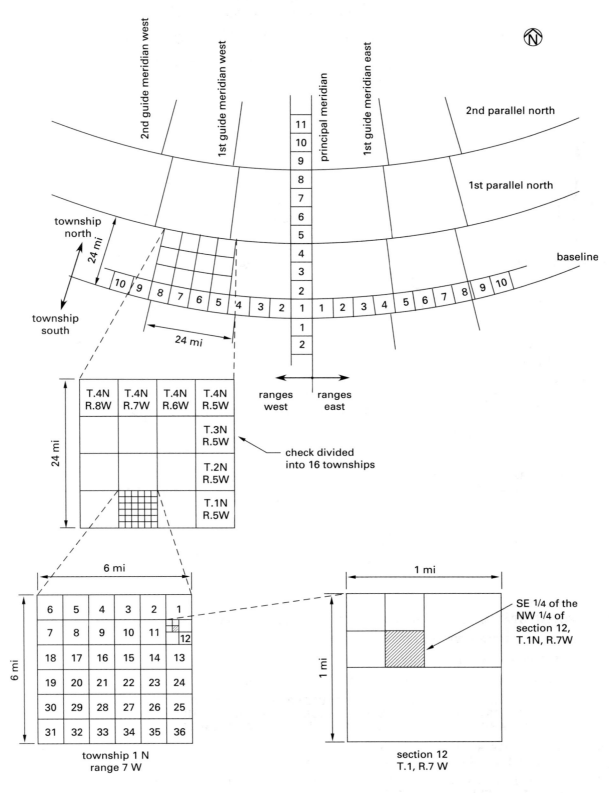

Figure 4.15 U.S. Survey System

BOUNDARY SURVEY
LOT 18, BLOCK 8, SCANLOCH SUBDIVISION
GRAND COUNTY, COLORADO

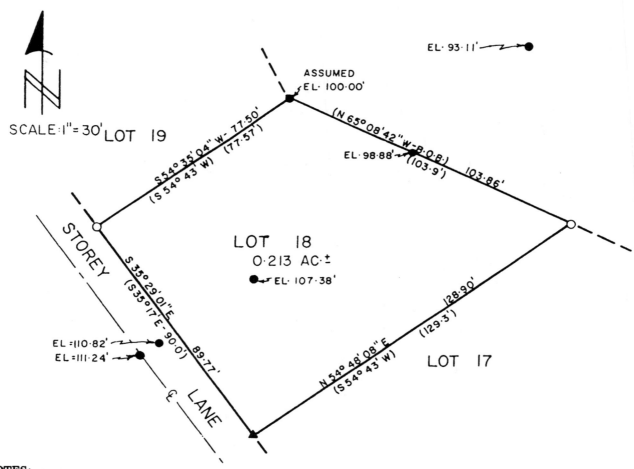

NOTES:

■ FOUND STANDARD BLM BRASS CAP MARKED AP—81 DATED 1950.

○ SET No. 4 REBAR WITH ALUMINUM CAP L. S. No. 11415.

▲ FOUND 1¼" IRON PIPE IN CONCRETE.

● CALCULATION POINT ONLY, NOTHING FOUND OR SET.

( ) BEARINGS AND DISTANCES AS PER RECORD PLAT RECEPTION No. 759621, GRAND COUNTY RECORDS, COLORADO. ALL OTHER BEARINGS AND DISTANCES ARE ACTUAL FIELD MEASUREMENTS.

B.O.B. THE BASIS OF BEARING FOR THIS SURVEY IS THE NORTHWESTERLY BOUNDARY LINE OF LOTS 17 & 18. SAID BEARING IS N65°08'42"W.

ELEVATIONS ARE ASSUMED FROM BRASS CAP NORTHEAST CORNER OF LOT 18 AP. 81—1950, ELEVATION = 100.00'.

Figure 4.16 Typical Boundary Survey Description

With all types of property descriptions, the area of the parcel is also included, usually in acres (hectares), one acre containing 43,560 ft². Remember, too, that one section contains 640 ac, and one quarter of a quarter section contains 40 ac. A *hectare* (ha) is 10 000 m².

OTHER DESIGN CONSIDERATIONS

In addition to the factors already discussed, many other design considerations can influence the location, orientation, and configuration of a building, as well as other features of the site design. One of the most important is the context of the surrounding development. The design of a building should be sensitive to the scale, massing, and fenestration patterns of nearby buildings. The design should also consider any functional adjacency requirements with other structures or outdoor activities. For example, the entry to a student union building should be located near the existing, primary campus circulation routes.

Views are also an important consideration. Pleasant, desirable views can be used to advantage, as seen either from important spaces within the building or from outdoor spaces. Undesirable views can be avoided by planning the building so service spaces or less-important spaces face them. Off-site sources of noise can be similarly avoided by minimizing windows near the noise source.

Quite frequently, buildings are located in order to fall on an important axis with surrounding structures or to complete the enclosure of a major outdoor space. The site-planning process should not overlook these kinds of symbolic criteria.

SAMPLE QUESTIONS

1. What is especially important in designing roads for drainage?

    A.   runoff
    B.   crown
    C.   catch basin
    D.   sheet flow

2. What term describes a land measure that is 6 mi on a side?

    A.   section
    B.   check
    C.   township
    D.   range

3. Wastewater flows because of differences between what?

    A.   catch basins
    B.   storm sewers
    C.   drain inlets
    D.   inverts

4. Assuming the building site shown is surrounded on four sides by city streets, which building and road layout is most appropriate for the site topography?

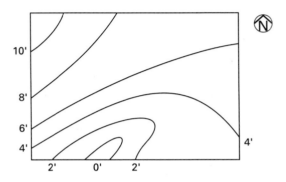

A.

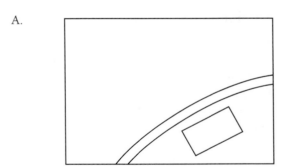

B.

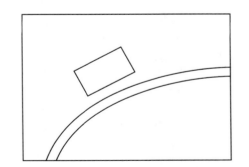

C.

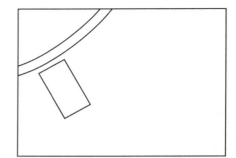

D.

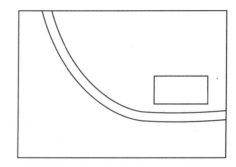

5. Which of the following statements is INCORRECT?

A. A 1¹/₂% slope is suitable for rough paving.

B. Landscaped areas near buildings should have at least a 2% slope away from the structure.

C. A safe sidewalk would slope 2¹/₂%.

D. Roads in northern climates can safely have up to a 12% grade.

6. Which of the following would result in the best site circulation?

I. planning the service entry drive separate from the automobile entry and drive

II. making parking areas oversized to accommodate pedestrian circulation

III. designing all two-way roads at least 24 ft wide

IV. limiting parking area traffic to a single entrance away from pedestrian walks

V. laying out walks parallel to parking areas

A. I, III, and IV

B. I, III, and V

C. II, IV, and V

D. I, III, IV, and V

7. Property can best be described with

A. metes and bounds

B. reference to a section and township

C. location within a subdivision

D. all of the above

8. Potential overheating of a medical clinic in a temperate climate could be minimized by

A. designing an overhang for the west and east sides of the building

B. planning a building shape to minimize the surface area of south-facing walls

C. having a landscape architect specify deciduous trees near the south elevation

D. all of the above

9. The contour lines in the sketch shown indicate

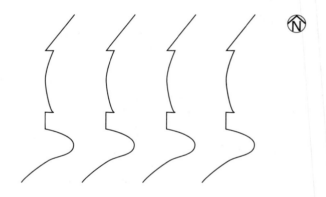

A. a sidewalk sloping down from east to west with a berm on the south side

B. a road with drainage in the middle and a sidewalk and berm on the south

C. a swale adjacent to a walking path sloping from northeast to southwest

D. a curbed street sloping up from west to east next to a drainage ditch

10. If land is limited, which of the following is the best way to plan parking lots?

A. two-way circulation with 90° parking on both sides of a drive

B. 30° parking on both sides of a one-way loop system

C. combining service circulation with parking at a 45° angle

D. 90° parking on one side of a one-way circulation drive

SECTION 2: MECHANICAL AND ELECTRICAL SYSTEMS

HUMAN COMFORT AND MECHANICAL SYSTEM FUNDAMENTALS

Nomenclature

ϵ	emissivity	n/a	n/a
A	area of a building assembly	ft^2	m^2
C	conductance	Btu/hr-ft^2-°F	W/m^2·K
e	emittance	hr-ft^2-°F/Btu	m^2·K/W
k	conductivity (for 1 in thickness)	Btu/hr-ft^2-°F	W/m·K
q	total heat loss through a building assembly	Btu/hr	W
q_v	sensible heat loss or gain due to infiltration or ventilation	Btu/hr	W
R	resistance	hr-ft^2-°F/Btu	m^2·K/W
Δt	temperature difference between indoor and outdoor air	°F	°C
U	coefficient of heat transmission	Btu/hr-ft^2-°F	W/m^2·K
V	volume flow rate of outside air	ft^3/min	L/s

DEFINITIONS

British thermal unit (Btu): the amount of heat required to raise the temperature of 1 lbm of water by 1°F. In SI units, energy is measured in joules, J. One joule is a newton-meter, or the force of 1 N acting through a distance of 1 m. One joule is $^1/_{4.184}$ of the amount of heat required to raise the temperature of a gram of water by 1°C. One Btu equals about 1.055 kJ.

Coefficient of heat transmission: the overall rate of heat flow through any combination of materials, including air spaces and air layers on the interior and exterior of a building assembly. It is the reciprocal of the sum of all the resistances in the building assembly.

Conductance: the number of British thermal units per hour that pass through 1 ft^2 of homogeneous material of a given thickness when the temperature differential is 1°F. In SI units, conductance is the rate at which watts pass through 1 m^2 of material when the temperature differential is 1K (Celsius).

Conductivity: the number of British thermal units per hour that pass through 1 ft^2 of homogeneous material 1 in thick when the temperature differential is 1°F. In SI units, conductivity is the rate at which watts flow through 1 m^2 of material 1 m thick when the temperature differential is 1K (Celsius).

Dew point: the temperature at which water vapor in the air becomes saturated and begins to condense to drops of water

Dry-bulb temperature: the temperature of the air-water mixture as measured with a standard dry-bulb thermometer

Enthalpy: the total heat in a substance, including latent heat and sensible heat

Insolation: the total solar radiation on a horizontal surface

Latent heat: heat that causes a change of state of a substance, such as the heat required to change water into steam. The amount of heat required to change the state of a substance is much greater than the heat required to raise the temperature of the substance (sensible heat). The average value of latent heat per pound of moisture is 1061 Btu (1120 kJ).

Resistance: the number of hours needed for 1 Btu to pass through 1 ft^2 of material or assembly of a given thickness when the temperature differential is 1°F. It is the reciprocal of conductance. In SI units, resistance is the number of hours needed for 1 W to pass through 1 m^2 of material or assembly of a given thickness when the temperature differential is 1K (Celsius).

Sensible heat: heat that causes a change in temperature of a substance but not a change of state. For example, the sensible heat required to raise the temperature of 1 lbm of water from 50°F to 100°F (10°C to 38°C) is 50 Btu (53 kJ). In contrast, the latent heat required to change water at 212°F (100°C) to steam at the same temperature is 1061 Btu (1120 kJ).

Specific heat: the number of Btus (joules) required to raise the temperature of a specific material by 1°F (1K). Specific heat is a measure of a material's capacity to store heat as compared with the storage capacity of water.

Wet-bulb temperature: the temperature of the air as measured with a sling psychrometer. The wet-bulb temperature is a more critical measure of heat in high humidity because it is an indicator of stress when the human body is near the upper limits of temperature regulation by perspiration.

HUMAN COMFORT

Human comfort is based on the quality of the following primary environmental factors: temperature, humidity, air movement, temperature radiation to and from surrounding surfaces, air quality, sound, vibration, and light. For each of these factors there are certain levels within which people are comfortable and can function most efficiently. Acoustics and lighting are reviewed in later chapters. This section discusses human comfort relative to the thermal environment. Ch. 6 deals with the mechanical systems used to modify internal environments to maintain human comfort.

Human Metabolism

The human body is a heat-producing machine. It takes in food and water and, through the metabolic process, converts these to mechanical energy and other bodily processes necessary to maintain life. Because the body is not very efficient in this conversion, it must give off excess heat in order to maintain a stable body temperature. The body's heat production is measured in metabolic units, or *mets*. A met is the energy produced per unit of surface area per hour by a seated person at rest. One met is 18.4 Btu/hr-ft² (58.2 W/m²). Given the average surface area of an adult, this means that at rest the human body gives off about 400 Btu/hr (117 W). This increases to around 700 Btu/hr to 800 Btu/hr (205 W to 235 W) for moderate activities like walking and work, and up to 2000 Btu/hr (586 W) for strenuous exercise.

The body loses heat in three primary ways: convection, evaporation, and radiation. It can also lose heat by conduction, but this accounts for a very small portion of total body heat loss. *Convection* is the transfer of heat through the movement of a fluid, either a gas or liquid. This occurs when the air temperature surrounding a person is less than the body's skin temperature, around 85°F (29°C). The body heats the surrounding air, which rises and is replaced with

cooler air. Heat loss through *evaporation* occurs when moisture changes to a vapor as a person perspires or breathes. *Radiation* is the transfer of heat energy through electromagnetic waves from one surface to a colder surface. The body can lose heat to a cooler atmosphere or to a cooler surface. *Conduction* is the transfer of heat through direct contact between two objects of different temperatures.

The body loses heat (or is prevented from losing heat) through these four processes in various proportions depending on the environmental conditions. If the body cannot lose heat one way it must lose it another. For example, when the air temperature is above the body temperature of 98.6°F (37°C), there can be no convection transfer because heat always flows from a high level to a low level. This is dictated by the second law of thermodynamics. The body must then lose all its heat by evaporation. Figure 5.1 illustrates how the total amount of heat generated at rest is transferred depending on the surrounding temperature.

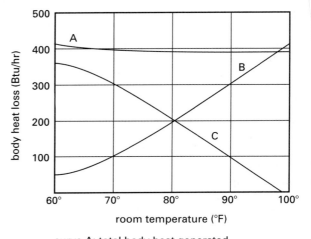

curve A: total body heat generated
curve B: body heat loss by evaporation
curve C: body heat loss by convection and radiation

Figure 5.1   Body Heat Generated and Lost at Rest

The sensation of thermal comfort depends on the interrelationship of many factors. Some of these include air temperature, humidity, air movement, surface temperature, clothing, and ventilation. These are discussed in the following sections. Other factors that are more difficult to quantify objectively include personal metabolic rate, age, and psychological variables such as light, color, and aroma.

Air Temperature

Temperature is the primary determinant of comfort. It is difficult to precisely state a normal range of comfortable temperature limits because the range depends on many factors including the humidity levels, radiant temperatures, air movement, clothing, cultural factors, age, and sex.

However, a general comfortable range is between 69°F and 80°F (20°C to 27°C), with a tolerable range from 60°F to 85°F (16°C to 29°C), depending on relative humidity.

A value called the *effective temperature* (ET) that attempts to combine the effects of air temperature, humidity, and air movement has been developed.

Dry-bulb temperature is measured with a standard thermometer. Wet-bulb temperature is measured with a *sling psychrometer*, a device that consists of a thermometer with a moist cloth around the bulb. The thermometer is swung rapidly in the air, causing the moisture in the cloth to evaporate. In dry air, the moisture evaporates rapidly and acquires latent heat, which produces a low wet-bulb temperature. A large difference between the wet-bulb temperature and the dry-bulb temperature indicates low relative humidity. In moist air, less moisture evaporates from the cloth, so the wet-bulb temperature is higher.

Humidity

Relative humidity is the ratio of the percentage of moisture in the air to the maximum amount the air can hold at a given temperature without condensing. Comfortable relative humidity ranges are between 30% and 65%, with tolerable ranges between 20% and 70%. Relative humidity is particularly important in the summer months because as the air temperature rises, the body can lose less heat through convection and must rely mostly on evaporation. However, as the humidity rises, it is more difficult for perspiration to evaporate; hence, a person feels much hotter than the air temperature would indicate.

Air Movement

Air movement tends to increase evaporation and heat loss through convection. This is why a person will feel comfortable in high temperatures and humidities if there is a breeze. It also explains the windchill effect when a tolerable cold air temperature becomes unbearable in a wind. Wind speeds from 50 ft/min to about 200 ft/min (0.25 to 1.02 m/s) are generally acceptable for cooling without causing annoying drafts.

Surface Temperature

Because the body gains or loses heat through radiation, the temperature of the surrounding surfaces is an important factor in determining human comfort. If the surface temperatures of the surroundings are colder than the surface temperature of the skin, about 85°F (29°C), the body loses heat through radiation; if the surrounding surfaces are warmer than the skin, the body gains heat. The rate at which radiation occurs depends on the surface temperatures of the body and the nearby object, the viewed angle, and the emissivity.

The *viewed angle* is the solid angle formed between the measuring position and the outer edges of the object. For example, when sitting close to a fireplace, a person experiences relatively high radiant heat because the fireplace occupies a large angle of view relative to the body. When the person sits across the room, the same fireplace occupies a much smaller angle of view, so it will not feel as warm.

The *emissivity* (ϵ) of an object is a measure of its ability to absorb and then radiate heat. Technically, the emittance of an object is the ratio of the radiation emitted by a given object or material to that emitted by a blackbody at the same temperature. Shiny objects or materials have very low emissivity, so they do not absorb or radiate heat as well as black objects. The shiny foil on many insulation materials is an example of using emissivity to reduce heat transfer.

To determine the effects of surface temperatures on comfort, all room surfaces, and their temperatures and positions, must be taken into account. The value used to calculate these factors is the *mean radiant temperature* (MRT). The MRT is a weighted average of the various surface temperatures in a room and the angle of exposure of the occupant to these surfaces, as well as of any sunlight present.

The MRT is an important comfort factor in cold rooms or in the winter because as the air temperature decreases, the body loses more heat through radiation than by evaporation, as shown in Fig. 5.1. Even a room with an adequate temperature will feel cool if the surfaces are cold. Warming these surfaces and providing radiant heating panels are two ways to counteract this effect.

Another way to factor in the effects of surface temperatures on human comfort is with operative temperature. *Operative temperature* is an average of the air temperature of a space and the mean radiant temperature (MRT) of the space. It can be measured with a *globe thermometer*, which is a thermometer inside a black globe. This type of thermometer can account for both the air temperature and radiant effects from surrounding surfaces.

Clothing

Clothing acts as an insulator, moderating the effects of conduction, convection, and radiation. Nearly all measurements and standards for human comfort are based on wearing clothing. To quantify the effects of clothing the unit of the Clo was developed. One Clo is about equal to the typical American man's business suit or about 0.15 Clo/lbm (0.35 Clo/kg) of clothing.

Ventilation

Ventilation is required to provide oxygen and remove carbon dioxide, to remove odors, and to carry away contaminants. The amount of ventilation required in a room depends on the activity involved, the size of the room, and whether smoking is involved. For example, a gymnasium needs a higher ventilation rate than does a library. The model codes give minimum requirements for ventilation, either by specifying minimum operable window areas, minimum mechanical ventilation rates, or both. The UBC states these requirements in each of the chapters dealing with specific occupancy groups.

Building codes specify the minimum amount of fresh, outdoor air that must be circulated in cubic feet per minute and the total circulated air, also in cubic feet per minute (liters per second). Mechanical systems are designed to filter and recirculate much of the conditioned air, and also to introduce a certain percentage of outdoor air along with the recirculated air.

Where exhausting of air is required, such as in toilet rooms, kitchens, and spaces where noxious fumes are present, additional requirements are given. Codes state minimum exhaust rates in cubic feet per minute (liters per second) per square foot of floor area or state how often a complete air change must be made. In these situations, the ventilation system must exhaust directly to the outside; none of the exhausted air can be recirculated.

MEASUREMENT SYSTEMS

Because the relationships between temperature, humidity, radiation, and other factors are complex, various methods have been developed to show these relationships and to assist in designing mechanical systems. Two of the more common methods are discussed in the following sections.

Comfort Charts

Comfort charts show the relationships among temperature, humidity, and other comfort factors. A simplified version is shown in Fig. 5.2. It shows the comfort zones for both winter and summer for temperature zones in the United States (about 40° latitude) for elevations below 1000 ft (300 m) above sea level, and for people normally engaged in sedentary or light work.

The tolerable humidity limits of about 20% and 75% are shown, but limits between 30% and 65% are preferred. The chart shows that as humidity increases, the air temperature must decrease to provide the same amount of comfort as is felt with lower humidity levels.

As the temperature drops below the recommended levels, radiation in the form of sunshine or mechanical radiation is needed to maintain comfort. The lower the temperature, the more radiation is required. As the humidity and temperature increase, air movement is required to maintain comfort levels.

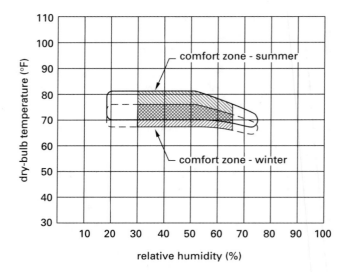

Figure 5.2 Comfort Chart for Temperate Zones

Psychrometric Chart

The psychrometric chart is a graphical representation of the complex interactions between heat, air, and moisture. The study of the water vapor content of air is known as *psychrometry*. Because warm air can hold more moisture than cold air can, and because the amount of moisture in the air (humidity) affects human comfort, especially at high temperatures, there must be a way to calculate the amount of heat and moisture that must be either added or removed by HVAC systems. The psychrometric chart is the tool used to make the necessary calculations.

Figure 5.3 shows a simplified version of the psychrometric chart. For illustrative purposes, it does not show all the graph lines that are present on the full chart. The vertical lines show dry-bulb temperatures, while the lines sloping from upper left to lower right show wet-bulb temperatures. The curved lines represent relative humidity from 0% to 100%. The 100% line is also known as the *saturation line* or *dew-point line*. This shows when water vapor will form when saturated air comes in contact with any surface at or below the air's dew-point temperature. At 100% relative humidity, the wet-bulb and dry-bulb temperatures are the same.

Along the upper-left side of the chart is a scale representing *enthalpy*, or the total amount of both sensible and latent heat in the air-moisture mixture. Its lines run approximately parallel to the wet-bulb temperature lines and are in units of Btu/lbm (kJ/kg) of dry air. The *enthalpy line* is used to determine the total amount of heat that must be either removed (in cooling) or added (in heating) from conditioned air. This is more than just the heat represented by air temperature (sensible heat), because the latent heat contained in the moisture in the air must also be removed or added.

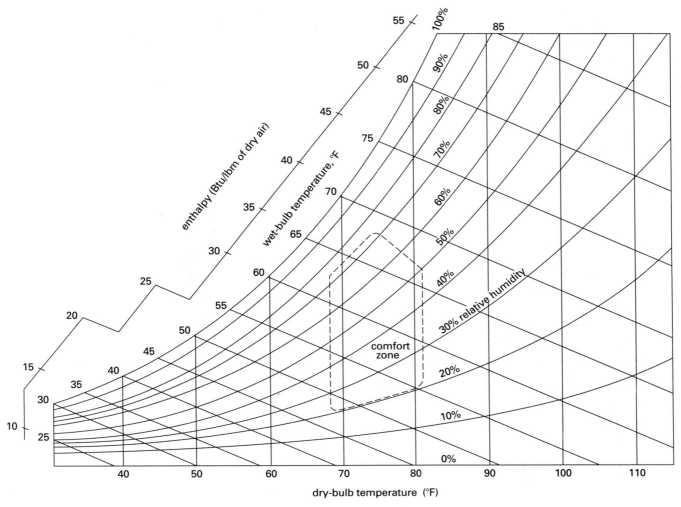

Figure 5.3 Psychrometric Chart

The amount of moisture that must be removed or added can also be read along a horizontal scale at the right side of the chart. These lines are not shown in the simplified version of Fig. 5.3, but represent the *humidity ratio*, or the amount of moisture by weight within a given weight of air.

The psychrometric chart illustrates why evaporative coolers only work in hot, dry climates. An *evaporative cooler* (swamp cooler) reduces the temperature of the air but does not reduce the enthalpy (total heat). For example, select the wet-bulb temperature line of 70°F (which is nearly parallel to the enthalpy lines) where it crosses the vertical dry-bulb temperature line of 90°F. Follow it up and to the left until it crosses the vertical 80°F dry-bulb temperature line. The chart shows that without changing the enthalpy and dropping the air temperature 10°F, the humidity has increased from about 40% to more than 60%.

In addition to providing a wide range of information for HVAC design, the psychrometric chart can also be used to plot the comfort zone based on combinations of temperature and humidity. This also is shown in Fig. 5.3.

EXTERNAL AND INTERNAL LOADS

In order to maintain human comfort, a building must resist either the loss of heat to the outside during cold weather or the gain of heat during hot weather. Any excess heat gain or loss must be compensated for with passive energy conservation measures or with mechanical heating and cooling systems.

External factors that cause heat loss include air temperature and wind. External factors that cause heat gain include air temperature and sunlight. Internal factors that produce heat loads include people, lights, and equipment.

Heat is transferred between the outside and inside of a building through conduction, convection, and radiation. *Conduction* is the transfer of heat through direct contact between molecules. *Convection* is the transfer of heat through the movement of air. *Radiation* is the transfer of heat energy through electromagnetic waves from one surface to a colder surface.

Heat Loss Calculations

In order to determine the size of a heating system for a building, the total amount of heat lost per hour must be calculated. Heat is lost in two basic ways: through the building envelope and through air infiltration. The *building envelope* consists of the walls, roof, doors, windows, and foundation. Each of the materials or groups of materials comprising these building elements resists the transfer of heat that occurs through the processes of conduction, convection, and radiation.

Every material has a unique property known as its *conductivity*, k, which is the amount of heat lost through 1 ft² of a 1 in thickness of the material when the temperature differential is 1°F. *Conductance*, C, is the same property, but when the material is a thickness other than 1 in. The *resistance*, R, of a material, is the number of hours needed for 1 Btu to pass through a material of a given thickness when the temperature differential is 1°F. In SI units conductivity, k, is the rate at which watts flow through 1 m² of material when the temperature differential is 1K (Celsius). Resistance, R, in SI units is the number of hours needed for 1 W to pass through 1 m² of material or assembly of a given thickness when the temperature differential is 1K (Celsius).

Conductance and resistance are related by the formula

$$R = \frac{1}{C} \qquad 5.1$$

Values for k, C, and R for various materials are given in standard reference texts as well as in the American Society of Heating, Refrigerating, and Air-Conditioning Engineers (ASHRAE) *Handbook of Fundamentals*. If any heat loss calculations are required on the exam, the necessary tables will be included with the online reference materials.

When a building assembly consists of more than one material, the value used to calculate heat loss is the coefficient of heat transmission, U. However, the value of U is not simply the sum of all the conductances of the individual materials. Instead, the coefficient of heat loss must be calculated according to the formula

$$U = \frac{1}{\Sigma R} \qquad 5.2$$

The amount of heat loss through one unit of area of building material or assembly is dependent on the coefficient of

heat transmission of the material or assembly and the temperature differential between the inside and outside. For an entire area of one type of material, this value is multiplied by the total area to get the total heat loss. The formula is

$$q = UA\Delta t \qquad 5.3$$

In order to calculate the heat loss for an entire room or building, the heat losses of all the different types of assemblies—walls, windows, roofs, and so forth—must be determined and then added together.

Example 5.1

Find the coefficient of heat transmission for the wall assembly shown.

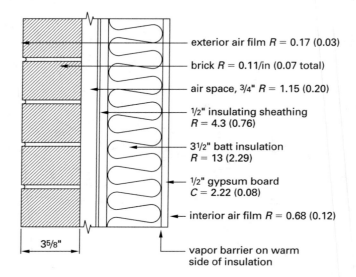

exterior air film $R = 0.17$ (0.03)
brick $R = 0.11$/in (0.07 total)
air space, 3/4" $R = 1.15$ (0.20)
1/2" insulating sheathing $R = 4.3$ (0.76)
3½" batt insulation $R = 13$ (2.29)
1/2" gypsum board $C = 2.22$ (0.08)
interior air film $R = 0.68$ (0.12)
vapor barrier on warm side of insulation
3⅝"

The R- and C-values for the various components are given. However, they must all be converted to conductances for the thicknesses used. Remember that air spaces and the thin layer of air on the exteriors and interiors of buildings have some thermal resistance. If the brick has an R-value of 0.11 hr/Btu-ft²-°F per inch and is 3⅝ in thick (3.625), then its total R-value is 0.40 hr/Btu-ft²-°F. The conductance of the gypsum board is 2.22 Btu/hr-ft²-°F, so its resistance is ¹/₂.₂₂, or 0.45.

The summation of the R-values of the assembly is

	R-value	
	(hr/Btu-ft²-°F)	(hr/W-m²·K)
exterior air film	0.17	0.03
brick	0.40	0.07
air space	1.15	0.20
sheathing	4.30	0.76
insulation	13.00	2.29
gypsum board	0.45	0.08
interior air film	0.68	0.12
ΣR	20.15	3.55

The overall coefficient of transmission is then

$$U = \frac{1}{\Sigma R}$$

$$= \frac{1}{20.15} \text{ Btu/hr-ft}^2\text{-}°F \quad \left(\frac{1}{3.55} \text{W/m}^2\text{·K}\right)$$

$$= 0.05 \text{ Btu/hr-ft}^2\text{-}°F \quad (0.28 \text{ W/m}^2\text{·K})$$

The value for Δt is determined by subtracting the outdoor design temperature from the desired indoor temperature in the winter, usually 70°F (21°C). Outdoor design temperatures vary with geographical region and are found in the ASHRAE Handbook or are set by local building codes.

One important aspect of heat loss calculations and the use of the psychrometric chart is to determine the dew point of the moisture in the air to avoid condensation on interior surfaces and especially inside building construction. For example, air at 70°F (21°C) and 35% relative humidity has a dew point of 41°F (5°C). Moisture will condense on surfaces at or below this temperature.

In Ex. 5.1, if the outdoor temperature is 0°F (−18°C) and the indoor temperature 70°F (21°C), somewhere inside the wall assembly the temperature is 41°F (5°C) or less. Water vapor from inside the building permeating the construction would condense on this surface, damaging the wood construction and possibly negating the effectiveness of the insulation. To avoid this problem, a vapor barrier must be placed on the warm side of the insulation, as shown in Ex. 5.1. Vapor barriers can be thin plastic films, or they can be a part of sheathing or insulation batts.

Heat loss through infiltration will be discussed in a separate section.

Heat Gain Calculations

There are several sources of heat gain in buildings. There is, of course, heat gain produced when the outside temperature is high and heat is transferred by conduction, convection,

and radiation, just as with heat loss. Heat gain through infiltration is also a factor when outside temperatures are high. In addition, heat is produced by the radiation of the sun on glazing, by the building's occupants, by lighting, and by equipment such as motors.

The percentage of heat generated by each of these factors varies with the occupancy of the building. For example, a residence is dominated by gains from the building envelope and through glazing. The number of occupants and lighting is negligible. A large office building, however, has a great many occupants, each producing a minimum of 400 Btu/hr (117 W) at rest, a large number of light fixtures, and a significant amount of equipment. The ratio of room and wall surface may be quite low for such an office building compared with a residence. Because of these types of conditions, it is not unusual in many occupancies for air conditioning to be required even in the winter months.

Heat gain through the building envelope is calculated in a manner similar to heat loss, using the overall coefficient of heat transmission and the area of the building assembly (as shown in formula 5.3), but the temperature differential is not used directly. Instead, a value known as the *design equivalent temperature difference* (DETD) must be used. This value, calculated through complex formulas, takes into account the air temperature differences, effects of the sun, thermal mass storage effects of materials, colors of finishes exposed to the sun, and the daily temperature range. These values are published in tables produced by ASHRAE.

Heat gain through glazing can be a very significant factor. It is calculated by multiplying the area of the glazing by the *design cooling load factor* (DCLF). Like the design equivalent temperature difference, the DCLF takes into account several variables that affect how solar heat gain occurs, including the type of glazing, the type of interior shading, and the outdoor design temperature. Design cooling load factors are also published by ASHRAE.

The occupants of a building produce two kinds of heat: sensible heat and latent heat in the form of moisture from breathing and perspiration. Sensible heat gain from occupants can be assumed to be about 225 Btu/hr (66 W), although this varies slightly with occupancy type. Total sensible heat is calculated by multiplying the number of occupants by 225 Btu/hr (66 W).

Heat gains from lighting can be found by using the fact that one watt equals 3.41 Btu/hr. Simply multiply the total wattage load of the building's lighting by 3.41. For fluorescent and other discharge lights, the energy used by the ballast must also be included. A rule of thumb is to multiply the Btu/hr generated by these types of fixtures by 1.25. In SI units, watts can be used directly.

Heat generated by equipment such as motors, elevators, appliances, water heaters, and cooking equipment can be a significant factor in commercial buildings. The methods of calculating such heat are complex and depend on variables such as horsepower ratings and efficiencies of motors, load factors, and any latent heat produced.

Latent heat must be accounted for in calculating heat gains because, for cooling purposes, moisture in the air (latent heat) must be removed to maintain a comfortable relative humidity level while the sensible heat level is being reduced. In heat-gain calculations, latent heat gain is either accounted for separately or by multiplying the total sensible heat gain in a building by a certain percentage derived through experience. Latent heat gain in residential and many other occupancies is about 30% of the sensible heat gain.

One effective passive method to mitigate the effects of heat gain from solar radiation and air temperature is to use building materials with high mass. Materials such as masonry, concrete, and tile slow the transmission of heat into a building. During the day, these materials absorb the heat energy and store it. During the night, when the air temperature is cooler than the surface of the mass, much of this energy is lost to the atmosphere instead of being transmitted into the building.

Infiltration

Infiltration is the transfer of air into and out of a building through open doors, through cracks around windows and other openings, through flues and vents, and through other gaps in the exterior construction. Unless a building is well sealed, infiltration can account for more heat loss than does transmission through the walls and roof. However, no building is perfectly sealed; there is always some infiltration.

Heat loss through infiltration is calculated by the formula

$$q_v = V(1.08)\Delta t \qquad 5.4$$

The factor of 1.08 Btu-min/ft^3-°F-hr accounts for the specific heat of air, that is, the amount of heat that air at a certain density can hold. The value of V can be calculated in detail based on the air lost through cracks, doors, and other openings, or it can be estimated with the use of tables that give air changes per hour based on certain criteria.

In SI units, the formula is

$$q_v = V(1200 \text{ J·s/m}^3\text{·°C·h})\Delta t \qquad 5.5$$

q_v is in watts, V is liters per second, and Δt is in degrees Kelvin (or Celsius). The factor of 1200 accounts for the specific heat of air.

Calculating sensible heat gain through infiltration is similar to calculating heat loss. The total heat gain is found by multiplying the total area by an infiltration factor. If a building is being mechanically ventilated, however, the volume of air being introduced into the building is multiplied by the amount of heat that must be extracted both to cool the air and to remove excess humidity (latent heat). In humid climates, the energy required to do this can be substantial.

CLIMATIC TYPES AND DESIGN RESPONSES

From the standpoint of human comfort, buildings are designed to moderate the effects of climate. When passive design strategies cannot maintain conditions of temperature and humidity within the comfort zone, additional active or mechanical means are used.

With today's technology, HVAC systems can provide comfort regardless of how a building is designed. However, relying only on mechanical systems without regard to passive design strategies appropriate to the local climate increases costs, wastes energy, contributes to pollution, and ignores the often desirable regional characteristics of architecture.

In the United States and Canada there are four basic climatic types, or zones: cool, temperate, hot-humid, and hot-arid. These are shown in Fig. 4.4. Each climate has a set of both passive and active design responses that are most appropriate. The *cool zone* includes all of Canada, the northern part of the middle United States, and the mountainous regions of Wyoming and Colorado. The *temperate zone* includes most of the middle latitudes of the United States, including the northwest and northeast areas of the country. The *hot-humid zone* includes the southeastern parts of the country, and the *hot-arid zone* stretches from southern California across the desert southwest to portions of southern Texas.

In cold climates, buildings should ideally minimize the exposed surface area to reduce heat loss. This generally suggests buildings with cubical shapes and those built partially underground. Northern exposure should be minimized, as should door and window openings. Entries should have air locks, and landscaping and building design should block winter winds. Because of extremes of temperature and little direct sunlight in the winter, passive solar heating is usually not appropriate. Mechanical heating and active solar heating are required.

In temperate climate zones, heat loss in the winter can be significant, so northern exposure should be minimized and winter winds should be blocked to reduce heat loss. However, solar heat gain is desirable in the winter, so building lengths should be oriented east and west to maximize southern exposure. In the summer, the same south-facing sides of buildings should be shaded with deciduous trees and mechanical devices like awnings to protect from unwanted heat gain. To mitigate the effects of daytime heating, it is best to provide for nighttime ventilation for the exhaust of hot air. Solar heating, both active and passive, works well in many locations without excessive cloud cover.

Hot-humid climates are the most difficult to design for without mechanical cooling. Buildings should be planned for the maximum amount of natural ventilation using narrow floor plans with cross ventilation; large, open windows; porches; and breezeways. Shading with vegetation (without blocking ventilation) or with double roofs is required. Building materials should be thermally lightweight so they do not store daytime heat and release it at night.

In hot-arid climates, shading from direct sunlight is also required, but the wide variations between day and night temperatures can be used to advantage by employing materials with high thermal mass so daytime heat is released at night. The same mass cools at night for daytime comfort. Night ventilation is very useful to remove heat built up during the day. If sufficient water is available, pools can reduce local air temperature through evaporation. Roof ponds for one- or two-story buildings provide this type of evaporative cooling as well as high thermal mass. Evaporative coolers work well in arid climates because an increase in humidity with a decrease in air temperature is desirable.

SAMPLE QUESTIONS

1. Heat gain is most affected by which of the following?

I.   motors
II. sunlight
III. people
IV. fluorescent lighting
V.   humidity

    A. II and III
    B. II, III, and V
    C. I, II, III, and IV
    D. all of the above

2. A sling psychrometer measures

    A. one of the factors shown in the psychrometric chart
    B. dry-bulb temperature
    C. relative humidity
    D. the level of the dew point in humid climates

3. Heat is lost through insulating glass by what process?

    A. convection
    B. conduction
    C. conductance
    D. radiation

4. In calculating solar heat gain, what value must be known in addition to the area of the glass?

    A. mean radiant temperature
    B. design cooling factor
    C. equivalent temperature difference
    D. coefficient of heat transfer

5. A high value of what property is desirable in heat loss calculations?

    A. conductance
    B. conductivity
    C. enthalpy
    D. resistance

6. Weatherstripping is a good energy conservation strategy because it affects what?

    A. effective temperature
    B. thermodynamics
    C. ventilation
    D. infiltration

7. Select the INCORRECT statement.

    A. Relative humidity is a measure of thermal comfort.
    B. People feel more comfortable in the winter if the MRT is high.
    C. There are differences in comfort level between different cultural groups.
    D. The range of comfortable dry-bulb temperature is dependent on air movement.

8. A roof covers an area 40 ft wide and 80 ft long. With heavy insulation, the resistance has been calculated as 38 and the design equivalent temperature difference is 44. The design temperature is $-5°F$ and it is desired to maintain a 70°F indoor temperature. What is the heat loss through the roof?

    A. 3661 Btu/hr
    B. 5455 Btu/hr
    C. 5824 Btu/hr
    D. 6240 Btu/hr

9. Melting ice requires

    A. enthalpy
    B. sensible heat
    C. dew-point temperature
    D. latent heat

10. What would be the best design strategy for passive cooling during the summer in a hot-humid climate?

    A. Design a series of pools and fountains to cool by evaporation.
    B. Include broad overhangs to shield glass and outdoor activities from the sun.
    C. Orient the building to catch summer breezes.
    D. Use light-colored surfaces to reflect sunlight and solar gain.

HVAC SYSTEMS

ENERGY SOURCES

Regardless of what energy conservation measures are adopted for a building, either the primary or backup energy source will be one of the conventional fuels. The selection of fuel type depends on the fuel's availability and dependability of supply, its cost, cleanliness, convenience of storage, and requirements of the equipment needed to use it. For example, in an urban area steam may be readily available as a by-product of a local utility company, whereas in a suburban area oil may have to be the energy source. In some parts of the country electricity is inexpensive and readily available; in other locations its use for heating is cost prohibitive.

Natural Gas

Of all the fossil fuels, natural gas is the most efficient. It is clean burning and relatively low in cost. Depending on geographic location and local market conditions, however, it is not always available, or the price may fluctuate widely. In remote locations it may not be available at all. It has a heating value of about 1050 Btu/ft^3 (39 100 kJ/m^3).

Propane is one type of gas that can be used in remote areas or where natural gas is not available. It is delivered and stored in pressurized tanks and has a heating value of about 21,560 Btu/lbm, or 2500 Btu/ft^3 (93 150 kJ/m^3).

Oil

Oil is widely used in some parts of the country, but because it is a petroleum product, its cost and availability are dependent on world and local market conditions. It must be stored in or near the building where it is used, and the equipment needed for burning it is subject to more maintenance than that used for gas-fired boilers.

Oil is produced in six grades for residential and commercial heating use: no. 1, no. 2, no. 4, no. 5 light, no. 5 heavy, and no. 6. The lower the number, the more refined and the more expensive the oil. No. 2 fuel oil is the grade most commonly used in residential and light commercial boilers, whereas no. 4 and no. 5 grades are used in larger commercial applications. The heat value for no. 2 oil is from 137,000 Btu/gal to 141,000 Btu/gal (38 200 kJ/L to 39 300 kJ/L), and that for no. 5 is from 146,800 Btu/gal to 152,000 Btu/gal (40 900 kJ/L to 42 400 kJ/L).

Electricity

Electricity has the advantages of being easy to install, low in installation cost, simple to operate, easy to control, and flexible in zoning; and it does not require storage facilities, exhaust flues, or supply air. Its primary disadvantage is its cost in most parts of the country compared with other fuels. Because most electric utilities now charge more for peak use as well as total electricity consumed, heating during a cold period can be very expensive.

Electricity is ideal for radiant heating, either in a ceiling or in individual panels. It can be used in baseboard units as well as to operate electric furnaces for forced air systems. One of its most prevalent uses is for supplemental space heating. Electricity has an equivalent heating value of 3413 Btu/kW (3600 kJ/kW).

Steam

Steam is not considered a basic fuel as are gas and oil, but in many urban locations it is available from a central plant or as a by-product of the generation of electricity. Once piped into a building, it is not used directly for heating but can be used to heat water for water or air heating systems and to drive absorption-type water chillers for air conditioning.

Heat Pumps

A *heat pump* is a device that can either heat in the winter or cool in the summer. It works by transferring heat from one place to another, using the principles of refrigeration as discussed in a later section. In the summer a heat pump acts as a standard air conditioner, pumping refrigerant to the condenser, where it loses heat, and then to the evaporator indoors, where it absorbs heat. By means of a special valve, the refrigerant flow is reversed in the winter so that the heat pump absorbs available heat from the air outside and transfers it to the indoor space.

Because of this process, however, the efficiency of a heat pump for heating decreases as the outdoor air temperature decreases. Below about 40°F (4°C), a heat pump is not competitive with oil or gas as an energy source. It is more effective in mild climates where winter temperatures are usually moderate. For supplemental heating, electrical resistance coils are often placed in supply ductwork.

To extend its efficiency, a heat pump can be connected to a solar energy system. With this approach, solar energy provides heat when the outdoor temperature is between 47°F and 65°F (8°C and 18°C). Below the lower extreme, a heat pump automatically turns on and provides heat until the temperature becomes too cold for its efficient use. Then both systems are used: the heat pump to preheat air and the solar energy system to raise the temperature high enough for space heating. Electrical resistance heating is also available for very cold or cloudy days.

Natural Energy Sources

Other energy sources include solar (either passive or active), photovoltaic, geothermal, wind, and tidal. These are described in Ch. 7. Of these, solar energy is the one that has been developed to the point where it is readily available and efficient for residential and some commercial uses.

Photovoltaic panels are available, but the cost per kilowatt hour is high, and their general use is limited. This is changing as more research is conducted and more efficient panels are manufactured. Refer to Ch. 7 for more information on photovoltaics.

Use of the other natural energy sources is still in the research and development stage and is limited to large-scale generation rather than use with individual buildings.

Selection of Fuel Sources

In addition to the considerations mentioned previously in regard to the selection of a fuel source, the number of degree days in a building's location and the efficiency of the fuel must be taken into account.

Degree days are a measure of the approximate average yearly temperature difference between the outside and the inside in a particular location. The number of degree days for a day is found by taking the difference between an indoor temperature of 65°F (18°C) and the average outside temperature for a 24-hour period. For example, if the 24-hour average is 36°F, then the number of degree days is 65 − 36 = 29. The values for each day of the year are added to get the total number of degree days for the year. Degree days are used to calculate yearly fuel consumption, to size some passive solar energy systems, and to factor into other heating computations.

Because different fuel types convert energy into heat with varying levels of efficiency, efficiency is an important consideration in the selection of fuel, assuming all fuels are available. Table 6.1 shows the typical efficiency ranges of several fuels.

Table 6.1

Approximate Efficiencies of Fuels

fuel	efficiency (%)
natural gas	70–80
propane	70–90
no. 2 oil	65–85
anthracite coal	65–75
electricity	95–100

ENERGY CONVERSION

Whatever type of fuel is selected for heating and cooling, it must be converted into a useful form for distribution throughout a building. This usually requires additional energy, such as electricity, to operate fans, motors, and other components of the system. This fact applies to conventional fuels as well as to natural energy sources such as active solar energy systems.

Heat Generation Equipment

Two of the most common devices for converting fuel to heat are the furnace and the boiler. *Furnaces* burn either gas or oil to heat air, which is then distributed throughout the building. *Boilers* burn gas or oil to heat water, in some instances, using steam as the fuel.

A furnace burns fuel inside a combustion chamber around which air is circulated by a fan. As the cool air from return air ducts passes over the combustion chamber, it is heated for distribution to the building. The hot exhaust gases pass through a flue that is vented to the outside. Replaceable filters are used on the return air side of the furnace to trap dust and dirt in the system.

Forced air furnaces may be of the upflow, downflow, or horizontal type. In an *upflow furnace*, the return air is supplied at the bottom of the unit and the heated air is delivered to the bonnet above the furnace where it is distributed through ductwork. A *downflow furnace* operates in exactly the opposite way and is used in cases where ductwork is located in a basement or crawl space and the furnace is located on the first floor. A *horizontal furnace* is designed to be used in areas where headroom is limited, such as in crawl spaces.

Boilers convert fuel to hot water or steam. The fuel source can be gas, oil, electricity, or steam. In the typical boiler, tubes containing the water to be heated are situated within the combustion chamber where the heat exchange takes place. As with furnaces, the gases and other products of combustion are carried away through breeching into the flue or chimney. Of course, if the primary fuel source is electricity or steam, there is no need for an exhaust flue.

Principles of Refrigeration

There are two types of refrigeration processes that can produce chilled air or water: compressive refrigeration and absorption. A third type, evaporative cooling, can be used to produce cool air in some climates.

Compressive refrigeration is based on the transfer of heat during the liquefaction and evaporation of a refrigerant. As a refrigerant in a gaseous form is compressed, it liquefies and releases latent heat as it changes state. As the same liquid expands and vaporizes back to a gas, it absorbs latent heat from the surroundings into the gas. These principles are used in the basic refrigeration cycle shown in Fig. 6.1.

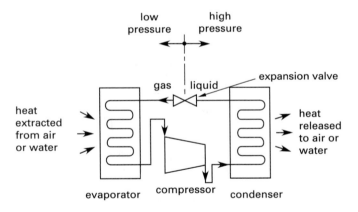

Figure 6.1 Compressive Refrigeration

In the past, refrigerants such as Freon were used in compressive refrigeration. However, these compounds contain chlorofluorocarbons (CFCs) that contribute to depletion of the earth's ozone layer when leaked into the atmosphere. As a consequence, new refrigerants such as hydrofluorocarbons (HFCs) have replaced CFCs.

There are three basic components of a compressive refrigeration cycle: the compressor, the condenser, and the evaporator. The *compressor* takes the refrigerant in a gaseous form and compresses it to a liquid. The refrigerant passes

through the *condenser* where the latent heat is released. This is usually on the outside of the building, and the heat is released to the outside air or to water. The refrigerant flows out of the condenser into the *evaporator* where it is allowed to expand. As it expands, it vaporizes back to a gas. In the process of vaporizing, it absorbs heat from the surroundings (either air or water) and then enters the compressor where it is cycled through the process again.

For many small cooling units, air is forced over the evaporator coils with a fan, and it is this cool air that is circulated through the space. However, water is a much more efficient medium to carry heat than is air. In larger units and in large buildings, water is pumped over the evaporator coils to produce chilled water, which is then pumped to remote cooling units where air is circulated over the chilled water pipes. On the condenser side, water is used to extract the heat from condenser pipes and carry it to remote cooling towers where the heat is released to the air.

Refrigeration by absorption produces chilled water and is accomplished by the loss of heat when water evaporates. This evaporation is produced in a closed system by a salt solution that draws water vapor from the evaporator. See Fig. 6.2.

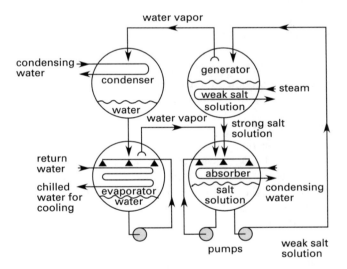

Figure 6.2 Absorption Cooling

As the salt solution absorbs water, it dilutes and must be regenerated by boiling off the water and returning the strong salt solution to the absorber. This is most often done with steam, but it can also be done with high-temperature water produced by solar collectors. The water boiled off in the generator is returned to a liquid state in the condenser and then returned to the evaporator. Both the condenser and absorber require condensing water, which removes the waste heat and carries it to cooling towers. Absorption systems are less efficient than compressive systems and are most often used when waste heat is available for energy input to the generator.

A third type of conditioning is *evaporative cooling*. Water is dropped over pads or fin tubes through which outdoor air or water is circulated. As the free water is evaporated to vapor, heat is drawn from the air or circulating water, which is then distributed to the indoor spaces. This type of cooling only works in hot-arid climates where the outdoor air has a low enough humidity level to allow the moistened air to evaporate. It is more economical than refrigeration cooling in some instances because it uses only one motor instead of three. An evaporative cooler is also simpler in construction and operation because it needs no refrigerant line and uses fewer parts.

A "ton of refrigeration" is a term used to describe the capacity of a refrigeration system. It is the cooling effect obtained when 1 ton of 32°F ice melts to water at 32°F in 24 hours. This is equivalent to 12,000 Btu/hr (3516 W). In general, the required capacity of a refrigeration machine can be determined by dividing the total heat gain in Btu/hr by 12,000.

HVAC SYSTEMS

HVAC systems can be categorized by the medium used to heat or cool a building. The two primary methods of transporting heat are air and water. Electricity can also be used directly for heating. Some systems use a combination of media. This section outlines some of the more common systems with which an examinee should be familiar.

Direct Expansion

The simplest type of system is the *direct expansion system* (DX), also known as an *incremental unit*. This is a self-contained unit that passes nonducted air, which is to be cooled, over the evaporator and back into the room. The condenser uses outdoor air directly, so these units are typically placed in an exterior wall.

Smaller units with $\frac{1}{3}$ ton to 2 ton capacities are adequate for individual rooms, whereas larger units with more than a 2 ton capacity can serve several rooms in a single zone. With the addition of a heating coil, a DX system can serve both heating and cooling functions. Ventilation comes directly from the outside. Direct expansion units can be through-wall types, roof mounted, or packaged.

All-Air Systems

All-air systems cool or heat spaces by conditioned air alone. Heat is transported to the space with supply and return air ducts. The most basic type of all-air system is the constant-volume *single-duct system*. This is typically used in residential and small commercial applications. Air is heated (and

cooled, if required) in a central furnace (and air conditioner) and is distributed throughout the building in ductwork at a constant volume. One centrally located thermostat controls the operation of the furnace. Return air ducts collect cooler air and return it to the furnace for reheating.

This type of system is simple and easy to operate, but it cannot be zoned so that different rooms or areas of the building receive varying amounts of heat (or cooling). The only control possible is by adjusting dampers on each supply air register to adjust the amount of heated (or cooled) air coming into a room. The need for individual zone or room control is one reason many homes use hydronic, or all-water systems.

For larger buildings there are four basic types of all-air systems.

Variable air volume system. For large buildings and situations where temperature regulation is required, humidity control is needed, and energy conservation is a concern, a variable air volume (VAV) system is often used. See Fig. 6.3.

With this system, air is heated or cooled as required in a central plant and distributed to the building at a constant

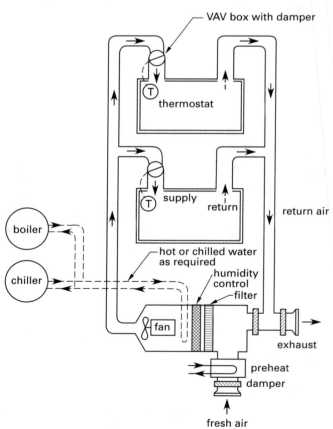

Figure 6.3 Variable Air Volume System

temperature through a single duct. At each zone, a thermostat controls a damper that varies the volume of conditioned air entering the space to respond to the user's needs. Dampers on the return air side of the system allow variable amounts of fresh air (up to 100%) to be introduced into the building for ventilation and for cooling when outdoor conditions make it unnecessary to mechanically condition the air. This system is somewhat limited in its ability to compensate for extremes in simultaneous heating and cooling demands in a building, but it offers a very efficient means of air conditioning large internal-load-dominated buildings.

Dual-duct (high-velocity) system. Where more flexibility is required, a high-velocity dual-duct system can be used. This system provides two parallel ducts, one with hot air and one with cool air. These two streams of air are joined in a mixing box in proportions to suit the temperature requirements of the conditioned space. A thermostat controls pneumatic valves in the mixing box to create the proper mixture. Figure 6.4 shows a simplified diagram of this type of system.

Because both hot and cool air is available anywhere in the building, a dual-duct system can respond to varying requirements. For example, during a cold day on the north

side of a structure with a high percentage of glazing, heating may be required. On the south side of the same building the combination of solar heat gain, lighting, and occupancy may create a need for cooling. Because the air travels at a high velocity, about 3000 ft/min (15 m/s), the ducts can be smaller, which saves space in high-rise buildings.

In spite of these advantages, a high-velocity dual-duct system has some disadvantages. It is inherently inefficient because both hot and cool air have to be supplied winter or summer, and previously cooled air may need to be heated or previously heated air may need to be cooled. In addition, the high velocity requires larger, more powerful fans to move the air, which requires more energy. Finally, the high velocity can cause noise problems in the ductwork. Initial cost is high because of the quantity of ductwork.

Reheat (constant-volume) system. A reheat system takes return air and fresh outdoor air and cools and dehumidifies the mixture, which is then distributed in a constant volume at low temperature throughout the building. At or near the spaces to be conditioned, the air is reheated as required by the cooling load of the space. See Fig. 6.5.

Reheating of the air is accomplished most often with heated water, but it can also be done with electricity. If the reheating equipment is located near the conditioned space, the unit is called a *terminal reheat system.* If the reheating coils are located in ductwork to serve an entire zone, the unit is

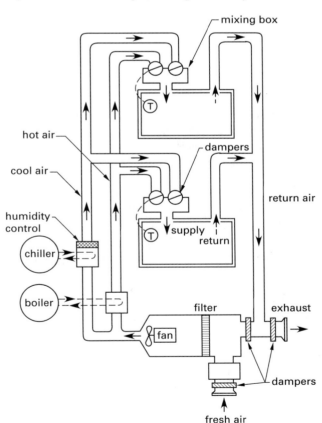

Figure 6.4 High-Velocity Dual-Duct System

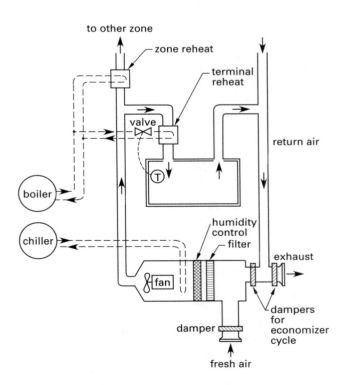

Figure 6.5 Constant Volume with Reheat

called a *zone reheat system*. Thermostats control valves in the water supply line to regulate the temperature.

In many cases, an *economizer cycle* is used. This allows outdoor air to be used for cooling when temperatures are low enough. The economizer works by adjusting dampers on the return air ducts and fresh air intakes.

The advantages of the reheat system are that humidity and temperature can be carefully controlled, and that the low supply temperature equates to smaller duct sizes and lower fan horsepower. However, a reheat system does use more energy than some systems because the primary air volume must be cooled most of the time, then reheated.

Multizone system. A multizone system (Fig. 6.6) supplies air to a central mixing unit where separate heating and cooling coils produce hot and cold air streams. These are mixed with dampers controlled by zone thermostats, and the resulting tempered air is delivered to the zones.

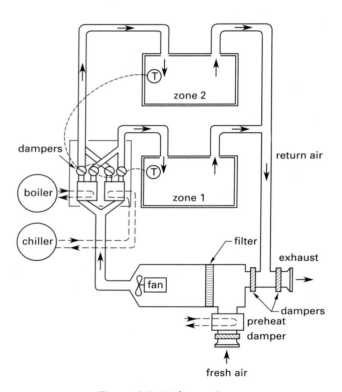

Figure 6.6　Multizone System

Multizone units offer the same advantage as dual-duct systems in that simultaneous cooling and heating of different zones can be accommodated. The main disadvantage is that the amount of duct space increases rapidly as more zones are added. This system is usually only used for medium-sized buildings or where a central mixing unit is located on each floor.

All-Water Systems

An *all-water system* uses a fan coil unit in each conditioned space. The fan coils are connected to one or two water circuits. Ventilation is provided with openings through the wall where the fan coil unit is located, from interior zone air heating, or by simple infiltration. In a two-pipe system, either hot or chilled water is pumped through one pipe and returned in another. In a four-pipe system, as shown in Fig. 6.7, one circuit is provided for chilled water and one for hot water. There are two supply pipes and two return pipes. A three-pipe system uses a single return pipe for both hot and cold water.

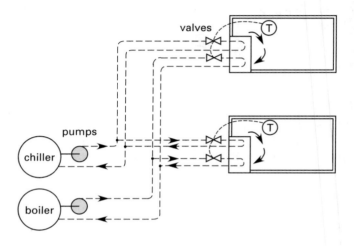

Figure 6.7　Four-Pipe All-Water System

All-water systems are an efficient way to transfer heat and are easily controlled, with a thermostat in each room regulating the amount of water flowing through the coils. However, humidity control is not possible at the central unit.

Air-Water Systems

Air-water systems rely on a central air system to provide humidity control and ventilation air to conditioned spaces. However, the majority of the heating and cooling is provided by fan coil units in each space. Air-water systems are often used where return air cannot be recirculated, such as in hospitals and laboratories. In these cases, 100% outside air is supplied, and return air is completely exhausted to the exterior.

With an induction system, shown in Fig. 6.8, air is supplied throughout the building under high pressure and velocity to each induction unit, where the velocity and noise are attenuated before the air passes over the coils and is heated or cooled as required. The water supply system may be either a two- or four-pipe system. Thermostatic control is provided by regulating the amount of water flowing through the coils. Another type of air-water system uses a fan-coiled unit for primary heating and cooling but has a separate air supply to provide humidity control and ventilation. See Fig. 6.9.

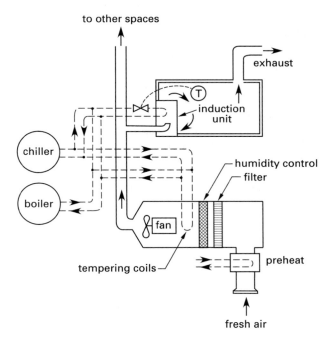

Figure 6.8 Air-Water Induction System

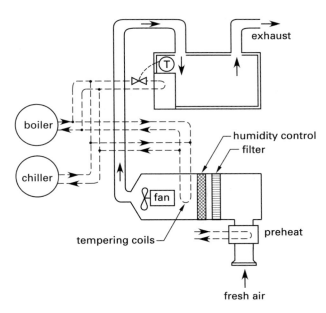

Figure 6.9 Fan Coil with Supplementary Air

Electric Systems

Electric heating is most often accomplished by laying a grid of wires in the ceiling of a room to provide radiant heating. Electric baseboard radiators are also available. This type of system provides a uniform, clean, inconspicuous form of heating that can easily be controlled with a separate thermostat in each room. No space is required for piping or ductwork. The big disadvantage is that electric heat is generally not economical except in areas where electricity is inexpensive. Most often, electric heat is used for supplemental heating in localized radiant panels or where water or air systems need a boost in temperature.

Selection of Systems

Selecting the most appropriate HVAC system for a building depends on several, interrelated variables. These include the following.

- use profile of the building
- building scale
- control requirements
- fuels available
- climatic zone
- integration with building structure and systems
- flexibility required
- economics

The first consideration in selecting an HVAC system is the anticipated use and occupancy of the building. Some occupancies, such as office buildings or retail stores, need a flexible system to account for changes during the life of the building and for different requirements of multiple tenants. Variable air volume or induction systems satisfy this requirement. Buildings with multiple uses or that are subject to simultaneous variations in heating or cooling loads may require a dual-duct system or multizone system. Occupancies such as hospitals and laboratories will require systems like induction or fan coils with supplementary air so that all air supply is 100% fresh with complete exhaust to the outside.

The size of the building helps determine whether to use a central system or individual units. If the air conditioning load is under about 25 tons, direct expansion units or heat pumps can usually be used, either rooftop mounted or the through-wall variety. For larger cooling needs, a central station is more economical and provides the required flexibility.

The third consideration is the kind of control that is required. Hotels, motels, apartments, and some office buildings need the ability for individual room or area thermostatic control, whereas other buildings such as theaters need less individual control.

Although chillers, boilers, and furnaces that operate with a variety of fuels are available, the designer will likely select an HVAC system according to which system is most readily and economically available. If steam is adjacent to the building site, for example, absorption-type chillers may be more appropriate than refrigeration equipment.

The climatic zone will also affect the system selection. If the proposed building is in a hot-arid climate, the requirement for dehumidification will not be as great, so an all-water system may be appropriate. Locations that experience a wide swing in temperatures during the day may need a dual-duct system or four-pipe system to provide flexibility and quick response as outdoor conditions change.

The consideration of integrating the mechanical system with other building systems is one with which the architect is most closely involved. The system must work with the building's structure; the location of the mechanical equipment room; provisions for piping and duct runs; the location and appearance of terminal units, such as fan coils or induction boxes; the choice of return air methods, either ducted or above a suspended ceiling; the means of air supply and location of supply air diffusers; and the locations and appearances of air intakes or exhaust grills on the exterior of the building.

In addition, the mechanical system may have to be integrated with the method of fire protection and smoke control required for the structure. For example, smoke control in a high-rise building can be accomplished by providing a separate fan room on each floor. In the event of fire, the air supply on the fire floor can be switched off and all return air can be exhausted to the outside. At the same time, the dampers on the floors above and below the fire floor can be switched to provide full pressurization, keeping the occupants safe and preventing the spread of smoke.

Flexibility is another important selection consideration for buildings that must change internally or that will be added onto in the future. All-water systems or air-water systems can be sized to accommodate the ultimate capacity of the building. Expansion is then a simple matter of extending the piping runs from the central heating and cooling plant.

Economic decisions involve initial costs of an HVAC system, its long-term maintenance, and the cost of operating the system. Speculative developers may want a low initial-cost system, whereas people owning and occupying a structure will be more concerned with the long-term energy efficiency of the system, including the cost of fuel. Usually, a life-cycle cost analysis of several alternatives is required in order to make an informed decision.

SYSTEM SIZING

Calculating the size of an HVAC system involves determining the required capacity of the heating and cooling equipment, determining the size of the mechanical spaces to house the equipment, and figuring the space needs and layout of the distribution system of pipes and ducts.

System Capacity

The primary determinants in sizing equipment are the total heat gains and losses the building will experience in the most extreme conditions. These are calculated according to the procedures discussed in Ch. 5, and then equipment is selected to offset these gains or losses. In some cases, cooling equipment is undersized slightly to lower initial costs, with the knowledge that some occasional minor extremes in indoor design temperature will be tolerated.

Mechanical Room Space Requirements

For preliminary sizing of mechanical rooms for medium- to large-sized buildings using all-air or air-water systems, allow from 3% to 9% of the gross building area. This includes space for boilers, chillers, fans, and related pumps and piping. All-water systems will require about 1% to 3% of the total gross area.

Boilers and chillers require rooms long enough to allow for the removal of the tubes, so the room has to be slightly longer than twice the length of the equipment. Equipment rooms need to be from 12 ft to 18 ft (4 m to 6 m) high.

Ductwork Distribution and Sizing

Supply ductwork for all-air and air-water systems must run from the central air handling unit to each terminal unit or supply air diffuser. Because ductwork can occupy a significant amount of space, a logical, simple, and direct route must be planned and coordinated with the other building systems. Either round or rectangular ducts are used. Round ducts are the most efficient and produce the least amount of pressure loss for air delivered, but rectangular ducts make better use of available space above ceilings and in vertical duct chases.

In most cases, main trunk ducts can follow the path of circulation systems because these must serve every space just as hallways do. The ductwork can be located above the ceiling in the corridors or between structural beams. Some structural systems, such as open-web steel joists, allow ductwork to run both parallel and perpendicular to the direction of the structure.

In air ducts, there is a loss of pressure due to the friction of the air moving through the ducts, fittings, registers, and other components. The pressure required to overcome this friction loss is called the *static head* and is measured in inches (mm) of water. As this pressure increases, larger ducts and fans are required to overcome it, resulting in higher initial costs as well as higher operating costs.

For preliminary sizing of low-pressure duct space, allow about 3 ft² to 6 ft² for every 1000 ft² (0.3 m² to 0.6 m² for every 100 m²) of floor space served for both vertical and horizontal duct runs. This figure includes supply and return ducts. Of course, high-pressure supply ducts will require less space.

ENERGY CONSERVATION

In many cases, it is possible to minimize reliance on HVAC systems by applying various mechanical techniques. These techniques can involve mechanical system components, heat transfer methods, building automation systems, or building commissioning.

Mechanical System Components

The amount of energy used by HVAC systems in buildings ranges from 40% to 60% of the overall energy consumption in the building, depending on the building type, climate, design, and other variables. Because some type of mechanical system is always required in large buildings and most small buildings, it is reasonable to include energy-efficient mechanical systems in an overall strategy for energy conservation and sustainability.

In order to make standard HVAC equipment described in previous sections more efficient, the National Appliance Energy Conservation Act of 1987 established minimum efficiency standards for both small and large heating and cooling equipment. The performance of this equipment is rated based on various standards including annual fuel utilization efficiency, the coefficient of performance, the energy efficiency ratio, the integrated part load value, and the seasonal energy efficiency ratio. These standards are defined in the Definitions section at the end of this chapter.

In addition to using more efficient equipment, reliance on standard HVAC systems can be minimized by the application of various mechanical techniques and devices to conserve energy. Following are some of the commonly used methods, many of which involve various methods of heat transfer.

Economizer Cycle

An *economizer cycle* uses outdoor air when it is cool enough to mix with recirculated indoor air. This reduces the energy required for refrigeration and is useful when the outdoor air temperature is about 60°F (16°C). An economizer cycle is basically a mechanical substitute for the open window, with the advantages of filtering the air and providing more even distribution. It has the added advantage of providing fresh air into the building to improve indoor air quality. As the temperature drops, less outdoor air is introduced because it would need to be heated. The control system balances the need for fresh air intake with the outdoor temperature and other variables of the heating system. For large, commercial buildings where internal loads and heat gain require cooling even in winter months, an economizer cycle can save significant amounts of energy.

Dual-Condenser Chillers

For refrigeration equipment, two condensers are used instead of one. When building heating is not needed, a heat rejection condenser sends heat to the cooling towers. When heat is needed, a separate heat recovery condenser sends excess heat to fan coil units or other devices. The building automation system controls how the system operates based on outdoor temperature and heating and cooling needs of the building. Another option is to use multiple chillers with units of varying sizes instead on one large chiller. This option allows the system to operate more efficiently by using the best sized chiller for the load.

Gas-Fired Absorption-Based Chillers

Conventional air-conditioning chillers of the centrifugal or reciprocating type are powered by electricity and use the compressive method (with HCFCs or other refrigerants) as described earlier in this chapter. Absorption-type chillers do not rely on ozone-depleting refrigerants. They are commonly powered by natural gas, which is generally a lower-cost fuel than electricity. Where potential power sources such as steam or high-temperature water from an industrial process are available, these may be used instead of natural gas. Although absorption chillers are not as efficient as electrically driven chillers, have a higher initial cost, and reject more heat to cooling towers, they may be more efficient for large buildings, especially in areas where electricity costs are high and where low-cost heat sources from steam or industrial processes are available. As an added benefit, equipment can be selected to provide hot water for heating.

Solar-Powered Absorption Cooling

Absorption chillers can be even more efficient (and sustainable) if they are powered by hot water from solar collectors. Standard flat-plate solar collectors can supply water from 175°F to 195°F (79°C to 91°C), which may prove less costly than running compressive-type chillers with electricity, even though the efficiency is low. Efficiency can be increased by using parabolic concentrating solar collectors to provide higher-temperature water.

Direct-Contact Water Heaters

A *direct-contact water heater* heats water by passing hot gases directly through the water. Natural gas is burned to provide the flue gases that transfer sensible and latent heat to the water. As a further efficiency, a heat exchanger on the combustion chamber reclaims any heat lost from the chamber. Although the gases are in direct contact with the water, the water is considered safe for human consumption. These types of heaters can be up to 99% efficient when the inlet water temperature is below 59°F (15°C). They have the added advantage of producing low emissions of carbon monoxide and nitrous oxides. Because direct-contact water heaters are a high-cost alternative, they are best used where there is a continuous demand for hot water, such as for food processing, laundries, and industrial purposes.

Recuperative Gas Boilers/ Boiler Fuel Economizers

A *recuperative gas boiler* recovers the sensible and latent heat from the high heat of exhaust flue gases that would normally be discharged to the atmosphere. Recuperative gas boilers are designed to cool flue gas temperatures enough to achieve condensation. The reclaimed heat is used to preheat the cold water entering the boiler or to preheat combustion air. Efficiencies can be increased from a high of only 83%, with standard gas boilers, up to 95%. Some systems also have reduced emissions of carbon monoxide and nitrous oxides. Installation is also easier than with standard flues because, since the final emitted flue gases are cool, plastic vent pipe can be used.

Displacement Ventilation

Displacement ventilation is an air distribution system in which supply air originates at floor level and rises to return air grilles in the ceiling as shown in Fig. 6.10. Because the supply air is delivered close to users, it does not have to be cooled as much, resulting in energy savings. Displacement ventilation is a good system for removing heat generated by ceiling-level lights and for improving indoor air quality, because these systems typically use a high percentage of outdoor air. This system can also be used in conjunction with personal temperature control and flexible underfloor wiring.

Most displacement ventilation systems use an access flooring system to provide space for underfloor ducting and to allow rearrangement of supply air outlets as the space layout changes. However, this makes displacement ventilation appropriate only for new construction, where the additional floor-to-floor height can be set to accommodate the 12 in (300) or more required for ductwork and where the elevations of stairway landings and elevator stops can match the elevation of the access floor.

A variation of this system uses supply air outlets located low on exterior walls, but this system only works for spaces next to the exterior wall to a depth of about 16 ft (5 m).

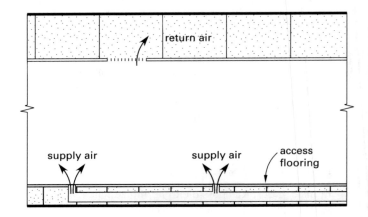

Figure 6.10 Displacement Ventilation

Water-Loop Heat Pumps

Water-loop heat pumps compose a heating and cooling system that uses a series of heat pumps (described earlier in this chapter) for different zones of a building, which are all connected to the same piping system of circulating water. See Fig. 6.11. The water loop is maintained at a temperature between 60°F and 90°F (between 15°C and 32°C). When some zones are cooling and dumping heat into the loop and other zones are heating and extracting heat from the loop, no additional energy has to be added or removed. Only when most of the units are in the same mode does the water in the loop have to be cooled or heated with a cooling tower or boiler. Automatic valves at the cooling tower and boiler direct the water as required.

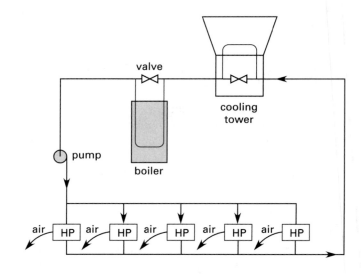

Figure 6.11 Water-Loop Heat Pump System

This system is very efficient where there is a simultaneous need for heating and cooling in different parts of the building. It also reduces piping costs over two or four pipe water heating systems. It is not appropriate for buildings where cooling loads are small.

Thermal Energy Storage

Thermal energy storage uses water, ice, or rock beds to store excess heat or coolness for use at a later time. Thermal storage makes it possible to manage a building's energy needs over climatic temperature swings throughout the day or week, and it allows the use of less expensive, off-peak energy costs to cool. For example, in the summer, chillers can cool water at night when utility rates are typically lower and the cooling needs of the building are not as great as they are during the day. During the next day, the stored coolness can be used to minimize the energy required for cooling. Heat and coolness can be stored in water, rocks, or other appropriate thermal masses. Coolness can be stored in these media as well as in ice. Ice has the advantage of being able to store sensible heat as well as the latent heat of fusion of ice. So, for a given amount of heat capacity (coolness), ice will occupy about eight times less space than that occupied by water.

Heat Transfer

The desire for energy conservation is not always compatible with the need for indoor air quality (IAQ). Historically, initial efforts at increasing energy conservation resulted in tightly sealed buildings with reduced infiltration of fresh air and reuse of conditioned air. This led to problems with human comfort, sick building syndrome, and other building-related illnesses. One of the ways to alleviate some indoor air quality problems is to introduce more outdoor air through the ventilation system while exhausting used, conditioned air. However, heating or cooling incoming air requires energy. The solutions to these incompatible requirements for energy conservation and IAQ involve various methods of heat transfer. The following are all based on the concept of heat exchange from a source where heat (or coolness) is not wanted to a place where it is desirable.

Energy Recovery Ventilators

Energy recovery ventilators, also called *air-to-air heat exchangers*, reclaim waste energy from the exhaust air stream and use it to condition the incoming fresh air. The energy required to condition the incoming air can be reduced from 60% to 70%. Energy recovery ventilators are especially efficient in very cold, hot, or humid climates, where the temperature differential between indoor and outdoor air is high. They are generally not justified in temperate climates. They are also most efficient in buildings with continuous occupancy, such as hotels, hospitals, and others that operate more than eight hours a day.

Three common devices are used to make air-to-air heat exchange: flat-plate heat recovery units, energy transfer wheels, and heat pipes. Energy transfer wheels and heat pipes are described in the following separate sections. *Flat-plate heat recovery units* have two separate ducts of various designs—one for incoming air and one for exhaust air of various designs—separated by a thin wall that facilitates the heat transfer. These types of recovery ventilators can only exchange sensible heat and offer no humidity control themselves.

Three conditions should be met when using energy recovery ventilators. First, the fresh air intake must be kept as far away from the exhaust outlet as possible, to avoid sucking contaminated indoor air back into the building. Second, exhaust air that contains excessive moisture, grease, or other contaminants should be separated from the heat-exchanger air. Third, in cold winter conditions, a defroster in the device may be needed to prevent the condensate in the exhaust air from freezing.

Energy Transfer Wheels

Energy transfer wheels, also called *enthalpy heat exchangers*, transfer heat between two air streams through the use of a heat exchanger wheel consisting of small openings through which the air passes. The wheels are impregnated with lithium-chloride or other proprietary substances. They are typically used in commercial buildings. The advantage of energy transfer wheels over other types of heat exchangers is that they can transfer latent heat (humidity) as well as sensible heat. In winter operation, warm, humidified exhaust air is transferred to the cool, dry incoming air. In summer operation, the cool exhaust air removes some of the heat from the hot incoming air. In addition, the humidity in the hot incoming air is transferred to the exhaust stream before the incoming air enters the building. See Fig. 6.12.

Energy transfer wheels conserve energy, reduce the cooling load, and minimize the need to humidify indoor air during the winter. Some units have a transfer efficiency up to 80%.

Heat Pipes

A *heat pipe* is a self-contained device that transfers sensible heat energy from hot exhaust air to cool outdoor air. As the hot exhaust air passes over the heat pipe, it vaporizes a refrigerant inside the pipe, which passes to the area of cool incoming air. As the refrigerant condenses, it gives off heat to the incoming air, warming it. The refrigerant then passes back to the hot side by capillary action through a wick material in the heat pipe. For heat pipes to work, the incoming and outgoing air streams must be adjacent.

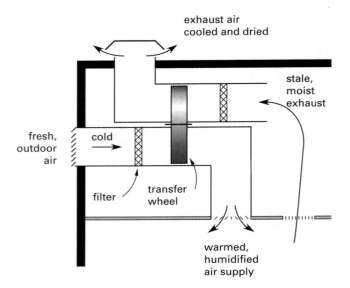

Figure 6.12 Energy Transfer Wheel

Water-to-Water Heat Exchangers

Water-to-water heat exchangers, sometimes called *runaround coils*, use water or some other liquid transfer medium to exchange heat. The main advantage of this type of system is that the incoming and exhaust air streams do not have to be adjacent. In winter operations, this type of system simply pumps a heat-transfer fluid from coils over which the hot exhaust air passes to coils over which the cool incoming air passes. In summer, the flow uses the cooled indoor air to reduce the temperature of the hot incoming air. These types of systems are commonly used in large buildings and eliminate the possibility that incoming air could be contaminated with exhaust air. The efficiency of water-to-water heat exchangers ranges from 50% to 70%.

Extract-Air Windows

An *extract-air window* uses a double-paned insulated glass unit over which another pane of glass is placed on the inside of the building. Air is drawn up between the inside pane and the main window unit and is extracted into the return-air system. This has the effect of warming the glass in winter and cooling it in summer to maintain a comfortable radiant temperature and eliminate the need for a separate perimeter heating system.

Ground-Coupled Heat Exchangers

Ground-coupled heat exchangers heat or cool outside air by circulating it through pipes buried in the ground. In the summer the air can be used directly if the outdoor air is higher than the ground temperature. In the winter the system can preheat air for an energy recovery ventilator (to prevent frosting) or for a standard fan-coil heating unit. Ground-coupled heat exchangers are typically only suitable

for low-rise buildings. Their disadvantage is the long runs of pipes they require for efficient operation. Because the air is forced through the pipes, the energy saved with the system must outweigh the energy required to run the fans. An alternative to this type of system that uses geothermal energy is the ground-source heat pump, described in Ch. 7.

Building Automation Systems

A *building automation system* (BAS) is a computer-based integrated system used to monitor and control building systems. The systems included in a BAS will vary depending on the complexity of the building and the needs of the owner, but they typically include HVAC, energy management, lighting control, life safety, and security. Other systems that may be part of a BAS include vertical transportation, communications, material handling, and landscape irrigation. A BAS reduces energy costs through better systems management, allows for monitoring of large, complex buildings, reduces the number of personnel needed to supervise a large building, improves occupant comfort, and provides detailed documentation of all aspects of the building's subsystems. If problems arise, the BAS notifies the building systems manager and outside authorities, if necessary.

The energy conservation component of a BAS, the energy management system (EMS), detects environmental conditions both inside and outside the building, monitors the status of all equipment (including temperature, humidity, and flow rates), and optimizes the control of the equipment (including start and stop times and operational adjustments).

Building Commissioning

Building commissioning is the process of inspecting, testing, starting up, and adjusting building systems and then verifying and documenting that they are operating as intended and meet the design criteria of the contract documents. Commissioning is an expansion of the traditional testing, adjusting, and balancing (TAB) that is commonly performed on mechanical systems, but with a greatly broadened scope over a longer time period.

Building commissioning begins during the design phase with the determination of which systems will be commissioned and what the criteria will be for acceptance, and the preparation of specifications to precisely outline the requirements for subsequent phases. The most important part of commissioning occurs during the construction phase when the various building systems are started up and tested to see if they meet the design criteria. Incorrectly functioning equipment is adjusted, corrected, or repaired as required. The operation and maintenance of the controls and equipment are demonstrated, and training is conducted for the building operators (owner). During this phase a commissioning report is also prepared to summarize the results of the construction-phase commissioning and to provide detailed operation and maintenance manuals for each of the systems. Finally, commissioning should be carried through a post-occupancy phase. Ideally, this should occur one year after initial occupancy to again verify that the systems are operating as intended under normal occupancy and operating conditions. Adjustments and corrections should take place at this time if necessary.

The building systems that require commissioning depend on the complexity of the building and the needs of the owner. They may include some or all of the following.

- mechanical systems (including heating and cooling equipment, air handling equipment, distribution systems, pumps, sensors and controls, dampers, and cooling-tower operation)

- electrical systems (including switchgear, controls, emergency generators, fire management systems, and safety systems)

- plumbing systems (including tanks, pumps, water heaters, compressors, and fixtures)

- sprinkler systems (including standpipes, alarms, hose cabinets, and controls)

- fire-management and life-safety systems (including alarms and detectors, air handling equipment, smoke dampers, and building communications)

- vertical transportation (including elevator controls and escalators)

- telecommunication and computer networks

Because large-building commissioning is a complex process, a knowledgeable person should be assigned responsibility for coordinating the efforts of everyone on the team. This may be the building contractor, the construction manager, or an independent commissioning agent. The people who should participate in building commissioning include

- the architect

- the mechanical, electrical, and plumbing engineers as well as other design consultants as appropriate

- the general contractor

- the various subcontractors for mechanical, electrical, fire protection, and so on

- the owner, owner's operation personnel, and owner's maintenance personnel

- others directly involved with the process, including the owner's agent, code officials, and construction manager

DEFINITIONS

Actuator: a device in a building control system that receives commands from a controller and activates a piece of equipment

Annual fuel utilization efficiency (AFUE): the ratio of annual fuel output energy to annual input energy. This includes nonseasonal pilot-light input losses.

Coefficient of performance (COP): a unitless number that is a rating of the efficiency of heating or cooling equipment. It is derived by dividing the steady-state rate of energy output (or the rate of heat removal, in the case of cooling equipment) of the equipment by the steady-state rate of energy input to the equipment. The output and input values must be in equivalent units, such as watts out to watts in.

Controller: a device that measures, analyzes, and initiates actions in a building control system

Deadband: in a building control system, the range of temperature within which neither heating nor cooling is called for

Energy efficiency ratio (EER): the ratio of net cooling capacity in Btu/hr to the total rate of electrical input in watts under designated operating conditions

Energy management system (EMS): a computer-based system used to monitor and control facility energy use. An EMS is typically part of a building automation system.

Ground-coupled cooling: a method of cooling a building by direct contact with the earth or by circulating air through underground tunnels to cool it

Heating seasonal performance factor (HSPF): a measure of the performance of a heat pump operating in the heating cycle. See also *Seasonal energy efficiency ratio*.

Home energy rating system (HERS): a standardized system for rating the energy efficiency of residential buildings using the HERS Council Guidelines and the Mortgage Industry HERS Accreditation Procedures. A HERS score is a numeric value between 0 and 100 indicating the relative energy efficiency of a given home as compared with the HERS Energy-Efficient Reference Home.

Integrated part load value (IPLV): the single-number figure of merit based on part load EER or COP expressing part load efficiency for air conditioning and heat-pump equipment on the basis of weighted operation at various load capacities for the equipment, as determined using the applicable test method in the Appliance Efficiency Regulations

Relative solar heat gain (RSHG): the ratio of solar heat gain through a window, corrected for external shading, to the incident solar radiation. This heat gain includes directly transmitted solar heat and absorbed solar radiation, which are conducted or convected into the space.

Seasonal energy efficiency ratio (SEER): the total cooling output of a central air conditioning system or heat pump in the cooling mode, measured in Btu/hr (W), during its normal usage period for cooling divided by the total electrical input in watt-hours, as determined by specific test procedures

SAMPLE QUESTIONS

1. A building under design in a temperate climate will have some areas that require cooling and others that require simultaneous heating. To minimize energy use, the best devices to employ would be

    A. energy recovery ventilators
    B. heat pipes
    C. recuperative fuel economizers
    D. water-loop heat pumps

2. During building commissioning, which of the following members of the building team would most likely be present?

I.   civil engineer
II. electrical engineer
III. elevator contractor
IV. general contractor
V.   owner

    A. I, II, and IV
    B. II, IV, and V
    C. I, II, III, and IV
    D. II, III, IV, and V

3. A developer in a midsized Arizona city is planning to build a small shopping mall for resale. The mall will consist of 40,000 ft^2 of rentable area on one level surrounding a small enclosed courtyard. Existing utilities adjacent to the site include water, sanitary sewer, storm sewer, natural gas, and electricity. Which of the following would be most important in the selection of an HVAC system for this project?

I.   flexibility
II. climatic zone
III. economics
IV. the tenant's preference
V.   building scale

    A. I, II, and V
    B. II, III, and IV
    C. II, III, and V
    D. all of the above

4. A seven-story office building is to have a variable air volume system. The building will have 105,000 ft^2 of net space and an estimated 126,000 ft^2 of gross area. About how much space should be allowed for HVAC systems?

    A. 2500 ft^2
    B. 3800 ft^2
    C. 6300 ft^2
    D. 7600 ft^2

5. Select the INCORRECT statement.

    A. A health center would probably use no. 4 or no. 5 fuel oil.
    B. Heat pumps rely on solar energy more than on electricity.
    C. Natural gas has a higher heating value than does propane.
    D. Electricity is not a good choice for powering boilers in remote areas.

6. A main trunk duct is to be placed above a suspended ceiling and below the structural framing. Ceiling space for the duct is not a problem. Assuming equal capacities, which of the following shapes of ducts would be best to use?

    A. rectangular, with the long dimension horizontal
    B. rectangular, with the long dimension vertical
    C. square
    D. round

7. A standard gas furnace has all of the following EXCEPT

    A. a flue
    B. a damper
    C. a combustion chamber
    D. filters

8. The heat gain for a building has been calculated at 108,000 Btu/hr. What size compressive refrigeration machine should be specified?

    A. 9 tons

    B. 12 tons

    C. 36 tons

    D. 54 tons

9. An economizer cycle

    A. only cools as much chilled water as required by the demand load

    B. uses outdoor air to cool a building

    C. automatically reduces the amount of time the compressor runs

    D. uses air and water to cool the condenser coils

10. The cooling system for a restaurant kitchen must remove

    A. sensible heat only

    B. latent heat only

    C. sensible and latent heat

    D. sensible heat and latent heat at 30% of sensible heat

ENERGY EFFICIENCY AND ALTERNATIVE ENERGY SOURCES

This chapter covers passive design methods for energy efficiency and the use of alternative energy sources. The careful use of both these strategies can greatly reduce reliance on mechanical systems, reduce operating costs, improve human comfort, and reduce the use of fossil fuels.

Additional sustainable design issues and building techniques are discussed in Ch. 8. Sustainable design techniques that can be employed during the pre-design and site planning processes are discussed in Chs. 2 and 4. Energy conservation techniques that incorporate features into HVAC systems to make them more efficient are discussed in Ch. 6. Refer to Ch. 10 for information on energy efficiency in electrical systems.

PART 1: ENERGY EFFICIENCY

BUILDING ORIENTATION

By orienting a building correctly, an architect can maximize solar heat gain in the winter (if desired), reduce solar heat gain in the summer, encourage cooling with prevailing winds, minimize exposure to cold winter winds, and optimize daily use of the prevailing climate. Preliminary siting decisions based on climatic influences are discussed in Ch. 4.

Selecting the optimum building orientation for energy efficiency is often difficult because of the interrelated and sometimes conflicting requirements for factors such as heat gain, protection from overheating, daylighting, use of photovoltaic and solar heating panels, use of beneficial cooling breezes, protection from cold winds, and the practical aspects of site topography and the building program. However, all other constraints being equal, building orientation for energy conservation attempts to balance the overheated and underheated periods during the year while also considering daily temperature fluctuations.

Many studies have been done to determine optimum building orientation. While they differ in the exact angle, they all recommend that rectangular buildings be oriented with the long direction generally east-west to minimize the intense east and west solar radiation while taking advantage of the heating potential of south-facing surfaces in the winter. During the summer months the sun is higher in the sky and strikes south-facing walls higher, so there is less incident radiation, and what incident radiation there is can be shaded easily. Considering the slightly lower morning temperatures, a rectangular building is best oriented slightly east of south as shown in Fig. 7.1. The exact angle of the south face varies slightly depending on the climatic region

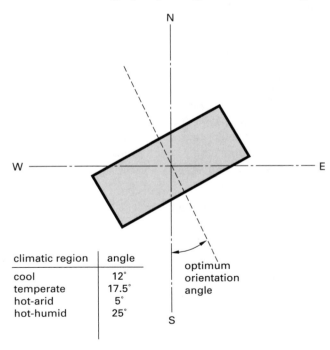

climatic region	angle
cool	12°
temperate	17.5°
hot-arid	5°
hot-humid	25°

Figure 7.1 Optimum Building Orientation

but is approximately 15° east of south. In hot-arid and hot-humid climates the building may have to be rotated slightly off these axes to pick up the cooling breezes of the local climate.

In cold climates, a building's entrance can be located on the leeward side, to avoid winter winds. In temperate climates, entrances should be located on the south side to make them more inviting and capitalize on the natural snow-melting effects of the sun. In hot climates, the long side of a building can be oriented to catch cooling breezes.

BUILDING SHAPE

As with building orientation, building shape is the result of many interrelated and sometimes conflicting requirements and programmatic needs. However, considering just the aspect of energy conservation, some general guidelines for building shape can be established.

Building shape can affect energy use in a number of ways. Because both heating and cooling loads depend on the thermal conductance of the walls and roof and the areas of those surfaces, any building that minimizes the total area will generally use less energy. A cubic building has the least surface for the volume contained. See Fig. 7.2(a). (A sphere is the ideal shape because it encloses the most volume for the least surface area, but it is not practical for buildings.) A two-story building is better than a one-story building of the same floor area. However, the goal of minimal surface area must be balanced with the gains provided by other building shapes that utilize solar heating, natural ventilation, and similar techniques. Minimizing surface area generally works best in cold climates.

As described in the previous section, the advantage of a rectangular building is that its long face can be oriented toward the south, for solar heating and to minimize heat gain on the east and west. Long, thin buildings also make it easier to utilize daylighting and to capture prevailing winds for natural ventilation. Larger buildings may require courtyards and rambling shapes for daylighting and ventilation. See Fig. 7.2(b).

Looking at energy efficiency in greater detail, the ideal shape of a building will depend on its climatic region and whether it is an external-load-dominant building or an internal-load-dominant building.

External-load-dominant buildings (also known as *skin-load dominant buildings*) are those whose energy use is determined mainly by heat loss or gain through the exterior envelope (or skin). These types of buildings generally have few occupants per unit area and a small amount of heat gain from lighting, equipment, and people. Examples of these

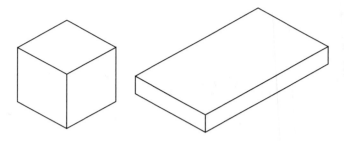

(a) For same floor area, cubic buildings have less surface area.

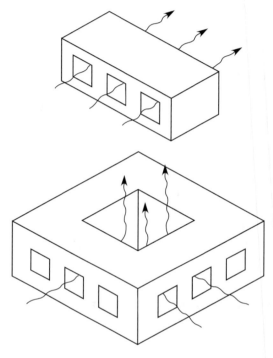

(b) Thin sections are best for natural ventilation and daylighting.

Figure 7.2   Building Shape Affects Energy Use

types of buildings include houses, apartments, condominiums, and warehouses.

Internal-load-dominant buildings are those whose energy use is driven by high heat gain from occupants, lighting, and equipment. Examples of these types of buildings include office buildings, hospitals, retail stores, schools, and laboratories. In most cases, building shape for internal-load dominant buildings influences the energy efficiency less than it would for external-load-dominant buildings. The exception would be if the building shape were being used for extensive daylighting or other passive or active energy conservation techniques.

Figure 7.3 illustrates a generalized summary of the optimum building shapes, based on type of load, for each of the four climatic regions of the United States. See Fig. 4.4 for a map of the climatic regions in the United States.

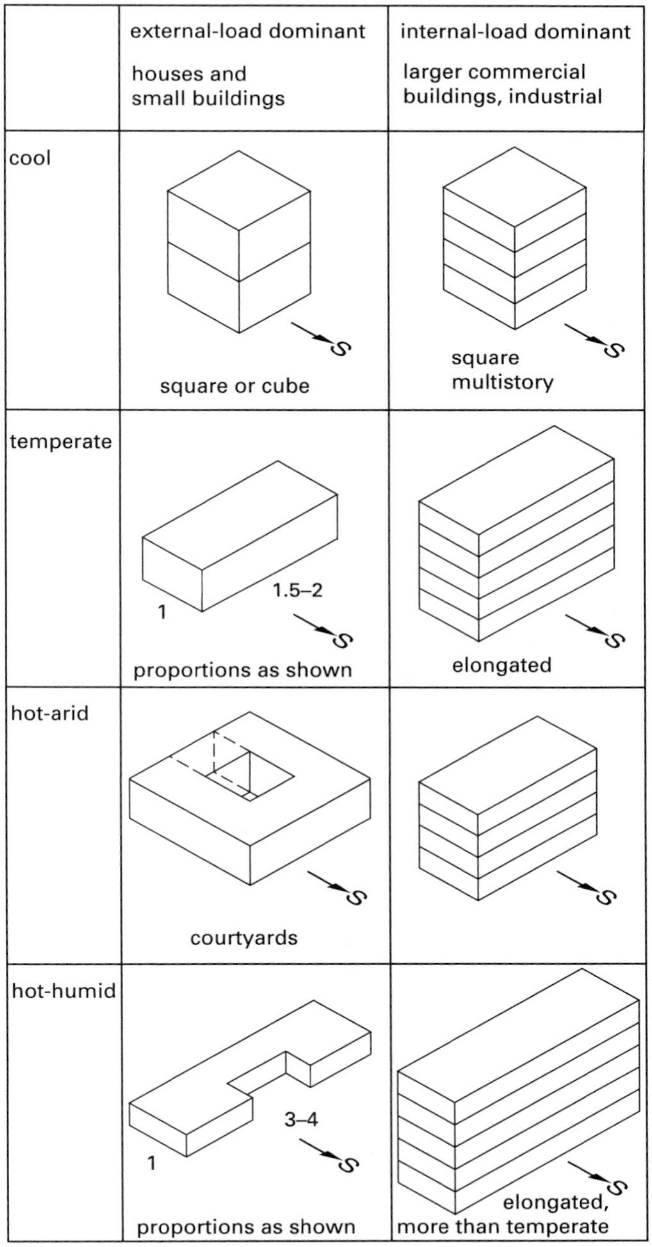

	external-load dominant houses and small buildings	internal-load dominant larger commercial buildings, industrial
cool	 square or cube	 square multistory
temperate	 proportions as shown	 elongated
hot-arid	 courtyards	
hot-humid	 proportions as shown	 elongated, more than temperate

Figure 7.3 Building Shapes Based on Climate Type and Type of Load

For the cool and cold regions a square or cubic shape generally works best because the extremes of winter temperature suggest the skin area should be minimized in both types of load-dominant buildings. For the same floor area, a two-story house is better than a one-story house.

For temperate climates shape has less of an effect, but a building elongated in the east-west direction has some advantages for winter solar heat gain, daylighting, and minimum heat gain in the summer.

For hot-arid regions a more square shape is best, but the plan should include open courtyards for external-load-dominant buildings or massive, multistory buildings for internal-load-dominant buildings.

For hot-humid regions shapes elongated in the east-west direction are preferable to allow breezes, provide natural cooling, and minimize severe heat gain from the east and west directions. Courtyards and broad overhangs are also useful.

LANDSCAPING

Trees and shrubs should be located such that they moderate the microclimate and maximize the energy efficiency of the building. For example, simply protecting a house or other external-load-dominant building from the effects of a cold wind can reduce the heating load substantially, sometimes up to one half.

Deciduous trees can be used on the south side of a building to provide the building with shade in the summer and allow solar heating in the winter. However, because even a deciduous tree will block some solar radiation in the winter, a building that depends on passive solar heating or solar panels may need to be exposed on the south side.

The effect of using trees to shield a building from undesirable winds is highly variable depending on the types of trees, the width of the row, how densely the trees are planted, and tree height. As mentioned in Ch. 2, a very deep row of trees can reduce wind velocities substantially. However, most site designs only have space for a single or double row of trees. In general, a row of trees of a certain height will decrease the velocity of the wind between 30% and 40% at a distance about five times the height of the trees. Trees planted next to a building may reduce wind velocity between 20% and 60%, depending on the density of the trees. The effect of trees on reducing wind velocity decreases greatly at about 10 times the tree height and is negligible beyond 20 times the tree height. In most cases evergreen trees are more effective at blocking wind than are deciduous trees. Evergreens should certainly be used for blocking winter winds.

Trees can also be used to direct desirable cooling breezes. Refer to Chs. 2 and 4 for more information on using landscaping to improve energy efficiency.

BUILDING SHADING

Building shading should be used selectively to minimize unwanted solar heat gain in the summer and maximize heat gains in the winter. This can be done naturally with deciduous trees or with horizontal or vertical shading devices. The shading devices can be either fixed or moveable. If daylighting is used, horizontal blinds can both shade glass and provide reflective surfaces to direct sunlight into a building.

The orientation of a building's façade determines the most effective type of shading device. South-facing façades require moderate overhangs or horizontal louvers, while east- and west-facing façades should be protected with vertical louvers. Southeast- and southwest-facing façades may require either a very wide overhang or vertical louvers, or both. Of course, fixed exterior shading devices will usually be supplemented with interior window coverings. See Fig. 7.4.

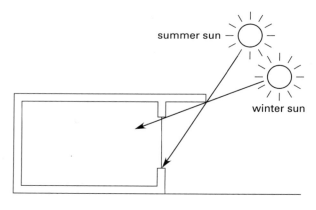

(a) horizontal shading on south

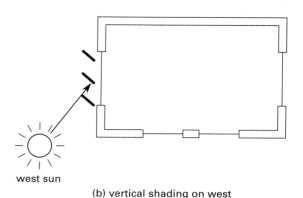

(b) vertical shading on west

Figure 7.4   Building Shading

EARTH SHELTERING

Burying a portion of a building underground has several advantages. Below a few feet the temperature of the earth is fairly stable. It is cooler in the summer and warmer in the winter than is the air aboveground. Therefore, heat gain and heat loss are minimized, and the impact of extreme outdoor air temperatures is lessened. Earth sheltering also protects a structure from cold winter winds. Additional advantages include natural soundproofing, less outside maintenance, and better protection from high winds, hail, and tornados.

There are three variations on the earth-sheltered design. The first design type is built aboveground and has earth bermed against the walls on one or more sides. The second design is similar to the first, but is built into the side of a hill, ideally with the north side built into the hill and the south side exposed for solar heating, views, and daylight. The east and west sides may be partially or completely buried. In either of these first two designs, the roof may also be covered with earth. The third type of earth-sheltered design is completely buried below grade with a courtyard in the middle to allow for access, daylight, an outdoor living area, and ventilation.

Usually, earth sheltering is only used on a portion of a building while the south side of the building is exposed. This approach combines the advantages of earth sheltering with the need to permit desirable heat gain and admit light.

Some of the practical considerations of earth-sheltered designs include the following.

- Ideally, there should be a natural slope to the land so earthmoving can be minimized.

- The soil should be granular. Gravel, sand, or sandy loam are all appropriate soils. Clay soils are not appropriate for earth-sheltered designs because they do not drain well and can expand with moisture. The site should be tested for radon concentrations.

- The groundwater level must be below the building, and positive drainage away from the building should be maintained.

- Extra care must be taken to waterproof the underground portions adequately.

- Even though earth-sheltered designs do not require much insulation, the insulation must be correctly designed to keep the indoor temperature comfortable and prevent condensation from forming on cool inside walls in a humid environment.

- With fewer windows on all sides, the building will need adequate ventilation to control humidity and maintain good air quality.

GREEN ROOFS

A *green roof*, also called a *vegetated roof cover*, *garden roof*, or *eco-roof*, is a thin layer of vegetation installed on the top of a roof. The advantages of a green roof can include the following.

- conserves energy by reducing cooling and heating costs

- reduces storm runoff

- absorbs carbon dioxide

- reduces ambient air temperatures

- filters the air and binds dust particles

- reduces the heat island effect normally caused by roofing

- protects the roofing from ultraviolet light degradation, temperature extremes, wind, and hail

- adds acoustical insulation

- adds aesthetic appeal to the roof

A variety of types of green roofs can be designed—from simple low-growing grasses and flowers in a thin layer of soil to complex groupings of grass, flowers, shrubs and trees in a layer of growing media 12 in (300) or more deep. Green roofs are generally divided into two major types: extensive and intensive. *Extensive green roofs* use soil less than 6 in (150) deep supporting meadow grasses, sedums, herbs, and perennials. *Intensive green roofs* use thicker soil and support complex landscapes, including shrubs and small trees along with ponds and fountains. If required by the climate, a subsurface irrigation system is installed.

Although there are many variations in design and detailing, a typical intensive roof is constructed as shown in Fig. 7.5. All green roofs must be constructed over a structural deck strong enough to hold the wet weight of the assembly. Depending on the type of system used, green roofs may weigh from 12 psf to 100 psf (60 kg/m^2 to 500 kg/m^2). This means that green roofs should typically be used only in new buildings where the structure can be designed correctly from the beginning. However, it may be possible to place lighter green roof systems over existing structures without additional support.

The steps involved in constructing a green roof are as follows.

1. A waterproof membrane is placed over the structural deck. This may be made of one of a variety of materials and may include polyvinyl chloride (PVC), ethylene propylene diene monomer (EPDM), thermoplastic polyolefin (TPO), or a polymer modified bituminous membrane.

2. If required, a root barrier is placed over the waterproofing. Some materials, such as PVC, EPDM, and TPO, are inherently root resistant.

3. Insulation is placed over the root barrier. Insulation helps prevent water stored in the growth media from extracting heat in the winter, and it adds thermal insulation. Some systems use a retention layer over the insulation to provide a long-term water supply.

4. A drainage layer is installed over the insulation to allow water that is not absorbed to flow to drains or scuppers. Green roofs should be constructed on decks with a minimum 1.5% slope. The maximum recommended slope is 30%, but on steep slopes stabilization panels, battens, and other devices must be used to prevent the growing medium from shifting.

5. A filter fabric above the drainage layer prevents the fine particles of the soil or growing medium from entering and clogging the drainage layer. Materials used for filter fabric include polypropylene or polyethylene mats or water-resistant polyester fiber mats.

6. Finally, the growth medium is placed in thicknesses from 2 in (50) to 12 in (300) or more. The growth medium is not just soil but an engineered mixture of soil plus organic and mineral additives, such as peat, sand, lava, expanded clay, and others. The growth medium is designed for the types of plants that will be used.

The actual plant material varies widely depending on whether an extensive or intensive system is planned, the local climate, the maintenance that will be available, and the aesthetic needs of the project. A drip irrigation system is usually recommended instead of a spray system.

A project can receive LEED™ credit for having a green roof if it covers at least 50% of the total roof area. LEED is an acronym for Leadership in Energy and Environmental Design, a program of the U.S. Green Building Council designed to encourage the implementation of sustainable building practices. Buildings receive credits for various sustainable design practices and are then awarded a LEED certificate if they accumulate enough points. Refer to the section on Building Rating Systems in Ch. 8 for more information on LEED.

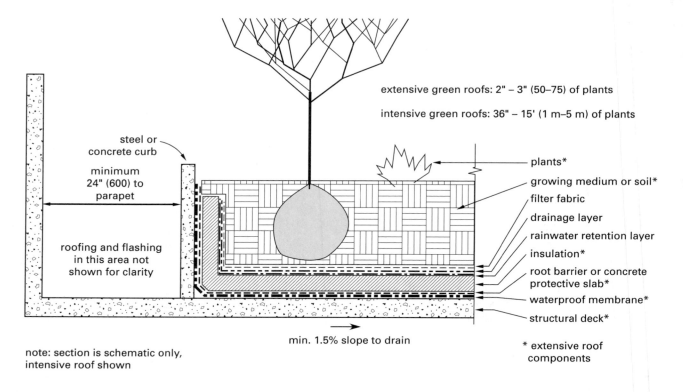

steel or concrete curb

minimum 24" (600) to parapet

roofing and flashing in this area not shown for clarity

extensive green roofs: 2" – 3" (50–75) of plants

intensive green roofs: 36" – 15' (1 m–5 m) of plants

plants*
growing medium or soil*
filter fabric
drainage layer
rainwater retention layer
insulation*
root barrier or concrete protective slab*
waterproof membrane*
structural deck*

min. 1.5% slope to drain

note: section is schematic only, intensive roof shown

* extensive roof components

Figure 7.5 Green Roof Construction

AIR LOCKS

A vestibule entry system is desirable in cold and temperate climates and can be beneficial in hot climates where a building is mechanically cooled. In addition to preventing cold drafts from entering when an exterior door is opened, air locks minimize heat loss when people enter and leave a building. In lieu of a vestibule, revolving doors can be used.

INSULATION AND WEATHER SEALING

One of the most basic passive energy conservation techniques is to adequately insulate and seal a building against air infiltration. How much insulation to use, in terms of cost considerations, depends on the climate. But the money spent on insulation, weatherstripping, and caulking is generally recovered within a few years in the majority of buildings. In addition to reducing heat flow, adequate insulation also keeps wall and ceiling surfaces warmer, raises the mean radiant temperature so the comfort level is increased, and improves acoustic qualities.

Insulation

Insulation is made from a variety of materials and is available in several forms. Commonly used materials include fiberglass, mineral wool, polystyrene, polyisocyanurate, polyurethane, and cellulous. Other materials that have not been traditionally used include cementitious foam, autoclaved aerated concrete, straw panels, straw-bale construction, and plastic fiber. Insulation is available as loose fill, batts, rigid foam boards, spray-on foam, and as part of other construction assemblies, like structural insulated panels.

Prior to selecting the type and form of insulation, the required R-value must be determined. The local or state building codes will either prescribe R-values or reference their locations in a model energy code, such as the *International Energy Conservation Code*, or in ASHRAE Standard 90.1. For example, the International Residential Code provides a prescriptive table that gives building envelope thermal component criteria for ceilings, walls, floors, basement walls, perimeter slabs, and crawl space walls based on the climatic zone and the number of heading degree days. Commercial buildings may be subject to energy budgets.

However, for increased energy savings, a life-cycle analysis can be made comparing the initial cost of installing more insulation of various types (and costs) with the long-term energy savings based on local fuel costs and other factors. Most insulation types also require a vapor barrier to be effective.

Insulation that requires chlorofluorocarbons (CFCs) or hydrochlorofluorocarbons (HCFCs) in its production should not be used, because CFCs are ozone-depleting compounds. However, today all closed-cell polyurethane foam insulation made is produced with a non-CFC gas as the blowing agent. When possible, use foamed-in-place insulations that use carbon dioxide (rather than pentane or hydrochlorofluorocarbons) in the manufacturing process.

Refer to Ch. 8 for more information on insulation and sustainability and Ch. 18 for more information on specific insulation types.

Super Insulation

Super insulation is simply the technique of providing higher levels of insulation than normally used, tightly sealing all joints and cracks, and preventing any thermal bridges between the outside and inside, such as through studs. All portions of the building are carefully detailed so that every piece is insulated. Gaps, such as electrical outlets on exterior walls, are avoided or placed inside the insulation. In many cases, exterior walls have to be made thicker than required to accommodate the added insulation. For homes this means using 2 × 6 studs instead of 2 × 4 studs.

Transparent Insulation

Transparent insulation consists of a relatively thick layer of polycarbonate honeycomb material, acrylic foam, or fiberglass sandwiched between layers of glazing. It is used to admit light while providing a high degree of insulation. It can also be used over another thermal mass material to trap solar heat and then slow the loss of the stored heat back into the atmosphere. Although good for diffusing light, transparent insulation cannot be used where a view is desired.

Moveable Insulation

Moveable insulation is typically used on windows that provide passive solar heating. The insulation is removed during sunlight hours and replaced at night or during cloudy weather to prevent heat loss. This type of insulation can be manually operated, power operated, or set to work automatically. Common types of moveable insulation include roll-down shutters, insulated shades, swinging panels of insulation, and expanded polystyrene beads blown between panes of glass.

Air Barriers

An *air barrier* is the part of a building envelope system that controls the movement of air into and out of a building (infiltration and exfiltration). An effective air barrier is important for three reasons. First, it conserves energy by conditioning unwanted infiltrating air until it meets indoor requirements and preventing conditioned indoor air from being lost to exfiltration. From 25% to 40% of the heating energy used by buildings is lost due to infiltration. Second, it blocks out infiltrating air, which may contain pollutants. Third, by controlling air movement an air barrier helps minimize the migration of moisture, which can condense and contribute to mold growth and degradation of building materials.

Air pressures that cause infiltration and exfiltration can be caused by wind pressure, stack pressure, and HVAC fan pressure. *Wind pressure* puts positive pressure on the side of the building it is hitting and negative pressure at the corners and on the lee side. *Stack pressure* is caused by a difference in atmospheric pressure at the top and bottom of a building due to temperature differences. In cold climates, cold air at the bottom of a building flows in and rises as it warms. The opposite occurs in warm climates with air conditioned buildings. *Fan pressure* is caused by the pressure created by the HVAC system.

A material used in an air barrier system must have an air permeability not exceeding 0.004 cfm/ft^2 under a pressure differential of 0.3 in of water (0.02 L/s/m^2 under 75 Ps). Some materials meeting this requirement include $1/2$ in thick gypsum wallboard, foil-faced urethane insulation, glass, metal, urethane foam, modified bituminous self-adhering membranes, cement board, and foil-faced urethane insulation, among others. In addition to using acceptable materials, an air barrier system must provide a continuous plane of air tightness, with all moving joints made flexible while still being sealed. The system must be designed and constructed to seal the joints of materials and the joints where different materials meet.

An air barrier is not the same as a vapor barrier, which is designed to prevent movement of water vapor out of a building in cold climates and into a building in hot-humid climates. However, many materials can serve as both a moisture and air barrier. Air barriers are especially important in moisture control because air flow has the ability to transport hundreds of times more water vapor through air leaks than does simple vapor transmission.

At the time of this writing many states had adopted a code requirement for airtight envelopes, but it was not yet a provision in the International Building Code.

GLAZING

Historically, glazing has been one of the weak points in constructing energy efficient buildings. Glazing materials were limited to double-paned glass, tinted glass, reflective glass, and a few other glass types. Today however, there are numerous glazing products that can balance the often conflicting requirements that glass must offer views, admit daylight, provide for solar heating, and insulate against extremes of temperature. For example, glass that will admit more than 70% of visible light while blocking nearly 95% of the infrared spectrum is available for daylighting use. Refer to Ch. 19 for more information on glazing types.

Glass can be a major source of heat loss and heat gain in a building. This is true because heat movement through glass occurs by both convection and radiation, and standard float glass has little resistance to either. In the winter the low insulative value of float glass results in large heat losses, whereas in summer the same glass can be a significant source of heat gain by radiation unless it is shaded. A single pane of glass has a U-value of about 1.11 Btu/ft²-hr-°F (6.3 W/m²·K).

Insulating glass is one product used to control heat loss through glazing. This is glass with two or, in some cases, three panes of glass separating a sealed air space or partially evacuated space that acts as an insulator. U-values decrease to about 0.57 Btu/ft²-hr-°F (3.2 W/m²·K) for a ¹/₄ in (6) air space. However, air currents within the air space still allow heat loss by convection. In addition, some of the desired solar heat gain through the glass is lost by radiation as objects in the building get warm and begin to emit infrared radiation that passes back outside.

Double glazing can be made more efficient at stopping heat transfer by convection by using an inert gas fill instead of a vacuum. Typically, argon gas is used because is offers good thermal performance at a low cost. Alternately, krypton gas can be used, but it costs about 200 times more than argon. Krypton is more efficient than argon when the space between glass panes is small, around ³/₈ in (9). A double-glazed unit with argon gas in a ¹/₄ in (6) space has a U-value of about 0.52 Btu/ft²-hr-°F (2.9 W/m²·K). However, the gas can leak out over time at a rate of approximately 0.5% to 1% per year.

Historically, heat gain was first controlled with tinted, reflective, or heat-absorbing glass that lowered the shading coefficient (SC) and solar heat-gain coefficient (SHGC), thereby reducing the solar heat gain. Refer to the Definitions section at the end of this chapter for a description of SC and SHGC. However, because about 50% of the incident solar radiation on glass is in the visible spectrum and about 50% is in the infrared spectrum, tinted and reflective glass also reduced the visible light transmittance. This reduced or eliminated the use of daylighting to conserve energy, darkened the view out, and generally resulted in darker-appearing interiors, especially on cloudy days. These glass types also eliminated the use of solar heat gain when it was desirable.

Some of the more-effective glazing types developed for heat-gain control are described in the following sections.

Low-ε Glazing

Another glazing type is *low-emittance*, or *low-ε glass*. This is double glazing with a thin film or coating placed somewhere in the glazing cavity. The film or coating allows both visible and near-infrared radiation to be transmitted through the glass. However, as objects in the room are heated and emit long-wave radiation, the film or coating prevents the loss of this heat; instead, the heat is reflected back into the room. When used with an argon gas fill to reduce convection, low-ε window units provide a very efficient fenestration. For example, a double-glazed unit with argon gas in a ¹/₄ in (6) space with a low-ε coating (ε = 0.15) has a U-value of about 0.36 Btu/ft²-hr-°F (2.0 W/m²·K). With a ¹/₂ in (13) space, the U-value drops to approximately 0.28 Btu/ft²-hr-°F (1.6 W/m²·K).

Spectrally Selective Glazing

Spectrally selective glazing transmits a high proportion of the visible solar spectrum while blocking heat from the infrared portion of the spectrum, up to 80%. Used with a low-ε coating, a double-glazed window can achieve an SHGC of approximately 0.25. These types of glazing materials are especially good for buildings that have a long cooling season and that require high light levels.

Super Windows

Super windows are glazing units that combine two low-ε coatings with gas-filled cavities between three layers of glass. With a U-value of 0.15 Btu/ft²-hr-°F (0.8 W/m²·K) or less, these units can actually gain more thermal energy than they lose over a 24-hour period in winter.

Other glazing technologies are currently being developed that allow glazing to serve the multiple functions of daylighting, view, maximizing heat gain when wanted, and minimizing heat loss in winter. For example, thermochromic glass becomes translucent when it reaches a certain temperature.

Switchable Glazings

Switchable glazings are chromogenic fenestration products that change their characteristics based on particular environmental conditions or through human intervention. They include the following types of products.

Electrochromic glazing consists of a multilayered thin film, applied to glass, that changes continuously from dark to clear as low-voltage electrical current is applied. This type of glazing allows variable transmittance in the visible portion of the spectrum while reflecting in the infrared spectrum, thereby reducing solar heat gain. The voltage can be controlled manually or automatically. Refer to Ch. 19 for more information on this type of glazing.

Photochromic glazing darkens under the direct action of sunlight, in the same way that some sunglasses do. As the light intensity increases, the window becomes darker. Although offering the advantage of automatic action, this type of glazing does not offer the control of electrochromic glazing. For example, there could be times when clear glazing is desirable, such as on a cold, sunny day.

Thermochromic glazing changes darkness in response to temperature. Like photochromic glazing, this technique offers less control than electrochromic glazing does.

Transition-metal hydride electrochromics make it possible to have a glazing material that changes from transparent to reflective. These products are based on coatings of nickel-magnesium instead of the oxides used in other electrochromic materials.

DOUBLE ENVELOPE

The double envelope concept involves constructing two glazed layers as the outer skin of a building. In a double envelope system these two glazed layers are typically separated by about 2 ft to 3 ft (600 to 1000) and incorporate some type of sun control (louvers, blinds, or shades) and either a passive or active ventilation system. Sometimes the system may include devices to redirect sunlight and thus enhance daylighting of the interior spaces.

The outer shell moderates the effects of the environment and provides a cavity between itself and the inner shell, which can be passively heated or not, depending on the climate and needs of the overall building design. Air flowing between the layers can exhaust excessive heat buildup directly to the outside in hot weather or can be redirected to a heat exchanger to warm incoming air in cold weather.

Although the cost is significantly more than that of a single envelope façade, the advantages of a double envelope system include reduced cooling loads, enhanced sun control, reduced operating costs, optimized daylighting, and enhanced air quality when natural ventilation is used.

When a new outer layer of glazing is built around an existing building, the system is known as a *dynamic buffer zone*. These types of systems are constructed primarily to prevent and control condensation that may result from remodeling and upgrading the existing building with higher humidity levels. In this type of system the space between the existing building and the new façade is ventilated with dry, preheated air during winter months.

DAYLIGHTING

Electric lighting and the cooling it requires typically account for 30–40% of a commercial building's total energy use and can sometimes range as high as 50%. In addition to providing energy savings and a sustainable design, daylighting can increase occupant satisfaction and increase productivity. Well-daylighted spaces can make it easier to lease space and reduce tenant turnover.

In order to make daylighting feasible and cost effective, several conditions must be met. First, there must be sufficient views of the sky. This may preclude the use of daylighting in dense urban sites or for houses or small buildings nestled among tall trees. Second, glazing must transmit enough light. This is usually not a problem in new building design, but it may be problematic in remodeling or historic building renovations where glazing cannot be changed. Finally, the daylighting design must be coordinated with artificial lighting control and mechanical systems design.

One concept often used in daylighting calculations is the *daylight factor* (DF). This is the ratio, expressed as a percentage, of the indoor illuminance at a point on a horizontal surface to the unobstructed exterior horizontal illuminance. Direct sunlight is excluded. The daylight factor can be calculated and compared with recommended daylight factors for various tasks. These range from about 1.5% for ordinary visual tasks to about 4% for difficult visual tasks such as drafting.

Daylighting Variables

Many variables must be accounted for in designing for daylighting. These include the compass orientations of the façades utilizing daylight, the brightness of the sky (which is affected by solar altitude, cloud conditions, and time of day), the area of the glass, the height of the head of the glass, the transmittance of the glass, the reflectance of both room surfaces and nearby outdoor surfaces, and obstructions such as overhangs and trees. Figure 7.6 illustrates some of the variables of daylighting design.

The advantages of daylighting must be weighed against the potential problems. These include unwanted heat gain or loss as glass area is increased, glare, and imbalanced lighting if side lighting is too strong. The issue of control must also be addressed because daylighting does not conserve energy if electric lights are not switched off. Normally, automatic switching is used to overcome this problem.

Building Design

The preliminary design of a building can have a significant impact on daylighting. Generally, buildings or portions of buildings where daylighting is to be optimized should be long and narrow and oriented with the long dimension in the east-west direction. Buildings with deep façades can provide a space for shading devices and light shelves. If the building is one or two stories, the glazed areas should be located away from tall trees or other obstructions. Light-colored surfaces on the exterior of the building should be used to reflect more daylight. Within the limits of cost, the building should also have high ceilings. This increases the penetration of daylight into the interior and makes it easier to incorporate light shelves into the design.

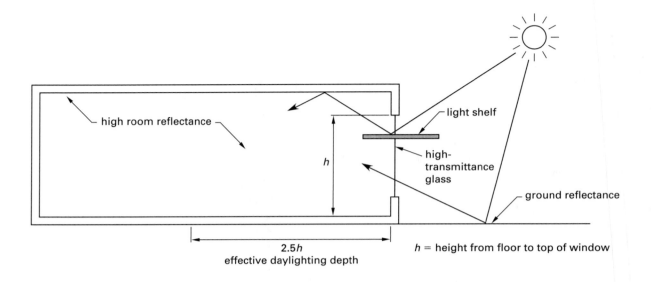

Figure 7.6   Daylighting Variables

Window Design

Two of the most important variables to consider when designing windows for daylighting are the height of the window head above the floor and the effective aperture (EA). The head of the window should be as high above the floor line as possible. With a standard window having no overhang protection or light shelf, the effective daylighted zone extends about 1.5 times the window head height into the room. With a light shelf, the effective daylighted zone is from 2.0 to 2.5 times the window head height.

The *effective aperture* combines the variables of light transmittance and window-to-wall ratio. The *visible light transmittance* (VLT) is the percentage of light that passes through a glazing material. The *window-to-wall ratio* (WWR) is the net glazing area in a room or space divided by the gross exterior wall area. It does not include window frames or mullions.

Small, punched windows have low WWRs while large, continuous windows have high WWRs. Generally, an EA of between 0.20 and 0.30 provides good daylighting. Thus, if the glazing has a low VLT, the size of the window should be increased.

For best uniform light distribution, use continuous windows (instead of punched windows) with solid wall between them.

Light Shelves

One of the problems with large, high windows for daylighting on the south side of a building is the resultant glare and heat gain of direct sun. One of the most effective ways to solve this problem is by using a light shelf. A *light shelf* is simply a horizontal surface placed above eye level that reflects direct daylight onto the ceiling while shading the lower portions of the window and the interior of the room. A light shelf also has the desirable effect of distributing the light more evenly from the window to the back of the room. This is diagrammed in Fig. 7.7.

Light shelves also provide a practical dividing point for using glass with a higher VLT above the shelf while using a tinted glass below for glare control. However they are designed, light shelves should have a diffuse or highly reflective surface.

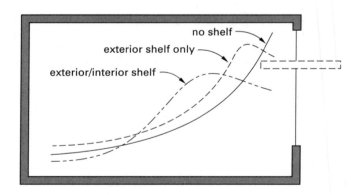

Figure 7.7   Effect of Light Shelf

Glazing Selection

Historically, one of the biggest problems with daylighting was trying to balance the need for a high VLT against the need for glare control and unwanted heat gain. To control heat loss through convection, a glazing unit with a low

U-value is desirable. To control gain from the sun's radiation, a low SHGC is desired. Generally, some type of tinted glass was used. Today however, spectrally selective glazing can be used, which gives a fairly high VLT with a good SHGC.

For glare control, a glass with a VLT value from 50% to 70% with the lowest possible SHGC is a good choice. If glare control is critical and if the size of the glazing area can be increased to achieve an EA between 0.20 and 0.30, a glazing product with a lower VLT can be selected.

Shading

As mentioned in a previous section, some type of shading is always required on windows, regardless of the compass orientation of the façade under consideration. Exterior shading devices are generally more effective than interior systems at blocking solar heat gain, although some type of interior window covering is usually required for occupant control and for those times when glare is excessive or the inside space needs to be darkened. Interior shading by itself has limited ability to control solar heat gain.

For daylighting applications, horizontal shading above the window on the south side of a building provides effective control. If a sufficient projection cannot be provided, a series of horizontal shades can be provided along the height of the glazing, but this is often expensive and blocks views. If light shelves are used they should be partially inside and partially outside the building.

Room Design

In addition to requiring shading and the correct size, position, and type of glazing, effective daylighting requires considerations related to room design. The reflectance of interior surfaces should be as high as possible. Minimum reflectances should be 80% for ceilings, 50% to 70% for walls, and 20% to 40% for floors. The wall facing the window should always be as light as possible to improve light distribution.

Furniture and equipment placement must be coordinated to make optimum use of the daylight. Low furniture should be used to ensure that light is not blocked from reaching the farther reaches of the space. Tasks that required higher light levels should be located closer to the windows. Computer monitors should be positioned such that they avoid reflected glare; that is, away from windows, with the screen oriented approximately perpendicular to and tilted slightly away from the window. Partial partitions can also be used to darken the area immediately around the screen.

Top Lighting

Top lighting with daylight involves using light pipes, skylights, roof monitors, sawtoothed roofs, or sloped glazing. Providing another source of daylight is advantageous because it is easier to evenly distribute the light, and because daylight can be provided to a larger portion of the building. Obviously, top lighting only works in one-story buildings, low-rise stepped-back buildings, or on the top floor of a multistory building.

Control of direct sunlight is often more difficult using these types of devices. One good product for providing light without direct sunlight is an insulated glazing panel or transparent insulation as described previously. These diffuse the light and keep heat loss to a minimum.

Light Pipes

Light pipes are round or square tubes with highly reflective interior coatings that extend from the roof to the space to be lighted. Sunlight is captured through a clear plastic dome and directed down to a translucent diffusing plate at the bottom. Light pipes are available in diameters from 10 in to 16 in (250 to 400). These devices are a relatively inexpensive way to bring natural light to the interior of a building, but their obvious limitation is that they only work in a space near the roof.

A project can receive LEED credit for achieving a minimum daylight factor of 2% in 75% of all space occupied for critical visual tasks. Additional credit is given if 90% of all regularly occupied spaces have a direct line of sight to vision glazing.

PART 2: ALTERNATIVE ENERGY SOURCES

Using alternative energy sources is one of the best ways to improve a building's sustainability while decreasing the building's life-cycle costs. Although most buildings designed to use alternative energy sources have a higher initial cost, they have relatively short payback periods. In addition, a project can receive LEED credit for supplying at least 5% of the building's total energy use with on-site renewable energy systems, such as solar energy, geothermal, wind, biomass, and bio-gas strategies. Another credit is given for supplying 10% of the building's total energy use, and yet another for reaching 20%.

SOLAR DESIGN

Good solar design can have a tremendous impact on energy conservation because of the vast amount of solar energy that strikes the earth every hour. In addition to providing energy for building heating and cooling and for water heating, the sun's light can be used for daylighting and electrical generation via photovoltaic cells.

Design Basics

Like most natural phenomena, daylighting is highly variable, and using it for building design requires an understanding of how it varies during different times of the year and day and in different geographical locations.

The sun's position varies by season because of the relationship between it and the earth. In fact, the seasons are a result of the change in angle between the earth and sun. The north-south axis of the earth is tilted at an angle of 23.5° relative to the north-south axis of the sun. This is called the *declination angle* (or simply the declination) of the earth and remains constant as the earth revolves around the sun during a one-year period.

As shown in Fig. 7.8, when the axis of the earth is tilted toward the sun it is summer in the northern hemisphere. This is when the rays of the sun are closest to perpendicular in relation to the surface of much of the northern part of the earth—when we consider the sun "highest" in the sky and when the northern hemisphere receives the most solar radiation. During the winter months the earth is tilted away from the sun, decreasing its angle relative to the horizon and reducing the amount of solar energy striking the earth. The times of maximum tilt are December 21 for the winter solstice and June 21 for the summer solstice. On March 21 and September 21, the tilt of the earth is sideways in relation to the sun, and day and night are of equal lengths. These times are called the *spring equinox* and *fall equinox*, respectively.

Seasonal variation determines how high above the horizon the sun is at any given time during the day. The other variable that determines the apparent height of the sun above the horizon is the latitude of the observer on the earth. At the equator, or 0° latitude, the surface of the earth is closer to perpendicular than at 90° latitude, or at the north pole.

The position of the sun as viewed from the earth is described by two angles, the azimuth and the altitude. See Fig. 7.9. The *azimuth* angle is the compass orientation of the sun. For solar design purposes this is usually the number of degrees either east or west of due south. For example, if the sun is halfway between south and west, the azimuth is 45° west of south. Sometimes, azimuth angle is measured in a 360° circle with due north being 0°, due east being 90°, south at 180°, and west at 270°. The *altitude* angle is the apparent height of the sun as measured from the horizon (which is 0° to directly overhead, which is 90°).

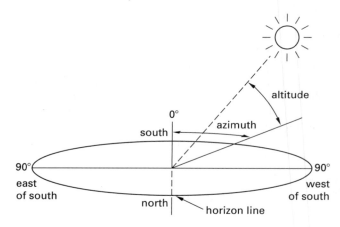

Figure 7.9   Sun Angles

Because the earth follows a repetitive pattern around the sun during a year, the position of the sun at any location on earth on any given day and at any given time can be calculated with various formulas. A simpler and quicker method is to use sun charts or solar plots similar to that shown in Fig. 7.10. Some types of sun charts use a circular format, but the same information is available from them. Sun charts plot the altitude and azimuth at different times during a

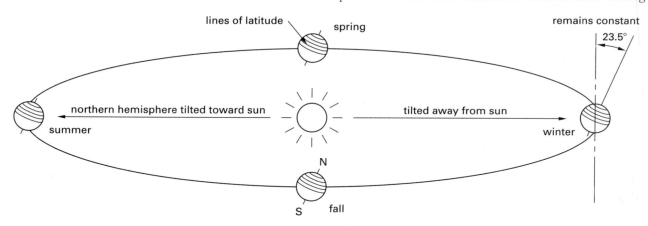

Figure 7.8   Seasonal Variation of Sun Angle

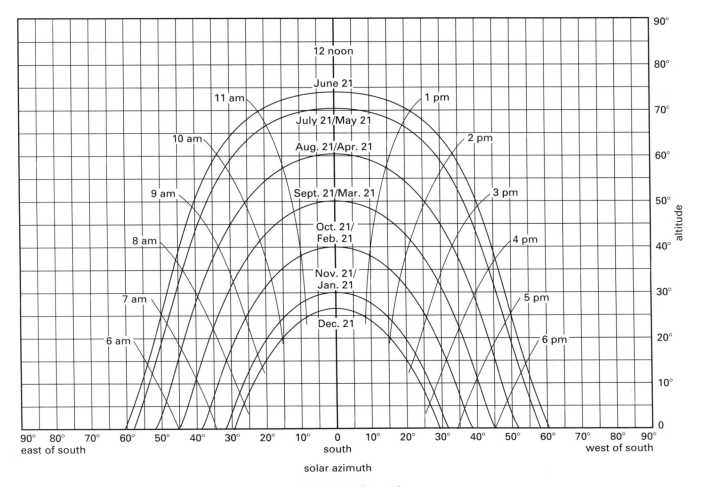

Figure 7.10 Typical Sun Chart

day. Several lines are used to represent the sun at yearly time intervals (usually the 21st day of each month). Because the latitude affects altitude angles, a separate sun chart is required for every latitude. However, to reduce the number of charts, latitudes are usually plotted for every 2°, 5°, or 10° of latitude, depending on what level of accuracy is required.

Sun charts can be used to determine the best design for overhangs and other shading devices and to plot the shading effects of surrounding structures and vegetation on a building using solar heating or daylighting. Such a plot is called a *shadow mask*. There are also computer programs that provide the same kind of information.

Charts and tables are also available that give the amount of solar radiation in Btu/ft²-day (W/m²·day) for different geographical locations for use in designing passive and active solar energy systems.

Passive Solar Design

There are several generic types of passive solar heating systems. A *passive solar energy system* simply means that solar energy is collected, stored, and distributed without the use of mechanical equipment. The following general categories describe the most commonly used passive solar design techniques. See Fig. 7.11.

Direct gain systems collect heat through south-facing glass and store the heat in high-mass materials such as concrete floors, masonry walls, tile, stone, or terrazzo. See Fig. 7.11(a). During nighttime hours the high-mass materials slowly release the heat gained during the day. To make this system effective, the glass area must be well insulated at night or the glazing must be low-ε glass. In order to be efficient, glazing used for passive solar heating should have a U-factor of less than 0.35 Btu/ft²-hr-°F (2.0 W/m²·K). Because moveable, nighttime insulation is not very efficient and requires human intervention, newer glazing materials can be used instead. The mass areas should be dark colored

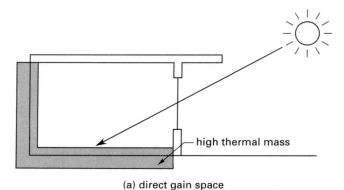

(a) direct gain space

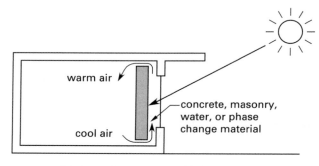

(b) thermal storage wall (Trombe wall)

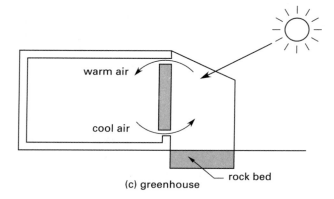

(c) greenhouse

Figure 7.11 Passive Solar Heating Types

A *thermal storage wall* is placed directly behind a south-facing glass wall and collects solar energy during the day for release at night, similar to a direct gain system. Most thermal storage walls are vented, which allows cool air to circulate in the space between the glass and wall, heat, and travel by convection up and over the wall and back into the space. A common form of thermal storage wall as diagrammed in Fig. 7.11(b) is the *Trombe wall*, which is constructed of masonry with vents at the top and bottom to allow thermocirculation. Thermal storage walls can also be constructed of water containers or phase change materials. Water is better than concrete or masonry because it has a higher specific heat and can store more energy than masonry. *Phase-change materials* are used to prevent overheating or wide swings in temperatures that can occur with concrete, masonry, and water. Phase change materials are typically eutectic salts that change from a solid to a liquid at a fairly low temperature, around 70°F (21°C). They store large amounts of heat because they store latent heat as they undergo the phase change from solid to liquid. At night, the heat is released as they change state from liquid to solid.

Greenhouse designs include large glazed areas on the south side of the building with a heavy thermal mass wall separating the greenhouse and the remainder of the structure. A rock bed or high thermal mass floor is built in the greenhouse. While the greenhouse often overheats and is subject to heat loss at night, the stored heat thermocirculates into the rest of the building at night. See Fig. 7.11(c).

Roof ponds store heat in large water-filled bags on the roof of a building. In winter during the day, the bags heat up. At night, insulation is moved over the roof pond, which loses its heat downward into the building. The same system can be reversed in the summer to cool the building by radiation. During the night the insulation is removed from the pond, so the heat collected from the building during the day is lost upward, away from the building.

Convective loop systems place the solar collector below the space so that air is circulated by natural convection as the warm air rises and cool air falls back to the collector. Convective loop systems are often used to circulate water.

Active Solar Design

Active solar energy systems use pumps, fans, ducts, pipes, and other mechanical equipment to collect, store, and distribute solar energy. In order of use, active solar systems are used for domestic and process water heating, space heating, space cooling, and electricity generation, although generation of electricity is still limited due to the expense of photovoltaic cells. One of the most common categories of active systems, which may be thought of as a "passive system with active assist," is when one of the types of passive systems described

and free of rugs, wall hangings, and other materials that would interfere with the storage and release of heat.

Indirect gain systems are similar to direct gain systems except that the thermal mass is not in direct sunlight. Rather, the mass is heated during the day by room air temperature and reflected sunlight. Indirect gain systems are less efficient than direct gain systems; they require about four times the amount of mass. However, they can be used in conjunction with direct gain systems to even out the temperature variations in different parts of the building.

previously is used with ductwork and fans to distribute the heated air without relying solely on natural convection.

For a typical active solar system, three components are required: the collector, a storage device, and a distribution system.

Collectors may be either flat-plate collectors or focusing collectors. *Flat-plate collectors* consist of a network of pipes located on an absorptive black surface with low emissivity below a covering of glass or plastic. The pipes carry the heat transfer fluid, which is generally water with antifreeze but can also be air or other liquids. *Focusing collectors* are parabolic-shaped reflectors that focus the incoming radiation to a single pipe that carries the heat-transfer medium. Because the reflectors focus the sun's energy, focusing collectors operate at a much higher temperature than do flat-plate collectors. However, they must be continuously aimed at the sun for maximum benefit, so they are usually attached to mechanisms that automatically track the path of the sun.

Storage devices are usually water for water systems or rock beds for air systems. Phase change materials can also be used, but are more expensive.

Distribution components are the same as for standard HVAC systems: ducts for air, pipes for water, and associated fans, pumps, registers, and control devices.

When solar energy is used for water heating it may be in either an open loop or closed loop. In an open loop, the water to be used is heated directly in the solar collector. In a closed loop, water or some other transfer medium is heated in the collector and circulated to a heat exchanger where the actual water to be used is heated by the transfer medium. A closed loop is often employed because antifreeze can be added to the water that circulates through the collectors. Refer to Ch. 9 for more information on solar water heating.

When solar energy is used for space heating, either air or water can be used for the transfer medium. If air is used, the heated air is circulated to a rock bed, normally under the building, where the heat is stored. At night, fans circulate cool air over the rock bed, where the air warms and is distributed to the building. If water is used as the transfer medium, it is stored in a large tank and then, when needed, it is pumped to baseboard heaters, radiant panels, or a heat exchanger in a forced air furnace.

Solar energy can be used for cooling if high enough temperatures are reached in the transfer medium. The heated water is used as the energy source for absorptive cooling, as diagrammed in Fig. 6.2.

WIND

Wind power offers an extremely sustainable method of generating electricity from a renewable and free source. There are many commercial wind farms across the United States and Canada that help reduce the need for fossil-fuel-burning power plants. However, wind energy is generally not appropriate for individual building use. Wind machines are costly, and most jurisdictions will not allow their use on urban or suburban sites. Of course, they are only appropriate for windy locations.

Even where a wind generating system can be installed, in most cases, the electricity must be used as it is generated. Using wind energy to charge batteries has limited use for most building sites. Some power companies will purchase excess electricity when it is placed back in the utility power grid.

GEOTHERMAL

Broadly speaking, geothermal alternate energy sources encompass a broad range of heat sources from the earth, including hot springs. Practically, geothermal energy involves the use of *ground-source heat pumps* (GSHPs) that use the relatively constant temperature of the earth. These are electrically powered systems that work like air-source heat pumps by either extracting heat from the ground in winter or giving off excess heat to the ground in summer. The heat from the ground is increased through the use of a vapor-compressor refrigeration cycle.

GSHPs can be used for space heating and cooling and for preheating water for domestic hot water. They can save from 20% to 50% on energy consumption for space heating and cooling and up to 50% on water heating.

Although the initial cost is higher than that of conventional equipment, long-term costs are lower, and they reduce the need for fossil fuel-based energy. They can be used for both residential and commercial buildings; however, they are most effectively used in buildings that require significant space and water heating and cooling over extended hours of operation. These include homes, multi-family buildings, schools, and similar uses.

The main feature of a GSHP is the assemblage of durable plastic pipes buried in the ground, either vertically or horizontally, depending on the space available and the geology of the site. About 400 ft (120 m) of pipe are required for every 12,000 Btu/hr (3500 W) of heating or cooling capacity needed. In the heating mode, water is pumped through the plastic tubing in the earth to the heat pump, where the water's heat is increased. The GSHP can then be used to preheat water or exchange heat in a water-water or water-air heat exchanger. The cycle is reversed for cooling.

PHOTOVOLTAICS

Photovoltaics is the direct conversion of sunlight into electricity. Photovoltaic (PV) cells are made from various types of semiconductor materials and deposited or arranged on a variety of materials in flat panels. There are also concentrator systems that focus sunlight on cells, but these are generally limited for use in large-scale power generation. The cells convert the sunlight into direct current (DC), which is converted into alternating current (AC). The electricity is used immediately, stored in batteries, or sold back to the power utility if the system is connected to the power grid.

Photovoltaics has many advantages. It reduces the demand on nonrenewable energy sources, such as coal- or gas-fired power plants. It can reduce energy costs because the power is generated on-site and the excess can, in many states, be sold back to the utility. It produces electricity with no pollution and comes from a free resource. Disadvantages include a higher initial cost, the need for solar access, low winter production, no production during night hours, and sometimes the requirement for storage batteries. In addition, some local jurisdictions, especially homeowners' associations, may limit the use of photovoltaics.

The development of PV technology is ongoing, and the efficiency is increasing while the cost is decreasing. Manufacturers now provide 20-year warranties for PV cells. The use of this technology continues to grow, with some states offering tax rebates or other financial incentives to make their use more feasible.

There are three types of photovoltaic cells in use: crystalline, polycrystalline, and thin-film. Crystalline cells are the most widely used. Polycrystalline cells are less expensive than crystalline but produce less power. Thin-film cells can be deposited onto other materials such as glass, metal, or plastic, making them ideal when they need to be integrated with other building materials. However, thin-film cells only produce as little as one-third the power of crystalline PV cells.

Photovoltaic cells are assembled into arrays and can be placed on a building in one of two ways. The PV arrays can be constructed in frames and attached to the roof, walls, or elsewhere as a distinct visual element. Newer technology now allows the cells to be built into other building materials, such as shingles, metal roofing, membrane roofing, and glass. When used on a roof, the ideal angle for the PV array is determined as the latitude of the building plus or minus 15°.

DEFINITIONS

Balance-point temperature: the outdoor temperature at which a building makes a transition from a heating need to a cooling need

Daylight factor (DF): the ratio, expressed as a percentage, of the indoor illuminance at a point on a horizontal surface to the unobstructed exterior horizontal illuminance. Direct sunlight is excluded.

Effective aperture: the product of visible transmittance multiplied by the window-to-wall ratio

Ground light: visible light from the sun and sky, reflected by exterior surfaces below the plane of the horizon

Light shelf: a horizontal element positioned above eye level and designed to reflect daylight on the ceiling for improved daylighting effectiveness

Net metering: the requirement that a utility pay and charge equal rates regardless of which way electricity flows as part of the utility grid. Thus, excess electricity generated with photovoltaics or wind systems can be sold back to the utility.

Radiative cooling (or *Nocturnal cooling* or *Night-cooled mass*): a passive or active design strategy that uses thermal mass to collect and store heat during the day for release at night. This works best in climates where there is a significant difference between daytime and nighttime temperatures, such as the southwest or in temperate climates.

Shading coefficient (SC): the ratio of the solar heat gain through a glazing product to the solar heat gain through an unshaded $1/8$ in thick (3), clear, double-strength glass under the same set of conditions. This is a value for the glass only and does not include the frame. The SC is a value between 0.0 and 1.0. Because this rating includes only the glass, the solar heat gain coefficient is considered a more accurate rating.

Solar heat-gain coefficient (SHGC): the ratio of the solar heat gain through a fenestration to the total solar radiation incident on the glazing. Solar heat gain includes directly transmitted solar heat and absorbed solar radiation, which is then reradiated, conducted, or convected into the space. This rating includes the effects of the frame and glass spacer. The SHGC is a value between 0.0 and 0.87.

Visible light transmittance (VLT): the fraction of visible light that passes through a glazing material

Window-to-wall ratio: the net glazing area (glass only, not including frame or mullions) in a room or space divided by the gross exterior wall area

Workplane: the assumed height at which work is performed, usually considered to be at desk height, 30 in (760) above the floor

SAMPLE QUESTIONS

1. The Indian Pueblo in Taos, New Mexico, illustrates which of the following climatic design principles?

    A. skin-dominant loading
    B. sun shading
    C. volume utilization
    D. wind effect

2. Air barriers are designed to stop infiltration and exfiltration caused by all of the following EXCEPT

    A. wind pressure
    B. stack pressure
    C. HVAC fan pressure
    D. vapor pressure

3. Which of the following is NOT a photovoltaic cell type?

    A. crystalline
    B. polycrystalline
    C. thin-film
    D. transparent

4. The greatest degree of protection from cold winter winds can best be achieved with

    A. air locks
    B. earth sheltering
    C. green roofs
    D. landscaping

5. The best measure to use when evaluating how well a glazed window prevents heat gain is with the

    A. daylight factor
    B. shading coefficient
    C. solar heat-gain coefficient
    D. window-to-wall ratio

6. A ground-source heat pump would not be appropriate

    A. on a site with extensive subsurface rock
    B. for a midsized commercial building
    C. for multi-family housing
    D. in a hot-arid climatic region

7. A massive brick wall behind glazing on the south side of a house would be used for a

    A. direct gain system
    B. greenhouse design
    C. passive system with active assist
    D. Trombe wall

8. The apparent angle of the sun above the horizon is the

    A. altitude
    B. azimuth
    C. declination
    D. latitude

9. For a room with a standard window whose head is 8 ft above the floor, daylighting could be used for illumination for a distance from the window of approximately

    A. 8 ft
    B. 12 ft
    C. 16 ft
    D. 20 ft

10. Glass that changes darkness in response to a change in the level of daylight is

    A. chromogenic
    B. electrochromic
    C. photochromic
    D. thermochromic

SUSTAINABLE DESIGN

Sustainability encompasses a wide range of concepts and strategies. Although specifics vary, a general definition of *sustainability* includes meeting the needs and wants of the present generation without harming or compromising the ability of future generations to meet their needs.

For architecture, *sustainable design* (also called *green building*, *environmental design*, or *ecological design*, among other terms) involves many planning, design, operational, and reuse concepts that together can create functional, healthy, nonpolluting, and environmental friendly buildings without compromising practical requirements or human comfort. In addition, the long-term costs are no greater, and are often less, than those of comparable buildings designed without sustainability in mind.

This chapter reviews the sustainable design issues that have not been covered elsewhere.

SITE DEVELOPMENT

The first step in developing a sustainable building project is to disturb the natural site as little as possible, by minimizing the building footprint, parking, and other development. The natural topography must be respected, and climatic conditions must be considered. All of these will affect the final building form. Additionally, development should take place to make the best use of community services such as public transportation, utilities, and pedestrian paths. Buildings should not be developed on sites designated as prime farmland, in floodplains, on or within 100 ft (30 m) of wetlands, on land designated as habitat for threatened species, or on land that was previously public parkland. A project can receive LEED™ credit for meeting these requirements. LEED is an acronym for Leadership in Energy and Environmental Design, a program of the U.S. Green Building Council designed to encourage the implementation of sustainable building practices. Buildings receive credits for using various sustainable design practices and are then awarded a

LEED certificate if they accumulate enough points. See the section on Building Rating Systems later in this chapter for more information on LEED.

Refer to Ch. 2 for more information on how sustainability practices affect project concepts. Refer to Ch. 4 for more information on how topography, utilities, climate, and alternative energy systems and new material technologies affect project concepts. See Ch. 7 for information on energy efficiency and alternative energy sources.

WATER USE

Water use in sustainable design involves a variety of issues. These include controlling and directing storm water runoff, preventing erosion and contamination of runoff, using rainwater, employing gray water, and practicing general water conservation through a variety of strategies, including low-flow plumbing fixtures.

When discussing water use for sustainability in architectural design there are four classifications: potable water, rainwater, gray water, and black water. *Potable water* is treated and is suitable for drinking. *Gray water* is wastewater not from toilets or urinals. *Black water* is water containing toilet or urinal waste, although some jurisdictions may include water from kitchen sinks and laundry facilities in the category of black water.

In an ideal situation, each of these types of water would be kept separate, and rainwater and gray water would be used for irrigation and for flushing toilets. With suitable treatment, black water could be used for irrigation. Both gray water and black water could be run through heat exchangers to preheat cold water for final heating in a water heater. However, because of high initial costs and strict local and state health regulations, making extensive use of gray water and black water is seldom feasible, especially in an urban or suburban setting.

Storm Runoff and Erosion Control

The first consideration in sustainable design of water use should be to protect existing watersheds on a site and on the surrounding areas and waterways. Improper water control during and after construction can create one or more of the following problems.

- increased load on local storm sewer systems

- increased potential for flooding

- pollution of waterways with sediment, road salts, petroleum products, fertilizers, heavy metals, and pathogenic bacteria

- erosion of sites and waterways

- erosion of stream banks

- accelerated soil creep or landslides

- stream warming

- loss of aquatic biodiversity

All development sites should have a storm water management plan. *Storm water management* is the use of structural or nonstructural practices designed to reduce storm water runoff pollutant loads, discharge volumes, and peak flow discharge rates.

During construction, erosion must be controlled while natural surfaces are stripped and subjected to building conditions. Most states and local municipalities have regulations to control erosion and sediment. Silt fences, sediment traps or basins, vegetated buffer strips, hay bales, and other methods are used to control water flow and pollutants onto adjacent property and ultimately into natural waterways.

The final constructed site should minimize the impervious coverage of development, utilize the natural filtration and cleansing action of soils and plants, and capture and control excessive runoff. Some of the common ways of doing this are to use pervious paving, develop constructed wetlands, or build grass-lined swales. *Pervious paving* can be manufactured grids of concrete, plastic, or other materials that allow grass or other ground covers to grow through, or it can be porous asphalt or concrete.

Refer to the definitions at the end of this chapter for additional terms related to storm water management. Additional guidelines for sustainable site design are given in Ch. 2.

Rainwater Collection

If local regulations allow, rainwater can be collected and used for irrigation and, in some cases, for nonpotable uses such as flushing toilets. Rainwater collection also reduces the amount of site runoff that can burden a storm sewer system. The effectiveness of a rainwater collection system is limited by the amount of rain some geographic regions receive and the quality of rainwater in air-polluted locations. 1 in of rain per square foot of roof area is about 0.6 gal (25 mm/m^2 is about 2.3 L).

A *rainwater collection system* is composed of a water collection system, a storage cistern, and a water distribution system. The water collection system is commonly the roof area of the building. If a roof is used, the materials should be selected to avoid contamination of the water or the addition of sediment. Good choices are metal, clay, and concrete tile. Avoid using asphalt shingles or lead-containing materials such as flashing. Steep roofs are better than low-sloped roofs because they are scoured by winds and collect less dust and debris. Devices can be used to divert the first flush of water during a rainfall, to prevent it from entering the cistern.

For irrigation use, the runoff can be filtered first with screens on the gutters and then with simple graded screens, paper filters, or sand filters. Additional treatment may be needed for use in flushing toilets and similar nonpotable applications.

After the rainwater is collected it is stored in a *cistern*. Cisterns can be made from fiberglass, steel, or concrete. They must be watertight and covered to prevent contamination. If cisterns can be located above the area of use, water can flow by gravity; otherwise, small pumps are used to distribute the water.

To calculate the amount of rainwater available, the horizontal area of the catchment area is multiplied by the average annual rainfall for a region and reduced by some amount, typically 75%, to account for evaporation and other losses.

Gray and Black Water Systems

Gray water recycling is the collection, treatment, storage and distribution of wastewater from sources that do not contain human waste, such as showers and sinks. Depending on the treatment methods and local health regulations, gray water may be used for irrigation, toilet flushing, vehicle washing, janitorial cleaning, cooling, and similar uses.

Gray water systems are generally only cost effective in new construction where separate piping can easily be installed and where the ratio of the demand for nonpotable to potable water is relatively high, such as for laundries and car washes. Other cost considerations include the net reduction in water consumption, the price of potable water, and economies of scale.

Even if gray water is only used for irrigation, health regulations may require that it be filtered and be applied subsurface, using drip or other methods rather than sprinklers. Any type of gray water system should have interceptors to prevent the flow of grease and hair into the system.

If gray water is not reused directly, the heat it carries can be run through heat exchangers to preheat potable water flowing to a water heater. This can reduce energy demand, increase the availability of hot water, allow downsizing of heated water storage, and lower energy costs. Heat recovery systems are best for buildings that have large domestic hot water needs such as restaurants, laundries, apartments, and arenas. Heat exchangers can either be a *direct system*, where the gray water flows past a coil of cold water, or a *tank system*, where the gray water is held around coils of incoming cold water. The tank system has the ability to extract more heat from the gray water, but requires periodic maintenance. Both systems require protection against contamination of the potable water supply. One way of doing this is with a double-walled heat exchanger. Building officials and health departments must be consulted to determine the local requirements for these types of systems.

Black water recycling is the collection, treatment, storage and distribution of wastewater from nearly any source, including from toilets and urinals. Because of the obvious contamination, black water requires more extensive treatment before use. Generally, black water recycling is not cost effective except on a large scale, although commercial systems are available for single-building use.

Plumbing Fixtures

The simplest method of water conservation for sustainable design is to reduce the amount of treated water used. This can easily be accomplished with low-flow toilets, showerheads, and faucets. Currently, 1.6 gal (6 L) toilets are mandated by law in the United States, and toilets that use even less water are available. Using various designs with air pressure tanks or vacuum systems, some toilets use as little as 1.5 qt (1.4 L) of water with each flush. Low-consumption appliances are also available that reduce water use without compromising function. For example, a front-loading washing machine uses less water than does a top-loading model.

ALTERNATIVE ENERGY SOURCES AND ENERGY EFFICIENCY

Alternative energy sources refer to renewable sources such as solar or wind power. While it is seldom possible to use only alternative energy sources in all buildings or for all of a building's energy needs, using them can substantially reduce reliance on depletable sources, such as fossil fuels, and can reduce pollution. Energy efficiency refers to a reduction in the consumption of energy. Both of these topics are discussed in Ch. 7. Energy efficiency using conventional fuels and mechanical systems is discussed in Ch. 6. Refer to Ch. 11 for more information on how sustainability can be improved with electrical and lighting systems.

MATERIALS

The selection and use of materials in a building represents a significant part of the total sustainability of a building project. As with energy consumption and other sustainability issues, material selection must be made with consideration of the entire life cycle of the building. However, sustainability issues must be considered along with the traditional concerns of function, cost, appearance, and performance.

Life-Cycle Assessment

A *life-cycle assessment* (LCA) provides the methodology to evaluate the environmental impact of using a particular material or product in a building. There are commonly four phases to an LCA. These are

- defining the goals and scope of the study

- performing an inventory analysis

- performing an impact assessment

- performing an improvement analysis, or interpretation, and reporting the results of the study

The first step in the process is to determine the purpose and goals of doing the study. Limits of the study and the units for study must also be established so alternatives can be compared and the framework for data acquisition can be developed.

The *inventory analysis* is often the most difficult part because it involves determining and quantifying all the inputs and outputs of the product under study. These might include the energy required to obtain the raw materials and process or manufacture them, the energy of transportation, the need for ancillary materials, and the pollution or waste disposal involved in the manufacturing, use, and disposal processes. The ability to recycle the material is also considered. Some of the criteria used for evaluating building materials are given in the next section.

The *impact assessment* attempts to characterize the effects of the processes found in the inventory analysis in terms of their impacts on the environment. The analysis may include such things as resource depletion, generation of pollution, health impacts, or effects on social welfare. For example, the energy required to produce a product may necessitate the addition of electrical generating capacity, which in turn may produce both waterborne and airborne pollution.

Finally, the *improvement analysis* is a way to suggest how to reduce the environmental impact of all the raw materials, energy, and processing required to produce the product or construction activity.

There are four main stages of a product's life cycle: raw-material acquisition, manufacturing, use in the building, and disposal or reuse. The potential individual elements of each stage are as follows.

Raw-Material Acquisition

- acquisition of raw materials and energy from mining, drilling, or other activities

- processing of raw materials

- transportation of raw materials to processing points

Manufacturing

- conversion of processed raw materials into useful products

- manufacturing or fabrication of materials into the final product

- packaging of the product

- transportation of the finished product to the job site

Use and Maintenance

- installation or construction of the product into the building

- long-term use of the product throughout its life or the life of the building

- maintenance and repair of the product throughout its life

Disposal

- demolition of the product used in the building

- conversion of the waste into other useful products

- waste disposal of the product

- reuse or recycling of the product if not disposed or converted

At any point in the life cycle of a building material or product (but most commonly during inventory analysis) consideration must be given to all the inputs and outputs of the material or product under study. These include the energy and other resources required to acquire, process, or use the product and the materials released to the air, water, and land as a result of its use. A model for analyzing these effects is shown in Fig. 8.1.

This model is helpful in directing the required collection of data. Inputs for energy are typically in units such as British thermal units or megajoules, inputs for raw materials are in pounds or kilograms, and water is commonly in gallons or liters. Output is typically given by weight, in pounds or kilograms.

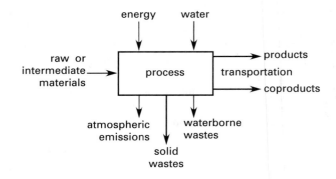

Figure 8.1 Life-Cycle Inventory Model

Criteria for Evaluating Building Materials

Some of the criteria for evaluating how sustainable a product or construction process is include the following. Of course, not all the criteria will apply to every product.

- *Embodied energy.* The material or product should require as little energy as possible for its extraction as a raw material, initial processing, and subsequent manufacture or fabrication into a finished building product. This includes the energy required for transportation of the materials and products during their life cycle. The production of the material should also generate as little waste or pollution as possible.

- *Renewable materials.* A material is sustainable if it comes from sources that can renew themselves within a fairly short time. LEED credits are given for using rapidly renewable building materials and products for 5% of the total value of all building materials and products used in the project. These include products typically made from plants that are harvested within a 10-year cycle or shorter. Products that meet this criterion include wool carpets, bamboo flooring and paneling, straw board, cotton batt insulation, linoleum flooring, poplar OSB, sunflower seed board, and wheatgrass cabinetry.

- *Recycled content.* The more recycled content a material has, the less raw materials and energy are required to process the raw materials into a final product. Each of the three types of recycled content should be considered: post-consumer materials, post-industrial materials, and recovered materials.

- *Energy efficiency.* Materials, products, and assemblies should reduce the energy consumption in a building.

- *Use of local materials.* Using locally produced materials reduces transportation costs and can add to the regional character of a design. A building can receive LEED credit for using 20% of building materials and products that are manufactured regionally within a radius of 500 mi. Additional credit is available for using 50% or more of local materials and products.

- *Durability.* Durable materials will last longer and generally require less maintenance over the life of a product or building. Even though initial costs may be higher, the life cycle costs may be less.

- *Low volatile organic compounds* (VOC) *content.*

- *Low toxicity.* Materials should be selected that emit little or no harmful gasses such as chlorofluorocarbons (CFCs), formaldehyde, and others listed on the EPA's list of hazardous substances.

- *Moisture problems.* If possible, materials should be selected that prevent or resist the growth of biological contaminants.

- *Water conservation.* Products should reduce water consumption in a building and in landscaping.

- *Maintainability.* Materials and products should be able to be cleaned and otherwise maintained with only nontoxic or low-VOC substances.

- *Potential for reuse and recycling.* Some materials and products are more readily recycled than others. Steel, for example, can usually be separated and melted down to make new steel products. On the other hand, plastics used in construction are difficult to remove and separate.

- *Reusability.* A product should be reusable after it has served its purpose in the original building. This type of product becomes a salvaged material in the life cycle of another building.

Use of Salvaged Materials

Salvaged materials should be used as much as possible. This includes items such as doors, window units, cabinetry, furnishings, and equipment. There may be extra costs involved in preparing salvaged materials for reuse, but these costs can be offset by savings on new materials and the costs associated with their production or disposal. Reusing materials, such as brick or timber from old buildings, can even add to the aesthetic appeal of a new building.

Concrete

Concrete is generally not a sustainable material, because the manufacture and production of portland cement requires substantial energy and raw material consumption and produces environmental emissions. However, when properly constructed, concrete does have a long life, and it can be recycled as crushed aggregate for highway base, fill, and subsequent concrete manufacture. By itself, concrete does not emit any appreciable air pollutants. However, some concrete admixtures (such as superplasticizers and water reducing agents) and form-release agents can produce odors and emissions.

The sustainability of concrete can be improved by incorporating fly ash admixtures, using recycled aggregates when possible, and using low-waste formwork. *Fly ash* is a waste material obtained from coal-fired power plants. It is used to increase concrete strength, decrease permeability, reduce temperature rise during placement, increase sulfate resistance, and improve the workability of concrete. It can be used to reduce the total amount of cement needed. In high-volume fly ash concrete, between 40% and 50%, and sometimes as much as 65% of the portland cement can be replaced by fly ash. Recycled aggregate can be used in some applications when its strength is sufficient for the purpose. Using lightweight aggregates such as pumice or perlite can lessen the need for standard aggregates, reduce the structural load, and improve insulation values. Finally, using steel forms or permanent rigid plastic foam forms can reduce the waste associated with standard wood forms. Rigid plastic foam forms have the additional advantage of improving the thermal resistance of foundation walls.

Autoclaved aerated concrete (AAC) is a lightweight, precast concrete made with aluminum powder as an extra ingredient, hardened in molds, and cured in an autoclave. It is formed into blocks, typically 10 in by 25 in (250 by 635) in thicknesses of 4 in, 8 in, or 10 in (100, 200, or 250). It can easily be cut and shaped with normal woodworking tools. ACC is used for nonloadbearing residential and light commercial walls. It provides excellent insulation value, reduced air infiltration, and improved acoustic qualities. ACC also requires less cement than does standard concrete.

Masonry

As with concrete, masonry (either concrete or clay based) and mortar require large amounts of energy and raw materials in their production. However, brick is a natural material and is generally manufactured close to the place of use and from locally quarried clay, reducing transportation costs. It is also a durable material with a long life. Like concrete, masonry produces no pollution or emissions once in place and provides excellent thermal mass. It can be recycled and, when placed in landfills, produces no toxic substances. Environmental impacts can be minimized by using fly ash, recycled aggregates (such as ground granulated blast furnace slag) and lightweight aggregates.

Metals

Although metals require large amounts of embodied energy for their production, they have a high potential for recycling. Steel is the most common metal used in buildings and is often recycled as scrap to produce more steel. Steel with a recycled content up to 30% or more is readily available. Aluminum is also widely used and is available with a recycled content of 20% or more. Copper has great value as a recycled material, and brass, bronze, and stainless steel can also be recycled, if separated.

Problems can arise with some metals that are plated or coated with chemicals. Electroplating processes produce high levels of pollution and byproducts. Alternatives to these processes include powder coatings and plastic polymer coatings. Whatever finish is applied, it should be readily removable to facilitate recycling.

Wood and Plastic

Lumber and wood products represent a large portion of both residential and commercial construction, from rough framing to furniture. This includes both softwoods and hardwoods from domestic and foreign sources. Deforestation, processing, and the manufacture of wood products represent a large ecological problem, but architects can minimize this by applying three sustainable strategies. These include using reclaimed wood, specifying sustainable or alternate materials, and using certified wood products.

Reclaimed wood is basically recycled wood from old buildings or structures that has been salvaged and prepared for a new use. Preparation may include removing nails and other fasteners, drying, and cutting or planing. In addition to being ecologically sound, reclaimed wood members have a unique visual character than many architects and clients find desirable.

Sustainable materials (or *alternate materials*) include a wide range of products. Standard solid-wood framing products can be replaced with engineered wood products such as wood I-joists, laminated veneer lumber, and structural insulated panels (SIPs). These products are discussed in Ch. 16. Panel products that use waste material, such as particleboard and medium-density fiberboard, are good sustainable products but often require adhesives and resins that outgas formaldehyde or other pollutants. These panels are typically made from urea formaldehyde. However, formaldehyde-free MDF or low-emission panels that use phenol-formaldehyde or urethane adhesives are available. These have a formaldehyde level of 0.04 ppm (parts per million) or less, which is below the commonly accepted level of 0.05 ppm. Another alternative to urea formaldehyde is methylene-diphenyl isocyanate (MDI). This resin does not emit toxic gasses during use and requires less dryer energy and lower press temperatures than do traditional binders.

Other innovative products can be used in some instances to replace rough lumber. Straw particleboard, for example, is made from wheat straw, a waste product from farming. The straw is milled into fine particles and hot pressed together with formaldehyde-free resins. It can be used for both construction and furniture making. Other agricultural products used are rice straw and bagasse, the residue from the processing of sugar cane. Some products also use post-consumer recycled waste paper for making building panels. A building can receive a LEED credit for using low-emitting materials such as wood and agrifiber products that contain no added urea-formaldehyde resins.

For finish carpentry and architectural woodwork many alternate products exist. Molding can be made from medium-density fiberboard or molded high-density polyurethane foam. Composite wood veneers are manufactured from readily available and fast-growing trees by slicing veneers, dying them, and gluing them back into an artificial "log." The manufactured log is then sliced. By varying the dye colors and how the artificial log is cut, a wide variety of veneers is possible, from those that look like standard wood to highly figured and colored products.

Certified wood products are those that use wood obtained through sustainable forest management practices. While there are many forest certification groups in North America, the most well known is the Forest Stewardship Council (FSC). This organization is an international body that oversees the development of national and regional standards based on basic forest management principles and criteria. It accredits certifying organizations that comply with its principles. The three groups the FSC currently accredits in the United States are the SmartWood Program of the Rainforest Alliance, the Forest Conservation Program of Scientific Certification Systems (SCS), and SGS Systems and Services Certification, Inc.

The FSC has ten basic principles and 56 individual criteria it uses to evaluate organizations for accreditation. It has also established additional regional criteria for different parts of the United States. The ten principles are as follows.

- Forest management must respect all applicable laws of the country in which they occur and must comply with FSC Principles and Criteria.

- Long-term tenure and use rights to the land and forests must be defined, documented, and legally established.

- The rights of indigenous peoples to own, use, and manage their land must be recognized and respected.

- Forest management practices and operations must maintain or enhance the long-term social and economic well-being of workers and local communities.

- Forest management must encourage the efficient use of the forest's products to ensure economic viability and environmental and social benefits.

- Forest management must conserve biological diversity, water resources, soils, ecosystems, and landscapes to maintain the ecological functions of the forest.

- A management plan must be written, implemented, and maintained.

- Monitoring must be conducted to assess the condition of the forest, yields, chain of custody, and management activities and their social and environmental impacts.

- Management activities in high-conservation-value forests must maintain or enhance the attributes that define such forests.

- Plantations must follow the first nine principles and the criteria that apply to plantations. Plantations should complement the management of, reduce pressures on, and promote the restoration and conservation of natural forests.

A building can receive a LEED credit for using at least 50% wood-based materials and products, certified in accordance with the FSC's Principles and Criteria. However, even though only a very small fraction of forests comply with FSC criteria, there are many other well-managed forests in North American and elsewhere.

Plastics identified as recyclable should be reserved and recycled. If possible, compostable plastics should be separated and identified as such. Recycled plastics have many uses. Polyethylene terephthalate (PET) from soft-drink containers, for example, can be used to manufacture carpet with properties similar to polyesters.

Plastic lumber is being used for decking, fencing, and other outdoor applications. This material may be either all plastic (a mixture of recycled plastic and pure high-density polyethylene (HDPE)), or a wood-plastic composite that is a mixture of recycled plastic resin (usually polyethylene) combined with wood fiber, which can be also be recycled material.

In addition to providing a use for post-consumer and post-industrial materials, plastic lumber is also an alternative to using chromated copper arsenate (CCA) pressure-treated wood, which can pose an environmental risk during disposal. Plastic lumber is durable, will not rot, absorb water,

or crack, and can be worked with standard woodworking saws and carbide blades. However, it is not suitable for loadbearing applications. Some wood-plastic composite lumber, on the other hand, has been graded for structural use.

Two new developments in plastic may improve the sustainability of this material type. The first is *bio-plastics*, specifically *polylactide* (PLA). This is a plastic derived from harvested corn that is biodegradable. It is currently used in fibers for carpet manufacture. The second is the development of *metallocene polyolefins*. This type of plastic allows polyolefins to be precisely manufactured to have specific properties. These may be a replacement for PVC and other plastics that are more harmful to the environment. They may be used for window frames, membrane roofing, siding, and wire sheathing.

Thermal Insulation and Moisture Protection

Materials for insulation and moisture protection are some of the most important for energy efficiency and the control of mold and other water-related problems. Very efficient plastic-based insulations with high thermal resistance are available, but these may cause problems with manufacturing (use of petroleum products and pollution), use (outgassing), and disposal. Because chlorofluorocarbons (CFCs) and hydrochlorofluorocarbons (HCFCs) have been phased out and replaced with other agents, the problem with ozone depletion has been reduced. Note than when CFCs were banned they were replaced with HCFCs, but these were phased out by the EPA in January of 2003.

Other types of insulation that are resource efficient and pose little danger for indoor air quality include the following. The conductivity of each is given in Table 18.1.

- *Cellulose insulation* containing at least 70% post-consumer paper waste is available in loose-fill form. It is manufactured without formaldehyde and with a nonhazardous fire retardant.

- *Mineral-fiber insulation*, which is made from steel mill slag or basalt rock, is available in rigid boards, batts, and loose-fill form.

- *Glass fiber insulation* containing 30% or more of post-consumer recycled glass is available in rigid boards, batts, and loose-fill form.

- *Vermiculite*, which is made from mica expanded by heat, is used for loose-fill applications. See the section on hazardous material mitigation later in this chapter for information on asbestos-containing vermiculite.

- *Perlite*, which is made from volcanic rock expanded by heat, is used as a lightweight aggregate for plaster and concrete and as loose-fill insulation.

- *Compressed straw* can be used as infill in structural insulated panels.

Refer to Ch. 18 for more information on insulation types.

Doors and Windows

Windows provide one of the best resources for sustainable design when they are used for daylighting, solar heat gain, and ventilation while maintaining good insulation qualities. New glazing products provide a variety of options to suit the individual needs of each building. In addition to controlling solar heat gain, glazing can have very high R-values.

In using any type of glazing, special consideration should also be given to the framing. If aluminum or steel is used, there should be a thermal break between the inside and outside surfaces. The energy efficiency of windows, doors, and skylights should be certified by an independent laboratory according to the standards of the National Fenestration Rating Council (NFRC) for U-factor, solar heat gain coefficient (SHGC), and visible light transmittance (VLT) coefficients. Windows may be certified with the Green Seal label if they meet the criteria given in Green Seal's standard GS-13.

Refer to Ch. 19 for more information on windows and glazing products.

Finishes

Interior finish materials provide a primary method of improving a building's sustainability because they are one of the main sources of potential indoor air pollution and they are typically replaced several times over the life of a building. Finish types are grouped according to the categories of adhesives, flooring, wall finishes, and ceiling finishes. The following sections give some of the more traditional finish materials as well as some alternative sustainable materials that are being used more frequently for both residential and commercial construction.

Adhesives

With many types of finishes, the potential problem is due to adhesives or coatings and not the finish material itself. Most adhesives emit gases because they contain plastic resins and other materials that can outgas. Three types of low-emission and zero-VOC adhesives can be used for installing carpet, resilient flooring, plastic laminates, sheet metal, wood veneers, and some types of wall coverings: dry adhesives that contain resins stored in capsules released by pressure, water-based adhesives containing latex or polyvinyl acetate, and natural adhesives containing plant resins in a water dispersion system. A building can receive a LEED credit for using adhesives and sealants with a VOC content less than that defined in the California South Coast Air Quality Management District (SCAQMD) Rule 1168, which is among the lowest VOC content standards in the country.

Flooring

When using carpet, there are three major considerations for sustainability: raw-material use, raw-material disposal, and indoor air quality. Good raw materials include polyester and nylon-blended carpet made from recycled soft-drink containers (PET) or wool. Although wool has a higher initial cost, it is a renewable resource, wears well, and may have a lower life-cycle cost when compared to less-expensive carpet that typically needs to be replaced more frequently. Carpet cushions made from recycled materials, such as tire rubber or synthetic and natural fiber from textile mill waste, should also be selected.

Disposal of carpet is a problem because of the total quantity that is placed in landfills, the fact that it does not decompose easily, the difficulty of separating the various components for recycling, and the costs of recycling compared with landfill disposal. Nylon 6, one type of nylon fiber, can be recycled easily. Although some manufacturers have made efforts to recycle used carpet, the amount is just a fraction of the total amount of carpet disposed. Generally, carpet tiles are more sustainable than broadloom carpet. This is because only a small number need to be replaced when they are damaged or worn, the adhesives used to apply them tend to offgas less than do broadloom adhesives, and several manufactures have programs to recycle the tiles.

Carpet can affect indoor air quality because of its construction and the adhesives used in direct-glue applications. Most carpet is made by bonding the face fiber to a backing with a synthetic latex resin. The latex can be replaced with fusion bonding, in which the face fiber is heat-welded to a sponge plastic backing. Carpets made with a needlepunching process also avoid the use of latex bonding. The Carpet and Rug Institute (CRI) has a voluntary testing program under which manufacturers have their carpet tested by an independent agency for four emissions: total volatile organic compounds, styrene, formaldehyde, and 4-phenylcyclohexene (4-PC). Carpet that passes the test criteria is allowed to carry the CRI IAQ carpet testing program label, or the "Green Label." The CRI also recommends that the ventilation system be operated at maximum capacity during and after installation for 48 to 72 hours. A building can receive a LEED credit for using carpet systems that meet or exceed the requirements of the CRI IAQ carpet testing program.

Vinyl flooring provides many benefits, including durability, easy cleaning, a wide choice of patterns and colors, and relatively low cost. However, it requires highly refined petro-chemicals for its manufacture and contains a large percentage of polyvinyl chloride (PVC) that can cause environmental problems during manufacture and disposal. Because of the high concentration of chlorine in the tile, hazardous substances can be given off if vinyl flooring is incinerated. Some vinyl tile is manufactured from recycled PVC, and one brand is made without chlorine. As with carpet, low-VOC adhesives should be specified for laying vinyl flooring.

Rubber flooring, both tile and sheet goods, made from recycled tires is available. This flooring is durable, slip-resistant, and resilient. However, because of the methods of manufacture and the binders that are used, recycled rubber flooring may give off indoor pollutants. This type of flooring should only be used where there is adequate ventilation, such as in outdoor sports areas, locker rooms, and other utility spaces.

Linoleum is available in tile or sheet form and can also be used for baseboards. Linoleum is made from natural, renewable products, including linseed oil, rosin, cork powder, and pigments. It is a durable floor material and is biodegradable, waterproof, fire resistant, naturally antibacterial, and does not generate static electricity. When used with low-VOC adhesives it emits only low levels of contaminants, less than those of vinyl flooring.

Cork flooring is made from a renewable resource, the bark of cork oak trees, which regenerates every nine to ten years. Cork forests are well managed and protected by the countries that have them. The only disadvantage to using cork as a natural material is that it must be imported from Mediterranean countries, increasing the transportation energy required. Although cork requires binders to hold the individual pieces together, the binders used today are phenol-formaldehyde, polyurethane, or all-natural protein products. Cork flooring using urea-formaldehyde should not be used. Cork can be finished with water-based urethanes with very low VOCs that provide durability along with water and chemical resistance. It should be installed with a water-based, low-VOC latex adhesive. Cork flooring is also an excellent absorber of sound.

Wood flooring offers many options for sustainable use. First, wood originating from well-managed forests can be selected. Both domestic and tropical hardwood is available from sustainable, FSC-accredited, certified sources. Second, veneered and laminated products using a plywood or MDF core can be used. Finally, salvaged solid-wood flooring is available. Whenever possible, prefinished flooring should be used to eliminate the need for sanding and finishing on the job site, which could create indoor air quality problems. If adhesives are required they should be low-VOC content types. On-site finishing should only use water-dispersed urethanes. Varnishes, acid-cured varnishes, or hardening oils for on-site finishing should be avoided.

As an alternate to standard wood floors, bamboo or palm wood can be used. Bamboo is a fast-growing grass that reaches maturity in three to four years. It is almost as hard and twice as stable as red oak or maple and is sold in tongue-and-groove strips prefinished with a durable polyurethane coating. Palm wood is harvested as a byproduct of commercial coconut plantations. It is harder than maple or oak and is also sold in tongue-and-groove strips and prefinished with polyurethane.

Ceramic tile is generally considered a sustainable material in spite of the high embodied energy required to produce it and the transportation costs to get it from the factory to the job site. It uses readily available natural materials, is very durable, produces practically no harmful emissions, and requires very little maintenance. Some tile is made from post-consumer or post-industrial waste products using from 25% to 100% recycled material. Cement mortars and grouts are also environmentally friendly and produce very few emissions. Avoid epoxy-modified grout, plastic adhesives with solvents, and sealers that contain VOCs.

Wall Finishes

Gypsum wallboard is manufactured with 100% recycled content for its paper faces and with some recycled content for the core. Some manufacturers mix recycled newspaper with gypsum as the core material. In addition, about 7% of the industry's total use of gypsum is synthetic gypsum. Synthetic gypsum is chemically identical to natural, mined gypsum but is a byproduct of various manufacturing, industrial, or chemical processes. The main source of synthetic gypsum in North America is *flue-gas desulfurization*. This is the process whereby power-generating plants (and similar plants) remove polluting gases from their stacks to reduce emission of harmful materials into the atmosphere. Synthetic gypsum represents an efficient application for refuse material. By itself, gypsum wallboard does not contribute in any significant way to indoor air pollution. However, adhesives, paints, and caulking can be pollution sources and should be specified carefully.

Disposal of gypsum wallboard is problematic because wallboard cannot be reused when taken out of an old building. Some gypsum wallboard plants are recycling old wallboard. However, the wallboard must be separated from other materials and be free of screws, nails, and lead paint. Currently, the cost of collecting and transporting the old wallboard is a disincentive for recycling. If the wallboard can be recycled, it is pulverized and can be worked into the ground as a soil additive.

Sisal wall covering is a natural material made from the fiber of the henequen plant. The branches are harvested and the fiber extracted, dyed, and spun into yarn. Although fairly rough and not suitable for wet areas, sisal wall covering (and floor covering) is durable, low maintenance, and reduces sound reflection and transmission. It should be applied with a zero-VOC adhesive and detailed to allow slight expansion and contraction with absorption and release of humidity.

Paints and other coatings require careful consideration in their selection and use. Although federal, state, and local regulations have eliminated coatings containing dangerous components such as lead and cadmium and have limited the use of volatile organic compounds, some commercial coatings may still contain them. Generally, paint sold now must conform to VOC limits set by the Environmental Protection Agency (EPA) as required by the Clean Air Act. The limits are set in the National Volatile Organic Compound Emission Standards for Architectural Coatings, 40 CFR Part 59. Many types of coatings are listed in the standard. For example, the VOC content of flat interior paint cannot exceed 250 g/L (2.1 lbm/gal), while non-flat interior paint cannot exceed 380 g/L (3.2 lbm/gal). (Enforcement of the rule is based on SI units.) California has stricter standards, limiting paint to 100 g/L (0.84 lbm/gal) for flat paint and 150 g/L (1.3 lbm/gal) for non-flat coatings. In the future these limits in California will be reduced even further.

A building can receive a LEED credit for using interior paints and coatings that comply with the VOC and chemical component limits of the Green Seal Standard GS-11. However, these standards are stricter for flat paint than are the EPA standards. Green Seal standards state that flat interior paint cannot exceed 50 g/L (0.42 lbm/gal).

Ceilings

Acoustical ceiling tile that uses recycled content of old tiles, newsprint, or perlite is available. Other material, such as clay and wood fibers, may also be used. Fiberglass ceiling panels are also available with recycled content. Recycled content varies but can be up to 95%, depending on the manufacturer and the product type. Old tile can be repainted if the correct type of paint and procedures are used. One manufacturer offers a recycling program that allows customers to ship old tile to their plant if the manufacturers' own tile is to be used as a replacement. The cost to recycle is typically less than the cost of sending the material to a landfill. The grid itself can be recycled as scrap steel.

However, tile may shed fiber if it is damaged or as it ages. This fiber can be collected by the HVAC system if the plenum is used as a return air space. Using separate ducts for return air or regular cleaning of the plenum with vacuums can alleviate some of the problem.

Furnishings

In addition to other sustainability issues, furnishings can be a significant source of formaldehyde in residential and commercial settings because of the particleboard, MDF, and coatings used in their construction. The following strategies can be used to improve sustainability through the selection and specification of furnishings.

- Use refurbished or reused office furniture.
- Consider using furniture made from steel, solid wood, and glass, which are all materials that can readily be recycled.
- Specify that furnishings can be fabricated with wood certified under standards established by the Forest Stewardship Council (FSC) or with reclaimed wood.
- Require that furnishings be fabricated with formaldehyde-free medium-density fiberboard or strawboard.
- Use furniture with cushions, workstation panels, and fabrics made with recycled PET (polyethylene terephthalate) from soda bottles.
- Look for fabrics with biodegradable and nontoxic dyes.
- Use finish coverings for furniture made of cotton, wool, ramie, blends, or other natural materials. Use chemical-free organic cotton fabrics.
- Use low-VOC finishes.
- Use powder coatings for finishes instead of standard paint.
- Require that cushions be foamed with CO_2-injected foam or other environmentally friendly materials.

INDOOR AIR QUALITY

Maintaining health is an important aspect of sustainable design, and one of the basic requirements of health is good indoor air quality (IAQ). In addition to simply maintaining health, the quality of indoor air affects a person's sense of well-being and can affect absenteeism, productivity, creativity, and motivation. Indoor air quality is a complex subject because there are hundreds of different contaminants, dozens of causes of poor IAQ, many possible symptoms building occupants may experience, and a wide variety of potential strategies for maintaining good IAQ. This section outlines some of the more important areas of knowledge with which you should be familiar. Because IAQ has become such an important topic in building design, there is no shortage of laws and standards devoted to regulating indoor air quality. Some of these are given at the end of this section.

Indoor Air Contaminants

Indoor air contaminants can be broadly classified into two groups: chemical contaminants and biological contaminants. Chemical contaminants include things such as volatile organic compounds, inorganic chemicals, tobacco smoke, and dozens of others, while biological contaminants include mold, pollen, bacteria, and viruses.

Volatile organic compounds (VOCs) are chemicals that contain carbon and hydrogen and that vaporize at room temperature and pressure. They are found in many indoor sources, including building materials and common household products. Common sources of VOCs in building materials include paint, stains, adhesives, sealants, water repellents and sealers, particleboard, furniture, upholstery, and carpeting. Other sources include copy machines, cleaning agents, and pesticides.

The Environmental Protection Agency has established regulations for VOCs in coatings. The final regulation on volatile organic compounds (VOCs) in architectural, industrial, and maintenance coatings was issued on September 13, 1998. This regulation listed the maximum content of VOCs in the various types of coatings. The maximum VOC levels of some common coatings were listed in the previous section. However, state laws also regulate VOCs, and each state may permit a different level. For example, the California South Coast Air Quality Management District has very strict limits on the volatile organic content of paints.

Formaldehyde is a colorless gas with a pungent odor. It is used in the preparation of resins and adhesives most commonly found in particleboard, wall paneling, furniture, carpet adhesives, and other glues used in the construction and furnishings industry. Formaldehyde is designated as a probable human carcinogen and causes irritant effects of the eyes and respiratory tract.

The maximum suggested or allowable exposure rates vary depending on the agency. ASHRAE recommends a maximum continuous indoor air concentration of 0.1 parts per million (ppm). OSHA specifies concentrations not to exceed 0.75 ppm in an 8-hour time period with a 2 ppm 15-minute short-term exposure. In order to qualify as Greenguard certified, a product cannot emit more than 0.05 ppm.

The problems associated with formaldehyde can most easily be solved by minimizing the source, using two or three coats of sealants, or airing out the building before occupancy.

There are potentially hundreds of organic and inorganic chemicals that may be harmful to humans. The California Office of Environmental Health Hazard Assessment has a list of 76 chemicals (at the time of this writing) that the state regulates along with the chronic inhalation reference exposure level (REL) for each, in micrograms per cubic meter ($\mu g/m^3$). These were developed as a result of California's Proposition 65, which was passed in 1986. Proposition 65 required businesses to provide a clear and reasonable warning before knowingly and intentionally exposing anyone to a listed chemical.

The Greenguard Environmental Institute also produces a list of products, chemicals in those products, and allowable maximum emission levels. Some of the common chemicals include VOCs, formaldehyde, aldehydes, 4-phenylcyclohexene, and styrene, as well as particulates and biological contaminates. In order to be certified by Greenguard, a product must meet these standards after being tested according to ASTM D5116 and D6670, the State of Washington's protocol for interior furnishings and construction materials, and the EPA's testing protocol for furniture.

Tobacco Smoke

Secondhand smoke, also called environmental tobacco smoke (ETS), is a mixture of the smoke given off by the burning end of a cigarette, pipe, or cigar and the smoke exhaled from the lungs of smokers. Secondhand smoke has been found to contain over 4000 substances, more than 40 of which are known to cause cancer in humans and many of which are strong irritants. The EPA and the California EPA have found that exposure to secondhand smoke causes increased risk for cancer and other serious health effects. In order to improve indoor air quality, smoking should either be banned completely from buildings and near entrances, or isolated smoking rooms should be constructed that have a separate ventilation system that vents directly to the outside.

Biological Contaminants

Potential biological contaminants in a building include the common problem of mold and mildew in addition to bacteria, viruses, mites, pollen, animal dander, dust, and insects. Even protein in urine from rats and mice is an allergen.

Molds and mildew are microscopic organisms, a type of fungi, that produce enzymes to digest organic matter. Their reproductive spores are present nearly everywhere. When exposed to the spores, people sensitive to molds and mildew may experience eye irritation, skin rash, running nose, nausea, headaches, and similar symptoms.

Mold spores require three conditions to grow: moisture, a nutrient, and a temperature range from 40°F to 100°F (4°C to 38°C). Nutrients are simply organic materials—which can include wood, carpet, the paper coating of gypsum wallboard, paint, wallpaper, insulation, and ceiling tile, among others—that serve as a nourishing food source for organisms. Because nutrients and a suitable temperature are always present in buildings, the only way to prevent and control mold is to prevent and control moisture in places where mold growth should be prevented.

CAUSES OF POOR INDOOR AIR QUALITY

There are four basic causes of poor indoor air quality. These include chemical contaminants from indoor sources, chemical contaminants from outdoor sources, biological contaminants, and poor ventilation. These factors may be present alone or combined with one or more of the others to produce the various symptoms of poor indoor air quality.

One of the most common sources of poor indoor air quality is chemical contaminants from indoor sources. These sources include all of the contaminants previously mentioned—VOCs, environmental tobacco smoke, respirable particles, carbon monoxide, and nitrogen dioxide, and so on. Lists of harmful chemicals can be found at one of the following sources.

- *Hazardous Chemicals Desk Reference*, Richard J. Lewis. New York: Van Nostrand Reinhold.

- National Toxicology Program. (Lists chemicals known to be carcinogenic.)

- International Agency for Research of Cancer (IARC). (Classifies chemicals that are known to be carcinogenic.)

- Chronic Reference Exposure Levels. California Office of Environmental Health Hazard Assessment. (Lists hazardous chemicals recognized by this office, with links to more information about each chemical.)

- California Health and Welfare Agency, Safe Drinking Water and Toxic Enforcement Act of 1986 (Proposition 65). (Lists chemicals known to cause cancer and reproductive toxicity.)

- California Air Toxics. California Environmental Protection Agency, Air Resources Board (ARB).

Chemical contaminants from outdoor sources are introduced to a building when air intake vents, windows, or doors from parking garages are improperly located, allowing pollutants from the outside (carbon monoxide, for example) to be drawn into the building. Indoor pollutants from exhausts and plumbing vents can also be sucked back into the building through improperly located air intakes.

Biological contaminants such as mold, bacteria, and viruses may develop from moisture infiltration, standing water, stagnant water in mechanical equipment, and even from insects or bird droppings that find their way into the building. These were discussed in the previous section.

Poor ventilation allows indoor pollutants to accumulate to unpleasant or even unhealthy levels and affects the general sense of well-being of building occupants. One of the most difficult aspects of providing proper ventilation is balancing the requirement for energy conservation. However, this problem can be solved by using heat exchangers and other methods described in Ch. 6. Some of the minimum levels of ventilation are given the following section on strategies for maintaining good IAQ.

SYMPTOMS OF POOR INDOOR AIR QUALITY

There are many symptoms of poor indoor air quality, from temporary, minor irritations to serious, life-threatening illnesses. They are generally grouped into three classifications: sick-building syndrome, building-related illnesses, and multiple chemical sensitivities. Problems with asbestos, lead, and radon are serious, long-term problems and are generally not grouped with these three classifications.

Sick-building syndrome (SBS) describes a condition in which building occupants experience a variety of health-related symptoms that cannot be directly linked to any particular cause. Generally, symptoms disappear after the occupants leave the building. Symptoms may include irritation of the eyes, nose, and throat; dry mucous membranes and skin; erythema (redness of the skin); mental fatigue and headache; respiratory infections and cough; hoarseness of voice and wheezing; hypersensitivity reactions; and nausea and dizziness.

Building-related illness (BRI) describes a condition in which the health-related symptom or symptoms of a building's occupants are identified and can be directly attributed to certain building contaminants. In the case of BRI, the symptoms do not immediately improve when the occupant leaves the building. Legionnaires' disease is an example of BRI.

Multiple chemical sensitivity (MCS) is a condition brought on by exposure to volatile organic compounds (VOCs) or other chemicals. People with MCS may develop acute, long-term sensitivity that shows symptoms each time they are exposed to the chemicals. These sensitivities can remain with some people for the rest of their lives. In many cases only a slight exposure to the chemical can be enough to produce symptoms.

STRATEGIES FOR MAINTAINING GOOD INDOOR AIR QUALITY

Methods of maintaining good indoor air quality that the architect can use or suggest to the building owner can be classified into four broad categories: eliminate or reduce the sources of pollution, control the ventilation of the building, establish good maintenance procedures, and control occupant activity as it affects IAQ.

Eliminate or Reduce Sources of Pollution

- Establish the owner's criteria for indoor air quality early in the project. This may be part of the programming process and should include the budget available.

- Select and specify building materials and furnishings with low emissions and VOCs. The standards listed in the next section provide guidance on choosing materials. Because it is not always possible to eliminate all sources of pollutants, set priorities by identifying materials that are the most volatile and that represent large quantities.

- Specify materials that are resistant to the growth of mold and mildew, especially in areas that may become wet or damp.

- Request emissions test data from manufacturers. This can be the material safety data sheets (MSDSs) from the manufacturer, or other data provided by the manufacturer. However, OSHA regulations require all manufacturers to develop and supply MSDSs for their products if they contain chemicals.

- Design the building envelope to properly control moisture.

- Prior to occupancy, the HVAC system in a new building or occupied space should be operated at full capacity for two weeks to reduce the emissions due to outgassing chemicals and moisture.

Control Ventilation

- During the programming phase, determine the owners' and occupants' requirements for ventilation. Also determine the energy conservation code requirements.

- Provide the minimum outdoor air ventilation as recommended by the American Society of Heating, Refrigerating, and Air-Conditioning Engineers for the specific activity of the building or individual space. These minimums, as given in ASHRAE Standard 62, range from 15 cfm/person to 60 cfm/person (8 L/s/person to 30 L/s/person). The absolute minimum now recommended is 15 cfm/person

(8 L/s/person). 20 cfm/person (10 L/s/person) is recommended for office spaces. The high range of 60 cfm/person (30 L/s/person) is used for smoking lounges.

- Locate fresh-air intakes away from loading docks, bus stops, or parking garages where carbon monoxide, carbon dioxide, nitrous-oxides, and odors can be drawn into the building.

- Avoid fresh-air vents near landscaped areas where irrigation moisture could be drawn into the building.

- Design the HVAC system with a high-efficiency air filtration system to rid outdoor air of particulates before it is introduced into the building system.

- Provide separate rooms and ventilation for equipment that emits high concentrations of pollutants. In an office, a high-volume copier might require a separate room. Health clubs, laboratories, and kitchens are other common locations for such equipment.

- When thermal insulation is required, place it on the outside of ductwork. Use acoustical insulation that is encapsulated for the inside of ducts.

- Design the HVAC system with local controls so building maintenance personnel can correct heating, cooling, and ventilating problems.

- Specify independent building commissioning and testing, adjusting, and balancing (TAB) of the HVAC system.

Establish Good Maintenance Procedures

Once a building is completed it is important that it be properly maintained. Of course, the architect has little control over this aspect of indoor air quality, but through the proper selection of materials, development of maintenance manuals, and establishment of operating guidelines, the architect, mechanical engineer, interior designer, and other design professionals can provide the building owner with the basis for proper maintenance.

- Select and specify building materials and finishes that are easy to clean and maintain.

- In the specifications, include requirements for warranties and maintenance contracts.

- Suggest that the building owner conduct post-occupancy evaluations at regular intervals to review procedures for maintaining good IAQ.

- In the specifications, require that the contractor assemble an operation and maintenance manual from the various suppliers of HVAC and electrical equipment giving performance criteria, operation requirements, cleaning instructions, and maintenance procedures.

- In the maintenance manual, include materials and procedures for regular cleaning of specified products, including furnishings. These should be low-emission products recommended by the manufacturer of each product or finish.

Control Occupant Activity

As with maintenance procedures, the architect has little control over occupant activity once the building is completed. However, the architect can suggest to the building owner methods of controlling occupant activity as it affects IAQ. The architect can also add long-term occupancy IAQ suggestions to the operation and maintenance manual.

- Suggest a no-smoking policy for the building.

- Suggest that the building owner or manager monitor individual space use to determine if major changes to occupant load, activities, or equipment occur. The building HVAC system may need to be adjusted accordingly.

- Install sensors for carbon dioxide (CO_2), carbon monoxide (CO), VOCs, and other products, which are connected to the building management system.

Indoor Air Quality Standards

The last few decades have seen the development of many laws, regulations, and standards enacted at the federal, state, and local level that attempt to control and improve indoor air quality. The Occupational Safety and Health Administration (OSHA) has also proposed rules for IAQ. Some of the more important laws and regulations with which architects should be familiar are listed here.

For a listing of additional regulations and industry standards related to sustainability, refer to the section later in this chapter.

- Clean Air Act (CAA) of 1970. This law regulates air emissions from area, stationary, and mobile sources. The law authorized the EPA to establish the National Ambient Air Quality Standards to protect public health and the environment. It has been amended several times since 1970 to extend deadlines for compliance and add other provisions.

- National Ambient Air Quality Standard. U.S. Environmental Protection Agency, 40 CFR 50. This standard implements part of the Clean Air Act.

- ASHRAE Standard 62-2001, *Ventilation for Acceptable Indoor Air Quality*. This is an industry standard and, as such, compliance with it is voluntary. However, most building codes incorporate all or a part of this standard by reference, thereby giving it the force of law. In addition to setting minimum outdoor air requirements for ventilation, the standard includes provisions for managing sources of contamination, controlling indoor humidity, and filtering building air, as well as requirements for HVAC system construction and startup, and operation and maintenance of systems.

- ASHRAE Standard 62.2-2003, *Ventilation and Acceptable Indoor Air Quality in Low-Rise Residential Buildings*. This is also a voluntary industry standard. The standard applies to single-family houses and multi-family buildings of three stories or less, including manufactured and modular houses. It defines the roles of and minimum requirements for mechanical and natural ventilation systems as well as the building envelope.

- National VOC Emission Standards for Architectural Coatings (40 CFR Part 59). This rule implements part of the Clean Air Act and sets limits on the amount of volatile organic compounds that manufacturers and importers of architectural coatings can put into their products.

- South Coast Air Quality Management District (SCAQMD) Rule 1113, Architectural Coatings. This rule limits the VOC content of architectural coatings used in the South Coast Air Quality Management District in California. The limits it sets are more restrictive than the national VOC emission standard published by the EPA. Rule 1168 limits the VOC content of adhesives and sealants.

- California Safe Drinking Water and Toxic Enforcement Act of 1986 (Proposition 65). This law prohibits businesses from discharging chemicals that cause cancer or reproductive toxicity into sources of drinking water and requires that warning be given to individuals exposed to such chemicals. The California Environmental Protection Agency's Office of Environmental Health Hazard Assessment (OEHHA) is the lead agency for the implementation of Proposition 65.

- Greenguard Environmental Institute. The Greenguard Environmental Institute (described later in this chapter) tests products following ASTM Standards D5116 and D6670, the EPA's testing protocol for furniture, and the State of Washington's protocol for interior furnishings and construction materials. Greenguard has a list of the emission levels that products must meet before they are certified by the organization.

- *Threshold Limit Values* and *Biological Exposure Indices*. American Conference of Governmental Industrial Hygienists (ACGIH). This document gives exposure limits for chemicals in the workplace called threshold limit values (TLV).

- ASTM D5116, *Standard Guide for Small-Scale Environmental Chamber Determinations of Organic Emissions from Indoor Materials/Products*. This guide describes the equipment and techniques suitable for determining organic emissions from small samples of indoor materials. It cannot be used for testing complete assemblages or coatings. Another standard, ASTM D6803, is used for testing paint using small environmental chambers.

- ASTM D6670, *Standard Practice for Full-Scale Chamber Determination of Volatile Organic Emissions from Indoor Materials/Products*. This practice details the method to be used to determine the VOC emissions from building materials, furniture, consumer products, and equipment under environmental and product usage conditions that are typical of those found in office and residential buildings. It is referenced by other standards or laws as a standard way to determine the level of VOC emissions.

- ASTM E1333, *Standard Test Method for Determining Formaldehyde Concentrations in Air and Emission Rates from Wood Products Using a Large Chamber*. This test method measures the formaldehyde concentration in air and the emission rate from wood products in a large chamber under conditions designed to simulate product use.

Recycling and Reuse

Recycling and reuse of materials and products is an important part of the total life cycle of a building. As many materials as possible should be recycled into other products or reused for their original purpose. In turn, new buildings should incorporate as many recycled and reused materials as possible to provide a market for those products. Ideally, all materials should be durable, biodegradable, or recyclable.

Adaptive Reuse

Adaptive reuse begins with reusing as much of the existing building stock as possible instead of constructing new buildings. Buildings can be either updated to conform to their original use or adapted to a new use. Turning an old warehouse into residences is a common example of adaptive reuse. A project can receive LEED credit for maintaining at least 75% of the existing building structure and shell, excluding window assemblies and nonstructural roofing material. Additional credit is also given for using at least

50% of the non-shell areas such as walls, doors, floor coverings, and ceiling systems.

On a smaller scale, individual products can be reused in new buildings. These include building elements such as plumbing fixtures, doors, timber, and bricks. For example, heavy timber can be reused by resawing and planing. In most cases, using these old materials adds to the architectural character of the new building. A project can receive LEED credit for using salvaged, refurbished, or reused materials, products, and furnishings for at least 5% of the total of all building materials. Additional credit is given for using 10%.

Reuse conserves natural resources, reduces the energy required to construct new buildings or products, lessens air and water pollution due to burning or dumping, and keeps materials from entering the waste stream.

Recycled Materials

Recyclability is the ability of a previously used material to be used as a resource in the manufacturer of a new product. Melting down old steel to manufacture new steel is an example of recyclability. Recycling materials is often difficult because of the problem of separating different substances so that they can be individually marketed. Most of this separating must be done by hand, and in some cases, such as with gypsum wallboard, the cost of separating all the component parts may be more than the cost of sending the material to a landfill.

Before selecting and specifying materials, the architect should ask product suppliers about the recycled content of their product. A project can receive LEED credit for using recycled materials if the sum of the post-consumer recycled content plus half of the post-industrial content constitutes at least 5% of the total value of the materials in the project. Additional credit is given for using 10%.

Recycling of consumer products can be encouraged by providing bins, recycling rooms, and other provisions as part of the building design. In some areas of the country local codes require that a portion of the trash area be reserved for recycling bins.

Building Disposal

If old products and materials cannot be reused or recycled, they must be burned or placed in a landfill for disposal. If a material is biodegradable it can break down quickly and return to the earth. Some materials, such as aluminum, most plastics, or steel, take a very long time to decompose naturally. A project can receive LEED credit for diverting at least 50% of construction, demolition, and land-clearing debris from landfill disposal to recycling or donation of usable materials to charitable organizations.

Biobased products may be used to minimize disposal problems while saving depletable raw materials. Biobased products are primarily made from plant or animal materials. Using biobased products also helps maintain good indoor air quality and provides a market for the rural economy. Some examples of biobased products include adhesives, composite panels, gypsum wallboard substitutes, ceiling tiles, carpet backing, and others. A project can receive LEED credit for using rapidly renewable building materials made from plants that are typically harvested within a 10-year cycle or shorter for 5% of the total value of all building materials used.

Hazardous Material Mitigation

Hazardous materials are chemicals or other biological substances that pose a threat to the environment or to human health if released or misused. There are thousands of products and substances that can be defined as hazardous. A few of the more common ones found in buildings are described in the following sections.

In many cases, building sites or existing buildings may be contaminated with harmful chemicals, mold, mildew, and so on. These contaminants need to be identified and removed in accordance with best practices and in compliance with federal, state, or local regulations.

Asbestos

Asbestos is a naturally occurring fibrous mineral found in certain types of rock formations. After mining and processing, asbestos consists of very fine fibers. Asbestos is known to cause lung cancer, asbestosis (a scarring of the lungs), and mesothelioma (a cancer of the lining of the chest or abdominal cavity). Oral exposure may be associated with cancer of the esophagus, stomach, and intestines. In buildings, exposure generally comes from asbestos that has become friable (easily crumbled) or that has been disturbed accidentally or by construction activities. Although generally not a problem in new construction, asbestos can be found in many types of existing building materials, including pipe and blown-in insulation, asphalt flooring, vinyl sheet and tile flooring, construction mastics, ceiling tiles, textured paints, roofing shingles, cement siding, caulking, vinyl wall coverings, and many other products.

Asbestos is regulated under two federal laws and one federal agency restriction: the Clean Air Act (CAA) of 1970, the Toxic Substances Control Act (TSCA) of 1976, and the U.S. Consumer Product Safety Commission (CPSC). Under authority of the TSCA, in 1989 the EPA issued a ban on asbestos. However, much of the original rule was vacated by the U.S. Fifth Circuit Court of Appeals in 1991. Products still banned include flooring felt, corrugated or specialty paper, commercial paper, and rollboard. The ban also prevents the use of asbestos in products that have not historically contained asbestos. Under authority of the CAA, the National Emission Standards for Hazardous Air Pollutants (NESHAP) rules for asbestos ban the use of sprayed-on or wet-applied asbestos-containing materials (ACM) for fireproofing and insulation. These rules took effect in 1973. NESHAP also bans the use of ACMs for decorative purposes. This took effect in 1978. The CPSC bans the use of asbestos in certain consumer products such as textured paint and wall patching compounds.

Testing for asbestos and mitigation efforts must be done by an accredited company following strict procedures. In many cases, if the asbestos has not been disturbed it can be left in place because the EPA and NIOSH (National Institute for Occupational Safety and Health) have determined that intact and undisturbed asbestos materials do not pose a health risk. The asbestos may be encapsulated to protect it from becoming friable or from accidental damage. During building demolition or renovation, however, the EPA does require asbestos removal. This must be done by a licensed contractor certified for this type of work.

Vermiculite

Vermiculite is a hydrated laminar magnesium-aluminum-ironsilicate that resembles mica. It is separated from mineral ore that contains other materials, including the possibility of asbestos. When heated during processing, vermiculite expands into worm-like pieces. In construction, it is used for pour-in insulation, acoustic finishes, fire protection, and sound-deadening compounds. Vermiculite obtained from a mine in Montana is known to contain some amount of asbestos. The mine was closed in 1990. It is still mined at other locations, but those have low levels of contamination. The current concern is with loose, pour-in insulation used in attics and concrete blocks.

The EPA recommends that attic insulation that may contain asbestos-contaminated vermiculite not be disturbed, and that any cracks in the ceiling be sealed. If the insulation must be removed, only a trained and certified professional contractor should perform the work.

Lead

Lead is a highly toxic metal that was once used in a variety of consumer and industrial products. Exposure to lead can cause serious health problems, especially to children, including damage to the brain and nervous system, slowed growth, behavior problems, seizures, and even death. In adults it can cause digestive and reproductive problems, nerve disorders, muscle and joint pain, and difficulties during pregnancy. Most exposure from lead comes from paint in homes built before 1978 or from soil and household dust that has picked up lead from deteriorating lead-based paint. The federal government banned lead-based paint from housing in 1978.

Federal law requires that anyone conducting lead-based paint removal be certified and that lead-based paint be removed from some types of residential occupancies and child-occupied facilities by a certified company using approved methods for removal and disposal. Removal of lead-based paint should not be done by sanding, propane torch, heat gun, or dry scraping. Sometimes, covering the wall with a new layer of gypsum wallboard or simply repainting is an acceptable alternative. Also, lead-coated copper used in flashing, sheet metal panels, gutters, and downspouts is no longer used due to the potential for soil contamination.

Radon

Radon is a colorless, odorless, tasteless, naturally occurring radioactive gas found in soils, rock, and water throughout the world. Radon causes lung cancer, with most of the risk coming from breathing air contaminated with radon and its decay products. Most radon exposure occurs in places where it accumulates, such as homes, schools, and office buildings, so most remedial work is done in existing buildings. Testing for radon is easy and can be done by a trained contractor or by homeowners with kits available in hardware stores or through the mail. The Environmental Protection Agency recommends that remedial action be taken if a radon level over 4 picocuries per liter (pCi/L) is found.

Remedial work should follow the radon mitigation standards of the EPA and ASTM E2121 and can include any or a combination of the following.

- sealing cracks in floors, walls, and foundations

- venting the soil outside the foundation wall

- depressurizing the voids within a block wall foundation (block wall depressurization)

- ventilating the crawl space with a fan (crawl-space depressurization)

- using a vent pipe without a fan to draw air from under a slab to the outside (passive sub-slab depressurization)

- using a fan-powered vent to draw air from below the slab (active sub-slab depressurization)

- using a fan-powered vent to draw air from below a membrane laid on the crawl-space floor (sub-membrane depressurization)

Polychlorinated Biphenyls (PCBs)

Polychlorinated biphenyls (PCBs) are mixtures of synthetic organic chemicals with physical properties ranging from oily liquids to waxy solids. PCBs were used in many commercial and industrial applications, including building transformers, fluorescent light transformers, paints, coatings, and plastic and rubber products. PCBs are known to cause cancer and other adverse health effects afflicting the immune system, reproductive system, nervous system, and endocrine system. Because of concerns regarding the toxicity and persistence of PCBs in the environment, their manufacture and importation were banned in 1977 under the Toxic Substances Control Act (TSCA) of 1976. While there are some exceptions on the use of PCBs, the TSCA strictly regulates manufacturing, processing, distribution, and disposal.

If PCBs are discovered in building components or on site, they must be handled by a certified contractor and disposed of by incineration, dechlorination, or placement in an approved chemical waste landfill.

Life-Cycle Cost Analysis

Life-cycle cost analysis (LCC) is a method for determining the total cost of a building or building component or system. It takes into account the initial cost of the element or system under consideration as well as the cost of financing, operation, maintenance, and disposal. Any residual value of the components is subtracted from the other costs. The costs are estimated over a length of time called the *study period*. The duration of the study period varies with the needs of the client and the useful life of the material or system. For example, investors in a building may be interested in comparing various alternate materials over the expected investment time frame, while a city government may be interested in a longer time frame representing the expected life of the building. All future costs are discounted back to a common time, usually the base date, to account for the time value of money. The *discount rate* is used to convert future costs to their equivalent present values.

Using life-cycle cost analysis allows two or more alternatives to be evaluated and their total costs to be compared. This is especially useful when evaluating energy conservation measures where one design alternative may have a higher initial cost than another, but a lower overall cost because of energy savings. Some of the specific costs involved in an LCC of a building element include the following.

- initial costs, which include the cost of acquiring and installing the element

- operational costs for electricity, water, and other utilities

- maintenance costs for the element over the length of the study period, including any repair costs

- replacement costs, if any, during the length of the study period

- finance costs required during the length of the study period
- taxes, if any, for initial costs and operating costs

The residual value is the remaining value of the element at the end of the study period based on resale value, salvage value, value in place, or scrap value. All of the costs listed are estimated, discounted to their present value, and added together. Any residual value is discounted to its present value and then subtracted from the total to get the final life-cycle cost of the element.

Note that a life-cycle cost analysis is not the same as a life-cycle assessment (LCA), described earlier in this chapter. An LCA analyzes the environmental impact of a product or building system over the entire life of the product or system.

Building Rating Systems

Leadership in Energy and Environmental Design (LEED) Certification

The Leadership in Energy and Environmental Design Green Building Rating System is a national consensus-based building rating system designed to accelerate the development and implementation of green building practices. It was developed by the U.S. Green Building Council, which is a national coalition of leaders from all aspects of the building industry, working to promote buildings that are environmentally responsible and profitable and that provide healthy places to live and work. In addition to developing the rating system, the full LEED program offers training workshops, professional accreditation, resource support, and third-party certification of building performance. In order for a building to be certified, certain prerequisites must be achieved and points earned for meeting or exceeding the program's technical requirements. Points add up to a final score that relates to one of four possible levels of certification: certified, silver, gold, and platinum. LEED is one of the primary building rating systems in the United States.

Leadership in Energy and Environmental Design BC

The Canada Green Building Council has adopted the United States' LEED program for use across Canada. The requirements are essentially the same except that SI units are used, reference is made to Canadian standards and regulations, protection of fish habitats is recognized, a few definitions are changed, and a few other minor modifications are made to tailor the requirements for Canada.

Building Research Establishment (BRE) Environmental Assessment Method

The Building Research Establishment is a British organization that provides research-based consultancy, testing, and certification services covering all aspects of the built environment and associated industries. The BRE Environmental Assessment Method (BREEAM) is a method of reviewing and improving the environmental performance of buildings. There are methods to review offices, industrial buildings, retail buildings, and homes.

BREEAM evaluates the performance of buildings in the areas of management, energy use, health and well-being, pollution, transportation, land use, ecology, materials, and water use. Credits are awarded in each area and added to produce a total score. The building is then given a rating of pass, good, very good, or excellent and awarded a certificate.

The BRE also runs a certified environmental profiling system that provides a measurement of the environmental performance of building materials and products.

Product Certification

Green Seal

Green Seal is an independent, nonprofit organization that strives to achieve a more sustainable world by promoting environmentally responsible production, purchasing, and products. Among other programs, Green Seal develops environmental standards for products in specific categories and certifies products that meet those standards. The organization meets the criteria of the International Organization for Standardization (ISO) 14020 and 14024 for ecolabeling. Green Seal's product evaluations are conducted using a life-cycle approach considering energy, resource use, emissions to air, water, and land, and health impacts of the product. The Green Seal is awarded to products that have less impact on the environment and also work well.

Greenguard

The Greenguard Environmental Institute is a nonprofit, industry-independent organization that oversees the Greenguard Certification Program. This program tests indoor products for emissions to ensure that they meet acceptable IAQ pollutant guidelines and standards. Products are tested for total VOCs, formaldehyde, total aldehydes, respirable particles, carbon monoxide, nitrogen oxide, and carbon dioxide emissions.

If the products meet the standards of Greenguard they are added to the Greenguard Registry. Products include building materials, furnishings, furniture, cleaning and maintenance products, electronic equipment, and personal care products. Greenguard also sets allowable emission levels for their testing, using the lesser value of levels established by the Environmental Protection Agency's procurement specifications, the state of Washington's indoor air quality program, the World Health Organization, and Germany's Blue Angel Program for electronic equipment.

Scientific Certification Systems (SCS)

Scientific Certification Systems is a private scientific organization established to advance both public and private sectors toward more environmentally sustainable policies. Under its Environmental Claims Certification program, SCS certifies specific product attributes such as biodegradability and recycled content. It also certifies environmentally preferable products, which are products that can have a reduced environmental impact when compared to similar products performing the same function. Building products that are certified include carpet, nonwoven flooring, composite panel products, adhesives and sealants, furniture, paints, and other wall coverings.

SCS also certifies forests if they are well managed under their Forest Certification Program as mentioned previously in the section on wood and plastic products.

ISO 14000

The International Standards Organization (ISO) is a nongovernmental organization comprised of national standards bodies from over 120 countries. ISO 14000 is a collection of standards and guidelines that cover issues such as product performance, product standards, labeling, environmental management, and life-cycle assessment as they relate to the environment. Several of the individual standards and guidelines are applicable to building products.

ISO 14020 describes a set of principles that must be followed by any practitioner of environmental labeling. ISO 14024 covers labeling programs and specifies the procedures and principles that third-party certifiers, or ecolabelers, must follow. These include requirements that an organization not have any financial interest in the products it certifies, conduct scientific evaluations using internationally accepted methodologies, and use a life-cycle approach when evaluating products. The ISO 14040 series of standards covers requirements for life-cycle assessments.

Regulations and Industry Standards Related to Sustainability

For a listing of standards and regulations that govern indoor air quality, refer to the previous section in this chapter.

- ASHRAE Standard 90.1, *Energy Standard for Buildings Except Low-Rise Residential Buildings*. This is a voluntary industry standard that gives information on minimum energy efficiency standards, building envelope requirements, zone isolation, floor, ceiling, and roof insulation, and power allowance calculation. It is written in mandatory enforceable language suitable for code adoption.

- ASTM E1991, *Standard Guide for Environmental Life Cycle Assessment of Building Materials/Products*

- ASTM E2114, *Standard Terminology for Sustainability Relative to the Performance of Buildings*

- ASTM E2129, *Standard Practice for Data Collection for Sustainability Assessment of Building Products*

- Green Seal, GS-11, product standard for paints

- Green Seal, GS-13, product standard for windows

- Toxic Substances Control Act (TSCA) of 1976. This law was enacted to give the Environmental Protection Agency the authority to track and regulate over 75,000 industrial chemicals produced or imported into the United States. It allows the EPA to ban the manufacture and import of those chemicals that pose an unreasonable risk.

DEFINITIONS

Coproduct: a marketable by-product from a process. Materials traditionally considered to be waste but that can be used as raw materials in a different manufacturing process are considered coproducts.

Demand control ventilation: a system designed to adjust the amount of ventilation air provided to a space based on the extent of occupancy. The system normally uses carbon dioxide sensors but may also use occupancy sensors or air quality sensors.

Detention: the temporary storage of storm runoff in a detention facility to control peak discharge rates and to provide gravity settling of pollutants. The detention facility is designed to provide for a gradual release of stored water at a controlled rate.

Drainage easement: the legal right granted by a landowner to a grantee, commonly a governmental entity, allowing the use of private land for storm water management

Embodied energy: the total energy required to extract, produce, fabricate, and deliver a material to a job site, including the collection of raw materials, the energy used to extract and process the raw materials, transportation from the original site to the processing plant or factory, the energy required to turn the raw materials into a finished product, and the energy required to transport the material to the job site

Fee in lieu: payment of money by a developer in place of meeting all or part of storm water performance standards

Hydrologic soil group (HSG): a classification system developed by the Natural Resource Conservation Service in which soils are categorized into four runoff potential groups. These groups range from A soils, with high permeability and little runoff production, to D soils, which have a high runoff potential

Infiltration: the process of percolating storm water into the subsoil

Post-consumer: referring to a material or product that has served its intended use and has been diverted or recovered from waste destined for disposal, having completed its life as a consumer item.

Post-industrial: referring to materials generated in manufacturing processes, such as trimmings or scrap, that have been recovered or diverted from solid waste. Also called *Pre-consumer materials*

Pre-consumer: see *Post-industrial*

Recovered materials: waste or by-products that have been recovered or diverted from solid-waste disposal. (Note: This term does not apply to materials that are generated from or reused within an original manufacturing process.)

Renewable product: a product that can be grown or naturally replenished or cleansed at a rate that exceeds human depletion of the resource

Sustainable: the condition of being able to meet the needs of the present generation without compromising the needs of future generations

Watercourse: any body of water including, but not limited to, lakes, ponds, rivers, and streams

Waterway: a channel that directs surface runoff to a watercourse or to a public storm drain

SAMPLE QUESTIONS

1.   Wood chips and sawdust made into panel products are examples of

    A.   post-consumer materials
    B.   post-industrial materials
    C.   recycled products
    D.   renewable products

2.   Which of the following agricultural products is NOT used in the production of panel products?

    A.   bagasse
    B.   poplar
    C.   rice straw
    D.   wheat straw

3.   The absolute minimum fresh air ventilation rate recommended by ASHRAE Standard 62 is

    A.   5 cfm/person (3 L/s/person)
    B.   10 cfm/person (5 L/s/person)
    C.   15 cfm/person (8 L/s/person)
    D.   20 cfm/person (10 L/s/person)

4.   Gray water would most appropriately be used for a

    A.   laundry
    B.   office
    C.   residence
    D.   restaurant

5.   An architect is evaluating various alternatives for a particular building product as they relate to sustainability. The architect would most likely use

    A.   an environmental impact study
    B.   a life-cycle assessment
    C.   an impact assessment
    D.   a matrix comparison chart

6.   A building can receive LEED credit if the carpet used meets the requirements of the

    A.   CRI IAQ program
    B.   Greenguard registry
    C.   Green Seal product standards
    D.   South Coast Air Quality Management District

7.   Buildings constructed prior to which year are likely to contain spray-on fireproofing and insulation containing asbestos?

    A.   1968
    B.   1970
    C.   1973
    D.   1978

8.   Certified contractors are required for all of the following hazardous materials EXCEPT

    A.   asbestos
    B.   lead
    C.   PCBs
    D.   radon

9.   A building that carries a gold rating has been designed and certified under which of the following systems?

    A.   Greenguard
    B.   Green Seal
    C.   ISO 14000
    D.   LEED

10. Storm runoff would best be minimized by using

    A. cisterns

    B. pervious paving

    C. rip-rap

    D. silt fences

PLUMBING SYSTEMS

WATER SUPPLY

Depending on geographic location, water is available from a variety of sources. It comes from rivers, lakes, wells, surface runoff, oceans, and even recycled wastewater. In some cases, water may be pure enough in its natural state for immediate human use. In most instances, however, it must be treated to remove impurities. Water suitable for human drinking is called *potable water*. If it is not suitable for drinking, it is called *nonpotable*, but this type of water may be used for irrigation, flushing toilets, and the like.

Two of the most common sources of large water supplies for cities are surface water and groundwater. Surface water comes from rain and snow that runs off into rivers and lakes. Groundwater is that which seeps into the ground until it hits an impervious layer of rock or soil. It then forms a water table that is tapped by drilling. Large regions of subsurface water are called *aquifers*.

Generally, the best sources for water are those that require little or no treatment, including water from deep wells, relatively clean rivers, and surface runoff. This type of water can be easily treated in most cases and can be made available in large quantities. However, with increasing pollution and the scarcity of water in some locations, greater use of treated seawater or recycled wastewater will be necessary. The means are available to do this, but the processing is more expensive than it is for other methods.

Water has many characteristics and can contain many types of chemical, biological, and physical contaminates. One common characteristic of all water is its pH level. The *pH level* is a measure of the relative acidity or alkalinity of water. It is based on a scale of 0 to 14, with a pH of 7 being neutral. Anything below 7 is considered acidic and can be corrosive; anything above 7 is considered alkaline. Knowing the pH of water is useful in determining necessary water treatment for corrosion, chemicals, and disinfection. For example, acidic water, along with entrained oxygen, can cause iron and steel pipes to rust. The problem can be corrected by adding a neutralizer to the washer. This raises the water's alkaline content.

Rainwater is slightly acidic in its natural state, but in many industrialized areas the acid level is greater due to sulfur and nitrogen compounds in the atmosphere. The compounds combine to form sulfuric or nitric acid and fall as "acid rain."

Another common characteristic of water is its hardness. *Hardness* is caused by calcium and magnesium salts in water. If untreated, hard water can cause clogged pipes and corrosion of boilers. It also makes laundry and other types of washing difficult because it inhibits the cleaning action of soaps and detergents.

Hard water is treated through an ion exchange process with a water softener. Hard water is piped into the softener, which contains zeolite. The calcium or magnesium ions are exchanged for the sodium ions in the zeolite. Periodically, the water softener has to be recharged by passing a brine solution through the zeolite. This is done automatically by the water softening equipment.

Other common water quality problems include turbidity, color, odor, biological contamination, and chemical contamination. *Turbidity* is caused by suspended material in the water—such as silt, clay, and organic material. Although it is not hazardous, turbidity is unpleasant and can be treated by filtration.

Color and odor problems are caused by organic matter, inorganic salts, or dissolved gases. Odor problems can be corrected with filtration through activated carbon. Color problems can be corrected with fine filtration or chlorination.

Biological contamination is potentially dangerous to health. Bacteria, viruses, and protozoa can all be present in contaminated water, and testing for them is difficult. One of the most common types is the coliform group that is found in human and animal waste. Biological contamination can be treated with chlorination.

Chemical contamination includes hundreds of hazardous materials including chemicals from industrial processes, mining, and pesticides. Some chemicals affect only the color and taste of water, but others are deadly. Treatment includes filtration, when possible, and other complex processes.

Private Water Supply

Private water supplies include wells, springs, or collected rainwater. The most common type, however, is the well, which is used for residences and small buildings where a municipal supply is not available. Wells are most commonly drilled or bored. A rotary bit is used for drilled wells, which is the only method possible for going through rock, and a bored well uses a rotary auger to make the hole.

Two of the most important considerations in drilling a well are depth and yield. The depth of a well may range from less than 25 ft (7.6 m), known as a *shallow well*, to several hundred feet. Of course, the depth affects the cost of the well, and there is no sure way of knowing prior to drilling how deep the well may have to be. Before drilling, the architect should talk to neighbors, local well drillers, and geologists in the area to see what their experience has been.

The *yield* of a well is the number of gallons per minute (gpm) it provides. A yield from 5 gpm to 10 gpm (0.3 L/s to 0.6 L/s) is about the minimum required for a private residence. If a yield is too low for the project, the system may need to include a large storage tank that can be filled during periods of low use, such as during the night, so enough water is available during peak periods.

As a well is drilled or bored, a pipe casing is lowered into the hole to prevent the hole from caving in and to prevent seepage of surface contamination into the well. The casing is a steel pipe from 4 in to 6 in (100 to 150) in diameter. Lower in the well, perforated casings are used to allow the water to seep into the well from which it is pumped out.

Pumps

Several kinds of pumps are used in wells, including suction, deep-well jet, turbine, and submersible. *Suction pumps* are only suitable for water tables less than 25 ft (7.6 m), while *deep-well jet pumps* can operate at depths from 25 ft to over 100 ft (7.6 m to over 30 m). *Turbine pumps* are used for high-capacity systems with deep wells. One of the most common types for moderate to deep wells serving private residences or small buildings is the *submersible pump*. This

type has a waterproof motor and pump that are placed below the water line and pump water to a pressure tank.

Jet pumps have the pump and motor aboveground and lift water by the venturi principle. Water is forced through a pipe in the well where a jet stream of small diameter is created in another pipe. The low pressure sucks up the well water and drives it to the surface. In both types of pumps, water is pumped to a pressure tank where air pressure circulates the water and operates fixtures.

In addition to the well itself and the pump, most well systems require some type of storage tank or pressure tank. Pressure tanks are required to maintain a constant pressure for use in the building and to compensate for brief peak use demand that exceeds the capacity of the pump. Pressure tanks also reduce the amount of time the pump must be running because small quantities of water can be used from the tank without the need for the pump to operate. As the pressure tank is emptied, a pressure gauge senses the loss and activates the pump. In a *jet (venturi) pump* system, an air volume control senses the depletion of the tank. When the yield of a well is too low to meet the demand, a larger storage tank may be used to provide water for normal use. During nighttime or low periods of use the pump slowly fills the tank.

Municipal Water Supply

Most cities get their water from rivers, lakes, or snow melt. In addition to the methods described earlier, water treatment typically involves first settling out heavy materials and coagulation (or flocculation) with a chemical such as alum. Suspended particles combine with the alum and settle out. The water is then filtered and treated with chlorine or some other chemical to kill organic materials. The water may also be aerated to improve its taste, and fluoride may be added to help prevent tooth decay. Other treatments can adjust the pH level.

Once the water is treated, it is piped through water mains at a pressure of about 50 psi (345 kPa), although this can vary from 40 psi to 80 psi (275 kPa to 550 kPa) depending on location and other factors. If the pressure is too high, a pressure-reducing valve is used between the water main and the building meter.

One of the first tasks in a building project is to determine the location of the water main, its size, its pressure, and the cost for tapping it. This information is available from the local water company. If a main is not adjacent to the property, the property owner is often required to extend the line at his or her own cost. If the water main is a substantial distance from the proposed building, the cost impact can be significant. The pressure in the line is needed to determine what kind of supply system can be used, as described in a later section.

WATER SUPPLY DESIGN

Designing a water supply system involves selecting the type of system; deciding on the type of piping, fittings, and fixtures of the system; and sizing the pipe. Each of these will be discussed in turn. Hot water supply system design is outlined in a later section.

Supply Systems

There are two primary types of water supply systems: the upfeed and the downfeed. The choice between the two is usually based on the height of the building and the pressure required to operate the fixtures.

Water supplied from a city main or from a pressure tank with a private well comes from the pipe under a certain pressure; in city mains it is about 50 psi (345 kPa). This pressure must be sufficient to overcome friction in the piping, fittings, meter, and static head, and still be high enough to operate fixtures. A flush valve, for example, requires from 10 psi to 20 psi (70 kPa to 140 kPa) to operate properly; a shower needs about 12 psi (80 kPa).

The static head is the pressure required to push water vertically, or the pressure caused at the bottom of a column of water. It requires 0.433 psi to lift up water 1 ft. Viewed another way, 1 psi will lift water 2.3 ft. In SI units, 1 m of head equals 10 kPa.

Example 9.1

How much pressure is lost in static head at a fixture 40 ft (12 m) above a water main with a pressure of 45 psi (310 kPa)? Ignoring friction loss, how much pressure is available to operate a fixture at this level?

If 0.434 psi is equivalent to 1 ft (10 kPa is equivalent to 1 m), then the pressure loss is

$$(40 \text{ ft}) \left(0.434 \; \frac{\text{lbf}}{\text{in}^2} \middle/ \text{ft} \right) = 17.36 \text{ psi} \qquad \text{[U.S.]}$$

$$(12 \text{ m}) \left(10 \; \frac{\text{kPa}}{\text{m}} \right) = 120 \text{ kPa} \qquad \text{[SI]}$$

Ignoring friction loss, the remaining pressure at the 40 ft (12 m) level is

$$45 \text{ psi} - 17.36 \text{ psi} = 27.64 \text{ psi} \qquad \text{[U.S.]}$$

$$310 \text{ kPa} - 120 \text{ kPa} = 190 \text{ kPa} \qquad \text{[SI]}$$

An *upfeed system* uses pressure in the water main directly to supply the fixtures. See Fig. 9.1(a). Because there is always some friction in the system and some pressure must be available to work the highest fixtures, the practical limit is about 40 ft to 60 ft (12 m to 18 m).

If the building is too tall for an upfeed system, a *downfeed system* is most often used. In this case, water from the main is pumped to storage tanks near the top of the building or at the top of the zone served and flows by gravity to the fixtures. See Fig. 9.1(b). The pressure at any fixture or point in the system is determined by the distance from the outlet of the tank to the fixture, using the equivalency of 0.434 psi for every foot (10 kPa for every meter).

The height of the zone served by a downfeed system is determined by the maximum allowable pressure on the fixtures at the bottom of the zone, allowing for friction loss in the piping. Depending on the fixture and manufacturer, this maximum pressure is from 45 psi to 60 psi (310 kPa to 415 kPa). Therefore, the maximum height of a zone is 60 divided by 0.434 psi, or about 138 ft ($^{415}/_{10}$ kPa, or about 41.5 m). Beyond this, pressure-reducing valves are required.

Conversely, the pressure at the fixtures at the top of a downfeed system is also of concern because there must be a minimum pressure to make fixtures work properly. For example, if a flush toilet needs 15 psi (100 kPa), then the water tank must be a minimum of $^{15}/_{0.434}$, or about 35 ft above the fixture ($^{100}/_{10}$, or about 10 m). Actually, the distance would have to be slightly greater to overcome friction loss in the piping.

In some cases, the lower floors of a high-rise building are served by an upfeed system and the upper floors are served by a downfeed system.

Another type of supply system that can be used for medium-sized buildings is the *direct upfeed pumping system*, or *tankless system*. Several pumps are used together controlled by a pressure sensor. When demand is light, only one pump operates to supply the needed pressure. As demand increases and is detected by the pressure sensor, another pump automatically starts.

Components and Materials

A water supply system is comprised of piping, fittings, valves, and other specialized components. Piping can be copper, steel, plastic, or brass. Copper is most commonly used because of its corrosion resistance, strength, low friction loss, and small outside diameter. Where the water is not corrosive, steel or galvanized steel pipe can be used, but these materials are more difficult to assemble because of their screw fittings. Steel pipe is available in different wall thicknesses that are indicated by schedule numbers. Schedule 40 pipe is the most commonly used.

Copper is available in three grades: K, L, and M. DWV copper is also used for drainage, waste, and vent piping that is not subject to pressure as supply pipe is, but it is rarely used. Type K has the thickest walls and comes in straight

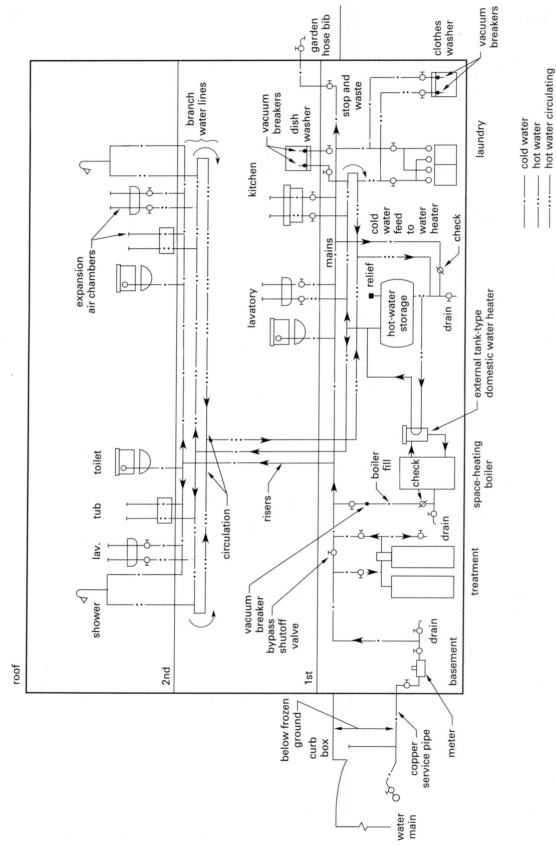

Figure 9.1(a)   Upfeed and Downfeed Systems

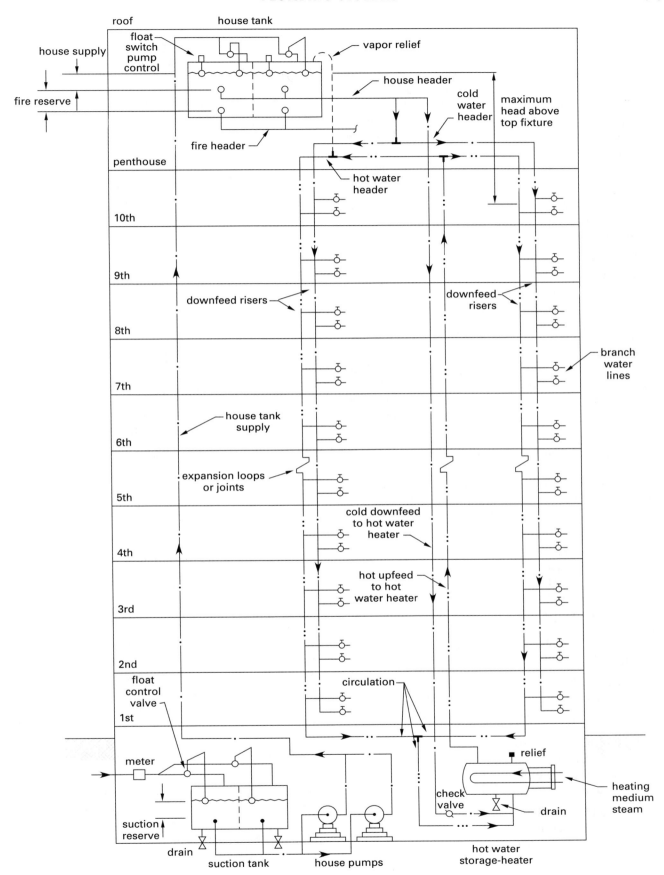

Figure 9.1(b) Upfeed and Downfeed Systems

lengths (hard temper) or in coils (soft temper). It is used for underground supply pipe where greater strength is required. Type L has thinner walls than type K and also comes in straight lengths or coils. It is the grade most commonly used for the majority of the plumbing system in a building. Type M is the thinnest of the three types and is available in straight lengths (hard temper) only. It is only used where low pressure is involved, such as branch supply lines, chilled water systems, exposed lines in heating systems, and drainage piping.

Plastic pipe has generally gained acceptance as a material suitable for supply piping, although some codes still restrict its use. Four types are used for cold water.

PE   polyethylene
ABS   acrilylonitrile-butadiene styrene
PVC   polyvinyl chloride
PVDC   polyvinyl dichloride

Of these, only PVDC is suitable for hot water.

Supply piping is connected with a variety of fittings, valves, and other components to form a complete system. Fittings connect pipes where lengths must be joined, where a change in direction occurs, where three pipes join, or where a change in size occurs. Fig. 9.2 shows some common fittings.

A *union* is a special fitting that connects two rigid sections of pipe and that can be easily unscrewed to allow for repairs or additions to the piping system. Unions are also used between piping and devices that may need to be replaced, such as water heaters. Adapters are also available that allow two different piping materials to be joined.

Fittings for steel and brass are made from malleable iron, cast iron, and brass and are threaded to receive the threaded pipe. Pipe compound or pipe tape is used to produce a watertight seal when the two are joined. Copper and plastic fittings are slightly larger than the pipe, to allow them to be slipped in. Copper joints are sealed by soldering, sometimes called sweating, and plastic pipes are sealed by using a solvent that "melts" the plastic together.

The connections between small-diameter pipes connecting bath and kitchen fixtures to supply line valves are often made with compression fittings. To make these types of connections, a flare nut is slipped over the copper tubing. Then, the copper end is flared slightly and fit onto a mating flange on the valve or faucet. The flare nut is then screwed onto the threads of the valve or faucet fitting, compressing the flanged tubing tightly against the mating flange.

Valves are used to control water flow. They are located at risers, horizontal branch lines, and pipe connections to fixtures and equipment, such as water heaters and sinks.

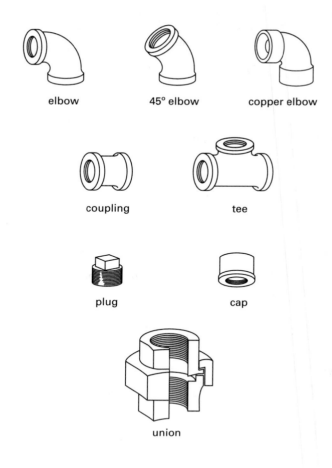

Figure 9.2   Plumbing Fittings

Valves allow selective shutdown of the system for repairs without affecting the entire building. Four common valve types are shown in Fig. 9.3.

The *globe valve* is used where water flow is variably and frequently controlled, such as with faucets or hose bibbs. A handle operates a stem that compresses a washer against a metal seat. Because the water must make two 90° turns, the friction loss in this type of valve is high. A *gate valve* seats a metal wedge against two metal parts of the valve. It is used where control is either completely on or off. Because there are no turns, it has a low friction loss. A *check valve* works automatically and allows water flow in only one direction where, for example, backflow might contaminate a potable water supply.

For water control at sinks and lavatories, a single-handle faucet is most commonly used. One handle controls both the hot and cold water supply and mixes the water to suit the temperature needs of the user. Valves are also available

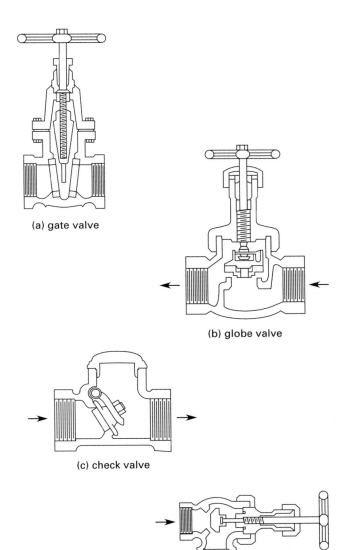

(a) gate valve

(b) globe valve

(c) check valve

(d) angle valve

Figure 9.3 Valves

that control temperature to prevent scalding and restrict flow to conserve water.

Other types of components include air chambers, shock absorbers, pressure reducers, and flow restrictors. Air chambers and shock absorbers are used to prevent *water hammer*. This is the noise caused when a valve or faucet is closed quickly, causing the water moving in the system to stop abruptly and the pipes to rattle. An *air chamber* is a length of pipe installed above the connection to the faucet that cushions the surge of water. A *shock absorber* performs the same function with a manufactured expansion device.

Pressure reducers, sometimes called *pressure regulators*, are required on fixtures if the supply pressure is too high, over about 60 psi (415 kPa). Because most fixtures only require from 5 psi to 15 psi (35 kPa to 100 kPa) to operate, higher pressures can cause excessive wear on the fixture. Pressure relief valves, on the other hand, are safety devices designed to open when pressure exceeds some predetermined maximum. They are used on water heaters and similar equipment where excessively high pressures could cause damage or explosion.

System Design

Designing a plumbing system involves sizing the pipes and laying out the required fittings, valves, and other components. As previously mentioned, there must be adequate pressure at the most remote fixture after deducting various pressure losses from the available pressure at the water main. Stated another way, the sum of all these values must be equal to or less than the water main pressure.

	pressure at most remote fixture
+	pressure loss from static head
+	pressure loss by friction in piping and fittings
+	pressure loss through water meter
=	total street water main pressure

The pressure required for fixtures can be found in Table 9.1. The pressure loss from static head is found by multiplying the total height by 0.434. (In SI units, multiply the height in meters by 10.) The water main pressure is found by consulting the local water company. What remains is to determine the pressure losses through the piping and water meter, which is most often a process of trial and error.

Table 9.1

Minimum Flow Pressure for Various Fixtures

fixture	minimum pressure	
	(psi)	(kPa)
standard lavatory	8	55
self-closing faucet	12	80
sink faucet, $^3/_8$ in	10	70
kitchen sink	8	55
service sink	8	55
flush-tank toilet	8	55
flush-valve toilet	15	100
flush-valve urinal	15	100
bathtub	8	55
shower	8	55
dishwasher	8	55
clothes washer	8	55
drinking fountain	8	55
hose bibb	8	55
fire hose	30	200

Pressure loss in pipes depend on the diameter of the pipe and the flow in gallons per minute. Pressure loss is due to friction within the pipe. For the same flow rate, the smaller the diameter of the pipe, the greater the friction. Likewise, for the same diameter pipe, the greater the flow rate, the greater the friction. The probable demand flow is found by first determining the demand load of the entire system or individual parts of the system. Probable demand is defined by fixture units; a fixture unit is a unit flow rate approximately equal to 1 ft³/min. Fixture units for various fixtures have been established and are listed in Table 9.2.

Because it is unlikely that all the fixtures in a building would be in use at the same time, tables or graphs are available that relate load (i.e., fixture units) to flow in gallons per minute (liters per second). The International Plumbing Code (IPC) uses a table, and the Uniform Building Code (UBC) uses graphs. In these tables or graphs, two sets of values are available, one for systems that primarily use flush-tank toilets and one for systems that use flush valves (which use more water). Table 9.3 shows a portion of the table used in the 2000 IPC for estimating demands. The values are based on experience and illustrate that flow does not increase in direct proportion to an increase in load.

Example 9.2

What is the flow rate for a group of plumbing fixtures in a small office building consisting of five flush-valve toilets, two ³/₄ in flush-valve urinals, four lavatories, two service sinks, and a drinking fountain?

From Table 9.2, the fixture units are calculated as follows.

toilets	(5)(10)	= 50
urinals	(2)(5)	= 10
lavatories	(4)(1.5)	= 6
sinks	(2)(2.25)	= 4.5
fountain	(1)(0.25)	= 0.25
total		70.75 fixture units

In Table 9.3, locate the demand for predominately flush valves, with a load of 70 fixture units. The demand is found to be about 58 gpm. Round up to 60 gpm.

Once the probable flow rate is known, other charts are used to relate flow, pipe size, and friction loss in static head in pounds per square inch per 100 ft length of pipe. The goal in pipe sizing is to select the smallest size that will do the job within the pressure loss limits. The smallest possible pipe size is desired because cost increases with pipe size. Several charts are available for different types of pipe. One such chart is shown in Fig. 9.4.

To use the chart, find the flow in gallons per minute determined from the fixture unit demand, and then read across to the intersection with one of the pipe diameter lines. If necessary, assume a pipe size at first, and then determine the total friction loss. If the total friction loss is too great, select a larger pipe size and perform the calculation again. Using Ex. 9.2, the pressure loss for 60 gpm in a 1¹/₂ in pipe is about 12 psi per 100 ft.

In this example, if a 1¹/₂ in pipe is used, the flow rate will be about 10 ft/sec (3 m/s). This, combined with the relatively high pressure drop of 12 psi per 100 ft (83 kPa per 30 m), would suggest that at least a 2 in (50) pipe should be used instead of a 1¹/₂ in pipe.

When using a chart like the one shown in Fig. 9.4, the velocity must be considered when selecting a pipe size. Above about 10 ft/sec (3 m/s) water in pipes is too noisy. In sound-sensitive situations anything above about 6 ft/sec (1.8 m/s) may be too noisy. The additional diagonal lines shown in Fig. 9.4 show the velocity, so this variable can be checked.

To find the total friction loss in the piping and fittings, calculate the total length of piping from the meter to the fixture under consideration. Friction loss in fittings is calculated by referring to tables that give the losses for various diameter fittings in equivalent lengths of pipe. Table 9.4 is one such table.

If the layout of the plumbing system has not been completely determined, it may be necessary to estimate the number and locations of fittings. Friction losses for pipes and fittings are then added together to get the total loss in pounds per square inch.

The final step is to calculate the loss through the water meter. Charts that relate pressure loss to meter size and flow rate in gallons per minute are also available for this. When the supply main is 1¹/₂ in (38) or greater, the typical meter size is one pipe size smaller than the main.

One critical part of plumbing design in large buildings is allowance for the expansion of piping. This is especially important in high-rise buildings where long lengths of piping are encountered. For example, a 100 ft length of copper pipe can expand well over ¹/₂ in with a 60° temperature change. PVC pipe expands 3.5 times more than copper pipe. Fig. 9.5 shows two common methods of providing for expansion.

Hot-Water Supply

Hot water is supplied by tank-type water heaters or boilers in which water is heated with gas, oil, electricity, or steam. In residences and small buildings, a single supply pipe is provided from the heater to the fixtures. This minimizes the cost of piping but can result in long waits for hot water when the fixture has not been turned on for a while. The

Table 9.2

Demand Weight of Fixtures in Fixture Units

fixture	occupancy	type of supply control	load values, in water supply fixture units (wsfu)		
			cold	hot	total
bathroom group	private	flush tank	2.7	1.5	3.6
bathroom group	private	flush valve	6.0	3.0	8.0
bathtub	private	faucet	1.0	1.0	1.4
bathtub	public	faucet	3.0	3.0	4.0
bidet	private	faucet	1.5	1.5	2.0
combination fixture	private	faucet	2.25	2.25	3.0
dishwashing machine	private	automatic		1.4	1.4
drinking fountain	offices, etc.	3/8″ valve	0.25		0.25
kitchen sink	private	faucet	1.0	1.0	1.4
kitchen sink	hotel, restaurant	faucet	3.0	3.0	4.0
laundry trays (1 to 3)	private	faucet	1.0	1.0	1.4
lavatory	private	faucet	0.5	0.5	0.7
lavatory	public	faucet	1.5	1.5	2.0
service sink	offices, etc.	faucet	2.25	2.25	3.0
shower head	public	mixing valve	3.0	3.0	4.0
shower head	private	mixing valve	1.0	1.0	1.4
urinal	public	1″ flush valve	10.0		10.0
urinal	public	3/4″ flush valve	5.0		5.0
urinal	public	flush tank	3.0		3.0
washing machine (8 lbs)	private	automatic	1.0	1.0	1.4
washing machine (8 lbs)	public	automatic	2.25	2.25	3.0
washing machine (15 lbs)	public	automatic	3.0	3.0	4.0
water closet	private	flush valve	6.0		6.0
water closet	private	flush tank	2.2		2.2
water closet	public	flush valve	10.0		10.0
water closet	public	flush tank	5.0		5.0
water closet	public or private	flushometer tank	2.0		2.0

For SI: 1 inch = 25.4 mm, 1 pound = 0.454 kg

For fixtures not listed, loads should be assumed by comparing the fixture to one listed using water in similar quantities and at similar rates. The assigned loads for fixtures with both hot and cold water supplies are given for separate hot and cold water loads and for total load, the separate hot and cold water loads being three-fourths of the total load for the fixture in each case.

water in the pipes cools and must be run until fresh hot water from the heater travels the distance to the fixture.

This problem can be solved with a two-pipe circulating system. All fixtures needing hot water are connected with a supply pipe and a return pipe. The natural convection in the system keeps the water slowly circulating; hot water rises to the uppermost fixtures and, as it cools, falls down to the water heater to be reheated. When a circulating system is used in long, low buildings or buildings where natural convection may not provide enough circulation, pumps are used.

The size of the water heater is based on the total daily and peak hourly hot-water demands of a building. The peak hourly demand can range from 0.4 gal (1.52 l) per person in a peak hour for an office building to 12 gal (45.5 l) per unit for a small apartment building. The peak hourly demand is used because at certain times of the day it is likely that most occupants will want hot water at the same time. For residences and small buildings, the capacity for the peak hourly demand will be the size of the water heater. For large buildings, a separate storage tank is required to meet demand, while a smaller boiler actually heats the water.

Table 9.3

Estimating Demand Based on Fixture Units

supply systems predominantly for flush tanks			supply systems predominantly for flush valves		
load	demand		load	demand	
(water supply fixture units)	(gallons per minute)	(cubic feet per minute)	(water supply fixture units)	(gallons per minute)	(cubic feet per minute)
1	3.0	0.04104			
2	5.0	0.0684			
3	6.5	0.86892			
4	8.0	1.06944			
5	9.4	1.256592	5	15.0	2.0052
6	10.7	1.430376	6	17.4	2.326032
7	11.8	1.577424	7	19.8	2.646364
8	12.8	1.711104	8	22.2	2.967696
9	13.7	1.831416	9	24.6	3.288528
10	14.6	1.951728	10	27.0	3.60936
11	15.4	2.058672	11	27.8	3.716304
12	16.0	2.13888	12	28.6	3.823248
13	16.5	2.20572	13	29.4	3.930192
14	17.0	2.27256	14	30.2	4.037136
15	17.5	2.3394	15	31.0	4.14408
16	18.0	2.90624	16	31.8	4.241024
17	18.4	2.459712	17	32.6	4.357968
18	18.8	2.513184	18	33.4	4.464912
19	19.2	2.566656	19	34.2	4.571856
20	19.6	2.620128	20	35.0	4.6788
25	21.5	2.87412	25	38.0	5.07984
30	23.3	3.114744	30	42.0	5.61356
35	24.9	3.328632	35	44.0	5.88192
40	26.3	3.515784	40	46.0	6.14928
45	27.7	3.702936	45	48.0	6.41664
50	29.1	3.890088	50	50.0	6.684
60	32.0	4.27776	60	54.0	7.21872
70	35.0	4.6788	70	58.0	7.75344
80	38.0	5.07984	80	61.2	8.181216
90	41.0	5.48088	90	64.3	8.595624
100	43.5	5.81508	100	67.5	9.0234
120	48.0	6.41664	120	73.0	9.75864
140	52.5	7.0182	140	77.0	10.29336
160	57.0	7.61976	160	81.0	10.82808
180	61.0	8.15448	180	85.5	11.42964
200	65.0	8.6892	200	90.0	12.0312
225	70.0	9.3576	225	95.5	12.76644
250	75.0	10.0260	250	101.0	13.50168
275	80.0	10.6944	275	104.5	13.96956
300	85.0	11.3628	300	108.0	14.43744
400	105.0	14.0364	400	127.0	16.97736
500	124.0	16.57632	500	143.0	19.11624
750	170.0	22.7256	750	177.0	23.66136
1,000	208.0	27.80544	1,000	208.0	27.80544
1,250	239.0	31.94952	1,250	239.0	31.94952
1,500	269.0	35.95992	1,500	269.0	35.95992
1,750	297.0	39.70296	1,750	297.0	39.70296

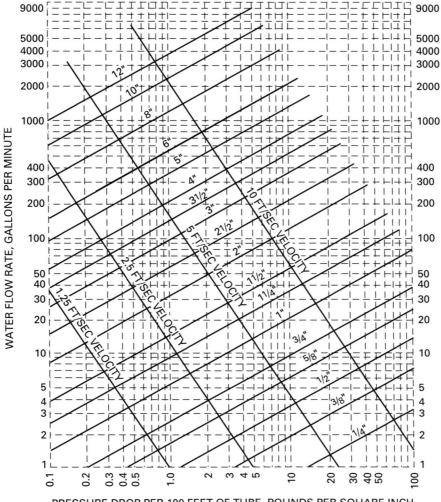

PRESSURE DROP PER 100 FEET OF TUBE, POUNDS PER SQUARE INCH

Note: Fluid velocities in excess of 5 to 8 feet/second are not usually recommended.

FIGURE E103A.2
FRICTION LOSS IN SMOOTH PIPE[a]
(TYPE L, ASTM B 88 COPPER TUBING)

For SI: 1 inch = 25.4 mm, 1 foot = 304.8 mm, 1 gpm = 3.785 L/m, 1 psi = 6.895 kPa,
1 foot per second = 0.305 m/s

a. This chart applies to smooth new copper tubing with recessed (Streamline) soldered joints
and to the actual sizes of types indicated on the diagram.

Figure 9.4 Flow Chart for Type L Copper Pipe

In addition to storage capacity, the *recovery rate* of a water heater is important. This is the number of gallons (liters) per hour of cold water that the heater can raise to the desired temperature.

The size of hot water piping is determined in a manner similar to that used for cold-water piping except that only the fixtures requiring hot water are used to calculate load. This value is multiplied by 0.75 (75%) and then looked up in Table 9.3 to find the flow rate. In no case can the pipe size

be less than the minimum sizes given in the plumbing codes.

Water heaters are set to keep the water at any desired temperature. Generally, this setting is the highest temperature that is required at the point of use. Recommended point-of-use temperatures range from 95°F (35.0°C) for therapeutic baths to 180°F (82.2°C) for commercial and institutional laundries and for sanitizing rinses for commercial dishwashers. Other common temperatures include 105°F

Table 9.4
Allowance in Equivalent Length of Pipe for Friction Loss in Valves and Threaded Fittings

fitting or valve	pipe sizes (in)							
	$\frac{1}{2}$	$\frac{3}{4}$	1	$1\frac{1}{4}$	$1\frac{1}{2}$	2	$2\frac{1}{2}$	3
45-degree elbow	1.2	1.5	1.8	2.4	3.0	4.0	5.0	6.0
90-degree elbow	2.0	2.5	3.0	4.0	5.0	7.0	8.0	10.0
Tee, run	0.6	0.8	0.9	1.2	1.5	2.0	2.5	3.0
Tee, branch	3.0	4.0	5.0	6.0	7.0	10.0	12.0	15.0
Gate valve	0.4	0.5	0.6	0.8	1.0	1.3	1.6	2.0
Balancing valve	0.8	1.1	1.5	1.9	2.2	3.0	3.7	4.5
Plug-type cock	0.8	1.1	1.5	1.9	2.2	3.0	3.7	4.5
Check valve, swing	5.6	8.4	11.2	14.0	16.8	22.4	28.0	33.6
Globe valve	15.0	20.0	25.0	35.0	45.0	55.0	65.0	80.0
Angle valve	8.0	12.0	15.0	18.0	22.0	28.0	34.0	40.0

For SI: 1 inch = 25.4 mm, 1 foot = 304.8 mm, 1 degree = 0.0175 rad.

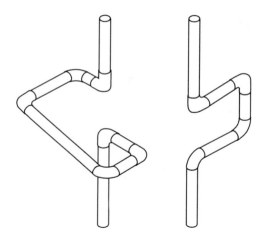

Figure 9.5 Expansion Devices for Hot-Water
Piping

(40.6°C) for hand washing, 110°F (43.3°C) for showers and baths, and 140°F (60.0°C) for residential dish washing and laundry. Above about 110°F (43.3°C), water becomes uncomfortable to the touch.

Water heaters are available in several configurations and heating methods as diagrammed in Fig. 9.6. First, there are two basic heating methods, direct and indirect.' brings the water directly into contact with heated surfaces that are warmed with flame, hot gases, electricity, or solar radiation. This is the method used for the typical residential tank-type water heater. *Indirect heating* uses an intermediary

transfer medium to heat the water. For example, in commercial applications where central steam is available, the steam can be piped to tubes within a tank containing the domestic hot water.

With either direct or indirect heating there are three basic types of equipment: storage tank, tankless, and circulating. Diagrams of these types of units using both direct and indirect heating are shown in Fig. 9.6. With the *storage tank system*, the same tank is used to both heat the water and store it for use. In the *tankless system*, water is quickly heated as it is needed and sent to where it is needed. One of the common variations of the diagram shown in Fig. 9.6 is the electric instantaneous water heater. These units are often used in remote locations where it is impractical or uneconomical to pipe hot water continuously. As the hot-water faucet is turned on, a high-capacity electric coil instantaneously heats cold water. With the *circulating system*, the water is heated in one place and stored in a separate tank until it is needed. This method is commonly used in solar-powered water heating systems and in many commercial applications.

In some cases it is impractical or very inefficient to use an indirect, tankless system. For example, heating domestic hot water in a furnace or boiler whose primary purpose is to provide space heating only works when the furnace or boiler is functioning. This means that the heating plant would have to work in the summer. In these cases, the heating plant provides only supplemental heating, and there is another source of heat for water heating only.

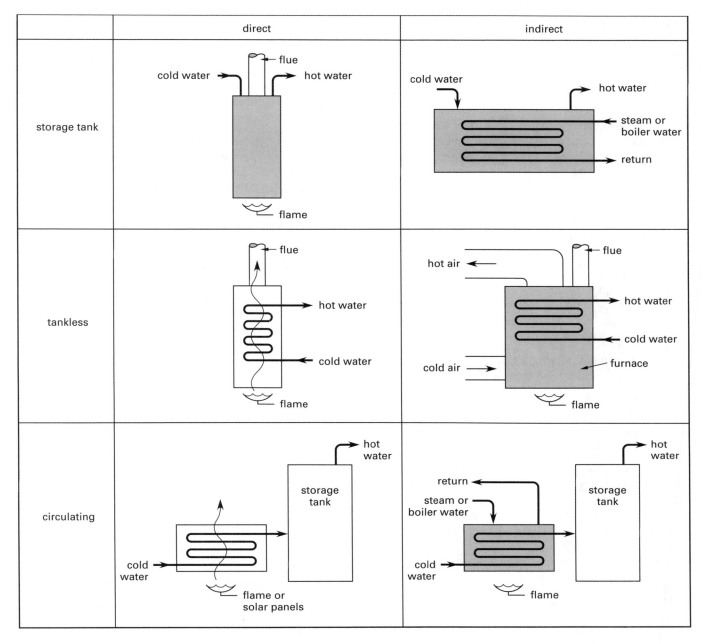

Figure 9.6 Water Heater Types

Solar Water Heating

Solar energy is commonly used to heat water for domestic use, industrial use, and swimming pools. Nearly all solar heating systems have certain components in common. These include some type of solar collector, a storage tank, associated piping to move the fluids, and a backup heater. If it is an active system it will use pumps and associated controls and sensors. The collectors are usually flat plate, but they can also be focusing collectors, or in the case of batch systems, they can be simply a black tank behind glass or plastic.

Many types of solar water heating systems exist, but they can be broadly classified by how the heat transfer occurs, how the heating fluid is circulated, and their means of protection from freezing.

Solar heat is transferred either directly or indirectly. In a *direct system*, or *open-loop system*, the water used in the building is the same water that is heated in the solar collectors. An *indirect system*, or *closed-loop system*, uses a separate fluid for collecting heat, which is then transferred to the domestic hot water. Direct systems have the advantages of simple design and operation and high efficiency, but they are subject to freezing. Indirect systems are easier to protect from freezing because the heat-collecting fluid can contain antifreeze, and these systems can also operate at a lower pressure than that required for the domestic hot water. However, a heat exchanger is required, which reduces efficiency.

The heating fluid is circulated either passively or actively. *Passive circulation systems* rely on gravity and the thermosiphoning action of heated water. They are simple and low-cost systems, but their storage tanks must be placed above the solar collectors, and the points of use must be close to the storage tanks. *Active circulation systems* use pumps to circulate the heat-collecting fluid. These systems are much more flexible and reliable but add costs for equipment and operation.

Protection from freezing is provided either by using a non-freezing medium (antifreeze solution or phase-change material) or by draining the fluid at night and during cloudy weather. Of course, direct or open-loop systems must use some type of drainage system.

Some of the common types of solar heating systems with which examinees should be familiar are listed here.

Batch system. A batch system (also known as a *breadbox heater*) heats water directly in a black-painted tank inside a glazed box. This passive system is simple, but it is subject to freezing and nighttime heat loss.

Thermosiphon system. A thermosiphon system relies on the natural movement of heated water to circulate the water in a passive, open-loop system. This system is also simple, but the storage tanks must be located above the collectors, and the piping must be kept simple to minimize pipe friction. To address the problem of freezing, a variation of this method uses a closed-loop system with antifreeze fluid.

Closed-loop active system. This is one of the most common types of systems for both residential and commercial applications. A separate, nonfreezing fluid is circulated by pumps through the solar collectors and into a heat exchanger where the domestic hot water is heated. A differential controller senses when the temperature of the collector is lower than that of the stored water and turns the pumps off. This system is flexible and provides control but suffers from some loss in efficiency because of the need for a heat exchanger.

Drain-down system. A drain-down system is a direct (open-loop), active system that solves the problem of freezing by automatically draining the water from the collectors when the outside temperature is near freezing. Because water is wasted whenever the system is drained, this method is best for climates with mild winters where the draining process would not occur frequently.

Drain-back system. The drain-back system is an indirect (closed-loop), active system that uses water as the heat-collector fluid. The heated water is pumped to a heat exchanger where a coil of domestic hot water is heated. When the controller senses the temperature is too low, it turns off the pump, and the collector water drains back into the solar storage tank.

Phase-change system. Hot water systems can also take advantage of phase-change materials as the collector fluid. As discussed in the previous chapter, phase-change materials store large amounts of latent heat as well as sensible heat.

SANITARY DRAINAGE AND VENTING

Drainage is separated into sanitary and storm drainage. *Sanitary drainage* comprises any drainage that may include human waste, whereas *storm drainage* involves only runoff from roof drains, landscaped areas, and the like. The two types of drainage are separated because storm drainage does not have to be treated. It can also easily overload the lines of a sanitary sewage disposal system and cause sewage to back up into a building. This section will discuss sanitary drainage only.

Sanitary drainage systems are sometimes further divided into the categories of gray water and black water. *Black water* is sewage including human waste, and *gray water* is sewage not including human waste, such as from kitchen sinks, dishwashers, and lavatories. In some conservation systems this distinction is made because gray water can often be recycled directly or with very little treatment for use in irrigation and for other purposes, whereas black water needs more extensive treatment prior to recycling or disposal.

Drainage Systems

A drainage system consists of a number of components designed to safely carry away sewage to a private or municipal disposal system. Beginning with an individual fixture, there are a number of components with which examinees should be familiar.

The first is the *trap*. With few exceptions, traps are located at every fixture and are designed to catch and hold a quantity of water to provide a seal that prevents sewage system gases from entering the building. When fixtures, such as toilets, have traps as an integral part of their design or where adjacent fixtures, such as a double kitchen sink, are connected, traps need not be installed. Traps are usually installed within 2 ft (600) of the fixture but may be installed at slightly greater distances depending on the size of the pipe. Occasionally, a house trap is installed at the point where the house drain leaves the building, but this is not always mandatory.

Traps are connected, of course, to the actual drainage piping, but they must also be connected to vents. *Vents* are pipes connected to the drainage system in various ways, vented to outside air, and designed to serve two primary purposes. First, they allow built-up sewage gases to escape instead of bubble through the water in the traps. Second, they allow pressure in the system to equalize so that discharging waste does not create a siphon that would drain the water out of the traps.

Air gaps are also used as a safety feature in sanitary drainage systems. If the potable water outlet was below the highest level of the overflow of a sink or tub, contaminated water in the sink could be siphoned back into the potable water supply lines. To prevent this, faucets are always mounted with their outlets at least 2 in above the highest possible level of waste water.

On fixtures where the water supply is below the rim of the fixture (on a flush-valve toilet, for example) a device called a *vacuum breaker* is used to prevent siphonage by closing when backward water pressure is present.

Figure 9.7 shows a simplified diagram of a typical drainage and vent system. From the trap, sewage travels in fixture branch lines to a vertical stack. If the stack carries human waste from toilets, it is called a *soil stack*. If the stack carries wastes other than human waste, it is known as a *waste stack*.

Vents from individual fixtures are connected above the fixtures in two ways. If a vent connects to a soil or waste stack above the highest fixture in the system, the portion of the stack above this point is known as a *stack vent*. The stack vent extends through the roof. Multistory buildings use a separate pipe for venting. This is called a *vent stack* and either extends through the roof or connects with the stack vent above the highest fixture, as shown in Fig. 9.7.

The stacks connect at the bottom of the building to a horizontal drain. Within the building and to a point 3 ft (1 m) outside the building this is the *house drain* (also known as the *building drain*). From a point 3 ft (1 m) outside the building to the main sewer line or private disposal system, the horizontal pipe is the *house sewer* (also known as the *building sewer*). Cleanouts are provided at the intersections of the stacks and house drain to allow for maintenance of the drain.

Horizontal drains must be sloped to allow for gravity drainage. The usual minimum for branch lines of house drains and sewers is 1/4 in/ft (20 mm/m), but for pipes larger than 3 in (76), 1/8 in/ft (10 mm/m) is sometimes allowed. Changes in direction must be made with easy bends rather than right-angle fittings.

Components and Materials

Piping for drainage systems may be DWV (drainage, waste, and vent) copper, cast iron, or plastic. Plastic has become very popular because it is less expensive and less labor intensive to install than other types. Polyvinyl chloride (PVC) and acrilonitrile-butadiene styrene (ABS) plastic are suitable for DWV systems. Occasionally, vitrified clay tile may be used for building sewers if allowed by the local code, but the joints in these pipes allow tree roots to grow into them, so they are seldom used.

Cast-iron piping can be connected with hub and spigot joints or with hubless joints. In the hub and spigot fitting, the end of one pipe is slipped into an enlarged hub of another pipe, and the joint is sealed with a gasket. A hubless joint uses a gasket held in place with a stainless steel retaining clamp. Cast-iron pipe is required for the house sewer. Copper and plastic piping are joined, as is supply water piping.

Other parts of a drainage system may include the following components.

Backflow preventers or *backwater valves* prevent sewage from upper stories or from the building sewer from reversing flow and backing up into fixtures set at a lower elevation.

When plumbing fixtures must be below the level of the house drain and house sewer, a *sump pit* is installed. This device collects the sewage and pumps it to a higher level where it can flow by gravity into the sewer.

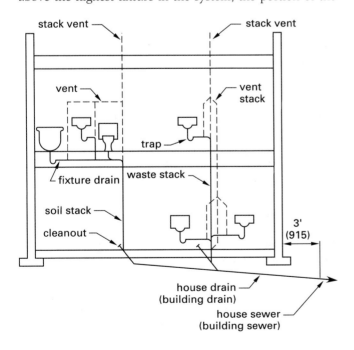

Figure 9.7 Drainage and Vent System

Floor drains collect water in shower rooms or in places where overflow is likely. Because some floor drains are seldom used, special care must be taken so that the water seal does not evaporate and allow sewer gases to penetrate the building. The traps of floor drains are usually required to have deeper seals than other types of traps.

Interceptors are devices that collect foreign matter at the source instead of allowing it to enter the sewer system. Some of the more common types include grease traps, plaster traps, and lubricating oil traps. Interceptors have provisions for periodic cleanout of the foreign matter.

System Design

The sizing of drainage pipes is based on the idea of fixture units (just as water supply piping is), although with different values of fixture units for each type of fixture. For example, a lavatory is assigned a drainage fixture unit of 1, and a public water closet is considered to have 6 fixture units. There are also certain minimum sizes of trap arms for individual fixtures: a single lavatory must have at least a 1¹/₄ in (32) drain and a single toilet must have at least a 3 in (76) trap arm. The minimum size for a vent is 1¹/₄ in (32). These values are given in tables from the plumbing code.

Design of a drainage system begins with the individual fixtures and branch lines and proceeds to the sizing of stacks and building drains. Tables in the plumbing code give the maximum number of fixture units and the maximum vertical and horizontal lengths of piping based on pipe diameter. It is thus a simple matter to accumulate fixture units served by a particular stack or drain and increase the size as needed as more fixtures are added to it.

The plumbing code also states the minimum sizes and lengths of vents based on fixture units connected. It also gives the maximum horizontal distance of trap arms based on size.

WASTE DISPOSAL AND TREATMENT

Once sewage leaves a building, it is transported by the house sewer to either a municipal collection system or a private disposal system. Private systems generally consist of a septic tank and a leaching field. The *septic tank* collects the sewage and allows the solid matter to settle to the bottom and the effluent (liquid portion) to drain into the distribution system, where it seeps into the ground. See Fig. 9.8.

The size of the septic tank is determined by the amount of daily flow. For residences this is usually based on the number of bedrooms and baths. For larger installations, it is based on the calculated sewage flow in gallons per day. The size and length of the leaching field system are based on the ability of the soil to absorb the effluent. A *leaching field* is an area where effluent seeps from the drain tiles into the soil.

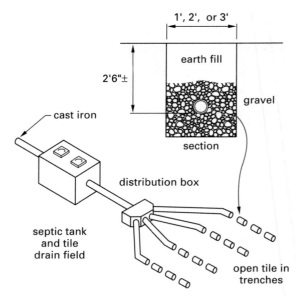

Figure 9.8 Private Sewage Disposal

This is determined by a percolation test, which measures the amount of time it takes water in a test hole to drop 1 in. Tables give the minimum length of piping in leaching fields based on percolation and volume handled.

Because there is the potential for septic tanks and leaching fields to contaminate potable water supplies—mainly wells—plumbing codes give minimum required distances between various parts of the system and other features of the site, such as wells, property lines, rivers, and buildings. For example, there must be a minimum of 100 ft (30.5 m) between a leaching field and a well, 50 ft (15 m) between a septic tank and a well, and 10 ft (3 m) between a leaching field and a building.

Where sewage is transported from a building to public sewer lines, the building sewer connects to a line in the street or other public right of way. From there, branch lines connect to larger main lines that eventually reach a sewage treatment facility. Manholes are provided for maintenance and inspection of the lines. They are located at every change in direction and at intervals of 150 ft (46 m).

STORM DRAINAGE

Water drainage from rain and snow melt is kept separate from sanitary drainage, as outlined in the previous section. This is to avoid overloading the sanitary drainage system, causing possible backup of sanitary sewer lines. In sparsely populated areas, storm drainage normally soaks into the ground or finds its way to rivers and lakes. In more populated areas with a higher percentage of roofed area and paved streets and parking lots, artificial systems are necessary to safely carry away storm water.

Private Systems

There are several methods for draining water from a private home. The first is the simplest and consists of collecting water from the roof in roof drains or gutters and leaders and simply letting it run onto the ground surrounding the house, where it soaks in. Splash blocks and other devices are used to carry the water far enough from the building to avoid excess water seeping into the foundation or eroding soil around the foundations.

If this is not adequate, drywells are connected to the drain leaders with underground pipes. A *drywell* is a large, porous, underground container where water collects and seeps into the soil. If a drywell is not adequate or the ground is not sufficiently porous, a *drain field*, similar to a leaching field, can be used. In addition to draining water from the roof, the land around the building must be graded to divert water away from the foundation.

Some communities require roof drains to be directly connected to the public sewer system.

Municipal Systems

A municipal storm sewer system is laid out in a manner similar to the sanitary sewage system, collecting runoff from street gutters, catch basins, and individual taps from private buildings and land developments. The system carries the water by gravity to natural drainage areas such as rivers, lakes, or oceans.

In some areas the potential runoff of rainwater from a storm may be too great for the storm system to handle. In this case, building regulations may required private owners to include a retention pond in their site plan. A *retention pond* is designed to contain the maximum expected runoff and then slowly release the water to the storm sewer system. Retention ponds may have a small outlet at one end, like a dam or drain to a low point in the middle of the pond, where a catch basin, or grate, covers the entrance to a pipe. This pipe transports the water to a storm sewer system or other natural drainage area.

Drains, Gutters, and Downspout Sizing

The sizes of horizontal drain pipes, gutters, and downspouts are determined based on the area of the roof or paved area drained and the maximum hourly rainfall. For gutters and horizontal piping, the slope of the pipe is also a factor, lower slopes requiring a greater size. Gutter slopes range from $1/16$ in/ft (5 mm/m) to $1/2$ in/ft (40 mm/m).

Rainfall rates are available from the local weather service or from published maps of the United States and Canada. When calculating the roof area of a sloped roof, the projected area is used. This is the horizontal area defined by the edges of the roof without regard to the slope. Based on the maximum hourly rainfall rate, roof area, and proposed slope of gutter, tables are created that give the minimum required diameter of gutter or roof leader.

FIRE PROTECTION AND LIFE SAFETY

Fire protection and life safety in buildings addresses three major objectives: the protection of life, the protection of property, and the restoration and continued use of the building after the fire. Life safety also involves the protection of people during emergencies other than fire, such as earthquakes, floods, terrorist threats, and similar disasters. However, this section only deals with life safety during fires.

Fire protection in buildings is accomplished in several ways.

- by preventing fires
- by early fire detection and alarm
- by providing for quick exiting of building occupants
- by containing the fire
- by suppressing the fire

Fire prevention includes limiting the products of combustion and other hazardous situations that could lead to starting a fire. Building codes address these concerns in a number of ways that include setting forth minimum flame-spread ratings and establishing flammability standards and similar constraints. These issues and those of exiting are outlined in Ch. 29.

Fire detection systems and alarms are critical, to provide sufficient warning for occupants to leave the building and to alert firefighters so that extinguishing efforts can begin before the fire spreads. Fire detection and alarms are covered in Ch. 10.

Fire containment is achieved through building materials, compartmentation, and smoke control. Fire suppression is achieved through sprinkler systems, standpipes, and other methods. These topics are reviewed in the following sections.

Compartmentation

Compartmentation is a critical concept in fire and life safety. The basic idea is to contain a fire and limit its spread, both to allow building occupants to escape and to protect other parts of the building that are not initially subject to the fire. In high-rise buildings, where it may not be practical to evacuate the building immediately, compartmentation can provide places of refuge where occupants can wait until the fire is extinguished or until they can exit safely. Compartmentation provides time for fire suppression, either by automatic sprinklers or by fire fighting personnel.

Compartmentation has been integral to building codes for a long time. Codes require fire separation between different occupancies, between use areas and exits, and between parts of a building when the maximum allowable area is exceeded. Separation is required both vertically, with fire-resistive floor-ceiling assemblies, and horizontally, with fire-rated walls. Any openings through fire assemblies must also provide protection for the spread of fire and smoke. These topics are covered in Ch. 29.

On a larger scale, the concept of compartmentation also applies to an entire building, so fire does not spread to adjacent structures. This is why building codes require certain fire ratings for exterior walls, limit the locations of buildings on a piece of property, and limit the size of or require protection of exterior openings when a building is near other structures or property lines. These requirements are also reviewed in Ch. 29.

On a smaller scale, structural members are isolated to protect them from the effects of fire and prevent structural collapse. In addition, the sizes of concealed areas above ceilings, in attics, in pipe chases, and under floors are limited to prevent the spread of fire, since a fire in these parts of a building would be especially difficult to extinguish. Fire stops in stud spaces between the first and second floors of a house are one important example of this kind of small-scale compartmentation.

Smoke Control

Because more deaths and injuries occur in fires due to inhalation of smoke and other gases rather than due to flame and heat exposure, smoke control is one of the most important aspects of fire protection. Smoke is particularly troublesome because many factors cause it to move rapidly through a building, well beyond the location of the fire. Smoke moves by the natural convection forces caused by differential air pressure between cool and warm air. In multistoried buildings, especially tall ones, the stack effect also pulls smoke through any vertical penetration such as stairways, elevator shafts, mechanical shafts, and atriums. Smoke spread is exacerbated by HVAC systems that can potentially distribute smoke a great distance from the original source.

There are several elements to smoke control. These include containment, exhaust, and, to a lesser degree, dilution. The same compartmentation that is used to contain fires is also used to contain the spread of smoke. Devices such as fire dampers, gaskets on fire doors, and automatic closing fire doors seal openings in fire walls. By containing smoke to one area of the building, places of refuge can be established. However, containment alone is not enough.

Because smoke is so deadly, it is always desirable to remove it from a building as quickly as possible. This helps keep it out of refuge areas, removes toxic smoke and gases, makes it easier to fight the fire, and helps control the path of the fire.

Some building codes provide for two types of control: passive and active. A *passive smoke control system* is one with a system of smoke barriers arranged to limit the migration of smoke. An *active smoke control system* is an engineered system that uses mechanical fans to produce pressure differentials across smoke barriers or to establish airflows to limit and direct smoke movement.

Passive smoke barriers can be partitions, doors with smoke seals, or curtain boards. A *curtain board* is a piece of construction suspended a minimum of 6 ft (1829) from the ceiling that restricts the passage of smoke and flame during a fire's initial stages. Curtain boards are commonly used in vented buildings and around escalator enclosures in conjunction with sprinkler systems to protect floor openings.

In one-story buildings of group F and S occupancies over 50,000 ft² (4645 m²) and in Group H occupancies over 15,000 ft² (1394 m²) in a single-floor area, automatic smoke and heat vents must be installed. These open automatically when their fusible links are subjected to excessive heat. Smoke vents must also be provided over stages more than 1000 ft² (93 m²) in area, in atria, and in other locations specified by the code.

The concept of active smoke control combined with compartmentation is illustrated in Fig. 9.9, which shows a diagrammatic plan of one floor of a high-rise building. A *high-rise* is defined as a building with a floor area more than 75 ft (22 860) above the lowest level of fire department vehicle access. When a fire starts in one zone and activates an alarm, several events take place. All open doors connected to automatic closing devices that provide communication between the two zones, such as those leading to the elevator lobby close. The supply air and return air ducts to the fire zone shut down, and exhaust to outside air is turned on, creating a negative pressure in the fire zone. In the other zone, return and exhaust air ducts are closed, and supply air is forced into the safe area. This creates a slight positive pressure in the refuge zone and prevents smoke from migrating in, even if doors are opened momentarily.

Stairways are also pressurized to prevent smoke from entering them. Vestibules are also pressurized at a level slightly higher than that of the fire floor but slightly less than that of the stairway. This arrangement provides a double protection of the stairway and also keeps smoke out of the vestibules, where the areas of refuge for wheelchair occupants are located and where the standpipe connections and fire department communication devices are located. This system of protection for stairways replaces the former "smokeproof enclosures" of previous codes.

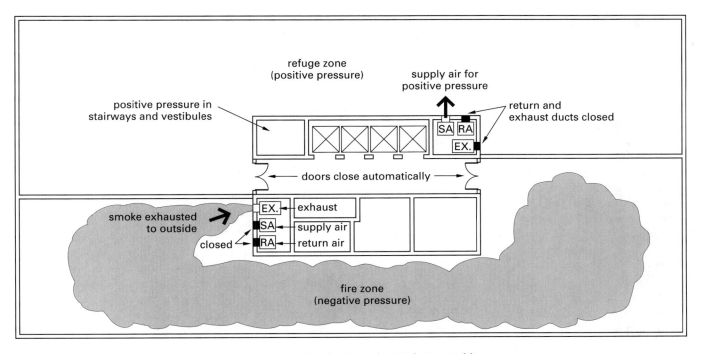

Figure 9.9 Smoke Control in High-Rise Buildings

Similar systems can be used for other building types, such as large shopping malls, buildings with atria, and large industrial buildings. The building code prescribes where smoke control must be installed and whether it must be active or passive.

Sprinkler Systems

Fire sprinkler systems are becoming more prevalent in construction because of increasingly more stringent building code regulations and because of the awareness of owners and insurance companies of the systems' ability to minimize property damage and improve life safety. For example, the IBC requires sprinklers in buildings over 75 ft (22 860) high.

There are four types of sprinkler systems: wet-pipe, dry-pipe, preaction, and deluge. *Wet-pipe systems* are the most common. They are constantly filled with water and respond immediately to a rise in temperature at any sprinkler head of from 135°F to 170°F (57°C to 77°C). The exact temperature trigger point depends on the normal temperature at the ceiling; fusible links are available for a range of temperatures. In most wet-pipe systems, flow detectors are placed on each zone of sprinkler piping. When a sprinkler head opens, the detector senses movement of water and sends a signal to an annunciator panel or fire control center so that fire fighting personnel know where the fire is.

Dry-pipe systems are used in areas subject to freezing. The pipes are filled with compressed air or nitrogen until one or more heads are activated, allowing water to flow. Alternately, a dry-pipe system can be activated by a valve connected to a fire alarm.

Preaction systems are similar to dry-pipe systems except that water is allowed into the system before any sprinkler head has opened. At the same time an alarm is activated. This system is used where damage from water might result. The early alarm allows the fire to be put out before any sprinkler head opens.

Deluge systems activate all the sprinkler heads in an area at once, regardless of where the fire is. All the sprinkler heads are open and the pipes are empty. Upon activation of an alarm, valves automatically open, flooding the space. Deluge systems are used in high-hazard areas where fire is likely to spread rapidly.

In tall buildings, water for a sprinkler system can either be supplied in a tank near the top of the building or zone, just as the water supply is, or can be supplied with pumps connected to an emergency power supply. When tanks are used, they are designed to provide fire fighting capability for a certain percentage of sprinklers for a given time until firefighters can arrive. Siamese connections are provided on the exterior of the building so the fire department can connect hose pumps to the sprinkler system.

The installation of fire sprinkler systems is governed by each local building code, but most codes refer to NFPA 13, Standard for the Installation of Sprinkler Systems, published by the National Fire Protection Association. This standard classifies the relative fire hazard of buildings into three groups: light, ordinary, and extra hazard. Each hazard classification is further divided into groups. The hazard classification determines the required spacing of sprinklers and other regulations.

For example, light hazard includes occupancies such as residences, offices, hospitals, schools, and restaurants. In these occupancies there must be one sprinkler for each 200 ft^2 (18.6 m^2), or 225 ft^2 (20.9 m^2) if the design of the system is hydraulically calculated. For open-wood joist ceilings, the area drops to 130 ft^2 (12.1 m^2). Maximum spacing between sprinkler heads is 15 ft (4.6 m) for the 225 ft^2 coverage requirement, with the maximum distance from a wall being one-half the required spacing.

Standpipes

Standpipes are pipes that run the height of a building and provide water outlets at each floor to which fire fighting hoses can be connected. They are located within the stairway or, in the case of pressurized enclosures, within the vestibule.

The IBC defines three classes of standpipes. Class I is a dry-standpipe system without a directly connected water supply and equipped with 2^1/$_2$ in (63.5) outlets for use by fire department personnel. Class II is a wet-standpipe system directly connected to a water supply and equipped with 1^1/$_2$ in (38.1) outlets and hoses intended for use by building occupants. Class III is a combination system directly connected to a water supply and equipped with both 1^1/$_2$ in (38.1) and 2^1/$_2$ in (63.5) outlets.

The IBC defines where each class of standpipe is required. Class III standpipes must be installed in buildings where the floor level of the highest story is more than 30 ft (9144) above the lowest level of fire department vehicle access, or where the floor level of the lowest story is located more than 30 ft (9144) below the highest level of fire department access. However, four exceptions allow Class I standpipes to be used. These include buildings equipped with a sprinkler system, open parking garages less than 150 ft (45 720) high, open parking garages subject to freezing temperatures, and basements that are sprinklered.

In buildings over 10,000 ft^2 (929 m^2) per story, Class I automatic wet or manual wet standpipes must be used where any portion of the building's interior area is more than 200 ft (60 960) of travel, vertically or horizontally, from the nearest point of fire department vehicle access. However, exceptions to this requirement include fully sprinklered buildings, Group A-4, A-5, F-2, R-2, S-2, or U occupancies, and cases where automatic dry and semiautomatic dry standpipes are allowed as provided for in NFPA 14, *Standpipe and Hose System.*

Other requirements given in the IBC cover Group A buildings, covered mall buildings, stages, and underground buildings.

Class I standpipes must be located at every level of a building within stairway enclosures or within the vestibule if the exit enclosures are pressurized. They are also required on each side of the wall adjacent to the exit opening of horizontal exits. Class II and III standpipes must be accessible and located so all portions of a building are within 30 ft (9144) of a nozzle attached to 100 ft (30 480) of hose.

Water is supplied in two ways: from storage tanks and through Siamese connections at ground level for connection with fire department groups.

Like a sprinkler system, the standpipes can be either dry or wet. In a wet system, the standpipes are constantly filled with water and are connected to a tank of water at the top of the building that provides a supply of water for immediate use. Once firefighters arrive, water is pumped from fire hydrants through the fire truck pumps to the standpipes. In a dry system, there is no water standing in the pipe. In the event of a fire, water must be charged with pumps in the building or by the fire department through Siamese connections.

Other Extinguishing Agents

Although sprinkler systems are the most common type of automatic extinguishing system, others are available.

Portable fire extinguishers are helpful for stopping small fires in the early stages of development. There are four general classes of extinguisher: A, B, C, and D. These classes correspond to the four fire types. Fires of type A involve ordinary combustibles of paper, wood, and cloth. Fire extinguishers for these fires contain water or water-based agents. B fires involve flammable liquids such as gasoline, solvents, and paints. B extinguishers contain smothering types of chemicals like carbon dioxide, foam, and halogenated agents. C fires involve electrical equipment, and the corresponding extinguisher contains nonconductive agents. Finally, class D fires involve combustible metals. Each type of fire must be fought with a suitable extinguisher. Combination extinguishers are also available for type A, B, and C fires.

Halogenated agents, commonly referred to as *halon*, are used where water might damage the contents of a room, like in computer installations. Halon is a gas that chemically inhibits the spread of fire. However, halon is a CFC gas that can damage the ozone layer, so alternate extinguishing agents will be used in the future.

Various types of foam can also be used to smother fires. Foam is commonly used where flammable liquid fires might occur, for example, in industrial plants or aircraft hangars.

Another type of extinguishing agent is actually a building material and acts passively in reaction to a fire. *Intumescent materials* respond to fire by expanding rapidly, insulating the surface they protect or filling gaps to prevent the passage of fire, heat, and smoke. They are available in the form of strips, caulk, paint, and spreadable putty. For example, a strip of intumescent material placed along the edge of one of a pair of fire doors will expand and seal the crack, substituting for an astragal that would otherwise be required. Intumescent paints can be applied to protect normally flammable wood.

SAMPLE QUESTIONS

1. What determines the size of a leaching field?

    A. percolation test
    B. yield test
    C. aquifer test
    D. water table test

2. What is an important concern in relation to a private water supply?

    A. fixture pressure
    B. hardness
    C. friction loss
    D. yield

3. What part of water supply design is affected by building height?

    A. fixture units
    B. pressure tank
    C. static head
    D. submersible pump

4. Select the correct statements.

I. Dry-pipe sprinkler systems are more efficient than wet-pipe systems.
II. Siamese connections serve both sprinklers and standpipes.
III. The hazard classification does not necessarily affect sprinkler layout.
IV. Standpipes must be located within stairways or vestibules of smokeproof enclosures.
V. Standpipes are required in buildings four or more stories high or those exceeding 150 ft.

A. I, II, and IV
B. II, III, and V
C. II, IV, and V
D. III, IV, and V

5. The pressure in a city water main is 57 psi. The pressure loss through piping, fittings, and the water meter has been calculated as 23 psi, and the highest fixture requires 12 psi to operate. What is the maximum height the fixture can be above the water main?

A. 9 ft
B. 24 ft
C. 50 ft
D. 78 ft

6. A house is being designed for a suburban location. The nearest water main is one block away (about 300 ft), and the city has no plans to extend the line in the near future. City and county regulations do permit the drilling of wells. What action should the architect recommend to the client regarding the water supply?

A. Estimate the cost of extending the municipal line, since the water quality is known and it would ensure a long-term supply. Consult with nearby property owners who plan to build in the area to see if they would be willing to share the cost of extending the line.
B. Drill a test bore to determine the depth, potential yield, and water quality of a well, and compare this information with the cost of extending the municipal line.
C. Assist the owner in petitioning the city to accelerate its plans for extending the water line to serve new development.
D. Consult with nearby property owners who use wells and with well drillers to estimate the depth and yield of wells in the area. Compare the estimated cost and feasibility of drilling with the feasibility of extending the municipal line at the owner's cost.

7. Which statements about drainage are correct?

I. Drains should always slope at a minimum of $1/8$ in/ft.
II. The vent stack extends through the roof.
III. Vents help prevent the drainage of water from traps.
IV. The house drain cannot also be called the building sewer.
V. Cleanouts are always a necessary part of a drainage system.

A. I, II, and V
B. I, III, and IV
C. II, III, and V
D. III, IV, and V

8. Water hammer is most likely to occur when

   A. the incorrect type of valve is used
   B. water suddenly stops because the flow is turned off
   C. expansion joints are not installed in water lines
   D. water flows backward against a check valve

9. Which of the following is one component of a plumbing system that is common to every building?

   A. stack vent
   B. vent stack
   C. backflow preventer
   D. house trap

10. Select the INCORRECT statement.

   A. Several types of plastic can be used for cold-water piping, but only PVDC is used for hot-water supply where allowed by local codes.
   B. Steel pipe is more labor intensive and requires more space than copper pipe in plumbing chases.
   C. Type M pipe is normally specified for most interior plumbing.
   D. ABS is suitable for water supply.

ELECTRICAL SYSTEMS

Nomenclature

d	distance	ft	m
E	illumination	fc	lux
I	current (electrical circuits)	A	A
I	luminous intensity (lighting design)	candlepower	cd
pf	power factor		
R	resistance	Ω	Ω
t	time	hr	h
V	voltage	V	V
W	power	W	W
Z	impedance	Ω	Ω
θ	angle	degrees	degrees

ELECTRICAL FUNDAMENTALS

Definitions

Ampere: the unit flow of electrons in a conductor equal to 6.251×10^{18} electrons passing a given section in 1 sec

Energy: the product of power and time, also called *work*

Impedance: the resistance in an alternating current (AC) circuit, measured in ohms

Ohm: the unit of resistance in an electrical circuit

Power factor: the phase difference between voltage and current in an alternating current circuit

Reactance: part of the electrical resistance in an alternating current circuit, caused by inductance and capacitance

Volt: the unit of electromotive force or potential difference that will cause a current of 1 A to flow through a conductor whose resistance is 1 Ω

Watt: the unit of electrical power

Basic Relationships

Electricity is the energy caused by the flow of electrons. A basic electric circuit consists of a conductor, the actual flow of electrons (current), an electric potential difference to cause the electrons to move (voltage), and some type of resistance to the flow of electrons. The circuit can be interrupted with a switch. These basic components are shown in Fig. 10.1.

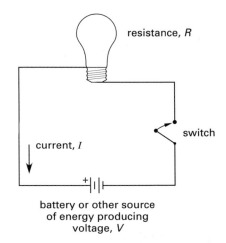

Figure 10.1 Basic Electric Current

Ohm's law relates current, voltage, and resistance in direct current (DC) circuits according to the formula

$$I = \frac{V}{R} \qquad 10.1$$

This states that the current in a circuit is directly proportional to the voltage and inversely proportional to the resistance.

In physics, power is the rate at which work is done or the rate at which energy is used. In electric circuits, power is expressed in watts. Wattage, in DC circuits, is the product of voltage and current, or

$$W = VI \qquad\qquad 10.2$$

Although this is the standard formula, a useful mnemonic way of remembering it is to think of PIE, or $P = IE$, power (wattage) equals current (I) times electromotive force (E), which is voltage.

Electrical circuits for alternating current are slightly different due to how alternating current is generated; they operate according to the principle of electromagnetic induction. This principle was discovered by Michael Faraday in 1831 and states that when a conductor is moved in a magnetic field, a voltage is induced. The direction of the movement determines the polarity of the voltage, either positive or negative. When a coil of conductor, or wire, is rotated within a magnetic field (or when the magnetic field is rotated around a fixed coil), a voltage of alternating polarity is produced. AC voltage is represented graphically with a sine wave as shown in Fig. 10.2. The *amplitude* of the wave represents the voltage, and the distance between peaks is one cycle. In the United States, alternating current is produced at a frequency of 60 cycles per second, or 60 Hz. In Europe and other countries the frequency is 50 Hz.

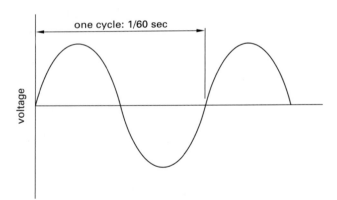

Figure 10.2 Sine Wave of Alternating Current

In AC circuits, resistance is known as *impedance*, which comprises resistance and reactance and causes a phase-change difference between voltage and current. The difference is represented by the power factor (pf) and can be a significant factor in calculating power in an AC circuit. For circuits with only resistive loads, such as incandescent lights or electric heating elements, the power factor is 1.0. Sometimes capacitors are used to improve the power factor.

For AC circuits, Ohm's law is similar to formula 10.1.

$$I = \frac{V}{Z} \qquad\qquad 10.3$$

Power in AC circuits is similar to formula 10.2 but with the power factor added.

$$W = VI(\text{pf}) \qquad\qquad 10.4$$

Example 10.1

Find the current in a 120 V circuit serving nine 150 W downlights.

Using formula 10.4 and rearranging,

$$I = \frac{W}{V(\text{pf})}$$

Because the power factor is 1.0 in this case,

$$I = \frac{(9)(150 \text{ W})}{(120 \text{ V})(1.0)}$$
$$= 11.25 \text{ A}$$

To determine the energy used in a system, simply multiply power times time, or

$$E = Wt \qquad\qquad 10.5$$

Energy can be measured in watt-hours but is more commonly measured in thousands of watt-hours, or kilowatt-hours, kWh.

There are two basic types of electric circuits: series and parallel. These are shown diagrammatically in Fig. 10.3. In *series circuits*, the loads (represented in the diagrams by zig-zag lines) are placed in the circuit one after another. The current, I, remains constant throughout the circuit, but the voltage potential changes, or drops, across each load. In a *parallel circuit*, the loads are placed between the same two points. The voltage remains the same, but the current is different across each load. However, adding up the individual currents results in a total current that is applied to the circuit as a whole.

Notice that if one load is removed in a series circuit (a lightbulb burned out) then the entire circuit is opened. This fact and the problem of voltage drops across individual loads are two reasons series circuits are not used in building construction.

Materials

The basic material of electrical systems is the conductor. Sizes of conductors are based on American Wire Gauge (AWG) and thousand circular mil (MCM) designations. AWG sizes range from 16 gauge to 0000 (4/0) gauge. Actual

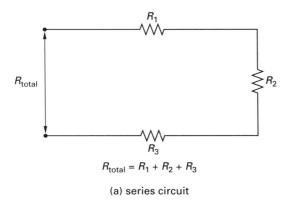

$$R_{total} = R_1 + R_2 + R_3$$

(a) series circuit

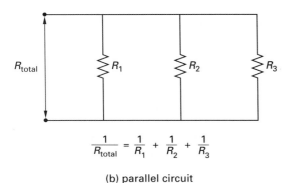

$$\frac{1}{R_{total}} = \frac{1}{R_1} + \frac{1}{R_2} + \frac{1}{R_3}$$

(b) parallel circuit

Figure 10.3 Basic Circuit Types

size of the conductor increases as the number designation decreases, so 16 gauge is the smallest at a 0.0508 in diameter, and 4/0 is the largest at a 0.460 in diameter. A single insulated conductor no. 6 AWG or larger, or several conductors assembled into a single unit, is referred to as *cable*. Conductors no. 8 AWG or smaller are called *wire*.

Cable larger than 4/0 gauge is designated with the MCM nomenclature. A circular mil is a derived area measurement representing the square of the cable diameter in thousandths of an inch (mils). The MCM cable sizes are 250, 300, 400, and 500. The current-carrying capacity (or *ampacity*) of a conductor is dependent on its size, the type of insulation around it, and the surrounding temperature.

There are many different types of conductors and insulating materials. The two basic conductors are copper and aluminum. Aluminum conductors must be larger than copper ones to carry the same amperage, but they are lighter and generally have a lower installation cost in large sizes. Copper is more cost effective in small- and medium-sized wire and cable. Aluminum conductors require special care in installation because joints can loosen and oxides can form, causing resistance and overheating. Because of these potential problems, aluminum is limited to primary circuits that are installed by skilled workers.

Some of the common cables, based on the type of insulation they use, are as follows.

Nonmetallic sheathed cable, also known by the trade name Romex™, consists of two or more plastic-insulated conductors and ground wire surrounded by a moisture-resistant plastic jacket. This type of cable can be used in wood-frame residential buildings and those not exceeding three stories, as long as it is used with wood studs and protected from damage by being concealed behind walls and ceilings. Because it does not require conduit, it is inexpensive to install.

Flexible metal-clad cable, also known by the trade name BX™, consists of two or more plastic-insulated conductors encased in a continuous spiral-wound strip of steel tape. It is often used in remodeling work because it can be pulled through existing spaces within a building.

The most common type of wire and cable is a single conductor covered with thermoplastic or rubber insulation. Several different types are available for different voltages and service conditions. This cable must be placed in metal conduit or other approved types of carriers.

When high currents are involved, the use of very large cables becomes expensive and awkward to tap into for transformers and branch circuits. Instead, rectangular bars of copper, called busbars, are used. When several busbars are assembled in a special metal housing, it is called a *busduct* or *busway*.

For commercial construction and large residential construction, individual conductors must be placed in metal conduit or other approved carriers. Conduit supports and protects the wiring, serves as a system ground, and protects surrounding construction from fire if the wire overheats or shorts.

There are three types of rigid steel conduit: rigid steel conduit, intermediate metal conduit, and electric metallic tubing. *Rigid steel conduit* is the heaviest and is connected to junction boxes and other devices with threaded fittings. *Intermediate metal conduit* (IMC) has thinner walls but the same outside diameter as rigid steel conduit. It is also installed with threaded fittings. *Electric metallic tubing* (EMT) is the lightest of the three and is installed with special pressure fittings because it is too thin to thread. It is easier and faster to install but cannot be used in hazardous areas. Flexible metal conduit is also available to minimize vibration transmission from equipment to the structure and for areas where installation of rigid conduit is not possible. It is commonly referred to as *flex*.

The number of conductors that can be placed in a conduit depends on the conductor type, the conductor size, and the size of the conduit. The purpose of limiting the number of conductors is to prevent damage from trying to pull too many conductors through a small space and to control the heat buildup inside the conduit. The National Electrical Code places certain limits on the length, number, and radius of bends in a conduit between pull boxes, to prevent damage to the conductors and make pulling the conductors easier. In most cases, there can be no more than four 90° bends between pull boxes.

Two additional types of power distribution that are often used in office buildings and wherever outlets must be changed frequently are underfloor raceways and undercarpet cable.

There are two varieties of underfloor raceways: underfloor ducts and cellular metal floors. *Underfloor ducts* are proprietary steel raceways cast into a concrete floor at regular spacing, usually about 4, 5, or 6 ft (1200, 1500, or 1800). Feeder ducts run perpendicular to the distribution ducts and carry power and signal wiring from the main electrical closet to each distribution duct. Preset inserts are placed along the distribution ducts at close intervals, and these are tapped wherever an outlet or telephone connection is required.

Cellular metal floors use the same basic concept but are actually part of the structural floor. They are essentially metal decking designed for use as cable raceways. Cellular floors differ from underfloor ducts in that the cells are closer together. Alternating cells can be used for power, telephone, and signal cabling. Cellular floors also have preset locations that can be easily tapped to install electrical outlets, telephone jacks, and computer outlets.

Under-carpet wiring is thin, flat, protected wire that can be laid under carpet without protruding. Cable for both 120 V circuits and telephone and signal lines is available. However, it must be used with carpet tiles so that it is readily accessible. Under-carpet wiring connects pedestals in the middle of the room that contain electrical outlets and telephone connections to junction boxes in nearby walls, where the wiring is connected to standard conduit-enclosed cable.

POWER SUPPLY

The most common form of electrical energy used in buildings is alternating current (AC). Direct current (DC) is used for some types of elevator motors and for low-voltage applications such as signal systems, controls, and similar equipment. Electricity is supplied by the local power company and distributed as described in the following sections. For emergency power, generators and batteries are used. These systems are also described in a later section.

Primary Service

Electrical service is provided by the utility company at the property line. It is the owner's responsibility to install and pay for wiring, metering, transformers, and distribution beyond that point, although most utility companies will, for a charge, extend the power supply from the line to the building's service entrance.

Service may be either overhead or underground. Underground service is more expensive but avoids the clutter of overhead wires and protects the lines from snow, wind, and other potentially damaging conditions. When overhead service is provided to smaller projects, the service cable is connected to a weatherhead at least 12 ft (4 m) above the ground. This is part of the conduit that leads to the meter and distribution panel.

There are several voltages that may be supplied to a building. Which one is used depends on what is available from the utility company at the property, what the electrical loads of the building are, and what types of transformers the owner may want to provide. In some cases, it is less expensive for the owner of a large commercial building to buy power from the utility company at higher voltages and supply the transformer than to pay a higher charge for lower voltages.

Power is supplied to buildings in several different voltages. The most common for residences and very small buildings is a 120/240 V, single-phase, three-wire system. It is used where the actual load does not exceed 80 A, although minimum service is considered 100 A. Figure 10.4(a) diagrams this system type, which consists of two hot wires, each carrying 120 V, and one neutral wire. Appliances, such as electric ranges and dryers, that need 240 V use the two hot wires, whereas 120 V service is obtained by tapping one hot wire and the neutral wire.

A system often used for larger buildings is the 120/208 V, three-phase, four-wire system. It is frequently used because it allows use of a variety of electrical loads. This system is shown schematically in Fig. 10.4(b).

For larger buildings, a 277/480 V, three-phase, four-wire system is used. It is the same as the 120/208 V system except for the higher voltages. The advantages to this system include smaller feeders, smaller conduit, and smaller switchgear. This is possible because of the higher voltages used and therefore the smaller currents the equipment has to carry. Buildings with this system have predominantly 277 V fluorescent lighting, which requires smaller wiring. Small, step-down transformers are used where 120 V service is needed for receptacles and other equipment.

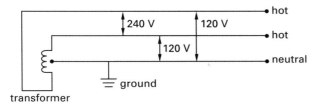

(a) 120/240 V, single-phase, 3-wire system

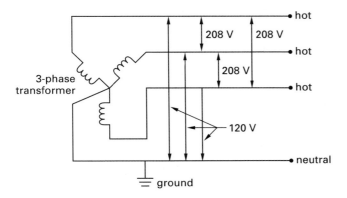

(b) 120/208 V, 3-phase, 4-wire system

Figure 10.4 Electrical Service Types

For very large commercial buildings and factories with a great deal of machinery, 2400/4160 V, three-phase, four-wire systems are available.

Transformers

Transformers are used to change alternating current voltages, either up or down. In most cases, power is supplied to a building at high voltage because the lines can be smaller and there is less voltage drop. The building owner must supply the transformer to provide one of the types of service described in the previous section. For residences and very small buildings, the utility company usually supplies step-down transformers to serve a small group of houses with 120/240 V service.

Transformers are rated on their kilovolt-amperes capacity (kVa) and described by their type, phase, voltage, method of cooling, insulation, and noise level. For cooling, transformers are either dry, oil filled, or silicone filled. When there is a possibility of fire, as with oil-filled transformers, the equipment must be placed in a fire-resistive transformer vault room. Because transformers generate a great deal of heat, the vault must be at an exterior wall and vented to the outside. Locating a transformer vault near the exterior wall also makes it easier to move the large, heavy device into place and replace it when necessary.

Metering and Load Control

Metering must be provided at a building's service entrance to allow the utility company to charge for energy used. For residences and other single-use buildings, one meter is typically used. For multiple-occupancy buildings, such as shopping centers and apartments, banks of meters are installed so that each unit can be metered independently. One of the reasons for this is to encourage energy conservation, because every tenant must pay for the energy used.

The most common meter is the watt-hour meter. This registers the use of power over time in kilowatt-hours. The meter is placed on the incoming power line in front of any master service switch so that it can operate continuously.

In order to encourage the conservation of energy and pay for the cost of providing power to customers, many energy companies levy energy charges based not only on the total amount of energy used (kilowatt-hours) but also on peak demand. The reasoning behind this is that if a customer uses a nominal amount of energy (power multiplied by time) over a billing period, but uses a great deal of energy only at certain times, the utility company must still provide facilities to supply the peak demand. The total amount of energy used can be relatively low even though the utility company must be ready to supply the occasional maximum amount.

To compensate for this, most utility companies make charges based on the maximum interval demand, the average amount of energy used in a certain time period, such as 15 min or 30 min. The ratio of the average power used to the maximum power demand is called the *load factor*. A low load factor implies an inefficient use of energy and a high demand charge.

From the user's standpoint, a building's electrical system should be designed to avoid peak electricity use. There are several methods of doing this, which are called *load control*. Other terms used include *load shedding*, *peak demand control*, and *peak load regulation*.

Manual and automatic devices are available to accomplish load control. With automatic load shedding, for example, a device automatically monitors the use of energy, and when a certain point is reached the device shuts off nonessential electrical loads. Such loads can include nonessential lighting, water heating, and space heating. Load scheduling can also be used if the energy consumption characteristics of the building are known. With this method, different electrical loads are automatically scheduled to operate at different times to control the peak demand.

Primary Distribution

For large buildings, a central electrical distribution center is required. Called the *switchgear*, this center consists of an assembly of switches, circuit breakers, and cables or bus-ducts that distribute power to other parts of the building. A transformer and metering are also often included with the switchgear. The equipment is usually housed in a separate room, depending on the type of transformer used and the security required.

Power coming through the meter and transformer is split into separate circuits, each with a master switch and circuit breaker to protect the circuit from overload or short circuits. From the switchgear, power is distributed to substations for further transforming and distribution, to motor control centers, to elevator controls, and to individual panel boxes as part of the secondary distribution system.

Secondary Distribution and Branch Circuits

Power from the main switchgear is distributed to individual panelboards where it is further split into individual branch circuits used for power, lighting, motors, and other electrical needs of the building. Secondary distribution involves the typical lower voltages of 120 V, 240 V, and 277 V. Secondary distribution is made with wires in conduit, various types of underfloor raceways, or flexible cabling systems.

Each circuit is protected with circuit breakers in the panelboard. These are rated for the amperage the circuit is expected to carry, ranging from 15 A and 20 A circuits for general lighting and power circuits to 100 amps or more for main disconnect switches or large loads.

There are two important kinds of protection for electric circuits: grounding and ground-fault protection. All new construction is grounded with a separate wire in addition to the hot and neutral wiring of each circuit. One of the primary purposes for providing a ground is to prevent a dangerous shock if someone touches an appliance with a short circuit and simultaneously touches a ground path such as a water pipe. The ground provides a path for the fault. The ground wire and the neutral wire are both grounded at the building service entrance to either a grounding electrode buried in the earth or in the foundation, or to a buried cold-water pipe.

A ground fault, however, can create other problems, because the current required to trip a circuit breaker is high and small current leaks can continue unnoticed until someone receives a dangerous shock or a fire develops. A *ground fault interrupter* (GFI) is a device that detects small current leaks and disconnects the hot wire to the circuit or appliance. GFIs can be part of a circuit breaker or installed as an outlet. They are required for outdoor outlets and in kitchens and bathrooms as well as other locations specified in the National Electrical Code. They are recommended on appliance circuits as well.

Wiring Devices

Wiring devices include those normally installed in outlet boxes such as receptacles, switches, and pilot lights. The most common receptacle for normal power distribution is the *duplex receptacle*, or *duplex outlet* as it is often called. It is also called a *convenience outlet* because it is designed for normal use by building occupants for portable lamps, clocks, electronic devices, appliances, and similar devices that operate at 120 V. Special receptacles are used for appliances and equipment that require higher voltages, such as electric ranges, dryers, and large copy machines. In addition, GFI outlets are provided for safety as described in the previous sections. These are sometimes called *ground-fault circuit interrupters* (GFCI). Electrical devices that are not plugged in but are connected to the building circuits in junction boxes are said to be *hard wired*.

A convenience outlet has two holes to receive the prongs of the plug supplying power and a third hole for the grounding prong. The grounding pole is connected to a green wire that is part of the wiring in the conduit. Alternately, the grounding pole of the outlet may be connected to the metal conduit that acts as the system ground. *Split-wired receptacles* can be installed so that one outlet is always energized but the other is controlled from a wall switch. This allows floor lamps and other devices that normally plug in to be controlled with a switch.

Outlets are normally mounted vertically from 12 in to 18 in (305 to 455) above the floor, although a minimum 15 in (380) mounting height is required for forward reach accessibility for persons in wheelchairs. In residential construction, outlets must be located no more than 12 ft (3660) apart, or such that no point is more than 6 ft (1830) from an outlet.

Most residential convenience outlet circuits are 15 A, but at least two 20 A appliance circuits must be provided for the kitchen, pantry, breakfast room, and dining room. The outlets serving the kitchen countertop area must be supplied from at least two different circuits, with no more than four outlets per 20 A circuit. The outlets in the kitchen must be located so that no point on a wall above a countertop is more than 24 in (610) from an outlet. There must also be at least one outlet between appliances and the sink so that no cord has to be draped across an appliance or the sink. Outlets within 6 ft (1830) of a sink must be of the GFCI type.

Switches are used to control power to lights, receptacles, and other electric devices. The most common is the toggle type, which simply switches on or off with a toggle, or lever. Other types that perform the same function include the rocker, push, and key. When one switch controls a light or other device it is called a *two-way switch*. When two switches are used to control the same device they are *three-way switches. Four-way switches* are used to control the same device from three or more locations. Other types of switches include dimmer switches, automatic timer switches, and programmable switches.

Low-voltage switching is also available. With this system, individual switches are operated on a 24 V circuit and control relays that provide the 120 V switching. Although more costly to install, low-voltage switching has several advantages over line-voltage switching. First, the same light or device can be controlled from several positions that are remote from each other. Second, a central control station can be set up to monitor the entire system and override local control. For example, pilot lights at the central station in a house can show which lights are on and which are off and allow switching from that station. Third, control devices such as timers and energy management systems can be wired to override local control. Finally, for large installations that require flexibility of control, low-voltage wiring and switches are a less expensive alternative to installing the same scope of line-voltage wiring and devices.

Emergency Power Supply

Emergency power is required for electrical systems that relate to the safety of occupants or community needs. This includes systems for exit lighting, alarms, elevators, telephones, and fire pumps, as well as equipment that could have life-threatening implications if power were lost, such as some medical equipment. Standby power, on the other hand, provides electricity for functions that the building owner requires to avoid an interruption in business. This often includes computer operations or industrial processes.

Emergency power is supplied by generators or batteries. Generators provide the capacity for large electrical loads for long periods of time, limited only by the available emergency fuel supply. However, they are expensive to install and must be maintained and checked periodically for proper operation.

Batteries are used for smaller loads for shorter time periods. Emergency lighting often consists of separate lighting packs with their own batteries, placed in strategic locations such as corridors and stairways. Large installations have racks of batteries in separate rooms connected to lights and other equipment with wiring.

LIGHTING FUNDAMENTALS

Light and Vision

Light is defined as visually evaluated radiant energy. Visible light is a form of electromagnetic radiation with wavelengths that range from about 400 nm (10^{-9} m) for violet light to about 700 nm for red light. White light is produced

when a source emits approximately equal quantities of energy over the entire visible spectrum.

When light strikes a surface it can be transmitted, reflected, or absorbed. If a material is transparent, such as window glass, most of the light is transmitted. The ratio of the total transmitted light to the total incident light is the *transmittance* or *coefficient of transmission*, expressed as a percentage. Clear glass has a transmittance of about 85%, whereas frosted glass has a transmittance between 70% and 85%. The remainder of the light is either reflected or absorbed. Material that allows the transmittance of light but not of a clear image is said to be *translucent*. In clear materials, light is *refracted*, or bent slightly, as it passes through the material. Refraction is the principle on which lenses are made, so light passing through the lens is bent toward the thicker part of the lens.

If a material allows no light to pass through, it is opaque, and all incident light is either reflected or absorbed. A flat, black material, for example, absorbs most of the incident light. A white material reflects most of the incident light. As with transmittance, the ratio of the total reflected light to the total incident light is the *reflectance* or *reflectance coefficient*, also expressed as a percentage. How light is reflected depends on the finish of the material it is striking. As shown in Fig. 10.5, reflection is specular, combined specular and diffuse, or diffuse. *Specular reflection* results from a smooth, polished surface, such as a mirror. The angle of incidence equals the angle of reflection. *Diffuse reflection* results from a uniformly rough surface. It appears uniformly bright, and the image of the source cannot be seen. *Combined specular and diffuse reflection* makes surfaces appear to be brighter at the point where the source is shining than in the surrounding areas.

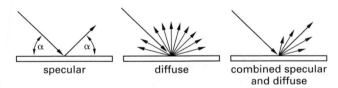

Figure 10.5 Light Reflections

Light is perceived through the eye and with the brain. In the process of seeing, light enters the eye through the pupil. See Fig. 10.6. The amount of light entering the eye is controlled by the iris. The lens focuses the image (upside down) on the retina, where the light stimulates cells that send messages to the brain for interpretation. The retina contains two types of cells: cones and rods. *Cones* are cells located near the fovea, or central portion of the retina. They are shaped like cones and are extremely sensitive to detail and color. However, they are located within only a 2° cone of vision around the line of sight. On the remainder of the retina are the cells

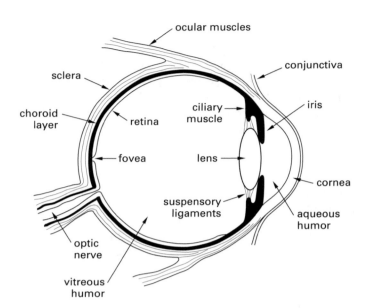

Figure 10.6 Human Eye

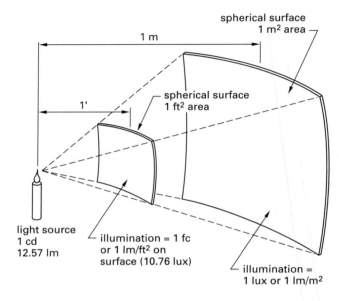

If surface has a reflectance of 50%,
then its reflected brightness is
1/2 footlambert (1.7 cd/m²).

Figure 10.7 Relationship of Light Source and
Illumination

shaped like rods. *Rods* are extremely sensitive to light and motion. On the other hand, they are not as good as the cones at discriminating color or detail. That is why in dim light people lose their sense of color vision; objects appear in varying shades of gray.

Definitions

Examinees should be familiar with the relationships between several illumination definitions. Figure 10.7 shows these units of light.

Candlepower: the unit of luminous intensity approximately equal to the horizontal light output from an ordinary wax candle. In the SI system of measurement, this unit is the *candela*.

Illuminance: the density of luminous flux incident on a surface in lumens per unit area. One lumen uniformly incident on 1 ft² of area produces an illuminance of 1 fc. In SI units, 1 lumen incident on 1 m² of spherical surface 1 m away produces 1 lux of illuminance.

Lumen: the unit of luminous flux equal to the flux in a unit solid angle of 1 steradian from a uniform point source of 1 candlepower. On a unit sphere (1 ft radius), an area of 1 ft² will subtend an angle of 1 steradian. Because the area of a unit sphere is 4π, a source of 1 candlepower produces 12.57 lm.

Luminance: the luminous flux per unit of projected (apparent) area and unit solid angle leaving a surface, either reflected or transmitted. By definition, the unit (in SI measurements now commonly used) is the candela per square meter (cd/m²), also called the *nit*. In the older

inch-pound system, the unit is the *footlambert*, where 1 footlambert is $1/\pi$ candlepower per square foot. Luminance takes into account the reflectance and transmittance properties of materials and the directions in which they are viewed. Thus, 100 lux striking a 1 m² surface with 50% reflectance would result in a luminance of 50 candelas per square meter. (In inch-pounds units, 100 fc striking a surface with 50% reflectance would result in a luminance of 50 footlamberts.) Luminance is sometimes called *brightness*, although brightness includes the physiological sensation of the adaptation of the eye, whereas luminance is the measurable state of object luminosity.

Luminous intensity: the solid angular flux density in a given direction measured in candlepower or candelas

Light Levels

Good lighting design involves providing both the proper quantity and proper quality of light to perform a task. This section discusses quantity; the next section discusses quality. Different visual tasks under different conditions require varying levels of illumination. The variables involved include the nature of the task itself, the age of the person performing the task, the reflectances of the room, and the demand for speed and accuracy in performing the task.

The Illuminating Engineering Society (IES) has established a method for determining a range of illumination levels in footcandles (lux) appropriate to particular design conditions. Various areas and activities are assigned an illuminance category, and these categories are used with other variables to establish the recommended task and background illuminances.

In order to conserve energy, most codes require designers to develop a power budget for a project based on the building type and to design lighting systems within that budget. This most often requires that the recommended illumination level be provided for task areas only and that general background illumination be less, about a third of the task level. Further, noncritical areas such as corridors are usually provided with less light than are the background levels.

Design Considerations

The quality of light is just as important as the amount of light provided. Important considerations are glare, contrast, uniformity, and color.

There are two types of glare: direct and reflected. *Direct glare* results when a light source in the field of vision causes discomfort and interference with the visual task. Not all visible light sources cause direct glare problems. The extent of the problem depends on the brightness of the source, its position, the background illumination, and the adaptation of the eye to the environment.

In order to evaluate the direct glare problem, the visual comfort probability (VCP) factor was developed. This factor is the percentage of normal observers who may be expected to experience visual comfort in a particular environment with a particular lighting situation. Although the calculations are complex, some simplifications are made, and many manufacturers publish the VCP rating for their light fixtures when it is used under certain conditions.

For most situations, the critical zone for direct glare is in the area above a 45° angle from the light source. See Fig. 10.8. This is because the field of vision (when looking straight ahead) includes an area approximately 45° above a horizontal line. Many direct glare problems can be solved by using a luminaire with a 45° cutoff angle or by moving the luminaire out of the offending field of view.

Reflected glare occurs when a light source is reflected from a viewed surface into the eye. If it interferes with the viewing task, it is also called *veiling reflection*. The effect of reflected glare is to decrease the contrast of the task and its background. For example, a strong light on paper with pencil writing can bounce off the relatively reflective graphite, making it almost as bright as the paper, and effectively obscuring the writing.

Veiling reflections are a complex interaction of light source and brightness, position of the task, reflectivity of the task, and position of the eye. One of the simplest ways to correct veiling reflections is to move the position of the task or the light source. Because the angle of incidence is equal to the

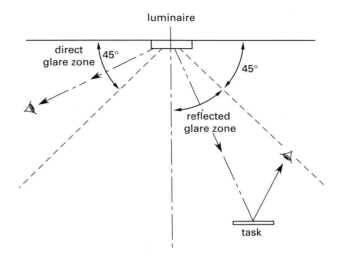

Figure 10.8 Glare Zones

angle of reflection, this is easy to calculate. It is not always possible to calculate, however, because the exact use of a room and its furniture arrangement are not always known. Another approach is to provide general background illumination and specific task lighting, the position of which can be controlled by the user.

Contrast is the difference in illumination level between one point and nearby points. Because contrast is the means by which people see, it is vital to the quality of an environment. A printed word on a page is only visible because it contrasts with the brightness of the surrounding paper. However, too much contrast can be detrimental. It is difficult to see fine detail on a small, dark object when the object is viewed against a bright background because the eye has adapted (the iris of the eye is smaller) to the brighter background and cannot admit enough light to see the darker object. The eye adapts by opening and closing the iris, but this causes eye strain and fatigue.

In most situations, brightness ratios should be limited to $1:\frac{1}{3}$ between the task and adjacent surroundings, to $1:\frac{1}{5}$ between the task and more remote darker surfaces, and to $1:10$ between the task and more remote lighter surfaces.

Uniformity of lighting affects a person's perception of a space as being comfortable and pleasant. Complete uniformity is usually not desirable except for certain tasks like drafting or machine shop work. Because people see by contrast, some amount of shade and shadow provides highlight and interest to a space.

Color in lighting is an interaction between the color of the light source (lamp or daylighting) and the color of the objects that reflect the light. Color in lighting is a complex subject but one that can affect people's comfort and impressions of an environment. For example, most people think of reds and yellows as "warm" colors and greens and blues as "cool" colors. Colors of light sources will be discussed in the next section, and the use of color in lighting design is covered in the following section.

LIGHT SOURCES

In addition to daylight, there are three types of light sources: incandescent, fluorescent, and high-intensity discharge. Some of the considerations that influence the type of light source used are its color rendition characteristics, initial cost, operating cost, efficacy, size, operating life, and ability to control its output from a luminaire. *Efficacy* is the ratio of luminous flux emitted to the total power input to the source and is measured in lumens per watt. It is an important measure of the energy efficiency of a light source. The amount of heat generated by a light source is also an important selection consideration because waste heat

usually needs to be removed or compensated for with the air conditioning system, which can add to the total energy load of a building. Some characteristics of common light sources are shown in Table 10.1. These are described in more detail in the following sections.

Some types of incandescent and fluorescent lamps that have traditionally been used in architectural applications are no longer manufactured in or imported into the United States. This is a result of the Energy Policy Act (EPACT) of 1992, which, among other things, set minimum standards for energy efficiency of these two sources of light. The deadline for final implementation was October 31, 1995. After this date certain classes of incandescent and fluorescent lamps had to meet minimum efficacy standards based on their wattage (minimum lumens per watt). These are described in more detail in the following two sections.

Table 10.1
Characteristics of Some Common Light Sources

lamp description	power (W)	initial luminous flux (lm)	color temp. (K)	CRI	approx. lamp life (hours)
incandescent					
A-19	100	1750	2500	100	750
old R-30	75	850	2500	100	2000
50PAR30	50	1100	2750	100	2500
old PAR 38	150	1730	2500	100	2000
fluorescent					
old F40T12CW	40	3150	4300	62	20,000
F32T8	32	2125	4100[1]	75	20,000
compact fluorescent	13	900	3000[1]	85	10,000
tungsten-halogen					
T-H PAR	150	2900	3000	100	3000
T-H PAR	250	5000	3000	100	2000
high-intensity discharge					
mercury-vapor					
100 M-V	100	4400	5500	40	24,000
metal-halide					
70 M-H	70	4900	3000	75	6000
150 M-H	150	12,000	4300	85	6000
high-pressure sodium					
HPS 100	100	5200	2800	70+	10,000

[1]Color temperatures from 2700K to 5000K are available in many fluorescent lamps.

Note: All figures are approximate and are for general comparison purposes only. Exact values vary with manufacturer.

Incandescent

An *incandescent* lamp consists of a tungsten filament placed within a sealed bulb containing an inert gas. When electricity is passed through the lamp the filament glows, producing light. Incandescent lamps are produced in a wide variety of shapes, sizes, and wattages for different applications. Some of the more common shapes are shown in Fig. 10.9. A typical designation of an incandescent lamp is a letter followed by a number, such as A-21. This means that the shape is the standard arbitrary shape and the diameter of the bulb at its widest point is $^{21}/_8$ in, or $^{25}/_8$ in.

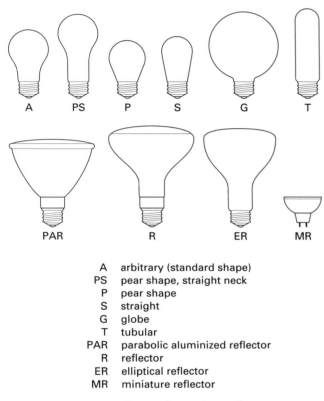

A	arbitrary (standard shape)
PS	pear shape, straight neck
P	pear shape
S	straight
G	globe
T	tubular
PAR	parabolic aluminized reflector
R	reflector
ER	elliptical reflector
MR	miniature reflector

Figure 10.9 Incandescent Lamp Shapes

Incandescent lamps are inexpensive, compact, easy to dim, can be repeatedly started without a decrease in lamp life, and have a warm color rendition. In addition, their light output can be easily controlled with reflectors and lenses. Their disadvantages include low efficacy, short lamp life, and high heat output. The combination of low efficacy and heat production makes incandescent lamps undesirable for large, energy-efficient installations. For example, a standard 150 W lamp produces less than 20 lm per watt, whereas a 40 W cool white fluorescent lamp has an efficacy of about 80 lm/W with much less heat output.

Another type of incandescent lamp is the *tungsten halogen*. Light is produced by the incandescence of the filament, but there is a small amount of a halogen, such as iodine or bromine, in the bulb with the inert gas. Through a recurring cycle, part of the tungsten filament is burned off as the lamp operates, but it mixes with the halogen and is redeposited on the filament instead of on the wall of the bulb as in standard incandescent lamps. This results in longer bulb life, low lumen depreciation over the life of the bulb, and a more uniform light color. Because the filament burns under higher pressure and temperature, the bulb is made from quartz and is much smaller than standard incandescent lamps.

Reflector (R) and *parabolic aluminized reflector* (PAR) lamps contain a reflective coating built into the lamp. This increases the efficiency of the lamp and allows more precise beam control. Both are available in *flood* (wide) and *narrow* (spot) beam dispersal patterns. PAR lamps are made with heavier glass and are also suitable for outdoor use.

Elliptical reflector (ER) lamps are an improved version of R lamps. They provide a more efficient throw of light from a fixture by focusing the light beam at a point slightly in front of the lamp before it spreads out. Its spread is slightly smaller than that of an R lamp. The design is used for downlights with deep baffles or with small openings so that less of the light's output is trapped in the fixture.

Low-voltage miniature reflector (MR) lamps are small tungsten-halogen lamps that are available in a wide variety of wattages (20 W to 75 W) and beam spreads. The regenerative halogen cycle provides consistently high output and a lamp life of from 2000 hr to 3000 hr. Typical color temperatures range from 2000K to 3400K, which makes many of them whiter than standard incandescent lights. MR lamps are available as MR-11 and MR-16. The numbers designate the diameter of the reflector in eighths of an inch. Therefore, an MR-16 is 2 in (50) across. MR-16 lamps are also available for use in 120 V circuits where they can be screwed directly into a socket without the need for a transformer.

Effective October 31, 1995, the Energy Policy Act of 1992 prohibits the manufacture or importation of several types of incandescent lamps that do not meet minimum energy standards. These include all medium-base PAR and R lamps of 40 W and higher. In place of these, some types of ER lamps and lower-wattage lamps can be used. Low-voltage and tungsten-halogen lamps can also be used in place of the old lamps.

Fluorescent

Fluorescent lamps contain a mixture of an inert gas and low-pressure mercury vapor. When the lamp is energized, a mercury arc is formed that creates ultraviolet light. This invisible light, in turn, strikes the phosphor-coated bulb, causing the bulb to fluoresce and produce visible light. The three types of fluorescent lamps are preheat, rapid start, and instant start, according to their circuitry. Preheat lamps have been supplanted by rapid-start types. These lamps maintain a constant low current in the cathode that allows them to start within about 2 sec. Instant-start lamps use a voltage high enough to start the arc in the tube directly without pre-heating of the cathode.

All fluorescent lamps have a *ballast*, a device that supplies the proper starting and operating voltages to the lamp and limits the current. Because ballasts produce noise and heat, their correct selection is critical for a successful lighting design. Ballasts are sound rated by letters. Class A is appropriate for spaces with the lowest ambient noise levels, and Class F is suitable only for noisy environments.

In recent years special ballasts have been developed to overcome some of the problems of standard ballasts and to meet more stringent energy conservation requirements. The most notable is the electronic ballast. This device produces high-frequency alternating current (from 25 kHz to 30 kHz as contrasted with 60 Hz of a standard ballast). Advantages include lower power consumption, silent operation, ease of dimming, and reduced flicker of the lamp.

Lamps are produced in tubular shapes. They are normally straight, but U-shaped and circular lamps are also produced. They are designated according to their type, wattage, diameter, color, and method of starting. Thus, F40T12WW/RS describes a fluorescent lamp, 40 W, tubular, $^{12}/_8$ in in diameter ($1^1/_2$ in [38]), warm white color, with a rapid start circuit. Like incandescent lamps, size is designated in eighths of an inch. A T8 lamp has a 1 in (25.4) diameter, for example. Fluorescent lamps come in a variety of lengths, 4 ft being the most common. 2, 3, and 8 ft lengths are also available as well as special U-shaped sizes. Compact fluorescent (CF) lamps have either a T-4 (10 mm) or T-5 (15 mm) glass envelope bent into a U shape or double U shape and mounted on a special base that houses the ballast and allows the lamp to be screwed into existing incandescent luminaires. Other CF lamps require luminaires specifically designed for them.

In the past, one of the objections to fluorescent lighting was that it was too "cold." Actually, lamps are available in a wide range of color temperatures, ranging from a "cool" FL/D (daylight) lamp of 6500K color temperature to a WWD (warm white deluxe) with a color temperature of 2800K, which has a large percentage of red in its spectral output.

Fluorescent lamps have a high efficacy (about 80 lm/W), relatively low initial cost, and long life. They come in a variety of color temperatures. They can also be dimmed, although fluorescent lamp dimmers are more expensive than their incandescent counterparts. Because fluorescent lamps are larger than incandescents, it is more difficult to

control them precisely, so they are usually more suitable for general illumination. However, with developments of smaller and brighter compact fluorescent lamps, several manufacturers now produce downlights with reflector designs for compact fluorescents that can replace traditional incandescent downlights.

The Energy Policy Act of 1992 prohibits the manufacture or importation of several types of fluorescent lamps that do not meet minimum energy standards. These include the standard F40T12 lamp, U-shaped lamps, and other full-wattage lamps. The F40T12 lamp has been replaced with a 32 W, T-8 lamp. This lamp has a higher efficacy and better color rendering than the old lamp. However, it requires an electronic ballast, so retrofitted fixtures have to include this as well as lamp replacement. The new T-8 fixtures also include relatively new triphosphor coatings, which give the lamps improved color rendering.

High-Intensity Discharge

High-intensity discharge (HID) lamps include mercury vapor, metal halide, and high- and low-pressure sodium. In the mercury vapor lamp, an electric arc is passed through high-pressure mercury vapor, which causes it to produce both ultraviolet light and visible light, primarily in the blue-green band. For improved color rendition, various phosphors can be applied to the inside of the lamp to produce more light in the yellow and red bands. Mercury lamps have a moderately high efficacy, in the range of 30 lm/W to 50 lm/W, depending on voltage and the type of color correction included.

Metal halide lamps, which produce about 50 lm/W to 100 lm/W, are similar to mercury lamps except that halides of metals are added to the arc tube. This increases the efficacy and improves color rendition but decreases lamp life.

High-pressure sodium (HPS) lamps produce light by passing an electric arc through hot sodium vapor. The arc tube must be made of a special ceramic material to resist attack by the hot sodium. High-pressure sodium lamps have efficacies from 80 lm/W to 140 lm/W, making them one of the most efficient lamps available. Color rendition is also acceptable for a wide variety of applications.

Low-pressure sodium lamps have an even higher efficacy, about 150 lm/W, but produce a monochromatic light of a deep yellow color. Therefore, they are suitable only for uses where color rendition is not important, such as street lighting.

LIGHTING DESIGN

Lighting design is both an art and a science. There must be a sufficient amount of light to perform a task without glare and other discomfort, but the lighting should also enhance the architectural design of the space or landscaping. Lighting must also be designed to minimize energy use, work with the HVAC design, and be cost efficient.

Lighting design is dependent on the fixtures, or luminaires, that are available to provide light. Thousands of different types of luminaires are available from hundreds of manufacturers, and each uses a different lamp in its own proprietary fixture to satisfy a wide range of needs. One of the basic elements of every luminaire is the way it delivers light to the space. This is shown graphically with a candlepower distribution curve, which shows how much light is output at all angles from the luminaire. A typical curve is shown in Fig. 10.10. In this example only one curve is shown for a downlight luminaire where the distribution is the same at all angles to the fixture. In contrast, a rectangular fluorescent luminaire typically distributes light differently in the direction parallel to the fixture and perpendicular to the fixture. In this case the candlepower distribution curve graph would have two slightly different curves. In some cases three curves are shown, the third being the distribution at a 45° angle to the fixture.

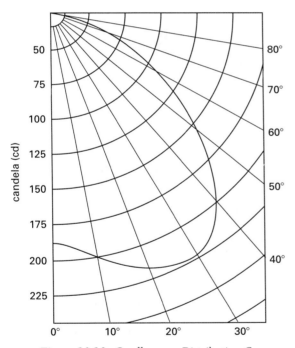

Figure 10.10 Candlepower Distribution Curve

Lighting Systems

There are several general types of lighting systems. The terms used to describe them can refer to individual luminaires or to the entire lighting installation. They are broadly described as direct, semidirect, direct-indirect, semi-indirect, and indirect. See Fig. 10.11.

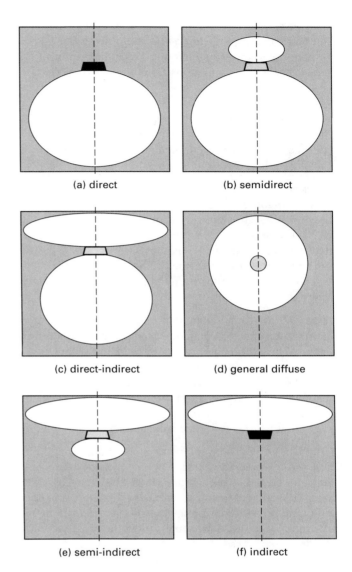

Figure 10.11 Lighting Systems

Direct lighting systems provide all light output on the task. A recessed fluorescent luminaire is an example of direct lighting. *Semidirect lighting* systems put a majority of the light down and a small percentage toward the ceiling. Obviously, fixtures for this type of system must be surface mounted or suspended. *Indirect lighting* systems throw all the light toward a reflective ceiling where it illuminates the room by reflection.

Another common system is *task-ambient lighting*. This approach to lighting design recognizes that it is inefficient to try to illuminate an entire room to the level required for individual tasks scattered around the room. Instead, a general background level of illumination is provided, and separate light fixtures are used to increase the light levels at individual workstations. This can be done with desk lamps, directed spotlights, or more fixtures near the tasks requiring more illumination. In addition to being energy efficient and responding to individual lighting needs, task-ambient systems usually create a more pleasant work environment.

Luminaire Types

Several general types of luminaires are available for lighting design. These are surface-mounted, recessed, suspended, wall-mounted, furniture-mounted, and freestanding fixtures, as well as accessory lighting.

Surface-mounted fixtures are among the most commonly used types for residential and commercial buildings. As the name implies, the luminaire is directly attached to the finished surface of the ceiling, directing all or a majority of the light into the room. These fixtures are used where there is not sufficient space above the ceiling to recess a fixture, or where fixtures are added after the ceiling has been constructed.

Recessed fixtures are used in both residential and commercial construction and include both incandescent and fluorescent lights. When the entire ceiling is made up of lighting, a luminous ceiling is formed. Recessed incandescents can be general downlights for overall illumination or wallwashers, which aim light in one direction only. Continuous, narrow strips of fluorescent luminaires can also be recessed next to a wall to wash the wall uniformly with light.

Luminaires dropped below the level of the ceiling are called *suspended fixtures*. These include direct incandescent or fluorescent fixtures, track lighting, indirect systems, chandeliers, and other types of specialty lights. Suspended mounting is required for indirect lighting systems. The fixture must be located far enough below the ceiling to allow for the proper spread of light to bounce off the surface. Suspended mounting is also used when the architect needs to get the source of light closer to the task area in a high-ceilinged room.

Wall-mounted luminaires can provide indirect, direct-indirect, or direct lighting. For general illumination, sconces direct most of the light toward the ceiling. Various types of adjustable and nonadjustable direct lighting fixtures are available that serve as task lighting, such as bed lamps. Cove lighting can also be mounted on a wall near the ceiling and will indirectly light either the ceiling or the wall depending on how it is shielded.

Furniture-mounted lighting is common with task-ambient systems. Individual lights are built into the furniture above the work surface to provide sufficient task illumination, whereas uplighting is provided by lights either built into the upper portions of the furniture or designed as freestanding elements.

Freestanding light fixtures include items such as floor lamps. These are available in thousands of different styles and sizes and can be custom designed and manufactured if needed. A freestanding light that directs most of its output to the ceiling is a *torchère*. For task-ambient lighting systems, freestanding kiosks contain high-wattage lights that provide indirect lighting by illuminating the ceiling.

Accessory lighting includes table lights, reading lamps, and fixtures that are intended for strictly decorative lighting rather than for task or ambient lighting.

Quality of Light

Lighting design requires the selection of luminaires, lamps, and fixture arrangement to provide the correct quantity of light. However, quality of light is just as important. (The topics of glare and contrast were discussed in a previous section.) Color quality depends on the color of the light source and its interaction with objects.

Every lamp has a characteristic *spectral energy distribution*. This is a measure of the energy output at different wavelengths, or colors. One such energy distribution curve is shown in Fig. 10.12.

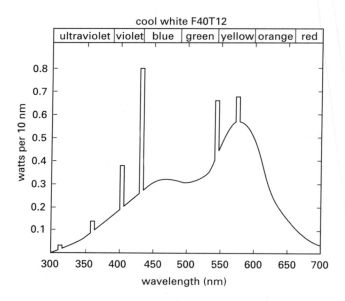

Figure 10.12 Spectral Energy Distribution Curve

Sources are also given a single number rating of their dominant color based on the temperature in degrees Kelvin to which a black-body radiator would have to be heated to produce that color. Lower temperatures, such as 3100K, are relatively warm colors like that of a warm white fluorescent light. Higher color temperatures, such as 5000K to 6000K, are cool colors with a high percentage of blue. A daylight fluorescent lamp has a color temperature of 6500K, for example.

Sources are also rated with a number known as the *color rendering index* (CRI). This is a measure of how closely the perceived colors of an object illuminated with a test source match the colors of the object when it is illuminated with daylight of the same color temperature. The maximum CRI rating is 100, so a light source with a rating of 85 or more is very good.

It is important to know the color characteristics of a light source when designing a lighting system because the light color can affect the colors of objects. For example, using a lamp with a high complement of blue and violet will make finishes and furniture of the warmer colors of red appear dull and washed out. Where color appearance is important, finishes and materials should be selected under the same lighting as will be used in the finished space.

Lighting Calculations

Lighting calculations involve determining the quantity of light in a space. These calculations can be complex because illumination is a result of several variables.

For point sources of light, the illumination on a surface varies directly with the luminous intensity of the source and inversely with the square of the distance between the source and the point. If the surface is perpendicular to the direction of the source, the illumination is determined by the formula

$$E = \frac{I}{d^2} \qquad 10.6$$

For surfaces that are not perpendicular to the source, the inverse square law of formula 10.6 must be adjusted to account for the angle. This relationship is shown in Fig. 10.13. The formula for finding the illumination on the horizontal surface is

$$E = \frac{I \cos \theta}{d^2} \qquad 10.7$$

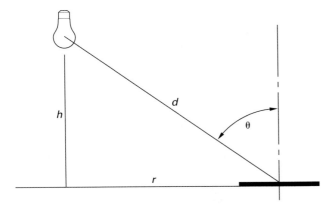

Figure 10.13 Illumination at an Angle to a Point Source

For spaces with several luminaires, other methods are used to calculate the illumination on the work surface or, knowing the desired illumination level, to determine the number of luminaires required. One of the most common is the zonal cavity method. This procedure takes into account several variables. They are

- the lumen output of the lamps used

- the number of lamps in each luminaire

- the efficiency of the luminaire. The rating given a particular luminaire is known as the *coefficient of utilization* (CU) and represents the fact that not all of the lumens produced by the lamps reach the work surface. The CU is a number from 0.01 to 1.00 that depends on the design of the light fixture as well as the characteristics of the room in which the fixture is placed, including the room size and surface reflectances. Manufacturers publish tables that give the CU for each of their luminaires under various conditions.

- the *light loss factor* (LLF). This is a fraction that represents the amount of light that will be lost due to several additional factors. Among these are lamp *lumen depreciation*, which is light loss with age, and *luminaire dirt depreciation*, which is light loss due to accumulated dirt on lamps based on the kind of environment in which they operate. Additional factors are lamp burnout, room surface dirt, operating voltage of the lamps, ambient operating temperature of the lamps, and accumulated dirt on the luminaire.

To calculate the number of luminaires required in a room to maintain a given illumination level, the following formula is used.

number of luminaires =
$$\frac{(\text{footcandles})(\text{area of room})}{(\text{number of lamps})(\text{lumen per lamp})(\text{CU})(\text{LLF})} \qquad 10.8$$

For complex spaces, manual calculation can be time consuming and error prone. Other tools are available. One is the *isolux chart* (sometimes called an *isofootcandle chart*), a diagram showing lines of equal illumination produced by a specific luminaire from a particular manufacturer. The chart is produced either by full-scale mock-ups of the luminaire or by computer simulation. If several fixtures are used, they can be moved around on a floor plan, and the illumination levels can be added to determine the total illumination at any given point.

Another calculation tool commonly used is computer simulation. Lighting design by computer is accurate and fast, and it allows the designer to try many alternatives that would not be possible with manual calculations. In addition, the computer gives more information than is common with manual calculation.

Energy Budgets

Most jurisdictions have code requirements concerning the maximum amount of power that can be consumed in a building for lighting. The maximum amount of power for a particular building type is determined according to certain procedures developed by the Illuminating Engineering Society, and the designer must work within the guidelines so that the total power budget is not exceeded. This allows for flexibility in design while conserving energy. Although the total power budget will vary with building type, a figure of approximately 2.3 W/ft^2 (25 W/m^2) is often considered a maximum.

Emergency Lighting

The IBC, National Electrical Code, and Life Safety Code all include provisions for emergency lighting. Because each jurisdiction differs slightly in its requirements, the local codes in force must be reviewed. Generally, however, all codes require that in the event of a power failure, sufficient lighting be available to safely evacuate building occupants.

Emergency lighting is required in exit stairs and corridors as well as in certain occupancies such as places of assembly, educational facilities, hazardous locations, and other places where occupancy loads exceed a given number. The usual minimum lighting level required is 1 fc (10.8 lux) at the floor level. Illuminated exit signs are also required in many situations.

As discussed in a previous section, the emergency power supply may come from batteries or a central generator connected to a separate emergency power circuit throughout the building.

SIGNAL AND SAFETY ALARM SYSTEMS

Contemporary buildings contain a complex variety of signal and communication systems. These are low-voltage circuits connecting various types of devices that make it possible for the building to function properly and that protect the occupants. In addition to communication systems such as telephone lines, building automation systems control the mechanical, electrical, and security systems from one central station and continuously monitor their operation.

Communication Systems

Communication systems include telephone systems, intercom systems, paging and sound systems, television, closed circuit television (CCTV), and most recently, computer systems, as well as local area networks (LANs) that allow the sharing of data on several computers within one building or in a complex of buildings.

Telephone systems are the most prevalent type of communication system. In most buildings, main telephone lines enter the structure in a main cable and connect to the terminal room where they are split into riser cables. These risers are generally located near the core and connect telephone equipment rooms on each floor. From these equipment rooms the lines branch out to serve individual spaces.

In the past, each floor would have one telephone equipment room that contained relay panels and other equipment. With the proliferation of separate telephone companies in recent years, each tenant space in a large building usually needs its own equipment room. The size of the room is dependent on the type of equipment used and the number of telephone lines connected.

Other types of communication systems are typically wired as the building is constructed. Cabling terminates at electrical boxes in the wall or floor with a jack into which individual equipment can be connected. Most signal cabling is run in metal conduit, such as electrical cable, unless the local building code allows it to be exposed. Conduit protects the cable and prevents it from burning in a fire and giving off dangerous gases.

Security Systems

Security systems include methods for detecting intruders, preventing entry, controlling access to secure areas, and notifying authorities in the event of unauthorized entry or other emergencies. The types of hardware and electronic devices that are used depend on the nature of the threat, the level of security desired, and the amount of money that can be devoted to the system. Following are some of the more common devices with which examinees should be familiar.

Intrusion detection. Security derived from intrusion detection devices can be classified into three types: perimeter protection, area or room protection, and object protection.

Perimeter protection secures the entry points to a space or building. These include doors, windows, skylights, and even ducts, tunnels, and other service entrances. Some of the more common types of perimeter protection are the following.

- *Magnetic contacts* are used on doors and windows to either sound an alarm when the contact is broken (door or window opened) or send a signal to a central monitoring and control station. These can be surface mounted, recessed into the door and frame, or concealed in special hinges.

- *Glass break detectors* sense when a window has been broken or cut by using either metallic foil or a small vibration detector mounted on the glass.

- *Window screens* in which fine wires are embedded can be used to set off an alarm when they are cut or broken.

- *Photoelectric cells* detect when the beam has been broken, by either a door opening or someone's passing through an opening. These can be surface mounted, but they are more secure and look better if provisions are made to recess them in the partition or other construction.

Area or room protection senses when someone is in a room or area within the device's field of coverage. These devices provide the advantage of warning of unauthorized entry when perimeter sensors have not been activated. Area intrusion devices include the following.

- *Photoelectric beams* warn of intrusion by sending a pulsed infrared beam across a space. If the beam is broken it can sound an alarm or send a signal to a monitoring station. Photoelectric beams can be focused in large and small areas alike.

- *Infrared detectors* sense sources of infrared radiation, such as the human body, compared with the normal room radiation. They are unobtrusive, but must have a clear field of view of the area they are protecting.

- *Audio detectors* identify unusual sounds in a space at levels above what is normally encountered. When that level is exceeded an alarm is sounded. Microphones can also be used to continuously monitor all sounds in a space through a speaker at a central monitoring station.

- *Pressure sensors* detect weight on a floor or other surface. Sensor mats can be separate fixtures laid over the existing floor finish or they can be placed under carpet or other building materials.

- *Ultrasonic detectors* emit a very high-frequency sound wave. When this is interrupted by an intruder, an alarm signal is activated. The range of ultrasonic detectors is limited to a space of about 12 ft (3.6 m) in height and 20 ft by 30 ft (6.1 m by 9.1 m) in area.

- *Microwave detectors* sense interruptions in the field of microwave radiation that these detectors emit. Their use is limited in interior construction, however, because the microwave radiation can penetrate most building materials and can be reflected by metal.

Object protection is used to sense movement or tampering with individual objects such as safes, artwork, file cabinets, or other equipment. Capacitance proximity detectors sense touch on metal objects; vibration detectors sense a disturbance of an object; and infrared motion detectors can determine if the space around an object is violated.

Access control. Access to secure areas can be controlled with a number of devices. The simplest is the traditional mechanical lock. High-security locksets are available that provide an additional level of security through the use of key types that are difficult to duplicate, special tumbler mechanisms, and long-throw dead bolts.

Because access and duplication of keys can be a problem even for the most secure mechanical lock, various types of electronic locks are available. These can not only selectively control access better than keys, but they can also monitor who enters and exits a door and record when the access was made.

Card readers are common electronic access control devices. When a valid card is passed through the reader, the plastic card's coded magnetic strip unlocks the door. Card readers can be connected to a central monitoring computer that keeps a log of which person's card was used to open the door and when the door was opened. The computer can be programmed to allow only certain cards to operate certain doors. Operation can be further limited to specific hours during the day and specific days of the week. If a card is lost or stolen, its access code can be quickly and easily removed from the system.

Numbered keypads operate in the same way by unlocking a door when the user enters the correct numerical code. However, numbered keypads do not provide the same flexibility as do magnetic cards. Numbered keypads can also include the keypad and knob or lever handle in one unit. These are not connected to a central station, but they do eliminate the key-control problem of standard locksets.

Card readers and other devices control the operation of one of several types of locking mechanisms. One type is the *electric lock*, which retracts the bolt when activated from the secure side of the door. Unlatching from the inside is done by a button or switch or by mechanical retraction of the bolt with the lever handle. Electric locks require an electric hinge or other power-transfer device to carry the low-voltage wiring from the control device to the door and then to the lock.

Electric strikes are also used. These replace the standard door strike and consist of a movable mechanism that is mortised into the frame. The latch bolt is fixed from the secure side of the door. On activation, the electric strike retracts, allowing the door to be opened. On the inside, the latch bolt can be retracted by mechanical means with the lever handle.

Doors can also be secured with *electromagnetic locks*. When activated, the lock holds the door closed with a powerful magnetic force. Card readers, keypads, buttons, or other devices deactivate the electromagnet. These can be designed to open on activation of a fire alarm or power failure.

New *biometric devices* are now available that can read individual biological features such as the iris or retina of the eye or a handprint, providing a counterfeit-proof method of identification. These devices are expensive but may be worth the cost when a very high level of security is required. Work is continuing on developing commercially available devices that can recognize voiceprints and fingerprints.

Notification systems. When intrusion is detected an alarm signal is triggered. This signal can activate an alarm such as a bell or horn, turn on lights, alert an attendant at a central control station, or be relayed over phone lines to a central security service. Combinations of all three notifications are also possible. If an office building has a central station, a building tenant may be able to connect special lease space security with the central station. When a central station is notified, the alarms are automatically recorded in the system.

Fire Detection and Alarms

There are four basic types of fire detection devices. The first is the *ionization detector*, which responds to products of combustion-ionized particles rather than to smoke. Ionization detectors are not appropriate where fires may produce a lot of smoke but few particles. Because they can detect particles from a smoldering fire before it bursts into flames, these devices are considered early warning detectors.

Photoelectric detectors respond to smoke, which obscures a light beam in the device. These are useful where potential fires may produce a great deal of smoke before bursting into flames.

Rise-of-temperature detectors sense the presence of heat and can be set to trip an alarm when a particular temperature is reached in the room. The major disadvantage is that flames must usually be present before the alarm temperature is reached. By that time it may be too late, because a fire can smolder and produce deadly smoke long before it reaches the flame stage.

There are also flame detectors that respond to infrared or ultraviolet radiation given off by flames. However, like rise-of-temperature detectors, they do not give an early warning of smoldering fires.

In many buildings, a combination of fire-detection devices must be used depending on the particular type of space in which they are placed. For example, an ionization device would not operate properly where air currents or other circumstances would prevent the products of combustion from entering the device.

The building code states the required types and locations of fire detectors. Detectors are required near fire doors, in exit corridors, in individual hotel rooms, in bedrooms, and in places of public assembly. They are also often required in main-supply and return-air ducts. Codes usually require them in other spaces based on a given area coverage.

When activated, fire detectors can be wired to trigger a general audible alarm as well as visual alarm lights for the deaf. They can also activate a central monitoring station or a municipal fire station. In large buildings with a central station, the detection of a fire also activates fire dampers, exhaust systems, the closing of fire doors, and other preventive measures as the alarm is being signaled to fire officials.

SAMPLE QUESTIONS

1. What steps could an architect take to increase the anticipated lighting level of a room if a selected fluorescent luminaire could not be replaced with another having a higher CU?

    A. Change lamp types.
    B. Suggest to the owner that the lamps be replaced often.
    C. Use finishes with a higher reflection value.
    D. all of the above

2. A spotlight shining perpendicular to a wall 15 ft away has a candlepower output of 3500 cd. The wall is painted to a reflectance of 75%. What is the luminance of the wall at the point perpendicular to the direction of light?

    A. 4.9 ftL
    B. 11.7 ftL
    C. 15.56 fc
    D. 55.7 fc

3. What precautions should be taken if aluminum conductors are used in a building?

I. Leads should be cleaned prior to making connections.
II. Special conduit should be specified.
III. Licensed electricians should be required to make the installation.
IV. All joints should be soldered.
V. Larger sizes should be used.

A. III and V

B. I, II, and III

C. I, III, and V

D. II, III, and V

4. Which of the following would an architect be most concerned about when designing the lighting for an office space with computer workstations and standard desks?

I. color-rendering index

II. visual comfort probability

III. veiling reflection

IV. reflected glare

V. task/surrounds brightness ratio

A. II, III, and IV

B. III, IV, and V

C. I, II, IV, and V

D. all of the above

5. High voltages are used in commercial buildings because

A. conductors and conduit can be smaller

B. a wider variety of loads can be accommodated

C. commercial buildings require more power

D. transformers can step down the voltages to whatever is required

6. Which would be the best location for a transformer for a large school building?

A. on the power pole serving the building

B. in a separate room at the exterior wall

C. outside, on a transformer pad close to the main switchgear

D. in a protective shed where power from the utility company enters the property

7. Which of the following would not be appropriate for fire protection in an elementary school?

A. ionization detector

B. temperature-rise detector

C. photoelectric detector

D. none of the above

8. Which of the following units would be used to measure the brightness of daylight coming through a window?

A. footcandles

B. candelas

C. footlamberts

D. candlepower

9. What combination of lighting would an architect probably recommend for a moderate-sized women's clothing store?

A. color-improved mercury lamps with metal halide accent lighting

B. limited natural daylight, warm white deluxe fluorescent for general illumination, and tungsten halogen for accent lighting

C. incandescent general lighting with low-voltage accent lighting on displays

D. daylighting for general illumination and PAR lamps for dressing areas and display lighting

10. Why should high-pressure instead of low-pressure sodium lamps be used in a storage warehouse?

A. They are less expensive.

B. They have a longer lamp life.

C. They can operate at higher, more efficient voltages.

D. They have better color-rendering properties.

ACOUSTICS

Nomenclature

a	coefficient of absorption	n/a
A	total acoustical absorption	sabins
c	velocity of sound	ft/sec (m/s)
f	frequency of sound	Hz (cycles per second)
I	sound intensity	W/cm^2
I_o	minimum sound intensity audible to the average human ear	10^{-16} W/cm^2
IL	sound intensity level	dB
NR	noise reduction	dB
P	acoustic power	W
r	distance from the source	cm
S	area of barrier or component between rooms	ft^2 (m^2)
t	coefficient of transmission	
T	reverberation time	sec
TL	transmission loss	dB
V	room volume	ft^3 (m^3)
w	wavelength	ft (m)
W	power	W

DEFINITIONS

Amplification: the increased intensity of sound by mechanical or electrical means

Articulation index: a measure of speech intelligibility calculated from the number of words read from a selected list that are understood by an audience. A low articulation index (less than 0.15) is desirable for speech privacy, whereas a high articulation index (above 0.6) is desired for good communication.

Attenuation: the reduction of sound

Decibel: 10 times the common logarithm of the ratio of a quantity to a reference quantity of the same kind, such as power, intensity, or energy density. It is often used as the unit of sound intensity according to the following formula.

$$\text{IL} = 10 \log \frac{I}{I_o} \qquad 11.1$$

dBA: the unit of sound intensity measurement that is weighted to account for the response of the human ear to various frequencies

Frequency: the number of pressure fluctuations or cycles occurring in 1 sec, expressed in Hertz (Hz)

Hertz: the unit of frequency; one cycle per second equals 1 Hz

Impact insulation class (IIC): a single-number rating of a floor-ceiling's impact sound transmission performance at various frequencies

Intensity: the amount of sound energy per second across a unit area

Intensity level: 10 times the common logarithm of the ratio of a sound intensity to a reference intensity. See definition of decibel.

Noise: any unwanted sound

Noise criteria (NC): a set of single-number ratings of acceptable background noise corresponding to a set of curves specifying sound pressure levels across octave bands. Noise criteria curves can be used to specify continuous background noise, achieve sound isolation, and evaluate existing noise situations.

Noise insulation class (NIC): a single-number rating of noise reduction

Noise reduction (NR): the arithmetic difference, in decibels, between the intensity levels in two rooms separated by a barrier of a given transmission loss. Noise reduction is dependent on the transmission loss of the barrier, the area of the barrier, and the absorption of the surfaces of the receiving room.

Noise reduction coefficient (NRC): the average sound absorption coefficient to the nearest 0.05, measured at the four one-third octave band center frequencies of 250, 500, 1000, and 2000 Hz

Octave band: a range of frequencies in which the upper frequency is twice that of the lower

Phon: a unit of loudness level of a sound equal to the sound pressure level of a 1000 Hz tone judged to be as loud

Reverberation: the persistence of a sound in a room after the source has stopped producing the sound

Reverberation time: the time it takes the sound level to decrease 60 dB after the source has stopped producing the sound

Sabin: the unit of absorption; theoretically, 1 ft² of surface having an absorption coefficient of 1.00 (1 m² of surface having an absorption of 1.00)

Sabin formula: the formula that relates reverberation time to a room's volume and total acoustical absorption.

$$T = (0.05)\left(\frac{V}{A}\right) \qquad 11.2$$

In SI units, the constant is 0.16 instead of 0.05.

Sound: a small compressional disturbance of equilibrium in an elastic medium, which causes the sensation of hearing

Sound absorption coefficient: the ratio of the sound intensity absorbed by a material to the total intensity reaching the material. Theoretically, 1.00 is the maximum possible value of the sound absorption coefficient.

Sound power: the total sound energy radiated by a source per second, in watts

Sound transmission class (STC): a single-number average over several frequency bands of a barrier's ability to reduce sound. The higher the STC rating, the better the barrier's ability to control sound transmission.

Transmission loss (TL): the difference, in decibels, between the sound power incident on a barrier in a source room and the sound power radiated into a receiving room on the opposite side of the barrier. The transmission loss varies with the frequency being tested.

FUNDAMENTALS OF SOUND AND HUMAN HEARING

Qualities of Sound

Sound has three basic qualities: velocity, frequency, and power.

The *velocity* of sound depends on the medium in which it is traveling and the temperature of the medium. In air at sea level the velocity of sound is approximately 1130 ft/sec (344 m/s). For acoustical purposes in buildings, the temperature effect on velocity is not significant.

Frequency is the number of cycles completed per second; it is measured in Hertz (Hz). One Hz equals one cycle per second.

Frequency and velocity are related by the following formula.

$$f = \frac{c}{w} \qquad 11.3$$

Power is the quality of acoustical energy as measured in watts. Because a point source emits waves in a spherical shape in free space, the sound intensity (watts per unit area) is given by the following formula.

$$I = \frac{P}{4\pi r^2} \qquad 11.4$$

Because 1 ft² equals 930 cm², the formula can be rewritten for English units as

$$I = \frac{P}{(930 \text{ cm}^2)(4\pi r^2)} \qquad 11.5$$

Inverse Square Law

The basic inverse square law is derived from formula 11.5 where sound intensity is inversely proportional to the square of the distance from the source.

$$\frac{I_1}{I_2} = \frac{r_2^2}{r_1^2} \qquad 11.6$$

Sound Intensity

The sensitivity of the human ear covers a vast range (from 10^{-16} W/cm² to 10^{-3} W/cm²). Because of this and the fact that the sensation of hearing is proportional to the logarithm of the source intensity, the decibel is used in acoustical descriptions and calculations. The decibel conveniently relates actual sound intensity to the way humans experience sound. By definition, zero decibels is the threshold of human hearing and 130 dB is the threshold of pain.

In mathematical terms, this relationship is expressed by the following formula.

$$IL = 10 \log \frac{I}{I_o} \qquad 11.7$$

Some common sound intensity levels and their subjective evaluations are shown in Table 11.1.

Loudness

The sensation of loudness is subjective, but some common guidelines are shown in Table 11.2. These are useful in evaluating the effects of increased or decreased decibel levels in architectural situations. For example, spending money to modify a partition to increase its sound transmission class by 3 dB probably would not be worth the expense because it would hardly be noticeable.

Addition of Decibels of Uncorrelated Sounds

Because decibels are logarithmic, they cannot be added directly. A detailed calculation can be performed, but a convenient rule of thumb gives results accurate to within 1%. Given two decibel values, use the values in Table 11.3 to add decibels.

For three or more sources, first add two, then add the result to the third number, and so on.

Example 11.1

Find the combined intensity level of two office machines, one generating 70 dB and the other generating 76 dB.

Use the rule of thumb shown in Table 11.3. The difference between 76 and 70 is 6; therefore, add 1 dB to 76, which gives 77 dB.

For the addition of several sources of identical value, use the formula

$$IL_{total} = IL_{source} + 10 \log (\text{number of sources}) \quad 11.8$$

Example 11.2

What would the sound level be in a room of eight typewriters, each producing 73 dB?

$$IL_{total} = 73 \text{ dB} + 10 \log 8$$
$$= 82 \text{ dB}$$

Human Sensitivity to Sound

Although human response to sound is subjective and varies with age, physical condition of the ear, background, and other factors, some common guidelines are useful to remember.

Table 11.1
Common Sound Intensity Levels

IL (dB)	example	subjective evaluation	intensity (W/cm²)
140	jet plane takeoff		
130	gun fire	threshold of pain	10^{-3}
120	hard rock band, siren at 100 ft	deafening	10^{-4}
110	accelerating motorcycle	sound can be felt	10^{-5}
100	auto horn at 10 ft	conversation difficult to hear	10^{-6}
90	loud street noise, kitchen blender	very loud	10^{-7}
80	noisy office, average factory	difficult to use phone	10^{-8}
70	average street noise, quiet typewriter, average radio	loud	10^{-9}
60	average office, noisy home	usual background	10^{-10}
50	average conversation, quiet radio	moderate	10^{-11}
40	quiet home, private office	noticeably quiet	10^{-12}
30	quiet conversation	faint	10^{-13}
20	whisper		10^{-14}
10	rustling leaves, soundproof room	very faint	10^{-15}
0	threshold of hearing		10^{-16}

Table 11.2

Subjective Change in Loudness Based on
Decibel Level Change

change in intensity level (dB)	change in apparent loudness
1	almost imperceptible
3	just perceptible
5	clearly noticeable
6	change when distance to source in a free field is doubled or halved
10	twice or half as loud
18	very much louder or quieter
20	four times or one-fourth as loud

Table 11.3

Addition of Decibels

when difference between the two values is:	add this value to the higher value:
0 or 1 dB	3 dB
2 or 3 dB	2 dB
4 to 8 dB	1 dB
9 dB or more	0 dB

The normal human ear of a healthy young person can hear sounds in the range of 20 Hz to 20,000 Hz and is most sensitive to frequencies in the 3000 Hz to 4000 Hz range. Speech is composed of sounds primarily in the range of 125 Hz to 8000 Hz, with most energy in the range of 100 Hz to 600 Hz.

The human ear is less sensitive to low frequencies than to middle and high frequencies for sounds of equal energy.

Most common sound sources contain energy over a wide range of frequencies. Because frequency is an important variable in how a sound is transmitted or absorbed, it must be taken into account in building acoustics. For convenience, measurement and analysis is often divided into eight octave frequency bands identified by the center frequency. These are 63, 125, 250, 500, 1000, 2000, 4000, and 8000 Hz. For detailed purposes, smaller bands are often used.

SOUND TRANSMISSION

Transmission Loss and Noise Reduction

One of the primary objectives of architectural acoustics is to reduce the transmission of sound from one space to another. Transmission of sound is primarily retarded by the

mass of the barrier. In addition, the stiffness of the barrier is also important. Given two barriers of the same weight per unit area, the one that is less stiff will perform better than the other.

There are two important concepts in noise reduction: transmission loss and actual noise reduction. *Transmission loss* (TL) is the difference (in decibels) between the sound power incident on a barrier in a source room and the sound power radiated into a receiving room on the opposite side of the barrier. This is the measurement typically derived in a testing laboratory.

Noise reduction (NR) is the arithmetic difference (in decibels) between the intensity levels in two rooms separated by a barrier of a given transmission loss. Noise reduction is dependent on the transmission loss of the barrier, the area of the barrier, and the absorption of the surfaces in the receiving room.

Noise reduction is calculated by the following formula.

$$\text{NR} = \text{TL} + 10\log\frac{A}{S} \qquad 11.9$$

In SI units, A is in metric sabins and S is in m². One metric sabin equals 10.76 English sabins.

This formula shows that noise reduction can be increased by increasing the transmission loss of the barrier, by increasing the absorption in the receiving room, by decreasing the area of the barrier separating the two rooms, or by some combination of the three.

The actual transmission loss of a barrier varies with the frequencies of the sounds being tested. Test reports, often published with manufacturers' literature, include the transmission loss over six or more octave bands. A single-number rating that is often used is the *sound transmission class* (STC). The higher the STC rating, the better the barrier (theoretically) in stopping sound.

There are many times when a partition will comprise two or more types of constructions, for example, a door in a wall or a glass panel in a wall. The combined transmission loss can be found by the following formula.

$$\text{TL}_{\text{composite}} = 10\log\frac{\text{total area}}{\Sigma tS} \qquad 11.10$$

In finding the value of t, if the value of the transmission loss of individual materials is known, the following formula can be used.

$$t = 10^{-(\text{TL}/10)} \qquad 11.11$$

Example 11.3

A conference room and an office are separated by a common wall 13 ft long and 9 ft high with an STC rating of 54. The total absorption of the office has been calculated to be 220 sabins. What is the total noise reduction from the conference room to the office?

$$\text{NR} = 54 + 10\log\frac{220 \text{ sabins}}{(9 \text{ ft})(13 \text{ ft})}$$
$$= 54 + 10\log 1.88$$
$$= 54 + 2.7$$
$$= 57 \text{ dB}$$

Notice that the second term of formula 11.9 can be a negative number, resulting in a noise reduction less than the transmission loss of the wall.

Example 11.4

What is the combined transmission loss of a wall 9 ft high and 15 ft long with a 3 ft by 7 ft door in it? Assume the TL of the wall is 54 dB and that the door, with full perimeter seals, is 29 dB.

total wall area: (9 ft)(15 ft) = 135 ft^2

area of door: 21 ft^2

area of partition: 135 ft $-$ 21 ft = 114 ft^2

t of partition = $10^{-5.4}$

t of door = $10^{-2.9}$

$$\text{TL}_{\text{composite}} = 10\log\frac{135}{(10^{-5.4})(114) + (10^{-2.9})(21)}$$
$$= 10\log 5012$$
$$= 37 \text{ dB}$$

Remember that STC ratings represent the ideal loss under laboratory conditions. Walls, partitions, and floors built in the field are seldom constructed as well as those in the laboratory. Also, breaks in the barrier such as cracks, electrical outlets, doors, and the like will significantly reduce the overall noise reduction.

In critical situations, transmission loss and selection of barriers should be calculated using the values for the various frequencies rather than the single STC average value. Some materials may allow an acoustical "hole," stopping most frequencies but allowing transmission of a certain range of frequencies. This often happens with very low or very high frequencies. However, for preliminary design purposes in typical situations the STC value is adequate.

Noise Criteria Curves

All normally occupied spaces have some amount of background noise. This is not undesirable, because some noise is necessary to avoid the feeling of a "dead" space and to help mask other sounds. However, the acceptable amount of background noise varies with the type of space and the frequency of sound. For example, people are generally less tolerant of background noise in bedrooms than they are in public lobbies, and they are generally more tolerant of higher levels of low-frequency sound than of high-frequency sound.

These variables have been consolidated into a set of noise criteria (NC) curves relating frequency in eight octave bands to noise level. See Fig. 11.1. Accompanying these curves are noise criteria ratings for various types of space and listening requirements. A representative sampling is shown in Table 11.4. Noise criteria curves can be used to specify the maximum amount of continuous background noise allowable in a space, to establish a minimum amount of noise desired to help mask sounds, and to evaluate an existing condition.

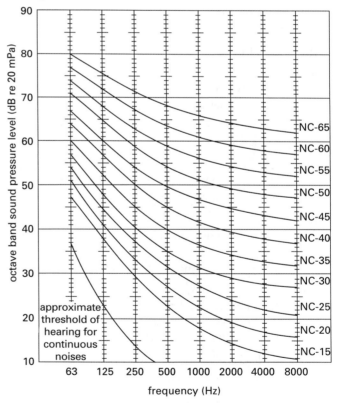

Figure 11.1 NC (Noise Criteria) Curves

For example, if the noise spectrum of an air conditioning system was plotted on the NC chart, as shown in Fig. 11.1, the noise criteria rating would be defined by that curve that

Table 11.4

Some Representative Noise Criteria

type of space	preferred NC (dB)
concert halls, opera houses, recording studios	15–20
bedrooms, apartments, hospitals	20–30
private offices, small conference rooms	30–35
large offices, retail stores, restaurants	35–40
lobbies, drafting rooms, laboratory work spaces	40–45
kitchens, computer rooms, light maintenance shops	45–55

was not exceeded by the air conditioning spectrum curve at any frequency.

When background noise conforms to a noise criteria curve, it usually still contains too many low-frequency and high-frequency sounds for comfort. A modification of the NC curves, called the *preferred noise criteria* (PNC), has been established that has sound-pressure levels lower than the NC curves on the low- and high-frequency ends of the chart.

Rules of Thumb

In addition to using calculations for acoustical design, many rules of thumb can be used for preliminary estimating and for noncritical situations.

- In general, transmission loss through a barrier tends to increase with the frequency of sound.

- A wall with 0.1% open area (from cracks, holes, undercut doors, etc.) will have a maximum transmission loss of about 30 dB. A wall with 1% open area will have a maximum of about 20 dB.

- A hairline crack will decrease a partition's transmission loss by about 6 dB. A 1 in² opening in a 100 ft² gypsum board partition can transmit as much sound as the entire partition.

- Although placing fibrous insulation in a wall cavity increases its STC rating, the density of the insulation is not a significant variable.

- In determining the required STC rating of a barrier, the guidelines in Table 11.5 may be used.

SOUND ABSORPTION

Fundamentals

Controlling sound transmission is only part of good acoustical design. The proper amount of sound absorption must also be included. Although sound intensity level

Table 11.5

Effect of Barrier STC on Hearing

STC	effect on hearing
25	normal speech can clearly be heard through barrier
30	loud speech can be heard and understood fairly well; normal speech can be heard but barely understood
35	loud speech is not intelligible but can be heard
42–45	loud speech can only be faintly heard; normal speech cannot be heard
46–50	loud speech is not audible; loud sounds other than speech can only be heard faintly, if at all

decreases about 6 dB for each doubling of distance from the source in free space, this is not the case in a room or semi-enclosed outdoor area. In a room, sound level decreases very near the source as it does in free space, but then it begins to reflect, and it levels out at a particular intensity.

In addition to reducing this intensity level of sound within a space, sound absorption is used to control unwanted sound reflections, improve speech privacy, and decrease or enhance reverberation.

The absorption of a material is defined by the coefficient of absorption, a, which is the ratio of the sound intensity absorbed by the material to the total intensity reaching the material. Therefore, the maximum absorption possible is 1—that of free space. Generally, a material with a coefficient below 0.2 is considered reflective, and one with a coefficient above 0.2 is considered sound absorbing.

The coefficient of absorption varies with the frequency of the sound, and some materials are better at absorbing some frequencies than others. For critical applications all frequencies should be checked, but for convenience the single-number noise reduction coefficient (NRC) is used. The NRC is the average of a material's absorption coefficients at the four frequencies of 250, 500, 1000, and 2000 Hz, rounded to the nearest multiple of 0.05.

The total absorption of a material is dependent on its coefficient of absorption and the area of the material.

$$A = Sa \qquad 11.12$$

Because most rooms have several materials of different areas, the total absorption in a room is the sum of the various individual material absorptions.

Noise Reduction Within a Space

Increasing sound absorption within a space will result in a noise reduction according to the following formula.

$$\text{NR} = 10 \log \frac{A_2}{A_1} \qquad 11.13$$

A_1 = total original room absorption in sabins

A_2 = total room absorption after increase of absorption

Note that this formula relates to overall reverberant noise level in a room and does not affect noise level very near the source.

Example 11.5

A room 15 ft by 20 ft with a 9 ft ceiling has a carpeted floor with a 44 oz carpet on pad (a = 0.40), gypsum board walls, and a gypsum board ceiling (a = 0.05). What would be the noise reduction achieved by directly attaching acoustical tile with a given NRC of 0.70 to the ceiling?

The original total absorption of the room is

floor: (15 ft)(20 ft)   = (300 ft²)(0.40) = 120 sabins

walls: (2 ft)(15 ft)(9 ft) = (270 ft²)(0.05) = 14 sabins

(2 ft)(20 ft)(9 ft) = (360 ft²)(0.05) = 18 sabins

ceiling: (15 ft)(20 ft)   = (300 ft²)(0.05) = 15 sabins

total = 167 sabins

The absorption after treatment is

ceiling: (15 ft²)(20 ft²) = (300 ft²)(0.70) = 210 sabins

Subtracting 15 from the old value and adding 210 as a new value, the net total is 362 sabins.

$$\text{NR} = 10 \log \frac{362}{167}$$

$$= 10 \log 2.17$$

$$= 3.4 \text{ dB}$$

Increasing the absorption by this amount helps a little, but the difference would be just perceptible (see Table 11.2). Tripling the absorption would be clearly noticeable.

Rules of Thumb

There are several rules of thumb related to sound absorption that are useful to remember.

- The average absorption coefficient of a room should be at least 0.20. An average absorption above 0.50 is usually not desirable, nor is it economically justified. A lower value is suitable for large rooms, while higher values are suitable for small or noisy rooms.

- Each doubling of the amount of absorption in a room results in a noise reduction of only 3 dB.

- If additional absorptive material is being added to a room, the total absorption should be increased at least three times (amounting to a change of about 5 dB, which is clearly noticeable). The increase may need to be more or less than three times to bring absorption to between 0.20 and 0.50.

- In adding extra absorption, an increase of 10 times is about the practical limit. Beyond this (representing a reverberant noise reduction of 10 dB), more absorption results in a decreasing amount of noise reduction and reaching the practical limit of 0.50 total average absorption coefficient.

- Each doubling of the absorption in a room reduces reverberation time by one-half.

- Although absorptive materials can be placed anywhere, ceiling treatment for sound absorption is more effective in large rooms, whereas wall treatment is more effective in small rooms.

- Generally, absorption increases with an increase in thickness of a porous absorber, except for low-frequency situations that require special design treatment.

- The amount of absorption of a porous type of sound absorber such as fiberglass or mineral wool is dependent on (1) the material's thickness, (2) the material's density, (3) the material's porosity, and (4) the orientation of the fibers in the material. A porous sound absorber should be composed of open, interconnected voids.

Reverberation

Reverberation is an important quality of the acoustical environment of a space. It is the one quality that affects the intelligibility of speech and the quality of conditions for music of all types. *Reverberation time* is the time it takes the sound level to decrease 60 dB after the source has stopped producing the sound. Reverberation time is found by the following formula.

$$T = 0.05 \left(\frac{V}{A} \right) \qquad 11.14$$

In SI units,

$$T = 0.16 \left(\frac{V}{A} \right)$$

Each type of use has its own preferred range of reverberation time, shorter times being best for smaller spaces and longer times working best for larger spaces. See Table 11.6.

Table 11.6

Recommended Reverberation Times

space	time (sec)
auditoriums (speech and music)	1.5–1.8
broadcast studios (speech only)	0.4–0.6
churches	1.4–3.4
elementary classrooms	0.6–0.8
lecture/conference rooms	0.9–1.1
movie theaters	0.8–1.2
offices, small rooms for speech	0.3–0.6
opera halls	1.5–1.8
symphony concert halls	1.6–2.1
theaters (small dramatic)	0.9–1.4

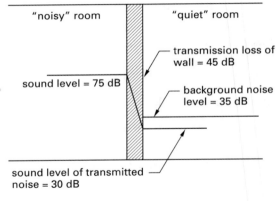

If transmitted sound level is below
the background level, the sound is not
perceptible.

Figure 11.2 Noise Reduction

SOUND CONTROL

Control of Room Noise

There are three primary ways sound can be controlled within a space: by reducing the level of the sound source, by modifying the absorption in the space, and by introducing nonintrusive background sound to mask the sound.

Reducing the level of the sound source is not always possible if the source is a fixed piece of machinery, if people are talking, or in similar situations. However, if the source is noise from the outside or an adjacent room, the transmission loss of the enclosing walls can be improved. If a machine is producing the noise, it can often be enclosed or modified to reduce its noise output.

Modifying the absorption of the space can achieve some noise reduction, but there are practical limits to adding absorptive materials. This approach is most useful when the problem room has a large percentage of hard, reflective surfaces.

In most cases, introducing nonintrusive background sound is desirable because it can mask unwanted noise. Some amount of background noise is always present. This may come from the steady hum of HVAC systems, business machines, traffic, conversation, or other sources. For example, in an office, if the sound level on one side of a partition with an STC rating of 45 is 75 dB and the background noise on the other side of the partition is 35 dB, the noise will not be heard (theoretically) on the "quiet" side of the wall. See Fig. 11.2. If the background noise level is decreased to 25 dB, then sounds will be heard.

This phenomenon is used to purposely introduce carefully controlled sound—often called *white sound*, *random noise*, or *acoustical perfume*—into a space rather than rely only on random background noise. Speakers are placed in the ceiling of a space and connected to a sound generator that produces a continuous, unnoticeable sound at particular levels across the frequency spectrum. The sound generator can be tuned to produce the frequencies and sound levels appropriate to mask the undesired sounds. White sound is often used in open offices to provide speech privacy and to help mask office machine noise.

Room noise can be reduced by adding absorption in the space. This is usually accomplished by adding some type of acoustic panels or upholstered walls. However, these types of panels are only effective for the higher frequencies and for speech. Controlling low-frequency and very high-frequency sounds within a room requires construction elements that can trap the longer, low-frequency wavelengths or control the very short high-frequency wavelengths.

Low-frequency control usually requires an allowance for thicker partitions or more space to apply detailing that absorbs low-frequency sound. Two typical methods for doing this include panel resonators and cavity resonators (also called *Helmholtz resonators*). See Fig. 11.3. The panel resonator absorbs low-frequency energy while reflecting mid- and high-frequency energy. Helmholtz resonators consist of a large air space with a small opening. As the sound strikes the resonator, the air mass inside the construction resonates at a particular frequency where the absorption is very great. However, the amount of absorption above and below the particular frequency drops off rapidly at higher and lower frequencies. A common type of cavity resonator is a concrete block wall constructed of special masonry units with narrow slits opening into the cavity of the block.

Control of Sound Transmission

As mentioned previously, control of sound transmission through barriers is primarily dependent on the mass of the barrier, and to a lesser extent on its stiffness. Walls and floors are generally rated with their STC value; the higher

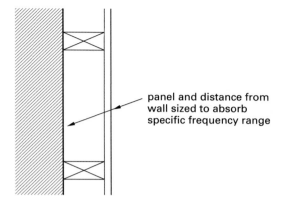

(a) vibrating panel

panel and distance from
wall sized to absorb
specific frequency range

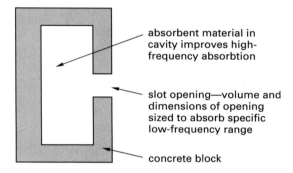

absorbent material in
cavity improves high-
frequency absorbtion

slot opening—volume and
dimensions of opening
sized to absorb specific
low-frequency range

concrete block

(b) volume resonator (Helmholtz resonator)

Figure 11.3 Details for Low-Frequency Sound
Absorption

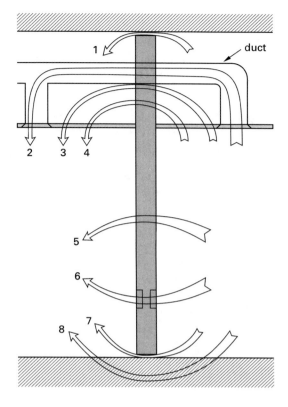

1 leaks between adjacent construction
2 flanking loss through duct
3 leaks at partition penetrations
4 flanking loss through ceiling into plenum
5 transmission and impact loss through partition
6 loss through outlets and other openings
7 leaks at floor/wall intersection
8 impact sounds through floor

Figure 11.4 Potential Sources of Sound Leaks
Through Partitions

the STC rating, the better the barrier in reducing transmitted sound. Manufacturers' literature, testing laboratories, and reference literature typically give the transmission loss at different frequencies.

In addition to the construction of the barrier itself, other variables are critical for control of sound transmission. See Fig. 11.4.

Gaps in the barrier must be sealed. Edges at the floor, ceiling, and intersecting walls should be caulked. Penetrations of the barrier should be avoided, but if absolutely necessary they can be sealed as well. For example, electrical outlets should not be placed back to back; rather, they should be staggered in separate stud spaces and caulked.

Penetrations of the barrier should be avoided. Pipes, ducts, and similar penetrations provide a path for both airborne sound and mechanical vibration. If they are unavoidable, they should not be rigidly connected to the barrier, and any gaps should be sealed and caulked.

"Weaker" construction within the barrier should be avoided or given special treatment. Construction with a lower STC

rating than the barrier itself will decrease the overall rating of the barrier. Doors placed in an otherwise well-built sound wall are a common problem and can be dealt with in several ways. The perimeter should be completely sealed with weatherstripping specifically designed for sound sealing at the jamb and head and with a threshold or automatic door bottom at the sill. The door itself should be as heavy as possible, preferably a solid-core wood door. Often, two doors are used, separated by a small air gap. See Fig. 11.5.

Interior glass lights can be designed with laminated glass set in resilient framing. Laminated glass provides more mass, and the plastic interlayer improves the damping characteristics of the barrier. If additional transmission loss is required, two or more layers can be installed with an air gap between them. See Fig. 11.6.

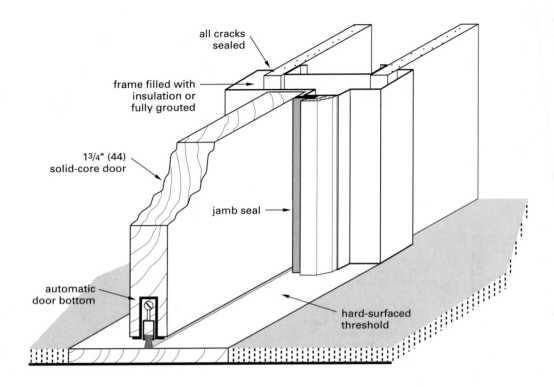

all cracks
sealed

frame filled with
insulation or
fully grouted

1³/₄" (44)
solid-core door

jamb seal

automatic
door bottom

hard-surfaced
threshold

Figure 11.5 Principles of Acoustic Control for Doors

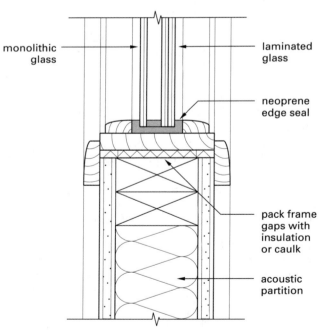

monolithic
glass

laminated
glass

neoprene
edge seal

pack frame
gaps with
insulation
or caulk

acoustic
partition

Figure 11.6 Glazing Assembly for Sound Control

Flanking paths for sound to travel should be eliminated or treated appropriately, including air conditioning ducts, plenum spaces above ceilings, hallways, and open windows in adjacent rooms.

Unusual sound conditions or frequencies must be given special consideration and design. Low-frequency rumbling or high frequencies are often not stopped, even with a wall with a high STC rating.

Speech Privacy

In many architectural situations, the critical acoustical concern is not eliminating all noise or designing a room for music, but providing for a certain level of privacy while still allowing people to talk at a normal level. In many cases, speech privacy is regarded as a condition in which talking may be heard as a general background sound but not easily understood.

Of course, speech privacy is subjective and depends on circumstances. People involved in highly confidential conversations may need greater privacy than those conducting normal, nonconfidential business in an open office. Also, one person may be annoyed by adjacent conversations more than another person.

Speech privacy is usually of greatest concern in office planning, and especially in open office planning. Because speech privacy in open offices depends on a complex interaction of many variables, two measures are used to evaluate open office acoustics: the articulation class (AC) and the articulation index (AI). Both of these test methods and rating systems have replaced the Speech Privacy Noise Isolation Class (NIC) and the Speech Privacy Potential (SPP) that were formerly used.

The *articulation class* (AC) gives a rating of system component performance and does not account for masking sound. The *articulation index* (AI) measures the performance of all the elements of a particular configuration working together: ceiling absorption, space dividers, furniture, light fixtures, partitions, background masking systems, and HVAC systems. It is used to objectively test speech privacy of open office spaces, either in the actual space or in a laboratory mock-up of the space.

The articulation index can be used to (1) compare the relative privacy between different pairs of workstations or areas, (2) evaluate how changes in open office components affect speech privacy, and (3) measure speech privacy objectively for correlation with subjective responses. The articulation index predicts the intelligibility of speech for a group of talkers and listeners, and the result of the test is a single number rating. The AI rating can range from 0.00 to 1.00, with 0.00 being complete privacy and 1.00 being absolutely no privacy where all individual spoken words can be understood. Confidential speech privacy exists when speech cannot be understood and occurs when the articulation index is at or below 0.05. Normal speech privacy means concentrated effort is required to understand intruding speech and exists when the AI is between 0.05 and 0.20. Above an AI of 0.20, speech becomes readily understood. Privacy no longer exists when the AI is above 0.30.

Both the articulation index and articulation class are intended only for open office situations with speech as the sound source of concern. However, the articulation index can be adapted for other open plans (like schools) and can be applied to measure speech privacy between enclosed and open spaces and between two enclosed rooms.

Speech privacy in areas divided by full-height partitions is usually achieved by sound loss through the partitions and, to a lesser extent, by the proper use of sound-absorbing surfaces. In open areas, such as an open-plan office, speech privacy is more difficult to achieve. There are five important factors in designing for speech privacy in an open area. All of these must be present to achieve an optimal acoustical environment.

1. The ceiling must be highly absorptive. The idea is to create a "clear sky" condition so that sounds are not reflected from their source to other parts of the environment.

2. There must be space dividers that reduce the transmission of sound from one space to the adjacent space. The dividers should have a combination of absorptive surfaces to minimize sound reflections placed over a solid liner (septum).

3. Other surfaces, such as the floor, furniture, windows, and light fixtures, must be designed or arranged to minimize sound reflections. A window, for example, can provide a clear path for reflected noise around a partial height partition.

4. If possible, activities should be distanced to take advantage of the normal attenuation of sound with distance.

5. There must be a properly designed background masking system. If the right number of sound-absorbing surfaces is provided, the surfaces will absorb all sounds in the space, not just the unwanted sounds. Background sound must then be reintroduced to maintain the right balance between speech sound and the background noise. This is referred to as the *signal-to-noise ratio*. If the signal-to-noise ratio is too great (as a result of either loud talking or minimal background noise), speech privacy will be compromised.

Control of Impact Noise

Impact noise, or sound resulting from direct contact of an object with a sound barrier, can occur on any surface, but it generally occurs on a floor and ceiling assembly. It is usually caused by footfalls, shuffled furniture, or dropped objects.

Impact noise is quantified by the *Impact Insulation Class* (IIC) number, a single-number rating of a floor-ceiling's impact on sound performance. A given construction is analyzed in accordance with a standardized test over 16 third-octave bands, and the results are compared with a reference plot much as noise criteria ratings are established. The higher the IIC rating, the better the floor's performance in reducing impact sounds in the test frequency range.

The IIC value of a floor can be increased by adding carpet, by providing a resiliently suspended ceiling below, by floating a finished floor on resilient pads over the structural floor, and by providing sound-absorbing material in the air space between the floor and the finished ceiling.

Control of Mechanical Noise

Mechanical noise is similar to impact noise in that the cause is due to direct contact with the barrier. However, mechanical noise occurs when a vibrating device is in continuous direct contact with the structure. There are several ways mechanical noise can be transmitted.

- Rigidly attached equipment can vibrate the building structure or pipes, which in turn radiate sound into occupied spaces.

- The airborne noise of equipment can be transmitted through walls and floors to occupied spaces.

- Noise can be transmitted through ductwork.

- The movement of air or water through ducts and pipes can cause undesirable noise. This is especially true of high-velocity air systems or situations where the air or water changes velocity rapidly.

Depending on the circumstances, mechanical noise can be controlled in several ways.

- Mechanical equipment should be mounted on springs or resilient pads (isolators).

- Connections between equipment and ducts and pipes should be made with flexible connectors.

- Where noise control is critical, ducts should be lined or provided with mufflers.

- Noise-producing equipment can be located away from quiet, occupied spaces.

- Walls, ceilings, and floors of mechanical rooms should be designed to attenuate airborne noise.

- Mechanical and plumbing systems should be designed to minimize high-velocity flow and sudden changes in fluid velocity.

ROOM ACOUSTICS

Reflection, Diffusion, and Diffraction

Reflection is the return of sound waves from a surface. If a surface is greater than or equal to four times the wavelength of a sound striking it, the angle of incidence will equal the angle of reflection. Wavelength, of course, varies with frequency according to formula 11.3. Assuming a velocity of 1130 ft/sec (344 m/s), Table 11.7 gives wavelengths of certain frequencies.

Reflection can be useful for reinforcing sound in lecture rooms and concert halls and for directing sound where it is wanted. It can be annoying, however, if it produces echoes, which occur when a reflected sound reaches a listener later than about $1/17$ sec after the direct sound. Assuming a sound

Table 11.7
Wavelengths Based on Frequency

frequency (Hz)	wavelength	
	(ft)	(m)
50	23.0	6.8
100	11.0	3.4
250	4.5	1.4
500	2.25	0.7
1000	1.13	0.34
2000	0.57	0.17
5000	0.23	0.07
10,000	0.11	0.034

speed of 1130 ft/sec (344 m/s), an echo will occur whenever the reflected sound path exceeds the direct sound path by 70 ft (21.3 m) or more.

Diffusion is the random distribution of sound from a surface. It occurs when the surface dimension equals the wavelength of the sound striking it.

Diffraction is the bending of sound waves around an object or through an opening. Diffraction explains why sounds can be heard around corners and why even small holes in partitions allow so much sound to be heard.

Room Geometry and Planning Concepts

There are many ways the acoustical performance of a building or individual room can be affected by floor plan layout and the size and shape of the room itself. In addition to designing walls and floors to retard sound transmission and for proper use of sound absorption, use the following suggestions to help minimize acoustical problems.

- Plan similar use areas next to each other. For example, placing bedrooms next to each other in an apartment complex is better than placing a bedroom next to the adjacent unit's kitchen. This concept is applicable for vertical organization as well as horizontal (plan) organization.

- Use buffer spaces such as closets and hallways to separate noise-producing spaces whenever possible. Using closets between bedrooms at a common wall is one example of this method.

- Locate noise-producing areas such as mechanical rooms, laundries, and playrooms away from "quiet" areas.

- Stagger doorways in halls and other areas to avoid providing a straight-line path for noise.

- Locate operable windows as far from each other as possible.

- If possible, locate furniture and other potential noise-producing objects away from the wall separating spaces.

- Minimize the area of the common walls between two rooms where a reduction in sound transmission is desired.

- Avoid room shapes that reflect or focus sound. Barrel-vaulted hallways and circular rooms, for example, produce undesirable focused sounds. Rooms that focus sound also deprive some listeners of useful reflections.

- Avoid parallel walls with hard surfaces in small rooms. In such situations, repeated echoes, called *flutter echoes*, can be generated that result in a perceived "buzzing" sound of higher frequencies. This is why small music practice rooms have splayed walls. Standing waves can also be produced in small rooms, when parallel walls are some integral multiple of one-half wavelength apart and a steady tone is introduced in the room.

SAMPLE QUESTIONS

1. Which of the following statements are FALSE?

I.   Sensitivity to sound varies between sexes.

II. People are generally more sensitive to middle and high frequencies than to low frequencies for sounds of equal energy.

III. Most healthy young people can hear sounds in the range of 15 Hz to 25,000 Hz.

IV. Practically all common sounds are made up of energy in a wide range of frequencies.

V.   Speech is composed of frequencies in the range of 125 Hz to 8000 Hz.

    A.   I and III
    B.   I and V
    C.   II and III
    D.   III and V

2. The construction assembly shown would be best for controlling which of the following kinds of acoustic situations?

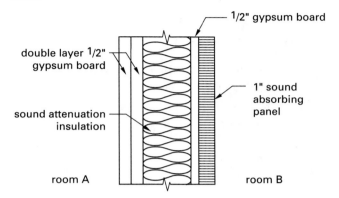

I.   impact noise

II. excessive reverberation in room B

III. transmission from room A to room B

IV. transmission from room B to room A

V.   mechanical vibration

    A.   I and II
    B.   II and III
    C.   II and IV
    D.   III and IV

3. In an office, a copy machine is found to produce 65 dB. A computer printer is added to the room, and it produces a sound intensity of 69 dB. What will be the resulting sound level?

    A.   70 dB
    B.   71 dB
    C.   72 dB
    D.   73 dB

4. What is the single number often used to evaluate the acoustic qualities of partitions?

    A.   noise reduction coefficient
    B.   sound absorption coefficient
    C.   noise insulation class
    D.   sound transmission class

5. What method is used to specify the maximum allowable intensity of background sounds?

    A.   noise reduction coefficient
    B.   noise criteria
    C.   sound intensity
    D.   inverse square law

6. What is one variable affecting reverberation time?

    A. decibel level
    B. frequency
    C. room volume
    D. sound intensity

7. Which of the following statements about noise reduction between two rooms is FALSE?

    A. Noise reduction increases with an increase in the transmission loss of the wall separating the two rooms.
    B. The stiffness of the wall has some effect on noise reduction.
    C. To improve noise reduction, place absorptive materials on both sides of the wall.
    D. An increase in wall area separating the two rooms is detrimental.

8. A room 15 ft wide by 20 ft long by 8½ ft high is finished with the following materials of listed absorptions.

	NRC	125	250	500	1000	2000	4000
floor, wood	0.10	0.15	0.11	0.10	0.07	0.06	0.07
walls, gypsum board	0.05	0.10	0.08	0.05	0.03	0.03	0.03
ceiling, acoustical tile	0.60	0.29	0.29	0.55	0.75	0.73	0.57
window, glass	0.15	0.35	0.25	0.18	0.12	0.07	0.04

On one wall there is a window 3½ ft high by 8 ft long. What is the total absorption of the room?

    A. 228 sabins
    B. 244 sabins
    C. 266 sabins
    D. 242 sabins

9. A material supplier states that adding a certain product to a wall assembly in a critical acoustical situation will increase the noise reduction (STC rating) between two spaces by more than 3 dB. How should the architect respond?

    A. Determine what the additional cost would be and then decide whether or not to use the product.
    B. Thank the supplier for stopping by but explain that the architectural firm probably will not be using the product because that amount of noise reduction does not make it worth the effort or cost.
    C. Specify the product as long as it does not affect the design or construction cost by more than 5%.

    D. Inquire whether some modification can be made to the product to increase its rating to 6 dB and say that then the architectural firm might consider it.

10. During a design development presentation to the building committee of a middle school, one of the teachers on the committee mentions that there might be a noise problem between the classrooms shown in the partial plan because the larger classroom will be used for open discussions, movies, lab work, and other loud activities. Both classrooms are scheduled to have gypsum board partitions, vinyl tile floors, and suspended acoustical ceilings.

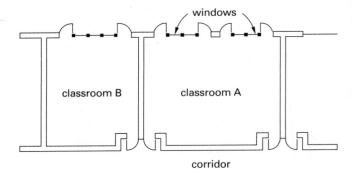

If cost is a consideration, what design changes should be suggested, in order of priority from most important to least important?

I. Substitute carpeting for tile in both rooms.
II. Move the operable windows near the separating wall so that they are not so close together, and change the direction of the swing.
III. Reroute the ductwork and conduit penetrations through the separating wall above the suspended ceiling, and write specifications to direct that any remaining penetrations be tightly sealed.
IV. Replan the layout so that there is a small audiovisual storage room between the classrooms.
V. Add an extra layer of gypsum board to each side of the separating partition, and specify that the cavity be filled with sound-attenuating insulation.
VI. Hire an acoustical consultant to determine the special frequency problems associated with the activities planned for the larger classroom, and design custom sound-absorbing surfaces and partitions accordingly.

    A. II, III, V, I, IV, VI
    B. III, II, V, I, VI, IV
    C. IV, II, III, V, VI, I
    D. V, III, II, I, IV, VI

SECTION 3:
BUILDING DESIGN/
MATERIALS AND METHODS

SITE WORK

Site work includes demolition and clearing of land, earthwork, installation of piles and caissons, paving and other types of surfacing, drainage, site improvements, and landscaping. Included in this chapter are those aspects of site work encountered on almost any architectural project.

SOIL

Because all aspects of site work depend on the nature of the soil, the architect must have a basic understanding of this element. *Soil* is the general term used to describe the material that supports a building. It is generally classified into four groups: sands and gravels, silts, clays, and organics.

Sands and gravels are granular materials that are low in plasticity. *Sand* consists of particles from about 0.002 in to $^1/_4$ in (0.05 to 6) in size. *Gravel* consists of rock particles from $^1/_4$ in to $3^1/_2$ in (6 to 89) in size. Both sands and gravels are very good bases for building foundations. In addition, they provide good drainage because of the voids between the individual particles.

Silt is fine-grained sedimentary soil composed of material smaller than sand but larger than clay. Silts behave as granular materials, but they are sometimes slightly plastic in their behavior.

Clays are composed of smaller particles than silts. Clays have some cohesion, or tensile strength, and are plastic in their behavior when wet. Clay is very unpredictable because it swells when it absorbs water and shrinks when it dries. In some cases silts and clays can provide an adequate base for foundations if soil investigations show they are stable. Generally, they make better foundations if they are mixed with other types of soil.

Organics are materials of vegetable or other organic matter and make poor bases for foundations.

In addition to these general types there are other commonly used terms for various types of soil. *Hardpan* refers to an unbroken mixture of clay, sand, and gravel. It is a good base for building foundations. *Shale* and *slate* are soft rocks with a fine texture. *Boulders* describe rocks that have broken off of bedrock. Finally, *bedrock* is the solid rock that forms the earth's crust. Bedrock has the highest bearing capacity of all soil types. Shale and slate make up the group with the second highest bearing capacity.

Soil Tests

Prior to design and construction, the exact nature of the soil must be determined. This is done with one of a variety of soil tests used to determine such things as the bearing capacity, water table level, and porosity. Porosity must be known if the land is to be used for private sewage disposal systems. Two of the most common soil tests for bearing capacity are borings and test pits.

With typical core borings, undisturbed samples of the soil are removed at regular intervals and the type of material recovered is recorded in a *boring log*. This log shows the material, the depth at which it was encountered, its standard designation, and other information, such as moisture content, density, and the results of any borehole tests that might have been conducted at the bore site. A typical boring log is shown in Fig. 12.1.

One of the most common borehole tests is the *Standard Penetration Test* (SPT), which is a measure of the density of granular soils and the consistency of some clays. In this test, a 2 in (51) diameter sampler is driven into the bottom of the borehole by a 140 lbm (63 kg) hammer falling 30 in (760). The number of blows, N, required to drive the cylinder 12 in (305) is recorded.

The recovered bore samples can be tested in the laboratory. Some of the tests include strength tests of bearing capacity, resistance to lateral pressure, and slope stability. In addition,

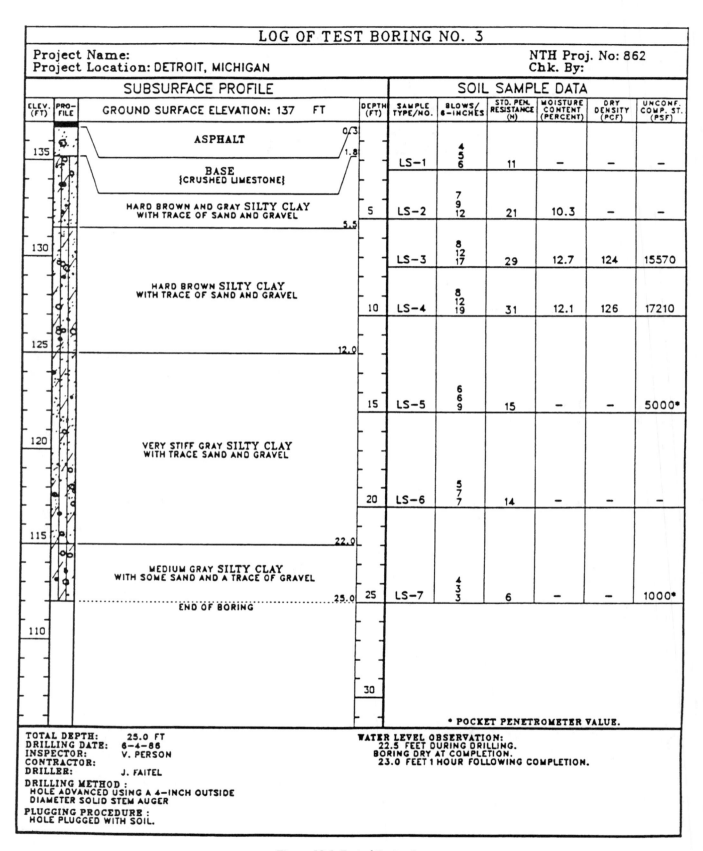

Figure 12.1 Typical Boring Log

compressibility, grain size, specific gravity, and density tests are sometimes performed. Because laboratory tests are expensive and not always necessary, they are not performed for every building project.

The number of borings taken at a building site is determined by many factors, such as the size of the building, suspected subsurface geological conditions, and requirements by local codes. Usually, a minimum of four borings is taken, one near each corner of the proposed building. If wide variations are found in the initial boring logs, additional tests may be warranted.

Test pits are the second common type of subsurface exploration. These are trenches dug at the job site that allow visual inspection of the soil strata and direct collection of undisturbed samples. Because they are open pits, the practical limit on depth is about 10 ft (3 m), so the soil below that depth cannot be directly examined.

The location of each test boring or test pit is shown on the plot plan and given a number corresponding to the boring log in the soil test report. Soil tests are usually requested by the architect but paid for by the owner. They are typically referred to in the specifications for information only. However, soil tests are not part of the contract documents.

Other types of tests include auger borings, wash borings, dry sample borings, and soil load tests. *Auger borings* raise samples of the soil by using a standard auger bit. The test is best used in sand or clay for shallow or intermediate depths because the auger cannot penetrate hard obstructions such as bedrock or hardpan soil.

Wash borings are made with a 2 in to 4 in diameter (50 to 100) pipe through which a water jet is maintained to force up the soil material. The resulting samples are so thoroughly mixed that analysis is difficult, but the test is useful for soils too hard for an auger test. Wash borings can extend down about 100 ft (30 m) or more.

Dry sample borings extract material by driving a pipe with a split sampling pipe on the leading edge about 5 in (125) into the soil. The pipe is lifted out, and the samples are removed for analysis. Subsequent samples are taken in approximately 5 in (125) increments.

Soil load tests involve building a platform on the site, placing incremental loads on it, and observing the amount of settlement during given time periods until settlement becomes regular after repeated loading. The design load is usually half the test load.

After the field sampling is done, the soil is tested in a laboratory and the soils engineer issues a report stating the results of the testing. From this the soils engineer gives the allowable soil bearing pressure and recommends a foundation type to use. Some of the properties that can be tested include the following.

Grain size and shape. These determine (for granular soil) the shear strength of the soil, its permeability, the likely result of frost action, and compaction ability.

Liquid and plastic limits. These values give the compaction and compressibility values for cohesive soil.

Specific gravity. This is used to determine void ratio, which determines compressibility of the soil.

Unconfined compression. The shear strength for cohesive soil is measured from this value.

Water content. This number is used to get the compressibility and compaction values for cohesive soil.

Soil Types

Soils are classified according to the *Unified Soil Classification System*. This system divides soils into major divisions and subdivisions based on grain size and laboratory tests of physical characteristics and provides standardized names and symbols. A summary chart of the USCS is shown in Fig. 12.2.

Bearing capacities are generally specified by the building code based on the soil type. Other bearing capacities may be used if acceptable tests are conducted that show higher values are appropriate.

Water in Soil

The presence of water in soil can cause several problems for foundations as well as other parts of the site. Water can reduce the load-carrying capacity of the soil in general, so larger or more expensive foundation systems may be necessary. If more moisture is present under one area of the building than another, differential settlement may occur, causing cracking and weakening of structural and nonstructural components. In the worst case, structural failure may occur. Improperly prepared soil can also cause heaving or settling of paving, fences, and other parts of the site.

Foundations below the groundwater line, often called the *water table*, are also subjected to hydrostatic pressure. This pressure from the force of water-saturated soil can occur against vertical foundation walls as well as under the floor slabs. Hydrostatic pressure creates two difficulties: it puts additional loads on the structural elements, and it makes waterproofing more difficult because the pressure tends to force water into any crack or imperfection in the structure. See Fig. 18.1 for a typical method of waterproofing a foundation.

course-grained soils more than 50% of material is larger that no. 200 sieve	gravels more than 50% of course fraction retained on No. 4 sieve	clean gravels less than 5% fines	GW	well-graded gravel
			GP	poorly graded gravel
		gravels with fines more than 12% fines	GM	silty gravel
			GC	clayey gravel
	sands 50% or more of course fraction passes No. 4 sieve	clean sands less than 5% fines	SW	well-graded sand
			SP	poorly graded sand
		sands with fines more than 12% fines	SM	silty sand
			SC	clayey sand
fine-grained soils 50% or more passes the no. 200 sieve	silts and clays liquid limit less than 50	inorganic	CL	lean clay
			ML	silt
		organic	OL	organic silt
	silts and clays liquid limit 50 or more	inorganic	CH	fat clay
			MH	elastic silt
		organic	OH	organic clay
highly organic soils	primary organic matter, dark in color, and organic odor		PT	peat

Figure 12.2 Unified Soil Classification System

Even if hydrostatic pressure is not present, moisture in the soil can leak into the below-grade structure if not properly dampproofed and can cause general deterioration of materials.

Soil Treatment

In order to increase bearing capacity, decrease settlement, or do both, several methods of soil treatment are used.

- *Drainage.* As mentioned in the previous section, proper drainage can solve several types of problems. It can increase the strength of the soil and prevent hydrostatic pressure.

- *Fill.* If existing soil is unsuitable for building, the undesirable material is removed and new engineered fill is brought in. This may be soil, sand, gravel, or other material as appropriate. In nearly all situations, the engineered fill must be compacted before building commences. Controlled compaction requires moisture to lubricate the particles. With all types of fill, there is an optimum relationship between the fill's density and its optimum moisture content. The method for determining this is the Proctor test, in which fill samples are tested in the laboratory to determine a standard for compaction. Specifications are then written that call for fill to be compacted between 90% and 100% of the optimum Proctor density; higher values are necessary for heavily loaded structures, and lower values are appropriate for other loadings. Moisture contents within 2% to 4% of the optimum moisture content at the time of compaction must also be specified. Fill is usually placed in lifts of 8 in to 12 in (200 to 300), with each lift compacted before placement of the next.

- *Compaction.* Sometimes existing soil can simply be compacted to provide the required base for construction. The same requirements for compaction of fill material apply to compaction of existing soil. One device used to compact large areas is the sheepsfoot roller.

- *Densification.* This is a type of on-site compaction of existing material using one of several techniques involving vibration, dropping of heavy weights, or pounding piles into the ground and filling the voids with sand. The specific technique used depends on the grain size of the soil.

- *Surcharging.* Surcharging is the preloading of the ground with fill material to cause consolidation and settlement of the underlying soil before building. Once the required settlement has taken place, the fill is removed and construction begins. Although suitable for large areas, the time and cost required for sufficient settlement often preclude this method of soil improvement.

- *Mixing.* In lieu of complete replacement of the soil, a layer of sand or gravel can be placed on less stable soil and mixed in, thus improving the soil's bearing capacity. By varying the type of added material, a soil with required properties can be created.

EARTHWORK

Earthwork includes excavating soil for the construction of a building foundation, water and sewer lines, and other buried items as well as modifying the site's land contours.

Excavation

Excavation is the removal of soil to allow construction of foundations and other permanent features below the finished level of the grade. It is usually done with machinery, although small areas may be excavated by hand. When a relatively narrow, long excavation is done for piping or for narrow footings and foundation walls, it is called *trenching*.

Because excavations can pose a hazard to workers, unshored sides of soil should be no steeper than their natural angle of repose or not greater than a slope of $1^1/_2$ horizontal to 1 vertical. Where this is not possible, the earth must be temporarily shored as discussed in the next section.

For large excavations, excess soil has to be removed from the site. However, to minimize cost, it is best to use the soil elsewhere on the site for backfill or in contour modification.

Grading

Grading is the modification of the contours of the site according to the grading plan. Rough grading involves the moving of soil prior to construction to approximate levels of the final grades. It also includes adding or removing soil after construction to the approximate final grades. In both of these operations, the grade is usually within about 6 in to 1 ft (150 to 300) of the desired level. Often, excavating is part of the rough grading as soil removed from the building is placed in low spots where the grade must be built up.

Finish grading is the final moving of soil prior to landscaping or paving, where the level of the earth is brought to within 1 in (25) of the desired grades. This operation is done with machines and by hand and often includes the placement of topsoil.

SHORING AND BRACING

For shallow excavations in open areas, the sides of the excavation can be sloped without the need for some supporting structure. However, if the depth increases or the excavation walls need to be vertical in confined locations, temporary support is required. There are two common methods of doing this.

The first method employs a system of vertical beams and horizontal timbers. See Fig. 12.3(a). Prior to excavation, steel wide-flange soldier beams are driven at 6 ft to 10 ft (1830 to 3050) intervals to a length slightly deeper than the anticipated excavation. As soil is removed, horizontal timbers 2 in to 4 in (50 to 100) thick, called *breast boards* or *cribbing*, are placed between the soldier beams so they bear against the inside face of the flange.

When the excavation reaches a certain point, holes are drilled diagonally into the earth or deeper rock. Rods or tendons are inserted into the holes and grouted into place.

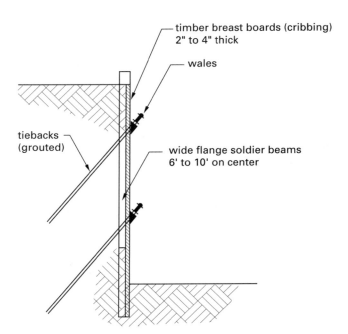

(a) soldier beams and breast boards

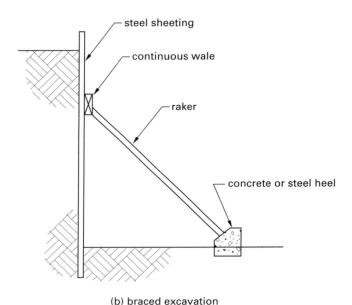

(b) braced excavation

Figure 12.3 Excavation Shoring

These tiebacks are connected to horizontal wales that hold the soldier beams back against the pressure of the excavation. As the excavation proceeds, more breast boards and tiebacks are added. The advantage of this method of shoring is that the excavation is free from bracing and allows drilling of piers, forming of foundation walls, and other construction to proceed unimpeded.

The second method uses vertical sheeting, either wood or steel, supported by diagonal braces, as shown in Fig. 12.3(b). Steel sheeting is composed of interlocking Z-shaped sections supported by continuous horizontal members called *wales*. The wales, in turn, are supported by diagonal rakers that are anchored to the bottom of the excavation with steel or concrete heels. For very small excavations, the diagonal rakers can be replaced with horizontal braces connecting opposite sides of the excavation.

Shoring and bracing are used to temporarily support adjacent buildings and other construction with posts, timbers, and beams when excavation is proceeding and to temporarily support the sides of an excavation.

Underpinning is a method to temporarily support existing foundations while they are being repaired or strengthened or when they are being extended to a lower level. Needle beams supported by the adjacent grade and hydraulic jacks are used to temporarily support the building while the new foundation is constructed.

SITE DRAINAGE

Water must be properly drained from a site to carry off excess rain and other surface water, to avoid leakage into the building, and to make other parts of the site, such as walks, parking areas, and outdoor activity areas, usable. There are two primary types of drainage to consider: subsurface and surface.

Subsurface Drainage

Water below ground can reduce the load-carrying capacity of the soil, cause differential settlement, and leak into a building. For these reasons, the site for a building must be examined and tested for potential water problems, and steps must be taken to drain excess water.

A small amount of moisture in the soil normally does not pose significant problems. However, if there is a high percentage of water in the soil or if the water table is high, these problems must be dealt with. The *water table* is the level below which the soil is saturated with groundwater. If any part of a structure is below this level, it is subject to hydrostatic pressure, putting additional loads on the structural elements of the foundation and making waterproofing more difficult.

In order to minimize subsurface water, the land around the building must be sloped to drain surface water before it soaks into the ground near the structure. A minimum slope of $1/4$ in/ft (6/305) is recommended. All water from roofs and decks should also be drained away from the building with gutters and drain pipes.

Below ground, perforated drain tile should be laid around the footings at least 6 in (150) below the floor slab to collect water and carry it away to a storm sewer system, drywell, or some natural drainage area. The drain tile is set in a gravel setting bed, and more gravel is placed above the drain. This is commonly known as a "French drain" or subdrain.

If hydrostatic pressure against the wall is a problem, a layer of gravel can be placed next to the wall. Open-web matting (geotextile material) can also be used. With either of these methods, when water is forced against gravel or matting, it loses its pressure and drips through the gravel or matting into the drain tile.

To relieve pressure against floor slabs, a layer of large gravel is placed below the slab. If the presence of water is a significant problem, the gravel layer is used in conjunction with a waterproofing membrane, and drain tiles are placed below the slab. See also Ch. 18.

Surface Water Drainage

Surface water should be drained away from a building by sloping the land and otherwise modifying the finish contours to divert water into natural drainage patterns or artificial drains. Gutters can be built into curbing to collect water from paved areas. In some cases, large paved or landscaped areas need to be sloped to drain inlets or catch basins that connect with storm sewers.

A drain inlet allows storm water to run directly into the storm sewer. A catch basin has a sump built into it so that debris will settle instead of flowing down the sewer. The sump can be cleaned out periodically. Large storm sewer systems require manholes for service access, located wherever the sewer changes direction, or a maximum of 500 ft (152 m) apart.

Refer to Chs. 2 and 4 for more information on sustainable design during the site analysis and design phases.

SITE IMPROVEMENTS

Site improvements include items not connected to the building, such as parking areas, walks, paving, landscaping, sprinkler systems, outdoor lighting, fences, retaining walls, and various types of outdoor furnishings.

Paving

Paving is used for parking areas, driveways, and large, hard-surfaced activity areas. Paving is normally constructed of concrete, asphaltic concrete, or unit pavers.

Concrete paving is placed on compacted soil or a gravel bed and is normally reinforced with welded wire fabric to resist temperature stresses. If heavy loading is anticipated, the concrete is often reinforced with standard reinforcing bars. Concrete paving should be a minimum of 5 in (127) thick, but the actual thickness required depends on the anticipated loading. Concrete paving is poured in sections, with joints between the sections. Expansion joints should be located every 20 ft (6100) separated with a $1/2$ in (13) premolded joint filler. Construction joints or control joints are placed where separate sections of concrete are poured, and they are intended to control the locations of the inevitable minor cracking that occurs in concrete.

Asphaltic concrete paving is a general term that includes several types of bituminous paving. The most common type of asphaltic concrete consists of asphalt cement and graded aggregates. This is laid on the base and rolled and compacted while still hot. Cold-laid asphalt is the same except that cold liquid asphalt is used. Before the asphalt is applied, a subbase of coarse gravel is overlaid with finer aggregate and compacted and rolled to the desired grade. The asphalt is laid over this base to a depth of 2 or 3 in.

Unit pavers can be any of a number of types of materials, including concrete, brick, granite, and flagstone. Unit pavers should be laid on a level, compacted base of sand over crushed gravel. For greater stability they may also be laid on a bituminous setting bed over a poured concrete slab. Figure 12.4 shows a typical unit paver section, and Fig. 12.5 shows common paving patterns.

Walks

Walks are common site improvements. Like paving, walks can be constructed of a number of materials, such as asphalt or brick, but the most common is concrete because of its strength and durability. Concrete walks should be laid over a gravel subbase with control joints every 5 ft (1500) and expansion joints every 20 ft (6100). These are usually 4 in (1500) thick. Additionally, expansion joints should be located where walks abut buildings, curbs, paving, and other permanent structures.

SAMPLE QUESTIONS

Sample questions for Chs. 12 through 21 are included in Ch. 22.

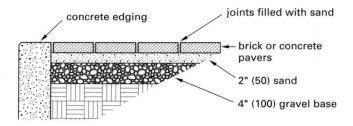

Figure 12.4 Unit Paving

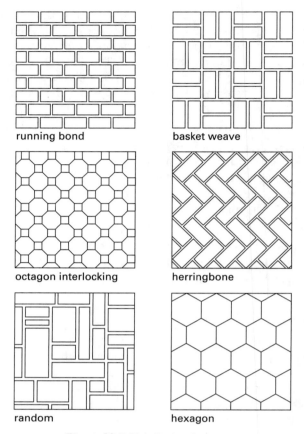

Figure 12.5 Unit Paving Patterns

CONCRETE

Concrete is one of the most versatile basic building materials. It is durable, strong, and weather resistant, and it can be formed into a wide variety of shapes and finished in a number of ways. It can be used in structural or nonstructural applications. Although concrete has many advantages, its use requires a knowledge of many variables and construction steps. These include formwork, reinforcing, placing, curing, testing, and finishing.

HISTORY OF CONCRETE

Concrete was first discovered by the Romans. As early as the third century B.C. Roman builders were using a mortar of lime and sand. Later, they discovered that by mixing pozzolana (a volcanic ash) with lime and water they would get a mixture that would set underwater. They mixed their new cement with stone and brick rubble to form walls, and cast it in wooden forms for vaults, arches, and domes.

Concrete was forgotten until the late eighteenth century when John Smeaton found that quicklime containing clay would harden under water. He used a primitive form of this mortar for a stone lighthouse. In 1824 Joseph Aspdin developed portland cement, the first manufactured hydraulic (able to set underwater) binding material. Reinforced concrete, or ferroconcrete as it was first known, was developed in the latter part of the century when both wire and bars were used to strengthen the construction.

Although some experimenting was done with concrete during the nineteenth century (the Paris Exhibition of 1867 used concrete in portions of the main building), it was not until the first two decades of the twentieth century that engineers and architects began to fully exploit the possibilities of the material.

The Swiss engineer Robert Maillart used concrete extensively in his bridges and industrial buildings. One of his best known works was Cement Hall, completed in 1939 in Zurich. It was a thinshell parabolic vault that fully exploited the possibilities of reinforced concrete.

Auguste Perret was another innovator with concrete. However, he used the material for structural frames in simple rectangular constructions. The area between the concrete frame was frequently filled in with other materials. A contemporary of Perret, Tony Garnier, envisioned using ferroconcrete as the basis for the buildings in his proposed town plan, the Cité Industrielle, designed between 1901 and 1904.

The engineer Pier Luigi Nervi used reinforced concrete for many of his most innovative structures. His stadiums at Florence, bridges, and airplane hangars use exposed concrete in daring and innovative forms. His most famous works include the Exhibition Building in Turin (1948) and the sports palace in Rome (1957). Nervi also experimented and used precast reinforced concrete units in many of his buildings.

Le Corbusier used concrete extensively in many of his later buildings. The apartment block at Marseilles (1946–1952), Ronchamp (1950–1954), and the Palace of Justice in Chandigarh (1953) are all examples of a master architect exploiting all the plastic possibilities of the material. Even Frank Lloyd Wright used reinforced concrete in many of his famous buildings such as Fallingwater, the Johnson Wax Company, and the Guggenheim Museum. Wright also experimented with concrete masonry units in his California concrete block houses in the 1920s.

FORMWORK

Formwork refers to the system of boards, ties, and bracing required to construct the mold in which wet concrete is placed. Formwork must be strong enough to withstand the weight and pressure created by the wet concrete and must be easy to erect and remove.

Types of Forms

Forms are constructed out of a variety of materials. Unless the concrete is finished in some way, the shape and pattern of the formwork will affect the appearance of the final product. Wood grain, knotholes, joints, and other imperfections in the form will show in their negative image when the form is removed.

Plywood is the most common forming material. It is usually $^3/_4$ in (19) thick and is coated on one side with oil, a water-resistant glue, or plastic to prevent water from penetrating the wood and to increase the reusability of the form. Oil on forms also prevents adhesion of the concrete so the forms are easier to remove. The plywood is supported with solid wood framing, which is braced or shored as required. Figure 13.1 shows two typical wood-framed forms.

Prefabricated steel forms are often used because of their strength and reusability. They are often employed for forming one-way joist systems, waffle slabs, round columns, and other special shapes.

Other types of forms include glass-fiber reinforced plastic, hardboard, and various kinds of proprietary systems. Plastic forms are manufactured with a variety of patterns embedded in them. These patterns are transferred to the concrete and constitute the final surface. Special form liners can also be used to impart a deeply embossed pattern.

For exposed architectural surfaces, a great deal of consideration must be given to the method and design of the formwork because the pattern of joints and form ties will be visible. Joints are often emphasized with rustication strips, continuous pieces of neoprene, wood, or other material that when removed shows a deep reveal in the concrete.

Form ties are metal wires or rods used to hold opposite sides of the form together and also to prevent their collapse. When the forms are removed, the wire remains in the concrete, and the excess is twisted or cut off. Some form ties are threaded rods that can be unscrewed and reused. Tie holes are made with cone-shaped heads placed against the concrete form. When these are removed, a deep, round hole is left that allows the tie to be cut off below the surface of the concrete. These holes can remain exposed as a design feature or can be patched with grout.

Special Forms

Most formwork is designed and constructed to remain in place until the concrete cures sufficiently to stand on its own. However, one method, called *slip forming*, moves as the concrete cures. Slip forming is used to form continuous surfaces such as tunnels and high-rise building cores. The entire form is constructed along with working platforms and supports for the jacking assembly. The form moves continuously at about 6 in to 12 in (150 to 300) per hour.

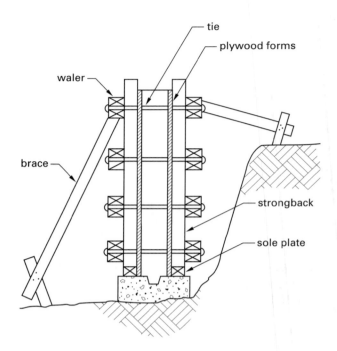

(a) wall formwork

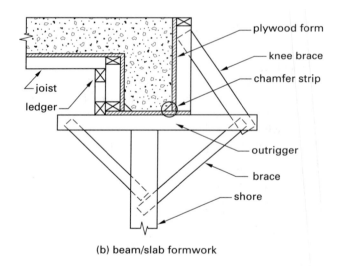

(b) beam/slab formwork

Figure 13.1 Concrete Formwork

Various types of jacking systems are used to support the form as it moves upward.

Flying forms are large fabricated sections of framework that are removed, once the concrete has cured, to be reused in forming an identical section above. They are often used in buildings with highly repetitive units, such as hotels and apartments. After forming the floor for a hotel, for example, the form assembly is slid outside the edge of the building where it is lifted by crane to the story above. Once that floor is poured, the process is repeated.

Economy in Formwork

Because one of the biggest expenses for cast-in-place concrete is formwork, the architect can minimize overall cost by following some basic guidelines. To begin with, forms should be reusable as much as possible. This implies uniform bay sizes, beam depths, column widths, opening sizes, and other major elements. Slab thicknesses should be kept constant without offsets, as should walls. Of course, structural requirements will necessitate variations in many elements, but it is often less expensive to use a little more concrete to maintain a uniform dimension than to form offsets.

Accuracy Standards

Because of the nature of the material and forming methods, concrete construction cannot be perfect; there are certain tolerances that are industry standards. Construction attached to concrete must be capable of accommodating these tolerances. For columns, piers, and walls, the maximum variation in plumb will be plus or minus $1/4$ in (6) in any 10 ft (3050) length. The same tolerance applies for horizontal elements such as ceilings, beam soffits, and slab soffits.

The maximum variation out of plumb for the total height of the structure is 1 in (25) for interior columns and $1/2$ in (13) for corner columns for buildings up to 100 ft (30 m) tall, while the maximum variation for the total length of the building is plus or minus 1 in (25). Elevation control points for slabs on grade can vary up to $1/2$ in (13) in any 10 ft (3050) bay and plus or minus $3/4$ in (19) for the total length of the structure.

For elevated, formed slabs the tolerance is plus or minus $3/4$ in (19). Finished concrete floors can be specified anywhere from plus or minus $1/8$ in in 10 ft (3 mm in 3 m) for very flat slabs to plus or minus $1/2$ in (13) for bullfloated slabs.

MOISTURE MIGRATION AND VAPOR BARRIERS

In all construction, water and moisture can cause a variety of problems. For concrete construction the potential problem of water migration through slabs on grade is one of the most significant. The problem of moisture is not as significant for suspended slabs; that is, those with an air space below them.

Moisture Migration Through Slabs on Grade

Moisture can migrate through slabs by capillary action or by movement of water vapor. Capillary action causes water to be drawn up through the slab through the forces of adhesion, surface tension, and cohesion. Water vapor moves from areas of high vapor pressure to areas of lower vapor pressure by the process of diffusion, which can occur in concrete and soil when water changes from a liquid to a vapor as it evaporates.

For slabs on grade, a vapor barrier is necessary to prevent the migration of moisture through the slab onto the surface of the slab or into the space above the slab. Moisture can cause damage to water-sensitive floor finishes, such as vinyl tile, and can create indoor air quality problems by supplying one of the necessary components of mold and mildew growth.

In addition to providing a vapor barrier, water problems inside the building can be minimized by specifying a low water-cement (w/c) ratio and, if possible, scheduling construction so that slabs have as much time as possible to cure and dry before any sealing or floor finishes are applied. Because it takes so long for the free water (that not used in the curing process) to evaporate out of the slab it is recommended that a maximum w/c ratio be set at 0.45 to 0.50. Ideally, concrete slabs should be allowed to cure and dry for a minimum of six weeks before resilient flooring is installed.

Vapor Barriers

The best way to stop the migration of moisture is with a vapor barrier placed directly below the concrete slab and on top of any sand cushion layer or subbase. This most recent recommendation is contrary to the traditional method of placing the vapor barrier under the sand cushion. However, the traditional method is no longer recommended, because the sand acts as a sponge to hold any water present during construction.

A *vapor barrier* is a thin sheet material, generally plastic, designed to prevent water vapor from passing through it. A *vapor retarder*, on the other hand, only slows the rate of water vapor transmission. A vapor barrier should have a permeance not exceeding 0.04 perm and be at least 10 mils thick. *Permeance* is a measure of a material's resistance to water-vapor transmission, expressed in perms. A *perm* is the passage of one grain of water vapor per hour through one square foot of material at a pressure differential of one inch of mercury between the two sides of the material (one nanogram per second per square meter per pascal of pressure difference).

REINFORCEMENT

Concrete is very strong in compression but weak in tension. As a result, reinforcing is required to resist the tensile stresses in beams, slabs, and columns, and to reduce the size of columns. There are two types of reinforcing steel for cast-in-place concrete: deformed bars and welded wire fabric for reinforcement of slabs.

Reinforcing Bars

Reinforcing bars, often called *rebar*, are available in diameters from $\frac{3}{8}$ in to $2\frac{1}{4}$ in (9.5 to 57), with $\frac{1}{8}$ in (3.2) increments up to $1\frac{3}{8}$ in (35). There are also two special large sizes of $1\frac{3}{4}$ in and $2\frac{1}{4}$ in (44.5 and 57). Bars are designated by numbers that represent the number of $\frac{1}{8}$ in increments in the nominal diameter of the bar. Thus, a no. 6 bar has a diameter of $\frac{6}{8}$ in, or $\frac{3}{4}$ in (19).

Because reinforcing steel and concrete must be bonded together to provide maximum strength, rebars are deformed to provide a mechanical interlocking of the two materials. Additional bonding is provided by the chemical adhesion of the concrete to steel and by the normal roughness of the steel. There are several different types of deformation patterns depending on the mill that manufactures the bar, but they all serve the same purpose. In order to clearly identify bars on the job site, standard designations have been developed for marking bars at the mill. These are shown in Fig. 13.2.

Rebars come in two common grades: grade 40 and grade 60. Grades 50 and 75 are also sometimes available. These numbers refer to the yield strengths in kips per square inch. Grade 60 is the type most used in construction. Wire for prestressing has a much higher tensile strength, up to 250 or 270 kips/in² (1724 or 1862 MPa). Rebars are classified as axle, rail, and billet; billet is the most commonly used.

In order to protect the reinforcing, there are certain minimum clearances between the steel and the exposed face of the concrete under various conditions. These are listed in Table 13.1. There are also minimum clearances between rebars to allow the coarse aggregate to pass through as the concrete is poured. If the concrete will be exposed to corrosive environments, specifically chlorides, in seawater or deicing salts, the rebars are coated with an epoxy compound or are galvanized.

Welded Wire Fabric

Welded wire fabric is used for temperature reinforcement in slabs and consists of cold-drawn steel wires, at right angles to each other, that are welded at their intersections. The wires are usually in a square pattern with spacings of 4 in or 6 in (102 to 152).

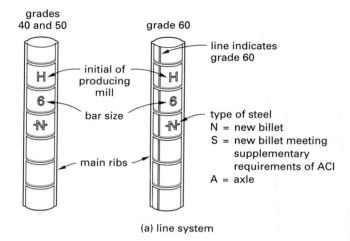

(a) line system

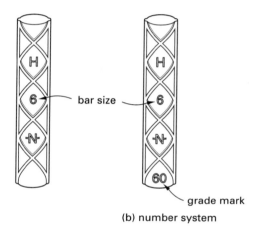

(b) number system

Figure 13.2 Reinforcing Bar Identification

Table 13.1

Minimum Concrete Protection for Reinforcement
(distance from edge of rebar to face of concrete)

location	distance (in)	(mm)
surfaces not exposed directly		
to the weather or ground:		
slabs and walls	$\frac{3}{4}$	19
beams and columns	$1\frac{1}{2}$	38
surfaces exposed to the weather		
or in contact with the ground:		
no. 5 bars and smaller	$1\frac{1}{2}$	38
larger than no. 5 bars	2	51
concrete poured directly on the ground	3	76

The system used to designate welded wire fabric consists of the size first and then the gage. The size is in inches and the gage is given in cross-sectional area in hundredths of a square inch. For example, 6 × 6–W1.4 × 1.4 means that the grid is 6 in by 6 in (150 m by 150 m), and the size of the wire is 1.4 hundredths of a square, or 0.014 in². The letter preceding the gage is either W for smooth wire or D for deformed wire. Refer to the next section for information on carbon fiber mesh.

Accessories

Before concrete is poured into the forms, various types of embedded items must be placed in addition to the reinforcing. These include welding plates for attachment of steel and other structural members, electrical boxes and conduit, sleeves for pipes to pass through the concrete, and other types of anchoring devices for suspended components and finish walls. Embedded items must be accurately placed and are temporarily held in position by wiring to the reinforcing, with nails, or with other proprietary devices until secured by the concrete.

Other accessories are used to hold the reinforcing bars in their proper locations. Intersecting reinforcing bars are wired together and held in place with spacers in walls and chairs in slabs. *Chairs* are metal wire devices placed on the form to hold the rebars above the bottom of the form at the proper distance.

CONCRETE MATERIALS

Basic Components

Concrete is a combination of cement, fine and course aggregates, and water mixed in the proper portions and allowed to cure to form a hard, durable material. In addition, admixtures are used to impart particular qualities to the mix. Because the strength of concrete depends on the materials and their proportions, it is important to understand the relationship between the constituent parts.

Portland cement is the binding agent in concrete. It is made from lime, silica, iron oxide, and alumina under strictly controlled conditions. It chemically interacts with water to form a paste that binds the other aggregate particles together in a solid mass. Cement is supplied in bulk or in 94 lbm bags containing one cubic foot.

There are five different types of cement, all used for specific purposes. Type I is called *standard cement*, or *normal cement*, and it is used for most general construction where the other types are not needed. Type II is called *modified cement*, and it is used in places where a modest amount of sulfate resistance is needed and where the heat of hydration needs to be controlled, such as in dams or other massive structures. Type III is *high-early-strength cement* and is used where a

quick set is needed. Type III also has a higher heat of hydration, so it is suitable for cold-weather concreting. Type IV, used in massive structures to minimize cracking, is called *low-heat cement*, and it is very slow setting. Type V is *sulfate resisting cement* and is used for structures that will be exposed to water or soil with a high alkaline content.

Although water is required for *hydration* (the chemical hardening of concrete) and to make it possible to mix and place the concrete into forms, too much water can decrease the concrete's strength. This is because excess water not used in the chemical process remains in the paste and forms pores that cannot resist compressive forces. Generally, for complete hydration to occur, an amount of water equal to 25% of the weight of the cement is required. An extra 10% to 15% or more is required to make a workable mix. The water itself must be potable, or drinkable, to ensure that it is free of any foreign matter that could interfere with adhesion of the aggregates to the cement paste.

For most concrete mixes the minimum water-cement ratio is about 0.35 to 0.40 by weight. Based on the weight of water, this works out to about 4 gal to 4.5 gal of water per 94 lbm sack of cement (15.1 L to 17 L per 42.7 kg sack). Because of the way water and cement interact, the water-cement ratio is the most critical factor in determining the strength of concrete. For a given mix, there should be just enough water to give a workable mix without being excessive. If too much water is added, *laitance* may develop. This is a chalky surface deposit of low-strength concrete. If additional concrete will be poured, the laitance must be removed in order for the new concrete to bond.

Aggregates consist of coarse and fine aggregates; fine aggregates are those that pass through a no. 4 sieve (one with four openings per linear inch [25 mm]). Because cement is the most expensive component of concrete, the best mix is one that uses a combination of aggregate sizes that fill most of the volume with a minimum amount of cement while still achieving the desired strength. Typically, aggregates occupy about 70% to 75% of the total volume of the concrete.

Generally, aggregates are sand and gravel, but others are used. Materials such as expanded clays, slags, and shales are used for lightweight structural concrete. Pumice or cinders are used for insulating concretes. Whereas standard concrete weighs about 150 lbm/ft³ (2400 kg/m³), lightweight mixes can range from 50 lbm/ft³ for insulating concretes to 120 lbm/ft³ for lightweight structural concrete (800 kg/m³ to 1920 kg/m³).

The size of coarse aggregates is determined by the size of the forms and the spacing between the reinforcing. In most instances, it should not be larger than three-fourths of the smallest distance between reinforcing bars or larger than one-fifth of the smallest dimension of forms, or more than one-third of the depth of slabs.

Proportioning

Several methods are used to specify the proportions of the concrete mix. One is to define the ratio of cement to sand to gravel by weight using three numbers such as 1:2:4, which means one part cement, two parts sand, and four parts gravel. In addition, the amount of water must also be specified. Another method is to specify the weight of materials, including water, per 94 lbm bag of cement. Yet another method, useful for large batch quantities, is to define the weight of the materials needed to make up one cubic yard of concrete.

The strength of the final mix is specified by the compressive strength of the concrete after it has cured and hardened for 28 days. This is known as the *design strength* of concrete. Typical specified design strengths, indicated with the symbol f'_c, are 2000 psi, 3000 psi (one of the most common), and 4000 psi (13 790, 20 680, and 25 580 kPa). Higher strengths, up to 12,000 psi (82 700 kPa), are now available for special applications but are more expensive than the standard mixes.

Admixtures

Admixtures are chemicals or other materials added to concrete to impart certain qualities. Admixtures are used to speed hydration, retard hardening, improve workability, add color, improve durability, and serve a variety of other purposes. Some of the more common admixtures are the following.

- *Air-entraining agents* form tiny, dispersed bubbles in the concrete. These agents increase the workability and durability of the concrete and improve its resistance to freezing and thawing cycles. They also help reduce segregation of the components during placing of the mix into forms.

- *Accelerators* speed up the hydration of the cement so that the concrete achieves strength faster. This allows faster construction and reduces the length of time needed for protection in cold weather.

- *Plasticizers* reduce the amount of water needed while maintaining the necessary consistency for correct placement and compaction. Reducing the water, of course, makes it possible to mix higher-strength concrete.

- *Retarders* slow down the setting time to help reduce the heat of hydration.

- *Waterproofing* agents decrease the permeability of the concrete.

- *Fly ash* is a waste material obtained from coal-fired power plants. It is used in concrete to increase strength, decrease permeability, reduce temperature rise, increase sulfate resistance, and improve workability. It can also be used to increase the total amount of cement needed. Refer to Ch. 8 for more information on how fly ash is used to make concrete a more sustainable material.

NEW CONCRETE PRODUCTS

Concrete continues to be improved through the use of new materials, admixtures, equipment, and construction techniques. Following are some innovations that are beginning to be adopted in mainstream construction practices.

Autoclaved Aerated Concrete

Autoclaved aerated concrete (AAC) is a precast concrete product manufactured by adding aluminum powder to concrete, hardening it in molds, and then curing the molds in a pressurized steam chamber (autoclave). The resultant blocks have about one-fifth the density of conventional concrete. They are typically manufactured in blocks 10 in (250) high by 25 in (635) long and in thicknesses of 4 in, 8 in, and 10 in (100, 200, and 250). The blocks are laid with a thin-set mortar and can be cut and shaped with woodworking tools. Unreinforced and reinforced panels of ACC are also produced for use as floor, roof, and wall panels.

As a sustainable material, AAC requires less material than does normal concrete and results in less construction site waste than does building with standard concrete block. It has very good sound-control qualities and thermal mass and has greater air tightness than do wood stud walls. It is resistant to insects, rodents, and mold. However, it does not have the strength of standard concrete, so construction is limited to nonloadbearing walls and low-rise structures. It must also be protected from the exterior environment with plaster, masonry, or some other exterior finish.

Self-Consolidating Concrete

Self-consolidating concrete (SCC) is a concrete mixture that can be placed purely by means of its own weight without the use of vibration. SCC is made possible with the use of a superplasticizer admixture called a polycarboxylate polymer. Because no vibration is required, SCC placement is accelerated, less labor is required, and productivity is increased. The concrete flows easily around dense reinforcement and provides a more uniform and smooth surface than does standard concrete, so less time is required to make minor cosmetic repairs. Because the concrete develops strength faster than conventional concrete, forms can be stripped sooner.

Carbon Fiber Concrete

Carbon fiber concrete uses epoxy-coated carbon fiber mesh in place of standard steel mesh for secondary steel reinforcement. It is used for precast panels, to make them thinner and lighter. Because carbon fiber is noncorrosive, less concrete cover is required. The resulting panels, in turn, require smaller foundations and support structures, reduce transportation costs, and speed the erection process.

The carbon fiber is manufactured by using industrial-grade carbon fiber and extruding it into ultra-thin fibers. The fibers are bundled together to form pieces resembling yarn, called tows. The tows are laid perpendicular to each other in a grid, with the intersecting tows bound together by a heat-cured epoxy resin. The resulting grid is about 0.04 in (1) thick. The various components of the grid can be modified to meet different strength requirements, with a typical grid having nearly seven times the tensile strength of standard steel mesh.

Poured Gypsum Decks

Poured gypsum decks are used for roofs and are similar to concrete in that a liquid mixture is poured on reinforcing material. In typical gypsum deck construction, purlins support fiber plank or rigid insulation. Wire mesh reinforcing is placed over this and gypsum poured on the assembly to a minimum depth of $2^1/_2$ in (64). Gypsum provides a highly fire-resistant roof deck.

Precast gypsum planks with tongue-and-groove edges are also available in 2 in and 4 in (50 and 100) thicknesses. They are reinforced with wire fabric and span up to 10 ft (3050).

CURING AND TESTING

Curing Concrete

Because concrete hardens and gains strength by curing through chemical reaction between the water and the cement rather than by drying, it is critical that the proper conditions of moisture and temperature be maintained for at least seven days and up to two weeks for critical work. If concrete dries out too fast, it can lose strength, up to 30% or more in some instances. With high-early-strength cements, of course, the time can be reduced. This is because concrete gains about 70% of its strength during the first week of curing, and the final 28-day design strength depends on the initial curing conditions.

There are many techniques for maintaining proper moisture levels, including covering with plastic, using sealing compounds, or continually sprinkling the surfaces with water.

Concrete must also be kept from freezing while curing or it will lose strength, sometimes as much as half. Because concrete produces heat while it cures (known as *heat of hydration*) it is often sufficient to cover the fresh material with insulated plastic sheets for a few days. In very cold conditions, Type III cement may be used and external heat supplied. In addition, the water and aggregate may be heated prior to mixing.

Testing Concrete

Because there are so many variables in concrete construction, the material must be continually tested at various stages to maintain quality. There are several tests with which the architect must be familiar: the slump test, the cylinder test, the core cylinder test, the Kelly ball test, the impact hammer test, and the K-slump test.

The *slump test* measures the consistency of the concrete, usually at the job site. In this test, concrete is placed in a 12 in high (305) truncated cone, 8 in (203) at the base and 4 in (102) at the top. It is compacted by hand with a rod, and then the mold is removed from the concrete and placed next to it. The distance the concrete slumps from the original 12 in (305) height is then measured in inches (mm). The amount of slump desired depends on how the concrete is going to be used, but it is typically in the range of 2 in to 6 in (51 to 152). Too much slump indicates excessive water in the mix, and a very small slump indicates that the mixture will be difficult to place properly.

The *cylinder test* measures compressive strength. As the concrete is being placed, samples are put in cylinder molds that are 6 in (152) in diameter and 12 in (305) high, and are moist-cured and tested in the laboratory according to standardized procedures. The compressive strength in pounds per square inch is calculated and compared with the f'_c value used in the design of the structure. Cylinders are tested at a specified number of days, normally 7 and 28 days. Seven-day tests are usually about 60% to 70% of the 28-day strength.

The *core cylinder test* is used when a portion of the structure is in place and cured but needs to be tested. A cylinder is drilled out of the concrete and tested in the laboratory to determine its compressive strength.

In the *Kelly ball test*, also known as the *ball penetration test*, a hemispheric mass of steel with a calibrated stem is dropped onto a slab of freshly laid concrete. The amount of penetration of the ball into the concrete is measured and compared to one-half the values of the slump test.

The *impact hammer test* is a nondestructive way to test concrete strength after it has hardened. A spring-loaded plunger is snapped against a concrete surface, and the amount of rebound is measured. The amount of rebound gives an approximate reading of the concrete strength. If this test is not accurate enough, then cylinder cores can be cut from hardened concrete and tested in the laboratory.

The *K-slump test* uses a $^3/_4$ in (19) tube that contains a floating scale. The tube is placed on the wet concrete, and the scale is pushed into the mixture and released. The distance the scale floats out is read directly and is a measure of the consistency of the concrete, comparable to the slump.

Testing Concrete for Moisture Content and Alkalinity

Because unwanted moisture in a slab on grade can create so many problems, as mentioned previously, the concrete should be tested for moisture level prior to the application of any critical finishes such as vinyl, rubber, linoleum, urethane, or wood. The flooring industry generally recommends that these types of flooring not be installed until the moisture emission from the concrete has reached a certain level. This maximum limit for moisture emission is 3.0 lbm per 1000 ft² per 24 hr (1.4 kg per 42 m² per 24 h) when exposed to 73°F and 50% relative humidity. There are several tests by which moisture level can be determined.

The *calcium chloride test* (sometimes called the *moisture dome test*) is one of the most common tests for moisture in concrete and is inexpensive and easy to complete. It also gives results in the same form that many flooring manufacturers use to determine if their products can be successfully installed. This test is made by placing a standard mass of calcium chloride below a plastic cover and sealing it to the concrete floor. After 60 to 72 hours, the calcium chloride is weighed to compare it with its pre-test weight. Through a mathematical formula, the amount of moisture the calcium chloride absorbed is converted to the standard measure of pounds per 1000 ft² per 24-hour period. One test should be conducted for every 500 ft² to 1000 ft² (46 m² to 93 m²) of slab area.

The *hygrometer test* (sometimes called the *relative humidity test*) determines the moisture emission by measuring the relative humidity (RH) of the atmosphere confined adjacent to the concrete floor. In this test a pocket of air is trapped below a vapor-impermeable box, and a probe in the device measures the RH. Test standards recommend that moisture-sensitive flooring not be installed unless the RH is 75% or less.

The *polyethylene sheet test* is a qualitative test conducted by sealing an 18 in by 18 in (460 by 460) sheet of plastic to the floor to trap excessive moisture. After a minimum of 16 hours a visual inspection is made of the floor and the sheet. The presence of visible water indicates the concrete is insufficiently dry for the application of finishes.

Similar to the sheet test is the *mat test*. This is also a qualitative method that uses a 24 in by 24 in (600 by 600) sample of vapor-retardant floor finish. The sample is applied with adhesive, and the edges are sealed with tape. After 72 hours a visual inspection is made. If the mat is firmly bonded or if removal of the mat is difficult, the level of moisture present is considered to be sufficiently low for installation of the flooring material.

The *electrical impedance test* uses proprietary meters to determine the moisture content of the concrete by measuring conductance and capacitance. Probes of the meter are placed on the concrete, and the percentage of moisture content in the slab is read out directly.

In addition to testing for moisture, the slab should be tested for pH level and alkalinity. *pH level* is a measure of the acidity or alkalinity of a material rated on a scale from 0 to 14 with 7 being neutral. Materials with a pH less than 7 are considered acidic while those above 7 are considered alkaline. The scale is logarithmic, so a material with a pH of 12 is actually ten times more alkaline than one with a pH of 11. Concrete normally has a pH of about 12.0 to 13.3. In addition to the alkalis within the concrete, excess alkalinity can also be carried from the soil below the slab through the migration of water vapor. This is another reason why vapor barriers are important. Although pH level is an indication of the presence of alkalinity, pH level and alkalinity are not synonymous. Two slabs can have the same pH level, but one can have a much higher alkalinity. Alkalinity cannot exist without moisture because the moisture causes the soluble alkalis in the concrete to enter into the solution. This is why it is important to first control moisture in slabs, as described previously.

Alkalinity in concrete can cause problems in two ways. High alkalinity on the surface of a slab can damage a tile installation by causing the adhesive to re-emulsify, or revert to its original liquid state. It can also cause problems with other coatings. At a level of about 9 or 10, most tile adhesives may begin to experience problems, although professional-grade adhesives can sometimes be used with a pH of 11. Surface alkalinity can be controlled with various proprietary coatings.

Alkalinity is also responsible for the phenomenon known as *alkali-silica reaction* (ASR). In this process strongly alkaline cement begins to dissolve sand and rock within the concrete. The chemical reaction produces a gel-like material that creates tremendous pressures in the pores of the concrete surface. These pressures, in turn, can buckle or blister floor finishes. The risk for ASR can be reduced by specifying aggregates that are not susceptible to ASR, by using low-lime cement, by proper curing, or by not finishing the concrete with a hard trowel surface.

A *pH test* is used to test the surface of concrete that will come in contact with flooring adhesives or other critical floor coatings. It is a simple test that uses a coated paper strip or a small pH meter. Once the pH level is known, it can be compared with the maximum pH recommended by the flooring manufacturer. A pH of 8.5 is considered ideal and about the minimum that concrete can have, with values up to 9.0 being acceptable.

In addition to the pH test, a *titration test* can be used to determine the level of alkalinity in concrete. This involves grinding portions of the concrete, mixing the resulting powder with demineralized water, and performing laboratory chemical analysis. A testing laboratory must perform this test.

PLACING AND FINISHING

Concrete Placement

Placing concrete involves several steps, from transporting the material from the truck or mixer to using the forms. First, the concrete must be conveyed to the formwork. This is done with bottom-dump buckets, by pumping, or in small buggies or wheelbarrows. Which method is used depends on the available equipment, the quantity of concrete, and the physical size and layout of the job. Concrete can even be placed underwater with a long, cylindrical steel chute called a *tremie*.

Once at the formwork, the concrete must be placed in such a way as to avoid *segregation*, which is the separation of the aggregates, water, and sand from each other. Dropping concrete long distances from the conveying device to the forms is one of the typical causes of segregation. Typically, 5 ft (1500) is the maximum distance that concrete should be dropped. Excessive lateral movement of the concrete in forms or slab work is another practice that should be minimized.

After placement, the concrete must be compacted to make sure the wet material has flowed into all the forms and around all the rebar, to make sure that it has made complete contact with the steel, and to prevent *honeycombing*, the formation of air pockets within the concrete and next to the forms. For small jobs, hand compaction can be used. More typically, it is done with vibrators.

As-Cast Finishes

Concrete can be finished in a variety of ways. The simplest is to leave the concrete as it is when the forms are removed. A *rough form finish* shows the pattern of the formwork and joints between forms. Defects and tie holes may be left unfinished or finished. This is the roughest finish and is usually used for concrete that will not be visible.

A *smooth form finish* is similar, but smooth forms of wood, metal, or hardboard are used, and joints and tie holes are planned so that they are symmetrical. Any fins left from concrete seeping into joints between forms are removed.

Architectural Finishes

Architectural finishes are used where concrete will be exposed and appearance is a consideration. There are several varieties of these finishes.

- *Form liner*. The concrete is shaped with liners of plastic, wood, or metal. Parallel rib liners are a common type. Joints and form tie holes are treated as desired—either left exposed or patched.

- *Scrubbed*. The surface of the concrete is wetted and scrubbed with a wire or fiber brush to remove some of the surface mortar and expose the coarse aggregate.

- *Acid wash*. The surface of the concrete is wetted with muriatic acid to expose and bring out the full color of the aggregate.

- *Water jet*. A high-pressure water jet mixed with air is used to remove some of the mortar and expose the aggregate.

Tooled and Sandblasted Finishes

Tooled finishes are produced by mechanically modifying the concrete surface.

- *Bush hammering*. A bush-hammered finish gives a rugged, heavy texture by removing a portion of the surface made with form liners. The type of texture depends on the form liner used.

- *Grinding*. This finishing technique smoothes out the surface of the concrete. It is similar to terrazzo in appearance.

- *Applied*. Applied finishes include the application of other materials, such as stucco, to the concrete.

- *Sandblasted finishes*. These are produced by removing surface material from the concrete. This exposes the fine and coarse aggregate to varying degrees, depending on whether the sandblasted finish is specified as light, medium, or heavy.

Rubbed Finishes

- *Smooth*. The surface of the concrete is wetted and rubbed with a carborundum brick to produce a smooth, uniform color and texture.

- *Grout cleaned*. Grout is applied over the concrete and smoothed out. This results in a uniform surface with defects concealed.

Concrete Slab Finishes

After a concrete slab is poured, the first finishing operation is to *strike off* the concrete by drawing a straightedge (metal or wood) across the forms to give a roughly level surface. If a smooth surface is required, the slab is then floated. This operation brings cement paste to the surface, where it is consolidated and smoothed over the coarse aggregate. *Floating* can be done with a wood or magnesium float or a bull float. *Floats* are simply hand-held wood or magnesium trowels. A *bull float* is similar to a standard float, but is wider and is attached to a long handle that allows finishers to smooth large concrete surfaces while standing away from the fresh concrete. At this point in the finishing operation the following finishes are available.

- If no further work is done after floating, the finish is called a *float finish*. It gives a sandpaper-like texture and is appropriate for exterior surfaces or where smooth surfaces are not required for other finish materials. A wood float gives a rougher finish texture than does a magnesium float.

- A *light steel troweled finish* is achieved by using a steel trowel several hours after floating. This further consolidates the concrete. Either hand trowels or large, mechanically driven rotary trowels may be used.

- A *hard steel troweled finish* continues the consolidation of the concrete and greatly densifies the top $^1/_8$ in (3) of the concrete, making a very smooth surface.

- After floating, a *broom finish* is created by running an industrial broom with medium bristles over the surface of the concrete. This process dislodges fine aggregate and products a rough-textured surface useful for slip-resistance on outdoor slabs.

- A *superflat floor finish* typically has a hard steel troweled finish, but mainly refers to the smoothness and levelness of a concrete slab. A superflat floor is commonly used in industrial warehouses where automated or special forklift vehicles are used to rapidly locate and retrieve materials from high-rack storage. Because of the small distances between the storage racks and the vehicles and the high reach of the lifts, the vehicle must travel on a very smooth, level floor.

JOINTS AND ACCESSORIES

Purposes and Types of Concrete Joints

There are four primary types of concrete joints: control, construction, expansion, and isolation. They all serve different functions and are constructed differently. See Fig. 13.3.

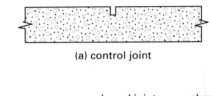
(a) control joint

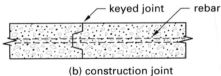
(b) construction joint

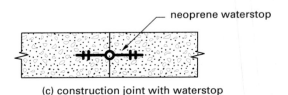
(c) construction joint with waterstop

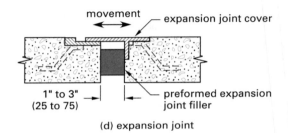
(d) expansion joint

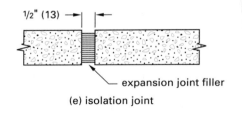
(e) isolation joint

Figure 13.3 Concrete Joints

Control joints create a weak section so that normal temperature and stress cracking occurs along the joint instead of at random. Control joints are normally formed by tooling when the concrete is still wet, by sawcutting, or by using premolded sections in the formwork. They are cut to a depth of one-fourth the slab thickness.

Construction joints occur wherever there are two successive pours; that is, wherever there is a new pour against a cured section of concrete. Because a construction joint creates a plane of weakness, it should be located at points of minimum shear. Normally, reinforcing extends from one pour to another to tie the two sections together. Construction joints are also a point where water leakage can occur. To prevent this, prefabricated waterstops can be inserted in the first pour that extend into the second pour, as shown in Fig. 13.3.

Expansion joints allow entire sections of a concrete structure to move independently of one another. The movement can be caused by shrinkage of the concrete or temperature changes. Because the movement can be cyclical, the expansion joint must be capable of moving in two directions. Expansion joints are complex fabrications, portions of which are embedded in the concrete and portions of which are exposed. In most instances, the expansion joint extends through the entire structure so there is no rigid connection between any two components of adjacent building sections.

Isolation joints also allow two adjacent sections to move independently of one another, but they are not as complex as expansion joints. Typically, they simply consist of two separate pours of concrete separated with a premolded joint material. They are often used to separate columns from slabs and slabs from foundations and other types of walls.

Inserts

Concrete inserts include a wide range of anchoring devices used to attach other materials and components to concrete construction. For example, *weld plates* are steel plates cast flush with the surface of concrete, to which steel members are welded. The weld plate is attached to a steel anchor that extends into the concrete for positive anchorage. In some cases, the anchors are welded to the reinforcing bars.

Concrete Sealers

Concrete sealers are proprietary products applied to concrete to protect against weather and water penetration, provide resistance to chemicals, to prevent dusting of the surface, or harden the surface. Other coatings are applied for decorative purposes. Some products help cure the concrete while sealing it.

There are two general types of concrete sealers: coating types and penetrating types. The coating types dry as a surface film and are made from a variety of materials including acrylics, urethanes, and epoxies. The penetrating types seep into the tiny pores of the concrete and include proprietary products made with silicones, silanes, and siloxanes. Because of the way they work, penetrating sealers do not wear off as some surface sealers do. Some proprietary formulations can be used to stop moisture and alkaline migration through an existing concrete slab.

PRECAST CONCRETE

Precast concrete consists of components cast in separate forms in a place other than their final position. Precast concrete can be cast on site or in fabricating plants where conditions can be more carefully controlled and where work can proceed regardless of the weather.

Beams and Columns

Precast concrete beams for buildings are usually rectangular, T-shaped, or L-shaped, as shown in Fig. 13.4. T-shaped and L-shaped beams allow the floor structure to be flush with the top of the beam and minimize the total depth needed for the structure. Two very efficient sections that are widely used are the single-T and double-T. These combine a deep section for efficient beam action and a wide flange for the floor structure. When T-sections are used, a topping slab is poured to cover the joints and provide a level floor. T-sections are often used with T-shaped and L-shaped beams in precast buildings.

Precast columns are usually rectangular in shape and cast with welding plates at the top and bottom. They are often cast with haunches that support beams, as shown in Fig. 13.4.

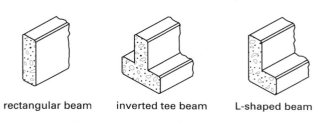

rectangular beam   inverted tee beam   L-shaped beam

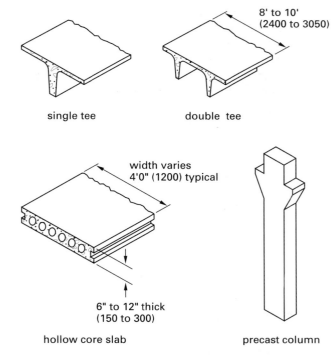

single tee   double tee

8' to 10'
(2400 to 3050)

width varies
4'0" (1200) typical

6" to 12" thick
(150 to 300)

hollow core slab   precast column

Figure 13.4 Typical Precast Concrete Shapes

Floor and Roof Panels

In addition to precast T-sections that serve as floor and roof structures, simple reinforced concrete slabs are cast for this purpose. For light loads and short spans, the slabs may be solid; for heavier loads and longer spans, hollow, cored slabs are used. These allow the depth of the slab to be increased for more efficient load-carrying capability while still minimizing weight. Cored slabs are 6 in to 12 in (150 to 300) thick and normally 4 ft (1200) wide. They can span up to 36 ft (11 m).

Lift slab construction is a technique for multistory construction in which entire floor sections are cast on the ground, one on top of another around pre-erected columns. The slabs are poured with a bond breaker between successive pours. Once cured, the slabs are lifted into place with jacks attached to the columns. The slabs are connected to the columns with weld plates. This type of construction minimizes the amount of formwork required and generally reduces total construction time.

Wall Panels

Wall panels can be cast in a variety of sizes and shapes. For greatest economy, the number of types of panels and openings should be minimized. Wall panels are generally 5 in to 8 in (125 to 200) thick (although they can be thicker) and long enough to span columns or beams. If the panels span beams, greater cost savings can be achieved in multistory buildings by casting panels to span two floors.

Wall panels can be cast in a precasting plant or on site. A typical method of building is with tilt-up construction. With this procedure the panels are cast in a horizontal position near their final location and lifted into place when sufficiently cured. In many cases the panels are cast directly on the building's floor slab with temporary boards forming the edges. A bond breaker is used to prevent the wall panel from sticking to the casting surface. A bond breaker may be a liquid solution or a sheet of plastic, but liquids result in a better finish.

PRECAST, PRESTRESSED CONCRETE

Prestressed concrete consists of members that have internal stresses applied to them before they are subjected to service loads. The prestressing consists of compressive forces applied where the member would normally be in tension. This effectively eliminates or greatly reduces tensile forces that the member is not capable of carrying. In addition to making a more efficient and economical structural section, prestressing reduces cracking and deflection, increases shear strength, and allows longer spans and greater loads. Prestressing is accomplished in one of two ways: pretensioning and post-tensioning.

Pretensioning

With this system, concrete members are produced in a precasting plant. High-strength pretensioning stranded cable or wire is draped in forms according to the required stress pattern, and a tensile force is applied. The concrete is then poured and allowed to cure. Once the concrete cures, the cables are cut and the resulting compressive force is transferred to the concrete through the bond between cable and concrete.

Post-Tensioning

In post-tensioned construction, hollow sleeves or conduits are placed in the forms on the site, and concrete is poured around them. Within the sleeves are high-strength steel tendons, which are stressed with hydraulic jacks after the concrete has cured. Once the desired stress has been applied, the ends of the cables are secured to the concrete and the jacks are removed. If the tendons are to be unbonded, no further action is taken. In bonded construction, the sleeves are removed and grout is forced into the space between the tendons and the concrete.

MASONRY 14

Masonry construction is one of the oldest building techniques known. It has survived through the centuries because of its many advantages: masonry is durable and strong, it can be formed into a variety of building shapes, and the raw materials are available in most parts of the world. Combined with modern materials such as improved mortars, reinforcing, and flashing, brick and stone remain timeless materials.

In simplest terms, masonry consists of an assembly of relatively small units of stone, burned clay, or other manufactured material held in place with mortar. Traditionally, masonry has been considered a material to be used to support loads in compression because stone, brick, and mortar have negligible resistance to tensile or bending forces. Horizontal spanning with masonry was always accomplished with some form of arch.

However, with steel reinforcing, high-strength mortars, steel lintels, and the like, brick and unit masonry can be used in an ever wider variety of situations, both horizontally and vertically. Philosophically, however, many designers still feel that since masonry is compressive by nature, it should be used in the traditional way.

MORTAR

Mortar is the cementitious material used to hold masonry units together. It must be compatible with the masonry units being used, the strength required, and the environmental conditions.

Components of Mortar

Mortar is a mixture of cement, lime, sand, and water. Normally, portland cement is used. Lime is added to plasticize the cement so that it is more workable, to add resilience, and to increase the water retention of the mortar. Resilience is important to accommodate movement caused by temperature change and brick swell. Water retention is important to improve the hydration of the cement as it sets.

Masonry cement is a prepared mixture of portland cement and pulverized limestone. It is not as strong or expensive as portland cement, but it has greater plasticity. It is suitable for low-rise building veneers and for interior, nonloadbearing applications.

Various other types of cements are available for special applications. One of the most common is nonstaining cement, which should be used for marble, limestone, terra cotta, cut stone, and glazed brick.

Types of Mortar

There are four basic types of mortar: Types M, S, N, and O. Each has a different proportion of cement, lime, and aggregate, and each has a different compressive strength. These are summarized in Table 14.1. Which mortar is specified depends on the type of masonry unit being used and the conditions of use. Generally, a job should never use a mortar that is stronger in compression than required. In addition, because lime helps retain water in the mortar for hydration, a mortar with a high lime content is appropriate for bricks with a high initial rate of absorption or for summer construction where evaporation is a factor. Table 14.2 summarizes some guidelines for mortar selection.

Grout

Grout is similar to mortar, but it is mixed to a pouring consistency and used to fill wall cavities or cores of hollow masonry units and to bond masonry to reinforcement. Grout may be fine or coarse. Coarse grout includes no. 4 aggregate (pea gravel). Fine grout is used when the dimensions of the space in which the grout is placed are less than 2 in (50).

Table 14.1

Types of Mortar

cement	type	portland cement	masonry cement M	masonry cement S	masonry cement N	hydrated lime or lime putty	aggregate ratio— measured in a damp, loose condition	min. average 28-day compressive strength (psi)	(kPa)
cement-lime	M	1		–		$\frac{1}{4}$		2500	17235
	S	1		–		over $\frac{1}{4}$ to $\frac{1}{2}$	not less than $2\frac{1}{4}$ and not more than 3	1800	12410
	N	1		–		over $\frac{1}{2}$ to $1\frac{1}{4}$	times the sum of the separate volumes of	750	5170
	O	1		–		over $1\frac{1}{2}$ to $2\frac{1}{2}$	cementitious materials	350	2410
masonry cement	M	1	_	–	1	–		2500	17235
	M	–	1	–	–				
	S	$\frac{1}{2}$	–	–	1	–		1800	12410
	S	–	–	1	–				
	N	–	–	–	1	–		750	5170
	O	–	–	–	1	–		350	2410

Table 14.2

Selection of Mortar

location	building component	mortar type 1st choice	alternate
exterior, above grade	loadbearing wall	N	S or M
	nonloadbearing wall	O*	N or S
	parapet wall	N	S
exterior, at or below grade	foundation walls, retaining walls	S	M or N
	pavements, walks, manholes		
interior	loadbearing walls	N	S or M
	nonloadbearing walls	O	N

*Use Type O mortar only where masonry is unlikely to be frozen when wet or unlikely to be exposed to high winds or other lateral loads.

BRICK

Types of Brick

A *brick* is a relatively small masonry unit made from burned clay, shale, or a mixture of these materials that is not less than 75% solid. The two basic types of brick are facing brick and building brick (also called *common brick*). As the name implies, *facing brick* is used for exposed locations where appearance and uniformity of size are important.

Building brick is made without regard to color or special finish.

Building brick is graded according to resistance to exposure: SW (severe weathering), MW (moderate weathering), and NW (negligible weathering). Among other things, these grades reflect the ability of brick to resist freeze-thaw cycles. Facing brick is available in SW and MW grades and is further classified into three types: FBS, FBX, and FBA. FBS is for general use where a wide range of color and variation in size are acceptable or required. FBX is used when a high degree of mechanical perfection, narrow color range, and minimal variation in size are required. FBA is nonuniform in color, size, and texture.

Hollow brick is also available in SW and MW grades. Like facing brick, hollow brick is further classified according to its appearance. HBS is for general use where a range of size and color variation are acceptable or desired. HBX is used when a high degree of mechanical perfection, narrow color range, and minimum variation in size are required. HBA is nonuniform in color, size, and texture.

There are many sizes of brick, but not all of them are available from all manufacturers. Some typical sizes are shown in Fig. 14.1 along with the common terms used to describe the various surfaces. The most common size is manufactured to an actual dimension of $3^5/8$ in thick, $2^1/4$ in high, and $7^5/8$ in long. With a mortar joint of $3/8$ in, this gives a modular size of 4 in thick and 8 in long. Three courses equal 8 in (200), the same as a standard concrete block course. Metric bricks are 90 mm wide and 190 mm long with 10 mm mortar joints.

Brick Coursing

Brick can be laid in a variety of patterns depending on which surface is oriented to the outside and what position it is in. Fig. 14.2 illustrates the methods of laying brick courses and the terms used to describe them. (A *course* is one continuous horizontal layer of masonry.)

The method of laying several courses in a wall is called the *bonding pattern*. A brick wall is stronger if the joints do not align and the bricks overlap. Before steel joint reinforcing was used, bonding patterns were a way to accomplish this and to tie several wythes of brick together. A *wythe* is a continuous vertical section of a wall one masonry unit in thickness. For example, a header course was designed to hold a two-wythe wall together, since the length of the brick was as long as the thickness of the double wall.

With joint reinforcement, metal wall ties, and veneer walls, bonding patterns are not as important as they once were for structural reasons, although overlapping bricks still form a stronger wall than do aligned joints. Some common bonding patterns are shown in Fig. 14.3.

Brick Joints

Joints are a critical part of any masonry wall. The mortar in the joints not only holds the entire wall together, it also prevents infiltration of water and air. Bricks should be set in full beds of mortar, on both the bed joints and head joints.

After the brick is laid, the joints must be tooled. *Tooling* imparts a decorative effect to the wall, but more important, it makes the joint more watertight by compressing the

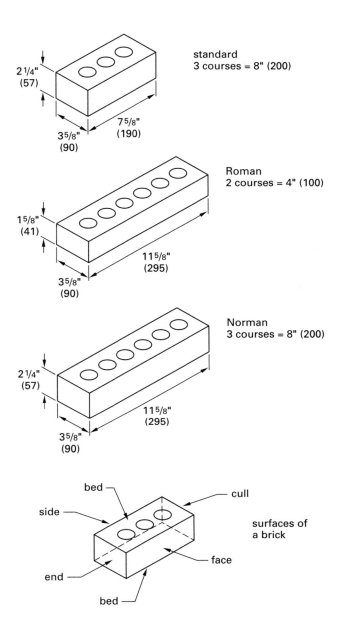

Figure 14.1 Sizes and Faces of Brick

mortar near the exposed surface. There are various types of mortar joints, as shown in Fig. 14.4, but only a few are recommended for exterior use because they shed water more effectively. These are the concave, flush, and vee joints. A weather-struck joint is sometimes acceptable for exterior use, but water running down the brick above the joint may not drip off and may instead run horizontally under the brick. If the joint is not tight, the water can be drawn through the joint by capillary action or by a pressure differential between the outside and inside of the wall.

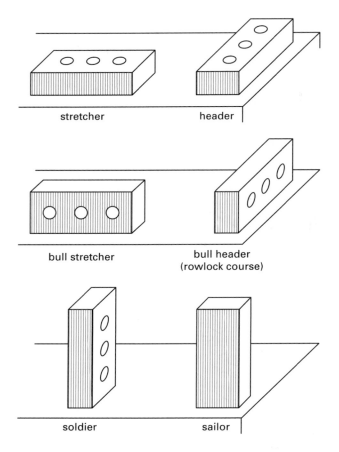

Figure 14.2 Brick Courses

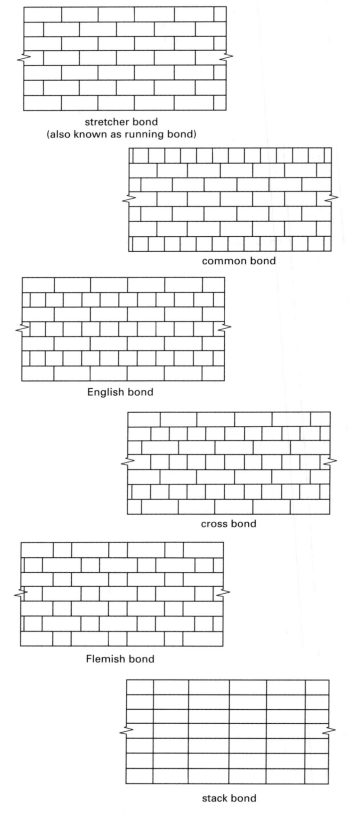

Figure 14.3 Brick Bond Patterns

In addition to the joints between individual masonry units, there must be horizontal and vertical joints to accommodate building movement caused by differential movement between materials and by temperature changes. If joints are not provided for such movement, cracking can occur in the joints or in the bricks themselves, resulting in water and air leakage and an unsightly appearance. In the worst case, stresses can be great enough without joints that the brick can crack and spall off.

There are several types of joints. Construction joints isolate the masonry from through-wall elements such as doors and windows. Control joints accommodate thermal expansion and contraction. Vertical control joints are constructed by separating two sections of masonry by about ³/₈ in to ¹/₂ in (10 to 13) and filling the joint with a backing covered with a sealant. In many cases, a neoprene gasket is placed within the wall between the two sections of masonry. Expansion joints are similar to control joints and accommodate expansion from swelling of the brick. Through-building expansion joints are much larger and are used to completely separate two sections of a building.

Major expansion joints are usually spaced every 100 ft to 150 ft (30 m to 45 m) in large buildings. Expansion and control joints are spaced about every 20 ft (6 m) and at places where the wall changes direction, height, or thickness.

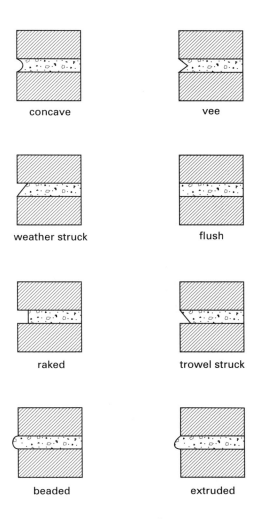

Figure 14.4 Brick Joints

Horizontal expansion joints should be placed below shelf angles that support intermediate sections of brick and below beams and slabs above brick. One such detail is shown in Fig. 14.5. These types of joints prevent excessive stress from being placed on the brick from the deflection of the angle or beam above.

Brick Construction

Although brick is a basic, simple construction material, it must be designed, detailed, and installed correctly in order to function properly. There are many types of brick and masonry walls. The more common ones are shown in Fig. 14.6.

A *single-wythe wall* consists of one layer of brick that acts as either a loadbearing or nonloadbearing wall. Because it is unreinforced, the maximum ratio of unsupported height or length to thickness cannot exceed 20:1 for a solid wall or 18:1 for a hollow masonry wall.

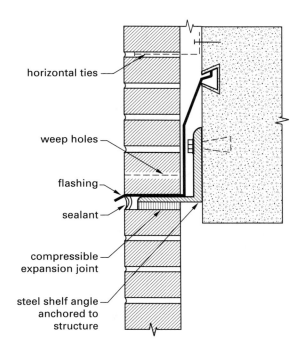

Figure 14.5 Typical Attachment of Brick Facing at Intermediate Floor

A *cavity wall* consists of two wythes of brick separated by an air space. The two sections must be tied together. This is most often done with galvanized metal wall ties or continuous horizontal reinforcement placed 16 in (400) on center vertically.

A *reinforced grouted wall* also consists of two wythes of brick, but the cavity contains vertical and horizontal reinforcing bars and is completely filled with grout. Compared with cavity walls, grouted walls can carry heavier loads, have higher unsupported heights, and are better able to resist lateral loading.

A *veneer wall* is a single wythe of brick attached to some other type of construction, normally a wood-frame wall, as shown in Fig. 14.6(d). In a veneer wall, the masonry is for decorative and weatherproofing purposes rather than for structural support.

One of the most important considerations in designing a brick wall is watertightness. In order to accomplish this, the brick and mortar must first be properly selected for the climate conditions and loading, as previously discussed. The brick joints must be tooled correctly to shed water and prevent expansion, and control joints must be located correctly to allow the wall to move without opening up cracks.

Next, the wall must be flashed and finished to prevent water from entering and to allow water that does enter to flow out. See Fig. 14.7. The tops of walls and parapets should be flashed and capped with coping, which should extend

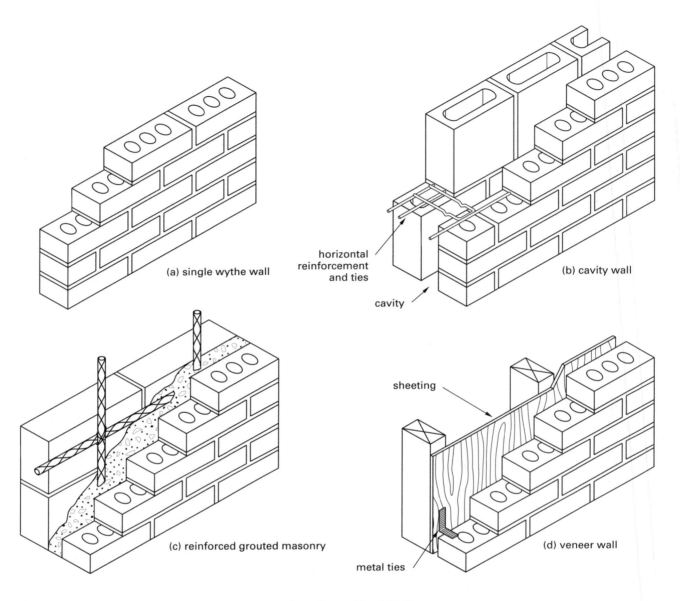

horizontal reinforcement and ties

cavity

(a) single wythe wall

(b) cavity wall

sheeting

(c) reinforced grouted masonry

metal ties

(d) veneer wall

Figure 14.6 Types of Brick Walls

beyond the face of the wall and include drips to allow water to drain off instead of run down the wall. The slope of the coping is called the *wash*.

Base flashing should be installed at the bottom of the exterior wythe, extend up about 8 in to 10 in (200 to 250), and be set in a reglet or masonry joint in the interior wythe, as shown in Fig. 14.7. Weep holes should be located 24 in (600) on center horizontally in the lowest course of brick to allow any water that penetrates the wall to drip out. This type of detail should also be used over windows and at shelf angles, as shown in Fig. 14.5.

Openings

Today, most openings in masonry construction are spanned with steel lintels. Steel lintels are often used because they are inexpensive and simple to install, and because their size and thickness can be varied to suit the span of the opening. Lintels should bear on each end of the supporting masonry such that the bearing capacity is not exceeded, but in no case should the bearing length be less than 6 in (150). However, there are several alternatives to steel lintels as shown in Fig. 14.8.

An arch is the traditional method of spanning a masonry opening because the compressive capabilities of the

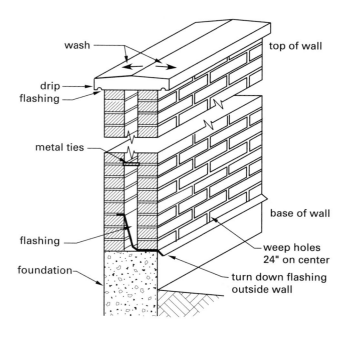

Figure 14.7 Brick Wall Construction

material are used. Alternately, a reinforced concrete beam
(see Fig. 14.8(c)) or a fully grouted and reinforced concrete
unit masonry bond beam (see Fig. 14.8(d)) can be used.

Regardless of the type of lintel used, there is always arch
action over the opening. This is shown diagrammatically in
Fig. 14.9. Unless a concentrated load or a floor load is near
the top of the opening, the lintel only carries the weight of
the wall above the opening in a triangular area defined by a
60° angle from each side of the opening.

Efflorescence

Efflorescence is a white, crystalline deposit of water-soluble
salts on the surface of brick masonry. It is caused when
water seeps into the masonry and dissolves soluble salts
present in the masonry, backup wall, mortar, or anything in
contact with the wall. The dissolved salts are brought to the
surface of the brick and appear when the water evaporates.
Although unsightly, efflorescence is usually not harmful to
the brick.

Efflorescence can be prevented or minimized by using
materials with few or no soluble salts, by forming tight
joints, and by detailing the wall to avoid water penetration.
Both brick and mortar can be specified to contain no or limited amounts of soluble salts. If efflorescence does occur, it
can be removed by dry brushing or by washing with a 5%
solution of muriatic acid. A simple water wash can also be
used, but this should be done in warm, dry weather so
additional moisture is not added to the problem.

Figure 14.8 Masonry Lintels

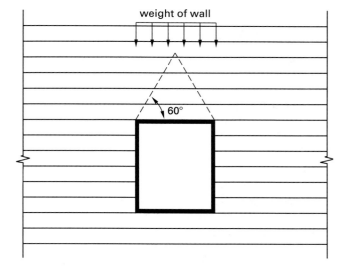

Figure 14.9 Arch Action in a Masonry Wall
over an Opening

Cleaning and Restoration

At the completion of a job, brick should be cleaned with a mild 5% to 10% solution of muriatic acid in water and then washed off with clean water. A stiff brush can be used to remove loose mortar pieces, stains, and efflorescence.

Restoration of brick is more difficult. Over time, many problems can develop with brick. It can be physically damaged, mortar joints can deteriorate, and the entire surface can become dirty and stained. Damaged units must be carefully removed and replaced with new brick that matches the existing surface as closely as possible. If mortar has fallen out, it must be replaced with a process known as *tuck pointing* or *repointing*. In this process, the mortar in the areas to be redone is removed to about $2^{1}/_{2}$ times the depth of the joint. The joint is then cleaned and wetted with water. New mortar is pressed into the joint with a special tuck-pointing tool. High-lime mortar is best and should be applied in layers; each one applied after the previous one becomes thumbprint hard.

There are several ways to clean brick. The one used should be selected for compatibility with the nature of the soiling, the amount of cleaning desired, the surrounding environment in which the cleaning must take place, and the type of brick involved. High-pressure water washing is often effective but can wash away mortar and create swirl marks across the surface of the wall. Simply scrubbing the wall by hand with a brush and water may be required for soft brick. Acid solutions and other types of chemicals may be used to remove stubborn dirt and stains, but this, too, is not always appropriate for some brick and can damage surrounding surfaces. Abrasive cleaning using sand, glass beads, or walnut shells can be used in certain circumstances, but this can erode both brick and mortar.

OTHER UNIT MASONRY

Unit masonry is a term used to describe various types of building products assembled with mortar, of which brick is one kind. Other types of unit masonry include concrete block, clay tiles, ceramic veneer, stone, terra cotta, gypsum block, and glass block.

Concrete Block

Concrete block is the common term for concrete unit masonry, also known as *concrete masonry units* (CMUs). This building product is manufactured with cement, water, and various types of aggregate, including gravel, expanded shale or slate, expanded slag or pumice, and limestone cinders.

Concrete block is classified as hollow, loadbearing; solid, loadbearing; hollow, nonloadbearing; and solid, nonloadbearing. Solid units are those that are 75% or more solid

material in any general cross section. Hollow units are those that are less than 75% solid material.

CMU dimensions are based on a nominal 4 in module with actual dimensions being $^3/_8$ in less than the nominal dimension to allow for mortar joints. Unit dimensions are referred to by width, height, and then length. One of the most common sizes is an 8 in by 8 in 16 in unit, which is actually $7^5/_8$ in wide and high and $15^5/_8$ in long. Common thicknesses are 4, 6, 8, 10, and 12 in, and common lengths are 8, 12, and 16 in. Concrete block is manufactured in a wide variety of shapes to suit particular applications. A few of the most common shapes are shown in Fig. 14.10. A metric block is 190 mm by 190 mm by 390 mm with 10 mm mortar joints.

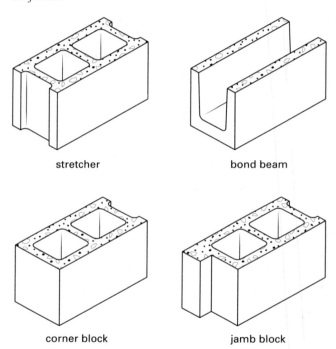

stretcher　　　　　　bond beam

corner block　　　　　jamb block

Figure 14.10 Typical Concrete Block Shapes

Concrete block walls can be either single or double wythe, but they are normally single thickness, for greater economy and speed of construction. The cores allow walls to be reinforced and grouted if additional strength is required for vertical or lateral load bearing. As with brick walls, horizontal reinforcing is required every 16 in (406) on center. Walls can simply be grouted if additional fire or sound resistance is required. Figure 14.11 shows a typical reinforced, grouted concrete masonry wall. It also shows the use of a bond beam at the top of the wall that can serve as a lintel over openings, to provide bearing for the floor and roof structure, and to resist lateral loads from floor and roof diaphragms.

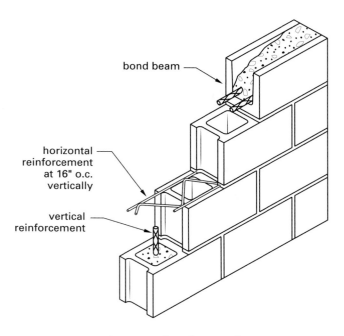

Figure 14.11 Reinforced, Grouted Concrete Masonry Wall

Because most concrete block walls consist of hollow units, it is important to understand equivalent thickness. *Equivalent thickness* is the solid thickness that would be obtained if the same amount of concrete contained in a hollow unit were recast without core holes. The value is calculated from the actual thickness of the block and the percentage of solid materials.

Example 14.1

What is the equivalent thickness of an 8 in thick concrete block that is 60% solids?

Actual thickness is $7^5/8$ in (7.625). Equivalent thickness is then

$$(7.625 \text{ in})(0.60) = 4.58 \text{ in}$$

Fire ratings for masonry walls are based on this value and the type of material used in the manufacture of the block. Building codes give the required equivalent thicknesses for various hourly fire ratings. The designer must determine whether the thickness and type of concrete block being used meet the required fire rating.

Detailing for concrete block and brick walls is especially important to prevent cracking, leaking, and structural instability. Adequate expansion and control joints should be provided, and recommended horizontal joint reinforcing should be installed as stated previously. In addition, the connection of other materials to the masonry must be well

detailed to maintain weather tightness and prevent other problems from developing.

One example of masonry detailing is shown in Fig. 14.12. This illustration shows a typical concrete block wall and parapet acting as a bearing wall for an open-web steel joist roof system. The concrete masonry is fully grouted and reinforced to provide the required bearing capacity, and a continuous bond beam with steel bearing plate is provided for attachment of the bar joist. Generally, the height of the parapet should not exceed three times its nominal thickness unless additional lateral support is provided. In this example the vertical reinforcing is continued into the parapet to anchor it to the rest of the wall and provide additional lateral support.

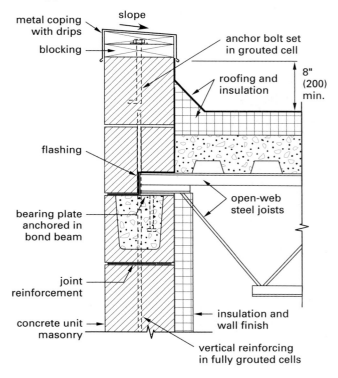

Figure 14.12 Reinforced Masonry Wall at Parapet

In this example a metal coping is used to keep water out of the wall, and it is sloped toward the roof to minimize the amount of water dripping on the side of the building. Alternately, a stone or precast concrete coping could be used if it is sloped and provided with drips to prevent water from seeping under its lower edge. To prevent leakage from moisture on the roof or from snow piled next to the parapet, the roofing is carried up under the coping. If the parapet is high, a counterflashing should be used with one edge fully embedded in a mortar joint. Additional flashing is used on the outside of the roof slab and joists.

Structural Clay Tile

Structural clay tile is made from burned clay and is formed into hollow units with parallel cells. Clay tile is available in loadbearing and nonloadbearing types and with glazed surfaces appropriate for finished exterior or interior walls.

Glazed structural clay facing tile is a loadbearing clay tile having a finish consisting of ceramic glaze fused to the body at above 1500°F (665°C). There are two grades of glazed structural tile: S grade (select) is for use with relatively narrow mortar joints, and SS grade (select sized) is for use where the variation of face dimensions must be very small.

Two types of structural clay tile are produced: side construction and end construction as shown in Fig. 14.13. Side construction tile is designed to receive its principal stress at right angles to the axis of the cells, and end construction tile is designed to receive principal stress parallel to the axis of the cells. Various sizes are produced in nominal 3, 4, 6, and 8 in widths and 6, 8, 12, and 16 in heights and lengths (76, 102, 152, and 203 mm widths and 152, 203, 305, and 406 mm heights and lengths).

Structural clay tile is used for loadbearing masonry walls that will be finished with other materials, as backup for exterior walls, and as nonloadbearing interior partitions. For interior partitions, glazed structural clay tile provides a wall with a hard, durable, decorative finish in one unit.

Terra Cotta

Terra cotta is a high-fired clay unit used for cladding and decorative purposes in building construction. Also known as *ceramic veneer*, terra cotta is made from enriched clay materials and fired at a high temperature which gives it a hardness and density that are not possible with other clay units. The base unit without the glaze is called the *bisque*. In most cases it is glazed to make it weather resistant and to provide a limitless range of colors.

Today, terra cotta is often manufactured to provide replacement pieces for building restoration. However, it has also gained popularity once again for new construction because it can be produced in a variety of custom shapes and sizes. Terra cotta can also be formed to look like stone, but with about one-tenth the weight of stone.

Terra cotta is manufactured by machine extrusion, by molding, or by hand carving for ornate work. The finished pieces are attached to a suitable substrate either by the adhesion method or the anchored method. For adhesion application, the back of the terra cotta is cast with dovetail slots and applied on a mortar bond. As with other veneer stone, building codes limit the maximum size of any one piece and the total weight to 15 lbm/ft² (73 kg/m²). Adhered units cannot exceed 1¼ in (32) in thickness.

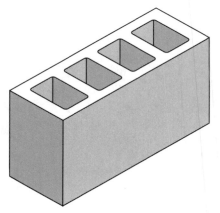

(a) end construction for loadbearing and nonloadbearing structural clay tile

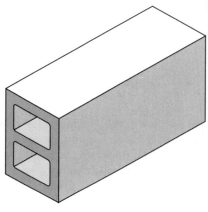

(b) side construction for structural clay facing tile

Figure 14.13   Structural Clay Tile

Anchored terra cotta is attached with stainless steel or galvanized metal anchors (usually 8-gage wire) and a full grout backing. The anchors must be at least 1¼ in (32) thick.

Because of the potential for glaze and base unit deterioration caused by moisture, terra cotta must be carefully detailed, flashed, and caulked to prevent water penetration. If moisture seeps between the bisque and the glaze, alternate freezing and thawing cycles can delaminate the glaze from the bisque. Water seeping into the clay body can also cause the clay to deteriorate.

Gypsum Block

Gypsum block or *tile* is solid or cored units cast of gypsum plaster that were previously used for nonloadbearing partitions and for fire protection of structural elements. They were available in thicknesses from 1½ in to 6 in with a standard face size of 12 in high and 30 in long. Gypsum block may be encountered when remodeling older buildings.

Glass Block

Glass block is manufactured as either a hollow or a solid unit with a clear, textured, or patterned face. The area inside the block is under a partial vacuum that improves the thermal insulating properties of the material. This property, along with the light-transmitting value and availability of obscuring patterns, makes glass block useful in both interior and exterior applications where a combination of light transmission, privacy, and insulation is needed. Solid block can also be used for flooring if it is correctly supported.

Generally, glass block does not provide rated fire resistance, but some assemblies are now available that qualify as 30-minute and 45-minute fire-rated enclosures in 1-hour walls. Underwriters Laboratories has classified some manufacturer's blocks for 60- or 90-minute ratings in openings up to 100 ft² (9.29 m²) if no dimension is greater than 10 ft (3050).

Glass block is manufactured in a nominal thicknesses of 3 in and 4 in and in face sizes of 6 × 6, 8 × 8, 12 × 12, and 4 × 8 (152 × 152, 203 × 203, 305 × 305, and 102 × 203). The two standard thicknesses are 3¹⁄₈ in and 3⁷⁄₈ in (79 and 98). The thinner block is commonly used for interior partitions. Other sizes are available from foreign manufacturers. Glass block is available in clear, textured, or patterned faces, and special blocks made by most manufacturers can be used to form 90° angles, end caps, and curves.

Glass block walls are laid in stack bond (with joints aligned rather than staggered) with Type S or N mortar and horizontal and vertical reinforcement in the joints. Because the coefficient of expansion of glass is a factor and the floor structure could experience deflection or some other building movement, it is recommended practice to provide expansion strips at the tops and sides of glass block partitions. Figure 14.14 shows typical detailing for the sill and head of an interior glass block wall.

Intermediate stiffeners are required when a glass block partition exceeds the maximum sizes allowed by the building code.

Because glass block cannot be loadbearing, individual exterior panels are limited to 144 ft² (13.4 m²) in total area and 15 ft (4572) in any direction. Interior panels are limited by code to 250 ft² (23.2 m²) and 25 ft (7620) in any direction. Each panel must be supported with suitable structure both horizontally and vertically and with expansion joints provided at the structural support points.

Cast Stone

Cast stone is a precast concrete building product made to simulate natural stone. It is a mixture of portland cement, sand, and light aggregates. It is often used as a substitute for limestone and other smooth-faced stones for facing panels,

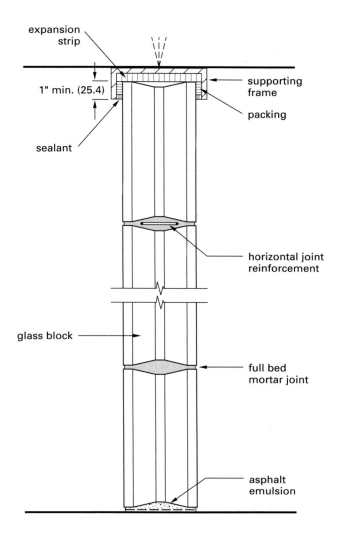

Figure 14.14 Glass Block Partition at Sill and Head

trim, ornaments, columns, moldings, and copings, among other architectural elements.

STONE

Stone is a construction material made from various types of naturally occurring rock. *Rock* is a geologic term meaning solid and unconsolidated material in the earth's crust; whereas small, quarried pieces of rock are called *stone*.

There are three classifications of rock: igneous, sedimentary, and metamorphic. *Igneous rocks* are formed from the solidification of molten rock. Granite is a type of igneous rock. *Sedimentary rocks* consist of consolidated products of rock disintegration, sea shells, and various clays and silts. Sandstone and limestone are examples of common sedimentary rocks. *Metamorphic rocks* are formed of either igneous or sedimentary rocks that have been altered by pressure or intrusion of molten rock or other liquids over a long period of time. Marble and slate are metamorphic rocks.

Types of Construction Stone

Stone is one of civilization's oldest building materials. In the past, stone has been used as both a structural material and a finish material; however, with the increased cost of stone and the labor to place it, solid stone is seldom used any longer for structural purposes. Stone is now used in the form of thin slabs for exterior and interior finish, as flooring, countertops, stair treads, and various types of trim pieces in masonry construction. Stone chips are widely used with cement for terrazzo.

Five of the most common stones used in construction include granite, marble, limestone, slate, and sandstone. Table 14.3 lists the most common uses of the various types of stone.

Stone Finishes

A wide variety of finishes is available for the different types of stone used in construction. Each type of stone has its own nomenclature, which is summarized in Table 14.4.

Stone finishes should be selected for the conditions under which they will be used. For example, highly polished surfaces are not appropriate for flooring or stairs where a small amount of water will make them very slippery. Rough finishes may not be appropriate for exterior walls in an environment where dirt and pollution may collect and be difficult to clean off.

Stone Coursing

Stone is classified by the way it is shaped and prepared prior to installation. Stone used with little or no shaping is called *rubble*, stone with slightly shaped edges resulting in vertical joints is called *squared stone*, and highly shaped stone is called *ashlar*. Ashlar is also referred to as *cut stone* and consists of thick pieces of stone.

Several methods are used to arrange stones in a wall. They are categorized into range, broken range, and random. *Range masonry* arranges stones in uniform courses for the entire length of the wall. In *broken range masonry*, stones are coursed for short distances. *Random masonry* is devoid of coursing or any attempt to align vertical joints. Figure 14.15 shows some common stone wall patterns.

Another commonly used classification of stone is *veneer stone*, so called because it is applied in relatively thin sheets, from 3/4 in to 1 1/4 in (19 to 32) thick, over a structural support system. With improved cutting methods, it is also possible to cut very thin slabs, about 3/8 in (10) thick, that can be mastic applied to a suitable backup wall. These tiles are

Table 14.3
Stones Used in Construction

types	uses
granite	exterior wall panels
	interior finish panels
	flooring
	base
	trim
	water courses
	countertops
	thresholds
	lintels
	windowsills
	stair treads
	hearths
	sculpture
	chips for terrazzo
marble	exterior wall panels
	interior finish panels
	flooring
	base
	trim
	toilet partitions
	thresholds
	tabletops
	stair treads
	hearths
	windowsills
	sculpture
	chips for terrazzo
limestone	exterior wall panels
	coping
	lintels
	sculptured trim
slate	flooring
	stair treads
	roofing
	blackboards
	countertops
sandstone	flooring
	exterior paving

Table 14.4

Types of Stone Finishes

marble finishes	
polished	a glossy surface that brings out the full color and character of the marble (not recommended for floor finishes)
honed	a satin-smooth surface with little or no gloss (recommended for commercial floors)
sandblasted	a matte-textured surface with no gloss (recommended for exterior use)
abrasive	a flat, nonreflective surface suitable for exterior use, stair treads, and other nonslip surfaces
wet-sand	a smooth surface suitable for stair treads and other nonslip surfaces

granite finishes	
polished	mirror gloss with sharp reflections
honed	dull sheen without reflections
fine-rubbed	smooth and free from scratches; no sheen
rubbed	plane surface with occasional slight "trails" or scratches
shot-ground	plane surface with pronounced circular markings or trails having no regular pattern
thermal (flame)	plane surface with flame finish applied by mechanically controlled means to ensure uniformity; surface coarseness varies, depending upon grain structure of granite
sandblasted, fine stipple	plane surface, slightly pebbled, with occasional slight trails or scratches
sandblasted, coarse stipple	coarse plane surface produced by blasting with an abrasive; coarseness varies with type of preparatory finish and grain structure of granite
8-cut	fine bush-hammered; interrupted parallel markings not over $3/32$ in (2) apart; a corrugated finish
6-cut	medium bush-hammered; markings not more than $1/8$ in (3) apart
4-cut	coarse bush-hammered; markings not more than $7/32$ in (5.5) apart
sawn	relatively plane surface, with texture ranging from wire sawn (a close approximation of rubbed finish) to shot sawn, with scorings $3/32$ in (2) in depth; gang saws produce parallel scorings; rotary or circular saws make circular scorings; shot-sawn surfaces are sandblasted to remove all rust stains and iron particles

limestone finishes	
smooth finish	machine finish producing a uniform honed finish; uses only select grade or standard grade
plucked	rough texture produced by rough planing the surface of the stone
machine tooled	finish made by cutting parallel, concave grooves in the stone with 4, 6, or 8 grooves to the inch; depth of the grooves range from $1/32$ in to $1/16$ in (0.8 to 1.6)
chat-sawed	coarse, pebbled surface that closely resembles the appearance of sandblasting; sometimes contains shallow saw marks or parallel scores; direction of score or saw marks will be vertical and/or horizontal in the wall unless the direction is specified
shot-sawed	coarse, uneven finish ranging from a pebbled surface to one rippled with irregular, roughly parallel grooves; steel shot used during gang-sawing rusts during process, adding permanent brown tones to the natural color variations
split face	rough, uneven, concave-convex finish produced by splitting action; limits stone sizes to 1 ft 4 in high by 4 ft 0 in long; available in ashlar or similar stone veneer only
rock face	similar to split face except that the face of the stone has been dressed by machine or by hand to produce bold convex projection along the face of the stone

commonly manufactured in small shapes, normally 12 in by 12 in (305 by 305) or similar sizes.

Stone Construction

Some types of stone work, such as steps, trim, coping, and belt courses, still employ cut stone, often called *dimension stone*. However, because the majority of stone wall finishes use veneer, it is important to know how such work is applied and anchored to structural backup walls. Many types of metal clamps and anchors are available for attaching cut stone and veneer stone to concrete, masonry, and

steel construction. A few of the common methods of anchoring and forming corner joints are shown in Figs. 14.16 and 14.17. In many cases, the space around the anchoring device between the back of the stone and the structural wall is filled with plaster of paris spots to plumb the stone and hold it away from the wall. The joints of stone should be filled with nonstaining portland cement mortar. Figure 14.18 shows a typical installation of stone veneer on a concrete frame building at the roof line.

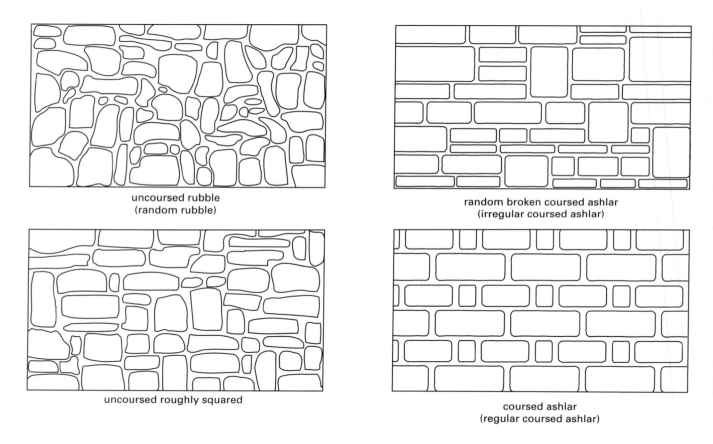

uncoursed rubble
(random rubble)

random broken coursed ashlar
(irregular coursed ashlar)

uncoursed roughly squared

coursed ashlar
(regular coursed ashlar)

Figure 14.15 Stone Patterns

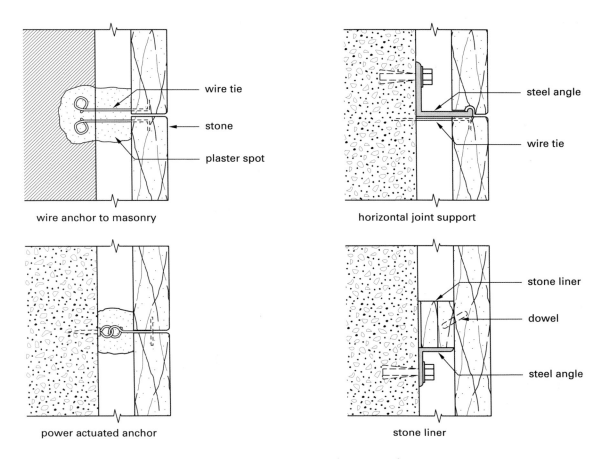

Figure 14.16 Veneer Stone Anchoring Details

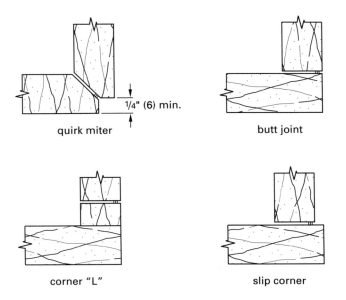

Figure 14.17 Veneer Stone Anchoring Details

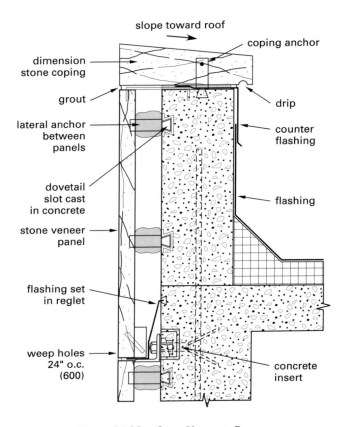

Figure 14.18   Stone Veneer at Parapet

METALS

Metals are the most versatile of all construction materials. Although they begin as natural elements, the process of refining, manufacturing, forming, and finishing metals allows an almost unlimited variety of forms and uses. Metals have been used in construction in a limited way for centuries, from the lead pipes of the Romans to the decorative grilles and doors of the English Medieval period. However, it has only been in the last 200 years that metals have seen widespread use in both structural and decorative applications.

HISTORY OF METALS

The first use of metals began over 3000 years before Christ when copper was produced by melting ores. Later, humans discovered that the copper could be strengthened by adding small amounts of tin to produce bronze. The Bronze Age continued until about 1200 B.C. when iron smelting was discovered and metal replaced bronze as the basic material for weapons, tools, and other utensils.

By the fourteenth century, cast iron was generally available in Europe, but its use in construction was largely restricted to door fittings, decorative grilles, and other small building parts. Structurally, iron chains were used by Brunelleschi to prevent the dome of Florence Cathedral from spreading (1463) and by Michelangelo for the same purpose on the dome of St. Peter's Cathedral (1585). Cast-iron pipes were used to supply water to the gardens at Versailles around 1664.

The invention that started the widespread use of iron in construction (and that helped fuel the Industrial Revolution) occurred when Abraham Darby introduced the use of coke for smelting the metal in 1709. Substituting coke for charcoal eliminated the impurities caused by charcoal and resulted in stronger, higher quality iron. By 1876 iron was being used for roof structures in France.

In 1779, Abraham Darby III made the first major use of cast-iron structural elements in a bridge over the river Severn at Coalbrookdale, England. Other cast-iron bridges followed this, and at about the same time cast-iron columns replaced wood columns in some English cotton mills.

As the nineteenth century began, cast-iron columns were commonly used for interior columns in the English mills. In other construction, the new material was being employed for railway station roofs, exhibition halls, and greenhouses. The first use of cast iron for both columns and I-beams for the entire framework of a building was in a cotton mill at Salford, Manchester. It was built by Matthew Boulton and James Watt. Although this building still used exterior masonry bearing walls, it is considered the precursor to the steel-framed buildings in Chicago during the latter part of the century.

Notable buildings during the first half of the century included the Royal Pavilion at Brighton by John Nash (1818), the Greenhouse of the Botanical Gardens in Paris by Rouhault (1833), and the Library of Saint Geneviève in Paris by Henri Labrouste (1843). At mid-century (1851), the Crystal Palace in London became the symbol of the age when Joseph Paxton designed the huge building using prefabricated parts and plate glass, which allowed the structure to be completed in only nine months. The Crystal Palace was followed by the Eiffel Tower, built for the Paris exhibition of 1889, and by the Halle des Machines, which used a 375 ft (114 m) arch formed of cast iron.

A major technical improvement in iron construction happened in 1856 when Henry Bessemer developed the Bessemer process for making steel inexpensively. Although the process was first used to make railroad rails, it produced better-quality steel (lower carbon content) and provided the raw materials for buildings that followed. In 1868 the open-hearth process improved on this further by shortening the time required for production and allowing scrap iron to be used in larger quantities.

In the United States in 1848, James Bogardus constructed a five-story factory in New York. This building was significant because it used cast-iron columns instead of masonry for the outside walls. Ten years later Bogardus designed a similar building for Harper and Brothers where he used an iron framework with large expanses of glass as infill.

The period from 1850 to the late 1880s was called the *Cast Iron Age* in the United States because of the widespread use of the material in New York, Chicago, Saint Louis, and elsewhere across the country.

In 1885 William Le Baron Jenney designed what is considered the first skyscraper. It was the ten-story Home Insurance Building in Chicago. The building utilized cast-iron columns for both the interior and exterior columns and employed the new Bessemer steel girders. In addition, the building was fireproofed.

Jenney also designed the Leiter Building in Chicago. This eight-story structure was one of the first where the architecture and engineering construction were integrated into one expression. The skeleton frame determined the form even though the exterior columns were protected by masonry. Other architects were quick to adopt the new iron and steel materials. Because most of the early and innovative work occurred in Chicago, the use of the iron skeleton came to be called "Chicago Construction."

As a strictly structural device, the steel skeleton was quickly adopted. Most architects during the latter half of the nineteenth and first half of the twentieth century still cloaked the steel in masonry and other materials. It was Mies van der Rohe who was one of the first architects to make the material and its structural purpose part of the form of the building. From his early studies for glass skyscrapers in 1919 to his later work, the steel frame was always elegantly detailed and shown, even if a false grid of steel had to be applied over the fireproofed structural frame. His most notable buildings include structures for the Illinois Institute of Technology in Chicago (from 1939 on) and the 860 Lake Shore Drive apartments (1951), also in Chicago.

BASIC MATERIALS AND PROCESSES

In their natural form, metals exist in combination with other elements and substances in metallic ores. *Smelting* is the process of refining the ores to extract the pure metal. Once the basic metal is obtained, it usually undergoes further treatment to eliminate any impurities that might affect its use.

Metals for construction are seldom used in their pure form but are combined with other elements to form alloys. The addition of other substances to the base metal imparts desirable characteristics. For example, adding chromium and nickel to steel makes the steel corrosion resistant, or stainless. It is the ability to form alloys that makes metals so versatile.

Fabricating Metals

Fabrication is the process of forming and shaping refined metal into the desired condition. The most basic fabrication method is *casting*, which has been used for centuries. In this process, molten metal is poured into a form where it is allowed to cool and harden into the desired shape. The iron columns used in the nineteenth century were cast shapes. Today, the casting process is still used for decorative shapes, pipe valves, and some hardware.

Rolling is the process of passing metal through rollers to produce the needed shape. Rolling can be done while the metal is hot or cold. Hot rolling tends to eliminate flaws in the metal, whereas cold rolling increases the metal's strength and elastic limit but decreases its ductility. Most of the structural steel shapes such as wide-flange beams and channel sections are hot rolled. Many smaller, relatively thin steel shapes are cold rolled for increased strength. All metals except iron can be formed by this method.

Extruding pushes metal through a die to form a shape. Many aluminum sections are formed this way, especially decorative sections and those used for door and window frames. One advantage to the extruding process is that if a sufficiently large quantity is required, special dies can be made and custom shapes extruded for a particular job.

Drawing is similar to extruding, but the metal is pulled through a die instead of being pushed through. The drawing process usually reduces the size of the piece or changes its shape and also improves the strength and surface qualities of the metal. Drawing is applicable for all metals except iron.

There are also many ways metal can be fabricated with mechanical forming. *Bending* changes the shape of tubes and extruded shapes by passing them through various kinds of rolling machines and presses. *Brake forming* takes plates and sheets of metal and makes successive one-directional bends to fabricate the shape. *Spinning* forms round shapes on a lathe. *Embossing* makes patterns on flat sheets of metal by passing them through a machine with the embossing pattern on rollers.

Part of the fabrication process of many metals includes some type of heat treatment. Thermal treatments are used to change the strength or workability of the material. Although any metal can be heat treated, the process is most often used with steel for various structural purposes.

Annealing is a process in which the metal is reheated and slowly cooled to obtain a more ductile metal, which will have improved its machinability and cold-forming characteristics.

Quenching involves heating the metal (most often steel) to a certain temperature and then rapidly cooling it by complete submersion in water or some other liquid. This strengthens the steel.

Tempering is similar to quenching but does not involve rapid cooling. It is also used to improve the strength and workability of steel.

Casehardening produces a hard-surface steel over a relatively softer core.

Finishing Metals

There are three general types of metal finishes. Not all of these finishes are used on all metals, but the classification helps in understanding the processes involved. Each metal type has its particular finishing systems and its own terminology, which will be discussed in the individual sections concerning each metal.

Mechanical finishes alter the surface of the metal in some way. This alteration may be as simple as the way the metal comes from the final forming process or may result from more refined finishing methods, such as grinding or buffing.

Chemical finishes are produced by altering the surface of the metal with some type of chemical process. They may simply clean and prepare the surface for other types of finishes or they may protect or color the metal. Anodizing of aluminum is one type of chemical finish in which the metal is immersed in an electrolytic bath and a current is applied to the metal. In the process, the finish, which can include various colors, becomes an integral part of the aluminum structure, producing a very durable surface.

Coatings are finishes that consist of applied materials that may be for protection of the metal or purely decorative. Coatings may be clear or opaque.

In deciding on the type of finish, several considerations should be reviewed. These include appearance, the amount of protection required, initial cost, long-term or life-cycle cost, and required maintenance.

Joining Metals

There are several methods of joining metals. The selection depends on the type of metal being joined, the working space available for the operation, and the final appearance desired.

All metals can be mechanically joined using accessories such as screws, bolts, and clips. It is common to use high-strength bolts in fastening structural steel. Bolts can also be used to fasten lighter metals such as aluminum and bronze. Bolts are useful when it is necessary to join two dissimilar metals. If potentially damaging galvanic action (electrolysis) might take place between the two metals, a plastic or rubber washer is used to separate them.

Screws can be used to join lightgage metal. Self-tapping screws are typically used to fasten metal or other materials to steel studs or other light framing. Screws are also appropriate for securing lightgage metals to other substrates, such as wood. However, heavier metals must be tapped with threads before screws can be used.

Welding is the joining of two metals by heating them above their melting point. When they cool, the metals physically form one piece of metal. Welding is commonly used for joining structural steel. Welding is not appropriate for thin metals or situations where appearance is important unless the weld can be ground smooth and finished to match the adjacent metal.

Brazing is the joining of two metals at an intermediate temperature using a nonferrous filler metal with a melting point that is above 800°F (427°C) but lower than welding. Brazing is usually used for brass, bronze, and some aluminums. It results in a clean joint, although some buffing may be required if a completely smooth joint is desired.

Soldering is the joining of two metals using lead-based or tin-based alloy solder filler metal that melts below 500°F (260°C).

Metals can also be fastened with adhesives. This method is usually reserved for small trim pieces and sheet stock where the strength of the bond is not critical. Normally, adhesives are used when fastening metals to other substrates such as plywood and particle board.

Properties of Metals

In selecting, detailing, and specifying metals, the architect must have a rudimentary knowledge of several of the unique properties of the various metals. These include gage sizing, galvanic action, and coefficients of expansion.

The thickness of large steel members is usually expressed in fractions or decimals of an inch. However, sheet steel and nonferrous metals of tubing, strips, and sheets are expressed with a gage number. Gage sizing to indicate the thickness of metal started in the early days of the metal industries and was based on the weight of a square foot of a metal. Obviously, the weight would depend on the density of the metal and whether there were any coatings, such as galvanized steel. To confuse matters, different companies had their own gages and different standards have been adopted over the years. As a result, gage is only a rough approximation of a metal's thickness. Even within the same company, the actual thickness may vary even though the gage is the same. Because of the variations, it is preferable to call out the actual thickness desired in decimals of an inch or in millimeters.

Galvanic action is the corrosion resulting when dissimilar metals come in contact with each other in the presence of an electrolyte such as moisture. In the process, called *electrolysis*, a mild electric current is set up between the two metals, gradually corroding one while the other remains intact.

The following list represents the galvanic series; the metals are listed in the order of their susceptibility to corrosion. The farther apart the metals are from each other on the list, the greater the possibility for corrosion when they are in contact.

- zinc
- galvanized steel
- aluminum
- steel and iron
- stainless steel
- lead
- tin
- copper alloys (brass, bronze)
- copper

To avoid galvanic action, use identical metals when they must be in contact, or separate the metals with nonconducting materials such as neoprene, plastic, or rubber. If these precautions are not possible, use metals as close to each other on the galvanic series as possible. Electrolysis is most severe in humid, marine environments where there is an abundance of seawater; it is less severe in dry climates.

Metals expand and contract with changes in temperature more than many other materials, so it is important to allow for changes in size when designing and detailing metal building components. Table 15.1 lists some of the coefficients of thermal expansion for various metals, along with a few other materials for comparison. Most often, slip joints or expansion joints are provided to accommodate such movement when the building assembly is primarily composed of metal. When metal is used within other materials, such as an aluminum frame within a concrete opening, allowances must be made for the differential movement.

Table 15.1

Coefficients of Thermal Expansion for Metals
(Temperature Range 68°–212°F (20°–100°C))

metal	coefficient of expansion $\times 10^{-6}$ in/°F	$\times 10^{-6}$ mm/°C
structural steel	6.5	11.7
copper, alloy 110	9.3	16.8
stainless steel, 302	9.9	17.8
commercial bronze, alloy 220	10.2	18.1
red brass, alloy 230	10.2	18.1
aluminum	12.8	23.1
lead	15.9	28.6
other materials		
wood	2.7	4.9
glass	5.1	9.2
concrete	5.5	9.9

FERROUS METALS

There are two major classifications of metals: ferrous and nonferrous. *Ferrous metals* are those that contain a substantial amount of iron; *nonferrous metals* are those that do not. The primary types of ferrous metals used in the construction industry include iron, steel, stainless steel, and other special steel alloys.

Wrought and Cast Iron

All ferrous metals contain a majority of iron, some carbon, and other elements in the form of impurities or components mixed with the iron to form an alloy. The amount of carbon and other elements determines the strength, ductility, and other properties of the ferrous metal.

Wrought iron is iron with a very low carbon content (less than about 0.30%) and a substantial amount of slag. It is similar in chemical composition to low-carbon steel, but most of the impurities are in the slag, which is mechanically mixed with the iron. Because of its low carbon content, wrought iron is soft, ductile, and resistant to corrosion. Its use in construction is limited to ornamental iron work such as gates, grilles, and fences.

Cast iron is iron with a carbon content above 2%. With this high percentage of carbon, it is very hard, but brittle. Cast iron was used extensively in the nineteenth century for columns and beams in such structures as the Crystal Palace, mill buildings in New England, and some of the early commercial buildings in New York City.

Cast iron with a low silicon content is called white cast iron and has little use in construction unless it is processed in such a way as to produce malleable iron. Cast iron with a high silicon content is called *grey cast iron* and is used for various types of castings such as plumbing valves, pipes, and hardware.

Steel

Steel is one of the most widely used metals because of its many advantages, which include high strength, ductility, uniformity of manufacture, variety of shapes and sizes, and ease and speed of erection. *Ductility* is a property that allows steel to withstand excessive deformations due to high tensile stresses without failure. This property makes steel useful for earthquake-resistant structures. Steel is used in a variety of structural and nonstructural applications including columns, beams, concrete reinforcement, fasteners of all types, curtain wall panels, interior finish panels and trim, pipes, flashing, and electrical conduit.

Because steel is manufactured under carefully controlled conditions, its composition, size, and strength can be uniformly predicted. Therefore, steel structures do not have to be overdesigned to compensate for manufacturing or erection variables as do concrete or timber structures.

In spite of the advantages, however, steel does have properties that must be accounted for. Most notable are its reduction in strength when subjected to fire and its tendency to corrode in the presence of moisture. Steel itself does not burn, but it deforms when exposed to high temperatures. As a result, steel must be protected with fire-resistant materials, such as sprayed-on cementitious material, gypsum board, or concrete. This adds to the overall cost but is usually justified when the many advantages are considered.

As with any ferrous material, steel will rust and otherwise corrode if not protected. This can be prevented by including other elements in the steel to resist corrosion (stainless steel is an example of a material that uses this method) or by covering the steel with paint or some other type of protective coating.

Steel is composed primarily of iron with small amounts of carbon and other elements that are part of the alloy, either as impurities left over from manufacturing or deliberately added to impart certain desired qualities to the alloy. In medium-carbon steel used in construction, these other elements include manganese (from 0.5% to 1.0%), silicon (from 0.25% to 0.75%), phosphorus, and sulfur. Phosphorus and sulfur in excessive amounts are harmful because they affect weldability and make steel brittle.

The percentage of carbon present affects the strength and ductility of steel. As carbon is added, the strength increases but the ductility decreases. *Low-carbon steel* contains from 0.06% to 0.30% carbon, *medium-carbon steel* has from 0.30% to 0.50% carbon, and *high-carbon steel* contains from 0.50% to 0.80% carbon. *Standard structural steel* has from 0.20% to 0.50% carbon.

The most common type of steel for structural use is ASTM A36, which means that the steel is manufactured according to the American Society for Testing and Materials (ASTM) specification number A36. The yield point for this steel is 36 ksi (248 MPa). Other high-strength steels include A242, A440, and A441 steel, which have yield points of 46 ksi or 50 ksi (317 MPa or 345 MPa).

Stainless Steel

Stainless steel is a steel alloy containing a minimum of 11% chromium. In addition, nickel is often added to increase the corrosion resistance and improve cold workability. Additional trace elements such as manganese, molybdenum, and aluminum are added to impart certain characteristics.

Stainless steel is highly corrosion resistant and stronger than other architectural metals. Its resistance to corrosion results from the formation of a chromium-oxide film on the surface of the metal. If the film is scratched or otherwise damaged it will re-form as the metal is exposed to oxygen in the air.

Of the nearly forty types of stainless steel produced, only eight are used for building purposes, six for products, and two for fasteners. They are labeled by number designation of the American Iron and Steel Institute (AISI) and include the following, which are the most commonly used in construction.

- *Type 302.* This contains 18% chromium and 8% nickel and has traditionally been one of the most widely used stainless steel types. It is highly resistant to corrosion, very strong and hard, and can be easily fabricated by all standard techniques.

- *Type 304.* Type 304 has largely replaced type 302 for architectural uses because of its improved weldability. Its other properties are identical to 302.

- *Type 301.* This alloy is similar to type 302, but with slightly smaller amounts of chromium and nickel. It is still very corrosion resistant. Its advantage is its improved work-hardening properties, which can result in very high tensile strengths.

- *Type 316.* For extreme corrosive environments such as industrial plants and marine locations, this type is often used. It has a higher percentage of nickel than the other alloys and includes molybdenum.

- *Type 430*. This type does not contain any nickel, so it is less corrosion resistant than the other types. Its use is generally limited to interior applications.

Stainless steel is available in a variety of forms including sheets, wire, bars, and plates. Structural shapes of H sections, channels, tees, and angles are also available, as are custom extrusions. Stainless steel can be finished in a variety of ways, including mechanical and coatings.

The most common polished finishes for architectural work include the following.

- *No. 3 finish*: an intermediate, dull finish, coarser than no. 4.

- *No. 4 finish*: a general-purpose polished finish that is dull and prevents mirror reflection. It is one of the most frequently used architectural finishes.

- *No. 6 finish*: a dull satin finish.

- *No. 7 finish*: a highly reflective polished surface.

- *No. 8 finish*: the most reflective finish, used for mirrors and reflectors. It is seldom used for general architectural applications; a no. 7 finish is usually used instead.

There are also patterned finishes available that are produced by passing a sheet between patterned rollers. Color coatings are also available. Organic coatings consist of acrylic or other plastic-based enamels, which are fairly elastic, that can be applied to the metal prior to forming. Inorganic coatings such as porcelain enamel are less elastic but add color to the metal.

Other Alloy Steels

Various elements can be added to steel to impart certain qualities. In addition to stainless steel as described, many types of alloy structural steel are produced, which are designated by specification numbers of the American Society of Testing and Materials (ASTM).

ASTM A36 is the most common type of structural steel. It has a minimum yield point of 36,000 lbm/in^2 (248 MPa) and a carbon content from 0.25% to 0.29%. ASTM A440 is a high-strength structural steel used for bolted or riveted structures. ASTM A441 is a high-strength, low-alloy manganese vanadium steel intended for welded construction.

Weathering steel is an alloy that contains a small amount of copper. When exposed to moisture in the air or from rain, it develops a protective oxide coating with a distinctive sepia-colored finish. It is used in structures where it is difficult to maintain the steel, or it is used simply for its appearance. However, because small amounts of oxide are carried off by rain, structures using weathering steel should be detailed so the runoff does not stain other materials.

NONFERROUS METALS

Nonferrous metals are those that do not contain iron. The types most often used in construction include aluminum, copper, and copper alloys such as bronze and brass. Other nonferrous metals such as zinc, lead, and gold are of limited use in their pure state or are used in conjunction with other metals and materials.

Aluminum

Aluminum is an abundant element. The primary source of aluminum is bauxite, which is hydrated oxide of aluminum and iron with small amounts of silicon. Aluminum by itself is soft and weak; however, alloying it with manganese, zinc, magnesium, and copper improves its strength and hardness.

Aluminum is used in a wide variety of applications including structure, wall panels, curtain walls, window and door frames, and other decorative uses. In most uses, its high strength-to-weight ratio makes aluminum a desirable building material. It can be formed by casting, drawing, and rolling, although it is most often formed by extruding.

Aluminum can be finished mechanically, chemically, and with coatings. Mechanical finishes include the following.

- *Buffed finishes*: smooth specular and specular.

- *Directional textured finishes* (satin sheen with tiny, parallel scratches): fine satin, medium satin, coarse satin, hand rubbed, and brushed.

- *Nondirectional textured finishes* (formed by abrasion methods, not applicable to thicknesses under 1/4 in): extra-fine matte, fine matte, medium matte, coarse matte, fine shot blast, medium shot blast, and coarse shot blast.

- *Patterned finishes*: formed by rollers and other methods.

Chemical finishing for aluminum is usually an intermediate process for some other final finishing such as cleaning, etching, or preparing for some other coating.

Coating finishes for aluminum include the most familiar *anodizing process*, which is an electrochemical process that deposits an integral coating on the metal. It is called an anodic coating and can include the familiar silvery color of aluminum or a number of colors in the black and brown ranges. The problem with this finish is that it can be scratched.

Other finishes include impregnated color coatings such as baked enamel, vitreous coatings, powder coatings, and laminated coatings.

Aluminum can be joined by screwing, bolting, welding, brazing, soldering, adhesive bonding, and with concealed fasteners. Welding, brazing, and soldering should only be used when the joint is concealed or prior to final finishing. Adhesive bonding should be limited to thin material in situations where high strength is not required.

One of the primary disadvantages of aluminum is the amount of energy required for its refining and manufacture. Although the material is recyclable, the amount of embodied energy to install a finished product into a building is considerable.

Copper and Copper Alloys

Copper is widely used in construction because of its resistance to corrosion, its workability, and its high electrical conductivity. The two primary alloys of copper are bronze and brass. Bronze, by definition, is an alloy of copper and tin, whereas brass is an alloy of copper and zinc. However, traditional nomenclature calls many true brasses by the name bronze. The confusion is clarified by referring to the alloys by their standard designation numbers developed by the Copper Development Association (CDA) or by the Unified Numbering System (UNS). Table 15.2 lists some of the alloys used in construction, including their number designations and common names as well as their nominal compositions.

Copper and copper alloys are used in a variety of applications. Of course, copper is used for electrical wiring because of its high electrical conductivity. The copper alloys are also used for hardware, curtain walls, piping, gutters, roofing, window and door frames, wall panels, railings, and many other ornamental purposes.

Copper and copper alloys can be formed by casting, rolling, bending, brake forming, extrusion, spinning, and several other methods. They are joined by mechanical fasteners, brazing, and adhesive bonding.

As with aluminum, copper alloys can be finished several ways using the three methods of mechanical finishes, chemical finishes, and coatings.

Mechanical finishes include buffed, directional textured (in a variety of grain sizes), nondirectional textured, and patterned.

Chemical processing is usually used as an intermediate step in a total finishing process, but it can also be used to color the copper alloy.

Coatings can involve clear organic coatings, metallics, and oils and waxes. Although one of the advantages of copper, brass, and bronze is their ability to resist corrosion, if left unprotected many of the alloys develop a patina that is very different in color from the original finish of the metal. The

Table 15.2

Composition and Description of Copper Alloys

alloy	UNS no.	name	nominal composition
110	C11000	copper	99.9% copper
220	C12200	commercial bronze	90% copper 10% zinc
230	C23000	red brass	85% copper 15% zinc
260	C26000	cartridge brass	70% copper 30% zinc
280	C28000	Muntz metal	60% copper 40% zinc
385	C38500	architectural bronze	57% copper 40% zinc 3% lead
655	C65500	silicon bronze	97% copper 3% silicon
745	C74500	nickel silver	65% copper 25% zinc 10% nickel

distinctive green color of aged copper is the most notable example. In some cases, this is undesirable, especially in interior applications. To prevent this, various types of thin, clear organic coatings can be applied to the metal. In other situations, a coat of oil or wax can bring out the rich luster of the metal, although continued maintenance is required.

One special alloy, used primarily for roofing, is Monel metal (a trade name), which is a combination of copper and nickel with small amounts of other elements. It is also highly resistant to corrosion and is easily worked.

Miscellaneous Nonferrous Metals

Zinc is resistant to corrosion and is sometimes used for sheet roofing and flashing. Zinc fasteners are also made. The metal is more commonly used for coating steel to produce galvanized steel.

Lead is also resistant to corrosion and is occasionally used to cover complex roofing shapes because it is very easy to form around irregularities. However, its density makes it ideal for acoustical insulation, vibration control, and radiation shielding. An alloy of 75% lead and 25% tin can be used to plate steel for roofing. This is known as *terneplate*.

STRUCTURAL METALS

Steel Shapes

The two metals used in structural applications are steel and aluminum, although steel is by far the most common. The structural use of aluminum is limited to small structures or minor portions of structures. Steel is used for beams, columns, and plates; in lightgage framing such as steel studs; for floor and roof decking; as prefabricated truss joists; and for many types of fasteners.

Structural steel comes in a variety of shapes, sizes, and weights, giving the designer a great deal of flexibility in selecting an economical member that is geometrically correct for any given situation. Figure 15.1 shows the most common shapes of structural steel.

Wide-flange members are H-shaped sections used for both beams and columns. They are called wide flange because the width of the flange is greater than that of standard I-beams. Many of the wide-flange shapes are particularly suited for columns because the width of the flange is very nearly equal to the depth of the section, so they have about the same rigidity in both axes.

Wide-flange sections are designated with the letter W followed by the nominal depth in inches (millimeters) and the weight in lbm/ft (kg/m). For example, a W18 × 85 is a wide flange nominally 18 in deep and weighing 85 lbm/ft. Because of the way these sections are rolled in the mill, the actual depth varies slightly from the nominal depth.

American Standard I-beams have a relatively narrow flange width in relation to their depth, and the inside faces of the flanges have a slope of one in six. Unlike the wide flanges, the actual depth of an I-beam in any size group is also the nominal depth. The designation of depth and weight per foot for these sections is preceded with the letter S. These sections are usually used for beams only.

American Standard channel sections have a flange on one side of the web only and are designated with the letter C followed by the depth and weight per foot. Like that of the American Standard I-beams, the depth is constant for any size group; extra weight is added by increasing the thickness of the web and the inside face of the flanges. Channel sections are typically used to frame openings, to form stair stringers, or in other applications where a flush side is required. They are seldom used by themselves for beams or columns because they tend to buckle due to their asymmetrical shape.

Structural tees are made by cutting either a wide-flange section or I-beam in half. If cut from a wide-flange section, a tee is given the prefix designation WT and, if cut from an

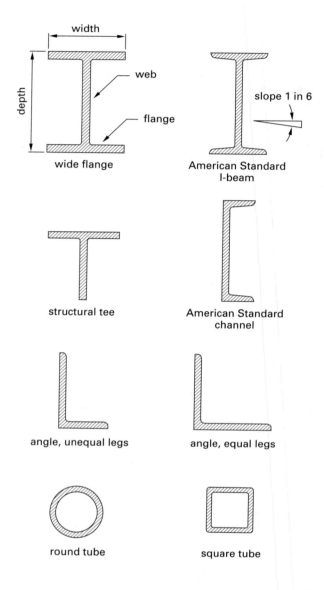

Figure 15.1 Structural Steel Shapes

American Standard I-beam, it is given the designation ST. A WT9 × 57, for example, is cut from a W18 × 114. Because they are symmetrical about one axis and have an open flange, tees are often used for chords of steel trusses.

Steel angles are available with either equal or unequal legs. They are designated by the letter L followed by the lengths of the angles and then followed by the thicknesses of the legs. Angles are used in pairs as members for steel trusses or singly as lintels in a variety of applications. They are also used for miscellaneous bracing of other structural members.

Square and rectangular tube sections and round pipe are also available. These are often used for light columns and as members of large trusses or space frames. *Structural tubing* of various sizes is available in several different wall thicknesses, while *structural pipe* is available in standard weight, extra strong, and double-extra strong. Each of the three weights has a standard wall thickness depending on the size. Pipe is designated by its nominal diameter, although the actual outside dimension is slightly larger, while the size designation for square or rectangular tubing refers to its actual outside dimensions. Standard designations for structural steel shapes are summarized in Table 15.3.

Table 15.3
Standard Designations for Structural Shapes

structural shape	example of standard designation
wide flange shapes	W 12 × 22
American Standard I-beams	S 12 × 35
miscellaneous shapes	M 12 × 11.8
American Standard channels	C 15 × 40
miscellaneous channels	MC 12 × 37
angles, equal legs	L 3 × 3 × 3/8
angles, unequal legs	L 3 × 4 × 1/2 LLV[1]
structural tees—cut from wide flange shapes	WT 7 × 15
structural tees—cut from American Standard I-beams	ST 9 × 35
plate	PL 1/2 × 10
structural tubing	TS 8 × 8 × 0.03750
pipe	pipe 4 std.

[1]LLV and LLH are used on drawings to indicate the orientation of the long leg of the angle: long leg vertical and long leg horizontal, respectively.

Finally, steel is available in bars and plates. *Bars* are considered any rectangular section 6 in (152) or less in width with a thickness of 0.203 in (5.2) and greater or sections 6 in to 8 in (152 to 203) in width with a thickness of 0.230 (5.8) and greater.

Plates are considered any section over 8 in (203) in width with a thickness of 0.230 in (5.8) and over, or sections over 48 in (1220) in width with a thickness of 0.180 in (4.6) and over.

Open-Web Steel Joists

Open-web steel joists are standardized, shop-fabricated trusses with webs composed of linear members and chords of back-to-back steel angles. The chords are typically parallel, but some types have top chords that are pitched for roof drainage. See Fig. 15.2.

There are three standard series of open-web joists: the K-series, the LH-series, and the DLH-series. The typical spans and depths of each are summarized in Table 15.4. The depths in the K-series increase in 2 in (50) increments, and the depths in the LH- and DLH-series increase in 4 in (100) increments. The standard designation for an open-web joist consists of the depth, the series designation, and the particular type of chord used. For example, a 36LH13 joist is 36 in (914) deep and of the LH-series, with a number 13 chord type. Within any size group, the chord type number increases as the load-carrying capacity of that depth of joist increases.

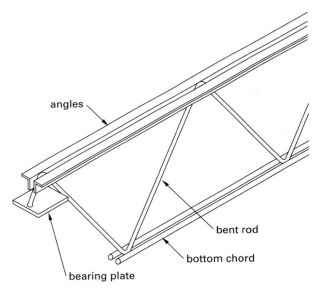

Figure 15.2 Open-Web Steel Joist

Table 15.4
Open-Web Steel Joists—Spans and Depths

series	name	span limits (ft)	(m)	depths in series (in)	(mm)
K	standard	8–60	2.4–18.3	8–30	203–762
LH	long span	25–96	7.6–29.3	18–48	457–1220
DLH	deep long span	89–144	27.1–43.9	52–96	1321–2438

Open-web steel joists have many advantages for spanning medium to long distances. They are lightweight and efficient structural members, they are easy and quick to erect, and the open webbing allows for ductwork and other building services to be run through the joists rather than under them. In addition, a variety of floor decking types can be used, from wood systems to steel and concrete decks. They can easily be supported by steel beams, by masonry or concrete bearing walls, or by heavier open-web joist girders.

There are also various types of composite joists that use wood top and bottom chords with steel webs. These are ideal for wood-frame buildings where wood decking is used and where spans exceed the limits of standard wood joists.

Metal Decking

Metal decking is available in steel or aluminum, although steel is the more common form. Steel decking consists of formed panels that are laid over steel beams or open-web steel joists to serve as formwork for poured concrete slabs. Before the concrete is poured, the decking also provides a convenient working deck during construction.

Steel decking is available in a wide variety of types, shapes, depths, and gages to satisfy nearly any span and loading condition. A few of the more common shapes are illustrated in Fig. 15.3. Decking is available that simply serves as a form for concrete or that is deformed to bond with the concrete and act as a composite structural material. Cellular decking provides structural support as well as raceways for power and communication cabling.

Lightgage Metal Framing

Lightgage metal framing consists of steel members with thicknesses from 10 gage to 25 gage. It is used for interior partitions, exterior bearing and nonbearing walls, joists, rafters, and similar framing. Unlike structural steel, lightgage framing comes in shapes more suitable for lighter loads and easier handling. Lightgage framing is noncombustible, is easily cut and assembled, and does not shrink or otherwise decay.

Manufacturers supply a variety of shapes, sizes, and gages for various uses. Most commonly, lightgage framing is used for interior partitions in noncombustible buildings. However, joists and deeper studs are used for floor and roof framing, as well as for some bearing wall applications. Some of the common shapes of lightgage framing are shown in Fig. 15.4.

Framing used for interior partitions ranges from 20 gage to 25 gage (0.87 to 0.48). Studs are available in depths of $1^5/8$, $2^1/2$, $3^5/8$, 4, and 6 in (41.3, 63.5, 92.1, 101.6, and 152.4). For higher walls, bearing walls, and exterior walls, heavier gages and depths are available. Joists are available in depths

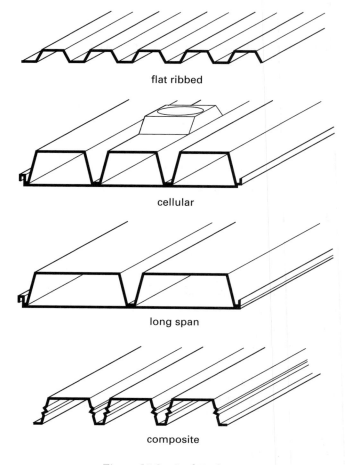

flat ribbed

cellular

long span

composite

Figure 15.3   Steel Decking

from 6 in to 14 in (152 to 356) and in thicknesses from 10 gage to 20 gage. Lightgage joists and rafters are capable of spanning up to 40 ft (12.2 m).

Lightgage framing is erected with screws, bolts, or welds depending on the thickness of the member and its application.

METAL FABRICATIONS

In addition to structural metals, there are individual building components fabricated partially or entirely of steel, aluminum, or other metals that belong in the category of "metals." These include items such as spiral stairs, expansion joints, gratings, and ladders.

Spiral Stairs

Spiral stairs have a closed circular form with wedge-shaped treads supported from a central, minimum-diameter column (usually 4 in [100]). Standard prefabricated spiral stairs are commonly made from steel. Treads can be exposed steel, hardwood over a steel support, recessed steel pans for infill with concrete or stone, or particleboard over

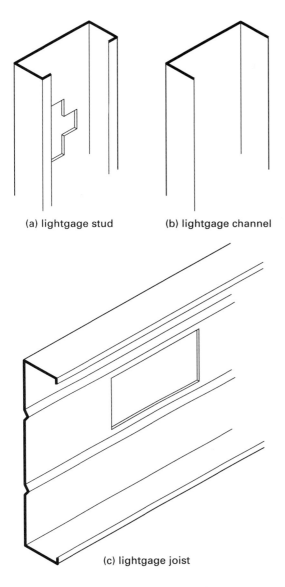

(a) lightgage stud   (b) lightgage channel

(c) lightgage joist

Figure 15.4   Lightgage Metal Framing

a steel support that can be finished with carpet or resilient flooring. Handrails can be specified as steel pipe, wood, or other ornamental metal. Custom spiral stairs can be fabricated of nearly any combination of steel, wood, and other ornamental metal. Spiral stairs are available in standard diameters from 3 ft 6 in to 7 ft 0 in, in 6 in increments (1067 to 2134, in 152 increments).

Spiral stairs can be fabricated with 22.5°, 27°, and 30° treads, with 30° treads being the most common. This means that there are twelve treads in a full 360° turn or three treads for each quarter circle of the stair. The riser height is set between $7\frac{1}{2}$ in and $9\frac{1}{2}$ in (190 to 240) to make up the total floor-to-floor height so each riser is the same and headroom is adequate. At the top of the stair, a square landing is used to make the transition between the stair and the rest of the floor when a square opening is used. Depending on the floor-to-floor dimension, a spiral stair must be planned so the first riser at the bottom and the last riser at the top are situated so people enter and exit the stair traveling in the right direction.

Expansion Joints

Expansion joint cover assemblies are fabrications designed to allow for major movement between independent structural units of the building. They are different from control joints or expansion joints in that the movements between adjacent portions of a building are significant—on the order of $\frac{1}{2}$ in (13) to several inches.

Expansion joints separate two sections of a building completely and continuously, from the foundation through floors, walls, and the roof. Two examples of expansion joint cover assemblies are shown in Fig. 15.5. The first, Fig. 15.5(a), illustrates an expansion joint between two floor slabs; Fig. 15.5(b) shows the separation between a floor and wall. Expansion joints that provide for lateral movement only or for both lateral and vertical movement are available. Seismic expansion joints are also available, but they require special engineering study to determine what type and amount of movement must be accommodated.

Other Miscellaneous Metal Fabrications

Other common miscellaneous metal fabrications include gratings, steel ladders for service areas, stair treads, pipe handrails and guardrails, sheet metal enclosures, prefabricated utility stairs, and protective steel bollards, bumpers, and corner guards.

ORNAMENTAL METALS

Ornamental metals include a wide variety of both functional and decorative products, such as handrails, guardrails, and elevator interiors. Metal may also be used for custom doors and door facings, partition and architectural woodwork facing, building directories and kiosks, signs, custom light fixtures, ceilings, or as part of nearly any construction assembly. The decorative options available to the architect are almost limitless. The most commonly used ornamental metals include stainless steel, the copper alloys of bronze and brass, and aluminum. Carbon steel, copper, iron, and porcelain enamel are used less frequently.

Stainless steel and copper alloys are available in several stock forms that fabricators use to construct custom assemblies. Some of the common shapes for brass and bronze are shown in Fig. 15.6. Sheet and bar stock are also available in a number of thicknesses.

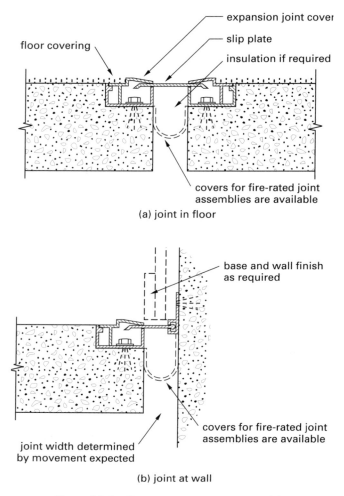

(a) joint in floor

(b) joint at wall

Figure 15.5 Expansion Joint Cover Assemblies

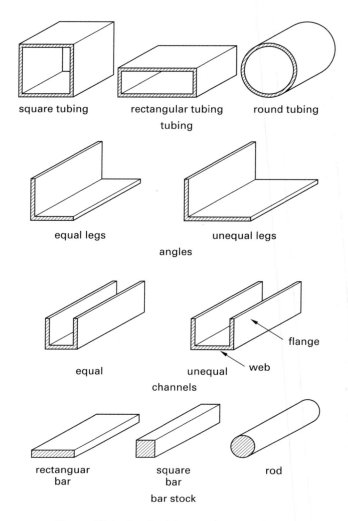

Figure 15.6 Standard Brass and Bronze Shapes

Detailing Stainless Steel

Custom details for stainless steel are developed in the same way as for plain carbon steel or any other metal. Combinations of bar, plate, tubing, sheet stock, and other shapes are detailed to nearly any configuration and in any combination. Stainless steel can be joined by welding, mechanical fasteners, and in some cases, with adhesives. For the smoothest joint, welding is preferred. However, the finish specified must make it possible to smooth and work the weld to match the adjacent finish. Some rolled and proprietary finishes cannot be matched after shop welding. When mechanical fasteners such as screws, bolts, and rivets are used, they should also be stainless steel to prevent galvanic action and rust stains caused by carbon steel fasteners. Adhesives are typically used to laminate sheet stock to other materials. In order to simplify fabrication and minimize cost, the smallest sizes and gages that satisfy the application should be used.

Detailing with Brass and Bronze

As with stainless steel, basic shapes are used to fabricate custom assemblies by various forming and fastening methods. Brass can also be extruded and cast. Extrusion is common for door and window frames, railings, and trim, whereas casting is used to manufacture hardware and plumbing fixtures.

Brass can be fabricated to any size required, but it is more economical to design and detail ornamental brass using standard shapes (see Fig. 15.6) and sizes whenever possible. Hexagonal and octagonal tubing is also available on special order as well as some T-shapes, Z-shapes, and proprietary shapes. Note that square and rectangular tubing, channels, and angles of brass have sharp corners as contrasted with the rounded corners of stainless steel and regular steel tubing, channels, and angles. Although there are some standard shapes and sizes, several manufacturers use brass to fabricate proprietary shapes and products. For example, several manufacturers produce lines of brass railings for bars, guardrails, and handrails, including brackets and other accessories for a complete installation.

Brass and bronze can be formed into an unlimited number of shapes and sizes, and different pieces can be fastened to fabricate nearly any type of detail. Brass and bronze can also be combined with other materials such as wood, plastic, and stone to construct specialty items. However, standard shapes, sizes, and metal alloys should be used to minimize cost and fabrication difficulty. Following are some general guidelines for designing and detailing with these metals.

For details with large expanses of smooth, flat sheet stock, the gage of metal must be thick enough to avoid oil canning or showing other surface imperfections. A minimum of 10-gage brass (0.1019 in [2.588]) is used when large areas are unsupported or unbacked. If the sheet has an embossed pattern, thinner material is used because the patterning imparts stiffness to the sheet. When brass is laminated to particleboard or other backing, sheets as thin as 20 gage (0.032 in [0.813]) are used. Items that are fabricated of brake-formed brass are from 14- or 12-gage (0.0640 or 0.0808 in [1.62 or 2.05]) metal.

Brass and bronze are joined with mechanical fasteners, adhesives, or by brazing or soldering. Mechanical fasteners include screws, bolts, rivets, and various types of clips in compatible alloys. In most cases the appearance of metalwork is improved if mechanical fasteners are concealed. If the installation makes it impossible to conceal fasteners, their type, size, and location should be given careful consideration based on the final installed position.

Adhesives are used for laminating sheets onto backing material or to join smaller pieces to other materials when exposed fasteners would be objectionable. Unless some additional mechanical fastening device can be incorporated into a detail, adhesive bonding should not be used alone where the metal has to support forces other than its own weight.

Brass can be joined by brazing, soldering, or welding as discussed in the earlier section on joining metals. Of the three methods, brazing is most often used for joining brass for architectural purposes. If possible, brazed joints should be concealed because the filler metal does not exactly match the brass.

Perforated Metal

Perforated metal is sheet metal that has been punched with a regular pattern of holes. Standard perforations include round and square holes as well as slots in a wide range of patterns, hole sizes, and hole spacings. For interior applications, perforated metals are used for space dividers, railing guards, shelving, furniture, supply air and return air grills, coverings for acoustical panels, custom light fixtures, or any specialty fabrication that can be constructed with sheet metal.

Architectural Mesh

Architectural mesh is a specialty metal that is most often used for elevator cab interiors, but it can be creatively applied in other architectural applications such as wall panels and door facings. Architectural mesh is formed by "weaving" thin strips of metal or heavy wire and then grinding off a portion of one face to reveal a highly textured but relatively flat surface. The final surface appearance depends on the type of weave, the type of metal used, and how much is ground off. Stainless steel and brass are the most commonly used materials.

STRUCTURAL AND ROUGH CARPENTRY

There are two broad categories of wood use in construction: rough carpentry and finish carpentry. *Rough carpentry* includes the structural framing, sheathing, blocking, and miscellaneous pieces necessary to prepare the building for finish work. Most rough carpentry is hidden once construction is complete, but exposed lumber such as heavy timber beams, glued-laminated members, and outdoor deck frames is considered rough carpentry.

As the name implies, *finish carpentry* includes the exposed, finished pieces of lumber necessary to complete a job, including such things as window and door trim, base, wood paneling, cabinets, and shelving. Finish carpentry work is normally done on the job site, but it also includes architectural woodwork, which is the fabrication of wood items in a manufacturing plant. Finish carpentry and architectural woodwork are reviewed in Ch. 17.

This chapter includes a general review of wood as a structural material. However, methods for calculating sizes of members and fasteners are not included.

When discussing wood as a construction material, several terms are often used interchangeably, but there is a distinction. Wood is the fibrous substance forming the trunk, stems, and branches of the tree. Lumber is the product of sawing, planing, and otherwise preparing wood to be used as construction members. Timber is lumber with a 5 in (127) minimum sectional dimension.

CHARACTERISTICS OF LUMBER

Lumber is a very versatile building material and has many advantages—it is plentiful, relatively low in cost, easy to shape and assemble, has good thermal insulating qualities, and is aesthetically pleasing. As a natural material, however, it lacks the uniform appearance and strength that manufactured materials have. Also, because of its cellular structure,

it is susceptible to dimensional changes when its moisture content changes.

These disadvantages can be overcome with some of the manufactured wood products available today. A few examples of these products are plywood, glued-laminated timber, and plywood web joists.

Types and Species

There are two general classifications of wood: softwood and hardwood. These terms have nothing to do with the actual hardness of the wood, but refer to whether the wood comes from a coniferous tree or a deciduous tree. *Conifers* (softwood) are cone-bearing, needle-leaved trees that hold their foliage in the winter, such as fir, spruce, and pine. Deciduous (hardwood) trees are broad-leaved trees that lose their leaves in the winter, such as oak, walnut, and maple. Softwoods are used for structural and rough carpentry because of their greater availability and lower cost. Finish carpentry and architectural woodwork utilize both hardwoods and softwoods.

There are literally hundreds of species of softwood and hardwood available throughout the world. However, only a few are used in the United States for rough carpentry, primarily due to local availability and cost. For example, southern pine is used in the southeastern portion of the United States, whereas Douglas fir or Douglas fir-larch is used in the western region. Other commonly used species for rough carpentry include hem-fir, eastern white pine, and hemlock. Redwood and cedar are commonly used for exterior applications where resistance to moisture is required.

Strength

The strength of lumber is dependent on the direction of the load relative to the direction of the wood's grain. Lumber is strongest when the load is parallel to the direction of the grain, such as with a compressive load on a wood column. Wood can resist slightly less tensile stress parallel to the grain and even less when compressive forces are perpendicular to the grain.

Wood is weakest when horizontal shear force is induced, which occurs when bending forces are applied to a beam and the fibers tend to slip apart parallel to the grain. Allowable forces used in structural calculations are lowest for horizontal shear, and this quite often governs the design of bending members.

Defects

Because wood is a natural material, there are several types of defects that can be present in lumber. There are also many types of defects that can occur during manufacture. These affect the strength, appearance, and use of lumber and are reflected in how an individual piece of lumber is graded. Figure 16.1 shows some of the more common wood defects.

- *Knots* are the most common natural defect. A knot is a branch or limb embedded in the tree that is cut through in the process of lumber manufacture. Knots are classified according to quality, size, and occurrence. There are over 10 different types of knots.

- A *check* is a separation of the wood fibers occurring across or through the annual growth rings, a result of improper seasoning.

- A *pitch pocket* is an open area between growth rings that contains resin.

- A *shake* is a lengthwise separation of the wood that usually occurs between or through the annual growth rings.

- A *split* is similar to a check except that the separation extends completely through a piece of lumber, usually at the ends.

- A *wane* is the presence of bark or absence of wood from any cause on the edge or corner of a piece of lumber.

Warping is a common manufacturing defect. A *warp* is any variation from a true or plane surface and is usually caused by the natural shrinkage characteristics of wood and uneven drying during processing. A *bow* is a deviation parallel to the length of the lumber in line with the lumber's flat side. A *crook* is a deviation parallel to the length of the lumber perpendicular to the flat side of the piece. A *cup* is a deviation from true plane along the width of the board.

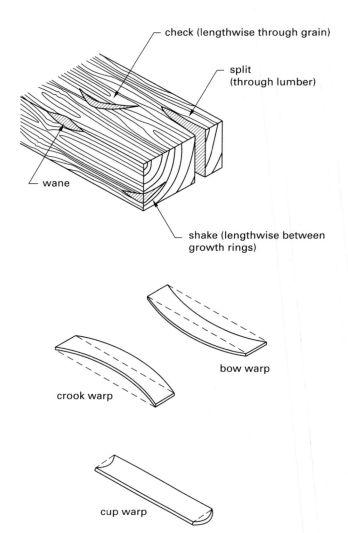

Figure 16.1 Common Wood Defects

Grading

Because a log yields lumber of varying quality, the individual sawn pieces must be categorized to allow selection of boards that are best suited for a particular purpose. For structural lumber, the primary concern is the amount of stress that a grade of lumber of a specific species can carry. For finish lumber, the primary concern is the appearance of the wood and how it accepts stain, paint, and other finishes. Load-carrying ability is affected by such things as size and number of knots, splits, and other defects.

Grading of lumber used for structural and rough carpentry purposes is done under standard rules established by several agencies certified by the American Lumber Standards Committee. The grading is done at the sawmill, either by visual inspection or machine, if the lumber is to be used for structural purposes. The resulting allowable stress values are published in tables that are used when making structural calculations.

There are two primary classifications of softwood lumber: "yard lumber," used for structural purposes and rough framing, and "factory and shop lumber," used for making door frames, windows, and finish items.

Yard lumber is further classified as boards, dimension, and timber, as shown in Fig. 16.2. Dimension lumber and timber are the two classifications used for structural purposes, and these are further classified into groups based on nominal size and use. With this system the same grade of lumber in a species may have different allowable stresses depending on which category it is in. This can be confusing, but it is critical in selecting the correct allowable stress for a particular design condition.

The five size groups (based on nominal dimensions) are as follows.

1. 2 in to 4 in (51 to 102) thick, 2 in to 4 in wide. This includes members such as 2 × 2s.

2. 2 in to 4 in (51 to 102) thick, 4 in (102) wide. This is the category for 2 × 4s, which are usually subdivided into grades of construction, standard, and utility.

3. 2 in to 4 in (51 to 102) thick, 5 in (127) wide and wider. This includes wood members such as 2 × 6s, 2 × 8s, and the like, but not 2 × 4s.

4. *Beams and stringers.* Beams and stringers are defined as members 5 in (127) wide and wider, having a depth more than 2 in (51) greater than the width.

5. *Posts and timbers.* Posts and timbers are defined as members 5 in by 5 in (127 by 127) and larger, with a depth not more than 2 in (51) greater than the width.

These five size categories are further subdivided into smaller groups such as select structural, no. 1, no. 2, and so on. The exact nomenclature and method of subdivision vary with each grading agency and the wood species.

Machine-stress-rated lumber is based on grade designations that depend on the allowable bending stress and modulus of elasticity of the wood.

Factory and shop lumber for boards (less than 1 in [25] nominal thickness) is graded according to defects that affect the appearance and use of the wood. Exact classifications vary with the grading agency and the species of lumber, but in general factory and shop lumber is divided into select and common grades. The three select grade categories are B & Better, C Select, and D Select, with B & Better being the best and free of knots.

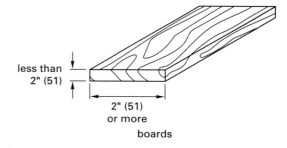

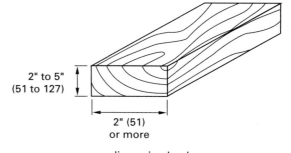

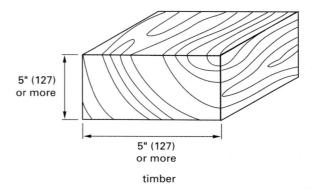

Figure 16.2 Yard Lumber Types

Common grades available include no. 1, no. 2, no. 3, no. 4, and no. 5—no. 1 common being the best. The individual grades are determined by the size and character of the knots.

Dimensioning

Lumber for rough carpentry is referred to by its nominal dimension in inches, such as 2 × 4 or 2 × 10. However, after surfacing at the mill and drying, its actual dimension is somewhat less. Table 16.1 gives the actual dimensions for various nominal sizes of sawn lumber.

Lumber is ordered and priced by the board foot. This is a measure of a quantity of lumber equal to a piece 12 in wide by 12 in long by 1 in thick. Nominal sizes are used so an actual sized piece of lumber ³/₄ in thick, 11¹/₄ in wide, and 2 ft long contains 2 board feet.

Table 16.1
Nominal and Actual Sizes of Lumber

nominal size	standard dressed size (in, width × depth)
1 × 2	³/₄ × 1¹/₂
1 × 4	³/₄ × 3¹/₂
1 × 6	³/₄ × 5¹/₂
1 × 8	³/₄ × 7¹/₄
2 × 2	1¹/₂ × 1¹/₂
2 × 4	1¹/₂ × 3¹/₂
2 × 6	1¹/₂ × 5¹/₂
2 × 8	1¹/₂ × 7¹/₄
2 × 10	1¹/₂ × 9¹/₄
2 × 12	1¹/₂ × 11¹/₄
4 × 4	3¹/₂ × 3¹/₂
4 × 6	3¹/₂ × 5¹/₂
4 × 8	3¹/₂ × 7¹/₄
4 × 10	3¹/₂ × 9¹/₄
4 × 12	3¹/₂ × 11¹/₄
4 × 14	3¹/₂ × 13¹/₄
6 × 6	5¹/₂ × 5¹/₂
6 × 8	5¹/₂ × 7¹/₂
6 × 10	5¹/₂ × 9¹/₂

For the wood to be considered dry lumber, its moisture content cannot exceed 19%. To be grademarked "kiln dry," its moisture content cannot exceed 15%. Design values found in structural tables assume that the maximum moisture content will not exceed 19%. If it does, the allowable stresses must be decreased slightly.

Wood shrinks most in the direction perpendicular to the grain and very little parallel to the grain. When considered perpendicular to the grain, wood shrinks most in the direction of the annual growth rings (tangentially) and about half as much across the rings (radially). See Fig. 16.3. The position in the log where a piece of lumber is cut also affects the wood's shrinkage characteristics.

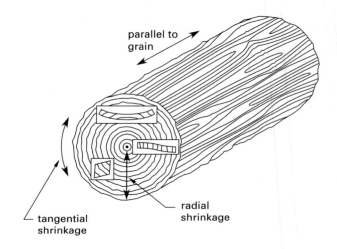

Figure 16.3 Wood Shrinkage

In detailing wood, an allowance must be made for the wood's shrinking and swelling during use, regardless of its initial moisture content. Of particular importance is the accumulated change in dimension of a series of wood members placed one on top of the next. The shrinkage of an individual member may not be significant, but the total shrinkage of several pieces may result in problems such as sagging floors, cracked plaster, distortion of door openings, and nail pops in gypsum board walls.

FRAMING

Framing is the assembly of lumber and timber components to construct a building. Because of code restrictions, structural limitations, and construction techniques, most wood construction is limited to small to moderate-sized buildings. This section discusses light frame construction; the next section reviews heavy timber construction used for larger structures.

Moisture Content

Moisture content is defined as the weight of water in wood as a fraction of the weight of ovendry wood. It is an important variable because it affects the amount of shrinkage, weight, and strength of the lumber, as well as the withdrawal resistance of nails.

Moisture exists in wood both in the individual cell cavities and bound chemically within cell walls. When the cell walls are completely saturated but no water exists in the cell cavities, the wood is said to have reached its *fiber saturation point*. This point averages about 30% moisture content in all woods. Above this point the wood is dimensionally stable, but as the wood dries below this point it begins to shrink.

When wood is used for structural framing and other construction purposes, it tends to absorb or lose moisture in response to the temperature and humidity of the surrounding air. As it loses moisture it shrinks, and as it gains moisture it swells. Ideally, the moisture content of wood when it is installed should be the same as the prevailing humidity to which it will be exposed. However, this is seldom possible so lumber needs to be seasoned, either by air drying or kiln drying, to reduce the moisture content to acceptable levels.

Light Frame Construction

Light frame construction uses small, closely spaced members such as 2 × 4 or 2 × 6 studs for walls and partitions and nominal 2 in (51) thick members for floor and roof joists. Beams may be built-up sections of nominal 2 in lumber, or heavy timber or steel.

Two systems of wall framing include the platform frame (also called *western framing*) and the balloon frame. The essential difference is that the platform frame uses separate studs for each floor of the building, with the top plates, floor joists, and floor framing of the second level being constructed before the second-floor wall studs are erected. The balloon frame uses continuous wall studs from foundation to second-floor ceiling. Figure 16.4 shows the two types of framing systems.

One advantage of the platform frame is that each floor can be completed and used for constructing the next floor, and shorter studs cost less. The advantage of the balloon frame is that vertical shrinkage is minimized because most of the construction is parallel to the direction of the grain where wood shrinkage is the least.

When wood joists are framed into masonry walls instead of wood stud walls, they must rest on metal hangers attached to wood ledger strips anchored to the masonry or be fire cut, as shown in Fig. 16.5. A fire cut is required to prevent the masonry from being pushed up and out if the wood member should collapse during a fire.

Framing Openings

Openings in wood construction are required for doors, windows, stairs, and similar conditions. Because light frame construction consists of many small, closely spaced members carrying the loads, eliminating any of these studs or joists affects the structural integrity of the building. As a result, framing of openings must be capable of transferring loads from one cut member to other members. Two typical methods of framing vertical and horizontal openings are shown in Fig. 16.6. The size of header over a window opening depends on the span and usually consists of a double 2 in wide member (commonly expressed as 2 ×) bearing on studs at either side of the opening.

Plywood

Plywood consists of sheets of thin veneer glued together to form a rigid panel. Sheets are made in standard 4 ft by 8 ft sizes in thicknesses of $1/4$, $3/8$, $1/2$, $5/8$, and $3/4$ in. These are the most readily available, although other panel sizes and thicknesses are available. Metric plywood is 1200 mm by 2400 mm.

Plywood is graded in two ways. The first is by span rating and is used for most structural applications, including

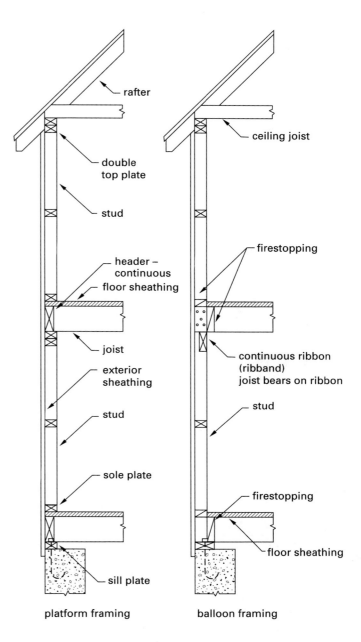

platform framing   balloon framing

Figure 16.4 Light Frame Construction

sheathing. The span rating is a measure of the strength and stiffness of the plywood parallel to the face grain. The rating consists of two numbers, such as $32/24$. The first number gives the maximum spacing in inches for roof supports under average loading conditions, and the second number gives the maximum spacing in inches for floor supports under average residential loading. These spacings are allowed if the face grain is perpendicular to the direction of the supports and if the panels are continuous over three supports.

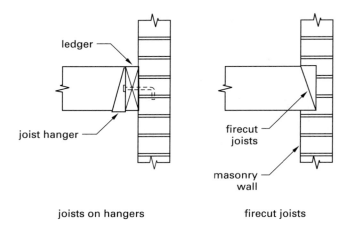

Figure 16.5 Wood Framing into Masonry

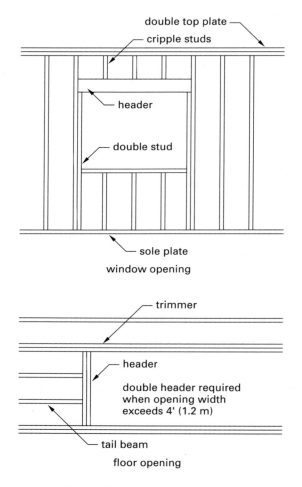

Figure 16.6 Framing for Openings

Plywood for structural uses is also classified according to the species of wood used. There are five groups. Structural I plywood is made only from woods in group 1; Structural II can be made from woods in groups 1, 2, and 3.

The other way plywood is graded is by the quality of the face veneer. Veneer grades are classified by the letters N, A, B, C, and D. *N grade* is intended for a natural finish and is made from all heartwood or all sapwood. It is free from defects but is only available on special order. *A grade* is smooth and paintable with few knots or other defects and is the best grade commonly available. *B grade* allows for plugged knotholes but has a smooth surface. *C grade* allows small knotholes and some splits, and *D grade* allows for larger knotholes. Plywood should be specified with exterior glue for outdoor locations.

Special types of plywood are also produced. These include patterned panels for exterior finish siding, marine plywood that has special glues, and overlaid plywood with a surface of resin-impregnated paper to provide a smooth surface.

Sheathing and Miscellaneous Wood Framing Members

Sheathing is thin panel material attached to framing to provide lateral support, increase rigidity, and provide a base for applying exterior finishes. For structural purposes, sheathing most often consists of plywood or particleboard nailed to the wood studs or joists. In situations where lateral stability is not critical, insulating sheathing may be used.

Particleboard is composed of small wood particles, fibers, or chips of various sizes mixed together in a binder and formed under pressure into a panel. Like plywood, it is available in several thicknesses in 4 ft by 8 ft sheets and is available in low-, medium-, and high-density forms. Metric particleboard sheets measure 1200 mm by 2400 mm. Particleboard is generally preferred for backing and framing of finish carpentry and architectural woodwork because it is less expensive and more dimensionally stable than plywood.

Oriented strand board (OSB) is an engineered panel product manufactured from precision-cut wood strands a maximum of 4 in (100) long and 0.0027 in (0.068) thick. The strands are arranged in layers at right angles to one another, much like plywood, and bonded with resin waterproof glue under heat and pressure. OSB is available in several thicknesses and sizes from standard 4 ft by 8 ft (1200 by 2400) size to much larger sizes, up to 8 ft by 28 ft (2400 by 8400). The primary strength of OSB panels is along the orientation of the chips on the face layer, which is generally parallel to the length of the panel. Although OSB is more susceptible to delamination than is plywood, it is still acceptable for use as sheathing with short-term weather exposure because of the waterproof glue used.

Medium-density fiberboard (MDF) is a panel product made from wood particles reduced to fibers in a moderate-pressure steam vessel and then combined with a resin and bonded together under heat and pressure. It is the most dimensionally stable of the mat-formed panel products. MDF has a smooth, uniform, and dense surface that makes it useful for painting, thin overlay materials, veneers, and high-pressure decorative laminate.

Hardboard is a panel product composed of inter-felted fibers consolidated under heat and pressure to a density of 31 lbm/ft³ (497 kg/m³) or more. It is available sanded on one or both sides and either tempered or untempered. Tempered hardboard has a greater hardness, stiffness, and weight than the untempered type.

Blocking is wood framing installed between main structural members such as studs or joists to provide extra rigidity or to provide a base for nailing other materials. For example, short pieces of lumber are often placed perpendicular to joists under the locations of interior partitions. Edge blocking is also placed at the intersection of wall and ceiling framing to provide a nailing base for the application of gypsum wallboard.

Bridging is bracing between joists that prevents the joist from buckling under load. Bridging may be solid wood blocking, 1 × 3 (actual 19 in by 64 in) wood cross members, or metal cross bridging. It is installed at intervals not exceeding 8 ft (2440) unless both the top and bottom edges of the joists are supported for their entire length.

Firestops are barriers installed in concealed spaces of combustible construction to prevent the spread of fire caused by drafts. Allowable materials include nominal 2 in thick wood members, gypsum board, or mineral wool. In most cases, wood blocking is used. The building code specifies where and when firestops must be installed, but in general firestopping is used in concealed spaces between floors, between a floor and ceiling or attic space, between floors under stairs, and in vertical openings around vents, chimneys, and ducts between floors.

ENGINEERED WOOD PRODUCTS

Engineered wood products include a wide range of components that are either constructed of standard wood elements (such as factory-built trusses made from 2 × 4s) or that use waste products or smaller pieces of wood to create new construction components (such as laminated veneer lumber). In some cases, wood products are used in conjunction with other materials, such as metal fasteners or insulation. Engineered wood products have the following advantages.

- better use of natural resources
- an improved product without typical wood defects
- increased strength for a given size compared with standard wood products
- consistent size and strength

Plywood Web Joists

Plywood web joists are like wood I-beams. They are fabricated with a plywood or an oriented strand board web piece fitted into grooves of chord members made of solid wood or laminated veneer lumber. They are manufactured in the same depths as standard solid wood joists and deeper. For the same depth they have a much higher load-carrying capacity than do wood joists, and they make very efficient use of wood products and only require wood from second- or third-growth timber forests. Other advantages include minimal shrinkage, ease of handling, and uniformity of size and shape. See Fig. 16.7(a).

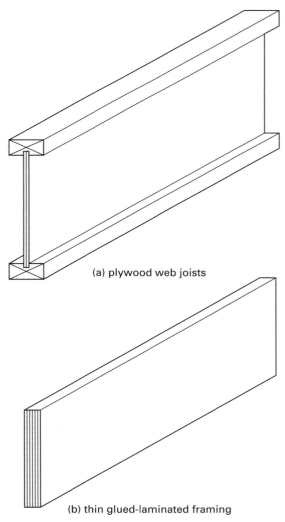

(a) plywood web joists

(b) thin glued-laminated framing

Figure 16.7 Prefabricated Structural Wood

Laminated Veneer Lumber

Laminated veneer lumber, sometimes called *thin glued-laminated framing*, is fabricated by gluing thin veneers of lumber together to build up a strong, rigid, dimensionally stable framing member than can be used like solid framing lumber. See Fig. 16.7(b). Laminated veneer lumber can be used for headers or beams and in place of studs.

Trusses

Wood trusses are factory-made assemblies consisting of relatively small wood members (normally 2 × 4s or 2 × 6s) held together with toothed plate connectors. They are available for residential and light commercial construction and can be fabricated with parallel top and bottom chords for floor framing or with sloped upper chords for roof framing. Common spacing is 24 in (600) on center. Depending on the depth of the truss and loading, floor trusses can span up to about 40 ft (12 m), and roof trusses can span up to about 70 ft (21 m). Some of the common types of trusses are shown in Fig. 16.8.

Structural Insulated Panels (SIPs)

A *structural insulated panel* (SIP) is a composite building unit consisting of two outer skins bonded to an inner core of rigid insulating material. Most SIP panels are composed of $^7/_{16}$ in (11) oriented strand board (OSB) facings with a core of molded expanded polystyrene (EPS). Other facings may include plywood, aluminum, cement board, and gypsum wallboard. However, not all units with other facings have undergone testing for building code approval. Other core materials include extruded polystyrene (XPS), urethane foam, and even compressed straw. CFC gases previously used to produce the insulation have been replaced with environmentally friendly processes.

SIPs are available in thicknesses from $4^1/_2$ in (114) to $12^1/_4$ in (311) and sizes from 4 ft by 8 ft (1200 by 2400) up to 9 ft by 28 ft (2740 by 8530). Larger sizes are also possible from some manufacturers. Custom sizes are available and are normally used to speed construction and avoid waste. They are used for residential and light commercial construction and can be used for walls, floors, and roofs.

SIPs have the following advantages.

- decreased construction time (about one-third less than for stick-built buildings)

- improved insulation value with no thermal bridges (whole-wall R-values of R14 for a $3^1/_2$ in (90) core vs. R9.6 for 2 × 4 studs with fiberglass insulation)

- reduced air infiltration

- stronger than conventional stud and sheathing construction

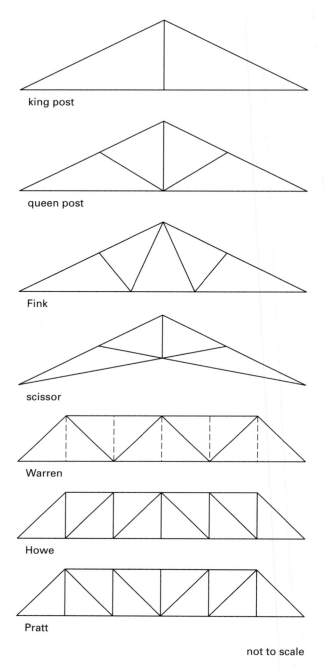

Figure 16.8 Types of Trusses

- very flat walls for subsequent finishes

- dimensional stability

Because of their composite construction, SIPs have strength in compression, bending, shear, and uplift. The erection of SIPs is accomplished by slipping the SIPs over wood plates attached to the floor. Wood splines at the vertical joints are used to fasten one panel to the next. Panels come with vertical and horizontal chases for wiring. Additional space can be made for piping or other electrical equipment by simply using a saw or hot wire to cut away the required insulation.

As a green product, SIPs require less wood than do conventional houses, use renewable resources for the facings, improve thermal performance, and reduce construction waste. Some manufactures recycle cutouts, trimmings, and EPS foam. The foam cores and water-based adhesives used have no formaldehyde content and are inert plastics. The amount of formaldehyde emitted by the OSB is less than 0.1 part per million (ppm), which is well below acceptable levels established by the U.S. Department of Housing and Urban Development.

Common coordination concerns include detailing a vapor barrier on the inside of the panel, providing seismic anchors where required, and detailing termite shields in geographical areas where they are required.

HEAVY TIMBER CONSTRUCTION

Heavy timber construction consists of exterior walls of non-combustible masonry or concrete and interior columns, girders, beams, and planking manufactured of large solid or laminated timbers. The Uniform Building Code requires that interior columns be at least 8 × 8 (203 × 203) in nominal size and that beams and girders supporting floors be at least 6 in (152) wide and 10 in (254) deep. Girders framed into masonry walls must be fire cut similar to the joists shown in Fig. 16.5. Floor decking must be at least 3 in (76) in nominal thickness with no concealed spaces below. Roof decking must have at least a 2 in (51) nominal thickness.

Due to the expense and limited availability of large, solid timbers today, new heavy timber construction is most typically built with glued-laminated members.

Glued-Laminated Construction

Glued-laminated wood members, or *gluelams* as they are usually called, are built up from a number of individual pieces of lumber glued together and finished under factory conditions for use as beams, columns, purlins, and other structural components. Gluelams are used where larger wood members are required for heavy loads or long spans and simple sawn timber pieces are not available or cannot meet the strength requirements. Gluelam construction is also used where unusual structural shapes are required and appearance is a consideration. In addition to being fabricated in simple rectangular shapes, gluelam members can be formed into arches, tapered forms, and pitched shapes.

Gluelam members are manufactured in standard widths and depths. In most cases, $1^1/_2$ in (38) actual depth pieces are used, so the overall depth is some multiple of $1^1/_2$, depending on how many laminations are used. If a tight curve must be formed, $3/_4$ in (19) thick pieces are used.

Standard actual widths are $3^1/_8$, $5^1/_8$, $6^3/_4$, $8^3/_4$, $10^3/_4$, and $12^1/_4$ in. See Fig. 16.9.

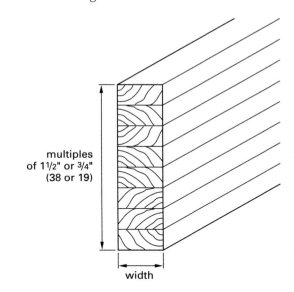

nominal width	actual width (in)	(mm)
4″	$3^1/_8$″	79
6″	$5^1/_8$″	130
8″	$6^3/_4$″	171
10″	$8^3/_4$″	222
12″	$10^3/_4$″	273
14″	$12^1/_4$″	311

Figure 16.9 Glued-Laminated Beams

Because individual pieces can be selected free from certain defects and seasoned to the proper moisture content, and because the entire manufacturing process is conducted under carefully controlled conditions, the allowable stresses for gluelam construction are higher than those for solid, sawn timber. Although gluelam beams are usually loaded in the direction perpendicular to the laminations, they can be loaded in either direction to suit the requirements of the design.

For structural purposes, gluelams are designated by size and a commonly used symbol that specifies the stress rating. Gluelams are available in three appearance grades: industrial, architectural, and premium. These do not affect the structural properties but only designate the final look and finishing of the member. Industrial grade is used where appearance is not a primary concern, whereas premium is used where the finest appearance is important. Architectural grade is used where appearance is a factor but where the best grade is not required.

Planking

Wood planking, or *decking* as it is often called, is solid or laminated timber that spans beams. It is available in nominal thicknesses of 2, 3, 4, and 5 in (51, 76, 102, and 127) with actual sizes varying with the manufacturer and whether the piece is solid or laminated. All planking has some type of tongue-and-groove edging so the pieces fit solidly together and load can be distributed among adjacent pieces. Unlike sheathing, planing is intended to span greater distances between beams rather than between closely spaced joists. Common spans range from 4 ft to 20 ft (1200 to 6000), depending on the planking thickness and loads carried.

In addition to satisfying the code requirements for heavy timber construction, planking has the advantages of easy installation, attractive appearance, and efficient use of material, because the planking serves as floor structure, finish floor, and finish ceiling below. Its primary disadvantage is that there is no place to conceal insulation, electrical conduit, and mechanical services.

FASTENERS

There are many types of fasteners used for carpentry, including nails, screws, bolts, and fabricated metal fasteners.

Nails

Although they are the weakest of wood connectors, nails are the most commonly used connectors in light frame construction. The types used most frequently for structural applications include common wire nails, box nails, and common wire spikes. *Wire nails* range in size from six penny (6d) to sixty penny (60d). *Box nails* range from 6d to 40d—6d nails are 2 in (51) in length, and 60d nails are 6 in (152) long. Common wire spikes range from 10d (3 in long) to $8^1/_2$ in long and $^3/_8$ in diameter (76 to 216 mm long and 10 mm diameter). For the same penny weight, box nails have the smallest diameter, common wire nails the next largest diameter, and wire spikes the greatest diameter.

For engineered applications, that is, where each nailed joint is specifically designed, there are tables of values giving the allowable withdrawal resistance and lateral load (shear) resistance for different sizes and penetrations of nails depending on the type of wood used. The more typical situation of most nailed wood construction is simply to use nailing schedules found in the building code. These give the minimum size, number, and penetration of nails for specific applications such as nailing studs to sole plates, joists to headers, and so forth.

There are several orientations that nails (as well as screws and lag screws) can have with wood members, which affect the holding power of the fastener. The preferable orientation is to have the fastener loaded laterally in side grain where the holding power is the greatest. The least desirable orientation is to have the nail or fastener parallel to the grain.

Screws

Wood screws are available in sizes from no. 0 (0.060 in shank diameter) to no. 24 (0.372 in shank diameter) and in lengths from $^1/_4$ in to 5 in (from 1.5 to 9.5 diameter, in lengths from 6 to 127). The most common types are flat head and round head. Because screws have a threaded design, they offer better holding power and can be removed and replaced more easily than nails. As with nails, screws are best used laterally loaded in side grain rather than in withdrawal from side grain or end grain.

Lead holes, slightly smaller than the diameter of the screw, must be drilled into the wood to permit the proper insertion of the screw and to prevent splitting of the wood.

A lag screw is threaded with a pointed end like a wood screw but has a head like a bolt. It is inserted by drilling lead holes and screwing the fastener into the wood with a wrench. A washer is used between the head and the wood.

Sizes range from $^1/_4$ in to $1^1/_4$ in (6 to 32) in diameter and from 1 in to 16 in (25 to 406) in length. Diameters are measured at the nonthreaded shank portion of the screw.

Bolts

Bolts are one of the most common forms of wood connectors for joints of moderate to heavy loading. Bolt sizes range from $^1/_4$ in to 1 in (6 to 25) in diameter and from $^1/_2$ in to 6 in (13 to 152) in length. Washers must be used under the head and nut of the bolt to prevent crushing the wood and to distribute the load.

The design requirements for bolted joints are a little more complicated than those for screwed or nailed joints. The allowable design values and the spacing of bolts are affected by such variables as the thicknesses of the main and side members, the ratio of bolt length in the main member to the bolt diameter, and the number of members joined.

Metal Fasteners

Because wood is such a common building material, there are dozens of types of special fasteners and connectors especially designed to make assembly easy, fast, and structurally sound. Hardware is available for both standard sizes of wood members and special members such as wood truss joists. Some of the common types of connection hardware are shown in Fig. 16.10.

In addition to the lightweight connectors shown in Fig. 16.10, there are special timber connectors used for heavy timber construction and for assembling wood trusses. Two of the most common types are split rings and

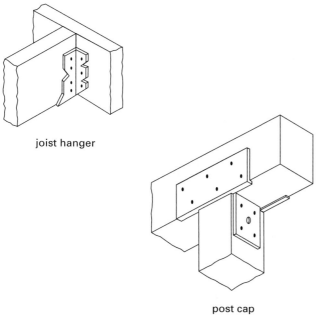

joist hanger

post cap

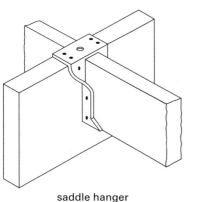

saddle hanger

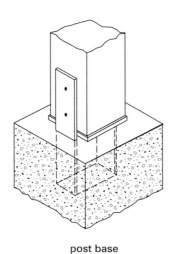

post base

Figure 16.10 Special Connection Hardware

shear plates. Split rings are either 2½ in or 4 in (64 or 102) in diameter and are cut through in one place in the circumference to form a tongue and slot. The ring is beveled from the central portion toward the edges. Grooves are cut in each piece of the wood members to be joined so that half the ring is in each section. The members are held together with a bolt concentric with the ring, as shown in Fig. 16.11(a).

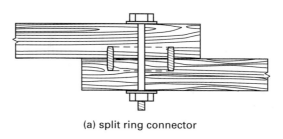

(a) split ring connector

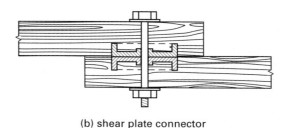

(b) shear plate connector

Figure 16.11 Timber Connectors

Shear plates are either 2⅝ in or 4 in (67 or 102) in diameter and are flat plates with a flange extending from the face of the plate. There is a hole in the middle through which either a ¾ in or ⅞ in (19 or 22) bolt is placed to hold the two members together. Shear plates are inserted in precut grooves in a piece of wood so that the plate is flush with one surface. (See Fig. 16.11(b).) Because of this configuration, shear plate connections can hold together either two pieces of wood or one piece of wood and a steel plate.

Split ring connectors and shear plates can transfer larger loads than can bolts or screws alone and are often used in connecting truss members. Shear plates are particularly suited for constructions that must be disassembled. Gang nail connectors are used in trusses also.

WOOD TREATMENT

As a natural material, wood is relatively durable if kept dry. Some woods, such as redwood, have naturally occurring resins that make them resistant to moisture and insect attack. However, most wood is subject to damage and decay from a number of sources and must be protected. The most common sources of attack and damage include fungi when moisture is present, insects such as termites and marine borers, and fire.

Preservatives may be applied by brushing, dipping, or pressure treatment. The most effective method is pressure treatment because the preservative is forced deep into the cells of the wood. For some applications such as marine use and protection from some insects, pressure treatment is the only satisfactory method to specify.

There are three basic types of wood preservatives: creosote, oil-borne preservatives, and waterborne preservatives. *Creosote* is a distillate of coal tar and is effective protection against insects. It is insoluble in water and is relatively easy to apply. Creosote is used mainly to protect railroad ties, marine timbers, and roadway guard posts. It is not used in building applications.

Oil-borne preservatives include *pentachlorophenol (penta)*. This preservative is used to treat utility poles and cross arms, fresh water pilings, and bridge timbers. It is applied by brushing, dipping, or pressure treating. Penta is generally not used in building applications; however, it is sometimes used on glue-laminated beams supporting long spans in sports arenas and over swimming pools, and for similar applications.

Waterborne preservatives are the type most commonly used in residential, commercial, and industrial buildings. The types used today include *ammoniacal copper quaternary* (ACQ), also called alkaline copper quat, copper azole, and sodium borate (SBX), and variations of these three basic types. These types of treatments are clean, odorless, and nonstaining, and they leave the wood paintable. They provide protection against termites and decay. Work is continuing to develop preservatives that are totally free of metals.

Two other chemicals that have traditionally been used are chromated copper arsenate (CCA) and ammoniacal copper zinc arsenate (ACZA). However, these have been shown to be harmful to health and the environment because of their arsenic content. Chromated copper arsenate (CCA) for residential and general consumer use was phased out by the Environmental Protection Agency on December 31, 2003. Evidence had shown that arsenic could leach out of the treated wood and that disposal by burning could release toxic substances.

ACQ and copper azole are more corrosive than is CCA to fasteners and some flashing. Fasteners and connecters compatible with the chemical preservative used should be specified. Fasteners should be type 304 or 316 stainless steel or hot-dip galvanized products with a minimum G90 coating; that is, 0.90 oz/ft^2 (Z 275, 275 g/m^2). Aluminum flashing should not be used with wood treated with these preservatives. Preservatives with borates will leach out of wood when exposed to moisture, so applications with borates are limited to areas protected from moisture and not in contact with the ground. When cuts are made to treated wood, the exposed areas should be treated with a copper naphthenate solution containing at least 2% copper.

FINISH CARPENTRY AND ARCHITECTURAL WOODWORK

Finish carpentry is the final exposed-wood construction done on the job site. It is usually nonstructural in nature. This class of work includes exterior wood siding, interior trim, door and window framing, stair framing, shelving and cabinetry, paneling, and similar finish items.

Although finish carpentry overlaps somewhat with architectural woodwork, the latter term refers to finish lumber items fabricated in a manufacturing plant and brought to the job site for installation. Architectural woodwork items normally include fine finished cabinetry, wall paneling, custom doors, and other items that can be better made under controlled factory conditions.

FINISH CARPENTRY

Wood Species and Grading

As stated in Ch. 16, wood is classified as softwood or hardwood. *Softwoods* are those cut from coniferous trees, and *hardwoods* are those coming from deciduous trees. Finish carpentry employs both. Lower cost interior trim is usually made from the better grades of pine and fir, but when appearance is important, hardwoods such as oak, mahogany, or birch are used. Hardwoods are used almost exclusively for architectural woodwork because of their superior appearance and durability.

There are hundreds of domestic and imported wood species available for finish carpentry and architectural woodwork. However, because of cost and availability, only a few are generally used for finish carpentry and several dozen are used for architectural woodwork. Some of the common hardwood species include red and white oak, ash, walnut, cherry, mahogany, birch, poplar, and maple.

Finish carpentry lumber is graded differently than are architectural woodwork and structural lumber. The grading varies slightly from species to species, but in general the Western Wood Products Association (WWPA) classifies finish lumber into selects, finish, paneling, and commons, along with grades for siding and what the WWPA terms alternate boards. Selects are divided into B & Better (the best grade in this category), C Select, and D Select. Finish is subdivided into superior, prime, and E grades. Western red cedar, redwood, and a few other domestic species have their own grading rules. These grades are summarized in Table 17.1.

In addition to these grades, finish lumber may be specified as heartwood or sapwood. *Heartwood* comes from the center of the tree and sapwood from the perimeter. In some species, such as redwood, there is a marked color variance and resistance to decay between the two types of lumber. In some circumstances it is important to differentiate between the two.

For many types of softwood trim there is another category called *fingerjointed*. This is not really a grade but a method of manufacturing lengths of trim from shorter pieces of lumber. The ends of the short pieces are cut with finger-like projections, glued, and joined together. Fingerjointed material is less expensive than continuous molding but is only appropriate for a paint finish where the joints will be covered.

Lumber Cutting

The way lumber is cut from a log determines the final appearance of the grain pattern. There are three ways boards (also called *solid stock*) are cut from a log. Thin veneers are sliced in similar ways, but these are discussed in the next section on architectural woodwork. The three methods used are plain sawing (also called *flat sawing*), quartersawing, and rift sawing. These methods are illustrated in Fig. 17.1.

Plain sawing makes the most efficient use of the log and is the least expensive of the three methods. Because the wood is cut with various orientations to the grain of the tree, plain

Table 17.1
Selected Grades for Appearance Grades of Western Lumber

grade category	grades	description
selects	B & Better	Highest quality of select grade lumber available, with many pieces absolutely clear and free of defects.
	C Select	Appearance only slightly less than B & Better. Recommended for high-quality interior trim and cabinet work with natural stain or enamel finishes.
	D Select	Allows more defects than C Select grade but is suitable where finish requirements are less exacting.
finish	Superior; Superior VG	Highest quality of finish grade lumber available, with many pieces absolutely clear. Used for high quality trim and cabinet work where natural, stain, or enamel finishes are used and the finest appearance is required. Can be specified as VG for vertical grain.
	Prime; Prime VG	Allows slightly more defects than Superior, but can be used where finishing requirements are less exacting. Can be specified as VG for vertical grain.
	E	Boards in this grade can be cut in such a way as to produce pieces of Prime or Superior grades. E grade boards must contain two-thirds or more of such cuttings 2 in (50) or wider and 16 in (406) or longer.
paneling	any select or finish grade	C Select or any other grade can be used to produce paneling.
	selected 2 common for knotty paneling	Grade reserved for knotty paneling made from no. 2 Common grade boards (not shown in this table).

Note: Additional grades are available, but they are commonly used for other architectural purposes.

sawing results in a finished surface with the characteristic cathedral pattern shown in Fig. 17.1.

Quartersawing is produced by cutting the log into quarters and then sawing perpendicular to a diameter line. Because the saw cut is more or less perpendicular to the grain, the resulting grain pattern is more uniformly vertical. Not only does this result in a different appearance than plain sawing, but quartersawn boards also tend to twist and cup less, shrink less in width, hold paint better, and have fewer defects.

As illustrated in Fig. 17.1, quartersawn boards cut from the edges of the log do not have the grain exactly at a 90° angle to the saw cut as do those in the middle. For an even more consistent vertical grain, *rift sawing* is used. With this method, the saw cuts from a quartered log are always made radially to the center of the tree. Because the log must be

shifted after each cut and because there is a great deal of waste, rift cutting is more expensive than quartersawing.

Because of the limited availability of some species of wood and the expense of making certain cuts, not all types of lumber cutting are available in all species. In some cases, for a particular species, a veneer cut (discussed in the next section) will be available, but not the corresponding solid stock cut. The availability of cuts in the desired species should be verified before specifications are written.

Wood Siding

Wood siding consists of individual boards applied horizontally, diagonally, or vertically. When the siding is applied over wood sheathing (either plywood or particleboard), a layer of building paper is placed under the sheathing to minimize air infiltration and improve the water resistance of the wall. When the siding is applied over fiberboard or

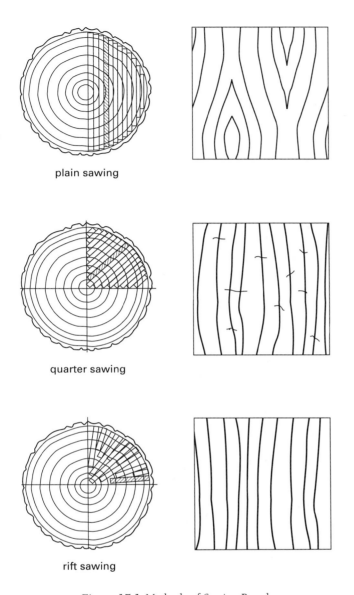

plain sawing

quarter sawing

rift sawing

Figure 17.1 Methods of Sawing Boards

insulating sheathing, an air infiltration barrier of high-density polyethylene is often used under the siding. This allows moisture vapor to pass through but minimizes air leakage.

Wood siding is milled from redwood, cedar, Douglas fir, pine, and several other species. Some, such as redwood and cypress, are naturally resistant to moisture and require less protection than varieties like pine. Siding comes in several shapes, as shown in Fig. 17.2. All are milled to allow one board to overlap.

Wood Stairs and Trim

The construction of wood stairs is considered a finish carpentry item. Stairs can range from simple utilitarian assemblies to elaborate, ornate, crafted works. A simple form of

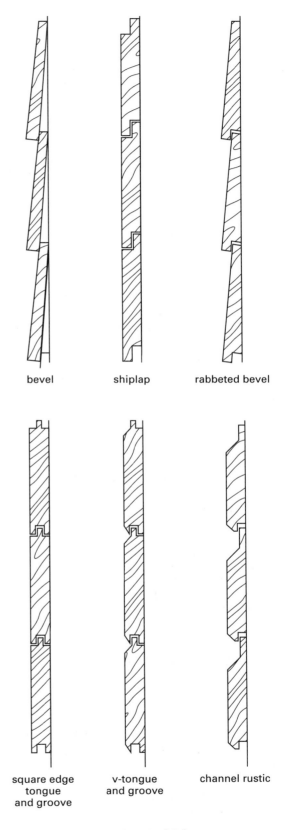

bevel   shiplap   rabbeted bevel

square edge   v-tongue   channel rustic
tongue   and groove
and groove

Figure 17.2 Wood Siding

stair construction is shown in Fig. 17.3 with the primary construction elements identified.

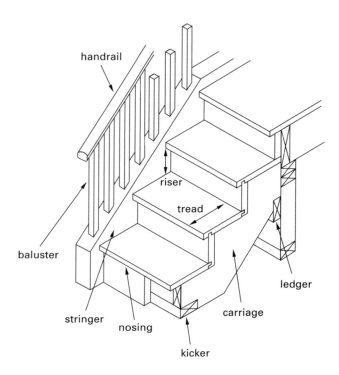

Figure 17.3 Typical Stair Construction

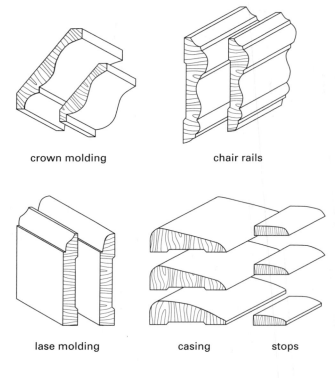

Figure 17.4 Interior Trim

Interior and exterior trim is used to finish off the joints between dissimilar materials, close construction gaps between building elements, and provide decorative treatment. Simple, rectangular shapes are used for a great deal of construction trim, but there are dozens of standard, shaped molding pieces used for particular applications. Some of the more common types of interior trim are shown in Fig. 17.4.

More ornate molding sections can be built by using a combination of standard shapes or by having a millshop make a cutting blade that is used to shape special profiles.

ARCHITECTURAL WOODWORK

Architectural woodwork is custom, shop-fabricated lumber components used for interior finish construction, which includes cabinetry, paneling, custom doors and frames, shelving, custom furniture, and special interior trim. Architectural woodwork makes it possible to produce superior finish carpentry items because most of the work is done under carefully controlled factory conditions with machinery and finishing techniques that could never be duplicated on a job site.

Lumber for architectural woodwork and the quality of constructed woodwork items are graded differently than rough carpentry or finish carpentry. Standards for architectural woodwork are set by the Architectural Woodwork Institute (AWI) and are published in AWI's *Architectural Woodwork Quality Standards* booklet.

Lumber is classed as Grade I, II, and III and is based on the percentage of a board that can be used by cutting out defects. There are also limitations on the types of defects that are allowed in any grade.

Construction standards, tolerances, and the finished appearance of completed components are specified as premium, custom, and economy grades. These grades apply to doors, cabinets, paneling, and other woodwork items. For example, the maximum gap between a cabinet door and frame is $3/32$ in (2.4) for premium grade, $1/8$ in (3) for custom grade, and $5/32$ in (4) for economy grade. A complete description for each item in each grade is given in the *Architectural Woodwork Quality Standards* booklet.

Lumber and Veneers for Architectural Woodwork

Architects have a wider selection of solid stock and veneer for use in woodwork than for finish carpentry. Material comes from both domestic and foreign sources and varies widely in availability and cost.

Because of the limited availability of many hardwood species, most architectural woodwork is made from veneer stock. A *veneer* is a thin slice of wood cut from a log (as described in the next section) and glued to a backing of particleboard or plywood, normally ³/₄ in (19) thick.

Refer to Ch. 8 for more information on certified wood products and alternates to standard veneers.

Types of Veneer Cuts

Just as with solid stock, the way veneer is cut from a log affects its final appearance. There are five principal methods of cutting veneers, as shown in Fig. 17.5. Plain slicing and quarter slicing are accomplished the same way as cutting solid stock, except the resulting pieces are much thinner. Quarter slicing produces a more straight-grained pattern than does plain slicing because the cutting knife strikes the growth rings at approximately a 90° angle.

With *rotary slicing*, the log is mounted on a lathe and turned against a knife, which peels off a continuous layer of veneer. This produces a very pronounced grain pattern that is often undesirable in fine quality wood finishes, although it does produce the most veneer with the least waste.

Half-round slicing is similar to rotary slicing, but the log is cut in half and the veneer is cut slightly across the annular growth rings. This results in a pronounced grain pattern showing characteristics of both rotary-sliced and plain-sliced veneers.

Rift slicing is accomplished by quartering a log and cutting at about a 15° angle to the growth rings. Like quarter slicing, it results in a straight-grain pattern and is often used with oak to eliminate the appearance of markings perpendicular to the direction of the grain. These markings in oak are caused by *medullary rays*, which are radial cells extending from the center of the tree to its circumference.

Because the width of a piece of veneer is limited by the diameter of log or portion of log from which it is cut, several veneers must be put together on a backing panel to make up the needed size of a finished piece. The individual veneers come from the same piece of log, which is called a *flitch*. The word "flitch" is sometimes also used to describe the particular sequence in which the veneers are taken off the log as it is cut. The method of matching veneers is discussed in the following sections.

Joinery Details

Various types of joints are used for woodwork construction to increase the strength of the joint and improve the appearance by eliminating mechanical fasteners such as screws. With the availability of high-strength adhesives, screws and other mechanical fasteners are seldom needed for the

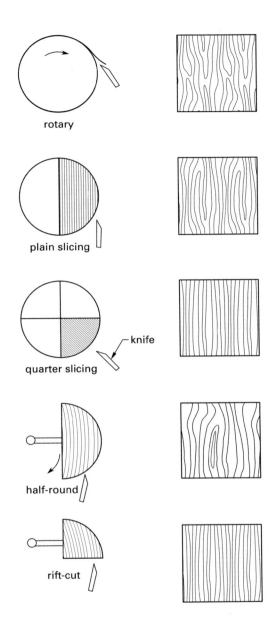

Figure 17.5 Veneer Cuts

majority of the work produced in the shop. Field attachment, however, often requires the use of blind nailing or other concealed fastening to maintain the quality look of the work. Some of the common joints used in both woodwork and finish carpentry are shown in Fig. 17.6.

Cabinetwork

Architectural woodwork cabinets are built in the shop as complete assemblies and are simply set in place and

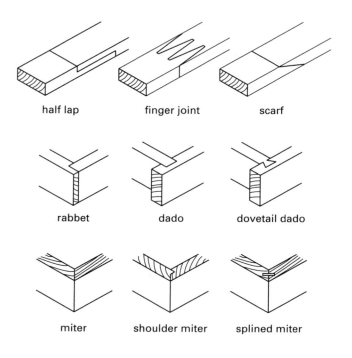

Figure 17.6 Wood Joints

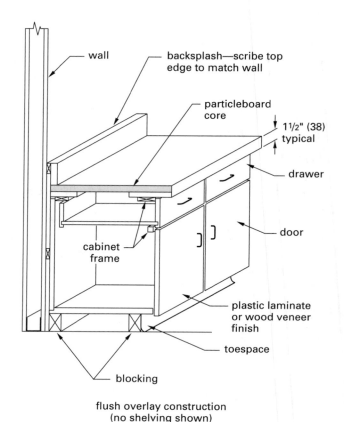

flush overlay construction
(no shelving shown)

Figure 17.7 Typical Wood Cabinet

attached to surrounding construction at the job site. There are several methods of detailing door and drawer fronts on cabinets, but the construction of the cabinet frames is fairly standard, as shown in Fig. 17.7.

Countertops are built separately from base cabinets and put in place in the field. This is because the countertops are built in single lengths that are much longer than any individual base cabinet. Building and installing the countertops separately also gives the installers the ability to precisely fit the countertop to the wall. This is most commonly done with a scribe piece on top of the backsplash or the back of the countertop. A *scribe piece* is an oversized piece of plastic laminate or wood that can be trimmed in the field to follow any minor irregularities of the wall. As with other woodwork components, there are hundreds of possible configurations to countertops including variations in width, materials, front edge shape and size, and backsplash shape and size. Some of the more common configurations are shown in Fig. 17.8. Figure 17.9 shows typical plastic laminate countertop edge treatments.

For both base and upper cabinets there are four basic categories of door and drawer front construction: flush, flush overlay, reveal overlay, and lipped overlay. These are shown in Fig. 17.10.

With *flush* construction, the face of a drawer or door is installed flush with the face frame. The primary disadvantage with this type of construction is its expense because of

the extra care required to fit and align the doors and drawers within the frame. Another disadvantage is that, with use, the doors and drawers may sag. This results in a nonuniform spacing between fronts and may cause some doors and drawers to bind against the frame.

With *flush overlay* construction, the fronts of the doors and drawers overlap the face frame of the cabinet. Edges of adjacent door or drawer fronts are separated only enough to allow operation without touching, usually about $^1/_8$ in (3) or less. Only doors and drawers are visible, and they are all flush with each other. As with flush construction, the millshop must take great care in aligning and fitting the doors and drawers so that the gap between them is uniform.

With *reveal overlay* construction, the edges of adjacent doors and door fronts are separated enough to reveal the face frame behind. This construction is less expensive than flush overlay construction because minor misalignments and sagging are not as noticeable. A variation is the *lipped overlay* construction in which part of the door or drawer overlaps the frame and covers the joint between the two pieces. See Fig. 17.10(d).

Upper cabinets are very similar in construction to base cabinets. The most notable exceptions are that they are not as

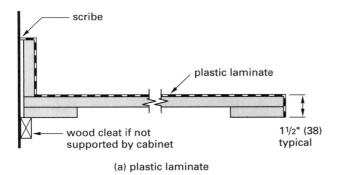

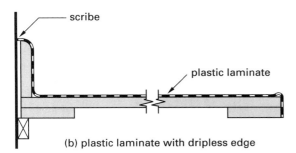

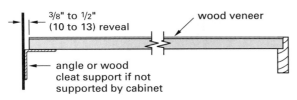

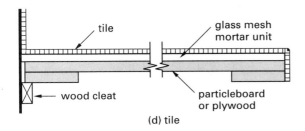

Figure 17.8 Typical Countertop Details

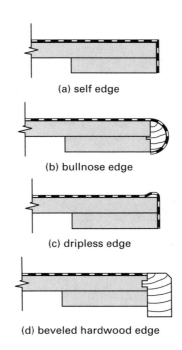

Figure 17.9 HPDL Edge Treatments

Flush Paneling

Architectural woodwork paneling includes flush or raised panel constructions used to cover vertical surfaces. As mentioned before, large, flat areas like paneling are built of thin wood veneers glued to backing panels of particleboard or plywood.

In addition to the way the veneer is cut, there are several methods of matching adjacent pieces of veneer and veneer panels in a room that affect the final appearance of the job. The three considerations, in increasing order of scale, are matching between adjacent veneer leaves, matching veneers within a panel, and matching panels within a room.

Matching adjacent veneer leaves may be done in three ways, as shown in Fig. 17.12. *Bookmatching* is the most common. As the veneers are sliced off the log, every other piece is turned over so that adjacent leaves form a symmetrical grain pattern. With *slip matching*, consecutive pieces are placed side by side with the same face sides being exposed. *Random matching* places veneers in no particular sequence, and even veneers from different flitches may be used.

Veneers must be glued to rigid panels to make installation possible. The method of doing this is the next consideration in specifying paneling. If the veneers are bookmatched, there are three ways, shown in Fig. 17.13, of matching veneers within a panel. A *running match* simply alternates bookmatched veneer pieces regardless of their width or how many must be used to complete a panel. Any portion

deep as base cabinets, and some design and detailing consideration must be given to the undersides of upper cabinets because they are visible. In addition, there must be some way to securely anchor the cabinet to the wall. In residential construction, the cabinet is attached to the wall by screwing through the cabinet back and wall finish into the wood studs. In commercial construction where metal studs are used, wood blocking is required in the stud cavity behind the wall finish. This blocking is installed as the studs are being erected and is attached to them with screws. The blocking provides a solid base for attaching the cabinets to the wall. Figure 17.11 shows a typical upper cabinet detail.

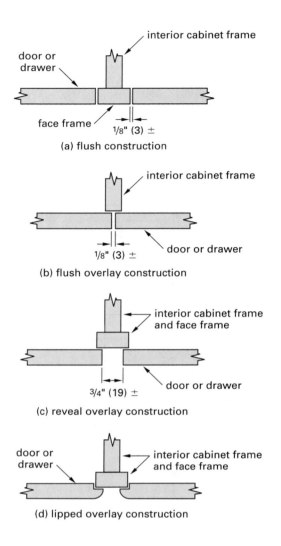

Figure 17.10   Types of Cabinet Door Framing

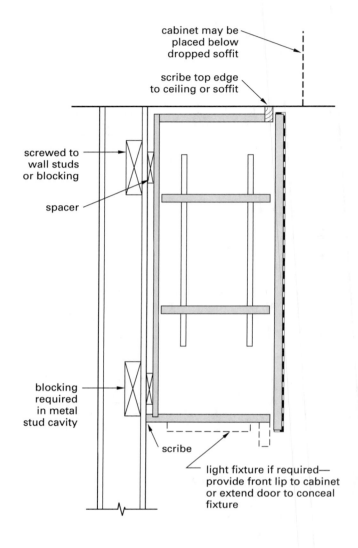

Figure 17.11   Typical Upper Cabinet

left over from the last leaf of one panel is used as the starting piece for the next. A *balance match* utilizes veneer pieces trimmed to equal widths in each panel. A *center match* has an even number of veneer leaves of uniform width so that there is a veneer joint in the center of the panel.

There are also three ways panels can be assembled within a room to complete a project. See Fig. 17.14. The first and least expensive is called *warehouse matching*. Premanufactured panels, normally 4 ft wide by 8 ft or 10 ft long (1200 wide by 2400 or 3000 long) are assembled from a single flitch that yields from six to twelve panels. They are field cut to fit around doors, windows, and other obstructions, resulting in some loss of grain continuity.

The second method, called *sequence matching*, uses panels of uniform width manufactured for a specific job and with the veneers arranged in sequence. If some panels must be trimmed to fit around doors or other obstructions, there is a moderate loss of grain continuity.

The third and most expensive method is called *blueprint matching*. Here the panels are manufactured to precisely fit the room and line up with every obstruction so that grain continuity is not interrupted. Veneers from the same flitch are matched over doors, cabinets, and other items covered with paneling.

Joints of flush paneling may be constructed in a number of ways depending on the finish appearance desired, as shown in Fig. 17.15. Paneling is hung on a wall with either steel Z-clips or wood cleats cut at an angle to allow the individual panels to be slipped over the hanger, which is anchored to the wall structure. These methods are also illustrated in Fig. 17.15.

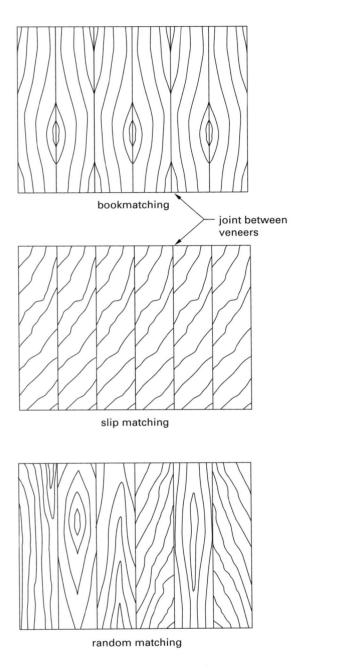

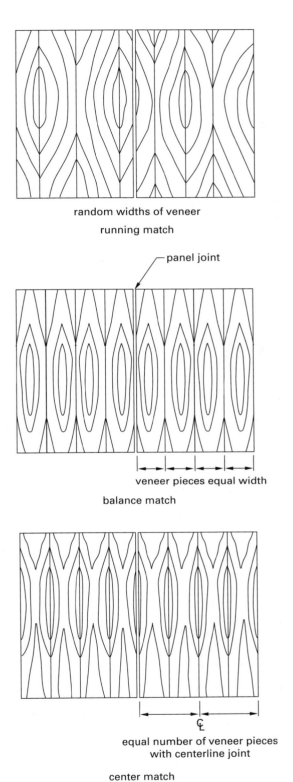

Figure 17.12   Veneer Matching

Figure 17.13   Panel Matching Veneers

Stile and Rail Paneling

Stile and rail panel construction consists of a frame of solid wood that contains individual panels. Along with various types of molding and matching doors, raised panel construction is used to detail a traditional wood-paneled room interior. See Fig. 17.16. Traditionally, the panels were also made from solid wood, but today it is more common for the panels to be veneered.

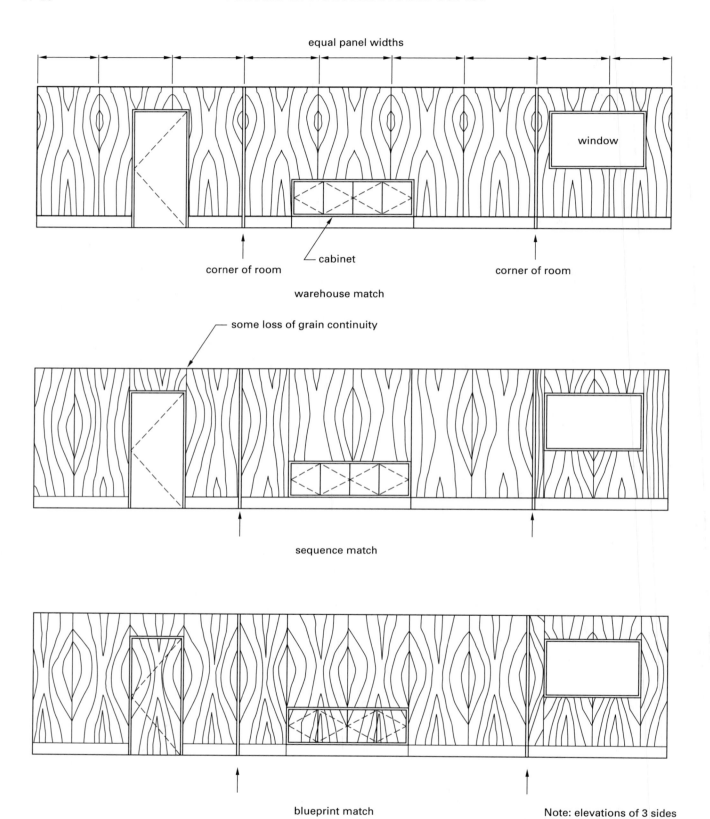

Figure 17.14   Matching Panels Within a Room

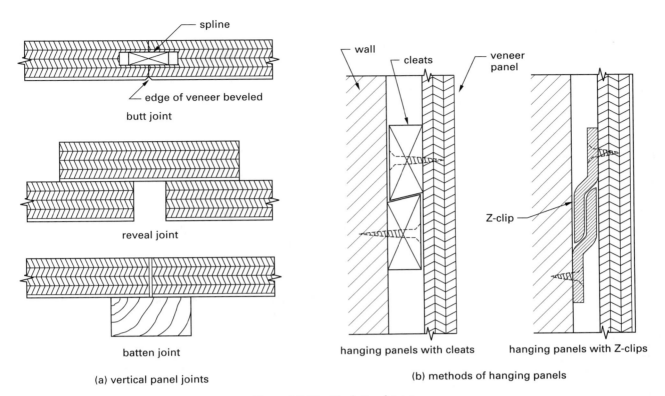

(a) vertical panel joints

(b) methods of hanging panels

Figure 17.15 Flush Panel Joints

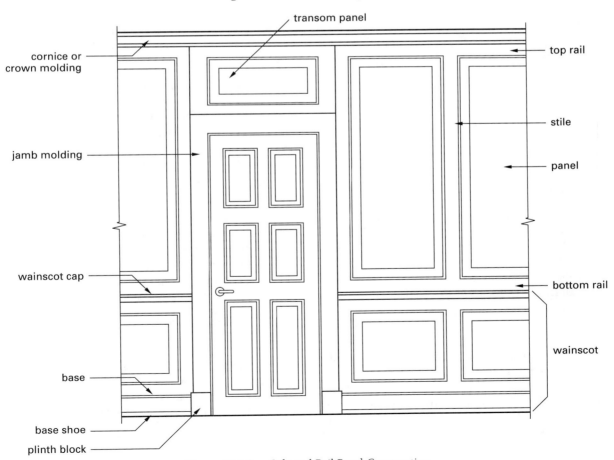

Figure 17.16 Stile and Rail Panel Construction

As shown in Fig. 17.17, the vertical frame pieces are called the *stiles*, and the horizontal members are the *rails*. The panels are held in place with grooves cut in the sides of the frames or with individual molding pieces, called sticking. The panels are set in the molding loosely to allow the panel to expand and contract with changes in the moisture content.

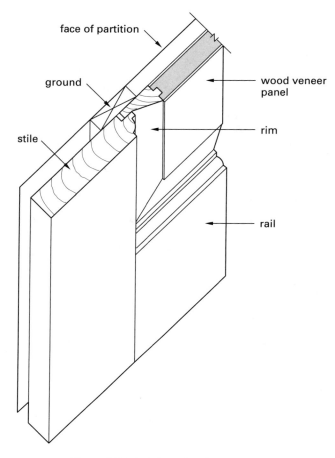

Figure 17.17 Stile and Rail Components

Stile and rail paneling may be hung on walls with wood cleats or metal Z-clips as with flush paneling, but if extensive molding is used the panels can be screwed to wood grounds behind the paneling and the fasteners concealed with the molding. Individual panels are joined with dowels or splines to keep the edges flush.

Laminates

A common finishing material used with architectural woodwork is *high-pressure decorative laminate* (HPDL). This is a thin sheet material made by impregnating several layers of kraft paper with phenolic resins and overlaying the paper with a patterned or colored sheet and a layer of melamine resin. The entire assembly is placed in a hot press under high pressure where the various layers fuse together. Plastic laminates are used for countertops, wall paneling, cabinets, shelving, and furniture.

Because laminates are very thin, they must be adhered to panel substrates such as plywood or particleboard. Smaller pieces can be glued to solid pieces of lumber. There are several types and thicknesses of plastic laminate, the most common being a general-purpose type that is 0.050 in (1.3) thick. It is used for both vertical and horizontal applications. A post-forming type, 0.040 in (1) thick, is manufactured so it can be heated and bent to a small radius.

When plastic laminate is applied to large surfaces of paneling, it must be balanced with a backing sheet to inhibit moisture absorption and to attain structural balance so that the panel does not warp.

There are several types of high-pressure decorative laminates manufactured for specific purposes. Although these generally cost more, they fill specific needs for some construction.

- *Colorthrough laminates.* These laminates are manufactured with decorative papers throughout the thickness so that the resulting sheet is a solid color. This eliminates the dark line visible at the edges of sheets when they are trimmed.

- *Fire-rated laminates.* These finishes comply with Class 1 or A ratings as long as the appropriate substrates and adhesives are selected.

- *Chemical-resistant laminates.* Special formulation of the laminate materials give these products additional resistance to strong chemicals found in laboratories, medical facilities, and photographic studios. They are available in horizontal as well as vertical thicknesses and can be post-formed for curved surfaces.

- *Static-dissipative laminates.* For areas where static control is required, such as in hospital operating rooms, electronic manufacturing plants, and computer rooms, these laminates provide a conductive layer in the sheet. When connected to suitable grounding they prevent the buildup of static charges and continuously channel them away.

- *Metal-faced laminates.* A limited number of metal finishes are available. They do not have the same wear resistance as real metal, so they should only be used on vertical surfaces subject to little abuse. They can be fabricated with standard woodworking equipment and cost much less than real metal. However, it is difficult to fabricate small, detailed items with finely crafted edges.

• *Natural wood laminates.* Thin veneers of actual wood are bonded to the standard type of laminate kraft papers and resins with this product. The laminate can be specified to provide untreated wood ready for finishing or with a protective layer of melamine resin.

Another type of laminate product is *thermoset decorative paneling.* It is made by pressing a decorative overlay from a thermoset polyester or melamine resin-impregnated saturated sheet onto a cellulosic substrate such as particleboard or medium-density fiberboard. This paneling differs from high-pressure decorative laminates in that its decorative surface is fused to the substrate of particleboard. (In contrast, the decorative surface of high-pressure laminates is a thin veneer that must be adhesive-bonded to another substrate.) Because the process is usually done with pressures lower than HPDLs, these products are sometimes called "low-pressure laminates" or melamine. The manufacturers that produce thermoset decorative panels form the American Laminators Association (ALA) and use the trade name Permalam® to identify these types of panels.

Because the decorative surface is part of the substrate, the potential problem of delamination is eliminated and the panels come ready to be fabricated. Generally, the cost of thermoset panels is less than HPDL in many cases. However, there are currently several disadvantages to thermoset decorative panels. The choices of colors, textures, and grades are limited. Thermoset panels cannot be post-formed for curves, and they should not be used for high-wear horizontal surfaces such as countertops. Only a limited number of Class I or A fire-rated panels is available from a few manufacturers. Thermoset panels are typically used for furniture, fixtures, and kitchen cabinets or where resistance to heavy use is not required.

Standing and Running Trim

Standing and running trim are similar to standard molding sections applied as finish carpentry items. Unlike moldings, however, standing and running trim are custom-fabricated to meet the requirements of a specific project.

Standing trim is woodwork of a fixed length, intended to be installed as a single piece of wood. Examples include door frame trim, door stops, window casings, and similar items. *Running trim* is woodwork of a continuing length that must be installed in several pieces fitted end to end, such as base molding, cornices, chair rails, and soffits. *Rails* are gripping or protection surfaces on corridor walls of hospitals and the like and guard rails at glass openings.

The *profile* of trim, or its *cross-sectional shape*, can be identical to the many standard shapes available in premanufactured molding, or custom profiles can be milled.

Solid Surfacing Material

Solid surfacing is a generic term for homogeneous, polymer-based surfacing materials. It can be formed into thick, flat sheets, or into shapes. It is frequently used for kitchen and bath countertops, sinks, toilet partitions, bars, and other areas where high-pressure plastic laminate might otherwise be used. It is available in a wide variety of colors and patterns. Standard thickness for countertops is $3/4$ in (19). Because the color is integral throughout the thickness of the material, scratches, dents, stains, and other types of minor damage can be sanded out or cleaned with a household abrasive cleanser. Because many of the available patterns resemble stone, it is often used as a lower cost, lighter weight substitute for stone tops.

Solid surfacing materials are easily fabricated and installed with normal woodworking tools. Edges can even be routed for decorative effects. When two pieces must be butted together, a two-part epoxy or liquid form of the material is used for a seamless appearance.

Moisture Content and Shrinkage

Shrinkage and swelling of lumber in architectural woodwork is not as much of a problem as for rough and finish carpentry because of the improved manufacturing methods available in the shop and the fact that solid stock and veneer can be dried or acclimated to a particular region.

However, some general guidelines should be followed. For most of the United States, the optimum moisture content of architectural woodwork for interior applications is from 5% to 10%. The relative humidity necessary to maintain this optimum level is from 25% to 55%. In the more humid southern coastal areas, the optimum moisture content is from 8% to 13%, and in the dry Southwest the corresponding values are from 4% to 9%.

Code Requirements

The various model building codes set limits on the flame-spread ratings of interior finishes based on the occupancy of the building and the use area within the building. In general, most of the model building codes regulate the use of woodwork as a wall or ceiling finish, but do not regulate the use of wood in furniture, cabinets, or trim. This includes cabinets attached to the structure.

Interior finish is defined in the IBC (and similarly in other model codes) as wall and ceiling finish including wainscoting, paneling, or other finish applied structurally or for decoration, acoustical correction, surface insulation, or similar purposes. Requirements do not apply to *trim*, which is defined as picture molds, chair rails, baseboards, and handrails; to doors and windows or their frames; or to materials that are less than $1/28$ in (0.91) thick cemented to the surface of walls or ceilings.

As discussed in Ch. 29, there are three flame-spread groupings. In the IBC these are A, B, and C, corresponding to flame-spread ratings of 0–25, 26–75, and 76–200, respectively.

Different wood species have different flame-spread ratings, but very few have ratings less than 75, so wood is generally considered a Class C material unless it is treated with a fire retardant. However, treating often darkens the wood and makes it difficult to finish.

FINISHES

Finish is used on woodwork to protect it from moisture, chemicals, and contact and to enhance its appearance. Woodwork can either be field finished or factory finished. Because more control can be achieved with a factory finish this is the preferred method, although minor cabinet and trim work is often field finished in single-family residential and small commercial construction. For high-quality woodwork, field finishing is generally limited to minor touch-up and repair.

Prior to finishing, the wood must be sanded properly and filled, if desired. On many open-grain woods such as oak, mahogany, and teak, a filler should be applied prior to finishing to give a more uniform appearance to the woodwork, but it is not required. Other types of surface preparation are also possible depending on the aesthetic effect desired. The wood may be bleached to lighten it or to provide uniformity of color. Wood may also be mechanically or physically distressed to give it an antique or aged appearance. Shading or toning can also be used to change the color of the wood and subsequent finishing operations.

Opaque Finishes

Opaque finishes include lacquer, varnish, polyurethane, and polyester. They should only be used on closed-grain woods where solid stock is used and on medium-density fiberboard where sheet materials are used.

Lacquer is a coating material with a high nitrocellulose content modified with resins and plasticizers dissolved in a volatile solvent. Catalyzed lacquers contain an extra ingredient that speeds drying time and gives the finish additional hardness.

Varnish is a material consisting of various types of resinous materials dissolved in one of several types of volatile liquids. Conversion varnish is produced with alkyd and urea formaldehyde resins. When a high solids content is specified, the finish becomes opaque.

Polyurethane is a synthetic finish that gives a very hard, durable finish. Although difficult to repair or refinish, polyurethane finishes offer superior resistance to water, to many commercial and household chemicals, and to abrasion. Opaque polyurethanes are available in sheens from dull satin to full gloss.

Polyesters are another type of synthetic finish that give the hardest, most durable finish possible. Opaque polyesters can be colored and are available only in a full-gloss sheen. Like polyurethanes, polyester finishes are very difficult to repair and refinish outside the shop, but they give very durable finishes with as much as 80% the hardness of glass.

Transparent Finishes

Transparent finishes include lacquer, varnish, vinyl, penetrating oils, polyurethane, and polyester.

Standard lacquers are easy to apply, can be repaired easily, and are relatively low in cost. However, they do not provide the chemical and wear resistance of some of the other finishes. Catalyzed lacquers for transparent finishes are more difficult to repair and refinish, but they are more durable and resistant to commercial and household chemicals. A special water-reducible acrylic lacquer is available if local regulations prohibit the use of other types of lacquers.

Conversion varnish has many of the same advantages of lacquer but can often be applied with fewer coats.

Catalyzed vinyl yields a surface that has the most chemical resistance of the standard finishes of lacquer, varnish, and vinyl. Vinyl is also very resistant to scratching, abrasion, and other mechanical damage.

Penetrating oil finishes are one of the traditional wood finishes. They are easily applied and give a rich look to wood, but they require re-oiling periodically and tend to darken with age. An oil-finish look can be achieved with a catalyzed vinyl.

As with the opaque finishes, both polyurethane and polyester provide the most durable transparent finishes possible. They are the most expensive of the finishing systems and require skilled applicators. Transparent polyurethanes are available in sheens from dull to full gloss, whereas polyesters are available only in full gloss.

Stains

Prior to applying the final finish, wood may be stained to modify its color. The two types of stains are water-based and solvent-based. Water-based stains yield a uniform color but raise the grain. Solvent-based stains dry quickly and do not raise the grain but are less uniform. Both are penetrating finishes and cannot be easily removed.

MOISTURE PROTECTION AND THERMAL INSULATION

Protecting buildings from water leakage and temperature transmission are two of the most troublesome technical problems an architect must solve. Water can leak into a building from underground moisture and groundwater and from precipitation on the roof and exterior walls. It can find its way into a building through a surface material such as roofing or a basement slab or through joints and penetrations between materials. Moisture can also be generated within a building from cooking, showering, or simple human habitation. This moisture must also be prevented from permeating the structure.

This chapter discusses the methods and materials used to protect a building from moisture and to control heat loss or heat gain.

DAMPPROOFING

Dampproofing is the control of moisture that is not under hydrostatic pressure. Dampproofing can apply to water-repellent coatings on concrete, masonry, and wood walls above grade, but in its most typical use the term describes the protection of slabs and foundation walls below grade that are subject to continuous exposure to moisture.

The following types of dampproofing may be used.

- *Admixtures.* Various types of admixtures can be added to concrete to make it water repellent. These include materials such as salts of fatty acids, mineral oil, and powdered iron. They may reduce the strength of the concrete, but they make it much less permeable to water.

- *Bituminous coatings.* These are asphalt or coal-tar pitch materials applied to the exterior side of the foundation wall. They may be brushed or sprayed on, can be applied either hot or cold (depending on the type), and should be applied to smooth surfaces.

They do not, however, seal cracks that develop after they are applied.

- *Cementitious coatings.* One or two coats of portland cement mortar can be troweled over the surface of masonry or concrete foundation walls. Mortar coatings are often used over very rough walls to provide a smooth surface for other dampproofing materials or by themselves. Powdered iron is often added as an admixture to the mortar. As the iron oxidizes it expands and limits the amount of shrinkage of the material, making a tighter seal.

- *Membranes.* These methods include built-up layers of hot- or cold-applied asphalt felts or membranes of butyl, polyvinyl chloride, and other synthetic materials. However, membranes are usually used for waterproofing walls subject to hydrostatic pressure, and their cost and difficulty of application is usually not warranted for simple dampproofing.

- *Plastics.* Silicone and polyurethane coatings are available, but they are usually reserved for above-grade dampproofing.

WATERPROOFING

Waterproofing is the control of moisture and water that is subject to hydrostatic pressure. This may include protecting structures below the water table. Waterproofing is a more difficult technical problem than is dampproofing because of the water pressure and the need to create a continuous seal over walls, slabs, and joints in the structure.

In most cases, waterproofing membranes are used on the exteriors of the walls and slabs. These may be built-up layers of bituminous saturated felts similar to roofing, or single-ply membranes of synthetic materials such as butyl, polyvinyl chloride, or other proprietary products. When membranes are used, they are subject to puncture during backfilling operations. For this reason, a protection surface is placed over the waterproofing prior to backfilling. Figure 18.1 shows a typical installation of a waterproofed slab and foundation wall.

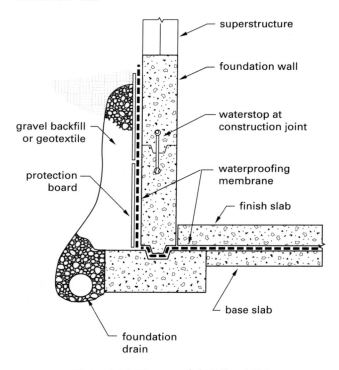

Figure 18.1 Waterproofed Wall and Slab

Joints in waterproofed walls are particularly subject to leakage. In concrete walls, *waterstops* are used to seal construction joints. Waterstops are dumbbell-shaped, continuous rubber or neoprene extrusions. Half of the waterstop is placed in the form during the first pour of concrete, and the other half is allowed to extend into the second pour.

Another method of waterproofing is the use of *bentonite panels*. These are flat packages of bentonite clay inside kraft paper packages. They are placed under slabs and against walls. After backfilling, the kraft paper deteriorates and the clay expands in the presence of moisture to form a waterproof barrier.

Of course, even when dampproofing or waterproofing a wall below grade, good construction design should include creating a positive slope away from the building to minimize water penetration around the foundation and provide some type of perimeter drainage if a heavy concentration of water is anticipated. This may include backfilling with gravel and placing perimeter foundation drains at the footing line, as discussed in Ch. 12. Hydrostatic pressure buildup can also be alleviated by using a geotextile matting over the waterproofing.

BUILDING INSULATION

Insulation is used to control unwanted heat flow, which can be from a warm building to a cold exterior or from a hot climate into a habitable space. Selecting and detailing insulation for buildings requires an understanding of the processes of heat gain and heat loss because different kinds of insulation are used to control these factors.

Methods of Heat Transfer

Heat is transferred in three ways: conduction, convection, and radiation. *Conduction* is the flow of heat within a material or between materials without displacement of the particles of the material. *Convection* is the transfer of heat within a fluid, either gas or liquid, by the movement of the fluid from an area of higher temperature to an area of lower temperature. Radiation is the transfer of heat energy through electromagnetic waves from one surface to a colder surface.

The best insulation is a vacuum. The next best insulation is air kept absolutely motionless in a space between two materials. However, this does not usually occur because convection currents carry warm air in one part of the space to the cooler parts of the space where heat is transferred by conduction. Most insulations are designed to create air pockets small enough to prevent convection but large enough to prevent the direct transfer of heat by conduction between the insulating materials.

Measuring Thermal Resistance

Thermal resistance is described with several terms, as outlined in Ch. 5. The quantity of heat used to measure transfer is the *British thermal unit* (Btu), which is the amount of heat required to raise the temperature of 1 lbm of water by 1°F. The basic unit of conductance is a material's k-value, or conductivity. This is the number of Btus per hour that pass through 1 ft² of homogeneous material 1 in thick when the temperature differential is 1°F. When the material is more than 1 in thick, the unit is *conductance*, or the C-value.

The more common term used is the R-value, or resistance of a material. Resistance is the number of hours needed for 1 Btu to pass through 1 ft² of a material of a given thickness when the temperature differential is 1°F. It is the reciprocal of conductance. Thus, the lower a material's k-value or C-value, the better its insulating qualities. Higher R-values also indicate a better insulating value.

In SI units, the joule (J) is the unit for energy, which is equal to $1/4.184$ of the amount of heat required to raise a gram of water by 1°C. 1 Btu equals 1.055 kJ. Conductivity is measured as the rate at which watts flow through 1 m² of homogeneous material when the temperature changes by 1K, which is the same as 1°C. Conductivity, k, in SI units is shown as W/m°K or W/m°C. Thermal resistance, *R*, in SI units is m²·K/W.

Another rating method for foam insulation products is *long-term thermal resistance* (LTTR). It has been found that, over time, the thermal resistance of foam insulation changes due to changes in cell gas composition caused by the diffusion of air into the foam cells and the diffusion of blowing agents out of the cells. This is sometimes called *thermal drift*. LTTR is the thermal resistance value of a closed-cell foam insulation product measured after storage for five years under prescribed laboratory conditions. This has been shown to be the equivalent to the time-weighted average resistance value over a 15-year service condition. Standard test methods apply to polyisocyanurate, extruded polystyrene, and sprayed polyurethane. The LTTR value is the one that should be used for heat-transfer calculations.

TYPES OF BUILDING INSULATION

The following sections describe several types of insulation used to control heat transfer by conduction, convection, and radiation. Types of insulation and their R-values are shown in Table 18.1.

Loose-Fill Insulation

Loose-fill insulation is produced as shreds, granules, or nodules and can be poured or blown into spaces to be insulated. Loose-fill insulation is used for places where it is difficult to install other types of insulation, such as in cells of concrete block walls, plumbing chases, and attics. It is also widely used in retrofit applications because it can be blown into wall and ceiling cavities where other types of insulation cannot be installed without great difficulty.

This type of insulation is made from several materials: rock or slag wool, cellulose, fiberglass, perlite, and vermiculite. All loose-fill insulation will settle somewhat after installation. Cellulose settles about 20% while rock wool and fiberglass only settle about 2% to 4%. Care must also be taken when installing thick layers in ceilings because too heavy of a load will cause ceiling drywall to sag. For example, the use of cellulose or rock wool is not recommended in ceilings with 1/2 in (13) wallboard on 24 in (600) centers. All loose-fill insulations require a vapor retarder or vapor barrier.

Rock wool is a fibrous material formed by blowing molten basalt rock under pressure. Slag wool is the most common type of "wool" and is made, in a similar way, from blast furnace slag. Both products use by-products that would otherwise be wasted.

Cellulose is shredded wastepaper or wood fibers. Cellulose loose-fill insulation contains more than 75% recycled materials. It requires less energy to produce than do other forms of insulation. By itself, cellulose is combustible, but chemicals are added to make it fire resistant and to inhibit the growth of fungus and repel rodents.

Fiberglass loose-fill insulation is made by spinning molten glass into fibers. It typically contains from 20% to 30% recycled materials.

Perlite is a volcanic rock expanded by heating.

Vermiculite is a hydrated laminar magnesium-aluminum-ironsilicate. When heated during processing it forms small worm-like pieces. Although it is a fairly good insulating material, some vermiculite may contain asbestos. See Ch. 8 for information on vermiculite as a hazardous material.

Batt Insulation

Batt insulation consists of fibrous material placed on or within a kraft paper carrier. The insulation is usually mineral fiber or glass fiber. In addition to providing a means of installation and holding the insulation in place, the kraft paper also serves as a vapor retarder. Some batt insulation also comes with a reflective surface. Batts are available that have a flame-resistant facing, for use in basement walls where the insulation will be left exposed.

Batts come in standard widths designed to fit within stud and joist spacings of 16 in (406) or 24 in (610) on center. It is either friction fitted or is attached by stapling the paper flanges to the studs. Various thicknesses are available to suit the size of the cavity and the R-value required.

Plastic fiber insulation is made from recycled plastic (PET) milk bottles and formed into batts similar to high-density fiberglass.

Board Insulation

Board insulation is made from a variety of organic or inorganic materials formed into rigid boards. Organic board insulation is made from wood, cane fiber, or straw sandwiched between coatings of bituminous material, paper, foil, or other materials. Rigid boards can also be made with perlite or cork. However, organic board insulation has generally given way to inorganic plastics, which have much higher insulating values, about two to three times greater than for most other insulating materials of the same thickness. Inorganic board insulation is made from molded expanded polystyrene, extruded expanded polystyrene, polyisocyanurate, or polyurethane.

Originally, polystyrene foams, polyisocyanurate, and polyurethane foams were made with CFCs as the blowing agent. CFS were phased out in 1996 and replaced, in many instances, with HCFCs. However, HCFCs also cause depletion of the ozone layer. Under provisions of the Clean Air Act of 1990, the production and importation of many of the

Table 18.1

R-Values for Insulation

insulation type	R-value/in (ft^2-hr-F/Btu)	R-value/mm ($m^2 \cdot K/W$)	R-value/m ($m^2 \cdot K/W$)
loose fill			
cellulose	3.2–3.8	0.022–0.026	22–26
fiberglass	2.2–2.7	0.015–0.019	15–19
perlite	2.3–2.7	0.016–0.019	16–19
rock wool	3.0–3.3	0.021–0.023	21–23
vermiculite	2.1	0.015	15
batts			
fiberglass, low density	3.1–3.5	0.021–0.024	21–24
fiberglass, high density	4.3	0.030	30
mineral wool	3.5	0.024	24
boards			
polyisocyanurate	5.6–7.7 (LTTR)*	0.039–0.053	39–53
polyurethane (2.0 lbm/ft^3)	6.5 (LTTR)	0.045	45
molded expanded polystyrene	3.8–4.4 (LTTR)	0.026–0.030	26
extruded expanded polystyrene	5.0 (LTTR)	0.035	30
straw	1.4–2.0	0.010–0.014	10
sprayed foam			14
polyurethane	5.0–7.0	0.035–0.049	35–49
polyicynene	3.6–4.0	0.025–0.028	25–28
soy-based polyurethane	3.7	0.026	26
sprayed fiber			
cellulose	3.5	0.024	224
fiberglass	3.0	0.021	21
rock wool	2.7	0.019	19
structural insulated panels	4.0–6.0	0.028–0.042	28–42
straw bales	2.4–3.0	0.017–0.021	17–21
autoclaved aerated concrete	1.1	0.008	8

*LTTR: long-term thermal resistance

Source: U.S. Department of Energy, Office of Energy Efficiency and Renewable Energy

highest ozone-depletion-potential HCFCs into the United States was banned, effective January 1, 2003. This included HCFC-141b. Two blowing agents being used as a replacement are hydrocarbon (HC) and carbon dioxide (CO_2).

Molded expanded polystyrene (MEPS) is a closed-cell material manufactured by mixing unexpanded polystyrene beads containing liquid pentane and a blowing agent. The mixture is heated to expand the beads, which are then injected into a mold to form a foam block. MEPS (or *beadboard* as it is sometimes called) is manufactured in various densities for roofing and wall insulation. These densities range from 0.7 lbm/ft³ to 3.0 lbm/ft³ (11 kg/m³ to 48 kg/m³), with 1.0 lbm/ft³ (16 kg/m³) being the density most commonly used for insulation. The spaces between the beads can absorb water, so a vapor retarder is required if moisture migration is a concern.

Extruded expanded polystyrene (XEPS) is a closed-cell material manufactured by mixing polystyrene pellets with various chemicals and then introducing a blowing agent. The resulting mass is forced through an extruder, where atmospheric pressure causes the mass to expand. Densities range from 1.4 lbm/ft³ to 3.0 lbm/ft³ (22 kg/m³ to 48 kg/m³). Although more expensive than MEPS, XEPS foams have a higher insulative value per unit thickness and a higher compressive strength than does MEPS. XEPS is used for residential sheathing and wall, foundation, and roof insulation. Because of its superior resistance to water absorption, XEPS is the only insulation recommended for protected membrane roof systems and below-grade insulation.

Polyisocyanurate (or *polyiso*, as it is commonly referred to) is a closed-cell foam that contains low-conductivity gas in the cells. Most polyiso made today is actually a mixture of rigid polyurethane and polyisocyanurate.

Polyurethane is a closed-cell foam made to a density of 2 lbm/ft³ (32 kg/m³). Most polyurethane foams are made without the use of HCFCs and have an R-value of 6.5 ft²-hr-°F/Btu to 7 ft²-hr-°F/Btu (0.045 m²·K/W to 0.049 m²·K/W). These types of foam boards are more expensive than the other foam boards.

Sprayed Foam Insulation

Sprayed foam insulation uses polyurethane or polyicynene as the base material. The components of the foam are mixed at the spray head, at which time they react immediately and expand to produce low-density foam that adheres to the cavity. Sprayed foam has an excellent R-value with the added advantages of conforming to the shape of the cavity and sealing all cracks and openings thoroughly.

As an alternate to petroleum-based polyurethane foams, there is a soy-based polyurethane foam that use products derived from soy beans. It is applied in the same way as other spray-on foams and has an R-value of about 3.7 ft²-hr-°F/Btu per inch (0.026 m²·K/W).

Sprayed Fiber Insulation

Sprayed fiber insulation includes cellulose, fiberglass, and rock wool mixed with an adhesive and a small amount of water to activate the adhesive. As with foam insulation, spray fiber insulation completely fills the cavities where it is installed and does a better job of filling voids than does batt insulation. Because the adhesive binds the fibers to each other and to the cavity, this type of insulation does not settle as loose-fill types do. However, because of the moisture in the spray mixture, sprayed fiber insulation must be allowed to dry thoroughly before being enclosed with gypsum wallboard or other finishes. This can take from a few days to several weeks, depending on the type of insulation, its moisture content, and the humidity when it was applied.

Cellulose is the most commonly used type of sprayed fiber insulation. It is combined with a fire retardant. Fiberglass sprayed on insulation is also known as a *blow-in-blanket system* (BIBS) and is the second most common type of sprayed fiber. It does not prevent air infiltration as well as sprayed cellulose does. Rock wool is commonly used for commercial building thermal insulation as well as fireproofing.

Radiant Barriers and Reflective Insulation

A *radiant barrier* is a single sheet of highly reflective material, usually aluminum, that faces an open air space. It is used to reduce the passage of thermal radiation, most often by blocking summer heat gain, but sometimes to help retain winter heat. To block heat gain, a radiant barrier is placed on the outside of conventional thermal insulation, such as on top of attic insulation. Heat radiated from the hot roof deck is reflected back toward the roof, reducing the heat that would normally strike the top of the thermal insulation. To block heat loss, the reflective barrier would have to face the heated side of the insulation. When a radiant barrier is combined with a backing of insulation it is called *reflective insulation*.

Reflective surfaces have two properties that make them good for insulation. The first is *reflectivity* (also called *reflectance*), which is a measure of how much radiant heat is reflected by the material. This is a number between 0 and 1. Sometimes it is given as a percentage between 0% and 100%. Thus, when a material has a reflectivity of 0.8, it means that 80% of the radiant energy striking the material is reflected. The second property is *emissivity* (also called *emittance*), which is a measure of how much energy is emitted. All materials give off, or emit, energy by thermal radiation as a result of their temperature. Emissivity is also measured on a scale of 0 to 1. For materials that are opaque, the sum of the reflectivity and the emissivity equals one.

To be effective, radiant barriers must have a minimum reflectivity of 0.9 and a maximum emissivity of 0.1, and they must face a ventilated air space. Some radiant barriers are manufactured with corrugations or folds that automatically provide an air space.

Insulated Concrete Forms

Insulated concrete forms (ICF) are systems of interlocking foam insulation blocks or panels that serve as forms for pouring concrete walls and that remain in place after the concrete has cured. The foam greatly increases the insulation value of the wall and serves as a backing for gypsum wallboard finish on the inside and sheathing and exterior finish on the outside. Building codes require that a fire-resistant material be used to cover the inside layer of foam; generally $^1/_2$ in (13) drywall is acceptable. Although ICFs are typically used for foundation walls, they can be used for the entire wall structure from the footings to the roof.

The foam is typically extruded expanded polystyrene (XEPS) and comes in a variety of configurations, from preformed interlocking blocks to large panels that are held in place with plastic ties. Reinforcing steel is installed before the concrete is poured.

Structural Insulated Panels

Structural insulated panels (SIPs) are composite building units consisting of two outer skins bonded to an inner core of rigid insulating material, most commonly expanded polystyrene (EPS). Approximate R-values for SIPs (including OSB on each side) range from R17 for a $3^5/_8$ in (92) core to R34 for a $7^3/_8$ in (190) core. Refer to Ch. 16 for more information on SIPs.

Vapor Retarders

A *vapor retarder* is a material used to slow the transmission of water vapor between spaces. Vapor retarders are not themselves insulation, but they play an important role in the effectiveness of other insulating materials.

Water vapor is produced in all buildings by human respiration and perspiration, by cooking, and by other activities that involve water. In addition, there is always a certain amount of humidity present in the air. Warm air is capable of holding more water than is cold air. If the temperature of the air containing a certain amount of water vapor drops, the relative humidity rises until the saturation point is reached. This is known as the *dew point*, the point at which water condenses from the vapor.

During a cold day, water vapor in the air can pass through many building materials into the wall and ceiling cavities. If the temperature is cold enough the water condenses, wetting the insulation and greatly reducing its effectiveness. In addition, the water can soak wood and other materials, promoting their deterioration.

To avoid this, vapor retarders are placed on the warm side of the insulation to prevent the water from reaching the dew-point temperature. Some vapor retarders are integral with the insulation; others, such as polyethylene films, are applied as separate sheets.

In addition to vapor retarders, air barriers are an important part of an energy-efficient building. Refer to Ch. 7 for more information on air barriers.

SHINGLES AND ROOFING TILE

Shingles and tiles are two of the oldest types of roofing materials. They consist of small, individual pieces of material placed in an overlapping fashion on a sloped surface in order to shed water.

Types of Roofs

Roofs are classified according to their shape. Some of the more common types are illustrated in Fig. 18.2, along with the common terms used to describe the various parts.

The amount of slope of a roof is designated by its *pitch*, which is the number of inches (mm) of rise for every 12 in (305) of horizontal projection or run. For example, a 5/12 pitch rises 5 in (127) vertically for every foot (305) of horizontal projection.

Not all roofing materials are appropriate for all pitches, although the exact pitch for any one material may affect how the roofing is detailed and installed. For example, low-slope roofs for asphalt shingles require a double layer of roofing felt rather than the normal single layer. Some general guidelines are given in Table 18.2.

When describing size, estimating, and ordering materials, roofing area is referred to in squares. A square is equal to 100 ft^2 (9.3 m^2).

Shingles

Shingles are small, rectangular, or other-shaped units intended to shed water rather than form a watertight seal. Asphalt shingles are made from a composition of felt, asphalt, mineral stabilizers, and mineral granules. They are available in a variety of colors and shapes and are laid over an asphalt-impregnated roofing felt that is nailed to solid wood sheathing.

Wood shakes are normally manufactured from cedar and are available in a variety of grades (no. 1, blue label being the best) and finishes including smooth face and handsplit face. A typical installation is shown in Fig. 18.3. Wood shingles

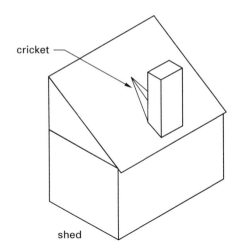

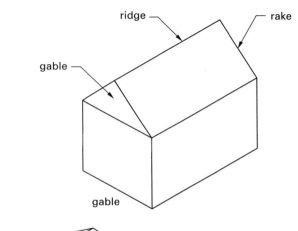

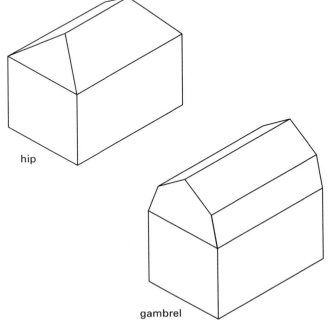

Figure 18.2 Roof Types

Table 18.2
Recommended Slopes for Roofing

| | slope—vertical rise | | | |
| | (in/ft) | | (mm/m) | |
roofing type	min.	max.	min.	max.
asphalt shingles, low slope	2	4	165	330
asphalt shingles, normal	4	12	330	1000
asphalt roll roofing	1	4	82	330
wood shingles	4	–	330	–
clay tile	4	–	330	–
slate tile	4	–	330	–
metal roofing	3	–	245	–
built-up roofing	$1/4$	1	20	82
single-ply membranes	$1/4$	6	20	490
(varies with type and				
method of attachment)				

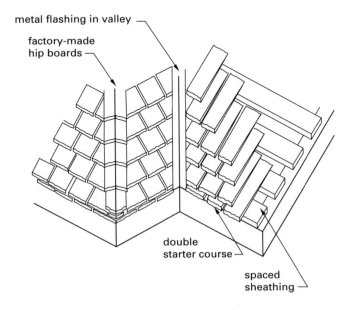

Figure 18.3 Wood Shingle Installation

are typically laid over spaced sheathing so that they can breathe without a buildup of moisture.

Wood shingles are laid so that only a certain portion of each shingle is visible. This is called the *exposure*, and the dimension varies with the pitch of the roof. The edges are staggered so that joints do not coincide, and 30 lbm asphalt felt is used as an underlayment.

Roofing Tile

Roofing tile consists of slate, clay tile, and concrete tile. Because each type is heavy (10 lbm/ft^2, or 49 kg/m^2, or more), the roof structure must be sized accordingly.

Slate tile is made by splitting quarried slate into rectangular pieces from 6 in to 14 in wide and from 16 in to 24 in long (152 to 356 wide and from 406 to 610 long). Slate tile is about $^1/_4$ in (6) thick. It is laid over 30 lbm asphalt-saturated roofing felt on wood or nailable concrete decking. The pieces are laid like other shingles, with the sides and ends overlapping, attached with copper or galvanized nails driven through prepunched holes in the slate. Slate is very expensive as a roofing material, but it is fire resistant and very durable; most slate roofs last over 100 years.

Clay tile, available in many colors, patterns, and textures, is made from the same clay as brick and is formed into various shapes. Like slate, it is laid on roofing felt over a sloped wood or nailable deck and attached by nailing through prepunched holes. Also like slate, clay tile is expensive, but very durable, fire resistant, and attractive. Some of the available shapes are shown in Fig. 18.4.

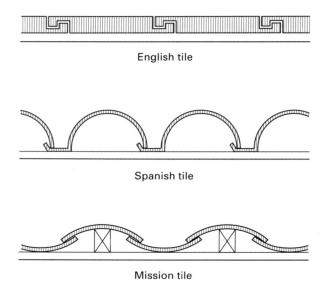

English tile

Spanish tile

Mission tile

Figure 18.4 Clay Roofing Tile Profiles

Concrete tile, manufactured from portland cement and fine aggregates, is available in several styles, some flat and others formed to look like clay tile. It is also available in several colors. Concrete tile is less expensive than clay tile, but it is still durable and fire resistant.

PREFORMED ROOFING AND SIDING

Sheet Metal Roofing

Metal roofing is durable, attractive, and can conform to a wide variety of roof shapes. Its disadvantages include high cost and the difficulty of installing it properly. Sheet metal roofs are fabricated of individual sheets of metal joined with various types of interlocking joints. Because of the high coefficient of expansion of metals used for roofing, these joints and other parts of the roofing system must be designed to allow for expansion and contraction.

Metals used for roofing include copper, galvanized iron, aluminum, and terneplate. *Terneplate* is steel sheet coated with lead and tin. Terne-coated stainless steel is also available. Other metals that are sometimes used include stainless steel, zinc, and lead. Stainless steel is expensive but very durable and maintenance free.

Copper roofs are popular because of their long life and the attractive green patina that forms after a few years of weathering. Copper is also a good metal roofing material because a wide variety of necessary roofing accessories such as gutters, flashing, and downspouts are also made in copper.

Metal roofs are installed over asphalt roofing felt laid on top of wood or nailable concrete decking. The one exception to the underlayment is for terne or tin roofs, which require a rosin-sized paper because the asphalt can react with the tin. The minimum slope for metal roofs is 3 in 12 (75 in 305).

In most cases, standing seams are made parallel to the slope of the roof and crimped tight. Flat seams are made perpendicular to the standing seams and soldered. These connect two pieces of metal along the slope of the roof, as shown in Fig. 18.5.

The roofing is held to the sheathing or decking with metal cleats attached to the roof and spaced about 12 in (305) apart. Continuous cleats are often used at the eaves, rakes (gable ends), and flashing. In all cases, cleats, nails, and other fasteners must be of the same type of metal to avoid galvanic action.

Preformed Roof and Wall Panels

Preformed panels are shaped pieces of metal or assemblies of metal facing with insulation between that are self-supporting and span intermediate supports. Roof panels span purlins, and wall panels span horizontal girts.

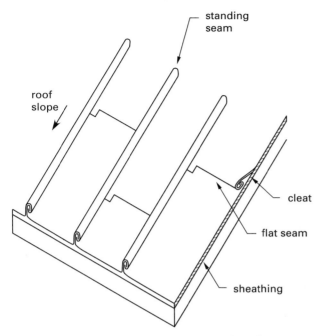

Figure 18.5 Standing Seam Metal Roof

The simplest preformed panels are simply corrugated or fluted sheets of metal of standard widths and varying lengths. They are assembled by lapping one corrugation at the edges and overlapping the ends. Preformed panels are also made as sandwich assemblies with insulation between two finished faces, joined with interlocking edges and a weather seal. Common widths are 24, 30, and 36 in (610, 760, and 910), although others are available. These types of sandwich panels are fabricated in lengths to match the requirements of the job and usually reach from the foundation to the roof framing in one-story buildings. If two panels must be placed end to end, they are butt-jointed with flashing between.

Preformed panels are made primarily from aluminum, galvanized steel, and porcelain enamel steel. They are attached to framing with screws, clips, and proprietary fasteners. They are durable, easy and quick to install, and do not require on-site finishing. For industrial buildings and some other types of structures, a sandwich panel can serve as the interior finish as well as the exterior finish. However, preformed panels are most economical when used on large, flat, unbroken expanses of walls or roofs.

MEMBRANE ROOFING

Membrane roofing includes those materials applied in thin sheets to nearly flat roofs. It also includes liquid-applied products that can be applied to any roof slope. Although some manufacturers claim that their products are suitable for flat roofs, every roof should have at least a $^1/_4$ in/ft slope

(6/305) to avoid standing water and the possibility of ponding. *Ponding* occurs when standing water causes a flat roof to deflect a little, allowing more water to collect, which causes more deflection, which in turn allows more water to collect. The process continues until the roof fails.

Built-Up Bituminous Roofing

Built-up roofing consists of several overlapping layers of bituminous saturated roofing felts cemented together with roofing cement. The bituminous material can be either asphalt or coal-tar pitch. The basic construction of such a roof is illustrated in Fig. 18.6.

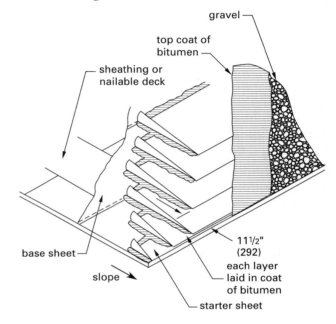

Figure 18.6 Three-Ply Built-Up Roof

Built-up roofs can be installed over nailable or non-nailable decks; the exact construction procedure changes slightly depending on which type is present. For nailable decks, a base sheet of unsaturated felt is nailed to the deck and covered with a coating of roofing cement. On non-nailable decks, the base sheet is omitted and a base coat is applied.

Three, four, or five layers of saturated roofing felts are then laid on top of each other, each layer bedded in roofing cement so that felt does not touch felt. The number of layers is determined by the type of deck used and the length of guarantee period desired. Five-ply roofs provide the most protection. A final coating of bituminous material is placed over the entire roof and covered with gravel or crushed slag. The purpose of the gravel is to protect the roofing from sunlight and other effects of weathering.

A variation of the built-up roof is the *inverted membrane roof*. Here, the built-up roof is placed on the structural decking and rigid, closed-cell insulation is placed over the roof rather than under it. The insulation is held down with gravel ballast. The purpose of this type of construction is to protect the membrane from the normal deleterious effects of expansion and contraction, drying, ultraviolet rays, and foot traffic that can cause leaks.

Built-Up Roofing Construction Details

As with any roof, built-up roofs must be designed to provide for positive drainage. As previously mentioned, the minimum roof slope should be $1/4$ in/ft (6/305). Nearly flat membrane roofs may be drained to interior drains, to perimeter drains, or to gutters on the low side of the roof. Crickets should be used to provide positive drainage in all directions. A *cricket* is a saddle-shaped projection on a sloping roof used to divert water around an obstacle. When a roof is surrounded on four sides with a parapet or walls, there should be *scuppers* (also called *overflow drains*) through the parapet, positioned with their low edge slightly above the top of the roof to provide a second means of drainage should the primary drains become clogged. These are usually required by building codes.

At the intersection of the roof and any vertical surface such as a wall or parapet, continuous triangular cant strips are placed in the intersection to provide positive drainage away from the joint and to give a smooth transition surface for the installation of the flashing at these points.

When objects project through a roof or roof-mounted equipment needs to be supported, the intersection of the roofing and these projections must be waterproofed. One traditional way to do this is to provide a *pitch pan*, a small metal enclosure around the projection that is filled with bituminous material. The pitch pan, however, is usually not recommended because of its tendency to leak. Projections should be treated like other joints and installed with cant strips and flashing. Roof-mounted equipment should be placed on wood curbs that are likewise flashed.

Single-Ply Roofing

Single-ply roofing is a single-membrane layer of various types of materials. Because the quality of built-up roofing is labor intensive and largely dependent on proper installation, single-ply roofing has come into widespread use. Although it too must be applied carefully, there are usually fewer installation problems. In addition, single-ply roofing is more resistant to slight building movement and the damaging effects of the weather.

There are several types of single-ply membranes. *Modified bitumens* are sheets about 50 mils (1.3) thick that are composed of bitumen, a chemical additive to enhance the elastic properties of the bitumen, and a reinforcing fabric to add tensile strength. The bitumen sheet is laid over insulation or

insulating decks with a separator sheet between the deck and the membrane. These sheets allow the roof to move independently of the structure, and some sheets are designed to allow water vapor from the building to escape to the perimeter of the roof. To anchor the membrane and protect it from ultraviolet degradation, the surface is covered with gravel ballast.

Other types of membranes fall into two categories: thermoset plastics and thermoplastics. *Thermoset plastics* are those that permanently harden when they are subjected to heat and then cured. They permanently lose their shape if heated again. *Thermoplastic materials*, also called *thermoplastics*, are those that can be repeatedly softened with heat and then harden again when cooled. Thermoset roofing includes EPDM and CSPE. Thermoplastic roofing includes PVC and TPO, as well as various hybrid blends.

Ethylene propylene diene monomer (EPDM) roofing is a thermoset plastic membrane manufactured in thicknesses of 0.045 in and 0.060 in (1.1 and 1.5). It has excellent resistance to weathering, heat, and fatigue, but is only available in black. Because it is a thermoset material, seams of EPDM roofing must be sealed with adhesive or pressure-sensitive tape. EPDM can be installed loose and covered with ballast, fully adhered with adhesive, mechanically fastened, or used in a protected membrane roof system. EPDM is one of the most common types of single-ply membrane roofing materials.

Chlorosulfonated polyethylene (CSPE) roofing, also known as *Hypalon*®, is also highly resistant to weathering and is available in white. It is applied fully adhered. CSPE has generally been replaced with PVC and TPO roofing.

Polyvinyl chloride (PVC) roofing is a thermoplastic roofing manufactured in thicknesses of 0.048 in, 0.060 in, and 0.072 in (1.2, 1.5, and 1.8). PVC membranes have excellent resistance to weathering (including hail), are easy to install, and are relatively inexpensive. Seams are heat welded. PVC can be installed loose and covered with ballast, fully adhered with adhesive, mechanically fastened, or used in a protected membrane roof system. It is available in white.

Thermoplastic polyolefin (TPO) roofing is a type of single-ply roofing made with a blend of polypropylene and ethylene propylene. It can be installed loose and covered with ballast, fully adhered with adhesive, mechanically fastened, or used in a protected membrane roof system. The mechanically attached system is used where high wind uplift is a concern and for reroofing applications. It has a low installed cost relative to EPDM.

Both PVC and TPO roofing materials are white, making them good choices for cool roof systems that are used to minimize heat transfer into a building and the subsequent energy required to cool it, as well as for minimizing the heat island effect. The heat island effect is the unnatural buildup of heat around buildings, especially in urban areas. Some jurisdictions, such as California, even require cool roofs to minimize interior heat gain and save energy. A new, white PVC or TPO roof will reflect approximately 78% of the radiant energy striking it, compared with about 6% for a black EPDM roof.

Because PVC and TPO membranes are themoplastics they can be recycled for roofing, while thermoset membranes, such as EPDM, cannot be reused for roofing. To be recycled EPDM roofing must be chopped up and mixed with another material to make product, such as rubber flooring.

The commonly used single-ply membranes are available with or without reinforcing. The reinforcing is typically polyester fibers, but some products use glass fiber reinforcing. Reinforced membranes have more dimensional stability and tear strength compared with nonreinforced membranes, and they have better puncture and wind load resistance. Reinforcing also helps the roofing lie flat for easier seaming. Reinforced membranes are good choices where high wind conditions exist and where heavy foot traffic is expected. Reinforced membranes are required where the roof is fully adhered or mechanically attached. Nonreinforced membranes have a higher elongation factor, which is good for accommodating substrate movement and to bridge small gaps in the substrate. Nonreinforced membranes are less expensive and are suitable for loose-laid and ballasted roof systems and where larger sheets are wanted.

Elastic Liquid Roofing

Liquid-applied roofings include butyl, *Neoprene®*, *Hypalon®*, and other products. They are applied in liquid form in one or two coats by brushing or spraying and are air-cured to form an elastic, waterproof surface. Liquid-applied membranes are also used for below-grade waterproofing on foundation walls, tanks, and pools, and for similar applications. These products are particularly suited for roofs with complex shapes such as thin-shell concrete domes.

FLASHING

Flashing prevents water penetration and directs any water that does get into construction back to the outside. Flashing is made of galvanized steel, stainless steel, aluminum, copper, plastic, and elastomeric materials. Material selection depends on the other metals or materials it is in contact with, the configuration of the joint, the durability desired, and the cost.

Flashing protects joints wherever water penetration is anticipated or where two dissimilar surfaces meet at an angle. This may include the areas where roofs intersect parapets, areas above windows, above steel lintels supporting masonry, between butt joints of preformed siding, and elsewhere. Figure 18.7 shows some common metal flashing details, and Fig. 18.8 illustrates flashing for single-ply roofing installations. Masonry flashing details are shown in Figs. 14.5 and 14.7. In all cases, the flashing detail should allow joint movement without destroying the integrity of the flashing connection.

ROOF ACCESSORIES

Roof accessories include items in addition to the roofing itself or flashing necessary to form a complete installation. Some examples of roof accessories are expansion joints, copings, roof hatches, smoke vents, and similar fabrications.

Expansion joints are required in buildings to allow for movement caused by temperature changes in materials and differential movement between building sections. They are required at frequent intervals in long buildings—about every 100 ft to 150 ft (30.5 m to 45.7 m) in masonry buildings and about every 200 ft (61 m) in concrete buildings. They should also be located at the junctions of T-, L-, and U-shaped buildings and where a low building portion abuts a higher, heavier section. Expansion joints are particularly important in roofs because of the extremes of temperature changes and the fact that joints in the roof are exposed to the most severe weathering conditions. Figure 18.9 shows some typical roof expansion joints. Refer to Chs. 13 and 14 for a discussion of joints for concrete and masonry structures.

Smoke vents are devices that allow excess smoke to escape in the event of a fire. Exact requirements for smoke vent locations and sizes are given in the various model building codes, but in general these vents must be located in hazardous occupancies, in certain business occupancies over 50,000 ft^2 (4645 m^2), over stages, and above elevator shafts. Vents are designed to release automatically in the event of fire, usually by being spring-loaded and connected to a fusible link.

CAULKING AND SEALANTS

Sealants are flexible materials used to close joints between materials. *Sealant* is the more correct term, but the word "caulking" (sometimes spelled "calking") is often used to designate low-performance sealants employed where little movement is expected, such as between a window frame and an exterior wall. Sealants must be capable of adhering to the joints while remaining elastic and weatherproof. There are several types of sealants, each with slightly different properties and uses under various conditions. Sealants are classified as low, intermediate, and high performance, depending on the maximum amount of joint movement they can tolerate. Low-performance sealants are used in

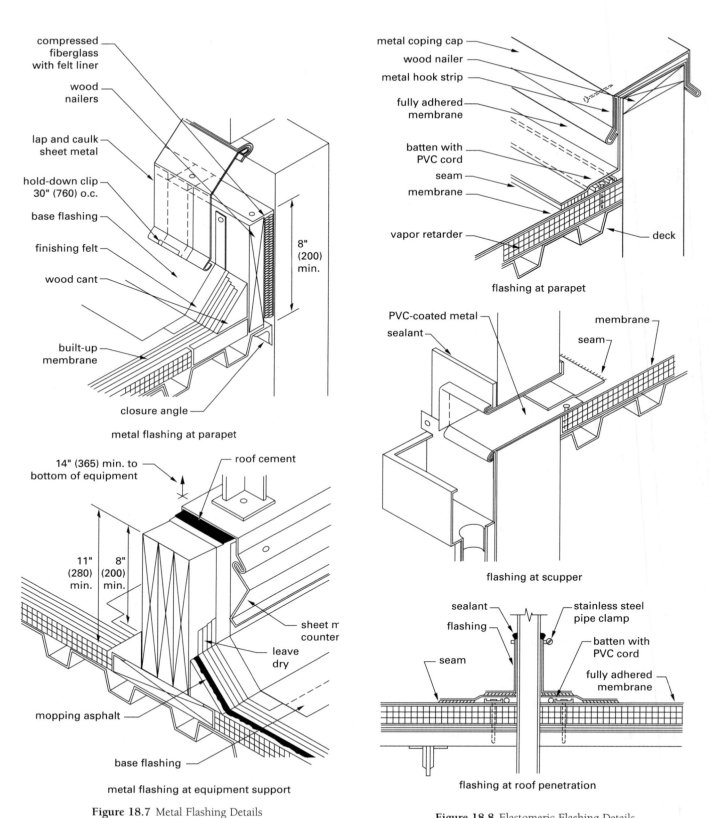

Figure 18.7 Metal Flashing Details

Figure 18.8 Elastomeric Flashing Details

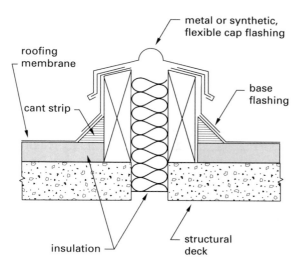

mid-roof expansion joint

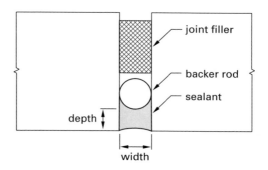

Figure 18.10 Typical Joint with Sealant

EXTERIOR INSULATION AND FINISH SYSTEMS

An *exterior insulation and finish system* (EIFS) is a cladding assembly consisting of a wet-applied cementitious finish over a rigid insulation board that is attached to building sheathing. Although portland cement stucco is included in these types of finish systems, the coating generally consists of various types of polymers (usually acrylics) or a mixture of cement and polymers. The exact formulation of an EIFS varies with each manufacturer, but there are three classifications: polymer based (Class PB), polymer modified (Class PM), and mineral based (Class MB). Class MB uses portland cement stucco in the traditional manner. A variation of the polymer-based system is the high-impact PB system, which is like the PB system but includes a heavy-duty fiberglass mesh and an additional layer of base coat.

Polymer-based systems use expanded polystyrene insulation with the base coat applied directly to the insulation with an imbedded fiberglass mesh. The base coat has a high percentage of polymeric binder, which gives the system a great deal of flexibility. The finish coat, like that of the polymer-modified system, consists of acrylic polymer, sand, pigments, and other additives.

Polymer-modified systems use extruded polystyrene that is mechanically fastened to the building sheathing and structure along with the reinforcing mesh. The base coats of PM systems are thicker, from $^3/_{16}$ in to $^3/_8$ in (5 to 10), and include a higher percentage of portland cement than does the PB system. As a result, control joints are needed in PM systems to limit cracking. They should be located from 10 ft to 12 ft (3000 to 3600) apart with no section exceeding 150 ft^2 (15 m^2) in area. PM systems are more resistant to impact than are standard PB systems, and the extruded polystyrene has a slightly higher thermal resistance than does the expanded polystyrene and is more resistant to water penetration.

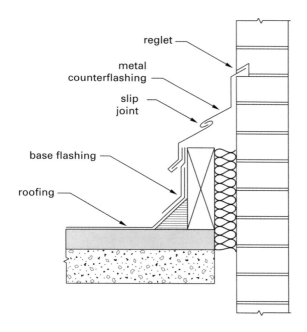

Figure 18.9 Expansion Joints

joints with ±5% movement, intermediate-performance sealants are used for joints with ±12.5% movement, and high-performance sealants are used for joints with up to about 25% movement.

The width and depth of a sealant are critical to its proper performance. See Fig. 18.10. The width is determined by the expected joint movement. The depth should be equal to the width for joints up to $^1/_2$ in (13) wide; for joints from $^1/_2$ in to 1 in (13 to 25), the depth should be $^1/_2$ in (13). For wider joints, the sealant depth should not be greater than one-half the width. Joint fillers are used behind the sealant to control the depth of the sealant. Table 18.3 lists some of the common sealant types and their properties.

Table 18.3

Comparative Properties of Sealants

sealant types	oil base	butyl	acrylic, water base	acrylic, solvent base	polysulfide, one part	polysulfide, two part	polyurethane, one part	polyurethane, two part	silicone	notes
recommended maximum joint movement, %	±5	±7.5	±7.5	±12.5	±12.5 to ±25	±25	±12.5 to ±15	±25	±25	(1)
life expectancy in years	5–10	10+	10	15–20	20	20	20+	20+	20+	
maximum joint width in inches (mm)	¼ (6)	½ (13)	½ (13)	¾ (19)	¾ (19)	1 (25)	¾ (19)	1–2 (25–50)	¾ (19)	(2)
weight shrinkage, %	10+	5–10	15	15	10	10	10	10	4	
adhesion to: wood	•	•	•	•	•	•	•	•	•	(3)
metal	•	•	•	•	•	•	•	•	•	
masonry	•	•	•	•	•	•	•	•	•	(3)
glass	•	•	•	•	•	•	•	•	•	
plastic		•	•	•					•	
curing time in days	120	120	5	14	14+	7	7+	3–5	5	
maximum elongation, %	15	40	60	60+	300	600	300+	400+	250+	
self-leveling available	n/a	n/a	•	•	•			•	•	
nonsag available	n/a	n/a	•	•	•	•	•	•	•	
resistance to: ultraviolet (see legend)	1–2	2–3	1–3	3–4	2	2–3	3	3	5	
cut/tear	1	2	1–2	1	3	3	4–5	4–5	1–2	
abrasion	1	2	1–2	1–2	1	1	3	3	1	
weathering	1–2	2	1–3	3–4	3	3	3–4	3–4	4–5	
oil/grease	2	1–2	2	3	3	3	3	3	2	
compression	1	2–3	1–2	1	3	3	4	4	4–5	
extension	1	1	1–2	1	2–3	2–3	4–5	4–5	4–5	
water immersion	2	2–3	1	1–2	3	3	1	1	3	

(1) Some high performance urethanes and silicones have movement capabilities as high as ±50%.
(2) Figures given are conservative. Verify manufacturers' literature for specific recommendations.
(3) Primer may be required.

Legend:
1 = Poor
2 = Fair
3 = Good
4 = Very good
5 = Excellent

DOORS, WINDOWS, AND GLAZING

19

With the materials and construction systems available today, doors and windows no longer simply serve to provide passage between spaces or to admit light. Openings can be selectively designed and specified to fulfill certain functions. For example, a window can admit light but be designed to minimize sound transmission while still providing security. Or a door passage can be designed as an unobtrusive, clear opening while still providing fire protection in the event of an emergency.

DOOR OPENINGS

Both metal and wood doors can serve a variety of functions. They can control passage, provide visual and aural privacy, maintain security, supply fire resistance and weather protection, control light, and serve as radiation shielding. It is important to understand what kind of control you want in order to select the most appropriate type of door. Considerations of durability, cost, appearance, ease of use, method of construction, and availability are also important in door selection.

There are three major components of a door system: the door itself, the frame, and the hardware. Each must be coordinated with the other components and be appropriate for the circumstances and the design intent.

The common parts of a door opening are illustrated in Fig. 19.1. To differentiate the two jambs, the side where the hinge or pivot is installed is called the *hinge jamb*, and the jamb where the door closes is called the *strike side* or *strike jamb*.

There is also a standard method of referring to the way a door swings, called the *door hand* or the *handing* of a door. Handing is used by specifiers, hardware suppliers, and manufacturers to indicate exactly what kind of hardware must be supplied for a specific opening. Some hardware will only work on a door that swings a particular way

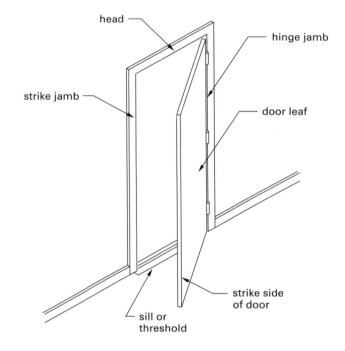

Figure 19.1 Parts of a Door

because of the way the strike side of the door is beveled. Hardware that can work on any hand of door is called *reversible* or *nonhanded*.

The hand of a door is determined from outside the door, as shown in Fig. 19.2. The exterior of a building is considered the outside, as is the hallway side of a room door, or the lobby side of a door opening into a room. In situations where the distinction is not clear, the outside is considered the side of the door where the hinge is not visible. When standing on the outside looking at the door, if the door hinges on the left and swings away from the viewer, it is a *left-hand door*. If it hinges on the right and swings away from the viewer, it is a *right-hand door*. If the door swings toward

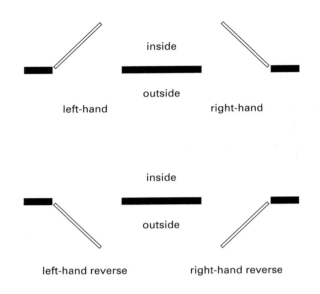

Figure 19.2 Door Handing

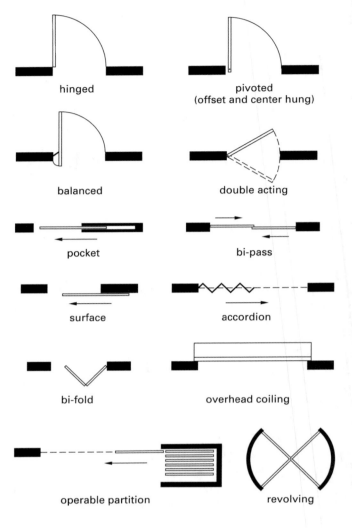

Figure 19.4 Door Classification by Operation

the viewer, it is considered a *left-hand reverse* or a *right-hand reverse*, depending on the location of the hinge or pivot.

A door can be classified by the function it serves, its operation, and the material from which it is made. Each type of classification is useful in its own way to help select the best type of door for a particular situation. Fig. 19.3 illustrates some of the common types of swinging doors, and Fig. 19.4 shows doors classified by type of operation. Table 19.1 summarizes some of the advantages and disadvantages of various door types.

METAL DOORS AND FRAMES

Door Types

The three most common types of metal doors are flush, sash, and louvered. *Flush doors* have a single, smooth surface on both sides; *sash doors* contain one or more glass lites;

and *louvered doors* have an opening with metal slats to provide ventilation. Paneled steel doors, which resemble wood panel doors, are also available with insulated cores for

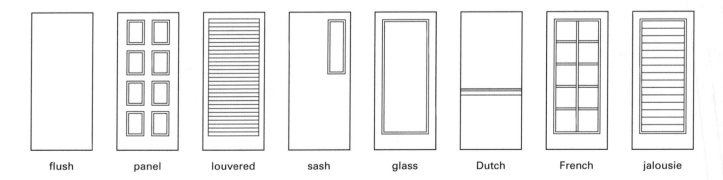

Figure 19.3 Types of Swinging Doors

Table 19.1
Door Type Advantages and Disadvantages

door operation type	advantages	disadvantages
swinging		
hinged	ease of use and installation inexpensive can be fire-rated wide variety of hinge styles	appearance of hinges sometimes undesirable
offset pivoted	ease of use closer can be part of pivot can be fire rated can accommodate very heavy doors minimal hardware appearance	more expensive than hinges floor closers require solid flooring and adequate thickness to accommodate closer
center-hung pivoted	ease of use closer can be part of pivot allows door to swing both ways support hardware fully concealed can be fire rated can accommodate very heavy doors	more expensive than hinges floor closers require solid flooring and adequate thickness to accommodate closer height limitations required to avoid bowing
balanced	little effort required to operate clear width reduced when open	expensive
double acting	easy operation both ways dangerous unless glass lite provided	cannot be used as exit door
pocket sliding	no operating space required difficult to seal against light or sound susceptible to sticking cannot be used as exit door	awkward for frequent use
bi-pass sliding	no operating space required difficult to seal cannot be used as exit door	awkward for frequent use
surface sliding	no operating space required cannot be used as exit door	appearance of hardware
bi-fold	minimum operating space cannot be used as exit door	awkward to use
accordion folding	useful for subdividing space inexpensive limited finishes and colors available	poor as a sound barrier cannot be used as exit door
operable partition	good for very large openings good sound barrier wide choice of finishes	expensive cannot be used as exit door
overhead coiling	automatic closing of large openings for security or fire separation cannot be used as exit door	visible when door closed requires large space for housing
revolving	accommodates large numbers prevents air infiltration types available for darkrooms	only appropriate for entrance doors requires large space; expensive cannot be used as exit door

residential use where energy conservation and durability are requirements in addition to a more traditional appearance.

Metal doors are available in steel, stainless steel, aluminum, and bronze, but other door materials are available on special order. The most common material is steel with a painted finish.

Construction

Steel doors, commonly referred to as *hollow metal doors*, are constructed with faces of cold-rolled sheet steel. 18-gage and 14-gage thicknesses are typically used, although 20-gage is available for light-duty doors. 16-gage is also available. The steel face is attached to cores of honeycomb kraft paper, steel ribs, hardboard, or other materials. The edges are made of steel channels, with the locations for hardware reinforced with heavier-gage steel. Mineral wool or other materials are used to provide sound-deadening qualities, if required.

Sizes

Although metal doors can be custom made in almost any practical size, standard widths are 2 ft 0 in, 2 ft 4 in, 2 ft 6 in, 2 ft 8 in, 3 ft 0 in, 3 ft 4 in, 3 ft 6 in, 3 ft 8 in, and 4 ft 0 in. Standard heights are 6 ft 8 in, 7 ft 0 in, and 8 ft 0 in. The standard thickness is 1¾ in.

In SI units, standard widths are 610 mm, 711 mm, 762 mm, 813 mm, 914 mm, 1016 mm, 1067 mm, 1118 mm, and 1219 mm. Standard heights are 2032 mm, 2134 mm, and 2438 mm. The standard thickness is 44 mm.

Frames

Steel door frames can be used for either steel doors or wood doors and are made from sheet steel bent into the shape required for the door installation. Frames are made from 12-, 14-, or 16-gage steel, depending on location and use. The frame is mortised for the installation of hinges and door strikes and is reinforced at these points with heavier-gage steel. Two of the most common frame profiles are shown in Fig. 19.5 along with some standard dimensions and the terminology used to describe the parts. Various types of anchoring devices are used inside the frame to attach it to gypsum board, masonry, concrete, and other materials. Where a fire rating over 20 minutes is required, steel frames are used almost exclusively, although some wood frames have higher ratings.

Steel frames are manufactured in three styles: one-piece, welded frames; knock-down (KD) frames, where the two jamb sections and head section are shipped to the job site as separate pieces; or slip-on frames. One-piece frames must be set in place before the partition is constructed, whereas knock-down and slip-on frames can be set after gypsum wallboard partitions are built. Slip-on frames are

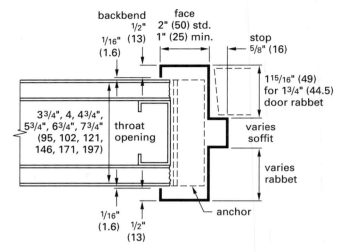

standard double rabbet

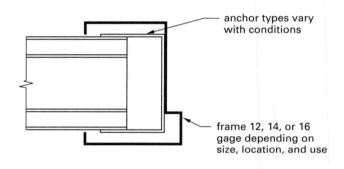

single rabbet

Figure 19.5 Standard Steel Door Frames

not available with welded corners and should be avoided if the appearance of a joint is objectionable.

Aluminum frames are used for both aluminum doors and wood doors. They are constructed of extruded sections and as a consequence can have thinner face dimensions and more elaborate shapes than are possible with bent steel.

Steel frames are painted, either in the shop or on site. Aluminum frames are anodized with the standard anodized colors, or they can be factory-coated with a variety of colors with baked acrylic paints and other finishes.

WOOD DOORS AND FRAMES

Wood doors are the most common types for both residential and commercial construction. They are available in a variety of styles, sizes, finishes, and methods of operation.

Door Types

Wood doors can be classed according to their operation, as shown in Fig. 19.4. *Swinging doors* are the most typical type, and they function by being hinged or pivoted on one side. They are relatively inexpensive, easy to install, and can accommodate a large volume of traffic. Double-acting doors swing in both directions when mounted on pivot hardware or special double-acting hinges.

Pocket sliding doors travel on a top track and move horizontally into a pocket built into the wall. They are good for limited space, but they are awkward to operate, and latching and sealing are difficult.

Bi-pass sliding doors also travel on a top or bottom rail and are often used for closet doors where space is limited. Bi-folding and multi-folding doors are also used for closets and other large openings where full access needs to be provided when the doors are open.

The two primary types of wood doors are the flush door and the panel door. See Fig. 19.6. *Flush doors* consist of a thin, flat veneer laminated to various types of cores as described. *Panel doors* consist of solid vertical stiles and horizontal rails that serve as a frame for flat or raised panels.

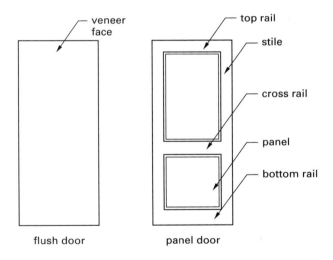

Figure 19.6 Types of Wood Doors

Construction

Wood doors are either hollow core or solid core. *Hollow-core doors* are made of one or three plies of veneer on each side of a cellular cardboard interior. The stile-and-rails frame is made of solid wood with larger blocks of solid wood where the locksets or latchsets are installed. Hollow-core doors are used in interior applications where only light use is expected and where cost is a consideration. They have no fire-resistance capabilities.

Solid-core doors are made with a variety of core types depending on the functional requirements of the door. Cores may be particleboard, stave core (solid blocks of wood), or mineral core for fire-rated doors. Solid-core doors are used for their fire-resistance properties, as acoustical barriers, for security, and for their superior durability. Solid-core doors may have a fire rating from 20 minutes to $1^1/_2$ hours. Mineral-core doors are used when fire ratings of $^3/_4$, 1, and $1^1/_2$ hours are required.

The face veneers of wood doors can be made from any available hardwood species using rotary-cut, plain-sliced, quarter-sliced, or rift-cut methods, just like wood panels. The veneers can be bookmatched, slip matched, or random matched, although bookmatching is the most common. Veneers of hardboard suitable for painting and plastic laminate are also available.

Sizes

Like metal doors, wood doors can be custom made to any size, but the standard widths are 2 ft 0 in, 2 ft 4 in, 2 ft 6 in, 2 ft 8 in, 3 ft 0 in, and 3 ft 4 in (610, 711, 762, 813, 914, and 1016). Standard heights are 6 ft 8 in and 7 ft 0 in (2032 and 2134), although higher doors, often used in commercial construction, are available. Hollow-core doors are $1^3/_8$ in (35) thick and solid-core doors are $1^3/_4$ in (44) thick; doors $2^1/_4$ in (57) thick are available for large, exterior doors and acoustical doors.

Frames

Frames for wood doors are made from wood, steel (hollow metal), and aluminum. A common wood frame jamb is illustrated in Fig. 19.7. Although the stop and casing are shown as rectangular pieces, several different profiles of trim are available and are frequently used.

The decision concerning the type of frame to use for a wood door depends on the appearance desired, the type of partition in which the opening is being installed, the fire-rating requirements, the security needed, and the durability desired. For example, wood frames may be used in 20-, 30-, and 45-minute fire door assemblies, but a 1-hour-rated door must be installed in a rated metal frame.

GLASS DOORS

Glass doors are those constructed primarily of glass with fittings to hold the pivots and other hardware. Sometimes they are called *all-glass doors*. Their strength depends on the glass rather than the framing. They are different from sash doors in that sash doors have a frame around all four sides of the door.

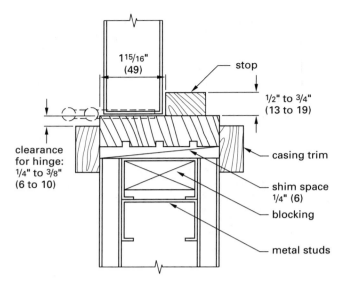

Figure 19.7 Standard Wood Door Frame

Components

Glass doors are generally constructed of $\frac{1}{2}$ in (13) or $\frac{3}{4}$ in (19) tempered glass with fittings and operating hardware as required by the installation. Common door sizes are 36 in (914) wide and 7 ft 0 in (2134) high, although many architects prefer to specify glass doors at the same height as that of the ceiling.

Some of the typical configurations are shown in Fig. 19.8. The minimum configuration requires some type of door pull and a corner fitting at the top and bottom to hold the pivots. In lieu of corner fittings, some manufacturers provide hinge fittings that clamp on the glass and support the door in much the same way as a standard hinged door. If a lock is required, the bottom fitting may be continuous across the door to allow for a dead bolt to be installed. Some architects prefer continuous fittings (sometimes called the shoes) on both the top and bottom.

Because a full glass door is a potential hazard and extra strength is required, the glass must be tempered. Any holes, notches, or other modification to the glass must be made before it is tempered.

Standard Assemblies

Glass doors can be used alone and set within a wall opening with or without a frame, or they can be installed between glass sidelights. If glass sidelights are used, the same type of fitting used on the door is generally used to support the sidelights. Although jamb frames of aluminum, wood, or ornamental metal can be used, they are not necessary, and the glass sidelights can be butted directly to the partition or held away a fraction of an inch.

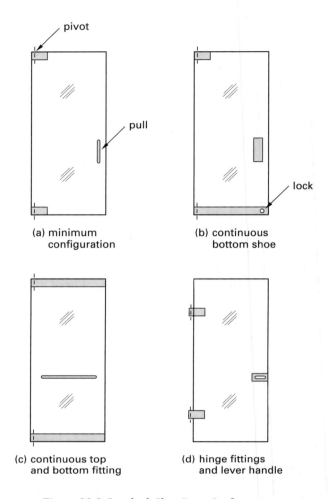

Figure 19.8 Standard Glass Door Configurations

Building Code Requirements for All-Glass Doors

Because all-glass doors cannot be fire rated, they cannot be used where a protected opening is required in a fire-rated partition. When they are allowed and serve as exit doors, the type of hardware used must conform to the requirements of the local building code. Some codes and local amendments are more restrictive than others and usually prohibit the use of a simple dead bolt in the bottom rail fitting. Instead, special panic hardware is available for glass doors that allows the door to be locked from the outside (and operated with card keys or keypads, if necessary), but still allows the door to be unlatched and opened from the inside in a single operation without any special knowledge or effort. See Fig. 19.9.

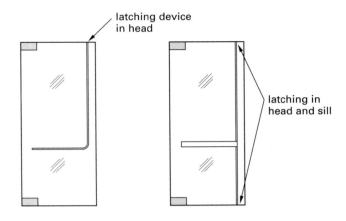

Figure 19.9 Glass Door Panic Hardware

SPECIAL DOORS

Special doors have a wide variety of applications where a special closing assembly is required. Some of the more common types of special doors include the following.

Revolving doors are assemblies of three or four leaves connected at a central point that rotate within an enclosure. They are used to control air infiltration and to allow large numbers of people to pass in and out. They are made of glass framed with aluminum, bronze, or other metals. In most cases, revolving doors do not count in determining the total exit width from a building or as a required exit. Some revolving doors are available with collapsing leaves that fold open if subjected to the force of a crowd of people pushing against them.

Overhead coiling doors are made from thin slats of metal that roll up into an enclosure above the head of the opening. They are used to close large openings such as industrial and garage doors, or as fire separations for large openings. They can be connected to fusible links so that they automatically close in the event of fire.

Sectional overhead doors also close large openings and are typically used for industrial buildings and garages. The door is made from individual sections of wood or metal that hinge as the door opens.

Other special doors include blast-resistant doors, sound-retardant doors, hangar doors, folding doors used to divide rooms, security doors, and cold-storage doors.

HARDWARE

Hardware includes the various types of finish hardware normally found on interior and exterior doors, weather stripping, electrical locking devices, and window operators.

Cabinet hardware and curtain and drapery hardware are classified as a different type and included with those items.

Functions of Hardware

Hardware is a vital part of any door opening assembly. In general, hardware can be grouped according to the function it serves based on the following list.

- Hanging the door: hinges, pivots, and combination pivots and closers

- Operating the door: handles, latchsets, push plates, and pull bars

- Closing the door: door closers and combination pivots and closers

- Locking the door: locksets, dead bolts, flush bolts, electric locks, and other special devices

- Sealing the door: weather stripping, sound seals, smoke seals

- Protecting the door: kick plates, corner protection, and similar materials

Hinges

Hinging is the most common method of attaching a door to its frame. Hinges are also referred to as *butts* because they are usually attached to the butt edge of a door. Hinges consist of two leaves with an odd number of knuckles on one leaf and an even number of knuckles on the other. The knuckles are attached with a pin. The pin and knuckles form the barrel of the hinge, which is finished with a tip.

There are four basic types of hinges: full mortise, half mortise, full surface, and half surface. These are shown in Fig. 19.10.

Full mortise is the most common type and has both leaves fully mortised into the frame and edge of the door. *Half-surface hinges* have one leaf mounted on the face of the door and the other leaf mortised into the frame. *Half-mortise hinge* leaves are surface-applied to the frame and mortised into the edge of the door. *Full-surface hinges* are applied to the face of both the door and frame. The various types of hinges are used when either the door or frame cannot be mortised. For example, a half-mortise hinge may be bolted or welded to a heavy steel frame.

There are also special types of hinges. *Raised barrel hinges* are used when there is not room for the barrel to extend past the trim. The barrel is offset to allow one leaf to be mortised into the frame. *Swing clear hinges* have a special shape that allows the door to swing 90° so that the full opening of the doorway is available. See Fig. 19.11.

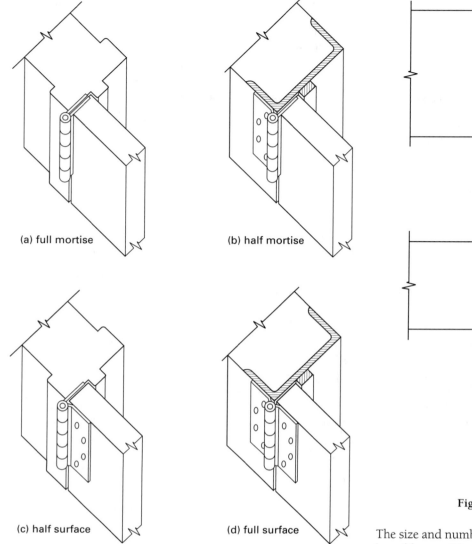

(a) full mortise   (b) half mortise

(c) half surface   (d) full surface

Figure 19.10   Common Hinge Types

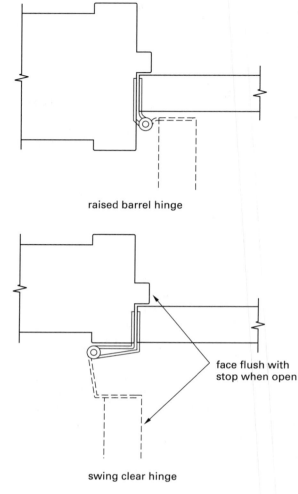

raised barrel hinge

face flush with
stop when open

swing clear hinge

Figure 19.11   Special Hinges

Without a swing clear hinge, standard hardware decreases the opening width by the thickness of the door when it is open 90°.

Hinges are available with or without ball bearings and in three weights. Which type to use depends on the door weight and frequency of use. *Low-frequency doors*, like residential doors, can use standard-weight, plain-bearing hinges. Most commercial applications require standard-weight, ball-bearing hinges. *High-frequency applications* such as office building entrances, theaters, and so forth, require heavy-weight, ball-bearing hinges. In addition, ball-bearing hinges are required for fire-rated assemblies and on all doors with closers.

The size and number of hinges for a door depend on a number of factors. The size is given by two numbers such as $4 \times 4^{1}/_{2}$. The first number is the length, which is the length of the barrel in inches, and the second number is the width, which is the dimension in inches when the hinge is open.

The width of the hinge is determined by the width of the door and the clearance required around jamb trim. One rule of thumb is that the width of the hinge equals twice the door thickness, plus trim projection, minus $^{1}/_{2}$ in (12.6). If a fraction falls between standard sizes, use the next larger size. Common hinge widths for $1^{3}/_{4}$ in (44) doors are 4 in and $4^{1}/_{2}$ in (102 and 114).

The length of the hinge is determined by the door thickness and the door width, as shown in Table 19.2.

The number of hinges is determined by the height of the door. Numbers of hinges are commonly referred to by pairs, one pair being two hinges. Doors up to 60 in (1500) high require two hinges (1 pair). Doors from 60 in to 90 in (1500

Table 19.2
How to Determine Hinge Heights

door thickness (in/mm)	door width (in/mm)	height of hinge (in/mm)
³/₄ to 1¹/₈ (19 to 29)	to 24 (610)	2¹/₂ (63.5)
1³/₈ (35)	to 32 (813)	3¹/₂ (89)
1³/₈ (35)	over 32 to 37 (over 813 to 940)	4 (102)
1³/₄ (44)	to 36 (to 914)	4¹/₂ (114)
1³/₄ (44)	over 36 to 48 (over 914 to 1219)	5 (127)
1³/₄ (44)	over 48 (over 1219)	6 (152)
2, 2¹/₄, 2¹/₂ (51, 57, 64)	to 42 (to 1067)	5 (heavy weight) (127)
2, 2¹/₄, 2¹/₂ (51, 57, 64)	over 42 (over 1067)	6 (heavy weight) (152)

to 2290) require three hinges (1¹/₂ pair), and doors 90 in to 120 in (2290 to 3050) require four hinges (2 pair).

Latchsets and Locksets

Latchsets and locksets are devices to hold a door in the closed position and lock it. A *latchset* only holds the door in place with no provision for locking. It has a beveled latch extending from the face of the door edge and automatically engages the strike mounted in the frame when the door is closed. A *lockset* has a special mechanism that allows the door to be locked with a key or thumbturn.

There are four types of latches and locks: mortise, preassembled, bored, and interconnected. These are shown in Fig. 19.12. Another type, the integral lock, is no longer produced in the United States, but is still found in older buildings.

A *mortise lock* or *latch* is installed in a rectangular area cut out of the door. It is generally more secure than a bored lock and offers a much wider variety of locking options. Mortise locks allow the use of a dead bolt and a latch bolt, both of which can be retracted with a single operation. A variety of knob and level handle designs can be used with the basic mechanism.

Preassembled locks and latches (also called *unit locks*) come from the factory as a complete unit. They are slid into a notch made in the edge of the door and require very little

adjustment. Preassembled locks are seldom used anymore, but they are often found in older buildings.

Bored locks and latches (also called *cylindrical locks or latches*) are installed by boring holes through the face of the door and from the edge of the door to the other bored opening. They are relatively easy to install and are less expensive than mortise locks, but they offer fewer operating functions than do mortise locks. They are generally used in residential and small commercial projects.

Interconnected locks have a cylindrical lock and a dead bolt. The two locks are interconnected so that a single action of turning a knob or lever handle on the inside releases both bolts.

With all types of latches and locks, either a doorknob or lever handle may be used to operate the latching device. In most cases, a lever handle is required to meet requirements for accessibility.

The distance from the edge of the door to the center line of the doorknob or pivot of a lever handle is called the backset. Standard backsets are 2³/₄ in and 5 in (70 and 127), although others are available on special order.

Other Types of Hardware

- *Pivots.* Pivots provide an alternative way to hang doors where the visual appearance of hinges is objectionable or where a frameless door design may make it impossible to use hinges. Pivots may be center hung or offset and are mounted in the floor and head of the door. See Fig. 19.13. For large or heavy doors, an intermediate pivot is often required for offset-hung doors only. Center-hung pivots allow the door to swing in either direction and can be completely concealed, but they allow only a 90° swing. Offset pivots allow the door to swing 180°.

- *Panic hardware.* This type of operating hardware is used where required by the building code for safe egress during a panic situation. Push bars extending across the width of the door operate vertical rods that disengage latches at the top and bottom. The vertical rods can be surface mounted or concealed.

- *Push plates and pull bars.* These are used to operate a door that does not require automatic latching. They are also used on doors to toilet rooms and commercial kitchens.

- *Closers.* Closers are devices that automatically return a door to its closed position after it is opened. They also control the distance a door can be opened and thereby protect the door and surrounding construction from damage. Closers can be surface mounted on the door or head frame or concealed in the frame

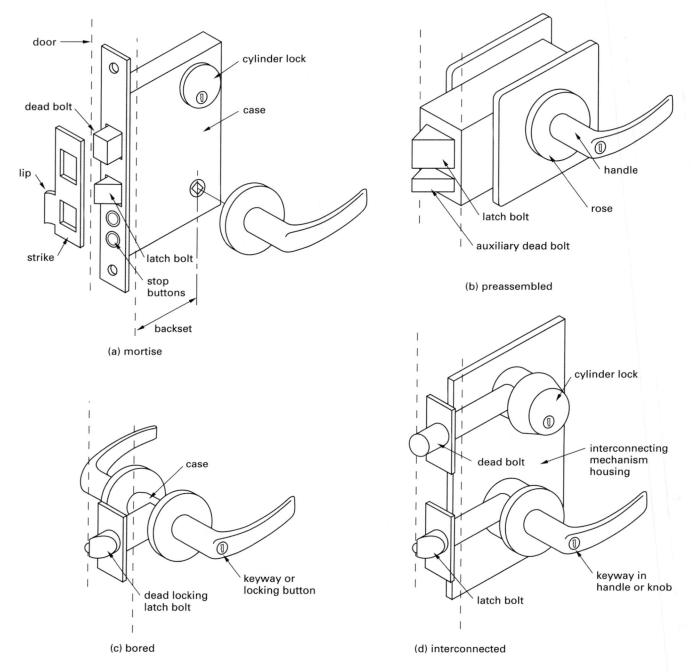

Figure 19.12   Types of Locksets

or door. Selection of a closer depends on the type, size, and weight of the door, the frequency of operation, the visual appearance desired, and the door height clearance required. Closers can also be integral with pivots mounted in the floor or ceiling, either center hung or offset.

Closers are available that have fire and smoke detectors built in so that a door may be held open during normal operation but will close when smoke is sensed.

- *Door stops and bumpers.* Some method of keeping a door from damaging adjacent construction should be provided. Closers will do this to some extent, but floor stops or wall bumpers provide more positive protection. These devices are small metal fabrications with rubber bumpers attached. See Fig. 19.14.

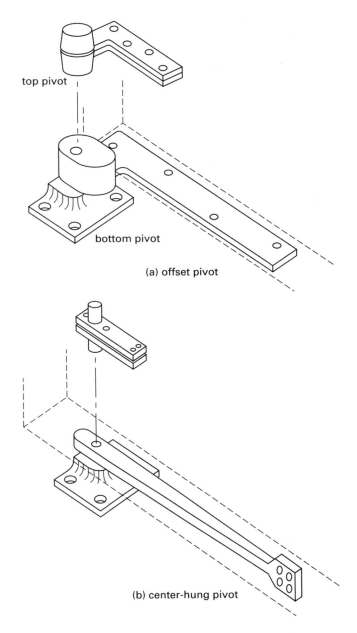

top pivot

bottom pivot

(a) offset pivot

(b) center-hung pivot

Figure 19.13   Door Pivots

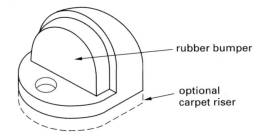

rubber bumper

optional carpet riser

(a) dome floor stop

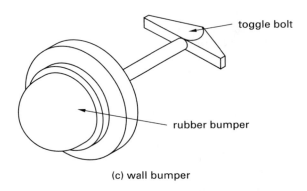

latch screws to door

(b) combination stop and hold open

toggle bolt

rubber bumper

(c) wall bumper

Figure 19.14   Miscellaneous Door Hardware

- *Astragals.* Astragals are vertical members used between double doors to seal the opening, act as a door stop, or provide extra security when the doors are closed. Astragals may be fixed or removable to allow for a wide opening when moving furniture.

- *Coordinators.* A door coordinator is a device used with double doors that are rabbeted or that have an astragal on the active leaf. The coordinator is mounted in or on the head of the frame, coordinating the closing sequence of the two doors so that

they close completely, rather than having the leaf with the astragal close first, preventing the other leaf from closing.

- *Flush bolts.* These are used on the inactive leaf of a pair of doors to lock the doors. They may be surface mounted or mortised into the edge of the door. The active leaf then closes to the locked inactive leaf, but both can be opened when needed. Flush bolts are not allowed on exit doors.

- *Automatic door bottoms.* These are devices that are mortised or surface applied to the bottom of the door to provide a sound or light seal. When the door is open the seal is up; as the door is closed a plunger strikes the jamb and forces the seal down.

- *Weather stripping.* Weather stripping is used along the edges and bottoms of doors to provide a tight seal against water and air infiltration. Various types of door seals are also used to provide light and sound protection on interior doors as well as sealing against the passage of smoke around fire doors. Different types of neoprene, felt, metal, vinyl, and other materials are used.

- *Thresholds.* These are used where floor materials change at a door line, where weather stripping is required, where a hard surface is required for an automatic door bottom, or where minor changes in floor level occur.

Electronic Hardware

Electronic hardware includes devices that control or monitor door openings using electric or electromechanical means. Local building codes must be consulted because some electronic hardware items do not qualify as allowable exit devices. If an exit door is electronically locked and controlled from the outside, most codes require that exiting be possible from the inside through a purely mechanical action on the locking device—that is, one that does not depend on any power supply or deactivation of the lock on the inside by the person exiting. Following are some of the most common types of electronic hardware.

- *Electric locks.* An electric lock maintains a mortise or bored lockset in the locked position until a signal is activated by some type of regulating device. Regulating devices can include wall switches, pushbuttons, card readers, key switches, computerized controls, automatic time devices, security consoles, and other sophisticated control devices. Electric locks can also be specified so that they automatically open if there is a power failure. In either case, the inside knob or handle mechanically unlatches the door for exiting at any time.

A variation of the electric lock is the electric latch. This device is normally in a position to hold the latchbolt of the lock so that the door cannot be opened. On activation, the electric latch pivots slightly, allowing the door to be opened. From the inside, the mechanical operation of the knob or handle retracts the latch, allowing exit regardless of the position of the electric latch. Electric latches have the advantage of not requiring any power to be run to the door; all wiring is done in the door jamb. Electric locks require the use of electric hinges or other power-transfer devices to make the low-voltage wiring connections from the door frame to the mechanism in the door.

- *Electric bolts.* Electric bolts are devices separate from the operating hardware of a door. They can be mounted in the strike jamb or head of a door. In the normal, locked position, a bolt extends from the unit into a strike in the door. A pushbutton, card reader, or other regulating device activates a solenoid that retracts the bolt. Fail-safe units are available that open when there is a power failure. Electric bolts are generally not allowed on exit doors because there is no sure way to mechanically open the door if the bolt does not retract.

- *Card readers.* Card readers are one type of regulating device that reads a magnetic code on a small plastic card when the card is inserted into the reader. If the reader detects a valid code, the switch is activated and the door is unlocked. Card readers can also be used to send a signal to a central monitoring computer that keeps track of whose card was used to open which door and when the entry was made. The computer can also control the times of day when a door can be opened by particular cards. Card readers are usually mounted on the partition near the door they control, but they can also be part of the lockset, as is typically the case in hotels.

- *Keypad devices.* An alternative to the card reader is the keypad, in which a coded number must be entered to gain access. These can be separate units mounted near the door or they can be part of the door knob or lever.

- *Magnetic hold-open devices.* Although exit doors must have closers, most codes allow them to be held in an open position if they can be closed automatically upon activation of a smoke detector or other approved fire signal. One method of doing this is to use a closer with an integral smoke detector as described previously. Another way is to use a magnetic hold-open device that is an electromagnet mounted on a wall or on the floor that contacts a metal plate attached to the door. Upon activation by a central alarm signal or smoke detector or upon a power failure, the electromagnet releases and the door closes.

Finishes

Hardware is available in a variety of finishes, the choice of which is dependent primarily on the appearance desired, but also on its ability to withstand use and weathering. The finish is applied over a base metal from which the hardware is made. For most hardware items this is not critical, but for hinges and other operating hardware it can be significant.

There are five basic metals: steel, stainless steel, bronze, brass, and aluminum. Fire-rated doors must have steel or stainless steel hinges, and hardware in corrosive environments may require stainless steel or bronze base metals with compatible surface finishes.

Hardware finishes have been standardized according to numbers developed by the federal government (U.S. designations) and the Builders Hardware Manufacturers Association (BHMA). These are listed in Table 19.3.

Table 19.3
Hardware Finishes

BHMA no.	US no.	BHMA finish description
605	US3	bright brass, clear coated
606	US4	satin brass, clear coated
611	US9	bright bronze, clear coated
612	US10	satin bronze, clear coated
613	US10B	satin bronze, dark oxidized, oil rubbed
618	US14	bright nickel, clear coated
619	US15	satin nickel-plated, clear coated
622	US19	flat black
623	US20	light oxidized, statuary bronze, clear coated
624	US20A	dark statuary bronze, clear coated
625	US26	bright chromium plate
626	US26D	satin chromium plate
627	US27	satin aluminum, clear coated
628	US28	satin aluminum, clear anodized
629	US32	bright stainless steel
630	US32D	satin stainless steel

BUILDING CODE REQUIREMENTS

Doors and hardware are highly regulated by the building codes. The requirements generally fall into three major categories: exiting requirements, fire-rated assemblies, and access requirements. Many of the exit door requirements are reviewed in Ch. 29. Additional regulations specifically related to doors and hardware are included here.

The building codes regulate under what circumstances a door must provide fire protection. If a partition must have a fire rating, the openings in that partition must also be fire rated. Typical places where fire-rated doors are required include openings in stairways, in fire-rated corridors, in occupancy separation walls, and in certain hazardous locations.

The codes consider not just the door but the entire collection of door, frame, and hardware to be the fire door assembly. Every part of the assembly must be rated to make an approved opening. Doors, frames, and hardware are tested by Underwriters Laboratories (UL) and Factory Mutual (FM) according to standard ASTM and NFPA tests. If the door meets the requirements of the standard fire test, a small metal label is attached to the door, indicating its class and hourly rating. Thus, a fire-rated door is also called a *labeled door*.

Doors are rated according to the time they can withstand the standard fire test and according to the rating of assembly in which they can be installed. Time ratings, summarized in Table 19.4, range from 20 minutes to 3 hours.

Table 19.4
Fire Door Classifications

use of partition	rating of partition or wall (hours)	required door assembly rating (hours)
exit access corridors	1	0.33
fire partitions	1	$^3/_4$
fire barriers (1-hour)		
shaft and exit	1	1
enclosure walls		
other fire barriers	1	$^3/_4$
fire walls and fire barriers	4	3
having a required fire-	3	3
resistance rating greater	2	$1^1/_2$
than 1 hour	$1^1/_2$	$1^1/_2$
exterior walls	3	$1^1/_2$
	2	$1^1/_2$
	1	$^3/_4$

The standard test for doors is NFPA 252. This test is described in Ch. 29.

All hardware on fire doors must be tested and approved for use on fire exits. Fire doors must be operable from the inside without the use of any special knowledge or effort. This provision is intended to prohibit the use of devices such as combination locks, thumb-turn locks, and multiple locks. Some occupants in a building may not be familiar with these, or similar, devices and may find them too difficult to operate during panic conditions or when visibility is low. The code does provide for some exceptions such as in residential units, places of detention, and a few other situations.

For certain occupancies, such as educational and assembly with an occupant load over 50, panic hardware is required. This is hardware that unlatches the door when pressure is applied against a horizontal bar rather than requiring a turning motion as with a level handle or doorknob.

Fire doors must be self-closing or automatic closing. A *self-closing door* simply has a closer or other device that returns it to the closed position after someone passes through. *Automatic closing doors* are those that are normally held open, but that automatically close upon activation of a smoke detector, fire-alarm system, or other approved device.

When fire doors are closed, they must be secured with an active latch bolt. This is to secure the door during a fire, preventing fire and gas pressure from pushing the door open.

Operating devices, including door handles, pulls, latches, and locks, must be installed on the door a minimum of 34 in (864) and a maximum of 48 in (1219) above the finished floor. The only exception is that locks used only for security purposes and not used for normal operation can be at any height.

The requirements for glazing in fire door assemblies vary depending on what type of wall or partition the door is located in.

When glass is installed in fire door assemblies, it must be wire glass set in metal frames or special fire-protection-rated glass. The size of the glass is limited in area and maximum dimensions as shown in Table 19.5. Wire glass has a fire rating of 45 minutes.

Other types of fire-protection-rated glazing and fire-resistance-rated glazing may be used in lieu of wired glass if it conforms to the size limitations of NFPA 80, *Standard for Fire Doors, Fire Windows*.

Additional requirements, based on the IBC, are listed here. Verify exact requirements with the model code used in the area where the work is being done.

- A fire-rated door assembly must have a label attached to the door and frame.

- A fire door must be self-latching.

- All hardware used must be UL listed.

- A fire door must be self-closing. In some cases the code permits the door to be held open if the hold-open or closer is connected to an approved smoke or fire detector.

- A fire door must use steel hinges of the ball-bearing type.

- If a pair of doors is used, astragals or other required hardware must also be used.

- Glass (if permitted) must conform in maximum area and construction to requirements of the local code. It must be wire glass or fire-rated glass and set in a steel frame with the glass stop made of steel.

- Louvers must conform to UL requirements for maximum size and construction.

Table 19.5
Maximum Size of Wire Glass in Fire-Protection-Rated Doors

use of door	fire rating	size of glass allowed		
		area	width	height
exit access doors in corridors	20 minute	no limit	no limit	no limit
exit access doors in other fire partitions	3/4 hour	1296 in² (84 m²)	54 in (1372)	54 in (1372)
exit doors in 1-hour vertical shafts and exit passageways	1 hour	100 in² (0.065 m²)	10 in (254)	33 in (838)
exit doors in 2-hour vertical shafts and 2-hour-rated fire barriers	1½ hour	100 in² (0.065 m²)	10 in (254)	33 in (838)

Accessibility requirements for doors and hardware include the following.

- Minimum width, clear of hardware, of an opened door must be 32 in (815).

- There must be adequate maneuvering clearance in front of and on the latch side of the door to operate it.

- There must be a minimum of 48 in (1220) between two doors in a series when they are open 90°.

- The maximum opening force required for various types of doors is specified by the code.

- Handles and latches must have a shape that is easy to grasp and use. This usually means lever handles or push-pull-type mechanisms.

- Thresholds with a change in level may have a vertical edge up to $\frac{1}{4}$ in (6.4) high, but must be beveled with a slope of 1:2 for heights from $\frac{1}{4}$ in to $\frac{1}{2}$ in (6.4 to 13).

WINDOWS

A *window* is an opening in a wall used to provide viewing, light transmission, solar heat (when desired), and ventilation. The standard nomenclature of a window is shown in Fig. 19.15, and the types of windows are illustrated in Fig. 19.16.

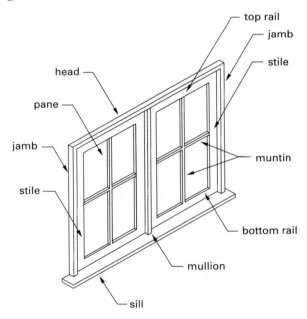

Figure 19.15   Parts of a Window

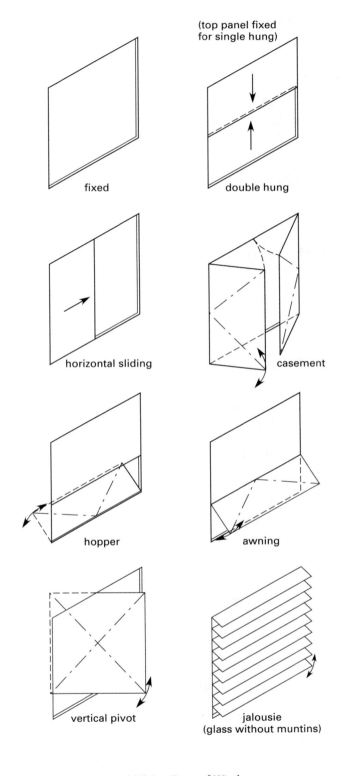

Figure 19.16   Types of Windows

Metal Windows

Metal windows are fabricated of aluminum, steel, or bronze. Aluminum is the most common metal window material because of its light weight, low cost, strength, and resistance to corrosion. A variety of finishes can be applied in the factory to make aluminum windows compatible with almost any building. Two disadvantages of aluminum are its susceptibility to galvanic action and its high heat conduction. However, both of these can be controlled. Galvanic action can be minimized or eliminated with the proper selection of fasteners and flashing; heat transmission and condensation can be prevented by specifying aluminum frames with thermal breaks. These are nonmetallic elements that connect the exterior and interior portions of a window.

Steel windows are fabricated from relatively small sections of hot- or cold-rolled steel. Because of steel's greater strength, frame sections are small compared with those aluminum. Steel windows are more expensive than aluminum ones and are used where high strength, high security, and a minimum profile size are required. They are shop painted or bonderized to improve the adhesion of site-applied paint.

Wood Windows

Wood windows are very popular because of the variety of types and sizes available, their appearance, their ease of installation, and their good insulating properties. These windows are delivered to the job site as complete manufactured units including the exterior trim. They are simply placed in a rough opening and secured to the framing. Installation of interior trim finishes the window opening.

Common types of wood windows include fixed sash, double hung, casement, and horizontal pivoted, either the awning or hopper types. Horizontal sliding units are also available. Materials used are usually pine and fir, although some other species, such as redwood and cypress, are occasionally used. Many manufacturers now provide clad wood windows. The exterior, exposed wood members are covered with a thin layer of steel or vinyl to minimize maintenance, and the interior portions are left exposed for painting or other types of wood finish.

Single-strength or double-strength glass is used for glazing windows, but most building codes now require glazing to be insulated glass in cold climates.

Skylights

Skylights are glazed openings in roofs that allow light to penetrate the interior. They are sometimes operable to allow for ventilation. Skylights may be glazed with glass or plastic, but if plastic is used it must adhere to building code restrictions on location and maximum size. If glazed with glass, the glass must be laminated or wire glass. If tempered or annealed glass is used, it must be protected from above and below with wire screening. These restrictions prevent injury to someone below if the glass breaks and falls.

A skylight should be mounted on curbs to raise the bottom edge above the roof surface, especially if the roof has a low slope. Because condensation of water vapor in a building can be a problem, skylight frames should be provided with a condensate gutter and weep holes, which allow collected water to drain to the outside.

Storefronts

Storefronts consist of extruded metal frames (usually aluminum), glass panels, doors, hardware, and miscellaneous fittings designed to be installed as one coordinated system. Storefront systems are used in one-story applications where the glass and its framing are supported within an opening rather than continuously supported across several floors as with curtain wall construction. Advantages of storefront systems include ease of construction, single-source supplying, light weight, coordinated elements, relatively low cost, and a range of styles, finishes, and sizes from which to choose.

GLASS AND GLAZING

Today's technology offers a wide variety of glass products to meet various glazing needs, ranging from simple, clear glass, to glass that can selectively transmit or reflect different wavelengths, or whose transparency can be switched on and off with electric current.

Glass is the term used to describe the actual material. Clear glass is a mixture of silica sand and small amounts of alkaline salts such as lime, potash, and soda. *Glazing* is the process of installing glass in the framing as well as installing the framing itself, or glass that has been installed through this glazing process.

Types of Glass

In selecting the type of glass to be used in a particular situation, several parameters must be considered. These include the amount of light to be transmitted, the degree of transparency, strength and security, sound isolation, insulating qualities, cost, availability, and special qualities such as radiation shielding. Following are the common types of glass available.

- *Float glass.* Float glass comprises the vast majority of glass produced in the United States. It is made by pouring molten glass on a bed of molten tin and allowing it to slowly cool, forming a smooth, flat surface. It is also called *annealed glass.*

- *Heat-strengthened glass.* This glass is produced by heating glass to about 1100°F (590°C) and slowly cooling it. Heat-strengthened glass has about twice the strength of annealed glass of the same thickness. This type of glass is used where the surface is subject to solar-induced thermal stresses and cyclic windloading.

- *Tempered glass.* Tempered glass is produced by subjecting annealed glass to a special heat treatment in which it is heated to about 1150°F (620°C) and then quickly cooled. The process sets up compressive stresses on the outer surfaces and tensile stresses inside the glass. This glass is about four times stronger than annealed glass of the same thickness. Tempered glass is available in thicknesses from $^1/_8$ in to $^7/_8$ in (3.0 to 21.0).

In addition to its extra strength for normal glazing, tempered glass is considered safety glass, so it can be used in hazardous locations (discussed in a later section). If it breaks, it falls into thousands of very small pieces instead of dangerous shards.

- *Laminated glass.* Laminated glass consists of two or more pieces of glass bonded together by an interlayer of polyvinyl butyral resin. When laminated glass is broken, the interlayer tends to hold the pieces together even though the glass itself may be severely cracked. This type of glass is used where very strong glazing is required. It can be bullet resistant and provides high security against intentional or accidental breakage. Like tempered glass, it is considered safety glazing and can be used in hazardous locations.

Laminated glass is also used where sound control is required. In addition to the sound control provided by the extra glass thickness, the interlayer has a damping effect on the otherwise rigid material. This glass is available in thicknesses from $^{13}/_{64}$ in to 3 in (5.2 to 76).

- *Tinted glass* or *heat-absorbing glass.* This is produced by adding various colorants to the glass material. The standard colors are bronze, gray, green, and blue. The purpose of tinted glass is to reduce the solar transmittance of the glass, which reduces the air conditioning load on the building, the brightness of the interior, and fading of fabrics and carpeting. Because tinted glass absorbs heat, it should not be used where portions of it are in direct sun and portions are shaded. The differential expansion and contraction (thermal load) will crack the glass. Because of this phenomenon, tinted glass is often heat strengthened or tempered.

One of the important variables for tinted glass, as well as other glass materials and sun blocking devices, is the *shading coefficient*. This is the ratio of the solar heat gain through a specific fenestration to the solar heat gain through a pane of $^1/_8$ in (3.0) clear glass under identical conditions. It is used when calculating heat gain. However, the shading coefficient is a value that represents the glazing only, not the frame or spacer effects. Today, most people refer to the *solar heat-gain coefficient* (SHGC) of a window. The SHGC is the ratio of the solar heat gain through glazing or a window compared to the total solar radiation incident on the glazing or window. The SHGC is a value between 0.0 and 0.87.

- *Low-iron glass.* Low-iron glass has a reduced amount of iron oxide, which gives a light-green cast to ordinary clear float glass. Low-iron glass offers exceptional clarity, optimal light transmission, and excellent color transmission.

- *Reflective glass.* Reflective glass is clear or tinted glass coated with an extremely thin layer of metal or metallic oxide. In insulating units, this reflective layer is placed on the inside of the exterior lite of glass. Its primary purpose is to save energy by reflecting solar radiation. In addition to this, the exterior of a building with reflective glass has a mirror-like surface that may have a desired aesthetic effect. Reflective coatings come in various silver, copper, golden, and earthtone shades that can be combined with the several colors of tinted glass.

- *Insulating glass.* Insulating glass is fabricated of two or three sheets of glass separated by a hermetically sealed air space of $^1/_4$ in to $^1/_2$ in (6 to 13). Insulating glass has a much lower U-value than that of single-thickness glass and is used almost exclusively in regions where heat loss is a problem. Insulating glass can be made with heat-strengthened, tempered, reflective, tinted, and laminated glass.

- *Patterned glass.* This specialty glass is made by passing a sheet of glass through rollers on which the desired pattern is etched, which may be on one or both sides. Vision through the panel is diffused but not totally obscured; the degree of diffusion depends on the pattern and depth of etch.

- *Wire glass.* Wire glass has a mesh of wire embedded in the middle of the sheet. The surface can be either smooth or patterned. Wire glass is used primarily in fire-rated assemblies where it is required by most building codes. It is approximately 50% stronger than annealed glass. Wire glass cannot be tempered and does not qualify as safety glazing for hazardous locations.

- *Spandrel glass.* Spandrel glass is used as the opaque strip of glass that conceals the floor and ceiling structure in curtain wall construction. It is manufactured by permanently fusing a ceramic frit color to the back of heat-strengthened or tempered glass. It is normally manufactured and installed as a single sheet with insulation behind.

- *Low-emissivity glass.* Low-emissivity glass, or *low-e glass* as it is sometimes called, selectively reflects and transmits certain wavelengths of the electromagnetic spectrum. It is manufactured by placing a very thin coating (just a few atoms) of metal or metal oxide on the surface of a piece of glass or a thin film. Low-e glass works by transmitting visible light and short-wave solar radiation but reflecting long-wave heat radiation from the air and warm objects.

  Thus, in a cold climate, low-e glass will admit solar heat gain during the day but prevent the built-up heat inside the building from escaping at night. In the summer, the same glass will reflect much of the ambient long-wave infrared heat away from the glass. In warm climates, low-e glass can be combined with tinted or reflective glass to prevent even more heat from being transmitted to the interior of the building.

  This type of glass is used in insulated units where it is placed on the interior surface of the inside lite to reflect building heat back to the inside before it crosses the air gap. Low-e glass can also be made by suspending a very thin layer of film in the center of the air gap, creating two air spaces. This is even more efficient than directly applying the coating to the glass, although glass made through this process is more easily damaged.

  An insulating low-e unit with $1/4$ in (6) thick glass has a U-value of about 0.31 (1.76 W/m^{2}K); an insulating unit with a low-e film suspended in the middle has a U-value of about 0.23 (1.31 W/m^{2}K). Standard double-pane insulating glass with a comparable air space has a U-value of about 0.42 (2.38 W/m^{2}K).

- *Energy-efficient glazing.* Some of the types of glazing products mentioned previously are used to variously keep heat out of a building, keep heat in, or limit the amount of light coming into a building. In the past, selecting one of these objectives meant compromising on one of the others. For example, using tinted or reflective glazing to limit heat gain reduced the visible light transmittance, which was detrimental to effective daylighting. Today, however, there are many glazing products on the market that allow the designer to meet all the requirements of energy efficiency simultaneously. Some are improvements on older technologies while some are new and experimental technologies. Refer to Ch. 7 for a more detailed discussion of these products and how they are used.

- *Electrochromic glazing.* This is a general term for a type of glazing that changes from either a dark tint or a milky white opaque to a transparent state with the application of an electric current. When the current is on, the glass is transparent; when current is off, the glass darkens or turns white (depending on which type it is). There are three distinct types of this glazing currently on the market, only one of which is technically known as electrochromic glazing. The other two types are suspended particle device (SPD) and polymer-dispersed liquid crystal film. The distinction is important because each of the three types on the market at the time of this writing have slightly different characteristics, although all three depend on the application of a low electric current to keep them clear.

  Electrochromic glazing uses an inorganic ceramic thin-film coating on glass and can be manufactured to range from transparent to heavily darkened (tinted). However, it is never opaque, so it cannot be used as privacy glass. It is intended for control of light, ultraviolet energy, and solar heat gain. The amount of tinting is not just an on or off condition; it can be controlled with a simple rheostat switch.

  Suspended particle device glazing (SPD) uses a proprietary system in which light-absorbing microscopic particles are dispersed within a liquid suspension film which is then sandwiched between two pieces of transparent conductive material. The appearance of the product can range from clear to partially darkened to totally opaque, so it can be used for privacy as well as for light control and energy conservation. It can also be variably controlled with a rheostat.

  Polymer-dispersed liquid crystal film glazing is fabricated by placing the polymer film between two pieces of glass. The transparency can range from transparent to cloudy white. In its translucent state it offers total visual privacy but still allows a significant amount of light to pass through so it cannot be used for exterior light control. All of the types of electrochromic glazing are very expensive, but the first two types do offer the potential for significant energy savings, in the range of 20% to 30%.

- *Fire-rated glazing.* Aside from wire glass, there are four additional types of glazing that can be used in fire-rated openings.

The first is a clear ceramic that has a higher impact resistance than does wire glass and a low expansion coefficient. It is available with a 1-hour rating in sizes up to 1296 in² (0.84 m²) and with a 3-hour rating in sizes up to 100 in² (0.0645 m²). Although some forms of ceramic glass do not meet safety glazing requirements, there are laminated assemblies that are rated up to 2 hours and are impact safety-rated.

The second type is a special, tempered fire-protective glass. It is rated at a maximum of 30 minutes because it cannot pass the hose-stream test, but it does meet the impact safety standards of both ANSI Z97.1 and 16 CFR 1201.

The third type consists of two or three layers of tempered glass with a clear polymer gel between them. Under normal conditions, the glass is transparent, but when subjected to fire, the gel foams and turns opaque, thus retarding the passage of heat. This product is available with 30-minute, 60-minute, and 90-minute ratings, depending on the thickness and number of glass panes used. There are restrictions on the maximum size of lites and the type of permitted framing.

The fourth type of glazing is glass block. However, not all glass block is rated. The glass block must have been specifically tested for use in fire-rated openings and be approved by the local authority having jurisdiction.

Installation Details

There are several ways glass can be framed. Some of the more common ones are shown in Fig. 19.17. The traditional way is to place the glass in a rabbeted frame, hold it temporarily with *glaziers points* (small triangular pieces of metal), and face putty the glass in place, as shown in Fig. 19.17(a). This method is labor intensive, and the putty dries and cracks with time and must be replaced often.

Although this method is still used for single-paned glass on small residential jobs, it has been largely replaced with other methods. The glazing putty has been replaced with glazing compounds of various types that are applied like caulking and with *glazing tape*, a semi-rigid, formed material that is placed between the frame and the glass. See Fig. 19.17(b).

Glazing stops are usually required for most installations. These are removable pieces of framing that allow the glass to be installed and removed easily if it must be replaced.

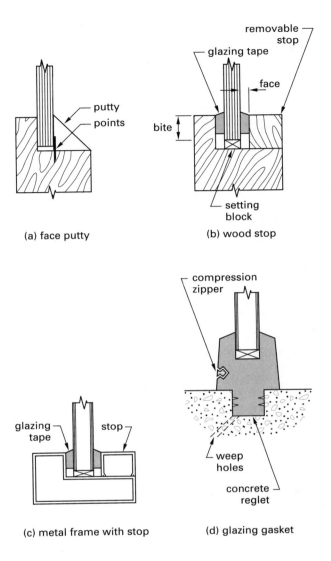

Figure 19.17 Methods of Glazing

Structural glazing gaskets are also used. They are fairly rigid strips of neoprene specifically designed to hold glass. Fig. 19.17(d) shows an application in a concrete reglet, but they can also be attached to metal frames. Once the glass is inserted, a compression strip is forced into a slot, which tightens the grip on the glass.

In all glazing installations, the glass should be placed on semi-rigid setting blocks of neoprene or other compatible elastomeric material. These prevent direct contact between the glass and frame and allow both to expand and contract and move without putting excessive stress on the glass.

Two dimensions of importance when installing exterior glazing are the face dimension and the bite, as illustrated in Fig. 19.17(b). Because glass is subject to wind loading and deflects, effectively pulling partially out of the frame, the bite must be sufficiently deep to hold the glass in place.

Some glazing installations may also be made with a *frameless glazing system*. With this method, the glass is supported at the top and bottom, and the edges are simply butt-jointed and sealed with silicon sealant. With structural glazing systems, the vertical and horizontal framing members are entirely behind the glass (on the interior of the building) and the glass is attached to it with silicon sealant. From the exterior, the installation presents a smooth, uniform appearance, broken only by the thin, butt-jointed glass units.

The required thickness of exterior glass depends on the size of the glazed unit and the wind loading. Tables in the building code give the minimum thicknesses for various types of glass according to these variables. The basic maximum allowable glass area, accounting for wind pressure and glass thickness, is based on float glass. Adjustment factors are provided by which the basic area is increased depending on other types of glass used. Tempered glass has the highest adjustment factor (4.00) of all the glass types. Heat-strengthened glass has an adjustment factor of 2.00; the factor for laminated glass is only 0.75.

Building Code Requirements for Glazing

Three primary glazing situations are regulated by the model codes. These are sizing of glass for wind loading, limitation on glass in fire-rated assemblies, and safety glazing subject to human impact in hazardous locations.

The codes specify the minimum thickness for glass depending on wind loading and the size of the glazed unit. The subject of maximum glass areas in fire doors was reviewed previously in this chapter.

For glass used in fire-resistance-rated partitions, the IBC differentiates between two types of glazing: fire-protection-rated glazing and fire-resistance-rated glazing.

Fire-protection-rated glazing is ¼ in thick wired glass in steel frames or other types of glazing that meet the requirements of NFPA 257, *Standard on Fire Test for Window and Glass Block Assemblies*. Such glazing must have a 45-minute rating and is limited to 1-hour-rated fire partitions or fire barriers when the fire barrier is used to separate occupancies or to separate incidental use areas. The amount of such glazing is limited to 25% of the area of the common wall within any room using the glazing. This limitation applies to partitions separating two rooms as well as a partition separating a room and a corridor. Individual lights of fire-protection-rated glazing cannot exceed 1296 in² in area (9 ft² or 0.84 m²) and any one dimension cannot be more than 54 in (1372). The IBC accepts ¼ in wire glass as meeting the requirements for a 45-minute rating without specific testing, but other glazing must meet the NFPA 257 test requirements for a 45-minute rating.

Fire-resistance-rated glazing is glass or other glazing material that has been tested as part of a fire-resistance-rated wall assembly according to ASTM E-119. This glazing definition allows the use of special fire-rated glazing that can have fire-resistive ratings up to 1½ hours. Refer to the previous section in this chapter for a discussion on these types of glazing products. This type of glazing may be used in partitions that must have a rating higher than 1 hour, although the glazing must have the same rating as the partition in which it is used. There are no size limitations.

In order to prevent injuries from people accidentally walking through glass doors or other openings, codes require safety glazing in hazardous locations. Hazardous locations are those subject to human impact, such as glazing in doors, glass doors, shower and bath enclosures, and certain locations in walls. A composite drawing of some situations where safety glazing is and is not required by the IBC is shown in Fig. 19.18. *Safety glazing* is considered to be tempered or laminated glass that meets the test requirements of the Code of Federal Regulations, 16 CFR 1201, *Safety Standard for Architectural Glazing Materials*.

CURTAIN WALL SYSTEMS

A *curtain wall* is an exterior wall system that is attached to the structural framework of a building and that carries no weight other than its own and wind loading that it transfers to the structure. Curtain walls can be made of preformed metal panels, precast concrete, and prefabricated marble, granite, or masonry panels, but they are usually built of aluminum framing and glass panels.

With aluminum and glass systems, the vertical mullions are attached to the floors or beams at every floor. Attachment devices allow the vertical mullions to be adjusted to provide a perfectly plumb and straight line for the entire height of the building. Horizontal mullions are attached to these vertical pieces according to the design of the system. Glass vision panels are used for window openings, whereas spandrel glass is used where floor and column lines must be concealed.

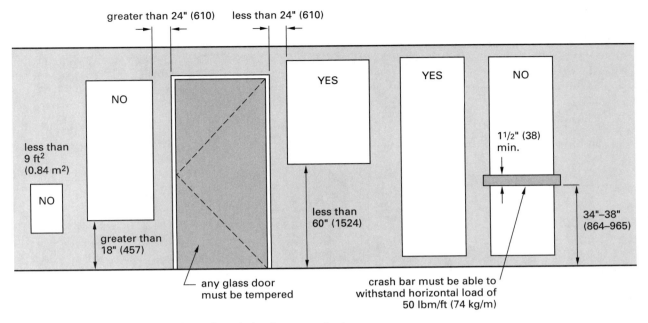

Figure 19.18 Selected Safety Glazing Locations

FINISH MATERIALS

LATH AND PLASTER

Plaster is a finish material made from various types of cementing compounds, fine aggregate, and water. It is applied over several kinds of base materials in two or three coats to form a smooth, level surface. Plaster is a term commonly used to describe various types of finish materials of this type used for interior applications, whereas stucco is a term reserved for exterior applications of plaster made with portland cement.

Plaster is made from gypsum and lime, aggregates of sand, vermiculite or perlite, and water. Vermiculite and perlite are used when a lightweight, fire-resistant plaster is needed. A special process is used to produce *Keene's cement*, which is a plaster that has a high resistance to abrasion and water penetration. It is used in wet areas or on walls subject to scratching or other abuse.

Stucco is made from portland cement, lime, sand, and water. It is used for exterior applications when a hard, non-water-absorbent plaster is needed. Portland cement plaster is also used as a backing for tile walls and as the scratch and brown coats under Keene's cement.

There are two common methods of applying plaster. The first is on metal lath that is attached to metal or wood studs. Metal lath is available in several types: expanded diamond mesh, paper-backed diamond mesh, flat-rib lath, and high-rib lath. See Fig. 20.1. Expanded diamond lath is a general-purpose type used for flat as well as curved surfaces. The paper-backed type has an asphalt-impregnated paper applied to it and is used as a base for portland cement plaster under ceramic tile. Rib lath is more rigid due to the one-way, V-shaped ribs about 4 in on center, and it is used for ceilings and solid partitions.

Metal lath provides a surface for the first coat of plaster to key into when the material flows around and behind the open mesh. This first coat is called the *scratch coat*. In

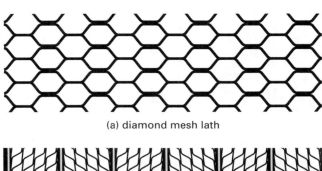
(a) diamond mesh lath

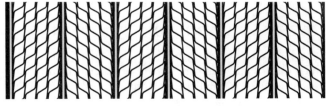
(b) flat-rib metal lath

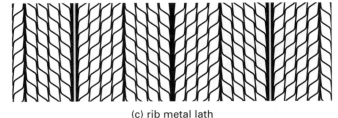
(c) rib metal lath

Figure 20.1 Expanded Metal Lath

standard plastering, the scratch coat is followed by the *brown coat* and then the final *finish coat*. The scratch and brown coats are about $^1/_4$ in (6) thick; the finish coat is about $^1/_8$ in (3) thick. Two-coat work combines the scratch and brown coats.

The other method of plastering uses *gypsum board lath* instead of metal lath. This is a special gypsum product specifically designed for plastering. Gypsum lath comes in 16 in by 48 in (906 by 1220) boards that are applied horizontally to studs, or it comes in 48 in by 96 in (1220 by 2440) sheets. One or two coats of thin veneer plaster are applied over the boards. Veneer plastering reduces labor over the traditional method because only one coat is needed.

Edges of plaster and stucco work must be finished with various types of metal trim pieces. These provide a termination point for the work and serve as screeds to give the plasterers guides for maintaining the required thickness. Common profiles include corner beads to protect outside corners; casing beads to trim doors, windows, and other openings; base screeds to finish plaster at the base of a room; and expansion joints to control cracking in the plaster or stucco surface. Stucco requires expansion joints at a minimum of every 10 ft (3000) or where it is likely to crack, such as at the corners of door and window openings.

In general, gypsum drywall systems have largely supplanted lath and plaster work because of their lower cost and faster construction sequence. However, plaster is still used where curved shapes are required and where a hard, abrasion-resistant surface is required. Stucco is still used for exterior applications regardless of the surface form of the building. Veneer plaster walls can be constructed to provide a 1- or 2-hour fire-rated partition.

GYPSUM WALLBOARD

Gypsum wallboard construction is one of the most common methods for building partitions in commercial and residential structures. It is inexpensive and can satisfy most of the performance requirements for partitions found in today's construction. *Gypsum wallboard*, also known as *drywall* or *sheetrock*, is made of a gypsum plaster core sandwiched between sheets of paper or other materials.

The advantages of gypsum wallboard include

- low installed cost
- quick and easy installation
- fire resistance
- sound control ability
- availability
- versatility: it can be used for partitions, shaft enclosures, ceilings, and so on
- ease of finishing and decorating
- ease of installation of doors, windows, and other openings

Gypsum Wallboard Materials

Gypsum wallboard is manufactured in panels 4 ft (1200) wide and 8, 10, 12, and 14 ft (2400, 3000, 3600, and 4200) long. Special 1 in (25) thick coreboard used for shaft enclosures is manufactured in 2 ft (600) widths. The length used depends on the requirements of the job, but contractors generally use the longest length practical to minimize the number of joints.

Standard gypsum wallboard is available in thicknesses of $1/4$, $3/8$, $1/2$, and $5/8$ in (6.4, 9.5, 13, and 16). There is also a $3/4$ in (19) thick product that carries a 2-hour fire rating. This allows a 2-hour-rated partition to be constructed with a single layer without resorting to a standard two-ply application.

The thickness used depends on the particular application, the spacing of the framing, and the building code requirements. For most commercial and high-quality residential work, $5/8$ in (16) thick wallboard is used. A $1/2$ in (13) thickness is commonly used in residential projects and for some commercial applications such as furred walls.

Other applications require different wallboard thicknesses. For example, a $3/8$ in (9.5) thickness is used in some double-layer applications or when wallboard is applied over other finished walls in remodeling work. A thickness of $1/4$ in (6.4) is used for forming curved surfaces and for providing new finishes over old wall and ceiling surfaces. Double-layer applications are used when additional fire resistance is required or for extra acoustical benefits.

Gypsum wallboard is available with square edges, tapered edges, and tongue-and-groove edges. The tapered edge is the most commonly used because the slight taper allows joint compound and tape to be applied without showing a bulge in the finished surface.

Other types available include Type X for fire-rated partitions, foil-backed for vapor barriers, water-resistant for use behind tile and in other moist conditions, exterior, backing board, abuse resistant, and predecorated with vinyl wall covering already applied.

Gypsum board is applied by nailing or screwing it to wood or metal framing, or with mastic when applying it to concrete or masonry walls. The joints are finished by embedding paper or fiberglass tape in a special joint compound and allowing it to dry. Additional layers of joint compound are added and sanded smooth after each application to give a smooth-finish wall surface. Various types of textured finishes can be applied, or the surface can be left smooth for the application of other wall coverings.

Because gypsum wallboard is produced in such large quantities, its manufacture, use, and disposal have an effect on the environment. Since the 1950s, gypsum wallboard manufacturers have been using recycled paper to manufacture the surfaces of wallboard. In addition, some manufacturers are using recycled newspaper mixed with gypsum as the core material, to yield a product that is more rigid than standard wallboard yet still maintains all the other advantages of the product. About 7% of the industry's total use of gypsum is synthetic gypsum. Synthetic gypsum is chemically identical to natural, mined gypsum, but is a by-product of various manufacturing, industrial, or chemical processes. The main source of synthetic gypsum in North America is *flue-gas desulfurization*. This is the process whereby power-generating plants (and similar plants) remove polluting gases from their stacks to reduce emission of harmful materials into the atmosphere. Using this by-product allows the efficient use of refuse material that would otherwise have to be discarded.

The larger environmental concern involves the disposal of used gypsum wallboard, which cannot be reused for its original purpose when it is ripped out of an old building or a renovation project. There are some gypsum wallboard plants around the country that are recycling old drywall. The only condition is that the wallboard must be free of screws, nails, asbestos, and lead paint. Currently, the cost of collecting, separating, and transporting the old wallboard is a disincentive for recycling.

Old wallboard can also be pulverized into pieces equal to or smaller than $1/2$ in size and worked into the ground as a soil additive. Farmers in California and parts of Colorado use recycled gypsum as a soil conditioner for grapes, peas, and peanuts. It is also possible to work the gypsum directly into the soil around a job site, as long as the land has adequate drainage and aeration and local and state regulations allow it.

Framing

Gypsum wallboard framing for vertical construction can be either wood or metal. Wood is used in residential construction, and metal studs are commonly used in commercial construction because they are noncombustible, lightweight, nonshrinking, and easy to work with. Occasionally, wood studs are used in smaller commercial projects. Metal framing *can* be used in residential construction, but residential contractors prefer wood. Wood stud walls are also used in residential work because they can double as loadbearing walls.

Wood framing for gypsum wallboard partitions consists of 2 × 4 wood studs (actual size $1^1/2$ in by $3^1/2$ in [38.1 × 88.9]) spaced 16 in (406) or 24 in (610) on center, although 16 in spacing is more common, especially for residential construction. These spacings are used because they are even subdivisions of the 4 ft width and 8, 10, and 12 ft lengths of gypsum wallboard. For ceilings, the wallboard is generally attached directly to wood joists or ceiling rafters, which are also spaced 16 in on center.

Metal framing is lightgage, galvanized steel formed in a variety of sizes and shapes. Although metal stud partitions are usually not loadbearing, they can be loadbearing if heavy-gage, structural steel studs are used.

Metal studs are available in several gages (thicknesses). The most common are 25 gage (0.0188 in [0.48]), 22 gage (0.0284 in [0.72]), and 20 gage (0.0344 in [0.87]). 25 gage is most often used for studs and other metal framing. Heavier gages are used for very tall partitions, when the partition has to support unusual loads, and when framing door openings. For loadbearing partitions, exterior walls, and other heavy loading conditions, structural steel studs of 12-, 14-, 16-, or 18-gage thickness are used.

Metal studs are manufactured into a C shape with small flanges, as shown in Fig. 20.2. Openings are pre-punched along the length to allow for the passage of electrical conduit, small pipes, and other wiring. Metal studs are available in depths of $1^5/8$, $2^1/2$, $3^5/8$, 4, and 6 in (41.3, 63.5, 92.1, 101.6, and 152.4).

Metal studs are placed vertically and, like wood studs, are spaced either 16 in or 24 in (406 or 610) on center, although 24 in spacing is common for most nonloadbearing commercial construction because it is more economical and minimizes construction time. Metal studs must be framed into runners at both the floor and ceiling as shown in Fig. 20.2. The runners are C-shaped metal fabrications without a flange. They have pre-punched holes and are the same widths as the studs. The runners are attached to the floor and upper support first, and then the studs are slipped into them and attached with self-tapping screws or with a crimping device. Other shapes of studs are also available for special uses such as stairway shaft framing.

The depth of the stud depends on the height of the partition, gage of the stud, number of layers of wallboard, and spacing of the studs. The most commonly used size is $2^1/2$ in, which is sufficient for normal ceiling heights and slab-to-slab partitions and also allows enough room for electrical boxes and small pipes. Metal studs are normally spaced 16 in and 24 in on center with $1/2$ in or $5/8$ in thick gypsum board screw applied.

Wallboard Trim

Like plaster walls, gypsum wallboard must have fabricated edging. This includes cornerbead, which is used for all exterior corners not otherwise protected, and various types of edge trim. These trim pieces are shown in Fig. 20.3 and are defined as follows.

- *LC bead*: edge trim requiring finishing with joint compound

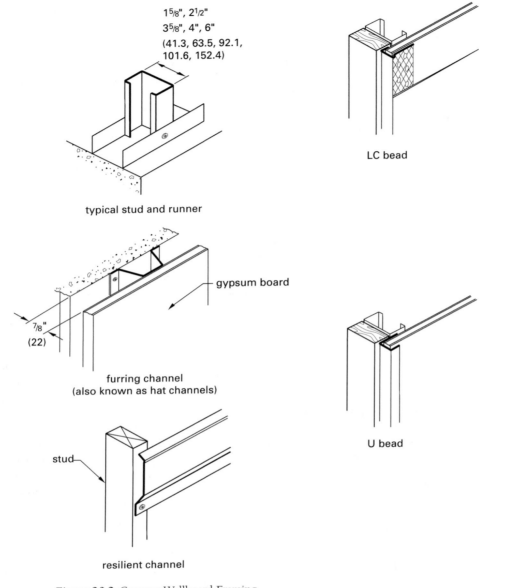

1⅝", 2½"
3⅝", 4", 6"
(41.3, 63.5, 92.1,
101.6, 152.4)

typical stud and runner

gypsum board

⅞"
(22)

furring channel
(also known as hat channels)

stud

resilient channel

Figure 20.2 Gypsum Wallboard Framing

LC bead

L bead

U bead

LK bead

Figure 20.3 Gypsum Wallboard Trim

- *L bead*: edge trim without a back flange; good for installation after the wallboard has been installed. It requires finishing with joint compound.

- *LK bead*: edge trim for use with a kerfed jamb. It requires finishing with joint compound.

- *U bead*: edge trim that does not require finishing with joint compound, but does have a noticeable edge. It is sometimes called *J metal* by contractors.

Two of the most common types of gypsum wallboard construction on metal framing are shown in Fig. 20.4. The standard partition is only built up to the suspended ceiling, whereas the slab-to-slab partition is used when a complete fire-rated barrier must be constructed or when sound control is needed. By adding additional layers of Type X wallboard, fire-resistive ratings of 2, 3, and 4 hours can be obtained. Gypsum wallboard is also used for ceilings and to provide fire protection for columns, stairways, and elevator shafts. It can also be used as a base for finishing by furring over other walls.

Glass-Reinforced Gypsum

Glass-reinforced gypsum (GRG) designates a broad class of products manufactured from a high-strength, high-density gypsum reinforced with continuous-filament glass fibers or

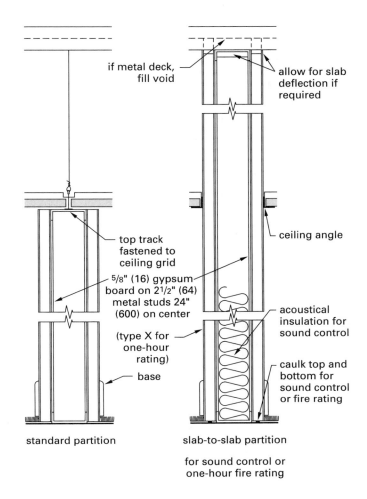

Figure 20.4 Gypsum Wallboard Partitions

(standard partition)

- top track fastened to ceiling grid
- 5/8" (16) gypsum board on 2 1/2" (64) metal studs 24" (600) on center
- (type X for one-hour rating)
- base

(slab-to-slab partition for sound control or one-hour fire rating)

- if metal deck, fill void
- allow for slab deflection if required
- ceiling angle
- acoustical insulation for sound control
- caulk top and bottom for sound control or fire rating

chopped glass fibers. It is also known as *fiberglass-reinforced gypsum* (FRG) and *glass-fiber-reinforced gypsum* (GFRG).

GRG products are used for decorative elements such as column covers, arches, coffered ceilings, ornate moldings, light troughs, and trim. They are premanufactured products made by pouring GRG into molds. After setting, the products are shipped to the job site for installation and final finishing. They can be finished with any kind of material that can be put on plaster or gypsum wallboard. An unlimited variety of shapes can be manufactured that would otherwise be too expensive or impossible to achieve with site-fabricated lath and plaster.

TILE

Tiles are small, flat finishing units made of clay or clay mixtures. The two primary types are ceramic tile and quarry tile. The advantages of tile include durability; water resistance (if glazed); ease of installation; ease of cleaning; a wide

choice of colors, sizes, and patterns; fire resistance; fade resistance; and the ability to store heat for passive solar collection.

Types of Tile

Ceramic tile is defined as a surfacing unit, usually relatively thin in relation to facial area, made from clay or a mixture of clay and other ceramic materials, having either a glazed or unglazed face, and fired above red heat in the course of manufacture to a temperature sufficiently high to produce specific physical properties and characteristics.

Quarry tile is glazed or unglazed tile, usually with 6 in² (3870 mm²) or more of facial area. It is made by the extrusion process from natural clay or shale.

Some of the common types of tile are glazed wall tile, unglazed tile, ceramic mosaic tile, paver tile, quarry tile (glazed or unglazed), abrasive tile, and antistatic tile.

Ceramic mosaic tile is tile formed by either the dust-pressed or extrusion method, 1/4 in to 3/8 in (6 to 10) thick, and has a facial area of less than 6 in² (3870 mm²).

Dust pressing uses large presses to shape the tile out of relatively dry clay. The extrusion process uses machines to cut tiles from a wetter and more malleable clay extruded through a die.

Classification of Tile

The United States tile industry classifies tile based on size: under 6 in² (3870 mm²) is *mosaic tile*; over 6 in² is *wall tile*. Glazed and unglazed nonmosaic tile made by the extrusion method is *quarry tile*; glazed and unglazed tile over 6 in² made by the dust-pressed method is called *paver tile*.

Tile is often classed according to its resistance to water absorption, as follows.

- *Nonvitreous tile*: tile with water absorption of more than 7.0%

- *Semivitreous tile*: tile with water absorption of more than 3.0% but not more than 7.0%

- *Vitreous tile*: tile with water absorption of more than 0.5% but not more than 3.0%

- *Impervious tile*: tile with water absorption of 0.5% or less

Imported tile is classified differently than tile produced in the United States. European manufacturers classify tile according to its production method (either the dust-pressed or extrusion method), its degree of water absorption, its finish, and whether it is glazed or unglazed.

The classifications of abrasion resistance are: Group I, light residential; Group II, moderate residential; Group III:

maximum residential; and Group IV, highest abrasion resistance—commercial.

Tile Sizes and Shapes

Ceramic mosaic tile is available in standard nominal U.S. sizes of 1 × 1 and 2 × 2 (25 × 25 and 50 × 50) with a nominal thickness of $1/4$ in (6). Some 2 × 1 tile is also available as well as tile in small hexagonal shapes. Glazed wall tile is manufactured in standard nominal sizes of $4^1/4$ × $4^1/4$, 6 × $4^1/2$, and 6 × 6 (108 × 108, 152 × 114, and 152 × 152) with a nominal thickness of $1/4$ in or $5/16$ in (6 or 8). Individual manufacturers may produce other sizes as well.

Most manufacturers produce a complete line of trim pieces for ceramic tile installation. These include cove base, bullnose, inside and outside corners, and other shapes most often required. The standard trim shapes are illustrated in Fig. 20.5.

Quarry tile is available in nominal flat sizes of 3 × 3, 4 × 4, 6 × 6, 8 × 8, 8 × 4, and 6 × 3 (75 × 75, 100 × 100, 150 × 150, 200 × 200, 200 × 100, and 150 × 75) with a nominal thickness of $1/2$ in (13). Trim pieces are similar in shape to that of wall tile.

Tile Installation

Tile must be installed on solid, flat substrates capable of supporting the weight of the material. There are two ways of doing this: with a full-mortar bed or with thinset mortar.

The traditional method of installing floor tile is to lay it in a thick bed of mortar. The tile and reinforced mortar bed are separated from the structural floor with a cleavage membrane (15 lbm roofing felt or 4 mil polyethylene film) to allow the two floors to move independently. This system should be used on floors where excessive deflection is expected and on precast and post-tensioned concrete floors. Because the mortar bed is reinforced with 2 in by 2 in (50 by 50), 16-gage welded wire fabric, the tile and bed are rigidly held together as a unit. In addition to providing for movement, the full-mortar bed allows for minor variations in floor level to be made up with the mortar. The tile can be set on the mortar bed while it is still plastic or on a cured mortar bed using a second coat of dry-set or latex-portland cement mortar. If a waterproof floor is required, a waterproof membrane can be used in place of the cleavage membrane. This is the preferred method for tile floors in commercial showers or where continuous wetting is present.

Thinset tile floors are laid on a suitable substrate, commonly a glass-mesh mortar unit specifically manufactured for tile installation. This is a cementitious panel nailed to the subfloor. The tile is laid on a thin coating of dry-set or latex-portland cement mortar with latex-portland cement

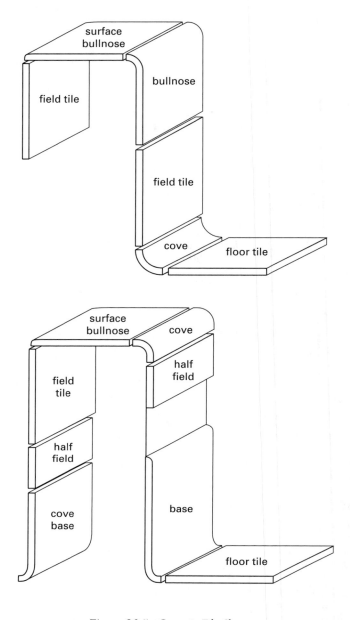

Figure 20.5 Ceramic Tile Shapes

grout. A standard sand and portland cement grout can also be used. When using thinset tile the subfloor must be level, free from dirt and other contaminants, and able to support the extra weight of the tile. If a subfloor deflects or moves in some way, a thinset tile installation will probably develop cracks.

Tile on walls can also be set with either the full-mortar bed or thinset method. The full-mortar bed method is typically used in commercial construction where extreme durability is required or in continuously wet areas, such as gang showers, laundries, pools, and tubs. For walls, instead of using welded wire fabric reinforcing, the base coat of portland cement plaster is attached to galvanized metal lath. Sometimes thinset methods are used in combination with waterproof cementitious backer boards for noncommercial construction.

TERRAZZO

Terrazzo is a composite material poured in place or precast that is used for floors, walls, stairs, and other construction elements. It consists of marble, quartz, granite, or other suitable chips, in a matrix that is cementitious, chemical, or a combination of both. Terrazzo is poured, cured, ground, and polished to produce a surface with a visible texture.

Terrazzo has many of the advantages of tile, which include durability, water resistance, ease of cleaning, a wide choice of patterns and colors, and fire resistance.

Types of Terrazzo

There are four basic types of terrazzo. *Standard terrazzo* is the most common type, using small chips no larger than ³/₈ in (9.5). *Venetian terrazzo* uses chips larger than ³/₈ in. *Palladiana terrazzo* utilizes thin random-fractured slabs of marble with standard terrazzo between. *Rustic terrazzo* has the matrix depressed to expose the chips.

An unlimited number of terrazzo finishes can be achieved by specifying various combinations of chips and matrix colors.

The most commonly used matrix is cementitious, a mixture of white portland cement, sand, and water. Modified cementitious matrices, mixing epoxy or polyacrylate with the portland cement, are used when additional chemical resistance or conductivity is required or when the installation is thinset. Resinous matrices of epoxy or polyester are used for thinset applications. Conductive floors are used where static electricity buildup must be avoided. Conductive matrices are black due to their carbon black content.

Installation of Terrazzo

Terrazzo can be installed on walls as well as on floors. The four common floor installations are shown in Fig. 20.6. The sand cushion method is the best way to avoid cracking of terrazzo, because the finish system is physically separated from the structural slab with a membrane. Because the underbed is reinforced, the terrazzo system can move independently of the structure. If floor movement or deflection is not anticipated, the bonded method can be used. Where the thickness of the installation is a problem, a monolithic or thinset method can be used.

Terrazzo is generally finished to a smooth surface with an 80-grit stone grinder, but it can be ground with a rough, 24-grit to achieve a more textured surface. Rustic terrazzo exposes some of the stone when the matrix is washed before

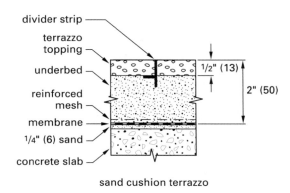

sand cushion terrazzo

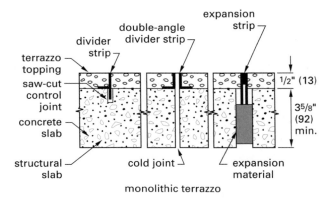

monolithic terrazzo

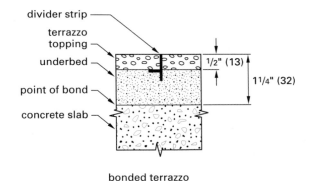

bonded terrazzo

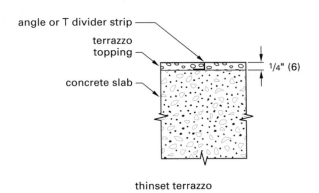

thinset terrazzo

Figure 20.6 Methods of Terrazzo Installation

it has set. Terrazzo is also available as precast floor tiles in 12 in and 16 in (300 and 400) squares. It is laid in a cement mortar like stone or ceramic tile.

STONE FINISHES

Stone is often used for interior finishes of walls and floors. Commonly used types include marble, granite, and slate for flooring. Interior veneer stone is about 3/4 in to 7/8 in (19 to 22) thick and is attached to wall substrates with stainless steel wires or ties. These are anchored to the substrate and hold the stone by being set in holes or slots cut into the back or sides of the panel. Lumps of plaster of paris, called spots, are placed between the substrate and the back of the stone panel at each anchor to hold the slab in place and to allow for precise alignment before they set.

Anchoring stone inside a building is simpler than exterior stonework because there is no wind load, precipitation, or freezing and thawing to contend with, and panels are seldom stacked above each other so that the weight of the panel can be carried by the floor. For high interior spaces many of the anchoring details are similar to those of exterior work, as shown in Fig. 14.16.

Thin stone tiles are also used for interior finishing. These are about 3/8 in (10) thick and come in sizes of 1 × 1 and 1 × 2 (300 × 300 and 300 × 600). They are used for flooring and wall finish.

When stone is used for flooring it may be installed in a number of ways. These are illustrated in Fig. 20.7. Like terrazzo, stone floors are subject to cracking if bonded to a subfloor that deflects excessively. To prevent this, a membrane is used so the subfloor and stone flooring can move separately. However, on rigid structures stone may also be thinset.

ACOUSTICAL TREATMENT

The three most common acoustical treatments for ordinary construction are ceilings, special acoustical wall panels, and carpeting. Special devices used in auditoriums and similar spaces are not discussed here.

Acoustical Ceilings

In contemporary commercial construction, the ceiling is almost always a construction system separate from the structure. This allows a smooth, flat ceiling surface for partition attachment, lights, and acoustical treatment. The space above the ceiling can be used for mechanical systems, wiring, and other services.

Acoustical ceilings consist of thin panels of wood fiber, mineral fiber, or glass fiber set in a support grid of metal framing that is suspended by wires from the structure above.

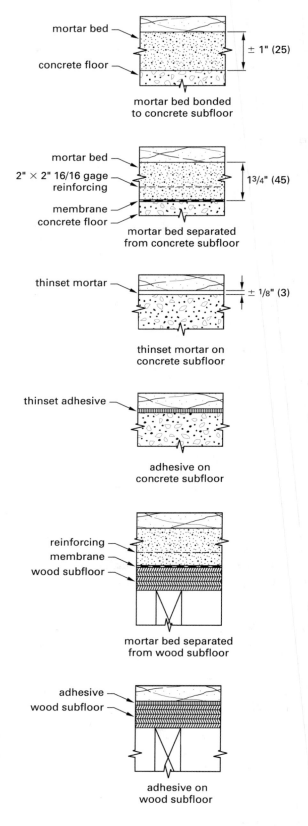

Figure 20.7 Stone Flooring Installation Methods

The tiles are perforated or fissured in various ways to absorb sound, which is the basis for the term "acoustical ceiling." It is important to remember that acoustical ceilings absorb sound, but they do not prevent sound transmission to any appreciable extent.

Acoustical ceiling tiles and the metal supporting grid are available in a variety of sizes and configurations. The most common type is the lay-in system in which tiles are simply laid on top of an exposed T-shaped grid system. See Fig. 20.8(a). A variation of this is the tegular system, which uses tiles with rabbeted edges, as shown in Fig. 20.8(b). Systems are also available in which the grid is completely concealed. These systems use 1 × 1 (300 × 300) or 1 × 2 (300 × 600) tile sizes. See Fig. 20.8(c). A typical lay-in acoustical system is shown in Fig. 20.9.

The most common tile and grid sizes for lay-in acoustical ceiling systems are 24 × 24 (600 × 600) and 24 × 48 (600 × 1200). Metric ceiling tiles are manufactured to a different size based on a 600 mm module, so they are exact multiples of 600 mm.

A 20 × 60 (500 × 1500) size is also available for use in buildings with a 5 ft working module, so three panels fit within one 60 in (1500) grid. This allows office partitions to be laid out on the 5 ft module lines without interfering with HVAC registers and with special 20 in by 48 in (500 × 1200) light fixtures located in the center of a module.

Other types of suspended systems that provide acoustical properties are also available. These include metal strip ceilings, wood grids, and fabric-covered acoustical batts. They all serve the same purpose: to absorb rather than reflect sound in order to reduce the noise level within a space.

Because suspended acoustical ceilings serve so many purposes in addition to acoustical control in today's construction, there are many elements that must be coordinated in their selection and detailing. These include determining required clearances for recessed lights; verifying clearances for ductwork; locating sprinklers, fire alarm speakers, smoke detectors, and similar items; and designing drapery pockets and other recessed fixtures.

In many cases, the space above a suspended ceiling is used as a return air plenum. Return air grilles are set in the grid, and return air is simply allowed to pass through the grilles, through the ceiling space, and back to a central return air duct or shaft that connects to the HVAC system. If this is the case, building codes require that no combustible material be placed above the ceiling and that all plastic wiring be run in metal conduit. Some codes allow wiring used for telephone, computer, low-voltage lighting, and signal systems to be exposed if it has an approved Teflon™-coated covering.

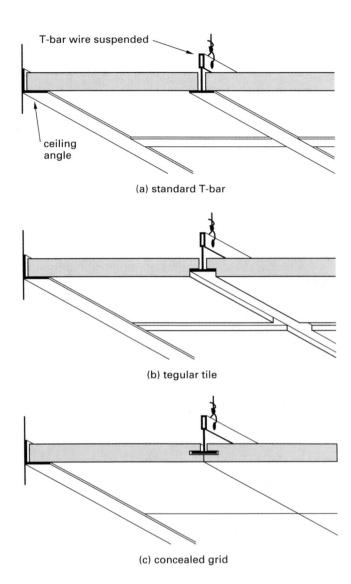

(a) standard T-bar

(b) tegular tile

(c) concealed grid

Figure 20.8 Standard Acoustical Ceiling Systems

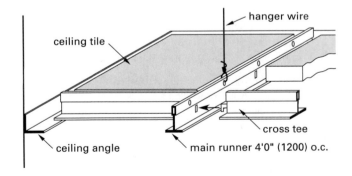

Figure 20.9 Lay-In Suspended Acoustical Ceiling

Suspended ceilings may be rated or nonrated. If they are fire rated, it means that they are part of a complete floor-ceiling or roof-ceiling assembly that is rated. Suspended ceiling systems by themselves cannot be rated. Rated acoustical ceiling systems consist of rated mineral tiles and rated grid systems, the latter of which include hold-down clips to keep the tiles in place and expansion slots to allow the grid to expand if subjected to heat.

Acoustical ceiling tiles are manufactured with varying degrees of recycled content utilizing newsprint, perlite, and ground-up pieces of old tiles. Recycled content may range for about 50% to nearly 90%.

Seismic Restraint for Suspended Ceilings

In some areas of the United States (including most of California and some portions of Idaho, Montana, Utah, Hawaii, and Alaska), special seismic-restraint detailing is required for suspended ceilings. Architects working on projects in these areas should verify the exact requirements based on the building code being used and the project's exact geographic location. When seismic restraint for suspended ceilings is required, certain criteria must be followed. Some of the more common criteria are as follows.

- Individual light fixtures and other types of equipment that are normally supported by the ceiling grid must be independently supported with wires.

- The actual weight of the ceiling system, including lights and air terminals, should be 2.5 lbm/ft² (12.2 kg/m²) or less.

- The ceiling system should not be used to provide lateral support for partitions. Instead, the partitions should be braced with detailing similar to that shown in Fig. 20.10.

- Ceiling angles should provide at least a 7/8 in (22) ledge, and there must be at least a 3/8 in (10) clearance from the edge of the tile to the wall. This is shown in Fig. 20.11.

- The perimeter main runners and cross runners must be prevented from spreading without relying on permanent attachment to the ceiling angle.

- For ceilings in very high-risk seismic zones, the suspension system must be a heavy-duty type and must have lateral force bracing 12 ft (3600) on center in both directions, with the first point within 6 ft (1800) of each wall. As illustrated in Fig. 20.12, these points of lateral bracing must provide support in all four directions and must have rigid struts connected to the structure above to prevent uplift as well as to support gravity loads. Additional wire supports are also required for all runners at the

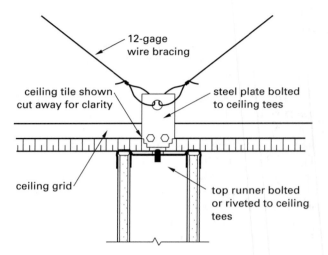

Note: All components and connections must be designed to resist design loads applied perpendicular to the face of the partition.

Figure 20.10 Partition Bracing for Zones 3 and 4

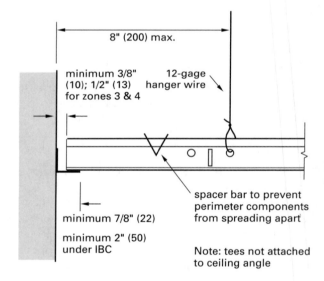

Figure 20.11 Detail of Runners at Perimeter Partition

perimeter of the room within 8 in (200) of the wall. Clearances from the end of the runners to the partition must be 1/2 in (13) instead of 3/8 in (9.5). The IBC now requires a minimum clearance of 3/4 in (19) in high-risk zones and a minimum 2 in (50) wide ceiling angle.

Acoustical Wall Panels

Sound-absorbent panels can be purchased or constructed for use in spaces that require acoustical treatment in

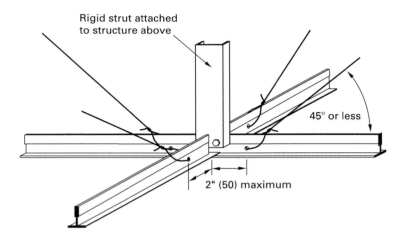

Figure 20.12 Ceiling Grid Bracing

addition to acoustical ceilings and carpeting. These are made from a sound-absorbent material such as fiberglass and are covered with a permeable material such as a loose-weave fabric. The acoustical material must be at least 1 in (25) thick in order to be effective.

WOOD FLOORING

Wood flooring offers a wide variety of appearances while providing a surface that is durable, wear resistant, and comfortable. It is available in several species and can be laid in dozens of different patterns.

Wood flooring is made from both hardwood and softwood, with the hardwoods predominating. Standard hardwoods used are red oak, white oak, maple, birch, beech, pecan, mahogany, and walnut. Softwoods used are yellow pine, fir, and western hemlock, among others.

Types of Wood Flooring

There are four basic types of wood flooring: strip flooring, plank flooring, block flooring, and solid block flooring. See Fig. 20.13.

Strip flooring is one of the most common wood flooring types and consists of thin strips from $3/8$ in to $25/32$ in (10 to 20) thick, of varying lengths, with tongue-and-groove edges. Most strip flooring is $2^1/4$ in (57) wide, but $1^1/2$ in (38) wide strips are also available. Strip flooring is used for residential and commercial wood floors for its appearance, warmth under foot, and resiliency, and where a durable floor is needed.

Plank flooring comes in the same thicknesses as strip flooring but is from $3^1/4$ in to 8 in wide (83 to 203). It is laid in random lengths with the end joints staggered. Plank flooring is

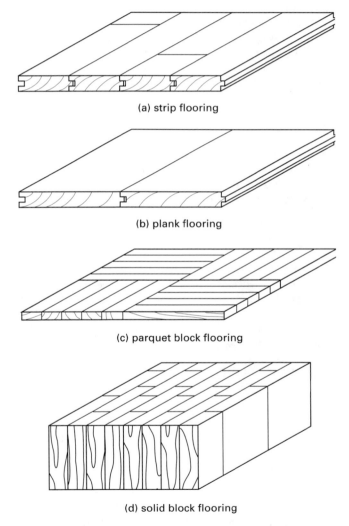

(a) strip flooring

(b) plank flooring

(c) parquet block flooring

(d) solid block flooring

Figure 20.13 Types of Wood Flooring

used primarily in residential applications where a larger scale is desired or to emulate wider, historic planking.

Block flooring is made of preassembled wood flooring in three configurations. Unit block flooring is standard strip flooring assembled into a unit held together with steel or wood splines. Laminated block flooring is flooring made with from three to five plies of cross-laminated wood veneer. Both types of block flooring are from $^3/_8$ in to $^{25}/_{32}$ in (10 to 20) thick, in varying lengths, depending on the manufacturer. Unit and laminated block flooring can be laid in any pattern, but herringbone is one of the most common.

Parquet flooring is made of preassembled units of several small, thin slats of wood in a variety of patterns. It is available either finished or unfinished, and some manufacturers make parquet with a cellular foam resilient backing with a factory-applied adhesive for residential "peel and stick" applications. Commercial applications use nonbacked units that are field finished. Parquet flooring is usually sold in 12 in squares, $^5/_{16}$ in thick (300 mm squares, 8 mm thick), for mastic application, although some manufacturers make other sizes. Parquet flooring is easier and less expensive to install than other types of flooring and can be installed in a wide range of designs.

Solid block flooring is made from solid end-grain blocks. These are solid pieces of wood 2, $2^1/_2$, 3, and 4 in thick (50, 64, 75, and 100) laid on end with adhesive. Solid block floors are very durable and resistant to oils, mild chemicals, and indentation. They are used for industrial floors or other heavy-duty commercial applications.

There are several variations of wood floors for special uses. These include resilient and relocatable floors. *Resilient floors* are wood strip floors laid on one of three types of systems described in the next section. They provide extra buoyancy for uses like dance and theater floors. *Relocatable floors* are systems of modular units, usually 4 ft^2 (1200 mm^2), that can be quickly installed and dismantled. They are used for athletic and institutional floors where the type of flooring needs to be changed frequently.

Grades of Wood Flooring

Wood flooring is graded differently than other wood products. Grading rules are set by the various trade associations such as the National Oak Flooring Manufacturers' Association, the Maple Flooring Manufacturers' Association, the Southern Pine Inspection Bureau, the West Coast Lumber Inspection Bureau, and the Western Wood Products Association.

Unfinished oak flooring is graded as clear, select, no. 1 common, and no. 2 common. Clear is the best grade with the most uniform color. Plain sawn is standard, but quarter sawn is available on special order. Lengths of pieces are

$1^1/_4$ ft (381) and up, with the average length being $3^3/_4$ ft (1143).

Beech, birch, and maple are available in first, second, and third grades along with some combination grades.

Species of Wood Flooring

In addition to the commonly used maple, oak, birch, and beech, there are many wood species, both domestic and imported, that can be used for flooring. Of the many available, two qualify as sustainable products: bamboo and palm wood.

Bamboo is not a tree, but a fast-growing grass that reaches maturity in three to four years. It can be used for flooring as well as for veneer and paneling. It can be obtained from managed forests where it is grown on steep slopes and in hill lands where other forms of agriculture are difficult to propagate.

Bamboo flooring is available in $^1/_2$ in (13) and $^3/_4$ in (19) thick strips about 3 in (76) wide or wider, depending on the manufacturer. It is milled with tongue-and-groove edges, so it can be installed like standard wood-strip flooring. It can be installed by nailing or with an adhesive.

Bamboo is almost as hard and twice as stable as red oak and maple. It is available in a natural color or a darker, amber color and is prefinished with a durable polyurethane coating.

Palm wood comes from coconut palms and is a by-product from commercial coconut plantations. Palm wood flooring is available in $^3/_4$ in by 3 in (19 by 76) wide strips with tongue-and-groove edges like those of standard strip flooring. It is harder and more stable than maple, red oak, and white oak. The flooring ranges from dark- to medium-red mahogany in color and is prefinished with polyurethane.

Finishes

Wood strip and plank flooring are usually installed unfinished for field sanding, staining, and finishing. Block flooring may come unfinished or prefinished. Parquet flooring is often impregnated with acrylic and irradiated for a very hard, durable finish. Wood may be stained and finished with wax, varnish, polyurethane, or a variety of other finishes.

Installation

Wood flooring must be installed over a suitable nailable base. Because wood swells if it gets damp, provisions must be made to prevent moisture from seeping up from below and to allow for expansion of the completed floor. Strip flooring is installed by blind nailing through the tongue. Figure 20.14 shows two methods of installing wood flooring over a concrete subfloor. In the first case, a sheet of $^3/_4$ in

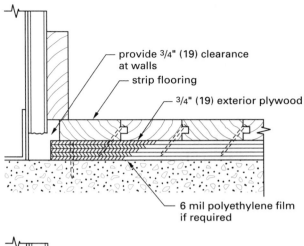

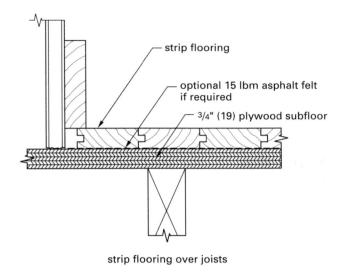

strip flooring over joists

Figure 20.15 Wood Flooring on Wood Framing

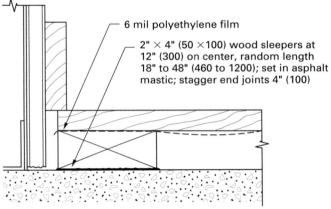

wood strip flooring over concrete

Figure 20.14 Wood Flooring Installation

(19) plywood is attached to the concrete to provide the nailable base. A layer of polyethylene film is laid down first if moisture may be a problem.

In the second case, the wood flooring is laid on wood sleepers. This method of installation not only gives a more resilient floor that is more comfortable under foot, but it also provides an air space so that any excess moisture can escape. In both instances, a gap of at least $^3/_4$ in (19) is left at the perimeter to allow for expansion and is concealed by the wood base.

Figure 20.15 shows the typical installation over wood framing with a plywood subfloor. A layer of 15 lbm asphalt felt may be laid to prevent squeaking and to act as a vapor barrier.

There are also resilient pads available that are used in place of sleepers for strip flooring installation. These provide an even more resilient floor and are often used for dance floors and gymnasium floors.

LAMINATE FLOORING

Laminate flooring is a variation of plastic laminate material. It is composed of a clear-wearing sheet over a melamine-impregnated decorative printed sheet with core layers of phenolic-impregnated kraft paper. These sheets are laminated to a high-density fiberboard core under heat and pressure and covered with a water-resistant backing sheet.

The decorative printed sheet can be made to resemble natural wood, tile, or stone, or can be printed in solid colors or even have photographic-quality images in it. Laminate flooring is available in planks (similar to wood-strip flooring but a little wider), square tiles, or rectangular blocks. It is about $^5/_{16}$ in (8) thick. It is normally laid on a cushioned foam underlayment with the tongue-and-groove edges glued together. A vapor barrier is normally required when laminate flooring is laid over a concrete floor.

Laminate flooring is hard, durable, and resistant to staining. It is gaining popularity where a less-expensive alternative to wood or other types of flooring is required. It can be used in most locations but is not recommended for rest rooms or other wet areas.

RESILIENT FLOORING

Resilient flooring is a generic term describing several types of composition materials made from various resins, fibers, plasticizers, and fillers and formed under heat and pressure to produce a thin material in either sheets or tiles. Resilient flooring is applied to a subfloor of concrete, plywood, or other smooth underlayment with mastic. Some resilient floorings may only be installed above grade; others may be placed below, on, or above grade.

Resilient flooring is available in tiles or in sheet form. Sheet flooring has several advantages over tile. Although it is more difficult to install, it provides a floor with fewer seams, which makes the floor easier to clean, more hygienic, and more resistant to moisture spills. Some types of sheet flooring even allow what few seams do exist to be sealed.

Vinyl Flooring

Vinyl tile is the term commonly used to refer to flooring based on polyvinyl chloride. It is a good, durable resilient flooring resistant to indentation, abrasion, grease, water, alkalis, and some acids. Vinyl comes in a variety of colors and patterns and is easy to install. It can be used below grade, on grade, or above grade. It must be installed over a clean, dry, smooth surface. It is slightly more expensive than vinyl composition tile.

Vinyl tiles are generally 12 in (300) squares, although some are available in 9 in (225) squares and larger sizes. Either $1/16$ in or $1/8$ in (1.6 or 3.2) thicknesses are available, but for commercial use and better residential floors, the $1/8$ in thickness is preferred.

Solid sheet vinyl, like solid vinyl tile, is a homogeneous nonlayered construction of polyvinyl chloride with color and pattern extending through the entire thickness. It is very durable and resistant to indentation and rolling wheeled traffic. Because the seams can be sealed with heat welding or solvent welding, it is an excellent floor for health care facilities, clean rooms, and industrial flooring.

Vinyl Composition

Vinyl composition tile is similar to vinyl tile but includes various type of fillers that decrease the percentage of polyvinyl chloride. Although composition tile costs less than homogeneous vinyl, it has less flexibility and abrasion resistance. Because of this, through-grain types are preferred. These are tiles where the color and pattern extend uniformly through the tile thickness. Normally, this tile is applied with mastic, but peel-and-stick types are available for residential applications. Tile is also available with an attached foam backing for greater resilience.

Rubber

Rubber flooring is made from synthetic rubber and offers excellent resistance to deformation under loads while providing a very comfortable, quiet, resilient floor. Rubber, however, is not very resistant to oils or grease, is hard to clean, and can be damaged by indentation of small objects. This flooring is available with a smooth surface or with a patterned, raised surface, which allows water and dirt to lie below the wearing surface, helping to prevent slipping or excessive abrasion. Rubber flooring is available in tiles or sheet form in several sizes and thicknesses.

Rubber sheet flooring has the same properties as rubber tile, but with fewer seams. The decorative types of flooring with raised patterns are usually specified in sheet form.

Linoleum

Linoleum is one of the traditional types of sheet flooring. It is composed of oxidized linseed oil or other binders, pigments, and fillers applied over a backing of burlap or asphalt-saturated felt. Linoleum is available as plain, battleship linoleum (which is a single color), or inlaid linoleum (which consists of multicolored patterns that extend through the thickness to the backing). Linoleum has very good abrasion and grease resistance, but it has limited resistance to alkalis. A light gage is used for residential floors and a heavy gage for commercial floors.

Cork

Cork flooring is available in tile form and is used where acoustical control or resilience is desired. However, it is not resistant to staining, moisture, heavy loads, or concentrated foot traffic. It should only be used above grade and must be sealed and waxed to protect the surface.

SEAMLESS FLOORING

Seamless flooring is a mixture of a resinous matrix, fillers, and decorative materials applied in a liquid or viscous form that cures to a hard, seamless surface. Depending on the type of matrix and specific mixture, the flooring is either poured or troweled on a subfloor. Some products are self-leveling; others must be worked to a level surface. Some products, such as epoxy terrazzo, are surface ground after they cure to produce a smooth surface.

Seamless flooring is a high-performance flooring used where special characteristics are required, such as extreme hardness, severe stain and chemical resistance, and high water resistance, and where cleanliness and ease of cleaning are required. It is used for industrial floors, commercial kitchens and food preparation plants, factories, clean rooms, laboratories, hospitals, correctional facilities, and parking garages.

Seamless flooring is applied in thicknesses from $1/16$ in to $1/2$ in (1.6 to 13), depending on the type of product. Mastics may be applied in thicknesses up to $1^1/2$ in (38). Seamless flooring is applied over a suitable base of concrete or wood subflooring with the material turned up at the walls to form an integral cove base.

CARPET

Carpet is a very versatile flooring material. It is attractive, quiet, easy to install, and requires less maintenance than many other types of flooring. If its material and construction are properly specified, it is appropriate for many interior uses.

Carpet is made from several fibers and combinations of fibers including wool, nylon, acrylic, polyester, and polypropylene. Wool, of course, is a natural material and overall one of the best for carpet. It is very durable and resilient, has superior appearance characteristics, and is easy to clean and maintain. Unfortunately, it is also one of the most expensive carpet fibers.

Nylon is an economical carpet material that is very strong and wear resistant. It has a high stain resistance and is easy to clean. However, its appearance is generally less appealing than that of other fibers.

Acrylic has moderate durability, but it has a more wool-like appearance than nylon. It is easy to maintain and has a fair crush resistance. Polyester has properties similar to those of acrylic.

Polypropylene (olefin) is used for indoor-outdoor carpet and has good durability and resistance to abrasion and fading, but it is less attractive than other carpet types and has poor resiliency.

Carpet is manufactured by tufting, weaving, needle punching, and fusion bonding. *Tufting* is the most common way of producing carpet and is done by inserting pile yarns through a prewoven backing. The tops of the yarns are then cut for cut pile carpet or left as is for level loop carpet. Weaving interlaces warp and weft yarns in the traditional manner, a method that produces a very attractive, durable carpet but is the most expensive method of manufacturing carpet. *Needle punching* pulls fibers through a backing with barbed needles. It produces carpet of limited variation in texture and accounts for a very small percentage of the total carpet market. *Fusion bonding* embeds fabric in a synthetic backing. It is used to produce carpet tiles as well as other carpet types.

The appearance and durability of carpet is affected by the amount of yarn in a given area, how tightly that yarn is packed, and the height of the yarn. The *pitch* of a carpet is the number of warp lines of yarn in a 27 in (685) width. The *stitch* is the number of lengthwise tufts in 1 in (25.4). The higher the pitch and stitch numbers, the denser the carpet. The *pile height* is the height of the fiber from the surface of the backing to the top of the pile. Generally, shorter and more tightly packed fibers result in a more durable carpet.

An important part of carpet installation is the *carpet cushion*, sometimes called *padding*. Cushion is not appropriate for all carpet installation (such as direct glue-down installation), nor is it required; however, it is recommended. Cushioning increases the life of the carpet, provides increased resiliency and comfort, helps sound absorption, lessens impact noise, and improves thermal qualities in some situations. Common cushion materials include sponge rubber, felt, urethane, and foam rubber.

Sponge rubber is made from natural or synthetic rubber and other chemicals and fillers with a facing on the top side. It is available in flat sheets or a waffled configuration.

Felt is available in four forms: hair, combination, fiber, and rubberized. Hair felt is composed of 100% animal hair. Combination felt is a mixture of animal hair and other fibers. Fiber felt is composed entirely of felt. Rubberized felt is any of the other three types with a rubberized coating on one side.

Urethane is manufactured in three different ways to produce prime, densified, or bonded sheets, each of which has a different range of densities. Thickness ranges from $1/4$ in to $3/4$ in (6 to 19).

Foam rubber is commonly applied as an integral backing to some carpet. It is natural or synthetic latex rubber with additives and with a backing on one side.

Carpet flammability is regulated in the building codes in two ways. The first limits the carpet's ability to ignite and sustain a fire if it is the first item ignited, and the second limits its flammability when subjected to the heat and flame of a fully developed fire. To prevent carpet from igniting and spreading fire when exposed to something like a dropped match, current federal law requires all carpet manufactured and sold in the United States to meet the requirements of ASTM D-2859, *Standard Test Method for Flammability of Finished Textile Floor Covering Materials*. This is more commonly known as the Methenamine Pill Test, or simply, the pill test. It is also known by its earlier designation, DOC FF-1. In this test a methenamine tablet is ignited in the center of a 9 in (229) carpet square. The distance the carpet burns beyond the center point is measured, and if the carpet burns to within 1 in (25) of the edge of an 8 in (203) distance from the center, the sample fails.

The second way of regulating carpet flammability is by limiting the degree to which a carpet sustains fire. This is done in the IBC with the flooring radiant panel test, NFPA 253 (which is discussed in the section on finishes in Ch. 29). Refer to Ch. 8 for more information on the sustainability aspects of carpet.

PAINTING

Painting is a generic term for the application of thin coatings of various materials to protect and decorate the surfaces to which they are applied. Coatings are composed of a *vehicle*, which is the liquid part of the coating, and the body and pigments if the coating is opaque. The vehicle has a non-volatile part called the *binder* and a volatile part called the *solvent*. The binder, along with the body, forms the actual film of the coating, and the solvent dissolves the binder to allow for application of the coating. The solvent evaporates or dries, leaving the final finish. The body of most quality paints is titanium dioxide, which is white. Pigments give paint its color.

Paints are broadly classified into solvent-based and water-based types. Solvent-based coatings have binders dissolved in or containing organic solvents, and water-based coatings have binders that are soluble or dispersed in water.

Clear, solvent-based coatings include varnishes, shellac, silicone, and urethane. When a small amount of pigment is added, the coating becomes a stain, which gives color to the surface but allows the appearance of the underlying material to show through. Stains are most often used on wood. For interior applications, clear coatings can be used. It is not necessary to have a pigment to protect an interior surface as is usually required for exterior surfaces.

Oil paints use a drying oil, or curing oil, as a binder. Linseed oil was traditional, but other organic oils have also been used. Today, synthetic alkyd resin is used as the drying oil. Oil paints are durable but have a strong odor when being applied and must be cleaned up with solvents such as mineral spirits. In addition, they cannot be painted on damp surfaces or on surfaces that may become damp from behind.

In many remodeling projects old paint must be removed. If the building is old enough to have lead-based paint, local regulations may require that the lead paint be removed from some types of residential occupancies by a licensed company using approved methods for removal and disposal. Sometimes, resheathing the wall is an acceptable alternative.

Latex paints are water based, with vinyl chloride or acrylic resins as binders. Acrylic latex is better than vinyl latex. Both can be used indoors as well as outdoors and can be thinned with water.

For more durable finishes, epoxy is used as a binder for resistance to corrosion and chemicals. Epoxies also resist abrasion and strongly adhere to concrete, metal, and wood. Epoxy is considered a high-performance coating and requires skilled applicators. The fumes are noxious, so special ventilation is usually required for on-site application.

Urethane is also considered a high-performance coating. It is used for its superior resistance to abrasion, grease, alcohol, water, and fuels. Interior applications most often include clear coverings for wood floors. Exterior applications include clear or pigmented paint for anti-graffiti coatings. Polyurethane paint is sometimes used for its strictly aesthetic qualities because it can have a very high-gloss finish with an almost glass-like sheen.

Successful application of coatings depends not only on the correct selection for the intended use, but also on the surface preparation of the substrate, the primer used, and the method of application. Surfaces must be clean, dry, and free from grease, oils, and other foreign material. Application can be done by brushing, rolling, or spraying. The amount of coating material to be applied is normally specified as either wet or dry film thickness in mils (thousandths of an inch) for each coat needed. The coating should be applied under dry conditions when the temperature is between 55°F and 85°F (13°C and 29°C).

As discussed in Ch. 8, all paints and other coatings must have volatile organic compounds (VOCs) that meet the requirements of the Clean Air Act. Most paints and common architectural coatings now meet the federal requirements. However, some specialized coatings may not, and these should be investigated before they are specified. Some jurisdictions, most notably California, have stricter standards.

VERTICAL TRANSPORTATION

Vertical transportation is a term that describes all the methods used to move people and materials vertically. This includes passenger and freight elevators, escalators, dumbwaiters, vertical conveyors, moving ramps, wheelchair lifts, and platform lifts, as well as stairs, ramps, and ladders.

HYDRAULIC ELEVATORS

Hydraulic elevators are one of the two major elevator types used for the movement of people and freight; the other is electric elevators. Hydraulic elevators are lifted by a plunger, or *ram*, set in the ground directly under the car and operated with oil as the pressure fluid. As a consequence, the cylinder for the ram must be extended into the ground to a depth the same as the elevator's full height.

Because the ram must be set in the ground and speed is limited, hydraulic elevators are only used for passenger and freight loads in buildings from two to six stories high, or about 50 ft (15 m). They have speeds much lower than those of electric elevators, traveling from 25 fpm to 150 fpm (0.13 m/s to 0.75 m/s) and are therefore not appropriate for moving large numbers of people quickly. Single-ram elevators have weight capacities from 2000 lbm to 20,000 lbm (1000 kg to 10 000 kg), and multiple-ram units can lift from 20,000 lbm to 100,000 lbm pounds (10 000 kg to 50 000 kg).

A few variations of the standard hydraulic elevator are available. The holeless hydraulic uses a telescoping plunger set in the shaft next to the cab. Lift is provided by applying force to the upper members of the car frame. Another type uses a roller chain mounted over a wheel mounted on top of the hydraulic plunger. With this type, the plunger is mounted above the ground in the side of the shaft.

ELECTRIC ELEVATORS

Electric elevators are the most common elevator type used for passenger service. They are capable of much higher lifts and greater speeds than hydraulic types and can be precisely controlled for accelerating and decelerating. The system employs a cab suspended by cables (known as *ropes*) that are draped over a sheave and attached to a counterweight. A motor drives the sheave, which transmits lifting power to the ropes by the friction of the ropes in grooves of the sheave. For this reason, electric elevators are also referred to as *traction elevators*. The common components of a traction elevator are shown in Fig. 21.1.

Electric passenger elevators travel from 250 fpm to 1800 fpm (1.25 m/s to 9 m/s) and have capacities from 2000 lbm to 5000 lbm (1000 kg to 2500 kg). Higher capacities are available for electric freight elevators.

Types

The two types of electric elevators are the gearless traction and the geared traction. *Gearless traction elevators* use a direct current (dc) motor directly connected to the sheave. The brake is also mounted on the same shaft. Gearless machines that are dependable and easy to maintain are used on high-speed elevators.

The *geared traction elevator* is used for slow speeds from 25 fpm to 450 fpm (0.13 m/s to 2.25 m/s). A high-speed dc or ac motor drives a worm gear reduction assembly to provide a slow sheave speed with high torque. With the many possible variations in gear reduction ratios, sheave diameters, motor speeds, and roping arrangements, geared traction machines provide a great deal of flexibility for slow-speed, high-capacity elevators.

Roping

Roping refers to the arrangement of cables supporting the elevator. The simplest type is the *single wrap*, in which the

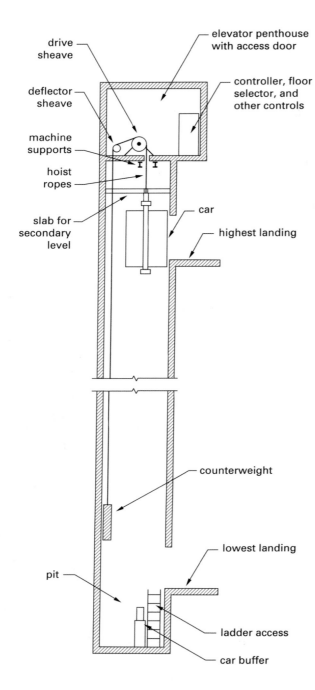

drive sheave

elevator penthouse with access door

deflector sheave

controller, floor selector, and other controls

machine supports

hoist ropes

slab for secondary level

car

highest landing

counterweight

lowest landing

pit

ladder access

car buffer

Figure 21.1 Traction Elevator

rope passes over the sheave only once and is then connected to the counterweight. For high-speed elevators, additional traction is usually required so that the rope is wound over the sheave twice. This is known as a *double-wrap* arrangement. The disadvantage to double wrapping is that there are more bends in the cable and consequently a shorter rope life.

When the rope is directly connected to the counterweight, the cable travels just as far as the car, only in the opposite direction. This is known as *1:1 roping*. When the rope is wrapped around a sheave on the counterweight and connected to the top of the shaft, the rope moves twice as far as the elevator cab. This is known as *2:1 roping* and requires that less weight be lifted. Therefore, a smaller, higher-speed motor can be used, which is desirable for speeds up to 700 fpm.

Operation and Control

Operation is the term used to describe the way the electrical systems for an elevator or group of elevators answer calls for service. *Control* describes the method of coordinating and operating all the aspects of elevator service, such as travel speed, accelerating and decelerating, door opening speed and delay, leveling, and hall lantern signals.

Many types of operating methods are available. The purpose of an operating system is to coordinate elevator response to signal calls on each floor so that waiting time is minimized and the elevators operate in the most efficient manner possible.

The simplest type of system is the *single automatic*. This was the first type of automated system for elevators without attendants and consists of a single call button on each floor and a single button for each floor inside the car. The elevator can only be called if no one is using it, and once inside, the passenger has exclusive use of the car until the trip is complete. This type of system has limited use, and is therefore best for small buildings with little traffic where exclusive use is desired.

The most common type of system for many buildings is the *selective collective operation*. With this system, the elevator remembers and answers all calls in one direction and then reverses and answers all calls in the opposite direction. When the trip is complete, the elevator can be programmed to return to a home landing, usually the lobby.

The selective collective system works well for light to moderate service requirements, but for large buildings with many elevators, *group automatic operation* is employed. This is simply the control of all elevators with programmable microprocessors to respond to calls in the most efficient manner possible, taking into account all the variables involved. In addition, such things as the time of day or day of the week can be included in the programming. This provides precise response to any building's needs.

Safety Devices

Modern elevators use many safety devices. The main brake on the sheave or motor shaft is normally operated by the control mechanism. If a power failure occurs, the brake is automatically applied. A governor also senses the speed of the car, and if the limit is exceeded, the brake is applied. There is also a safety rail clamp that grips the side rails if there is an emergency. In the pit of the elevator below the lowest landing, car buffers stop a car's motion if it over-travels the lowest stop; however, they are not designed to stop a free-falling elevator cab.

Hoistway door interlocks prevent the elevator from operating unless the hoistway door is closed and locked. In addition, various devices prevent the doors from closing on someone in their path. *Safety edges* are movable strips on the leading edge of the door that activate a switch to reopen the door if something contacts it. Photoelectric devices serve the same purpose. There are also proximity detectors that sense the presence of a person near the door and can stop the closing motion.

To prevent overloading of a car, sensors under the floor detect when the maximum weight is reached by deflection of the floor. This then makes a warning noise with additional loading and prevents the elevator from picking up any more people. Additional safety devices include multiple ropes, escape hatches in the top of the cab, alarm buttons on the car control panel, and telephones for direct communication in an emergency.

In the case of a power failure all cars will stop where they are, but most codes require that emergency power be available to operate at least one car at a time. This allows the unloading of occupied cars. Building codes require that if a fire alarm is activated, all cars return to the lobby without stopping and switch control to manual mode. The cars can then only be operated by fire fighting personnel using a manual key.

Elevators must also be accessible to the physically disabled. In lobbies this usually means visual signals that can be easily seen as well as audible signals indicating car approach, car landing, and directions of approach. Call buttons and raised and braille floor designations must be placed within certain height limitations. There is also a formula for calculating the minimum time between notification that a car has answered a call and the moment the doors of that car start to close, with a minimum time of 5 sec.

Elevator cars themselves must be sized to allow a person in a wheelchair to enter, maneuver within reach of the controls, and exit the car. Minimum clear door opening width is 36 in (915). All car controls must be no higher than 54 in (1370) for side approaches and 48 in (1220) for front approaches. The car controls must be designated by braille and by raised standard alphabet characters. Main entry floor, door open, door closed, emergency alarm, and emergency stop buttons must also be designated by standard raised character symbols.

ELEVATOR DESIGN

In simplest terms, elevator design involves selecting the capacity, speed, and number of elevators to adequately serve a particular building's population and then arranging the location of each elevator bank and the arrangement of the lobby. In addition, the roping method, machine room layout, control system, and cab decoration must be determined.

Capacity and Speed

Determining the number, capacity, and arrangement of elevators to serve a building is a complex process because there is an optimal interrelationship between the number of people to be served in a given time period, the maximum waiting time desired, cost, and particular requirements of the building. For example, a hospital elevator moves large numbers of people but also must have provisions for stretchers and large quantities of supplies. The elevator in a corporate headquarters building may handle a great deal of interfloor traffic, whereas one in an apartment building will primarily move people from the lobby up to their floors and back down again.

For most buildings the *handling capacity*, or number of people to be served, is usually based on a 5-minute peak period. For office buildings, this is usually the time in the morning when everyone is coming to work. The number of people a car can carry is a function of its capacity, which is measured in weight. Through experience, some general guidelines have been established for recommended capacities based on building types and rough building areas. These are shown in Table 21.1.

The capacities listed in Table 23.1 are in pounds. The equivalent SI units are approximate and are based on 1 kg being equal to 2.2 lbm. The corresponding SI units of elevator capacity are shown in Table 21.2.

The maximum number of passengers in a car is directly related to the capacity in weight. Table 21.3 gives the car passenger capacity based on weight capacity.

General recommended elevator speeds are also available based on the number of floors served and the general size of the building. The higher speed translates to shorter intervals, or waiting time, but there are some limits due to overall travel distance (number of floors). Higher-speed elevators also generally cost more. Recommended elevator speeds are shown in Table 21.4.

Number of Elevators Required

Based on the car capacity and speed, along with such particular characteristics of the elevator functioning as door opening and closing time, delays at stops, and so forth, the average round trip time can be calculated, and then the

Table 21.1

Recommended Elevator Capacities

building type	building size (lbm) small	medium	large	service elevator (lbm)
offices	2500/3000	3000/3500	3500/4000	4000–6500
garages	2500	3000	3500	–
retail	3500	3500	4000	4000–8000
hotels	3000	3500	3500	4000
apartments	2000/2500	2500	2500	4000
dormitories	3000	3000	3000	–
senior citizens	2500	2500	2500	4000

Table 21.2

Metric Equivalents of Elevator Capacity

capacity (lbm)	standard capacity (kg)
2000	1000
2500	1250
3000	1500
3500	1600
4000	2000
6500	3200
8000	4000

Table 21.3

Car Passenger Capacity

elevator capacity (lbm)	elevator capacity (kg)	maximum passenger capacity
2000	1000	12
2500	1250	17
3000	1500	20
3500	1600	23
4000	2000	28

Table 21.4

Recommended Elevator Speeds (in ft/min)

number of floors	small	medium	large	service
offices				
2–5	250	300/400	400	200
5–10	400	400	500	300
10–15	400	400/500	500/700	400
15–25	500	500/700	700	500
25–35	–	800/1000	1000	500
35–45	–	1000/1200	1200	700
45–60	–	1200/1400	1400/1600	800
over 60	–	–	1800	800
garages				
2–5	200			
5–10	200–400			
10–15	300–500			
hotels				
2–6	100–300			200
6–12	200–500			300
12–20	400–500			400
20–25	500/700			500
25–30	700/800			500
30–40	700–1000			700
40–50	1000–1200			800
apartments/dormitories, senior citizen housing				
2–6	100			200
6–12	200			200
12–20	300–500			200
20–25	400/500			300
25–30	500			300

handling capacity of one car in a given 5-minute period can be determined. The exact procedure for doing this is complicated and involves probability of number of stops, highest floor reached, and other variables.

The number of elevators required is then found by taking the total number of people to be accommodated in a 5-minute peak period and dividing by the handling capacity of one car. The *interval*, or average waiting time for an elevator to arrive, can then be checked to see if it is acceptable. Recommended intervals vary with the type of building. For diversified offices the time is between 30 and 35 sec. For hotels and apartments it is from 40 to 70 sec or more.

The speeds in Table 21.4 are in feet per minute. The equivalent SI units are approximate and are based on 1 m/sec being equal to about 200 fpm. These are listed in Table 21.5.

Location and Lobby Design

Elevators should be grouped near the center of a building whenever possible. At the lobby level, they should be easily accessible from the entrance and plainly visible from all points of access. In all but the smallest installations, there should be a minimum of two elevators so that one is available if the other is being serviced. Consideration should also be given to obvious traffic generators such as subway entrances, parking garage doors, and the like. Service elevators may be remotely located from passenger elevators as required by the building function.

Elevator lobbies should be designed so that it is easy to see all hall lanterns from one point and to minimize walking distance from any one point to the car that happens to arrive. This is especially important for barrier-free design. Adequate space must also be available so that people can wait without interfering with other circulation. There should never be more than eight cars in a group or more

Table 21.5
Metric Equivalents of Elevator Speed

speed	
(fpm)	(m/s)
100	0.5
200	1
250	1.25
300	1.5
400	2
500	2.5
700	3.5
800	4
1000	5
1200	6
1400	7
1600	8
1800	9

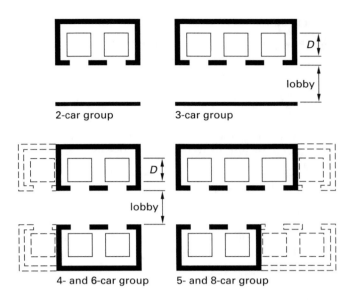

grouping	relative to D	but no less than	other
2 car	D		
3 car	$1.5 \times D$	6 ft (1800)	
4 car	1.5 to $2 \times D$	10 ft (3000)	4 cars in line $1.5 \times D$, min. 8 ft (2400)
5 car	1.5 to $2 \times D$	10 ft (3000)	
6 car	1.75 to $2 \times D$	10 ft (3000)	
8 car	$2 \times D$	max. 14 ft (4200)	lobby open both ends

Note: Maximum of 5'0" (1500) from center line of lobby to wall for barrier-free design

Figure 21.2   Elevator Lobby Space Requirements

than four cars in a line. Figure 21.2 shows the recommended lobby layouts for various numbers of cars and the minimum space requirements based on the depth of the car.

As buildings get taller and larger, the number of elevators required to adequately serve all floors increases, and the proportion of elevator shaft area to total floor area increases beyond economic levels. In addition, it becomes impossible for a single elevator to serve more than about 12 to 15 floors without exceeding acceptable waiting and total travel times. To solve these problems, several methods of elevatoring have been developed.

The first method simply divides the total number of elevators into banks that serve separate zones of the building. For example, the first bank may serve floors 1 through 14 while the second bank serves the lobby floor and floors 14 through 28. Additional banks can be added for taller buildings. Although this method keeps waiting and total travel times at acceptable levels, the elevator shafts still take up considerable floor space, especially on the lower floors.

The second method is the sky-lobby concept. One or more intermediate lobbies are placed in very tall buildings and large-capacity, high-speed elevators take people from the first floor lobby to the sky lobby where they transfer to elevators serving the upper floors. This method reduces the amount of space occupied by elevators, because the shafts do not extend the full height of the building. It also works well for multi-occupancy buildings such as those with apartments, offices, and parking.

The third method uses stacked, or double-deck, elevator cabs. At the main terminal level, traffic going to even-numbered floors is directed to one floor, and traffic going to odd-numbered floors is directed to an adjacent floor. This method effectively doubles shaft capacity, reducing the area required for elevators while decreasing the number of local stops.

Doors

Doors are an important part of elevator design because of their effect on passenger convenience and round-trip time. If a car makes 10 stops on a trip, a difference in opening and closing time of only 1/2 sec can add 10 sec to the interval time and make an otherwise satisfactory design unacceptable. Doors can be either center opening or side opening and single speed or two speed. Single-speed, center-opening doors are common and allow faster passenger loading and unloading than do side-opening doors.

Two-speed, side-opening doors have two leaves, one of which telescopes past the other as they move. Two-speed, center-opening doors have four leaves. The minimum opening width is 3 ft 6 in (1070), but 4 ft 0 in (1220) is better because it allows two people to easily and quickly enter or leave at the same time.

Machine Rooms

Machine rooms are best located directly above the hoistway and must provide adequate space for the motor, sheave, brake, controller board, speed governor, floor selector mechanism, and motor generator. All of these require minimum clearances for servicing and access. The exact size varies with manufacturer and type of elevator, but in general the machine room must be about as wide as the hoistway and from 12 ft to 16 ft (3660 to 4880) deeper than the hoistway.

Minimum ceiling height ranges from 7 ft 6 in (2290) to over 10 ft 0 in (3050). In addition to this dimension, the distance from the floor of the top landing to the underside of the machine room floor can be substantial, from about 15 ft to 30 ft (4570 to 9140) depending on the type, speed, and capacity of the elevator.

FREIGHT ELEVATORS

Freight elevators are designed and intended to transport only equipment and materials and those passengers needed to handle the freight. Elevator codes classify these elevators into five groups: A, B, C1, C2, and C3. Class A is for general freight, and no item can exceed one-fourth of the rated capacity of the elevator. The rating cannot be less than 50 lbm/ft^2 (240 kg/m^2) of platform area. *Class B* elevators are those used for motor vehicle loading and are rated at no less than 30 lbm/ft^2 (150 kg/m^2). *Class C* elevators are for industrial truck loading based on 50 lbm/ft^2 (240 kg/m^2). Class C1 includes the truck; Class C2 does not include the truck; and Class C3 is for concentrated loading with the truck not carried and with increments greater than 25% rated capacity.

Freight elevators are commonly available in capacities from 2500 lbm to 8000 lbm (1250 kg to 4000 kg), with some multiple-ram hydraulic elevators capable of lifting up to 100,000 lbm (50 000 kg). Speeds range from 50 fpm to 200 fpm (0.25 m/s to 1 m/s), with speeds up to 800 fpm (4 m/s) available for very tall buildings. With freight elevators, interval time is not as important as capacity, so the speeds are much less than those of passenger elevators.

ESCALATORS

Escalators are very efficient devices for transporting large numbers of people from one level to another. They are also useful for directing the flow of traffic.

Escalators are rated by speed and size. The industry standard speed is 100 fpm (0.5 m/s). A second speed of 120 fpm (0.6 m/s) is available for transportation and sports facilities but is not used often in other applications. Three sizes are available: 32, 40, and 48 in (800, 1000, and 1200).

The actual tread widths of these sizes are 24, 32, and 40 in (600, 800, and 1000), respectively. Because the 40 in size does not increase the capacity of a 32 in escalator in actual use, the two most common sizes are 32 in and 48 in (800 and 1200).

The actual observed capacity of people using escalators is somewhat less than the theoretical maximum capacity. This is because under crowded conditions, people tend to space themselves on every other step on 32 in models and on an average of every step on 48 in models. Observed capacity ranges from 2300 people per hour for a 32 in escalator to 4500 people per hour for a 48 in model.

Escalators are housed in a trussed assembly set at a 30° angle. The motors, drives, and other mechanisms extend below the treads and floor at both the top and bottom of the assembly, so this must be taken into account when calculating head height clearance and floor-to-floor heights. See Fig. 21.3.

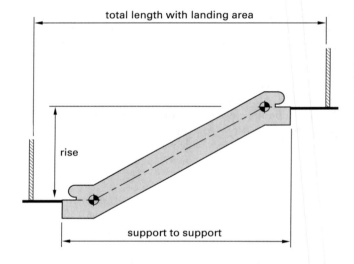

Figure 21.3 Escalator Configuration

If more than one floor is traversed by escalators, the directional flow of people should be maintained at each landing so that it is possible to get off one escalator, turn, and step onto the next without having to backtrack the length of the opening. In addition, there must be sufficient space for people to bunch as they are waiting to get on and to disperse once they get off.

STAIRS AND RAMPS

Stairs are one of the most basic types of vertical circulation—as old as buildings themselves. Because they affect the safety of all buildings in which they are used, they must be designed correctly.

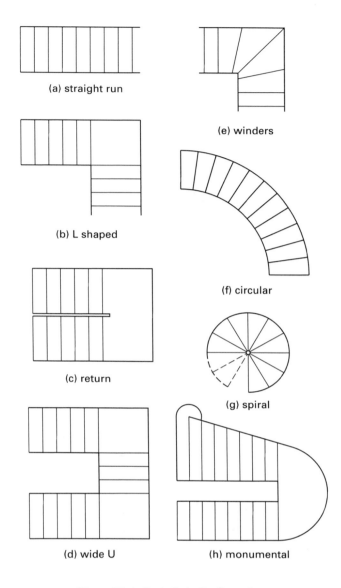

Figure 21.4 Basic Stair Configurations

may project from the face of the open side of the stair. L-shaped stairs can have equal or unequal legs.

Once the basic configuration of a stairway has been determined, the width, total run, and landing depths and widths determine how much space is required. Figure 21.5 shows the minimum dimensions for laying out a stairway in plan view, including a landing. The total run depends on the depth of the treads and the number of risers and landings that will be used.

The minimum width of any stair is 36 in (914), or 44 in (1118) when the occupant load exceeds 50. Handrails may project a maximum of $4^{1}/_{2}$ in (114) on both sides of a stairway.

In addition to the requirements shown in Fig. 21.5, building codes limit the use of special types of stairs. These include winding, circular, and spiral stairways. They are only allowed as private stairways in homes, apartments, condominiums, and the like.

Winding stairways have tapered treads that are wider at one end than at the other. See Fig. 21.6(a). When circular stairways have a smaller radius than is required by code, they are classed as winding stairways. When winders are used they should all be the same shape and size.

Circular stairways have sides shaped as a circular arc. The inside, smaller arc cannot be less than twice the width of the stair. See Fig. 21.6(b). If it is, the stairway is considered a winding stairway.

Stairways may be classified into two broad categories: those used for strictly utilitarian purposes, such as exit stairs, and monumental stairs designed to be a prominent design feature as well as provide vertical access. Whichever type is used, there are common design features that must be incorporated. This section elaborates on some of the basic building code requirements given in Ch. 29.

A stair's design and detailing begins with deciding on its basic configuration and shape, the approximate amount of space it requires, and the geometry of its layout. Some of the most common configurations are shown in Fig. 21.4. Each of these types has many variations. For example, a simple straight-run stair may be enclosed or partially open, it may be interrupted with several landings, or the landings

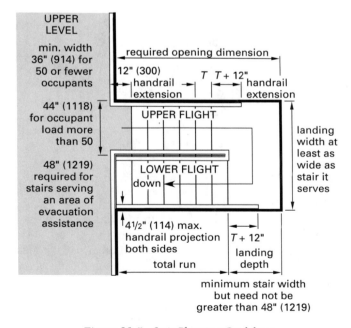

Figure 21.5 Stair Planning Guidelines

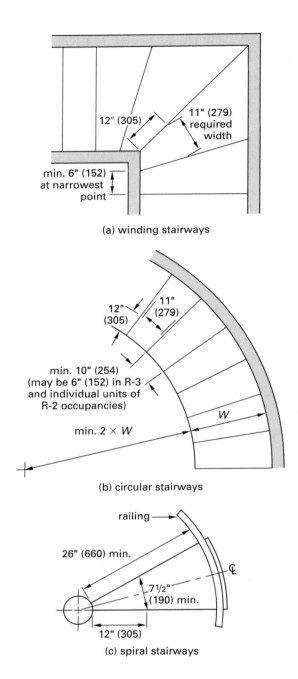

(a) winding stairways

(b) circular stairways

(c) spiral stairways

Figure 21.6 Building Code Requirements for
Nonstraight Stairs

Spiral stairs use wedge-shaped treads that radiate from a center support column, as shown in Fig. 21.6(c). The allowable riser height is greater than for other stairs; it must be enough to provide a minimum headroom height of 6 ft 6 in (1981) but cannot be greater than 9½ in (241).

For enclosed exit stairways with doors adjacent to landings, the codes require that the door not intrude into the required exit path more than a certain distance, either as the door is

opening or when the door is fully opened. IBC requirements are shown in Fig. 21.7. Although the dimensions in Fig. 21.7 do not include any allowance for evacuation assistance space, if it is required, these areas are normally provided in the building exit stairways.

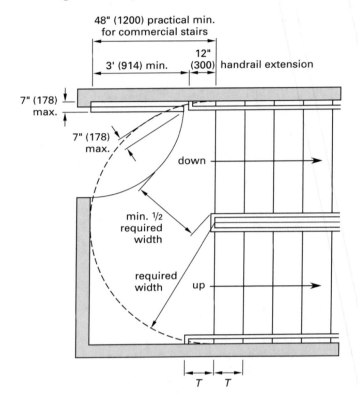

Figure 21.7 Building Code Requirements for
Enclosed Exit Stairs

The basic design and code requirements for vertical dimensions of stairs are shown in Fig. 29.8 along with the related discussion in that chapter.

Extensive research has determined the best dimensions for the rise and treads of stairs and the safest and most comfortable proportion between the two. The maximum rise and minimum tread dimensions of 7 in and 11 in (178 and 279), respectively, represent some of the most current research, including considerations for the physically disabled. Some researchers recommend that treads be even wider, from 12 in to 14 in (305 to 356). The tread of a stair is considered the horizontal projection of the distance from the edge of one nosing to the next. It does not include any part of the tread under the nosing.

Because stair dimensions are based on the normal stride of a person while ascending and descending a stair, various formulas have been used to determine one dimension based on the other. For example, a formula can be used to determine the total number of stairs when the total rise is known and the number of risers must be a whole number without exceeding 7 in or 8 in (178 or 203) on private stairways. Some of these formulas include the following (where R equals riser height and T equals tread depth).

$$2R + T = 25 \qquad 21.1$$

$$RT = 75 \qquad 21.2$$

$$R + T = 17 \qquad 21.3$$

$$T = 20 - \frac{4R}{3} \qquad 21.4$$

Some of these formulas are rather old and represent proportions that were comfortable for people who, on average, were slightly smaller than the average size of people today. Formula 21.1, for example, was developed in the seventeenth century and originally stipulated that twice the riser plus the tread be between 24 and 25. Now the minimum should be 25 and may be increased to 26. Of the four formulas, 21.1 gives the widest tread based on a given riser height if the value of 25 is used, and can be used in most designs. A wider tread is generally the safest, especially for descending stairs.

The total run of a stair is calculated by taking the total rise in inches (mm) and dividing by an estimated riser height, usually 7 in (178). If the result is not a whole number, the required number of risers is the next highest whole number. This number is then divided into the total rise to obtain the actual required riser height. The number of treads for a straight-run stair is one less than the number of risers, and this number is multiplied by the tread dimension to obtain the total required run.

The maximum distance between landings is 12 ft (3660); however, some research suggests that 9 ft (2740) is a better dimension, especially for the physically disabled. The top and bottom treads should have contrasting strips at nosings for visually impaired people.

Tread design is an especially important part of stair design. The important parts of treads include their depth, material, and nosing design. The depth of treads must be enough to provide safe footing for both ascending and descending as discussed previously. The material should be a nonslip surface, but not so rough that people get their feet caught on the nosing when descending. Any nonslip material designed into the nosing should be level with the rest of the tread.

Safe and accessible design requires that nosings not be abrupt and that they have a maximum rounded edge of $\frac{1}{2}$ in (13).

Ramps are another type of vertical transportation used for minor transitions between floor levels. The requirements for ramps are covered in Ch. 30.

MATERIALS AND METHODS— SAMPLE QUESTIONS

This chapter contains sample questions related to materials and methods of construction that are reviewed in Chs. 12 through 21. To treat this chapter as a sample test, allow about 50 minutes to answer the questions.

1. Which of the following is NOT a copper alloy?

 A. Monel metal

 B. Muntz metal

 C. nickel silver

 D. All are copper alloys.

2. For a large building being planned with a two-level basement used for meeting rooms, which of these water-related soil problems would be the most important to solve?

 A. uplift pressure on the lowest slab

 B. moisture penetration caused by hydrostatic pressure

 C. deterioration of foundation insulation

 D. reduced load-carrying capacity of the soil

Questions 3 and 4 refer to the following sketch.

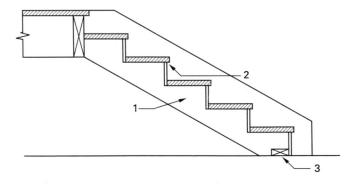

3. What is the purpose of the block shown at 3?

 A. to counteract the thrust of the stair

 B. to provide a nailing base for the riser board

 C. to give lateral stability to the vertical supports

 D. to help locate and lay out the stair

4. The parts identified as 1 and 2 are which of the following, respectively?

I. tread

II. nosing

III. carriage

IV. ledger

V. stringer

 A. III and I

 B. III and II

 C. IV and V

 D. V and I

5. Tempered glass is required in

 A. entry doors

 B. sidelights with sills below 18 in

 C. glazing within 1 ft of doors

 D. all of the above

6. If a soil is analyzed as being primarily silty, how should it be characterized?

 A. very fine material of organic matter

 B. rigid particles with moderately high bearing capacity

 C. particles with some cohesion and plasticity in their behavior

 D. smaller particles with occasional plastic behavior

7.   In the sketch shown, where should the vapor barrier be located?

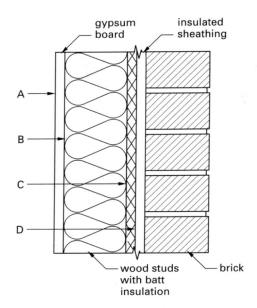

8.   What type of glass would probably NOT be appropriate for a 10-story building?

    A.   tempered
    B.   annealed
    C.   heat-strengthened
    D.   laminated

9.   A fire-rated gypsum board partition must always consist of

    A.   Type X gypsum board
    B.   full-height construction
    C.   attachment according to testing laboratory standards
    D.   all of the above

10. Which mortar type has the highest compressive strength?

    A.   M
    B.   N
    C.   O
    D.   S

11. What type of brick would most likely be specified for an eastern exposure in New Hampshire?

    A.   NW
    B.   FBX
    C.   MW
    D.   SW

12. In order to achieve the most uniform, straight-grain appearance in wood paneling, which of the following should be specified?

    A.   plain slicing
    B.   rotary slicing
    C.   quarter slicing
    D.   half-round slicing

13. Asphalt-impregnated building paper is used under siding to

    A.   improve thermal resistance
    B.   increase the water resistance of the wall
    C.   act as a vapor barrier
    D.   all of the above

14. Which area in the masonry wall assembly shown would be most susceptible to water penetration?

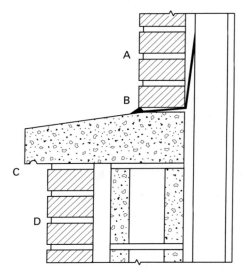

15. Expansion joints in concrete walks should be located at a maximum of what spacing?

    A.   5 ft
    B.   10 ft
    C.   20 ft
    D.   25 ft

16. Which of the following are characteristics of stainless steel?

I.   It cannot be welded.
II.   It should not be in contact with copper.
III.   It is an alloy of steel and chromium.
IV.   It is only available with mechanical and coated finishes.
V.   It is just as strong as bronze.

A. I, II, and III

B. II, III, and IV

C. II, IV, and V

D. III, IV, and V

17. The horizontal member that holds individual pieces of shoring in place is called a

A. wale

B. breast board

C. raker

D. none of the above

18. When the architect is on the job observing concrete placement, what is most likely to be of LEAST concern?

A. height of a bottom-dump bucket above the forms as the concrete is being placed

B. type of vibrator being used

C. location of the rebar in relation to the forms

D. method of support of the forms

19. A nominal 3 × 6 piece of lumber is classified as which of the following?

A. timber

B. board

C. dimension

D. yard

20. Select the INCORRECT statement from among the following.

A. The larger the pennyweight, the longer the nail.

B. Design values for bolts are dependent on the thickness of the wood in which they are located.

C. Split-ring connectors are often used for heavily loaded wood structures that must be disassembled.

D. In general, lag bolts have more holding power than large screws.

21. What cement would be used in slip-form construction?

A. Type I

B. Type II

C. Type III

D. Type IV

22. Which of the following most affects lumber strength?

A. split

B. wane

C. check

D. shake

23. What variable is used to measure the rate of heat transfer in a thickness of material?

A. conductivity

B. coefficient of heat transmission

C. resistance

D. conductance

24. Which of the following would be LEAST appropriate for insulating a steel stud wall?

A. polystyrene boards

B. rock wool

C. fiberglass batts

D. perlite boards

25. Three courses of a bull stretcher using a standard brick and standard mortar joints equal

A. 8 in

B. 12 in

C. 15 in

D. 18 in

26. Which of the sketches depicts a half-surface hinge?

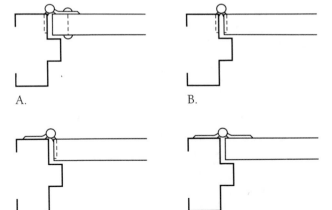

A.   B.

C.   D.

27. Select the INCORRECT statement concerning fire-rated door assemblies.

A. Hinges must always be the ball-bearing type.

B. Under some circumstances a closer is not needed.

C. Labeling is required for both the door and frame.

D. The maximum width is 4 ft 0 in.

28. Which of the following would be most appropriate for dampproofing an above-grade concrete wall with a moderately rough surface?

    A. cementitious coating
    B. bituminous coating
    C. synthetic rubber
    D. silicone coating

29. The depth of elevator lobbies serving four or more cars should generally not be less than

    A. 6 ft
    B. 1½ times the depth of the car
    C. 10 ft
    D. 3 times the depth of the car

30. Which of the following would probably NOT be reasons for using a copper roof?

I.   workability
II. resistance to denting
III. cost
IV. corrosion resistance

    A. I and II
    B. I and III
    C. II and III
    D. III and IV

31. If cracking occurred along the joints of a brick wall in a generally diagonal direction from a window corner up to the top of the wall, which of the following would most likely be the cause?

    A. lack of vertical control joints
    B. horizontal reinforcement placed too far apart
    C. poor grouting of the cavity
    D. inadequate mortar

32. What is used to keep water from penetrating an expansion joint at the intersection of a roof and wall?

    A. base flashing
    B. counterflashing
    C. sealant
    D. coping

33. The portion of paint that evaporates or dries is called the

    A. binder
    B. pigment
    C. solvent
    D. vehicle

34. In the partial plan of a concrete basement shown, what would be the best way to improve the economy of the concrete form work?

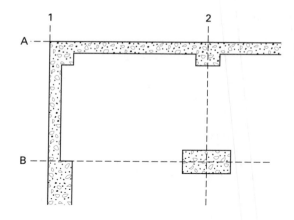

    A. Make the column square.
    B. Separate the pilaster at A2 from the wall.
    C. Form the pilaster at A1 with a diagonal.
    D. Make the wall along grid line 1 a uniform thickness.

35. Structural steel typically contains what percentage of carbon?

    A. above 2.0%
    B. from 0.50% to 0.80%
    C. from 0.20% to 0.50%
    D. from 0.06% to 0.30%

36. What is used to minimize corner chipping of concrete?

    A. chamfer strip
    B. hardeners
    C. rustication strip
    D. waler

37. In what part of a panel door is the lockset mounted?

    A. stile
    B. mullion
    C. keyway
    D. rail

38. What is the building code requirement for pairs of exit doors with astragals?

    A. weather stripping
    B. door stop
    C. coordinator
    D. flush bolts

39. What is the most important fire-resistance property of a CMU partition?

    A. overall width

    B. density

    C. joint reinforcement

    D. equivalent thickness

40. What is a requirement for a door opening in a masonry partition?

    A. bond beam

    B. arch action

    C. weep holes

    D. flashing

41. Galvanic action can be avoided by

    A. using neoprene spacers

    B. increasing the thickness of the materials

    C. reducing contact with dripping water

    D. all of the above

42. A geared traction elevator would be most appropriate for

    A. a 5-story medical office building

    B. a 16-story office building

    C. a 4-story department store

    D. an 8-story apartment building

43. In determining the width and gage of gypsum board framing, what are some of the important considerations?

I.   thickness of the gypsum board

II. spacing of studs

III. height of the wall

IV. size of piping and other built-in items

V.   number of layers to be supported

    A. I, III, IV, and V

    B. II, III, and IV

    C. II, III, IV, and V

    D. all of the above

44. Joining two metals with heat and a filler metal with a melting point above 800°F is called

    A. annealing

    B. soldering

    C. brazing

    D. welding

45. In the drawing shown, what is the purpose of the gravel?

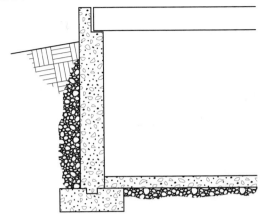

    A. to reduce hydrostatic pressure

    B. to keep the soil from direct contact with the concrete

    C. to provide a firm base for concrete bearing

    D. to hold the membrane in place and protect it

46. Which of the following statements about veneer stone is FALSE?

    A. It can be fabricated $^3/_8$ in thick.

    B. Copper or steel clamps are used to anchor the stone to the substrate.

    C. Only special types of portland cement mortar or sealants should be used in the joints.

    D. It can be supported on masonry, concrete, steel, or wood framing.

47. Which of the following is the most important consideration in detailing a wood-strip floor?

    A. flame-spread rating

    B. expansion space at the perimeter

    C. nailing method

    D. moisture protection from below

48. Which of the following are of most importance in wood frame construction?

I.   sheathing type

II. differential shrinkage

III. location of defects

IV. firestops

V.   headers

    A. I, II, and III

    B. I, II, and IV

    C. II, III, and V

    D. III, IV, and V

49. In the window elevation shown, what is represented at point 1?

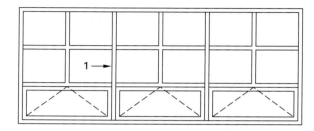

    A. mullion

    B. muntin

    C. stile

    D. rail

50. Which type of lock would be most appropriate for an entry door into an office suite?

    A. cylindrical lock

    B. unit lock

    C. mortise lock

    D. rim lock

51. Which of the following are true about built-up roofing?

I.   It may be applied on slopes from 0 in/ft to 1 in/ft.

II.   It is best applied only over nailable decks.

III.   The top layer should be protected from ultraviolet degradation.

IV.   Proper installation is more important than the number of plies.

V.   Roof insulation can be placed either above or below the roofing.

    A. I, III, and V

    B. II, III, and IV

    C. III, IV, and V

    D. I, II, IV, and V

52. Ceramic mosaic tile in a public shower room is best installed over

    A. water-resistant gypsum board

    B. a bed of portland cement mortar

    C. concrete block walls coated with a waterproofing membrane

    D. rigid cement composition board made for this purpose

53. What are two important considerations in designing a fire-rated ceiling?

I.   hold-down clips

II.   the structural slab

III.   thermal insulation

IV.   composition of the floor/ceiling assembly

V.   style of grid

    A. I and III

    B. I and IV

    C. II and IV

    D. III and V

54. What is the primary purpose of the voids in a cored slab?

    A. to allow electrical services to be concealed in the slab

    B. to make a more efficient load-carrying member

    C. to make erection easier

    D. to minimize weight

55. A reasonable elevator capacity for a medium-sized office building is

    A. 2000 lbm

    B. 3000 lbm

    C. 4000 lbm

    D. 6000 lbm

56. Select the INCORRECT statements about steel doors.

I.   Fire ratings up to $1^1/_2$ hours are possible.

II.   The frames are normally 12-, 14-, or 16-gage, depending on use.

III.   Steel doors must be used with steel frames.

IV.   Hinges or offset pivots can be used with steel doors.

V.   The standard thickness is $1^3/_8$ in.

    A. I and V

    B. II and IV

    C. I, III, and V

    D. II, III, and V

57. Which of the vertical joints shown would be appropriate for a concrete basement wall?

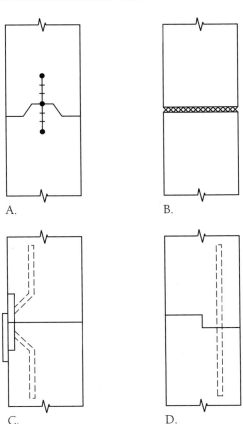

A.

B.

C.

D.

58. The allowable stress ratings for lumber in the building codes are based primarily on

    A. size groups

    B. species

    C. types of defects

    D. all of the above

59. Architectural woodwork for installation in the southwestern United States should have a maximum moisture content of

    A. less than 5%

    B. 4% to 9%

    C. 5% to 10%

    D. 8% to 13%

60. On floors subject to deflection, both terrazzo and granite installations should include

    A. a membrane

    B. a latex additive in the mortar

    C. thinset mortar

    D. a sand cushion

SECTION 4:
CONSTRUCTION DOCUMENTS AND SERVICES

CONSTRUCTION DRAWINGS AND DETAILS

Construction drawings represent the architect's final decisions concerning design, building methods, and construction technology. As such, they must show the technically correct ways of meeting the functional requirements of the design, such as keeping water out, distributing electricity, providing safe finishes, and satisfying thousands of other concerns. They must also clearly communicate the information to the contractor, material suppliers, and other people involved with the project. Finally, they must be coordinated with the specifications and the consultant's drawings. The drawings form part of the contract and are legal documents.

This chapter reviews some of the functional criteria for selecting materials and evaluating or developing details based on design development decisions and drawings. Whereas other chapters examine specific materials and construction techniques, this chapter takes a broader look at building technology. It also reviews some of the essentials in assembling a set of construction drawings and making sure they are correctly coordinated with the consultant's drawings and with the project specifications. Thorough coordination is vital in avoiding errors, cost overruns, and scheduling delays, as well as minimizing the architect's exposure to liability.

DEVELOPING AND EVALUATING CONSTRUCTION DETAILS

A building is a complex collection of component parts, all of which are connected to other parts in various ways. The manner in which an assembly of several parts is organized and connected is commonly referred to as a detail. A detail may be as simple as two bricks connected with a mortar joint or as complex as the intersection of a curtain wall, roof, ceiling, structural beam, and parapet consisting of dozens of different materials.

There are certain common functional characteristics involved with almost every category of construction detail, and the correctness of the assembly can be developed or evaluated based on these characteristics. For example, the intersection of a roof and a parapet must be designed to fulfill several functions, one of which is to drain water and avoid leakage into the structure. This holds true regardless of the roofing material or the method of wall construction. Different materials may influence certain aspects of the detail, but the intersection will always need a cant strip and positive drainage, and material expansion and contraction must be taken into account.

The following parameters cover most of the common characteristics that must be considered in a construction assembly's design or evaluation. Of course, not all of them relate to every detail, but combined with the specific information on materials given in other chapters, they should help candidates to make rational evaluations during the examination.

Compatibility with Design Intent

All building configuration begins with the desire to satisfy the program requirements and specific needs arising from these requirements. These needs and requirements must be balanced against practical considerations such as code requirements, cost, and material limitations, but even with these types of constraints there are many ways to design. Sometimes, during the long process of design and detailing, the original design intent gets lost in the practicalities of solving functional problems and making changes. A detail may work but may not look like what the client and designer originally intended.

Simple performance requirements can also be involved. This is simply the ability of the product to do its intended job. For instance, how well does an acoustical ceiling absorb sound? How slip resistant is a floor tile? In many cases, the criteria of performance can be judged against a standard test procedure.

The architect should constantly check the development of a detail against its original purpose, performance requirements, and desired appearance. For example, a client might have originally requested a simple, unobtrusive demountable partition system. Through material selection, cost analysis, and integration with other building systems, the final product may satisfy the requirements of demountability, sound transmission, cost, and finish, but may not have the clean, simple look the client wanted.

Structural Integrity

Structural integrity refers to the ability of a material or construction component to withstand the forces applied to it. These include not only the obvious natural forces of gravity, snow, wind, and seismic loading, but also other forces such as impact. The particular type of detail will determine what kinds of forces the detail must resist, and each force should be reviewed.

Some possible common forces on a detail are the following.

- live and dead loads
- wind loads
- seismic loads
- hydrostatic pressure
- forces induced by building movement
- loads induced by human use (for example, the forces produced on a door jamb through the hinge from door operation)
- loads created by one material acting as the substrate for another
- forces caused by accidental or intentional abuse
- strength properties of a material or assembly that may be necessary to resist various forces including compression, tension, shear, torsion, rupture, hardness, and impact

Safety

There are many aspects to safety, which is one of the most important elements of detailing, because the architect is responsible for protecting the health, safety, and welfare of the public. Be aware of safety concerns such as the following.

- *Structural safety.* Will the material or detail physically collapse or otherwise fail, causing harm?
- *Fire safety.* Is the material fire resistant enough for its intended use? Will it produce smoke or toxic fumes if burned? If it burns, will its failure lead to failure of adjacent construction?
- *Safety with human contact.* Is there a potential for harm when people come in contact with the material or detail? For example, will sharp edges cut people, wet floors promote slipping, or poorly designed stairs cause falls?

Security

Security is an important aspect of design today. Security can be viewed as providing protection against theft, vandalism, intentional physical harm, or a combination of all three. Common security concerns include residential and commercial burglary, employee pilferage, vandalism, sabotage or theft of company records and property, confinement of prisoners, protection of personnel, safety and confinement in psychiatric wards, abduction, and in extreme instances, terrorism.

In addition to physical barriers, security systems include methods for preventing entry, detecting intruders, controlling access to secure areas, and notification in the event of unauthorized entry or other emergencies. Refer to Ch. 10 for information on the many types of security devices.

Although the security consultant, equipment vendor, electrical engineering consultant, and contractor are responsible for designing and installing security systems and the power they need to operate, the architect is the person who must coordinate the efforts of the design team so their work fits within the overall design and construction of the project. Some of the important elements of security system coordination that may be included on the drawings and in the specifications include the following.

- Lighting required for surveillance and deterrence should be compatible with the general ambient lighting whenever possible. The electrical engineer or lighting designer should know what types of cameras are being used, in order to select the best lighting types. Lighting positions and details are shown on the architectural drawings, but detailed circuiting drawings will be produced by the electrical engineer.
- The architect must show on the architectural drawings adequate space and support for video cameras, monitors, access devices, controls, and other equipment. The actual electrical and signal circuiting will be shown on the electrical drawings.
- Conduit must be shown on the electrical consultant's drawings to accommodate signal system wiring, electric lock wiring, telecommunication wiring, and other wiring that may be provided by a separate contractor.

- Speakers that are required for public address and communication within secured areas should be shown on the architectural drawings and coordinated with other elements on the reflected ceiling plan.

- Power transfers for doors should be specified to met the necessary level of security, but should be concealed whenever possible.

Durability and Maintainability

Most building materials and details are subject to a wide range of abuses from both natural forces and human use. To the greatest extent possible, they must be able to withstand this abuse and be maintained and repaired throughout their lifetimes.

Exterior materials must have resistance to ultraviolet radiation, temperature changes, pollution, water, and atmospheric corrosion. Materials and details within human reach must be resistant to scratching and abrasion, impact, and marking.

All details must be maintainable. Can a material be cleaned easily? How will it look if it is not regularly maintained? How costly will the maintenance be? Can part of a detail be easily replaced or repaired?

Code Requirements

Of course, all details and building components must satisfy the requirements of the local building code and other statutory regulations. Checking for compliance should be an automatic reaction when developing or reviewing construction drawings. Many of these requirements have been discussed in other chapters, with reference to specific materials and areas of construction.

Construction Trade Sequence

Because all building requires the involvement of many trades and material suppliers, the best details are those that allow for construction to proceed directly from one trade to another in a timely fashion. Because labor is one of the biggest expenses of a building project, anything that can be done to minimize it saves money (within the bounds of adequate craftsmanship, of course). Organizing the detailing of a building to allow for a clear division of the labor trades can minimize interference and potential conflicts.

Each detail should be reviewed to see if its construction can proceed from one trade to another with the least amount of overlap. For example, in building a standard partition, the drywallers can install the metal framing. Then the electricians and plumbers can install conduit and piping. Then the drywallers can return, finish the wall, and leave, making way for the painters. Partition details that deviate from this standard sequence will take more time to complete and will be more costly.

Fabrication and Installation Methods

All construction details should be reviewed to ensure that they do not present building problems, such as limitations on the size and shape of assemblies due to transportation restrictions, the inability to move materials into proper position, installation difficulties, and interference with connections or construction. For example, swinging a steel beam into position and then having enough room to tighten the bolts requires certain minimum clearances. Installing a door frame in an opening requires shim space to compensate for possible deviations in plumb of the rough door opening.

Tolerances

All elements of construction are built to a different closeness to perfection. This level of perfection is typically represented by the lines and dimensions on the construction drawings. The amount of allowable variance from a given line, dimension, or size is known as *tolerance* and must be accounted for in detailing. Some construction items, such as woodwork, have a very small tolerance, sometimes as small as $1/64$ in (0.4), whereas other elements, such as poured concrete footings, may be oversized by as much as 2 in (51) and still be acceptable.

Tolerances for a great many construction components have been established by various trade organizations and are the accepted norms unless the architect specifies otherwise. However, requiring tighter tolerances than is industry standard usually requires better materials, more time, more labor, or a combination of all three. These also mean a higher cost.

Details should allow for expected tolerances. For example, a finished wood-panel wall installed over cast concrete must have enough space for shimming and blocking so that the final wall surface can be plumb, whereas the rough structural wall may be out of plumb by as much as $1/4$ in in a 10 ft height (6 mm in a 3050 mm height).

Clearances

A *clearance* is a gap or space designed to allow for the construction or installation of a material, construction element, or piece of equipment. Details must provide enough clearance to make construction possible. For example, the shim space around doors and windows is provided so the door or window unit can be slipped into the rough opening and leveled and plumbed before being attached to the framing. Structural steel connections made with bolts require sufficient room so an ironworker can use a pneumatic impact wrench.

Costs

There are three major elements of cost involved with building: materials, labor, and equipment. Other costs are overhead and contractor profit, which represent the initial costs of the structure and may change as the other costs fluctuate. However, there are life-cycle costs with which the architect and client must be concerned. What may be a low initial cost of an assembly may end up being a very expensive detail to maintain and ultimately replace. Refer to Ch. 8 for information on life-cycle cost analysis.

Cost control involves striking the proper balance between client needs, initial costs, and life-cycle costs. The client may want more than is affordable or may ask for the lowest initial costs without realizing that inexpensive materials will cost more in the long run. If the building is a speculative venture, low initial costs may be acceptable to the developer regardless of the consequences. It is up to the architect to make sure the client understands all the choices and ramifications of design and detailing decisions.

The cost of a portion of a building in proportion to the total cost is also an important concept to understand. If the entire building is going to cost $2 million, it does not make sense to spend a great deal of time and worry over saving $100 on one detail. On the other hand, if extensive research and study on a typical wall detail of the same building can save $30,000, then it is reasonable to make the effort. In another situation, saving a little money on quantity items is desirable. If just $100 can be trimmed from the construction of one hotel room, then saving this amount on a 2000-room hotel will add up to $200,000.

Of course, cost is directly related to the choice of materials, which is a function of the intended use, durability, strength, maintainability, and all the other considerations involved with designing a detail. Labor cost is largely determined by the effort required to build a detail so that, in general, construction costs can be minimized by developing simple details that still satisfy all other criteria. Equipment costs involve the purchase or rental of specialized machinery needed to build the project. Prefabricated concrete components may require large, expensive cranes to set them in place, but this cost may be more than offset by the savings in formwork and time delays involved with cast-in-place concrete.

Material Availability

Construction is a geographically localized industry. Not only does labor availability vary with location, but many different materials are found in different parts of the country. Of course, any material can be shipped anywhere else, but the cost may not be justified. Specifying southern pine for rough framing in Oregon does not make sense. Steel framing may be less expensive than concrete in parts of the country that are near mills, whereas the same steel building would be prohibitively expensive in other locales where concrete would be the logical choice.

Building Movement and Substrate Attachment

Because all details consist of a number of components connected with each other, it is important to understand that one material must provide an appropriate base for the attachment of another. This attachment may be done in one of three ways. The first is rigid, such as plaster fixed to lath: if one material moves, both move. The second is rigid but adjustable for installation, such as a curtain wall anchored to a floor beam. The third is flexible so that movement is allowed. An expansion joint is a typical example of this attachment.

Within each detail there must be space for the attaching device as well as clearance for workers. Problems with incompatible materials must also be considered, such as possible galvanic action or deterioration of one material from water leakage through another. If the materials are chemically bonded with sealants, mastics, paint, or other coatings, the base material must be compatible with the coating or the joining material.

In all cases, the detail must provide for expected building movement as discussed in other chapters. Movement is inevitable, whether it is from live, dead, or lateral loading; temperature changes; water absorption; or other forces. The amount of movement that will occur on a given detail varies, but it is always present.

Conformance to Industry Standards

Certain common methods of building are considered industry standards. These methods have been developed through practice and experience, from the recommendations of trade associations and testing organizations, and from building codes. A reinforced masonry wall should be built in a similar manner regardless of who designs it, who builds it, or what it is used for. The only things that may change to suit the particular needs of the building are the finish, the size of reinforcing, the type of mortar, and so on.

Conforming to these types of industry standards not only increases the likelihood that the detail will work, but also minimizes potential liability if something goes wrong. This is not to say that the architect should not try new design approaches or be creative in solving unusual technical problems, but that he or she should only do so when necessary.

Deviation from industry standards should be done only after precise definition of the performance requirements specified for the building assembly, after thorough research of the materials and construction techniques being proposed to meet the requirements, and by careful analysis of how the construction might actually perform. Then the final decision should be made by the client based on information and recommendations provided by the architect.

Resistance to Moisture and Weathering

Controlling moisture is one of the most troublesome areas of construction design and detailing and one of the most error prone. Specific methods of waterproofing are discussed in Ch. 20. Whenever water might be a problem, the detail should be carefully reviewed. These situations include all roofing details, exterior walls and wall penetrations, below-grade walls and slabs, pools, areas under and around showers and tubs, kitchens, mechanical rooms, and any other interior space where excess moisture is present.

Some of the considerations are as follows.

- *The permeability of the material itself.* Can it resist moisture, or must it be protected with a coating or by some other mechanical means?

- *The durability of the material.* Will aging, building movement, and other forms of deterioration cause the material to crack or break up, allowing water to penetrate?

- *Aggravating circumstances.* Will other conditions cause a normally water-resistant detail to leak? An exterior material may shed water but leak when wind-driven rain is forced in.

- *Joints.* Are joints constructed, flashed, and sealed so that water cannot enter? Will building movement damage the integrity of the joints?

- *Capillary action.* Are tiny joints or holes that can admit water inherent in the material? Brick mortar joints are a perfect example of this. The wrong type of joint can crack imperceptibly and let water that does not run off be sucked into the wall. A windowsill or coping without a drip can allow water to flow up the underside and into the structure.

- *Outlets.* If water does get into the structure, as is normal in some situations, is there a way for it to drain back out? Weep holes in masonry walls and curtain walls allow this to happen. A *weep hole* is a small opening or outlet in a wall or at the bottom of a window member through which accumulated condensation or water can drain to the exterior. Another example of a weep hole is the small extension of metal framing at the lower portion of skylights that collects the condensation that forms inside the glass and drips down.

- *Sealants.* Have the proper types of sealants been selected for the type of material used and for the expected movement of the joint? Is the backup material correct, and is the sealant installed with the correct dimensions?

In addition to precipitation, other forms of weathering include ultraviolet degradation, freeze-thaw cycles, and atmospheric corrosion. Materials must be selected to withstand the expected conditions.

Thermal Resistance

When necessitated by the detail's location, the detail's resistance to heat transfer, including both heat loss and heat gain, must be investigated. Of course, the resistance of the insulation must be checked, but in addition, the prudent architect will look for possible paths of air infiltration and insulation breaks where the full thickness of the insulation is not present. Exterior studs, pipes penetrating walls, and metal door frames are examples of areas where there is a weakness in the insulation value of the exterior wall.

Sustainability

With greater interest in the sustainability of buildings in general, architects must also review details, in particular, with an eye toward the environmental impact of details and how buildings are put together. Some of the same criteria for evaluating building materials that were discussed in Ch. 8 can be used as detailing guidelines for sustainability. These include the following.

- The embodied energy of the materials used in the detail should be as low as possible. This includes materials that are hidden, like blocking or bracing, as well as the obvious finish materials.

- As many of the materials and components as possible should be made from renewable materials or have recycled content.

- Details should reduce energy consumption in the building. Something as simple as adding insulation in a small gap in a detail could yield significant energy savings, especially if the detail is repeated dozens or hundreds of times in a building.

- As many of the materials and components as possible should come from local sources.

- Adhesives, cleaning compounds, and finishes should have low VOC content. For example, in some cases, mechanical fasteners can be used instead of construction mastics.

- If possible, the detail should be designed to allow for easy deconstruction so the individual components can be recycled.

Other Properties

There are many other properties of materials and construction details to review when developing or evaluating drawings. These are, when applicable, such things as acoustical properties, light reflection, abrasion resistance, resistance to termites and other insects, holding power of fasteners, resistance to fading, mildew resistance, color, and finish. Of course, no material will completely satisfy all criteria, but the architect must find the best balance.

ORGANIZATION AND LAYOUT OF CONSTRUCTION DRAWINGS

Construction drawings (also known as *working drawings*) are used more often than any other part of the contract documents. In addition to representing a correctly designed and detailed building, the drawings themselves must be accurately produced and organized to clearly communicate the architect's intent.

Organization of Construction Drawings

Construction drawings are organized in a generally standardized sequence, which has been established based on the normal sequence of construction and through practice. The drawings are usually organized in the following way.

- title and index sheet
- civil engineering drawings (if any)
- site drawings (landscape)
- architectural drawings
    - demolition plan (if any)
    - floor plans
    - reflected ceiling plans
    - roof plans
    - exterior elevations
    - interior elevations
    - building sections
    - wall sections
    - exterior details
    - interior details
    - schedules
- structural drawings
- plumbing drawings
- mechanical drawings
- electrical drawings
- other consultants' drawings, such as kitchen, acoustical, and so on

Some offices vary the exact sequence of individual sheets in the architectural portion, but the preceding method is typical. The intent is to present the information in a logical sequence so that the contractors and others can find what they need without confusion.

Sheet Organization and Layering

After the borderlines and title block are drawn, the remaining drawing area is commonly organized on a module system. The exact size of the module depends on office standards, the size of the drawing sheet, and how much of the sheet is allotted for the widths of the borderlines and the title block (usually drawn along the right side of the sheet). The typical drawing module is about 6 in square (150), but this varies slightly to provide an even division of modules within the confines of the borderline. Drawings are developed to fit within one or more modules. For example, a small detail may require only one module. A wall section may require a space one module wide and three modules high. A floor plan may require the entire sheet of modules.

Using such a system allows for the development and easy use of standard or master details that are drawn to fit within the module. This system works with either manual drafting or computer-aided drafting (CAD). A standard numbering system for the modules also makes it possible for individual drawings to be numbered early in the development of the construction drawings.

Layering of drawings is the term applied to the system of placing particular information on separate layers (or levels) in a CAD system. Layering allows information to be shown or hidden so that several drawings can be developed from one computer file of information. For example, the same partition layout layer can be used for the floor plan as well as the reflected ceiling plan of a building. Individual offices may have their own layering system or use the AIA CAD layering system.

Content and Coordination of Construction Drawings

Drawings should show the general configuration, size, shape, and location of the components of construction with general notes to explain materials, construction requirements, and dimensions, and with similar explanations of the graphic material. Detailed requirements for material quality, workmanship, and other items are contained in the technical specifications of the project manual. The following is a brief description of some of the more common items that should be included with the architectural drawings. This list is by no means inclusive.

- *Site plan*: vicinity map, property description, property line locations with dimensions and bearings, benchmarks, existing structures, new building location, landscaping, site improvements, fencing, roads, streets, right of way, drainage, and limit of the work of the contract
- *Floor plans*: building configuration with all walls shown, as well as dimensions, grade elevations at

the building line, construction to remain, references to other details and elevations, room names and numbers, door swings and door numbers, window numbers, floor material indications, plumbing fixtures, built-in fixtures, stairs, special equipment, vertical transportation, and notes as required to explain items on the plan

- *Roof plans*: roof outline, overall dimensions, dimensions of setbacks, slope of roof, drainage, reference to other drawing details, roof materials, penetrations through roof, and roof-mounted equipment

- *Reflected ceiling plans*: partitions extending to and through the ceiling; ceiling material and grid lines; ceiling height notes; changes in ceiling heights; locations of all lights (including exit lights), diffusers, access panels, speakers, and other equipment and ceiling penetrations; and expansion joints

- *Exterior elevations*: structural grid center lines, vertical dimensions, floor-to-floor heights, opening heights, references to other details, floor lines, elevations of major elements, grade lines, foundation lines (dashed), material indications and notes, symbols for window schedule, gutters, signs and windows, doors, and all other openings

- *Building sections*: vertical dimensions, elevations of the tops of structural components and finish floor lines, general material indications, footings and foundations, references to other details, ceiling lines, and major mechanical services

- *Wall sections*: dimensions to grid center lines, face of wall dimensions to other components, vertical dimensions from foundations to parapet relating all elements to top of structural elements, material indications with notes, all connection methods, mechanical and electrical elements shown schematically, roof construction, floor construction, and foundation construction

- *Interior elevations*: vertical dimensions to critical elements, references to other details, openings in walls, wall finishes, built-in items, and locations of switches, thermostats, and other wall-mounted equipment

- *Schedules*: room finish schedule, door schedule, window schedule, and hardware schedule are common schedules found on most drawings. Others are louver, architectural woodwork, piling, and equipment schedules.

- *Structural drawings*: footing and foundation plans, rebar layout, framing plans, major structural sections, detail sections, pier reinforcing schedules, and connection details. Based on information from the structural engineer, the architect incorporates the exact sizes of structural members in the architectural details to coordinate construction details and make sure that sufficient space is provided for construction, clearances, tolerances, and finishes. Generally, only the overall outline of piers, footings, foundation walls, structural walls, and framing is shown on the architectural drawings. Elevations for tops of beams, structural walls, and floors are shown on both sets of drawings.

- *Mechanical and plumbing drawings*: location of mechanical equipment; layout of ductwork, pipes, fixtures, and other major components; plumbing isometrics; details of mechanical room layout; details, such as ductwork connections and pipe support; and equipment schedules. Generally, mechanical and plumbing items are only shown on the architectural drawings where they interface with other construction. Examples include the locations of grilles and registers on the reflected ceiling plan, the locations of sprinkler heads on the reflected ceiling plan, plumbing fixtures, ducts and piping when part of an architectural section or detail, and other situations where coordination with other construction elements is important. Because of the obvious potential for conflicts when different offices complete different drawings, coordination between the architect and the consulting engineers is critical.

- *Electrical drawings*: power plans; lighting plans; telecommunication plans; signal and security systems; one-line diagrams; and transformer, equipment, and fixture schedules. The number of plans will vary depending on the complexity of the project. For example, for simple projects all telecommunication and signal work may be shown on the power plan. In other cases a separate plan is developed for each system.

The electrical drawings contain information concerning the exact circuiting of lighting and power outlets, including the number and size of conductors in each conduit, the sizes of conduits, and home runs to panel boxes. A *home run* is a graphic indication (using an arrowhead and the numbers of the circuits) that the line on the drawing connecting lights or outlets is connected to particular circuit breakers in a particular electrical panel box. This graphic device is used so that the entire line does not have to be drawn to the panel box, thereby avoiding clutter on the drawing.

As with mechanical and plumbing work, electrical elements shown on the architectural drawings are for coordination and location only. For example, where the location of power outlets is critical, the architectural drawings may include a separate power and telephone plan with exact dimensions. The locations of luminaires are also shown on the architect's reflected ceiling plan so they can be coordinated with other ceiling-mounted equipment and architectural features. Usually, no other electrical information is given on these drawings. However, in some cases, the architect may want to show the locations of switches on the reflected ceiling plan.

In addition to these overall views of the construction, there are corresponding details for all portions of the work.

Information Required by Building Departments

Building codes require that certain information appear on the set of construction documents submitted for plan review. Although the exact list of required information will vary from one jurisdiction to another, the following is required by the IBC and is typical of most codes.

- In general, construction documents must be of sufficient clarity to indicate the locations, nature, and extent of the proposed work and how it will conform to the code. This normally includes the standard types of drawings of floor plans, elevations, sections, and details for architectural, structural, mechanical, electrical, and other specialty construction as well as applicable schedules and written specifications.

- A site plan must be included to show the size and location of new construction and existing structures on the site, including distances from lot lines, established street grades, and the proposed finished grades. An accurate boundary survey must be shown.

- The drawings must show all portions of the means of egress. The number of occupants to be accommodated on every floor and in all rooms and spaces must be indicated.

- The exterior wall envelope must be shown in sufficient detail to determine compliance with code provisions. Manufacturing installation instructions may also have to be included to show that the weather resistance of the exterior wall envelope will be maintained.

- Fire protection shop drawings may have to be submitted to show conformance with the code.

- Structural calculations may have to be submitted.

In addition, the local authority having jurisdiction may want to see listed on the first sheet of the drawings some or all of the following information.

- names and addresses of all design professionals responsible for the work

- street address or legal description of the property

- square footage of the building

- building type and occupancy group or groups

- occupant load calculations

- the valuation of new construction represented by the plans and specifications

COORDINATION

Because the architectural construction drawings are only a part of the entire set of contract documents, they must be coordinated with other documents. Coordination is an ongoing effort during the design and production phases. Depending on how an individual office is organized, the responsibility may fall on the project architect, project manager, or job captain.

Coordination with Consultants' Work

On nearly all projects there will be several consultants working with the architect. Small- to medium-sized jobs will have structural, mechanical, and electrical consultants as a minimum. Larger projects may have additional consultants in fire protection, civil engineering, landscape architecture, food service, elevators, curtain walls, and interior design, among others.

Each discipline develops its own drawings, so coordination among everyone on the team is critical. Although all consultants must be diligent in their efforts to work with others, the primary responsibility for overall coordination is with the architect. In the office, this responsibility usually falls on the project manager, although in smaller firms or on smaller jobs the project architect may take on this task.

There are a number of ways to accomplish coordination during the design and production of contract documents. First, periodic meetings should be held to exchange information and alert everyone to the progress of the job. At these meetings, anyone may ask questions and raise issues that may affect the work of others. Second, progress prints or electronic files should be exchanged between the architect and the consultants for ongoing comparison of work being produced. Third, the project manager must be responsible for notifying all consultants, in writing, of changes made as they occur. If computer-aided drafting is being used, base sheets or electronic information can be exchanged according to the particular methods being employed. Finally, the architect must have a thorough method of checking and coordinating the entire drawing set prior to issue for bidding or negotiation.

Correlation with the Specifications

The architectural drawings must also be coordinated with the specifications. These components of the contract documents are complementary; they both give necessary information about the design of the project. Either component alone is incomplete. They should work together without duplication or overlap.

Specifications are part of the project manual and describe the types and quality of materials, quality of workmanship, methods of fabrication and installation, and general requirements related to the construction of the project. They are normally written after production of the drawings has started and materials have been selected. Because the specifications are usually written by someone not working on the drawings, there must also be close coordination within the architect's office. Again, this is usually the responsibility of the project manager. Specifications are discussed in more detail in Ch. 24.

If a computer-aided master specification system is used, there may be a sheet of drawing coordination notes produced by the system for each section of the specifications. These can be used for checking by the people producing the drawings.

SAMPLE QUESTIONS

1. Which of the following is probably of LEAST concern to a subcontractor?

    A. the number of times equipment must be brought to the job site

    B. the types of tools required to build a project

    C. workers' skill level needed to complete the work

    D. other trades that will be working on the same part of the construction

2. An architect is reviewing a decorative wood grille wall covering in a building lobby. The grille is attached to a gypsum board partition with metal clips. In what probable order of importance should the following items be checked?

I. the spacing and size of the screws holding the clips to the partition

II. the possibility of splintering due to the way the exposed surfaces are milled

III. the flame-spread rating

IV. the method of cleaning the grille based on design and finish techniques used

V. the local code requirements for surface finishes

    A. I, II, III, V, then IV

    B. III, V, II, IV, then I

    C. III, I, V, IV, then II

    D. V, III, I, II, then IV

Questions 3 and 4 refer to the accompanying Wall Detail at 2nd Floor.

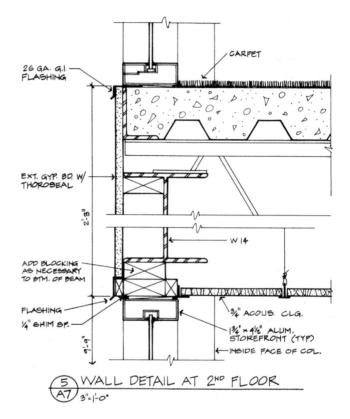

5 / A7   WALL DETAIL AT 2ND FLOOR   3"=1'-0"

3. If this detail is on an east-facing elevation in Boston, what recommendation should the architect make to the client?

    A. Modify the drip detail at the top of the window frame.

    B. Change the glazing.

    C. Add seismic fasteners for the suspended ceiling.

    D. Increase the shim space.

4. In the detail shown, which of the following would be of most concern?

    A. attachment of exterior materials to the structure

    B. possible water leakage

    C. lack of tolerance for the storefront system

    D. cracking from differential movement of materials

5. During design development for a small corporate head-quarters building, the client informs the architect that the estimated construction costs must be reduced. As far as the details are concerned, which of the following actions would most likely reduce costs?

I.   Design and specify larger tolerances.
II. Examine areas subject to maintenance and improve their quality.
III. Suggest changes that would make custom details closer to industry standards.
IV. Examine ways to reduce the number of pieces in the details.
V.   Try to reduce the number of different details involved in the project.

    A. I, IV, and V
    B. III, IV, and V
    C. II, III, IV, and V
    D. all of the above

6. Who is responsible for verifying that recessed down lights do not interfere with ductwork shown on the plans?

    A. architect
    B. electrical engineer
    C. lighting designer
    D. architect's drafting staff

7. For the project architect on a job, what is one way of ensuring that the client's design goals are being satisfied by the final set of construction documents?

    A. Hold periodic meetings with the project designer, job captain, and programmer to compare the current status of the drawings with schematic design documents.
    B. Have another architect in the office review the drawings for compliance with the original program report.
    C. Send the client periodic check sets of drawings, and request that any corrections be communicated to the architect's office within a set time period.
    D. Make a checklist of design requirements based on the original design goals, and give this to the people working on the job so that they have a constant reminder of the client's needs.

THE PROJECT MANUAL
AND SPECIFICATIONS

THE PROJECT MANUAL

The *project manual* is a bound book containing all contract and noncontract documents for a construction project, except the drawings. The project manual contains the technical specifications, but it also includes several other types of documents.

Organization of the Project Manual

The project manual is divided into four major parts: (1) bidding requirements; (2) parts of the contract itself, such as the agreement between owner and contractor, bond forms, and the like; (3) the general and supplementary conditions of the contract; and (4) the technical specifications.

A more detailed list of the project manual's contents might include some or all of the following.

- bidding requirements
  - invitation to bid
  - prequalification forms
  - instructions to bidders
  - information available to bidders
  - bid forms
- supplements to bid forms
  - bid security form
  - subcontractor list
  - substitution list
- contract forms
  - agreement (contract between owner and contractor)
  - performance bond
  - labor and materials payment bond
  - certificates of insurance
- general and supplementary conditions
  - general conditions of the contract (such as AIA form 201)
  - supplementary conditions
- technical specifications

Contracts, bidding documents, and general conditions of the contract are discussed in more detail in later chapters. This chapter focuses on the technical specifications.

Coordination with the Drawings

The technical specifications and the drawings are complementary. The drawings show the general configuration and layout of the building as well as the size, shape, and dimensions of the construction. General notes to explain the graphic representation are also included. The *technical specifications* describe the quality of materials and workmanship along with general requirements for the execution of the work, standards, and other items that are more appropriately described in written, rather than graphic, form.

The drawings, technical specifications, and other parts of the project manual must be coordinated to avoid conflicting requirements, duplication, omission, and errors. There are several areas of particular concern.

First, the specifications should contain requirements for all the materials and construction indicated on the drawings. The use of one checklist by both the specifications writer and the project manager or job captain is one way to accomplish this.

Second, the terminology used in both documents should be the same. If the term *gypsum board* is used in the specifications, the term *drywall* should not be shown on the drawings.

Third, dimensions and thicknesses should only be indicated on one document. If the thickness of flashing is included in the technical specifications, there is no need to note it on the drawings.

Fourth, notes on the drawings should not describe methods of installation or material qualities; these belong in the specifications.

When there is a conflict between the drawings and the specifications, the courts have held that the specifications are more binding and take precedence over the drawings.

SPECIFICATIONS

As previously described, specifications form part of the project manual and are legal documents. As such, they must be complete, accurate, unambiguous, and exact. Because of these needs and because specifications represent complex technical information, they are difficult to write correctly. Fortunately, some standard methods of preparing specifications are in general use. These will be described in the following sections.

In addition, master specifications are available that can be used as starting documents. A master specification is a prewritten text that includes the majority of requirements for a particular specification section. Master specifications are edited by deleting unnecessary portions, adding particular requirements for a specific job, and coordinating the requirements with other specification sections and other parts of the project manual. Master specifications are available in written form and on computer disk from various commercial sources.

Computer programs based on expert system technology are also becoming available. These generate specifications through interactive sessions with the specifier and with links to some computer-aided drafting software.

Types of Specifications

There are two broad categories of specifications: prescriptive and performance.

Prescriptive specifications (also called *closed specifications*), by specifying brand names, tell the contractor exactly what product or material to use. *Performance specifications* (also called *open specifications*) tell what results the final construction assembly should achieve, but give the contractor some choice in how they will be achieved. Most specifications fall somewhere between these two extremes.

The type of specification used will depend on several factors. Public projects almost always require open specifications in order to encourage competitive bidding. In other cases, it may be preferable to use a closed specification to ensure that only one particular product is used. Whether the job is bid or a negotiated contract may also affect the choice. With bidding, it might be best to allow the contractor as much choice as possible so that he or she can find the lowest price within the context of the specification requirements.

The following types of specifications are the ones most commonly used.

Types of Prescriptive (Closed) Specifications

Proprietary specifications are the most restrictive in that they call out a specific manufacturer's product. These give the architect complete control over what is installed. They are easier than other types to write and are generally shorter. However, they do not allow for competitive bidding, and by limiting products the architect may force the contractor to get materials that may be difficult or expensive to procure in a certain geographical area or that require excessive delivery time. Further, the burden is on the specifier to call out products that meet code requirements, are within the budget, and are technically correct.

A base bid with alternates is a type of specification that calls out a proprietary product but allows the substitution of other products that the contractor thinks are equal to the one stated. This is a dangerous method of specifying because the contractor may substitute a less expensive item that he or she thinks is equal but actually is not.

There are two variations of a base bid specification. The first lists several approved manufacturers of a product. The contractor is free to bid on any one listed. This type satisfies the requirements for public work where at least three different manufacturers must be listed, but it puts the burden on the architect to make sure that every one of the approved products or manufacturers listed is equal.

The second variation is a base bid with "approved equal" language. This specification states that one product or an approved equal must be used. This means that the contractor may propose a substitution, but it is subject to review and approval by the architect before it can be incorporated into the bid. Although this gives the contractor some freedom in looking for lower-priced alternates, it also puts the burden for finding them on the contractor. However, the responsibility for fairly and accurately evaluating the proposed alternates is placed on the architect or owner. During a hectic bidding period this can be a large burden, so the specifications should clearly state how much lead time the contractor must give the architect and how alternates will be evaluated.

Types of Performance (Open) Specifications

A *descriptive specification* gives detailed written requirements for the material or product and the workmanship required for its fabrication and installation. It does not mention trade names. In its purest form, a descriptive specification is difficult to write because the architect must include all the pertinent requirements for the construction and installation of the product.

A variation of the descriptive type is a reference standard specification. This describes a material, product, or process based on requirements (reference standards) set by an accepted authority or test method. For example, a product type can be required to meet the testing standards produced by such organizations as the American Society for Testing and Materials (ASTM), the American National Standards Institute (ANSI), or Underwriters Laboratories (UL). Reference can also be made to specific trade associations, such as the Architectural Woodwork Institute, the American Iron and Steel Institute, and the Gypsum Association.

For example, in specifying gypsum wallboard the architect can state that all gypsum wallboard products must meet the requirements of ASTM C36. This particular document describes in great detail the requirements for gypsum wallboard, so they need not be repeated. The document can instead refer to a generally recognized industry standard.

Reference standard specifications are fairly easy to write and are generally short. Chances for errors are reduced and liability is minimized by using industry standards and generally recognized building methods. However, the architect must know what is in the standard and how to refer to the appropriate part of the standard if it includes more provisions than are needed for the job.

A pure performance specification is a statement setting criteria and results required of the item being specified, which can be verified by measurement, test evaluation, or other types of assurance that the final result meets the criteria. The means of achieving the required results are not specified; they are left up to the person trying to meet the specification.

A true performance specification is often used for construction components when the specifier wants to encourage new ways of achieving a particular end result. For example, a movable partition system could be specified by stating its required fire rating, acoustical properties, finish, maximum thickness, tolerances, required size, and all the other required properties. It would then be up to the contractor and manufacturer to design and develop a system to meet the criteria.

Performance specifications are difficult to write because they require that the specifier know all the criteria, state the methods for testing compliance, and be prepared for the cost consequences.

Organization of the Technical Sections

The organization of the technical sections has been standardized through general adoption of the MasterFormat™ system. This was developed by the Construction Specifications Institute and Construction Specifications Canada to standardize the numbering and format of project-related information for use in specifying, cost estimating, and data filing. The most recent version is MasterFormat 04 and is a significant change from the previous 16-division organization that had been in use for several decades. The Construction Specifications Institute undertook the revision recognizing that the previous 16 divisions made it difficult to incorporate the increased use of building automation, signal systems, and electronic security and that the numbering system was not particularly well-suited for transportation, utility, marine, industrial, and process engineering construction.

The most recent MasterFormat division organization is shown in Fig. 24.1. There are major subgroups, with individual divisions within each subgroup. Many of the divisions are reserved for future use to allow the system to grow as new materials and technologies emerge. Most of the divisions in the Facility Construction Subgroup are essentially the same, with the same numbers as were assigned in the previous version. These include Divisions 03 through 14. Divisions 31, Earthwork, and Division 32, Exterior Improvements, are also typically used on architectural projects. The significant changes in the most recent version for architectural use include the following.

- Much of Division 01, General Requirements, covers the same material, but it has been expanded to allow for writing performance specifications for elements that overlap several specific work sections (the building envelope, for example).

- Division 02, Existing Conditions, now only covers what the name implies; namely, subsurface and other investigation, site remediation, selective demolition, and similar work. Actual site construction work groups, such as earthwork, site improvements, and planting, have been moved to the Site and Infrastructure Subgroup, Divisions 31, 32, and 33.

- Division 11, Equipment, is about the same except that equipment related to process engineering is now in the Process Equipment Subgroup, and equipment related to infrastructure is now in the Site and Infrastructure Subgroup. Most of the elements that are common to standard architectural work, such as library, audio-visual, and medical equipment, are still in Division 11.

- In Division 13, Special Construction, the work groups that deal with security access, building automation, detection and alarm, and fire suppression are now in various divisions of the Facility Services Subgroup. Special construction related to process engineering is now in the Process Equipment Subgroup.

Procurement and Contracting Requirements Group:

Division 00 – Procurement and Contracting Requirements

Specifications Group:

General Requirements Subgroup:
Division 01 – General Requirements

Facility Construction Subgroup:
Division 02 – Existing Conditions
Division 03 – Concrete
Division 04 – Masonry
Division 05 – Metals
Division 06 – Wood, Plastics, and Composites
Division 07 – Thermal and Moisture Protection
Division 08 – Openings
Division 09 – Finishes
Division 10 – Specialties
Division 11 – Equipment
Division 12 – Furnishings
Division 13 – Special Construction
Division 14 – Conveying Equipment
Division 15 – Reserved for future expansion
Division 16 – Reserved for future expansion
Division 17 – Reserved for future expansion
Division 18 – Reserved for future expansion
Division 19 – Reserved for future expansion

Facility Services Subgroup:
Division 20 – Reserved for future expansion
Division 21 – Fire Suppression
Division 22 – Plumbing

Division 23 – Heating, Ventilating and Air Conditioning
Division 24 – Reserved for future expansion
Division 25 – Integrated Automation
Division 26 – Electrical
Division 27 – Communications
Division 28 – Electronic Safety and Security
Division 29 – Reserved for future expansion

Site and Infrastructure Subgroup:
Division 30 – Reserved for future expansion
Division 31 – Earthwork
Division 32 – Exterior Improvements
Division 33 – Utilities
Division 34 – Transportation
Division 35 – Waterway and Marine
Division 36 – Reserved for future expansion
Division 37 – Reserved for future expansion
Division 38 – Reserved for future expansion
Division 39 – Reserved for future expansion

Process Equipment Subgroup:
Division 40 – Reserved for future expansion
Division 41 – Material Processing and Handling Equipment
Division 42 – Process Heating, Cooling, and Drying Equipment
Division 43 – Process Gas and Liquid Handling, Purification and Storage Equipment
Division 44 – Pollution Control Equipment
Division 45 – Industry-Specific Manufacturing Equipment
Division 46 – Reserved for future expansion
Division 47 – Reserved for future expansion
Division 48 – Electrical Power Generation
Division 49 – Reserved for future expansion

The Division Numbers and Titles used in this product are from *MasterFormat*™ 2004 Edition and the three part *SectionFormat*™ (1997 edition) outline, published by the Construction Specifications Institute (CSI) and Construction Specifications Canada (CSC), and are used with permission from CSI, 2004. For those interested in a more in-depth explanation of *MasterFormat*™ 2004 Edition and *SectionFormat*™ and their use in the construction industry contact:

The Construction Specifications Institute (CSI)
99 Canal Center Plaza, Suite 300
Alexandria, VA 22314
800-689-2900; 703-684-0300
CSINet URL: http://www.csinet.org

Figure 24.1 MasterFormat™ 04 Divisions

- Division 15 is now reserved for future expansion and all the mechanical and plumbing work groups are now in Division 22, Plumbing, and Division 23, Heating Ventilating and Air Conditioning, of the Facility Services Subgroup. See Fig. 24.1.

- Division 16 is now reserved for future expansion, and all the electrical work groups are now in Division 26, Electrical, and Division 27, Communications of the Facility Services Subgroup. See Fig. 24.1.

Another change in the new MasterFormat system is the use of six-digit numbers for individual specification sections instead of the previous five-digit numbers. In the new system the first two numbers represent the division numbers, with a leading zero used for the single-digit divisions (02, 03, 04, etc.). The next pair of numbers (digits three and four) represents the level-two hierarchy, and the last pair of numbers represents level three in the hierarchy. This change to a six-digit format allows for flexibility and room for expansion as new materials or technologies are added.

There are often several questions on the exam asking in which CSI MasterFormat section information on a particular material will be found. Know the names of the divisions, or at least those in the facility construction subgroup and the facility services subgroup, and generally what is included in them. Following are brief summaries of what is included in each division. Study these summaries along with the more detailed level-two divisions to get familiar with the correct locations of particular construction elements in the specifications.

- *Division 00, Procurement and Contracting Requirements*: This division covers requirements for bidding and contracting including bid solicitation, instructions to bidders, information available to bidders, bid forms, the agreement (contract), bonds and certificates, and general conditions of the contract, supplementary conditions, addenda, and modifications. These parts of the contract documents are discussed in Ch. 25.

- *Division 01, General Requirements*: This division includes requirements that are applicable to the entire project or all the individual technical sections. These include a summary of the work, how pricing and payment will be handled, alternates, value analysis, contract modification procedures, unit prices, construction progress documentation, submittal procedures (for samples, shop drawings, etc.), quality control, temporary facilities at the job site, product substitution procedures, owner-furnished items, special execution requirements, and final cleaning and protection of the work.

  The term *General Requirements* should not be confused with *General Conditions* of the Contract for Construction, as discussed in Ch. 25.

- *Division 02, Existing Conditions*: This division is now used to specify site remediation, site decontamination, subsurface investigation, surveying, and selective demolition, among other items related to existing conditions on a job site.

- *Division 03, Concrete*: This division covers all aspects of concrete, including forms, reinforcement, cast-in-place concrete, precast concrete, cementitious decks and underlayment, grouts, and concrete restoration and cleaning.

- *Division 04, Masonry*: This division covers all aspects of masonry, including brick, concrete block, stone, terra cotta, simulated masonry, glass block, and masonry restoration and cleaning.

- *Division 05, Metals*: The metals division includes all types of structural steel and other structural metals, ornamental metals, metal fabrications (metal stairs, ornamental ironwork, handrails, gratings, metal castings, and stair treads and nosings), as well as expansion joint covers and metal restoration and cleaning. Light-gage metal framing for partitions is located in Division 09.

- *Division 06, Wood, Plastics, and Composites*: This division covers typical structural wood framing, rough carpentry, finish carpentry, and architectural woodwork. It also includes structural plastics, plastic fabrications, wood and plastic restoration and cleaning, and the newer plastic wood and other specialty composite materials. Note that manufactured casework is in Division 12, Furnishings.

- *Division 07, Thermal and Moisture Protection*: This is the same as the previous edition of the MasterFormat and includes dampproofing and waterproofing, insulation, vapor retarders, air barriers, shingles, roof tiles, siding, membrane roofing, flashing, joint sealers, fire and smoke protection, and roofing specialties such as roof hatches, smoke vents, roof pavers, scuppers, and gravel stops.

- *Division 08, Openings*: This was formerly called Doors and Windows but contains the same elements as before, including metal doors and frames, wood doors and frames, specialty doors, storefronts, all types of windows, skylights, hardware, curtain walls, and glazing.

- *Division 09, Finishes*: The Finishes division covers all types of finish materials, including plaster, gypsum wallboard (including metal framing), all types of floor and wall tile, terrazzo, all types of flooring materials, acoustical ceilings and other types of decorative ceilings, wall coverings, acoustical treatments, paints, and other coatings.

- *Division 10, Specialties*: The specialties division covers a long list of items including visual display boards, toilet compartments, louvers, grilles, wall and corner guards, access flooring, pre-built fireplaces, flagpoles, signage, lockers, awnings, demountable partitions, storage shelving, exterior protection (sun screens, storm panels, etc.), and toilet and bath accessories.

- *Division 11, Equipment*: This division contains information for architectural equipment including vaults and security items, teller and security equipment, church-related equipment, library equipment, theater and stage equipment, musical equipment, mercantile equipment, checkroom equipment, vending machines, audio-visual equipment, loading-dock equipment, detention equipment, athletic equipment, medical equipment, mortuary equipment, and equipment for laboratories, planetariums, observatories, and offices.

- *Division 12, Furnishings*: Division 12 includes furniture, systems furniture, art, window treatments, accessories, multiple seating, and interior plants. Note especially that this division includes manufactured casework, whereas custom casework would be in Division 06.

- *Division 13, Special Construction*: Special construction covers air-supported structures, special-purpose rooms (clean rooms, saunas, planetariums, etc.), seismic control, radiation protection, lightning protection, pre-engineered structures, hot tubs, and kennels.

- *Division 14, Conveying Equipment*: Division 14 includes elevators, escalators, dumbwaiters, moving walks, and lifts.

- *Division 21, Fire Suppression*: This division contains specifications that were previously in Division 13 and includes detection and alarms and all types of fire-suppression systems, such as wet-pipe, dry-pipe, deluge, carbon dioxide, foam, pre-action, and dry chemical systems as well as standpipes and hoses. Note that fire-related materials (doors, fire-stopping, etc.) are in their respective divisions.

- *Division 22, Plumbing*: Plumbing for buildings has been relocated from the previous Division 15. Processing piping is now in the Process Equipment Subgroup.

- *Division 23, Heating, Ventilating, and Air Conditioning*: HVAC now has its own division, relocated from the previous Division 15.

- *Division 25, Integrated Automation*: This division contains specifications for the expanding technology of integrated automation, including energy monitoring and control, environmental control, lighting control, and similar topics.

- *Division 26, Electrical*: Electrical now has its own division, with specifications for communication, sound, and video in Division 27.

- *Division 27, Communications*: This division has been established for the expanding technologies and specialized nature of computer networks and all types of communications systems (cable, telephone, internet, sound systems, etc.).

- *Division 28, Electronic Safety and Security*: This division has also been established for the expanding technologies and specialized nature of security systems,

including intrusion detection, security access, video surveillance, and related topics.

- *Division 31, Earthwork*: Some of the specification items from the previous Division 2 have been moved to this division and include excavation and fill, grading, embankment, soil stabilization, erosion control, piles, caissons, and foundation walls. Most of the elements in this section are below-grade work.

- *Division 32, Exterior Improvements*: This division also contains specification items previously in Division 2 and includes mainly above-grade items like paving, utility types of fences and gates, site furnishings, play field equipment, and planting.

- *Division 33, Utilities*: Utilities contains previous Division 2 items such as water distribution, sanitary piping, septic tanks, subdrainage, storm drainage, ponds and reservoirs, and constructed wetlands.

Questions are especially difficult when they involve Divisions 10, 11, and 13. Use the following suggestions to help remember what item is in which division. Although the suggestions are sometimes superseded by exceptions, they may assist in categorizing the information. Generally, only the first two numbers (representing the division) have to be remembered if the answer choices give the full six-digit CSI number.

Division 10, Specialties, includes items that are not standard materials (like wallboard, flooring, finishes, and ceilings), are typically small scale, and are usually placed in a building in multiples. For example, visual display boards, lockers, wall and corner guards, and access flooring are typically not found in every building (they are "special"). They are small relative to the building and the spaces in the building. There is also usually more than one of them installed (more than one display board, more than one locker, and more than one corner guard).

Division 11, Equipment, includes items that are generally larger and more expensive than those in Division 10.

Division 13, Special Construction, includes much larger elements that can almost be thought of as a building within a building. Examples include air-supported structures, seismic control, and animal kennels.

Technical Section Outline and Format

The MasterFormat system also establishes a standard way of organizing any particular section. The first level of division within a section is the three-part format. This includes Part 1, General; Part 2, Products; and Part 3, Execution. All sections include these three parts; the specific articles within the parts vary with the type of material or product being specified.

Part 1 gives the general requirements for the section such as the scope of the section, submittals required, quality assurance requirements, warranties, project conditions, and specifications for the delivery, storage, and handling of materials.

Part 2 details the specifications for the materials and products themselves, including acceptable manufacturers (if applicable), standards and test methods to which the materials must conform, how items are to be fabricated, and similar concerns.

Part 3 tells how the products and materials are to be installed, applied, or otherwise put into place. This part also describes the examination and preparation required before installation, how quality control should be maintained in the field, and requirements for adjusting, cleaning, and protecting the finished work.

Figure 24.2 shows the SectionFormat™ outline, listing all the possible articles of each part.

Specifying for Sustainability

There are two main areas of a project's specifications where sustainability issues are addressed. The first is in Division 01, General Requirements, and the second is in all of the individual technical sections that cover specific materials and construction elements.

Division 01, General Requirements

In Division 01, there should be a separate specification section that applies to all the other specification sections and sets the goals and general direction of the project for sustainability and environmental quality. It is in this section that the contractor should be advised of the design requirements used by the architect and the rest of the design team in the preparation of the contract documents. These criteria can then be used if the contractor wants to propose substitutions or make enhancements.

Some of the specification articles in the general Division 01 specification section may include the following.

- A summary of the environmental goals of the project and the special requirements expected of the contractor. This summary generally includes requirements addressing three areas: resource-efficient materials and systems, energy conservation, and indoor air quality. These goals may be as simple or as complex as warranted by the project or the client's goals. If LEED™ certification is being sought, the individual credits required by LEED may be used to develop a list of requirements. Refer to Ch. 8 for information on LEED certification.

- Required submittals from the contractor. These may include manufacturer's certificates of recycled content, certification of wood products as coming from an accredited certifier (refer to Ch. 8 for information on wood certification), material emission testing reports, cleaning product information, and other documentation as may be required for LEED certification.

The architect should request that the contractor submit material safety data sheets for all products that may contain hazardous materials. A *material safety data sheet* (MSDS) is a listing of product safety information prepared by manufacturers and marketers of products containing toxic chemicals. In addition to giving the basic product components, MSDSs are required to list the health effects of the material; first aid, safe storage, and disposal guidelines; protective equipment required for handling; and procedures for handling leaks and spills. They are intended for use by employers and emergency responders rather than by consumers.

- Required tests and procedures for testing materials to verify that they comply with the requirements

- A list of hazardous materials and chemicals

- A list of definitions with which the contractor may not be familiar. These may be included in this section or in individual sections if they only apply to one material, such as "certified wood product."

- A list of sources of information for product certification or sustainability that the contractor can use. This may also include trade associations and specific regulatory agencies' names and addresses.

- Requirements for the packaging of materials with recycled products

- Requirements for construction activities to minimize pollution, dust, erosion, chemical emissions, spills, and water and moisture leaks. This could include a "no smoking" provision for the job site.

Individual Technical Sections

The individual technical sections of the specification should contain the sustainability requirements unique to each product, such as use of local products, recycled content, requirements for VOCs, energy efficiency, cleaning and maintenance requirements, certification by a third party, and the other material criteria mentioned in Ch. 8. Generally, the sections affected will include concrete, rough carpentry, architectural woodwork, plastic products, doors, windows, gypsum wallboard, acoustical ceilings, carpeting, resilient flooring, ceramic tile, wood flooring, paints and coatings, and toilet partitions. Others should be included as required.

PART 1 GENERAL

SUMMARY
 Section Includes
 Product Supplied But Not Installed
  Under This Section
 Products Installed But Not Supplied
  Under This Section
 Related Sections
 Allowances
 Unit Prices
 Measurement Procedures
 Payment Procedures
 Alternates
REFERENCES
DEFINITIONS
SYSTEM DESCRIPTION
 Design Requirements,
  Performance Requirements
SUBMITTALS
 Product Data
 Shop Drawings
 Samples
 Quality Assurance/Control Submittals
  Design Data, Test Reports,
  Certificates,
  Manufacturers' Instructions,
  Manufacturers' Field Reports,
  Qualification Statements
 Closeout Submittals
QUALITY ASSURANCE
 Qualifications
 Regulatory Requirements
 Certifications
 Field Samples
 Mock-ups
 Pre-installation Meetings
**DELIVERY, STORAGE,
AND HANDLING**
 Packing, Shipping, Handling,
  and Unloading
 Acceptance at Site
 Storage and Protection
 Waste Management and Disposal
PROJECT/SITE*CONDITIONS
 Project/Site*Environmental
  Requirements
 Existing Conditions

SEQUENCING
SCHEDULING
WARRANTY
 Special Warranty
SYSTEM STARTUP
OWNER'S INSTRUCTIONS
COMMISSIONING
MAINTENANCE
 Extra Materials
 Maintenance Service

PART 2 PRODUCTS

MANUFACTURERS
EXISTING PRODUCTS
MATERIALS
MANUFACTURED UNITS
EQUIPMENT
COMPONENTS
ACCESSORIES
MIXES
FABRICATION
 Shop Assembly
  Fabrication Tolerances
FINISHES
 Shop Priming, Shop Finishing
SOURCE QUALITY CONTROL
 Tests, Inspection
 Verification of Performance

PART 3 EXECUTION

INSTALLERS
EXAMINATION
 Site Verification of Conditions
PREPARATION
 Protection
 Surface Preparation
ERECTION
INSTALLATION
APPLICATION
CONSTRUCTION
 Special Techniques
 Interface with Other Work
 Sequences of Operation
 Site Tolerances
REPAIR/RESTORATION
RE-INSTALLATION
FIELD QUALITY CONTROL
 Site Tests, Inspection
 Manufacturers' Field Services
ADJUSTING
CLEANING
DEMONSTRATION
PROTECTION
SCHEDULES

*Project Conditions is the preferred term in the U.S.,
Site Conditions is the preferred term in Canada

The Division Numbers and Titles used in this product are from *MasterFormat*™ 2004 Edition and the three part *SectionFormat*™ (1997 edition) outline, published by the Construction Specifications Institute (CSI) and Construction Specifications Canada (CSC), and are used with permission from CSI, 2004. For those interested in a more in-depth explanation of *MasterFormat*™ 2004 Edition and *SectionFormat*™ and their use in the construction industry contact:

The Construction Specifications Institute (CSI)
99 Canal Center Plaza, Suite 300
Alexandria, VA 22314
800-689-2900; 703-684-0300
CSINet URL: http://www.csinet.org

Figure 24.2 SectionFormat Outline

For actual specifying in Part 2, Products, of each specification section, the architect can use several approaches. First, the architect can write a performance specification giving the requirements for recycled content, maximum emissions of chemicals, and other criteria and the testing standard by which products must be evaluated. As stated previously in this chapter, true performance specifications are difficult to write.

Another approach is to give a list of three to five approved products that the architect knows will satisfy the requirements of the specification section. This list can contain products that have the desired recycled content or are capable of being recycled, products that have low emissions of VOCs and other hazardous chemicals, and equipment that is low polluting. Along with this, a provision can permit the contractor to submit a proposed substitution if the contractor can prove that the substitution meets all of the requirements. This puts an additional burden on the architect during the bidding or negotiation phases, when time may be short for full consideration of such substitution proposals.

Finally, if there is only one product that meets both the sustainability and aesthetic and functional requirements of the project, a proprietary specification can be written. This is typically only possible for private work, where requirements for competitive bidding are not as strict as they are for public work. Even for private work, the number of proprietary specifications should be kept to a minimum.

Specification Writing Guidelines

As previously mentioned, specifications are legal documents as well as a tool for communicating technical information to the contractor. Because of this, they must be complete, accurate, and unambiguous. The language must be precise. Some of the important things to remember are the following.

- Know what the standards and test methods referred to include and what parts of them are applicable to your project. Make sure they are the most current editions.

- Do not specify the results with the methods proposed to achieve those results, since the result may be a conflict. For instance, specifying that a brick must have certain absorption characteristics according to an ASTM test method and then specifying a particular brick that does not meet the stated requirements will result in a specification that is impossible to comply with.

- Do not include standards that cannot be measured. For example, saying that the work should be done "in a first class manner" is subject to wide interpretation.

- Avoid *exculpatory clauses*. These are phrases that try to shift responsibility to the contractor or someone else in a broad, general way. An example is something like "contractor shall be totally responsible for all ..." Unless the clause is generally accepted wording or makes sense in the context of the specification, current legal opinion disapproves of such clauses, especially when they favor the person who wrote them.

- Avoid words or phrases that are ambiguous. The combination "and/or," for example, is unclear and should be replaced with one word or the other. The abbreviation "etc." is also vague; it may include undesirable factors, and it implies that a list can go on forever. The word "any" implies that the contractor has a choice. This can be acceptable if the architect wants to allow a choice, but this is usually not the case.

- Keep the specifications as short as possible. Specification writing can be terse, even sometimes omitting words such as "all," "the," "an," and "a."

- Describe only one major idea in each paragraph. This makes reading easier and improves comprehension; it also makes changing the specification easier.

SAMPLE QUESTIONS

1. Which of the following would NOT be found in a project manual?

    A. bid log
    B. subsurface soil conditions report
    C. sitework specification
    D. bid bond

Question 2 refers to the following excerpt from a specification.

Part 2—Products

2.01 Metal Support Material

General: To the extent not otherwise indicated, comply with ASTM C754 for metal system supporting gypsum wallboard.

Ceiling suspension main runners: $1\frac{1}{2}$ in steel channels, cold rolled.

Hanger wire: ASTM A641, soft, Class 1 galvanized, prestretched; sized in accordance with ASTM C754.

Hanger anchorage devices: size for 3 × calculated loads, except size direct-pull concrete inserts for 5 × calculated loads.

Studs: ASTM C645; 25 gage, $2^1/_2$ in deep, except as otherwise indicated.

ASTM C645; 25 gage, $3^5/_8$ in deep.

ASTM C645; 20 gage, 6 in deep.

Runners: Match studs; type recommended by stud manufacturer for floor and ceiling support of studs, and for vertical abutment of drywall work at other work.

Furring members: ASTM C65; 25 gage, hat-shaped.

Fasteners: Type and size recommended by furring manufacturer for the substrate and application indicated.

2.   In the given specification, which item is described as a performance specification?

    A.   fasteners

    B.   hanger wire

    C.   hanger anchorage devices

    D.   ceiling suspension main runners

3.   A performance specification

    A.   allows innovation by the contractor

    B.   requires more work by the architect

    C.   is not appropriate for normal building products

    D.   all of the above

4.   What is likely to occur if the drawings and specifications are not thoroughly coordinated?

I.   a decrease of the actual cost from the estimated cost because the contractor bid on a less expensive material shown on the drawings, although the same material was called out as a more expensive type in the specifications

II.   a lawsuit

III.   the need for a change order during construction, to account for modifications required to correct discrepancies in the two documents

IV.   a delay in construction

V.   an increase in cost because the contractor bid the least expensive choice between two conflicting requirements when the client wanted the more expensive option

    A.   I and III

    B.   I, III, and IV

    C.   II, IV, and V

    D.   III, IV, and V

5.   In specifying asphalt roofing shingles, which of the following types of specifications would probably NOT be used?

    A.   descriptive

    B.   base bid or equal

    C.   reference standard

    D.   base bid with alternate approved manufacturers

6.   Which of the following are generally true of specifications?

I.   Both narrowscope and broadscope sections can be used in the same project manual.

II.   For the contractor, drawings are more binding than the specifications if there is a conflict.

III.   Specifications show quality; drawings show quantity.

IV.   Proprietary specifications are the same as prescriptive specifications.

V.   They should not be open to interpretation if they are the base bid type.

    A.   I, III, and V

    B.   II, III, and IV

    C.   I, III, IV, and V

    D.   all of the above

7.   Requirements for library checkout equipment are found in which division of the MasterFormat specifications?

    A.   10100

    B.   11050

    C.   12450

    D.   13800

8.   The specification requirements for interior steel stud walls should be included in which MasterFormat division?

    A.   05

    B.   09

    C.   10

    D.   13

9.   The procedure for submitting shop drawings for architectural woodwork is specified in MasterFormat Division

    A.   01
    B.   06
    C.   09
    D.   12

10. Where would the requirements for testing a plumbing
system be located?

    A.   in a section of Division 1 of the specifications
    B.   in Part 1 of Section 22400, Plumbing
    C.   in Part 2 of Section 22400, Plumbing
    D.   in Part 3 of Section 22400, Plumbing

THE PRIMARY CONTRACTUAL DOCUMENTS

This chapter reviews the various approaches to project delivery and the primary contractual documents that formalize the delivery method selected. These include the Owner-Architect Agreement, the Owner-Contractor Agreement, and the general and supplementary conditions of the contract. Additional contractual documents, which include the drawings, specifications, change orders, and other types of forms, are discussed in other chapters. Remember that the various types of documents used in the project delivery process that may establish contractual relationships between the many parties involved should not be confused with the contract documents as formally defined.

The *contract documents* consist of the Owner-Contractor Agreement, the general conditions of the contract, the supplementary conditions of the contract (if any), the drawings, specifications, and addenda issued prior to execution of the contract, any other documents specifically listed in the agreement, and modifications issued after execution of the contract. A *modification* is a change order, a construction change directive, a written order issued by the architect for a minor change in the work, or a written amendment to the contract signed by both parties.

APPROACHES TO PROJECT DELIVERY

The term *project delivery* describes the entire sequence of events necessary to provide an owner with a completed building. It includes the selection of people who will design and construct the project, establishment of contractual relationships, and some method of organizing contractors to perform the work. This section reviews some of the elements of project delivery and discusses the three primary types.

Responsibility for Design and Construction

The traditional construction method available to owners is to hire an architect to design the project and a contractor to build the project. The architect acts as agent for the owner, looking after the owner's best interest with no financial stake in the project. The contractor, in turn, agrees to finish the project according to the plans and specifications for a fixed price within a certain time period. The owner has separate contracts with the architect and the contractor.

Another method is to have a single entity responsible for both designing and building a project. This approach allows review by construction experts during design and often includes a guaranteed cost. However, it eliminates the advantages of competitive bidding and can set up potential conflicts because the goals of designers are usually at variance with the goals of contractors. Both of these delivery approaches will be discussed later in this section.

Agency

One of the key concepts in the traditional relationships among the architect, owner, and contractor is that of agency. The legal concept of agency involves three parties: the principal, the agent, and the third party. The owner is the principal, the architect is the agent of the owner, and the contractor is the third party. The agent acts on behalf of the principal and has the authority to perform certain duties. In the performance of these duties the agent can legally bind the principal to the third party (contractor). It is therefore important that the architect understand the full extent of his or her authority and what duties are expected.

In contrast to an agent, the contractor is considered a vendor. A vendor supplies a specific product for a fixed price. Unlike the architect/agent, a vendor acts primarily in his or her own interest. Refer to Ch. 28 for more information on agency.

Contract Types

In nearly any building project, regardless of size, a number of contractual relationships are established between all the parties involved. Contract types are often classified by the primary relationship the owner has with the contractor (or contractors). This relationship is called the *prime contract*.

The most common type is the single prime contract, in which the owner has an agreement with a general contractor to build a project according to the plans and specifications. If other, specialized contractors are needed, then the general contractor subcontracts with these parties. Typical subcontractors are mechanical, electrical, plumbing, concrete, roofing, and the like. On large projects there are dozens of subcontractors and many sub-subcontractors. However, the general contractor is responsible to the owner and must coordinate the other subcontractors. The primary advantage of this method is that the owner has a single source of responsibility, which also makes the project easier for the architect to administer.

Another type is the *multiple prime contract*. With this method, major portions of the work, such as mechanical, electrical, and plumbing work, are contracted separately with the owner. Many specialty contractors favor this approach, but it makes the project more difficult for the architect to coordinate.

A third type of contract arrangement involves *many prime contracts*. This is usually applied in fast-track construction where one portion of the work needs to start before other elements are designed or ready to be priced. This arrangement is much more difficult to manage and often requires the use of a construction manager if the architect is unable to coordinate the effort.

Design-Award-Build

The design-award-build is the first and most traditional of the three common methods of project delivery. With this approach, the architect designs the project and prepares the construction drawings and specifications. These are used as the basis for costing the project and awarding a construction contract, either through competitive bidding or negotiation with one contractor. The contractor then builds the project, with the architect providing contract administration services. The owner has separate contracts with both the architect and contractor.

This method of project delivery is fairly simple because all the roles are well defined and the work proceeds in a linear fashion, from selection of the architect to final build out. Coordination problems are minimized, contract relationships are straightforward, and the owner can receive a fixed price before proceeding with construction. The disadvantage is that one phase must be completely finished before the next one proceeds. This can be a problem if the owner needs the building quickly or if extended design and construction times result in higher financing costs.

Fast-Track

When the overall time for design and construction must be compressed, a fast-track method can be used. This overlaps some of the design process with some of the construction process to reduce the total time needed for project delivery. For example, based on design development drawings, construction drawings and specifications can be completed for foundations, and this work can be begun before the architect has completed work on interior finish design. Fast-track construction requires many prime contracts and much more coordination, but it can substantially reduce the time and cost of a project.

With the fast-track delivery method, the owner may want to use the services of a construction manager (CM). A *construction manager* is a third party who advises on constructability issues, provides cost estimating during design, makes early material purchases, assists with contract negotiations, manages the construction contracts, and administers the design contracts during construction. A construction manager can also be used with standard design-award-build methods of project delivery, but this is not typical.

A construction manager can either be an independent third party who acts as the owner's agent (as does the architect) without any financial interest in the project or can be the construction contractor. If the CM is an independent advisor, the document that is used is often AIA A201Cma, General Conditions of the Contract for Construction, Construction Manager-Adviser Edition (CCA 5, Management Contract Form Between Owner and Construction Manager). If the CM is a contractor, then the CM may provide the services described in addition to being financially responsible for the construction of the project, often guaranteeing the total construction cost and completion time.

The advantages of using a CM include early advice on constructability of the design as it is developed, early cost estimating and value analysis, project scheduling, professional management of multiple contracts or fast-track construction, and in some cases, a guaranteed price and completion date.

The disadvantages of using a CM include the extra costs and the more complicated management structure of having one more person on the design and build team. These disadvantages can be minimized if the contractor acts as construction manager. However, when this occurs, the advantages of competitive bidding among general contractors is lost.

Whether the CM acts as an independent agent or as a contractor (vendor), there are three common methods for establishing the total cost of a project. The first is the *fixed-price method*, also known as the *stipulated sum* or *lump sum* method, where the contractor gives the owner a set price for completing the project. With this method the owner knows the final cost before construction begins and is not responsible for cost overruns. However, the owner does not share in any savings that the contractor may realize for whatever reason. The second method is the *guaranteed maximum price* (GMP). In this case the owner has a fixed, maximum price that the contractor (or construction manager) guarantees. If the project is completed for less than this amount, the client receives the cost savings. The third method is the *cost plus fee method*, where the owner pays the actual cost of construction (direct plus indirect costs) plus a fee that is agreed to before construction begins.

Design-Build

With the design-build method, the owner contracts with one entity to provide both design and construction services. The design-build firm then subcontracts with others as required. There are several variations of the design-build firm. It may have its own staff of architects and construction personnel. It may primarily have a construction staff and hire architects as subcontractors. It may be a joint venture of an architect and contractor. Or it may subcontract both architecture and construction.

The design-build approach offers the owner several advantages. It is a single source of responsibility, and administering the contract is direct. The owner also has a fixed price early in the process. In addition, the total time of design and construction is usually reduced over more traditional approaches.

There are also several disadvantages. First, the owner does not have as much control over design as with other methods, once the contract is signed. Second, because this is done after the contract is signed, there can be disagreements concerning what was supposed to be included in the design. Third, the design-build firm has control over the quality of the materials and construction methods used. Fourth, in order to get what is needed, the client must develop a specific set of performance requirements.

In many cases, the owner hires an architect to act as advisor. The architect acts as the owner's agent to help set up performance requirements, evaluate potential design-build firms, administer the contract, and evaluate the progress of the work against the contract and approved design.

Design-build contracts are typically used by owners who have building experience with multiple facilities and who have clearly defined needs that can be precisely stated in performance requirements.

OWNER-ARCHITECT AGREEMENTS

There are several types of owner-architect agreements published by the American Institute of Architects (AIA). The most common is AIA Document B141, Standard Form of Agreement Between Owner and Architect with Standard Form of Architect's Services (CCAC Document 6, Canadian Standard Form of Contract for Architectural Services). A 1997 revision to this document made significant changes to previous forms. This agreement is in two parts to allow architects to offer a broad range of services spanning the life of a project. The first part is an agreement form that contains initial information, responsibilities of the parties, terms and conditions, and compensation provisions. The first part applies to whatever services are defined in the second part. The second part, a services form, contains the architect's scope of services. Standard forms of this part can be used, or the architect can draft his or her own form to permit the agreement to be used for many different types of projects.

Additional AIA standard documents are available for small projects of limited scope, jobs where construction management services are performed, interior design services, and housing services.

Although AIA forms do not have to be used between either the owner and architect or the owner and contractor, they have been developed over many years and represent a general consensus concerning the rights and duties of the various parties involved with a construction project. A solid understanding of the provisions in the AIA documents should clarify the concept of standard contractual relationships. These are the contracts covered by the ARE.

Because the various agreements discussed in this chapter are lengthy and cover a great deal of material, it is advisable to read through the primary agreements prior to taking the exam. The remaining sections of this chapter will only highlight some of the more important provisions. They are based on AIA B141. Similar provisions are found in CCAC, Document 6.

Initial Information

The first article of the first part of AIA B141 requires the architect and owner to itemize the information and assumptions about the project, if known at the time of contract execution. Information includes the project's objective; the owner's program; the physical, legal, financial, and time parameters; and the key personnel for both the owner and the architect. The intent of this new article is to encourage communication at the beginning of the project.

The Architect's Responsibilities

The architect's responsibilities are spelled out in both the first and second parts of AIA B141. The first part contains responsibilities that apply to any type of professional service; responsibilities in the second part are unique to the scope of service as defined.

The first part of the agreement states that the architect must submit, for the owner's approval, a schedule for the performance of the architect's services, including time for (a) the owner's review, (b) the performance of the owner's consultants, and (c) the approval of submissions by authorities having jurisdiction. The time limits cannot be exceeded by the architect or owner except for reasonable cause.

The architect must maintain the confidentiality of information designated by the owner; must not engage in any activity that would compromise the architect's judgment; and must review all laws, codes, and regulations applicable to the architect's services. Finally, the architect is entitled to rely on the accuracy and completeness of information furnished by the owner; however, the architect must notify the owner if the architect becomes aware of any errors or omissions in such information.

The second part of AIA B141, Standard Form of Architect's Services: Design and Contract Administration, provides a method to define the architect's scope of services. Although the majority of it is written for standard building projects, it is flexible enough to be used for other types of service, such as programming, feasibility studies, and interior design. The second part most closely resembles the older (and now obsolete) five phases of service: work during schematic design, design development, construction documents, bidding or negotiation, and contract administration. The following are some of the more important provisions of this part of the agreement.

- *Project administration services.* The architect must manage the architect's own services and administer the project. This includes consulting with the owner, researching design criteria, attending project meetings, coordinating both the architect's and owner's consultants, and issuing progress reports. A *progress report* may consist of copies of correspondence, memos detailing the progress of the project, architect's field reports, minutes of meetings, or any other writings that keep the owner advised.

  The architect must prepare, and keep updated, a project schedule that identifies *estimated* milestone dates for decisions required of the owner, services furnished by the architect, time required for governmental and other approvals, completion of document provided by the architect, commencement of construction, and substantial completion. The project schedule is not the construction schedule, which is prepared by the contractor and only runs from commencement of construction to the proposed date for substantial completion.

The architect must also consider alternative materials and building systems, make presentations to the owner, submit design documents to the owner at intervals for the purposes of evaluation and approval by the owner, and assist the owner in filing documents required for approval of governmental authorities.

- *Evaluation of budget and cost of the work.* The architect must prepare a preliminary estimate of the cost of the work and update and refine it as design work progresses through the end of the preparation of construction documents. At each point, the cost estimate should be compared with the owner's budget. If the estimate exceeds the budget, the architect must make recommendations to the owner to adjust the project's size, quality, or budget, and the owner must cooperate with the architect in making the adjustments.

All cost estimates prepared by the architect represent the best professional judgment. However, neither the architect nor the owner warrants that bids or negotiated prices will not vary from the owner's budget or from any estimate that the architect has made. Only the contractor can guarantee prices.

- *Evaluation and planning services.* The architect must provide a preliminary evaluation of the information furnished by the owner, including information about the site, program, schedule, budget, and proposed method of contracting for construction. In this evaluation the architect should review the balance between quality, cost, and time. The architect should notify the owner of any impact that the budget, schedule, site, or method of contracting may have on the project.

- *Design services.* This article covers the bulk of the architect's standard services, including schematic design, design development, and construction document production, and describes generally what is involved in each of these design phases. At the end of each phase the owner's approval is a precondition that must be received before the architect can begin work on the next phase. When schematic designs are presented to the owner, the owner is not obligated to approve the scheme if it fails to match the agreed-upon program, budget, or time frame. However, the owner must act in good faith to work with the architect as revisions are made. During the construction document production phase the architect must *assist* the owner in the development and preparation of bidding documents and the conditions of the contract for construction. By assisting, it is clear that the architect is *not* providing legal services to the owner and is *not* a party to the Owner-Contractor Agreement.

- *Construction procurement services.* During this phase the architect must *assist* the owner in obtaining competitive bids or negotiated proposals and must *assist* in awarding the contract and preparing contracts for construction. With the contract language of *assist*, the architect is acting as an agent for the owner. The architect produces the bidding documents, distributes the documents, considers requests for substitutions, holds pre-bid conferences, answers questions, prepares addenda, and participates in the opening of bids. Similar requirements are defined if the project is negotiated with a contractor. Refer to Ch. 26 for more information on bidding procedures and documents and the architect's responsibilities during this phase of the work.

- *Contract administration services.* This article of the Owner-Architect Agreement outlines the responsibilities of the architect during the construction phase of the project.

The architect must make site visits at intervals appropriate to the stage of construction to generally determine whether, when completed, the project will be in accordance with the contract documents. The architect must keep the owner informed of the progress and endeavor to protect the owner against defects. However, the architect is not required to make exhaustive or continuous on-site inspections.

The architect is not responsible for the means of construction, building techniques, or safety precautions. These are the sole responsibility of the contractor. The only time this is not true is if the architect has actually specified means and methods of construction. (Note that this provision is in Document AIA A201, General Conditions of the Contract, not in AIA B141). Refer to Ch. 27 for more information on construction administration services and the architect's responsibilities during this phase.

The owner and contractor are supposed to communicate through the architect. Communications by and with the consultants are also supposed to be through the architect.

The Owner's Responsibilities

Under the first part of AIA B141, the owner must provide the architect with information such as program, schedule, and budget. The owner must also furnish the services of

consultants or authorize the architect to furnish these services as a change in services (see section on changes in services). In addition, the owner must furnish tests, inspections, and reports required by law or the contract documents, such as structural, mechanical, and chemical tests, along with tests for pollution or hazardous materials. The owner must also furnish all legal, insurance, and accounting services necessary for the project.

The second part of AIA B141, Standard Form of Architect's Services: Design and Contract Administration, requires the owner to provide three additional supporting services.

First, the owner must provide a program that gives the owner's objectives, schedule, constraints, and design criteria, including space requirements and relationships, special equipment, systems, and site requirements.

Second, the owner must furnish land surveys to describe the legal limits of the site, grades, locations of utilities, easements, right-of-way, and other aspects of a standard survey. The architect may assist the owner in procuring these services (using AIA Document G601, Land Survey Agreement), but this would be an expansion of the architect's standard services.

Third, the owner must furnish the services of a geotechnical engineer, which may include test borings, determinations of soil bearing values, percolation tests, evaluation of hazardous materials, and other investigations as may be required by the site and the project. A report with recommendations should be provided. The architect is entitled to rely on the accuracy of the geotechnical services. The architect may assist the owner in procuring these services and coordinating the necessary information (using AIA Document G602, Geotechnical Services Agreement). Note that the owner also has certain responsibilities under the terms of the General Conditions of the Contract, AIA A201 (CCDC 2). Those are summarized in the next section.

Terms and Conditions of the Contract

There are many other important provisions in the Owner-Architect Agreement. These include the following.

- *Instruments of service.* The drawings, specifications, and other documents, including those in electronic form, are instruments of service and belong to the architect, who retains the copyright on them. The owner is allowed to keep and use originals and copies in connection with the project, but cannot use them for other projects or for additional work on the project.

- *Waiver of consequential damages.* Both the architect and owner waive consequential damages, which limits claims to damages resulting directly from a breach of the agreement.

- *Hazardous material.* The architect and architect's consultants have no responsibility for the discovery, presence, handling, removal, or disposal of or for the exposure of persons to hazardous materials such as asbestos, PCBs, or other toxic substances.

- *Third-party claims.* One provision states that nothing in the agreement shall create a contractual relationship with a third party against either the architect or the owner. This is to reinforce the idea of *privity*, which states that one party to a contract is protected from claims from other parties with whom there is no direct contractual relationship.

- *Causes of action.* This clause provides a uniform date from which a statutes of limitation period will begin if legal actions are taken by either the architect or the owner. It is defined as either the date of substantial completion for acts or failures to act occurring prior to substantial completion *or* the date of issuance of the final certificate for payment for acts or failures to act occurring after substantial completion.

- *Waiver of rights.* This clause provides for a waiver of damages that are covered by property insurance during construction. It means that the owner and architect cannot sue each other for damages if they are covered by property insurance that is required by the Owner-Contractor Agreement. This is also known as a *waiver of subrogation.* A waiver of subrogation prevents the insurance company from suing any of the principal participants in the project (architect, contractor, subcontractors, engineers, and consultants) to recover what has been paid out for an insured loss.

- *Right to photograph.* The architect has the right to photograph the project and include photographs or other artistic representations of the design in the architect's promotional materials unless the owner has specifically notified the architect in writing that some or all of the portions the architect wants to photograph are confidential or proprietary information. Unless such notice has been given, the owner must give reasonable access to the completed project for photography.

- *Termination.* Either party can terminate the agreement on no less than 7 days' written notice if the other party fails substantially to perform according to the terms of the agreement. The architect is also allowed to suspend performance of services on 7 days' written notice to the owner if the owner fails to make fee payments when due. If the owner suspends work for more than 30 days or terminates the agreement, the architect must be compensated for services performed prior to termination or suspension. A new clause also allows the owner to terminate the contract without cause for the owner's convenience as long as the owner gives 7 days' written notice.

Cost of the Work

The *cost of the work* is defined as the cost at current market rates of labor and materials furnished by the owner and items specified or designed by the architect, including costs of management or supervision of construction provided by a separate construction manager or contractor, plus a reasonable allowance for overhead and profit. Construction cost does not include professional fees, land cost, financing costs, or other costs (such as land surveys) that are the responsibility of the owner.

The architect does not warrant that bids or negotiated costs will not vary from the owner's budge or from any estimate prepared by the architect. However, the architect must adhere to the owner's budget. If the budget is exceeded by the lowest bid or negotiated proposal, the owner has four choices: to increase the budget, to authorize rebidding or renegotiation, to terminate the project, or to cooperate in revising the project scope and quality. However, if the owner chooses to revise the project scope or quality, the architect must modify the documents for which the architect is responsible *without* any further compensation.

Change in Services

The *change in services* article allows the architect's services to be modified after the execution of the original agreement without invalidating the agreement, if both the owner and the architect agree in writing. The need for a modification can come about for several reasons. All are valid *except* for changes that are the fault of the architect. The events that may require a Change in Services, for which the architect must be compensated, include the following.

- changes in the instructions by the owner that require revisions to the drawings or specifications (instruments of service)

- revisions of codes, laws, or regulations that require changes in the drawings or specifications

- decisions of the owner not made in a timely manner

- significant changes in the project, including size, quality, complexity, the owner's schedule, budget, or procurement method

- failure of performance on the part of the owner or owner's consultants or contractors

- preparation for and attendance at public hearings, dispute resolution proceedings, or legal proceedings except where the architect is a party

- changes in information contained in the first article of the agreement, which includes the physical, financial, and legal parameters of the project; the program; the proposed construction procurement method; or the time parameters

Additional work by the architect that is also considered justification for a Change in Services includes the following, which are given in the second part of the AIA B141 document.

- reviews of contractor's submittals that are out of sequence from the original schedule

- responses to contractor's requests for information where such information is available to the contractor from a careful study of the contract documents and other information

- change orders and construction change directives requiring evaluation of proposals

- consulting related to the replacement of work caused by fire or other factors

- evaluation of excessive number of claims made by the owner's consultants, contractor, or others

- evaluation of substitutions proposed by the owner's consultants or contractors, and making revisions to the drawings and specifications

- preparation of design and documentation for alternate bid requests proposed by the owner

- contract administration services provided more than 60 days after substantial completion

Normally, the following services are not provided unless specifically listed in the agreement: programming, economic feasibility studies, site analysis and selection, landscape design, tenant planning, interior design, on-site project representation, construction management, and preparation of record drawings.

Mediation and Arbitration

When there is a claim or dispute, the standard agreement requires that mediation be undertaken before arbitration or litigation. *Mediation* is a process by which a neutral third party facilitates and assists the disputing parties to negotiate a settlement using preset rules established by the American Arbitration Association (AAA). If an agreement cannot be reached, the AIA B141 agreement requires that the dispute advance to arbitration. *Arbitration* is a formal, legally binding process for resolving disputes without litigation in a court of law. One or more arbiters with experience in the construction industry hear the disputing party's arguments and render a decision, which is binding. The arbitration proceedings are conducted according to rules and guidelines established by the AAA.

Compensation Methods

There are several methods of compensation that the owner and architect can negotiate. The following are the common types.

- *Stipulated sum (fixed fee).* This method states a fixed sum of money that the owner will pay to the architect for a specific set of services. The money is usually paid out monthly according to the proportion of the five basic phases of services previously described. With a stipulated sum, the architect must accurately estimate the cost for the office to do the job and still make a profit. Reimbursable expenses are in addition to fees for the basic services and include such things as postage, reproduction, transportation, long-distance communication, computer-aided design and drafting equipment time, renderings, and models.

- *Cost plus fee.* With this approach the professional is compensated for the actual expenses of doing the job plus a reasonable fee for profit. The actual expenses include salaries, employee benefits, direct expenses, and office overhead. Several variations of the cost-plus-fee approach are used.

  With the *multiple of direct personnel expense*, the direct salary of employees is determined and multiplied by a factor to account for normal and required personnel expenses such as taxes, sick leave, health care, and so on. This is then increased by a multiplier that includes provisions for overhead and profit. For example, if a particular person's direct personnel expense is calculated at $30.00 per hour and the multiplier is 2.5, then the cost to the client for that person is $75.00 per hour.

  Multiple of direct salary expense is similar, except that the multiplier is larger, to provide for employee benefits.

  Hourly billing rates simply build in the multiplier to the hourly rate so that the client only sees one number for each of the types of people working on the project.

- *Percentage of construction cost.* This method is not used as much as it once was. With it, the professional fee is tied to the cost of construction as a fixed percentage. However, from the client's standpoint, the architect may be encouraged to increase the cost of construction to increase the fee or, conversely, may lose any incentive to reduce construction cost. From the architect's standpoint, the percentage method may not be good because a low-cost project may require just as much work as, or more work than, an expensive project.

- *Unit cost method.* Fees are based on a definable unit, such as square footage, for such work as tenant planning in a leased building or on a per-house basis in a large residential project.

The choice of compensation method depends on several factors. The method used should fairly compensate the architect for the actual work required and the value of that professional service. It should also allow for the rising cost of providing services, which is especially important when the project will be of long duration. Finally, the client should be comfortable with the method and understand where the money is being spent.

OWNER-CONTRACTOR AGREEMENTS

Although the owner enters into an agreement directly with the contractor for construction of the project, the architect must be familiar with the various types of owner-contractor agreements. The variations of agreements are usually based on the method of compensation for the contractor. These will be discussed in a later section. One common document used is AIA Document A101, Standard Form of Agreement Between Owner and Contractor, where the basis of payment is a stipulated sum (CCDC 2, Stipulated Price Contract). Many of the provisions of this agreement are used in other agreement types and in non-AIA agreements between owner and contractor.

Identification of Contract Documents

The first article specifies that the contract documents include the agreement, the general and supplementary conditions of the contract, drawings, specifications, addenda, modifications, and other documents listed in the agreement. It makes reference to a later article in which all the documents are listed in detail. The purpose of this article is to include all the other documents by reference.

Basic Provisions

Some basic provisions are common to all contracts. These include a description of the work, the times of commencement and substantial completion, and the contract sum.

The work normally includes what is described in the contract documents, primarily the drawings and specifications. Any exclusions can be spelled out in the Owner-Contractor Agreement as well as in the contract documents when they are identified as being the responsibility of others.

The date of commencement is important because it is from this date that the construction completion time is measured. The date can be a specific calendar day or it can be when the contractor is given a notice-to-proceed letter by the owner.

The time of substantial completion is expressed with a specific calendar date or by a number of calendar days from the date of commencement. *Substantial completion* is defined as the stage in the progress of the work when the work or designated portion thereof is sufficiently complete in accordance with the contract documents so that the owner can occupy or utilize the work for its intended use.

Completion time may be extended as provided for in the general conditions when circumstances are beyond the control of the contractor. If a particular completion date is important to the owner, provisions for liquidated damages may be included. *Liquidated damages* are monies paid by the contractor to the owner for every day the project is late. They represent actual anticipated losses the owner will incur if the project is not completed on time. For example, if an owner cannot occupy the project and must pay double rent, the liquidated damages may be the amount of extra rent.

In many cases, a liquidated damages provision is accompanied by a bonus provision so that the contractor receives a payment for early completion. This too is usually based on a realistic cost savings the owner will realize for early completion. If a penalty clause is included (which is different from liquidated damages), a bonus provision *must* also be included.

The *contract sum*, of course, states the compensation the contractor will receive for the work. The various methods of compensation are discussed in a later section.

Progress Payments

Based on applications for payment submitted by the contractor, the owner makes periodic payments, usually monthly, to the contractor on account of the contract sum. The Owner-Contractor Agreement defines how these payments are to be made.

In the AIA A101 agreement, the amount due in any time period is based on the percentage of completed work and any materials purchased and in approved storage. The percentage is based on a schedule of values that the contractor submits to the architect, which allocates the total contract sum to various portions of the work such as mechanical, electrical, foundations, and so forth. A certain percentage of each payment, usually 10%, called the *retainage*, is withheld until final completion of the work.

In order to receive payment, the contractor must submit an application for payment to the architect listing the completed work and stored materials according to the schedule of values. The architect then reviews the application, verifies it, and recommends payment to the owner, who then makes payment. If there is work in dispute, the architect may choose not to certify payment of all or a portion of the amount until the problem is resolved.

Enumeration of Contract Documents

In this article, all of the documents are listed individually. Reference is made to the agreement itself, AIA Document A201, General Conditions of the Contract, any supplementary general conditions, each specification section, all the drawings, the addenda, if any, and any other documents made part of the contract.

Compensation Methods

There are several ways the contractor can be paid for the work, as mentioned in a previous section. One of the most common is the *stipulated sum*, which is a fixed price the owner agrees to pay the contractor for the work as shown in the contract documents. This is a simple way to arrange things, and owners like it because the cost is known when the bids are made or negotiation is completed. Competitive bidding always uses a stipulated-sum method.

Another method is the *guaranteed maximum price* (GMP). In this case the owner has a fixed, maximum price that the contractor (or construction manager) guarantees. If the project is completed for less than this amount, the client receives the cost savings. If the project costs exceed the GMP, the contractor must pay the excess.

Cost plus fee methods compensate the contractor for actual expenses of labor, materials, and subcontracts in addition to a fixed fee. Cost plus fee contracts have more flexibility than fixed fees and allow construction to proceed before design is complete. Their disadvantage is that the cost is not known, a problem that can be mitigated with such things as guaranteed maximums, target prices with incentives, and partial cost guarantees. Target prices establish a likely project cost, and the contractor may share in a percentage of savings below the target price or be responsible for a percentage over the price. Partial cost guarantees involve obtaining fixed prices from certain subcontractors or material suppliers.

Construction can sometimes be based on unit prices. Entire projects are seldom based this way, but portions of a project may be. For example, in cases where it is not possible to firmly establish quantities at the time of bid, a unit price can be set. This happens quite frequently with excavation where a cost per cubic yard of material is stated. The final quantity is then multiplied by this unit price to arrive at the total cost. In other cases where changes or additions are anticipated, the contractor can be requested to include unit prices in the bid. These can then be used to evaluate the possible cost consequences of making a change and as a check against the final cost of a change order.

GENERAL CONDITIONS OF THE CONTRACT

The General Conditions of the Contract, AIA Form A201 (CCDC 2), is one of the most important parts in the entire set of contract documents. It is incorporated by specific reference into the Owner-Architect Agreement as well as the Owner-Contractor Agreement. Obtain a copy of the General Conditions and read the entire document prior to the exam. Many of the most important provisions will be outlined in this section. Other portions that pertain to bidding and contract administration are discussed in the following two chapters.

General Provisions

Article 1 provides basic definitions used in the General Conditions of the Contract for Construction. One of the most important is that of the contract documents. As stated at the beginning of this chapter, the *contract documents* consist of the agreement between owner and contractor, conditions of the contract (general, supplementary, and special conditions), the drawings, the specifications, addenda issued prior to execution of the contract, other documents listed in the agreement, and modifications issued after execution of the contract. The contract documents do *not* include other documents such as the bidding documents.

It is clearly stated that the contract documents do not create a contractual relationship between the architect and contractor, between the owner and any subcontractor, between the owner and the architect, or between any other persons other than the owner and the contractor.

One of the definitions is that of the *Work*, which means the contractor's obligations to provide improvements to the project. It is important to distinguish what is the contractor's responsibility and to define what the property insurance covers. The Work is distinguished from the *Project*, which includes the work of the contractor as well as that of separate contractors or the owner's own forces. The Work may be the whole or a part of the Project.

The Owner

Article 2 outlines the duties, responsibilities, and rights of the owner. Among these is the responsibility of the owner to furnish evidence, at the request of the contractor, that financial arrangements have been made to fulfill the owner's obligations under the contract, in other words, to pay the contractor.

If the contractor makes a written request, the owner must give information necessary to give notice of or enforce mechanic's lien rights. This information usually means the legal description of the property and proof of legal title.

The owner must secure and pay for necessary approvals and permits required for construction of permanent structures or for changes in existing structures. Generally, these will be costs required *before* the execution of the contract, such as zoning permits, easements, assessments, environmental impact studies, and the like. However, these payments *do not* include those that the contractor must pay for after execution of the contract, such as building permits and other governmental fees and permits.

The owner must also furnish, free of charge, the necessary copies of the drawings and project manual required for the completion of the work. The contractor is also entitled to receive any information the owner has about the site conditions. The contractor has a right to rely on the accuracy of the information furnished by the owner.

If the contractor fails to correct work not in conformance with the contract documents or persistently fails to carry out such work, the owner may order the contractor to stop the work until the cause for the order is eliminated.

The owner also has the *right to carry out the work* if the contractor fails in his or her duties to correctly do so. In order to do this the owner must give written notice to the contractor demanding correction of the problem. The contractor has seven days from receiving written notice to begin to correct the problem. If the contractor has not acted within seven days, the owner may give the contractor a second notice, which should also state that the owner intends to carry out the work if the contractor fails to respond within three days. If there is no response, the owner can begin work while still retaining rights to arbitration or legal action for breach of contract. The owner may execute a change order or construction change directive deducting the cost of the work from the contract sum, including compensation for the architect's services. The architect must approve the owner's actions in regard to carrying out the work as well as the amount charged to the contractor.

The Contractor

Article 3 details the responsibilities of the contractor. Before starting the work the contractor must review and study the various drawings, specifications, other contract documents, and information furnished by the owner to facilitate the contractor's work. The contractor must also observe site conditions and take any field measurements necessary.

The contractor is not liable to the owner or architect for damage resulting from errors or omissions in the contract documents unless the contractor recognized such error and knowingly failed to report it to the architect. It is also not the contractor's responsibility to ascertain that the contract documents are in accordance with building codes, ordinances, and other regulations. However, if the contractor notices some variance, he or she must notify the architect and owner in writing. If the contractor does not give this notice and performs work knowingly in variance with some regulation, the contractor assumes full responsibility for such work.

The contractor is solely responsible for the means, methods, and techniques of construction and for coordinating the work under the contract. This includes making sure that work already performed is in proper condition to receive subsequent work. It also includes controlling his or her work force, coordinating the subcontractors, and being responsible to the owner for acts and omissions of all people performing work under the contract. However, if the contract documents include specific instructions concerning the means, methods, techniques, and procedures, the contractor is only responsible for job-site safety, not the results of the architect's specifications.

If the contractor wants to make a substitution, he or she can only do so with the consent of the owner, after evaluation by the architect, and in accordance with a change order.

A warranty clause states that the materials and workmanship furnished under the contract is of good quality, is free of defects, and conforms to the requirements of the contract documents. This warranty is in addition to other warranties that may be given by manufacturers or fabricators. This warranty clause is also *separate and distinct* from the one-year correction period that is outlined in a later article in the General Conditions on correction of work.

The contractor must secure and pay for the building permit and other permits, governmental fees, licenses, and inspections necessary for the execution of the work that are ordinarily obtained *after* the execution of the contract. The contractor must also pay sales, consumer, use, and similar taxes for work provided by the contractor.

When developing the contract sum, the contractor must include all allowances that are listed in the contract documents. An *allowance* is a set amount of money estimated by the architect to cover a particular material or piece of equipment when the cost for that material or equipment cannot be determined precisely at the time of the bid or negotiated proposal. It is, in effect, a placeholder so some amount of money can be reserved for the item. The article on allowances further states that the allowance shall cover the cost to the contractor of the allowance item delivered at the job site and all required taxes. However, the contractor must add to the allowance the cost for unloading, handling, and installing the item as well as costs for the contractor's overhead and profit. If the costs for the allowance are more or less than the original estimate, the contract sum is adjusted accordingly by change order.

The contractor is also obligated to provide a schedule for the owner's and architect's information, to keep it up to date, and to conform to it.

The contractor must keep at the job site one set of drawings, specifications, addenda, modifications, samples, and shop drawings for the contractor's own use as well as for reference by the architect. An important part of this article requires the contractor to maintain record documents. *Record documents* are marked-up construction drawings, specifications, and other documents that record exactly how the project was built, noting any changes or deviations from the original contract documents. The architect should include the exact requirements for record documents in Division 01 of the specifications.

The article regarding shop drawings, product data, and samples states that these items are *not* contract documents and that their purpose is to demonstrate the way in which the contractor proposes to conform to the information given and the design concept expressed in the contract documents. Refer to Ch. 27 for more information on submittals.

Part of the article on shop drawings, product data, and samples states that the contractor *can* be required to provide professional design services or certifications if *specifically required* to do so by the contract documents or if the contractor needs to provide such services in order to carry out the work of the contract. The architect must specify all performance and design criteria that such services must satisfy. This requirement is sometimes called *design delegation*, but legally it is a form of design allocation by the owner because there is no contractual relationship between the architect and the contractor. Design delegation allows the use of performance specifications for products and building assemblies or allows the contractor to select the best approach to completing the work. For example, specialized temporary shoring may be required to support cutting and patching operations for a portion of the work. The contractor is responsible for doing this but may require the services of a registered professional engineer to design the shoring according to the contractor's needs.

Under a section on indemnification it is stated that, to the extent provided by law, the contractor will indemnify and hold harmless the owner, architect, architect's consultants, and agents against claims, damages, and expenses arising out of performance of the work. However, this clause does not relieve the architect of his or her liability for errors in the drawings, specifications, or administration of the contract.

To *indemnify* is to secure against loss or damage. This clause is intended to protect the owner and architect against situations where a person is injured due to the negligence of the contractor or the contractor's agents. It also is intended to protect the owner and architect against claims from property damage other than to the work itself.

Administration of the Contract

Article 4 of the General Conditions states the architect's roles and responsibilities in contract administration. These are discussed in more detail in Ch. 27, but in general, this article provides for the typical duties the architect performs as follows.

The architect visits the site regularly to become familiar with the progress of the work and to determine whether it is proceeding in general accordance with the contract documents.

It is reiterated in one paragraph that the architect does not have control over construction means, methods, techniques, procedures, or safety precautions.

The architect has the authority to reject work that does not conform to the contract documents. However, this authority does not give rise to any duty or responsibility to the contractor, subcontractors, or others. In addition, the architect does not have the right to stop the work if something is wrong or the architect observes some safety problem. Instead, the architect should notify both the contractor and the owner.

The architect reviews shop drawings and other submission, but only for the limited purpose of checking for conformance with the design intent expressed in the contract documents.

The architect prepares change orders and may authorize minor changes in the work that do not involve adjusting either the contract sum or contract time and that are not inconsistent with the intent of the contract documents.

The architect interprets and decides on matters concerning the performance of the contract if the owner or contractor requests such interpretation.

The architect's decisions concerning matters related to aesthetic effect are final if consistent with the intent shown on the contract documents.

If there are claims or disputes, they are to initially be referred to the architect for a resolution, and the architect must follow certain procedures in deciding on the resolution. (These procedures are described in more detail in

Ch. 27.) If problems cannot be resolved through the architect, then the claims (except those relating to aesthetic effect) must be submitted to mediation as a condition precedent to arbitration or other legal proceedings.

Construction by Owner or by Separate Contractors

The owner has the right to perform construction on the project with the owner's own forces and to award separate contracts for certain work. However, exercising this right does require the owner to provide for coordination of his or her own forces and to act with the same obligations and rights as would any contractor.

The contractor must work with the other separate contractors and the owner in coordinating construction schedules when requested to do so and must follow the schedules. The contractor must also allow the owner and separate contractors the opportunity to store materials and perform their work. If the contractor discovers that construction by the owner or separate contractors will adversely affect his or her work, the contractor must promptly notify the architect. The contractor must pay the owner for any costs incurred by the owner for delays or defective construction of the contractor.

Changes in the Work

The General Conditions of the Contract allows for changes to be made in the work after execution of the contract. These changes are made by written change order, construction change directive, or minor change in the work.

A change order is based on a written agreement among the owner, contractor, and architect concerning the extent of the change and how it affects construction cost and construction time. A construction change directive only requires agreement between the owner and architect and may or may not be agreed to by the contractor. A minor change in the work can be made by the architect alone.

A construction change directive instructs the contractor to proceed with the required changes in the work even if the contractor does not agree with the basis for adjustment in contract sum or contract time. When final determination of cost and time changes is made through submittals by the contractor and review by the architect and owner, a change order is issued.

The exact procedures the architect must follow for making changes are described in Ch. 27.

Time

The *contract time* is the period from the starting date established in the agreement to the time of substantial completion, including any authorized adjustments. The contractor

is expected to proceed expeditiously with adequate work forces and to complete the work within the allotted time.

Payments and Completion

As mentioned previously, the contractor makes monthly applications for payment based on the percentage of work completed in accordance with a schedule of values allocated to various portions of the work. The architect reviews these applications and issues to the owner a certificate for payment or decides to withhold issuance if there are valid reasons. The exact procedures the architect must follow are described in Ch. 27.

Liens

A *mechanic's lien* is a claim by one party against the property of another party for the satisfaction of a debt and is a common method for an architect, contractor, or material supplier to gain payment. If a property carries a mechanic's lien, it cannot be sold or transferred until the lien is disposed of (or bonded), except through foreclosure. If a contractor does not pay a subcontractor or material supplier, and the subcontractor or material supplier files a mechanic's lien against the property, the owner becomes responsible for payment. If the lien is not paid, the property can be foreclosed by the lien holder, the lender, or a taxing entity.

Because the owner has no responsibility for paying subcontractors or material suppliers, the General Conditions of the Contract provides ways to protect the owner from liens. This is done by requiring the contractor to submit a release or waiver of liens to the owner before final payment is made or retainages of previous payments are released. The contractor must also furnish to the owner and architect an affidavit of payment of all debts and claims, and an affidavit of release of liens (a standard AIA form) stating that all obligations have been satisfied. The release or waiver of liens is attached to this affidavit.

The exact laws governing liens and the time period during which a lien may be filed vary from state to state, so the architect and owner must be familiar with local regulations.

Protection of Persons and Property

The contractor is exclusively responsible for on-site safety and precautions against damage to persons and property. This includes the contractor's employees, other people affected by the work, the work itself, and adjacent property. Provisions concerning the discovery of asbestos, PCBs, and other hazardous materials are also included. If such substances are found or suspected by the contractor, the contractor must stop work and report the conditions to the owner and architect in writing. The owner is then required to obtain the services of a licensed laboratory to verify the presence or absence of hazardous materials reported by the contractor. The owner is responsible for removal of discovered hazardous materials, after which time work can resume upon written agreement of the owner and contractor.

If any damage to the work is sustained due to inadequate protection, the contractor must repair or correct it. However, this does not include damages caused by acts of the owner or architect.

Insurance and Bonds

For the duration of the project, both the owner and contractor must maintain insurance to protect against various types of losses. The provisions for insurance are spelled out in the General Conditions of the Contract. Additional provisions as required by the unique nature of each project are included in the Supplementary General Conditions.

Although insurance is required, the architect is not responsible for giving advice to either the owner or the contractor on matters related to insurance and bonds. In fact, architects' professional liability insurance policies exclude such advice from coverage. Both the owner and contractor should receive advice from their respective legal counsels and insurance advisers as required.

The contractor must furnish liability insurance to provide coverage for the entities for whom the contractor is legally liable. This includes such coverage as workers' compensation, bodily injury or death of the contractor's employees and others, damages to the work, personal injury, motor vehicle insurance, and claims involving contractual liability. The contractor should require that all subcontractors carry similar insurance.

The amount of coverage should not be less than the limits of liability specified in the contract or required by law, whichever is greater. It must be maintained without interruption from the beginning of the work until the date of final payment.

At the beginning of the project, the architect should write a letter to the owner reminding him or her of the owner's responsibilities under the terms of the agreement and requesting that the owner determine, with his or her legal and insurance advisers, the type and amount of coverage required. This information, including the owner's requirements on bonds, should be given to the architect for use in assisting the owner with preparing the contract and bidding documents.

The architect should also have certificates of insurance from the contractor on file and should not issue any certificate of payment until such evidence is available or until he or she has been advised by the owner that such insurance has been obtained.

The owner must also purchase and maintain the liability insurance needed to protect the owner against claims and losses arising from operations under the contract. This includes insurance for property damage and loss of use.

The owner's property insurance protects against fire, theft, vandalism, and other hazards. It must be an all-risk policy that insures against all perils that are not otherwise specifically excluded. The amount of coverage must be for the full value of the work, which is usually the contract sum plus any subsequent modifications.

This article of the General Conditions also gives the owner the right to require the contractor to furnish bonds covering faithful performance of the contract. A *bond*, often fully labeled a *surety bond*, is an agreement by which one party, called the *surety* (the bonding company), agrees to be responsible to another party, called the *obligee* (the owner), for the default or debts of a third party, called the *principal* (the contractor). Bonds are simply a protection for the owner against default by the contractor. Bonds are discussed in more detail in Ch. 26.

Uncovering and Correction of the Work

If the contract documents state that certain portions of the work are to be observed by the architect prior to being covered or enclosed and the contractor proceeds with covering them, then the contractor must uncover them at no additional charge on request of the architect. If there is no specific mention of an item to be observed prior to covering, but the work is in accordance with the contract documents (the architect may still ask that it be uncovered), the cost is borne by the owner through a change order.

The contractor must correct work rejected by the architect for failing to conform to the requirements of the contract documents. The contractor must bear the cost of such corrections, including testing, inspections, and compensation for the architect's services connected with the corrections.

If the contractor does not correct the work, the owner has the right to have someone else correct the work. If this approach is used, the owner must first give the contractor one 7-day written notice that the work must be corrected or the owner will hire someone else to do the corrective work. The owner must then give another 3-day written notice to the contractor.

If the owner so chooses, he or she can accept nonconforming work as long as it meets code. Because this entails a change in the contract, it must be done by written change order, and if appropriate, the contract sum may be reduced.

Termination or Suspension of the Contract

Either the owner or the contractor may terminate the contract for valid reasons that are enumerated in the General Conditions of the Contract.

The contractor may terminate the contract if work has stopped for more than 30 days, through no fault of the contractor, for any of the following causes: a court order, an act of government, failure by the architect to issue a certificate of payment without giving a reason, repeated suspensions by the owner, or failure of the owner to provide proper evidence that financial arrangements have been made to fulfill the owner's obligations. Seven days' written notice is required.

If the architect certifies that sufficient cause exists, the owner can give seven days' written notice and terminate the contract if the contractor fails to supply enough properly skilled workers or proper materials, fails to make payment to subcontractors, disregards laws and ordinances, or is guilty of substantial breach of a provision of the contract documents. The owner may also suspend or terminate the work for convenience, without any cause.

SUPPLEMENTARY CONDITIONS OF THE CONTRACT

Because of the unique nature of construction projects, not every condition can be covered in a standard document such as the General Conditions of the Contract (CCDC 2). Each job must be customized to accommodate different clients, governmental regulation, and local laws. Information that is unique to each project can be included in one of four areas: the bidding requirements if it relates to bidding, the Owner-Contractor Agreement, the Supplementary Conditions if it modifies the General Conditions, and Division 01 (General Requirements) of the specifications. In most cases, supplementary conditions are not a separate document but are modifications made to AIA A201 (CCDC 2).

Some of the additional items that may be included in the Supplementary Conditions are

- permission for the architect to furnish the contractor with instruments of service in electronic form

- additional information and services provided by the owner

- cost for the architect to review the contractor's requests for substitutions

- provisions for the owner, instead of the contractor, to pay for utilities

- requirement that the contractor employ a superintendent to coordinate mechanical and electrical work

- provisions for fast-track scheduling

- reimbursement by the contractor for extra site visits by the architect, made necessary by the fault of the contractor

- additional protection for the owner against claims for additional time or for consequential damages

- requirements for more detailed information on costs and overhead

- additional requirements for payment procedures

- requirements for liquidated damages and bonuses

- additional requirements for bonding and insurance

There are additional items that can be included as part of the supplementary conditions, but the above list suggests what kinds of things are often included.

In addition to the supplementary conditions, a project may require special conditions. *Special conditions* are a separate section of the conditions of the contract and are written as a separate document to describe conditions that are unique to a particular project or project site. Special conditions would be written only once for unique conditions, while supplementary conditions could, for example, be used several times for the same client on different projects. They differ from the Supplementary Conditions of the Contract in that the supplementary conditions *modify the general conditions* to accommodate different clients, governmental regulations, and local laws.

SAMPLE QUESTIONS

1. Which of the following may the owner NOT do?

    A. stop work if the contractor's performance is not satisfactory or is in variance with the contract documents

    B. carry on the work and deduct costs normally due to the contractor for any corrections required because of unsatisfactory work

    C. stop the work if the architect reports safety problems on the site

    D. refuse, with good cause, to give the contractor proof that the owner can meet the financial obligations of the project

2.   During bidding, the client asks that the architect provide a full-time staff member on the job site during construction. The architect is entitled to extra compensation under what provision of AIA B141?

    A.   designated services

    B.   schedule of services

    C.   schedule of values

    D.   optional additional services

3.   The standard Owner-Architect Agreement separates the architect from the contractor with what?

    A.   agency

    B.   privity

    C.   mediation

    D.   indemnification

4.   What is used to encourage the contractor to finish the job or to satisfy mechanic's lien claims by subcontractors?

    A.   surety bond

    B.   liquidated damages

    C.   retainage

    D.   arbitration

5.   What fee method is preferable when a client is doing his or her first architectural project and does not yet have a program?

    A.   fixed sum

    B.   multiple of direct personnel expense

    C.   percentage of construction cost

    D.   unit cost based on square footage

6.   A project is about 60% complete when the owner begins receiving field reports from the architect stating that the contractor is failing to properly supervise the job, which is resulting in incorrect work. After several weeks of this the owner becomes worried and asks the architect for advice. What should be done if the work is being performed under the conditions of AIA Document A201?

    A.   After receiving the architect's field reports, the owner should stop the work and arrange for a meeting between the owner, architect, and contractor to determine the cause of the problems and what the contractor intends to do. If the contractor does not correct the work, the owner should carry out the work with other contractors and deduct the cost by change order from the original contractor's construction cost.

    B.   The architect should recommend that the owner give the contractor written notice of nonconformance with the contract documents and if, after 7 days, the contractor has not begun corrective measures, the owner should terminate the contract.

    C.   The architect and owner should discuss the problem to see if the owner would be willing to accept the nonconforming work in exchange for a reduction in the contract sum. If not, the owner should give 7 days' written notice to terminate the contract and find another contractor to finish the job.

    D.   The architect should, with the owner's knowledge, reject nonconforming work and notify the contractor that it must be corrected promptly. The architect should then remind the owner that the owner can have the work corrected after giving the contractor one 7-day written notice to correct the work and then an additional 3 days with a written notice.

7.   Which of the following describes agency?

    A.   The architect acts on behalf of the owner, making decisions, expediting the work, and taking on responsibilities the owner would normally have.

    B.   The architect mediates between the owner, the contractor, and vendors for the benefit of the owner.

    C.   The architect is the principal of the relationship and balances the needs of the contractor and the owner.

    D.   The architect works for the owner in certain designated areas with the authority to act on the owner's behalf.

8.   A client owns a large manufacturing plant and needs to expand to new facilities quickly and without interruption in production. The owner has arranged for a flexible line of credit to finance construction but wants to minimize project costs. The new facility will be very similar to the previous one, only sized for greater production capacity. Which type of construction should be recommended?

    A.   design-build

    B.   fast-track

    C.   multiple prime contract

    D.   design-award-build

9.   Which of the following are parts of the contract documents?

I.   an addendum
II. a change order
III. special supplementary conditions
IV. the contractor's bid
V.   a written amendment signed by owner and contractor

    A.   I, III, and V
    B.   I, II, III, and V
    C.   II, III, IV, and V
    D.   all of the above

10. Which of the following is NOT an accurate statement?

    A.   The architect is responsible for a defect in the work if he or she sees the defect but fails to report it to the contractor.
    B.   The owner has the sole right to make changes in the work but must do so through the architect.
    C.   The architect does not have to verify soil test reports given by the owner.
    D.   By the time construction documents are almost completed, the architect must still update the preliminary estimate of the cost of the work.

BIDDING PROCEDURES AND DOCUMENTS

Bidding is one of the primary ways contracts are awarded. After the architect has completed the contract documents, various acceptable or invited contractors review them and submit a price for doing the work. The contractor with the lowest bid is usually awarded the contract.

Competitive bidding is popular with many owners because it usually results in the lowest construction cost. For most public agencies, open public bidding is mandatory. However, it must be done within clearly defined guidelines to protect the owner from disreputable contractors and unethical bidding practices.

Bidding is in contrast to negotiation, in which the owner, with the assistance of the architect, works out the final contract price with one contractor. The contractor with which the owner negotiates may be selected in one of two ways. In the first, the owner may know precisely which contractor he or she wants to complete the project. This knowledge may come from having worked with the contractor before, through a referral, or by reputation. In the second method, the owner may select several possible contractors to be interviewed. Each of the contractors is interviewed, and one is selected based on qualifications, and possibly a fee proposal. If requested by the owner, the architect may assist in organizing and participating in the selection interviews and the negotiation process. During the negotiation process, the contractor may point out problems, make suggestions, or propose changes in the design or specifications to reduce the cost of the project. If the agreement is negotiated with a general contractor, the subcontracts may be open to competitive bidding.

BIDDING PROCEDURES

Through many years of practice the bidding procedure has generally been standardized and codified in various industry association documents. Everyone involved with the process knows the rules and what is expected of them. This chapter reviews the common procedures and documents used during this phase of the project delivery process. The duties of the architect are given in AIA Document B141 (CCAC Document 6).

Prequalification of Bidders

Bidding may be open to any contractor or restricted to a list of contractors who have been prequalified by the owner. The purpose of prequalification of bidders is to select only those contractors who meet certain standards of reliability, experience, financial stability, and performance. An owner contemplating the construction of a multimillion-dollar laboratory building would not be comfortable reviewing the bid of a small home contractor. Once these standards have been met, the owner is better able to review contractors' bids based primarily on price, personnel, and completion time.

Prequalification is usually based on information submitted by contractors concerning their financial qualifications, personnel, experience, references, size, bonding capability, and any special qualities that make them particularly suited for the project under consideration. For public work, when prequalification is allowed, it is usually based on the financial assets and size of the firm.

Advertising for Bids

There are two ways to notify prospective bidders. The first is by advertising in newspapers and trade journals, and the second is with an invitation to bid. With an *advertisement for bids*, the following information is published in one or more newspapers.

- the fact that a call for bids is being made
- the project name and location
- the name and address of the owner and architect

- a brief description of the project, including building type, size, principal construction materials and systems, and other pertinent information

- the date, time, and location the bids are due

- how and where bidding documents can be obtained, and deposit required, if any

- the locations where bid documents may be viewed

- the type and amount of bid bonds required

- the procedures for submitting bids

- whether or not the bids will be opened publicly

- other information as required, such as the owner's right to waive irregularities of the bidding process or to accept bids other than the lowest

Advertising for bids is usually required for public work, although much private work is also advertised if it is open bidding.

For prequalified bidders, an invitation to bid is sent to the prospective bidders. The invitation contains the same information listed previously for bid advertisements. Even with a prequalified list, there should be a sufficient number of bidders to encourage price competition.

Availability of Bid Documents

Bid documents are generally made available through the architect's office. Each bidder receives the required documents including prints of the drawings, specifications, bidding documents, bid forms, and other items as required. It is general practice to require that each bidder put down a deposit on each set of documents taken up to a certain number. After bidding, the deposit may be returned when the documents are returned in usable condition. In some cases the documents are loaned with no deposit required. Extra sets of documents over a certain number can be purchased by the contractor. In most large cities, documents are also put on file in a central plan room where subcontractors and material suppliers can review them. Electronic versions of the central plan room are also available.

Substitutions

During bidding, many contractors request that substitution for some of the materials specified be considered. This most often happens when there are proprietary specifications or a very limited list of acceptable manufacturers. The conditions under which substitutions will be considered and the procedures for reviewing submissions are clearly defined in the instructions to bidders, outlined later in this chapter.

Addenda

An *addendum* is a written or graphic document issued by the architect prior to the execution of the contract that modifies or interprets the bidding documents by addition, deletion, clarification, or correction. During the bidding process, there are always questions that need answers, errors that are discovered, substitutions that are made, and changes that the owner or architect decides to make. Addenda are instruments with which to do this. They are issued prior to bidding.

When an addendum is issued, it is sent to all registered bidders not later than 4 or 5 days before receipt of bids to give all the bidders ample opportunity to study the document and modify their proposals accordingly.

Prebid Conference

On some projects it is advantageous to hold a prebid conference. This is a meeting with the architect, owner, and bidders during which the bidders can ask questions and the architect and owner can emphasize particularly important conditions of the project. On very large projects, there may be separate conferences for mechanical subcontract bidders, electrical bidders, and so on. During these conferences, the architect should have someone take complete notes concerning the items discussed. A copy of the notes should be sent to all bidders whether or not they were in attendance. Answers to significant questions should be formalized in an addendum.

Bid Opening

In the instructions to bidders, the date, time, and place of the bid opening is included. Unless modified by addenda, the bid opening time and method of submitting the bids should be strictly observed. Bids received after the opening time should not be accepted unless none of the bids has been opened and there are no objections from those bidders present.

Most public bid openings are conducted by the architect with the owner and bidders present. The bids are read aloud, and the presence or absence of any required supporting documentation is noted. The architect usually prepares a bid log to note the base bid amount, amounts of alternates (if any), whether receipt of addenda was acknowledged, and other pertinent information. This should be made available to the bidders in either open or private bidding.

There should be no announcement of the apparent low bid at the bid opening; the architect should thank everyone for submitting and state that the submissions will be evaluated and a decision of award made within a certain time, usually 10 days. The decision should be sent to all the bidders.

If, after the bids have been opened, a bidder discovers and can support the claim that a clerical or mathematical error has been made, the bidder is usually allowed to withdraw the bid. If it was the low bid, the next lowest bidder is accepted.

Evaluation and Awarding of Bid

The architect assists the owner in evaluating the bids. This includes not only looking for the lowest proposed contract sum, but also reviewing prices for alternates, substitutions, lists of proposed subcontractors, qualification statements, and other documentation required by the instruction to bidders.

The owner has the right to reject any or all bids, to reject bids not accompanied by the required bid bond or other documentation (if required), and to reject a bid that is in any way incomplete or irregular.

If all of the bids exceed the project budget and the Owner-Architect Agreement fixes a limit on construction, the owner has one of four courses of action.

1. to rebid (or renegotiate if a negotiated contract)

2. to authorize an increase in the construction cost and proceed with the project

3. to work with the architect in revising the scope of the project to reduce construction cost

4. to abandon the project

Rebidding seldom results in any significant reduction in cost unless the bidding marketplace is changing rapidly. If the project is revised, the architect must modify the documents without any additional compensation. As discussed in a later section, alternates are often used as a flexible method of deleting or substituting alternative materials or construction elements to help reduce costs. Because the alternates are priced along with the base bid, the owner and architect can quickly evaluate the ramifications of selecting certain alternates.

BIDDING DOCUMENTS

Bidding documents are usually prepared by the architect using standard AIA forms or forms provided by the owner. Many commercial clients who engage in a great deal of building have developed their own forms and procedures, but they are typically similar in content to the AIA forms. The bidding documents are bound into the project manual, but they are *not* part of the contract documents.

The bidding documents usually include the following.

*   the advertisement or invitation to bid
*   instructions to bidders

*   supplementary instructions to bidders (if any)
*   bid forms
*   bid security information
*   performance bond, if required
*   labor and material payment bond, if required

Other documents that are sometimes added are qualification forms, a subcontractor list form, certificates of insurance, certificates of compliance with applicable laws and regulations, and information available to bidders, such as geotechnical data.

In addition to the bidding documents, which are not part of the contract documents, the bidding package also includes the drawings, specifications, general and supplementary conditions of the contract, special conditions (if any), addenda issued prior to the receipt of bids, and the form of agreement between owner and contractor.

Advertisement to Bid

As mentioned in the previous section, public bidding requires that bidding for the proposed building project be advertised in one or more newspapers and trade publications. If a list of prequalified bidders is being used, an invitation to bid is sent to those contractors. The advertisement or invitation to bid is also printed and bound into the project manual with the other bidding documents.

Instructions to Bidders

The instructions to bidders outline the procedures and requirements that the bidders must follow in submitting bids, how the bids will be considered, and submittals required of the successful bidder. AIA standard Document A701, Instructions to Bidders, is often used; other organizations produce similar forms. Instructions to bidders normally include the following items. (If the AIA form is being used and additional requirements must be included, it is suggested that supplementary instructions to the bidders be written.)

*   *Bidder's representations.* In making a bid, the bidder represents that he or she has read and understood the documents, reviewed the plans and specifications, and visited the site to become familiar with the conditions under which the work will take place, and that the bid is based on the materials, equipment, and systems required by the bidding documents, without exception.

*   *Bidding documents.* This article of the Instructions to Bidders states where the documents may be obtained, how many sets the bidders may have, and the amount of deposit, if any, for the documents. If the documents are returned within 10 days after receipt of bids, the deposit is returned. The cost of

replacing any missing or damaged documents is deducted from the deposit. The bidder winning the contract may keep the documents, and their deposit is returned. Normally, bidding documents are not issued directly to sub-bidders unless specifically stated in the advertisement or invitation to bid.

- *Interpretation or correction of bidding documents.* This article requires the contractor to carefully study the documents and examine the site and local conditions, and to report to the architect any errors, inconsistencies, or ambiguities discovered. If the bidders or sub-bidders need clarification or interpretation of the bidding documents, they must make a written request that must reach the architect at least seven days prior to the bid date. The architect must then issue any interpretations or corrections by addendum, which is sent to all bidders. Bidders must acknowledge receipt of all addenda on the bid form.

- *Substitutions.* The materials and products described on the drawings and specifications establish a standard for the work. If the bidder wants to propose a substitution, it must meet these standards. A bidder is required to submit a request for approval at least 10 days prior to the bid opening date. The request must include the name of the material or equipment for which the substitution is submitted, along with complete backup information about the proposed substitution. The burden of proof of the merit of the substitution rests with the bidder. The architect then reviews the submission and may either reject it or approve it. If approved, the architect issues an addendum stating this fact and sends it to all the bidders. No substitutions can be considered after the contract award.

- *Addenda.* Addenda were discussed previously. The Instructions to Bidders states that addenda must be transmitted to all bidders and made available for inspection wherever bidding documents are on file for that purpose. Addenda must be issued no later than four days prior to the date of bid opening.

- *Bidding procedures.* This article specifies how the bid form is to be filled in, what kind of bid security is to accompany the bid, and the procedure for submitting the bid. Bids are normally submitted in sealed envelopes, with the name of the party receiving the bid on the outside, along with the project name and the name of the entity submitting it. Bid security is described in a following section.

- *Modification or withdrawal of bid.* Bids may not be modified after the designated bid time and date. However, prior to that time a bid may be modified or withdrawn by making notice in writing over the signature of the bidder. The person receiving bids must date- and time-stamp the request. Withdrawn bids can be resubmitted if they are in full conformance with the Instructions to Bidders.

- *Consideration of bids.* The procedure for opening bids and reviewing them is explained in this article, including under what conditions bids may be rejected, how they will be evaluated, and conditions for award of the contract. The owner has the right to reject any or all bids. The owner also has the right to accept alternates in any order or combination and to determine the low bidder on the basis of the sum of the base bid and alternates accepted.

- *Post-bid information.* After the award of the bid, the contractor must submit to the architect a contractor's qualification statement, AIA Document A305 (CCDC 11), unless it has already been submitted as part of the bidding process. The contractor must also furnish to the owner the following.

  - a designation of the work to be performed with the contractor's own forces

  - the names of the manufacturers, the products, and the supplier of the principal items proposed for the project

  - the names of persons or companies proposed to perform major portions of the work

  If the successful bidder requests it, the owner must furnish to the bidder reasonable evidence that the financial arrangements have been made to fulfill the owner's obligations. This must be done no later than seven days prior to the expiration of the time for withdrawal of bids.

- *Performance bond and payment bond.* The required bonds and the time during which they must be delivered are outlined in this article. Normally, the cost of bonds is included in the bid number unless they are specifically required to be furnished after the receipt of bids and before execution of the contract. Performance and payment bonds are described in more detail in the following section.

Bid Forms

To ensure that all bids will be in identical form, there should be a standard form on which all the bidders enter the required information, making it easier to compare and evaluate the bids. The bid form should contain space for the amount of the base bid, written in both numbers and words, the price for the alternates (if any), unit prices (if any), and the number of calendar or work days in which the bidder proposed to complete the work. Space should be provided for the bidder to acknowledge receipt of any addenda. The bid form must be signed by someone legally empowered to bind the contractor to the owner in a contract.

Bid Security

Bid security is required to ensure that the successful bidder will enter into a contract with the owner. The form of the bid security may be a certified check, cashier's check, or bid bond. If the successful bidder does not enter into an agreement, the bid security may be retained to compensate for the difference between the low bid and the next lowest bidder. The amount of the bid security is either set as a fixed price or as a percentage of the bid; it is usually about 5% of the estimated cost of construction or the bid price.

Performance Bonds

A *performance bond* is a statement by a surety company that obligates the surety company to complete construction on the project should the contractor default on his or her obligations. If this happens, the surety company may complete construction by hiring another contractor, or it may simply supply additional money to the defaulting contractor to allow construction to proceed.

Performance bonds are usually mandatory on public work and advisable on private work. The cost of the performance bond is paid by the owner and is usually included in the amount of the construction price. The architect or owner must verify that the bond is written by a surety acceptable to issue bonds in the particular state where the construction is to take place. Some states will not accept so-called surplus-lines carriers who are not based in their state. In such cases the bond may be invalid.

Labor and Material Payment Bonds

Although a performance bond ensures the completion of the contract, it does not guarantee payment for labor and materials by the defaulting contractor. The result could be liens against the property or litigation by subcontractors and material suppliers. Because of this, a labor and material payment bond is usually required along with a performance bond to protect the owner against these possibilities.

COST CONTROL

Throughout the design process and up to completion of contract documents, the construction cost is only an estimate by the architect. It is only with bidding or final negotiation that the owner finally receives a firm price on the project. If the architect has been doing a reasonable job of tracking design changes and has a good idea of component costs, the bid price should be fairly close to the estimated amount.

Although the architect does not (and cannot) guarantee that the final construction cost will not vary from the estimate, there are several variables that can affect the final bid price.

Bidding in the Marketplace

By its very definition, bidding is a competitive activity. The price a contractor is willing to submit to an owner is, of course, dependent on the actual cost of subcontractor bids, the cost of the contractor's own labor and materials, the cost of equipment rental, the contractor's indirect costs, overhead, and profit.

Bidding is also affected by the construction marketplace, which is itself competitive. For example, if the local economy is depressed, contractors, subcontractors, and material suppliers may be willing to lower prices or reduce profit margins in order to get work and simply stay in business. In good times when work is plentiful, contractors are more selective about what jobs to bid on and what profit allowance to put in their bids. They are not as concerned about reducing prices to get jobs.

Both the architect and owner should be sensitive to these types of market conditions. If there is some flexibility in the owner's schedule, it can be advantageous to either delay or accelerate design and bidding to match favorable market conditions.

Effects of Documents on Bids

One of the variables over which the architect and owner have control is the set of contract documents. These can affect the amount of bids by what they contain and how they are put together, beyond just the amount and quality of construction they represent.

Poorly prepared drawings and specifications can raise questions in the mind of the contractor about what is specifically required, what may simply be implied, and what is omitted. To cover possible unforeseen items, the contractor may add extra money in the bid to cover these unknowns. On the other hand, a complete and clearly coordinated set of documents gives the contractor confidence in the scope and quality of the work. The contractor can then bid with more confidence only those items shown.

Alternates

An *alternate* is a request included in the bidding documents asking the contractor to supply a price for some type of variation from the base bid. This may be a change in materials or level of quality of a material, a deletion of some component, or the addition of some construction element. For example, the base bid may include carpet as a floor covering, whereas an alternate may be to substitute wood flooring for the carpet.

Alternates allow the owner some flexibility in modifying the cost of the project when the bids are in by varying the quantity or quality of the project. They also allow the owner to select certain options based on firm prices rather than on preliminary estimates.

Alternates are called *add-alternates* if they add to the base bid, or *deduct-alternates* if they reduce the base bid amount. Because alternates require more time for both the architect and bidders to prepare, they should be used carefully and should not be a substitute for conscientious cost estimating and reasonable design for the base bid amount.

For evaluating the bids, the selected alternates should be used to arrive at the lowest overall bid, but alternates should not be manipulated to favor one bidder over another.

Unit Prices

Unit prices are set costs for certain portions of work based on individual quantities. When required, they are listed on the bid form and provide a basis for determining changes to the contract. For example, a square foot cost for asphalt paving may be requested if the full extent of paving is unknown when bids are received. Even though the total cost may not be known, the unit costs of the bidders can be compared.

If unit prices are used when work is deleted from the contract, the amount of credit is usually less than the price for an additional quantity of the same item. Spaces should be provided in the bid form for both add and deduct amounts when applicable.

Allowances

As described in Ch. 25, an *allowance* is a set amount of money estimated by the architect to cover a particular material or piece of equipment when the cost for that material or equipment cannot be determined precisely at the time of the bid or negotiated proposal. For bidding, an allowance provides a way to allocate some amount of money for an item in the bid, even if the exact quantity or quality of the item is not known. The allowance (or allowances) is stated in the appropriate section (or sections) of the specifications, so all bidders are using the same amount in their bids. The contractor must add to the allowance the cost for unloading, handling, and installing the item as well as costs for the contractor's overhead and profit. If the costs for the allowance are more or less than the original estimate, the contract sum is adjusted accordingly by change order.

SAMPLE QUESTIONS

1. Which of the following would be used to formally incorporate a substitution into the work prior to the award of the contract?

    A. change order

    B. addendum

    C. alternate listing

    D. construction change directive

2. Which of the following are part of the bidding documents?

I. specifications

II. invitation to bid

III. list of subcontractors

IV. Owner-Contractor Agreement

V. performance bond

    A. II, III, and IV

    B. I, II, IV, and V

    C. II, III, IV, and V

    D. all of the above

3. At the time scheduled for a bid opening, a contractor comes rushing into the room three minutes late with a bid. None of the bids have been opened yet. What should the architect do?

    A. Refuse to accept the bid, stating that the deadline has passed.

    B. Since none of the bids have been opened yet, ask the other bidders if they would object to accepting the late bid.

    C. Accept the bid with prejudice.

    D. Accept the bid because none have been opened, but make a mental note to look on it with disfavor while you are evaluating it.

4. Which of the following statements about bidding is generally FALSE?

    A. Bidding procedures must be clearly and extensively outlined in the instructions to bidders because there are so many variations of the procedures.

    B. Bidding is nearly always necessary for federal government projects.

    C. Open bidding usually presents more problems than do other types.

    D. Competitive bidding takes more time than negotiation but can result in a lower construction cost.

5. A performance bond is designed to

    A. ensure that the subcontractors complete their work

    B. guarantee that the contractor will finish on time

    C. cover any possible liens that may be filed on the building

    D. protect the owner by having a third party responsible for completing the work if the contractor does not

6. If the lowest bid came in 20% over a client's construction budget, the architect should advise the client to

    A. increase the budget

    B. rebid the project using another list of contractors

    C. collaborate on revising the scope of the project to reduce cost

    D. accept all the deduct-alternates, to reduce the bid, and authorize a slight increase in construction cost to bring the two closer together

7. What variable affects a bid the most?

    A. the contractor's profit margin

    B. the influences of the construction marketplace

    C. labor and materials

    D. subcontract bids

8. The requirements for how a bidder should propose a substitution will be found in the

    A. advertisement to bid

    B. bidding procedures

    C. instructions to bidders

    D. general conditions

9. When the owner wants to make sure some amount of money is included in the bid before the exact amount of the item is known, the architect should use

    A. an allowance

    B. an add-alternate

    C. a material bond

    D. a unit price

10. The final responsibility of awarding a contract rests with the

    A. architect

    B. construction manager

    C. owner

    D. owner's legal counsel

CONSTRUCTION ADMINISTRATION SERVICES

Construction of the project is one of the most important phases of project delivery. It is the culmination of a great deal of planning, design, documentation, and organization. The architect should be closely involved with this phase of the project to the extent of his or her contractual responsibilities. During this phase the architect reviews and processes shop drawings and samples, manages requests for changes in the work, observes construction to make sure it is consistent with the contract documents, evaluates and processes the contractor's requests for payment, and administers the project closeout procedures.

SUBMITTALS

After the contract is awarded, the contractor is responsible for providing submittals called for in the contract documents. These include shop drawings, samples, and product data. The submittals are sometimes prepared by the contractor, but most often they are prepared by the subcontractors, vendors, and material suppliers.

Shop drawings are drawings, diagrams, schedules, and other data prepared to show how a subcontractor or supplier proposes to supply and install work to conform to the requirements of the contract documents. As such, they are usually very detailed, showing how portions of the work will be constructed.

A *sample* is a physical example of a portion of the work intended to show exactly how a material, finish, or piece of equipment will look in the completed job. Samples become standards of appearance and workmanship by which the final work will be judged.

Product data include brochures, charts, instructions, performance data, catalog pages, and other information that illustrate some portion of the work.

Although all submittals show in detail how much of the work is going to be built and installed, they are not contract documents.

When shop drawings and other submittals are prepared by the various subcontractors and material suppliers, they are sent to the general contractor, who is responsible for reviewing and approving them. By reviewing them, the contractor represents that field measurements have been verified, materials have been checked, and other construction criteria have been coordinated. Only after this review should the contractor transmit the submittals to the architect. If the submittals are not checked and signed by the contractor, the architect should immediately return them without review.

The architect's review of submittals is only for the limited purpose of checking for conformance with information given and seeing if they conform to the design intent. The architect is not responsible for determining the accuracy of measurements and completeness of details, for verifying quantities, or for checking fabrication or installation procedures. The architect's review does not relieve the contractor of his or her responsibilities under the contract documents.

If the submittals require the review of one of the architect's consultants, the architect forwards them to the consultant, who returns the submittals to the architect after review. The architect then reviews them and returns them to the contractor, who in turn returns them to the subcontractor or material supplier who prepared them. The architect may indicate that no exceptions are taken, that marked corrections should be made, that the submittals should be revised and resubmitted, or that they are rejected.

The architect must review submittals with reasonable promptness so as to cause no delay in the work, but neither the Owner-Architect Agreement nor the General Conditions of the Contract for Construction states a specific amount of time, except that the architect must act with reasonable promptness while allowing sufficient time, in the architect's professional judgment, to permit adequate review. The issue of time is generally dealt with in two ways. First, the General Conditions of the Contract for Construction requires that the contractor prepare a construction schedule for the project, which must include a schedule of submittals that allows the architect a reasonable amount of time for review. Second, the architect may, and should, indicate in the section on submittals in Division 01 of the specifications the procedure for making submittals, including the time that the contractor must allow for the architect's review. The contractor generally takes this time to establish the construction schedule.

According to the Owner-Architect Agreement, the architect must keep a log of submittals and copies of the submittals. The log should include the submittal name or other identification and the date the submittal was received by the architect. Other dates that must also be included on the log are the date the submittal was sent from the architect to the consultant (if necessary), returned to the architect, and subsequently returned it to the contractor. The action taken should also be noted.

Shop drawings are not a way for the architect to make changes in the design or refine details. Although minor corrections and changes can be made, the contractor may request a change order if the architect's modification of the shop drawings or samples results in an increase in project cost or time.

CHANGES IN THE WORK

During construction, changes in the work are usually required. They may be necessitated by errors discovered in the drawings, unforeseen site conditions, design changes requested by the client, rulings of building officials, or many other factors. During bidding and prior to contract award, changes are made by addenda. During construction, changes in the work are accomplished in one of three ways: by minor changes in the work, by construction change directive, or by formal change order.

Minor Changes in the Work

When a change does not involve a modification of the contract sum or time and is consistent with the contract documents, the architect may issue a written order directing the contractor to make a minor change. For example, moving a door opening over 6 in before it is framed would be a minor change. The architect may issue an order for such a minor change without the approval of either the owner or contractor.

Construction Change Directive

When a change needs to be made right away but the owner and contractor cannot agree on a price or time revision, the architect may issue a construction change directive. A *construction change directive* is a written order prepared by the architect directing a change in the work before the owner and contractor agree on an adjustment in contract cost, time, or both. The construction change directive gives the owner a way to unilaterally order changes to the contract without changing the terms of the contract. It is used in the absence of total agreement on the terms of a change order. The change in the work may involve additions, deletions, or other revisions. The construction change directive must be signed by both the architect and the owner but does *not* have to be signed by the contractor.

In addition to describing the changes required, the directive should include a proposed basis for determining the adjustment of cost or time or both. If the directive involves a cost adjustment, the architect's proposed basis of adjustment must be based on one of four methods: (1) a lump sum, properly itemized, (2) unit prices previously agreed to in the specifications, (3) costs to be determined by mutual agreement on a fixed or percentage fee, or (4) as provided for in a subsequent clause and summarized in the following paragraph.

Under provisions of the General Conditions of the Contract, the contractor must proceed with the work and advise the architect of the contractor's agreement or disagreement with the basis for cost and time adjustment. If the contractor agrees, the change is recorded as a change order. If the contractor disagrees, the architect determines the method and adjustment based on reasonable expenditures and savings of those performing the work. In addition to the actual cost of the work, the architect must include costs related to worker's benefits, equipment rental, supplies, premiums for bonds and insurance, field supervision, permit fees, and profit.

Change Orders

A *change order* is a document authorizing a variation from the original contract documents that involves a change in contract price, contract time, or both. Technically, it is issued by the owner because the owner has the agreement with the contractor, but it is prepared by the architect. It must be approved by the owner, architect, and contractor.

Any of the three parties may suggest a change order, but it is normally the architect who submits a proposal request to the contractor. This request is accompanied by supporting drawings or other documents as required to fully describe the proposed change. The contractor submits his or her quotation of price and time change. If these are acceptable to the owner, the formal change order document is prepared and signed by all three parties.

FIELD ADMINISTRATION

Once the project actually gets underway, the architect has a number of responsibilities under the Standard Form of Agreement Between Owner and Architect and in accordance with the General Conditions of the Contract.

Construction Observation

If made part of the architect's services in the Owner-Architect Agreement, the architect visits the site at intervals appropriate to the stage of construction or as agreed to in writing.

The purpose of the architect's observation is (1) to become generally familiar with the progress and quality of the work and to keep the owner informed, (2) to endeavor to guard the owner against defects and deficiencies in the work, and (3) to determine, in general, if the work is progressing in such a way that, when completed, it will be in accordance with the contract documents.

During construction observation, definite lines of communication among the parties are established by the General Conditions of the Contract for Construction. During this time the owner and contractor must communicate through the architect, unless otherwise provided in the Owner-Architect Agreement and the General Conditions. Communications between the contractor and consultants should also be through the architect. Communications between the architect and the subcontractors and material suppliers should be through the contractor.

The number and timing of visits to a job site are left to the judgment of the architect based on the size and complexity of the project, the type of construction contract being used, and the exact schedule of construction operations.

During each site visit the architect should make complete notes of the observations and include these in appropriate field reports.

A field report should include the following items.

- the report name and the architect's project number
- the field report number
- the date and time of the observation, and the weather conditions at the site
- the work currently in progress
- the number of workers present at the site or an estimate of the number, if the project is large
- observations made, including any problems

- an estimate of the conformance with the schedule and the estimated percent of completion
- items to verify and action or information required
- a list of any attachments, and the name of the person making the report

Copies of the field reports are sent to the owner, to keep him or her informed of the progress of the work, and to the contractor. Unless otherwise agreed to in writing in the Owner-Architect Agreement, the architect is not responsible for exhaustive or continuous on-site inspections, nor is the architect responsible for the contractor's failure to carry out the work, or for the means, methods, or techniques of construction, or for safety precautions on the job.

Rejecting Work

The General Conditions of the Contract gives the architect the authority to reject work that does not conform to the contract documents. Because rejecting work means extra time and expense for the contractor, the reasons for rejection should be carefully documented, and the owner should be kept informed of the situation. The architect has the authority to require inspection or testing of work, whether or not such work is fabricated, installed, or completed. However, this action does not give rise to any duty or responsibility of the architect to the contractor, subcontractors, or anyone else performing portions of the work. The contractor must promptly correct work rejected by the architect or work not conforming to the contract documents, whether discovered before or after substantial completion. The contractor pays for the cost of correcting such work.

Uncovering and Correction of Work

There are two situations where work may have to be uncovered. The first occurs when a portion of the work has been covered contrary to the architect's request or to specific requirements in the contract documents. In this case, the work must be uncovered for the architect's examination, and the cost for this, and for replacing it, is paid by the contractor. The second situation occurs when the architect has not specifically made a request to view a portion of the work and the work has already been covered. If the architect then requests that the work be uncovered and it is found that the work *does* conform to the contract documents, the owner must pay for the uncovering and replacement through a change order. If the work *does not* conform, it must be corrected and replaced, and the cost must be borne by the contractor. However, if the owner or a separate contractor caused the unsatisfactory work, the owner must pay the costs.

Safety

The contractor is solely responsible for safety on the job site. If the architect volunteers suggestions or directions concerning construction means and techniques in regard to safety issues, the architect may also assume legal responsibility and be held liable for accidents or other problems.

If the architect observes an obvious safety violation, he or she should call it to the attention of both the contractor (but not suggest how it can be corrected) and owner and should follow up with a notice in writing. If the safety problem is not corrected, the architect should notify both the contractor and the owner in writing.

Field Tests

When tests and inspections are required by the contract documents, or by laws, regulations, or orders of public authorities (building departments), the contractor is responsible for making arrangements with testing agencies acceptable to the owner or with the appropriate public authorities. The contractor pays for the tests and must give the architect timely notice of when and where the test is to be made so that the architect can observe the procedure.

If the architect, owner, or public authorities require additional testing beyond what is required in the contract documents, the architect should instruct the contractor to make arrangements, but only after written authorization from the owner. In this case, the owner pays for the tests.

Regardless of whether the tests were required originally by the contract documents or later by the architect or public authorities, if a test shows that a portion of the work does not conform to the contract documents (including violating building codes or other laws), then the contractor must pay all costs required to correct the problem, including those of additional testing and compensation for the architect's services.

Documentation

During the entire construction administration phase (as well as all phases of the architect's service), the architect should keep complete documentation of the progress of the job. This includes not only the standard forms used, such as change orders, certificates of payment, and the like, but also all correspondence, meeting notes, emails, telephone logs, and similar written material that records the who, what, why, when, and how of the project. This kind of documentation is critical if disputes arise or the client objects to fee payments for extra services of the architect.

Claims

There are usually disputes and claims on any construction project, and these typically occur during the construction phase. The General Conditions of the Contract specifically outlines the procedure to be followed if a claim or dispute arises.

A *claim* is a demand or assertion by the contractor or owner seeking payment of money, an extension of time, an adjustment or interpretation of the contract terms, or other relief from terms of the contract. Claims must be made by written notice to the other party and to the architect and must be initiated within 21 days from the occurrence of what prompted the claim or 21 days after the person making the claim first recognized the problem. Whoever makes the claim must substantiate it with documentation or other evidence.

The architect is responsible for reviewing claims and making decisions, such decisions being final but first subject to mediation, then arbitration. In the worst of cases, a claim may have to be decided by litigation.

If the owner or contractor has a dispute or makes a claim, the architect must take certain preliminary action within 10 days of receipt of the claim. Such action may include (a) requesting additional supporting data from the claimant, (b) suggesting a compromise, (c) accepting the claim, (d) rejecting the claim, or (e) advising the parties that the architect is unable to resolve the claim because of a lack of sufficient information, or that it would be inappropriate for the architect to resolve the claim.

In evaluating claims, the architect may consult with or seek information from either party or from anyone with special knowledge or expertise. The architect can ask the owner to authorize the retention of experts at the owner's expense. If the architect asks either the owner or the contractor to respond to a claim or provide additional information, that person must respond within 10 days and must either (1) give the response or information, (2) tell the architect when the response will be furnished, or (3) tell the architect that no supporting data will be provided.

The approval or rejection of a claim by the architect is final and binding on the parties but is subject to mediation and arbitration. A demand for mediation and arbitration must be made by the claiming party within 30 days from the date on which the party making the demand receives the final written decision from the architect on the claim. Mediation is a condition precedent to arbitration or the institution of other legal proceedings.

Although claims can arise from a multitude of conditions, there are two that are especially common.

- *Claims for additional time.* If the contractor feels that extra time is needed, he or she must submit the reasons for the request and include an estimate of the cost. If weather conditions are the basis for the claim, the contractor must submit evidence that weather conditions were abnormal for the time period, could not have been reasonably anticipated, and had an adverse effect on the construction schedule.

- *Claims for concealed or unknown conditions.* Sometimes there are surprises on the job site once construction begins. When this happens the contractor may make a claim for additional time or money. However, to be valid, the unknown conditions must meet two criteria: (1) they must be subsurface in nature or otherwise physically concealed, causing the site to differ from what is shown on the contract documents, or (2) they must be of an unusual nature that is different from what would ordinarily be found as part of construction activities for the project type. For example, test borings may indicate a standard type of soil, and the contractor may budget for normal excavation. If a large boulder is discovered that requires blasting or special excavation techniques, the contractor would be entitled to extra money and possibly an extension of the contract time. Claims of this type must be made within 21 days from first discovery.

Mediation and Arbitration

Arbitration is a method of resolving disputes between the owner and the architect and between the owner and the contractor. It is an alternative to the lengthy and costly procedure of litigation. The General Conditions of the Contract requires mediation and arbitration as the method of resolving claims between the owner and contractor if they are not resolved by the architect in the procedures outlined in the previous section or by mediation, which must be used before arbitration. Refer to Ch. 25 for more information on these two methods of dispute resolution.

The AIA standard documents require that arbitration proceedings be conducted under the Construction Industry Arbitration Rules of the American Arbitration Association and any applicable state laws.

Under arbitration, the two parties agree to submit their claims to an arbitrator or arbitrators and agree to abide by the arbitrator's decision. The arbitrator is knowledgeable in the construction industry and listens to evidence, reviews documents, and hears witnesses before making a decision.

Arbitration has the advantages over litigation of speed, economy, and privacy. However, unlike a trial, there are no rules of evidence and the decision cannot be appealed.

PROGRESS PAYMENTS

During the course of a job, the contractor requests periodic payments, usually monthly, against the total contract sum. Under the General Conditions of the Contract, the architect is responsible for making sure that the amounts requested are consistent with the amount of work actually done and the amount of materials stored.

Intermediate Payments

In order to receive periodic payment, the contractor must submit to the architect a notarized application for payment at least 10 days before the date established for each payment in the Owner-Contractor Agreement. This application should include the value of work done up to the date of the application, in addition to the value of materials purchased and in acceptable storage but not yet incorporated into the work.

In most cases, acceptable storage means stored at the site. However, if approved in advance by the owner, payment can also be authorized for materials and equipment suitably stored off-site at a location agreed to in writing. When the application for payment includes off-site storage, the amount must also include costs of applicable insurance, storage, and transportation to the site.

Certification of the application for payment constitutes a representation by the architect that the work has progressed to the point indicated and that, to the best of the architect's knowledge, information, and belief, the quality of the work is in accordance with the contract documents. Certification is not a representation that the architect has made exhaustive on-site inspections or that the architect has reviewed construction methods, techniques, or procedures. Further, certification is not a representation that the architect has reviewed copies of requisitions received from subcontractors and material suppliers or that the architect has determined how and for what purpose the contractor has used money previously paid.

The amount due to the contractor is based on the schedule of values that the contractor submits to the architect after the award of the contract. This allocates the total contract sum to various portions of work such as site work, foundations, framing, and so forth.

If the application for payment is approved, the architect signs it and sends it to the owner for payment. An amount, called the *retainage*, is withheld from each application until the end of the job or some other time during the work that is agreed on by both the contractor and the owner. The retainage gives the owner leverage in making sure the job is completed and can be used to provide money to satisfy lien claims.

The architect may withhold all or a portion of the applications for payment in order to protect the owner if the architect cannot represent that the amount of work done or materials stored is in conformance with the application. The architect may also withhold payment for any of the following reasons.

- defective work not remedied

- third-party claims or evidence of probability of third-party claims

- failure of the contractor to make payments to subcontractors

- reasonable evidence that the work cannot be completed for the unpaid balance of the contract sum

- damage to the owner or another contractor

- reasonable evidence that the work will not be completed on time and that the unpaid balance will not be sufficient to cover damages due to the delay

- persistent failure of the contractor to carry out the work in accordance with the contract documents

Final Payment

After the final punch list inspection, the contractor notifies the architect in writing that the work is ready for final inspection and submits a final application for payment. If, after a final inspection, the architect determines that the work is complete and acceptable under the conditions of the contract documents, a final certificate for payment is issued to the owner.

Before the certificate can be issued, however, the contractor must submit to the architect the following items.

- an affidavit that payrolls, materials, and other debts for which the owner might be responsible have been paid (AIA Document G706, Contractor's Affidavit of Payment of Debts and Claims, is often used)

- a certificate showing that insurance required by the contract documents to remain in force after final payment will not be canceled or allowed to expire without at least 30 days' written notice to the owner

- a written statement that the contractor knows of no reason that the insurance will not be renewable

- the consent of surety to final payment, if applicable (AIA Document G707, Consent of Surety Company to Final Payment, may be used for this purpose)

- any other data required by the owner that establish evidence of payment of obligations, such as releases and waivers of liens

If final completion is delayed through no fault of the contractor, the owner may, with certification by the architect, make partial payment for that portion completed without terminating the contract.

PROJECT CLOSEOUT

Project closeout is an important part of the construction administration phase. It is during this time that the building work is completed, the structure is made ready for occupancy, and all remaining documentation takes place.

The contractor initiates closeout procedures by notifying the architect in writing and submitting a comprehensive list of items to be completed or corrected. The contractor must proceed promptly to complete or correct these items. The architect then makes an inspection to determine if the work or a designated portion of it is substantially complete or if additional items need to be completed or corrected.

Substantial completion is the stage when the work is sufficiently complete in accordance with the contract documents so that the owner can occupy or utilize the work for its intended purpose. The date of substantial completion is important because it has legal implications. For example, in many states, the statute of limitations for errors possibly caused by the architect begins with the date of substantial completion. The date of substantial completion is also the termination of the contractor's schedule for the project. If there are bonuses or liquidated damages involved, they are based on this date.

The list of items made by the architect as a result of the inspection is called the *punch list*. It is during this inspection that the architect notes anything that needs to be completed or corrected if not in accordance with the contract documents. The contractor must correct these items, after which another inspection is called for. If the final inspection shows that the work is substantially complete, the architect issues a certificate of substantial completion. It is at this time that the final application for payment is processed.

In addition to completing the work, the contractor must also submit to the owner certain other items including the following.

- all warranties, maintenance contracts, operating instructions, certificates of inspection, and bonds

- all documentation required with the application for final payment (as described previously)

- a set of record drawings if required by the Owner-Contractor Agreement

- the certificate of occupancy as issued by the building department (part of the permit process originally paid for by the contractor)

- extra stock of materials as called for in the specifications

The contractor must also complete final cleaning, instruct the owner or owner's representatives in the operation of systems and equipment, complete the keying for locks and turn keys over to the owner, and restore all items damaged by the contractor.

If the work is not substantially complete based on the architect's inspection, the architect notifies the contractor of work that must be completed before a certificate of substantial completion can be prepared. The owner may wait for the entire project to be completed or, if appropriate, may agree with the contractor to occupy or utilize only a portion of the work.

The architect's services may terminate when the final certificate for payment is issued, if so described in the Owner-Architect Agreement. In the Standard Form of Architect's Services for Design and Contract Administration, administration services provided beyond the date of substantial completion are considered a change in service.

SAMPLE QUESTIONS

1. In what order should the following activities take place during project closeout?

I.   preparation of the final certificate for payment
II.   punch list
III. issuance of the certificate of substantial completion
IV.   notification by the contractor that the project is ready for final inspection
V.   receipt of consent of surety

    A. II, III, V, IV, then I
    B. II, IV, III, V, then I
    C. IV, II, V, I, then III
    D. IV, V, II, III, then I

2. Substantial completion indicates which of the following?

    A. The owner can make use of the work for its intended purpose, and the requirements of the contract documents have been fulfilled.
    B. The contractor has completed correcting punch list items.
    C. The final certificate for payment is issued by the architect, and all documentation has been delivered to the owner.
    D. all of the above

3. During a periodic visit to the site, the architect notices what appears to be an undersized variable air volume box being installed. What should the architect do?

    A. Tell the mechanical engineer to look at the situation during the next site visit by the engineer. Note the observation on a field report.
    B. Find the contractor and stop work on the installation until the size of the unit can be verified by the mechanical engineer and compared to the contract documents.
    C. Notify the owner in writing that the work is not proceeding according to the contract documents. Arrange a meeting with the mechanical engineer to resolve the situation.
    D. Notify the contractor that the equipment may be undersized, and have the contractor check on it. Ask the mechanical engineer to verify the size of the unit against the specifications and report to the architect.

4. When the project is 90% complete, the building department requires exit signs in addition to those shown on the approved plans. Which of the following instruments should the architect use?

    A. order for minor change
    B. addendum
    C. change order
    D. construction change directive

5. The contractor is solely responsible for which of the following?

I.   field reports to the owner
II.   field tests
III. scaffolding
IV.   reviewing claims of subcontractors
V.   reviewing shop drawings

    A. II and III
    B. III and IV
    C. I, II, and III
    D. II, III, and IV

6. Which of the following statements about submittals is FALSE?

    A. The architect must review them prior to checking by the contractor.
    B. The contractor is ultimately responsible for the accuracy of dimensions and quantities.
    C. They are not considered part of the contract documents.
    D. The contractor can reject them and request resubmittal.

7. If a contractor makes a claim for additional money for extra work caused by unforeseen circumstances, under AIA Document A201, when must the architect respond?

    A. within 5 days

    B. within 7 days

    C. within 10 days

    D. not until supporting data are submitted

8. Which of the following is NOT considered a submittal?

    A. mock-ups

    B. product data

    C. samples

    D. shop drawings

9. The architect's submittal log entries should include all of the following EXCEPT the

    A. action taken

    B. contract name

    C. date of receipt of the submittal

    D. date of forwarding to the consultant

10. A construction change directive requires the signature(s) of the

    A. architect only

    B. architect and contractor

    C. architect and owner

    D. architect, owner, and contractor

PROJECT AND PRACTICE MANAGEMENT

Project and practice management covers a wide range of services that the architect must apply throughout the entire design life cycle of a project. Most of these topics are covered in this chapter because construction documents and construction administration services are such a large part of project management, and most of the ARE test specifications related to this topic have been placed in the Construction Documents and Services division.

This chapter reviews the pertinent aspects of project and practice management that apply to all phases of the architect's work. The duties and responsibilities of the architect during construction administration are covered in Ch. 27. Also refer to Ch. 2 for more information on architectural practice and contracts during pre-design. Refer to Ch. 3 for a review of project budgeting, cost estimating, and scheduling during pre-design. Chapter 8 includes information on life-cycle cost analysis. Refer to Ch. 23 for information on the content and coordination of the architectural and consultant drawings. Project delivery methods, scope of services, and contracts are discussed in Ch. 25. Chapter 26 reviews the architect's role in construction procurement through the bidding or construction contract negotiation process.

PART 1: PRACTICE MANAGEMENT

Project and practice management are two of the most important services provided by an architect. Practice management refers to all the activities related to running a professional services business: business organization, human resources management, financial management, and marketing, as well as providing the actual services to complete projects, including project management.

BUSINESS ORGANIZATION

There are several types of organizational structures than an architect can use to conduct business. Each has its advantages and disadvantages and may be more or less appropriate depending on the number of people in the firm, the laws of the state or states where the firm is doing business, the type of practice, the size of business, and the level of risk the owner or owners want to take.

Sole Proprietorship

The simplest business type is the *sole proprietorship*. In this structure the company is owned by an individual and operates either under the individual's name or a company name. To set up a sole proprietorship, it is only necessary to establish a name and location for the business, open a company bank account, have stationery printed, and obtain whatever licenses are needed by the local jurisdiction. If employees are hired, other state (province) and local requirements must be met.

The advantages to this form of business include the ease of setting it up, total management control by the owner, and possible tax advantages to the owner because business expenses and losses may be deducted from the gross income of the business. The primary disadvantage is that the owner is personally liable for all debts and losses of the company. For example, if a client sues the designer, his or her personal income (and possibly co-owned property of a spouse), personal property, and other assets can be seized to pay any judgments. Another disadvantage is that it is more difficult to raise capital and establish credit as a sole proprietorship unless the owner's personal credit rating and assets are adequate. Because the business depends primarily on the work and reputation of the owner, it may be difficult to sell the business, and the company usually ceases to exist when the owner quits or dies.

Partnerships

With a *general partnership*, two or more people share in the management, profits, and risks of the business. Income from the business is taxed as ordinary income on personal tax forms. If necessary, employees can be hired as with any form of business.

Partnerships are relatively easy to form (a partnership agreement is usually advisable) and provide a business with the skills and talents of several people rather than just one, as with a sole proprietorship. In most cases, partnerships are formed because each of the partners brings to the organization a particular talent such as business development, design, or technical knowledge.

The primary disadvantage is that all the partners are responsible and liable for the actions of the others. As with a sole proprietorship, the personal assets of any of the partners are vulnerable to lawsuits and other claims. Because income is taxed at individual rates, this is another disadvantage of the partnership form. On a personal level, the partners may eventually disagree on how to run the business. If one partner wants to withdraw, the partnership is usually dissolved.

A variation of the general partnership is the *limited partnership*. This type of organization has one or more general partners and other limited partners. The general partners invest in the company, manage it, and are financially responsible, as with a general partnership. The limited partners are simply investors and receive a portion of the profits. They have no say in the management of the company and are liable only to the extent of their investment. Limited partnerships have generally given way to the limited liability company, described in a following section.

Corporations

Another common form of business organization is the *corporation*, sometimes called a *C corporation*. A corporation is an association of individuals created by statutory requirements and having an existence independent from its members. The formation and conduct of corporations are governed by the laws of individual states, and formal articles of incorporation must be drawn up by an attorney and filed with the appropriate state office in order to legally form a corporation.

Because a corporation is a separate legal entity, it is financially and legally independent from the stockholders. As such, the stockholders are financially liable only for the amount of money invested in the corporation. If the corporation is sued, the personal assets of the stockholders are not at risk. This is the greatest advantage of the corporate form.

Another advantage is that a corporation is generally taxed at a lower rate than are individuals, which can result in considerable savings. However, corporations are taxed at two levels: the corporation is taxed on the profit of the corporation and then shareholders are taxed on their dividends. Additionally, corporations have a continuity independent of changes in stockholders, deaths of members of its board of directors, or changes in the principles. It is also relatively easy to raise capital for corporations by selling stock in the corporation.

The primary disadvantages of a corporation are the initial cost and the continuing paperwork and formal requirements necessary to maintain the business. These, however, are usually outweighed by the reduced liability and tax benefits.

Variations on the corporate form include the subchapter S corporation and the professional corporation. A *subchapter S corporation* (also known as an *S corporation*) has certain eligibility requirements and offers all the advantages of a standard corporation, but the profits or losses are paid or deducted from the stockholders' personal income taxes in proportion to the share of stock they hold. This can be an advantage when there are losses or the tax rates of the state shift the financial benefits when the individual is taxed rather than the corporation.

Many states allow the formation of a *professional corporation* for professionals such as architects, lawyers, doctors, accountants, and interior designers. This form of business is similar to other corporations except that liability for malpractice is generally limited to the person responsible. However, each state has its own laws regarding the burden of liability in a professional corporation.

Limited Liability Companies and Limited Liability Partnerships

A *limited liability company* (LLC) and a *limited liability partnership* (LLP) are two hybrid business organizations that combine the advantages of the corporation and the partnership. The particular requirements of LLCs and LLPs vary according to the state in which the business is established, but basically, both are formed like a partnership where the investors are called members and those who manage are called managers. Unlike partnerships, it is possible to have nonmembers as managers. The company name must include LLC or LLP in the name.

The main advantage to these types of organizations is that liability is limited to a member's investment; a member has no personal liability. In addition, they are taxed as a partnership or corporation, as the owners decide, with only one level of taxation for members, unlike a C corporation. Generally, they are easier than a corporation to set up and operate.

Joint Ventures

A *joint venture* is a temporary association of two or more persons or firms for the purpose of completing a project. It is typically used by architectural firms when a project is too large or complex to be completed by one firm alone. It can also be used when one firm may not have the experience in a particular building type that the partnering firm has.

With joint ventures, a formal, written agreement should be developed that describes the duties and responsibilities of each firm, how profits and losses should be divided, and how the work will be done. Joint ventures are treated as partnerships and cannot be sued like a corporation can. Depending on the state (province) in which the joint venture operates, profits may be taxed as a partnership, or the individual members of the joint venture may be taxed separately.

OFFICE ORGANIZATION

In addition to the legal organization of the business, offices can be set up in various ways to complete projects. In the *departmental organization*, a project moves through the office from one department to another. There may be a marketing department, a design department, a specifications department, a contract documents department, and a construction administration department. While this type of organization is efficient and can take advantage of many types of specialists, communication among departments about any particular project can be a challenge. A departmental organization also discourages or makes it impossible for anyone to gain a breadth of experience or share their knowledge in other aspects of project planning and completion.

The *studio organization* is based on various smaller groups in the business, called studios. Each studio is responsible for completing an entire project, from initial planning to production and construction administration. Members of each studio have the necessary expertise to provide all or most of the work required of the project. Projects can be assigned to studios based on their expertise, or studios can be formed or dissolved as the need arises. For example, an office may have one studio to complete retail projects, another to do industrial work, and another to provide office planning. The advantages of the studio organization include close and immediate communication among members of the design team and the synergy that comes from sharing ideas and group problem solving. Studios also work well with a strong project manager system where the project manager has daily contact with the design and production teams as well as with the client. Sometimes the studio organization is combined with one or more departments that provide very specialized work, such as specification writing.

Smaller offices may work on a very informal basis in which the principal or the partners complete the client contact and design work and then hand off the production and administration to others in the office.

LEGAL ISSUES

There are a multitude of legal issues with which the architect should be familiar. These include not only contractual issues, but also issues such as office organizational structure, human relations, financial management, insurance, professional conduct, copyright, expert witness involvement, and obligations to the public. It is helpful to understand the fundamental principles on which contract language is based. Some of the more important ones are briefly described here.

Agency

The legal concept of *agency* is that one person, the "agent," acts on behalf of another, the "principal," in dealings with another, the "third party." In architecture, the agent is the architect, the principal is the owner or client, and the third party is the contractor. Legally speaking, when the agent consents to act on behalf of and represents the interest of the principal, the agent is empowered to create a legal relationship between the principal and third parties.

When the architect works with and conveys information to the contractor, the contractor may assume the architect has more authority than he or she has. The contractor may blame the architect for instructions the owner may not be aware of, and the owner may blame the architect for inadequately or incorrectly carrying out the wishes of the owner. The architect must be careful to act on the owner's behalf. The standard agreement forms and general conditions of the contract attempt to minimize potential problems by clearly defining duties and responsibilities of the various parties. This is one reason, for example, why change orders must be signed by the owner as well as the architect.

Duties

The law attempts to define what one person "owes" another in particular relationships, including contracts, by applying the term *duties* to a set of terms or requirements. Duties are important in the construction industry because of the multitude of formal (contractual) and informal relationships involved.

For the architect, there are three ways duty is established. The first is by the terms of a contract, whether written or oral. The standard forms of agreement established by the AIA (and Canadian organizations) attempt to outline the services and responsibilities of the architect as clearly as possible and state that these may not be extended without written consent of the owner. The second way duty is defined is by legislative enactment, such as building codes and architectural licensing laws. The third way duty is established is by the architect's conduct. Courts often look to the *implied duties* based on how the parties conduct themselves in the course of performing their work. Many situations may arise that are not covered by the contracts or general conditions. In these cases the architect is not free to act unilaterally without consultation with the client. The architect may be held liable for the consequences of either action or inaction.

Some examples of implied duties include the following.

- The architect has the duty to cooperate with the contractor. While some actions related to this duty are clearly stated in the contracts, others are not.

- The architect has the duty not to interfere with the contractor's work. Such interference includes actions that might cause delay or additional costs, or that cause the contractor to modify standard methods and procedures of construction.

- The architect has the duty to inform the contractor of relevant information that may affect progress of the job, including any problems or errors observed.

- The architect has the duty to assist the owner in coordinating the schedules and requirements of other contractors and vendors not under the control of the general contractor.

Liability, Negligence, and Risk Management

Liability is the legal responsibility for injury or damage to another person or property. Architects are constantly exposed to liability through their actions or inactions, or by simply being named as a responsible third party in other claims. One of the primary ways architects can be liable is through negligence. *Negligence* is the failure to use due care to avoid harming another person or property.

In order for an architect to be found negligent, three conditions must be met. First, there must be a legal duty established between the parties. Second, it must be shown that the architect breached that duty. Third, it must be shown that the breach of duty was the cause of the damage or injury suffered by the other party.

The architect is a person who represents himself or herself as having special knowledge and skill, and the law holds such professionals liable for their professional actions. However, the prevailing legal concept is that the professional is not expected to be perfect. The architect is only expected to exercise the degree of skill, knowledge, and judgment normally possessed by other professionals in similar circumstances in similar communities. The architect is expected to perform to the standards of the professional

community. That is, the architect should display the generally accepted knowledge and use the generally accepted practice and procedures of that community.

Although an architect cannot totally avoid liability, he or she can limit exposure to liability through good risk management. This involves the following procedures.

- Use well-written contracts and follow them thoroughly. Standard AIA (or Canadian) documents have been written to coordinate with each other and are based on decades of experience. If these cannot be used, employ an attorney to write your own contract or to review a client's contract.

- Maintain an active quality-control program. This should include a wide variety of elements, but the most important are establishing a well-defined program and set of objectives for the project; having standard checklists of procedures; using proven construction methods, details, and specifications; maintaining communication among everyone on the design and construction team (including the client); and making sure everyone in the office who works on the project understands the contractual obligations and their responsibilities.

- Document every decision, meeting, action, and observation throughout the entire life of the project. See the section under project management for more information on documentation. Documentation is invaluable in proving the sequence of events, who made a decision, and the standards of care the architect took to complete his or her work.

- Be very careful of last-minute changes and substitutions. About half of all claims and lawsuits are due to these types of actions, which result in modifications that the architect does not have time to fully research and consider.

- Carry sufficient liability insurance for the types of work the office does. See the following discussion on types of insurance.

- Follow the guidelines for avoiding third-party claims as discussed in the next section.

Exposure to Third-Party Claims

Through the concept of *privity*, the architect is theoretically protected from claims by parties with whom he or she has no direct contractual relationship. This is clearly stated in the General Conditions of the Contract for Construction, AIA A201 (CCDC 2), as an indemnification clause. An *indemnification clause* attempts to hold harmless both the owner and architect for any damages, claims, or losses resulting from the performance of any work on the project, whether by the contractor or others with whom the architect has no contractual relationship. However, in some cases courts may not support the enforcement of this clause for a variety of reasons, one of which may be that instructions the architect gave or failed to give were the primary cause of the damage or injury. In addition to making sure an indemnification clause is in the contract and general conditions, the architect can minimize third-party claims by doing the following.

- Do not include contract language that would expressly state or imply responsibility to provide management, supervision, coordination, or planning of construction, unless those services are specifically being provided.

- Be aware that actions or directions to the contractor during construction may imply that the architect's responsibility extends to portions of the work beyond what the contract requires. Do not give directions concerning methods of construction.

- Point out obvious construction safety problems to the contractor. Follow up in writing to both the contractor and owner. If the problems are not corrected, suggest to the owner that the owner stop construction until the problems are corrected.

Copyright

Copyright protection for an architectural work falls into two categories. The first is the traditional one and includes copyright for the drawings, specifications, and other pictorial or graphic representations of the architect's work. The second is for the building itself. This latter copyright protection was established under The Architectural Works Copyright Protection Act, which applies to buildings erected after December 1, 1990. With the current copyright protection, the copyright holder retains rights that include the graphic representation of a building as well as the overall form, arrangement, and composition of spaces and elements in the design. This means that an owner cannot make unauthorized copies of a building that was designed by the architect (copyright holder) or make derivative works. Derivative works are buildings designed after the original building that are either substantially similar to or modifications of the original building.

Generally, the architect owns the copyright unless the architect is an employee of the owner or the architect specifically assigns the copyright to the owner. This is something that should be clearly stated in the Owner-Architect Agreement. AIA Document B141 (CCAC Document 6) states that the architect is the owner of the instruments of service and shall retain all common law, statutory, and other reserved rights, including copyrights. In addition, the architect should specifically claim ownership rights of the building copyright.

To do this the Owner-Architect Agreement should state that these rights belong to the architect, and the architect should register the work with the U.S. Copyright Office. Although not technically required, official registration is advisable and allows the architect to bring a lawsuit for infringement, to collect attorneys' fees, and to recover statutory damages. Registration should be made within three months of "publication," or the construction of the building.

The architect can transfer copyright to the owner, if desired, or can grant a license to reproduce the building or a derivative work one or more times.

Insurance

There are many types of insurance, both required and optional, that pertain to doing business and completing a project. Each of the three primary parties to a project—the architect, owner, and contractor—must have certain kinds of insurance to protect against liability, property loss, and personal loss. Because the issue is so complex and the architect is not qualified to give insurance advice, it is best that the owner's insurance counselor give insurance recommendations for specific projects. The architect and contractor should also have their respective insurance advisers recommend needed insurance for their businesses.

Architect's Insurance

- *Professional liability insurance*: This type of insurance protects the architect in case some action by the architect causes bodily injury, property damage, or other damage. Sometimes called *malpractice insurance* or *errors and omissions insurance*, this coverage responds to problems resulting from things such as incorrect specifications, mistakes on drawings, and negligence. However, it excludes intentional wrongful acts, claims for cost estimates being exceeded, and claims arising from express warranties.

- *General liability insurance*: This includes a range of insurance to protect against claims of property damage, liability, and personal injury caused by the architect or employees, consultants, or other people hired by the architect. Sometimes the architect will also buy insurance to cover the possibility that contractors or subcontractors do not have their own valid insurance as they should.

- *Property insurance*: Property insurance protects the architect's building and its contents against disasters such as fire, theft, and flood. Even if office space is rented, property insurance protects the contents of the office.

- *Personal injury protection*: This protects the architect against charges of slander, libel, defamation of character, misrepresentation, and other torts. A *tort* is a civil wrong (as contrasted with a criminal act) that causes injury to another person.

- *Automobile insurance*: Automobile insurance covers liability and property damage to vehicles owned and used by the business and can include protection against claims made by employees using their own cars while on company business.

- *Workers' compensation*: This insurance is mandatory in all states and protects employees in the event of injuries caused by work-related activities.

Other types of insurance that the architect may carry include health and life insurance for employees, special flood insurance, valuable papers insurance, and business life insurance.

Owner's Insurance

As stated in A201, General Conditions of the Contract for Construction (CCDC 2), the owner is required to carry his or her own liability insurance as well as property insurance for the full insurable value of the work. This insures against physical loss or damage caused by fire, theft, vandalism, collapse, earthquake, flood, windstorm, or malicious mischief. It also provides for reasonable compensation for the architect's and contractor's services and expenses required as a result of insured losses. The policy must be the "all risk" type rather than the "specified peril" type. All-risk insurance is broader in coverage and includes all hazards except those that are specifically excluded by the policy. If the property insurance requires deductibles, the owner pays the costs not covered because of the deductibles. The insurance covers work stored off-site and portions of the work in transit. The owner is also required by the General Conditions to carry boiler and machinery insurance.

Contractor's Insurance

The General Conditions of the Contract require that the contractor carry insurance that will protect from the following types of claims.

- claims under workers' compensation

- claims for damages because of bodily injury, occupational sickness, or death of employees

- claims for damages of bodily injury or death to people other than employees

- claims for personal injury, which includes slander, libel, false arrest, and similar actions

- claims for damages other than to the work because of destruction of tangible property, including loss of use resulting from such damages

- claims for damages related to use of motor vehicles

- claims for bodily injury or property damage arising when an injury occurs after the job is complete and the contractor has left the site

- claims involving contractual liability insurance

PART 2: PROJECT MANAGEMENT

Project management is the coordination of the entire process of completing a job in the architect's office, from its inception to final move-in and post-occupancy follow-up. In most cases project management is the responsibility of one person. Another method of managing a project is with *partnering*. With this method, the various stakeholders of a project, such as the architect, owner, contractor, vendors, and others are brought into the decision making process. Partnering can produce much closer communication on a project and shared responsibilities. However, the day-to-day management of a project may be difficult with so many people involved. A clear line of communications and delegation of responsibility should be established and agreed to before the project begins.

PLANNING AND SCHEDULING

The project manager should be involved from the first determination of the scope of work and estimation of fees to the final follow-up. Planning involves setting requirements in three critical areas: time, fees, and quality. Time planning is scheduling the work required and making sure there are enough fees and staff to complete it. Methods of scheduling are discussed in Ch. 3.

A *fee projection* is one of the earliest and most important tasks that a project manager must complete. A fee projection takes the total fee the designer will receive for the project and allocates it to the schedule and staff members who will work on the project, after deducting amounts for profit, overhead, and other expenses that will not be used for professional time.

Ideally, fee projections should be developed from a careful projection of the scope of work, its associated costs (direct personnel expense, indirect expenses, and overhead), consultant fees, reimbursable expenses, and profit desired. These should be determined as a basis for setting the final fee agreement with the client. If this is done correctly, there should be enough money to complete the project within the allotted time.

There are many methods for estimating and allocating fees, including computer programs. Figure 28.1 shows one simple manual form that combines time scheduling with fee projections. In this example, the total working fee, that is,

Project: Mini-mall Project No.: 9274 Date: 10/14/2010
Completed by: JBL Project Manager: JBL Total Fee: $26,400

Phase or Task	Period 1 / 11/16–22	2 / 11/23	3 / 11/30	4 / 12/7	5 / 12/14	6 / 12/21	7 / 12/28	8 / 1/4	9 / 1/11	% of total fee	fee allocation by phase or task	person-hrs. est.
SD-design	1320	1320								10	2640	
SD presentation		1320								5	1320	
DD—arch. work			1980	1980						15	3960	
DD—consultant coord.			530	790						5	1320	
DD—approvals				1320						5	1320	
CD—plans/elevs.					1056	1056	1056	1056	1056	20	5280	
CD—details							2640	2640		20	5280	
CD—consultant coord.					440		440	440		5	1320	
CD specs.								1320	1320	10	2640	
CD—material sel.					660	660				5	1320	
budgeted fees /period	1320	2640	2510	4090	2156	1716	4136	5456	2376	100%	$26,400	
person–weeks or hours	53 / 1.3	106 / 2.6	100 / 2.5	164 / 4	108 / 2.7	86 / 2.2	207 / 5	273 / 6.8	119 / 3			
staff assigned	JLK	JLK AST JBC	JLK AST EMW-(1/2)	JLK AST JBC EMW	JLK AST EMW	JLK AST	JLK AST EMW →	JLK SBS BFD	JLK AST EMW			
actual fees expended												

Figure 28.1 Fee Projection Chart

the fee available to pay people to do the job after subtracting for profit, consultants, and other expenses, is listed in the upper right corner of the chart. The various phases or work tasks needed to complete the job are listed in the left-hand column, and the time periods (most commonly in weeks) are listed across the top of the chart.

The project manager estimates the percentage of the total amount of work or fee that he or she thinks each phase will require. This estimate is based on experience and common rules of thumb the design office may use. The percentages are placed in the third column on the right and multiplied by the total working fee to get the allotted fee for each phase (the figure in the second column on the right). This allotted fee is then divided among the number of time periods in the schedule and placed in the individual columns under each time period.

If phases or tasks overlap (as they do in the example in Fig. 28.1), total the fees in each period and place this figure at the bottom of the chart. This dollar amount can then be divided by an average billing rate for the people working on the project to determine an approximate budgeted number of hours that the office can afford to spend on the project

each week and still make a profit. Of course, if the number of hours exceeds about 40, then more than one person will be needed to do the work.

By monitoring time sheets weekly, the project manager can compare the actual hours (or fees) expended against the budgeted time (or fees) and take corrective action if actual time exceeds budgeted time.

Quality planning involves determining with the client what the expectations are concerning design, cost, and other aspects of the project. Quality does not simply mean high-cost finishes, but rather the requirements of the client based on his or her needs. These needs should be clearly defined in the programming phase of a project and written down and approved by the client before design work begins.

One useful technique for developing a schedule while at the same time involving all members of the design and construction team (including the client) is to complete a *full wall schedule*. With this process vertical lines are drawn 5 in apart on an entire wall, with the space between each line representing one week. The project manager develops a preliminary list of project tasks and who may be responsible for completing the tasks. Each task is written on two

3 × 5 index cards with one labeled "start" and one labeled "finish." The names of all the people responsible for tasks are placed along the left edge of the chart. Each person is asked to place the start and finish cards where they think the activity should be placed in the total schedule to indicate the time they need allotted for the task. This large, interactive schedule, serves as a starting point for discussion among everyone on the project team. Cards can be moved around easily, and once everyone agrees to the dates the schedule can be copied in a smaller format and used by everyone on the team.

MONITORING

Monitoring is keeping track of the progress of the job to see if the planned aspects of time, fee, and quality are being accomplished. The original fee projections can be monitored by comparing weekly time sheets with the original estimate. One way of doing this manually is shown in Fig. 28.2, which shows the same example project estimated in Fig. 28.1. Some project management software performs the same monitoring function.

In this chart, the budgeted weekly fees are placed in the table under the appropriate time-period column and phase-of-work row. The actual amounts of fees expended are written next to them. At the bottom of the chart, a simple graph is plotted that shows the actual money expended against the budgeted fees.

The project manager can also plot his or her estimate of the percentage of work completed to compare with money expended. If either line begins to vary too much above the estimate, the project manager must find the problem and correct it.

Monitoring quality is sometimes more difficult. At regular times during a project, the project manager, designers, and office principals should review the progress of the job to determine if the original problems are being solved and if the job is being produced according to the client's and design firm's expectations. The work in progress can also be reviewed to see whether it is technically correct and if all the contractual obligations are being met.

COORDINATING

During the project, the project manager must constantly coordinate the various people involved: the architect's staff, the consultants, the client, the building code officials, and firm management. The individual efforts of the staff must also be directed on a weekly, or even daily, basis to make sure the schedule is being maintained and the necessary work is getting done.

The coordination can be done by using checklists, holding weekly project meetings to discuss issues and assign work, and exchanging drawings or project files among the consultants.

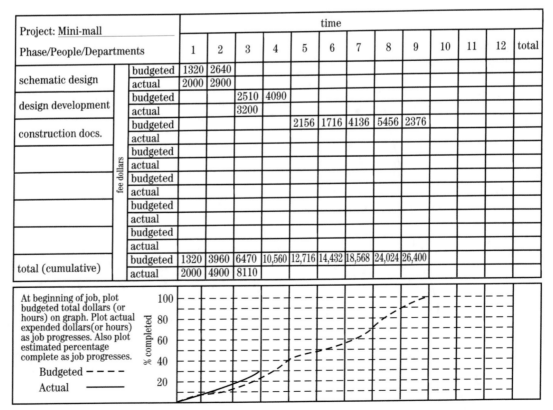

Project: Mini-mall Phase/People/Departments		time												
		1	2	3	4	5	6	7	8	9	10	11	12	total
schematic design	budgeted	1320	2640											
	actual	2000	2900											
design development	budgeted			2510	4090									
	actual			3200										
construction docs.	budgeted					2156	1716	4136	5456	2376				
	actual													
	budgeted													
	actual													
	budgeted													
	actual													
	budgeted													
	actual													
	budgeted													
	actual													
total (cumulative)	budgeted	1320	3960	6470	10,560	12,716	14,432	18,568	24,024	26,400				
	actual	2000	4900	8110										

At beginning of job, plot budgeted total dollars (or hours) on graph. Plot actual expended dollars(or hours) as job progresses. Also plot estimated percentage complete as job progresses.

Budgeted - - - -

Actual ———

% completed: 100, 80, 60, 40, 20

Figure 28.2 Project Monitoring Chart

DOCUMENTATION

Everything that is done on a project must be documented in writing. This documentation provides a record in case legal problems develop and serves as a project history to use for future jobs. Documentation is also a vital part of communication. An email or written memo is more accurate, communicates more clearly, and is more difficult to forget than a simple phone call, for example.

Most design firms have standard forms or project management software for documents such as transmittals, job observation reports, time sheets, and the like. Such software makes it easy to record the necessary information. In addition, all meetings should be documented with meeting notes. Phone call logs (listing date, time, participants, and discussion topics), emails, personal daily logs, and formal communications like letters and memos should also be generated and preserved to serve as documentation.

SAMPLE QUESTIONS

1. Which of the following is NOT a condition necessary for an architect to be found negligent to another party?

    A. It must be proven that the architect had a duty toward the other party.

    B. The architect must have violated a written contractual agreement.

    C. The architect must have committed a breach of duty.

    D. The damage must have been caused by a breach of duty on the part of the architect.

2. The business organization best suited to minimize the individual liability of the owners is a

    A. general partnership

    B. joint venture

    C. limited liability company

    D. limited partnership

3. About one third of the way through completion, a project manager notices that the fee expenditures are about 15% over budget. What is the first course of action the manager should take to ensure the project makes a profit?

    A. Determine what has caused the problem, and attempt a solution.

    B. Notify the client that fees may need to be increased.

    C. Alert the firm owners, and ask for direction to correct the problem.

    D. Modify the remainder of the project schedule and fee allocation.

4. A tort may arise from

    A. criminal activity of the architect

    B. unauthorized downloading of software

    C. negligence of the architect

    D. theft by an employee of an architect

5. What is NOT an advantage of a sole proprietorship?

    A. ease of establishment

    B. liability is limited to the owner's investment

    C. management control by the owner

    D. tax advantages

6. In a typical agency working relationship established by standard AIA (Canadian) documents, the agent is the

    A. architect

    B. contractor

    C. legal advisor

    D. owner

7. The architect can best involve all members of the project team with a

    A. flow diagram meeting

    B. full wall schedule

    C. Gantt chart

    D. project monitoring chart

8. At the beginning of a project the owner asks the architect to recommend the types of insurance the owner will need to carry for the duration of the project. How should the architect respond?

    A. Give the owner the AIA document on project insurance.

    B. Suggest the standard insurance types, and advise the owner about optional insurance.

    C. Tell the owner that the owner's insurance agent should make the recommendations.

    D. Arrange a meeting with the architect's insurance counselor and the owner.

9. Project management related to monitoring fees and completion is most often done

    A. daily

    B. weekly

    C. biweekly

    D. monthly

10. The office organization that would give individual employees the most job satisfaction is

    A. departmental

    B. pyramidal

    C. sole proprietorship

    D. studio

SECTION 5:
BUILDING REGULATIONS

BUILDING CODES AND REGULATIONS

Some of the most important subject areas tested in the ARE include building codes and regulations. In all divisions of the exam the candidate is required to apply knowledge of various regulations and codes to specific areas of practice such as pre-design, building design, structures, mechanical and electrical systems, and material selection.

Because there are several model codes being used in the United States and Canada, and because each local jurisdiction may amend a model code or write their own, the ARE tests the candidate's knowledge of general principles common to all of the model codes. The *ARE Guidelines*, published by NCARB, recommends that the candidate be familiar with the latest edition of one of the model code series. This includes the model code itself and related codes, such as the Uniform Mechanical Code, which is part of the series related to the Uniform Building Code (UBC). Refer to the section on model building codes later in this chapter for a listing of the currently existing model codes.

In the Building Planning and Building Technology divisions, the candidate is given specific code requirements that are very similar to most model code requirements, but that may not be exactly like a particular model code. They apply only to the test division being taken.

This chapter is based on the International Building Code (IBC), which was first published in 2000. Many local and state jurisdictions around the United States and elsewhere have adopted the IBC or will adopt it soon, replacing their use of the Uniform Building Code, the Standard Building Code, or the BOCA National Building Code.

Building codes differ from zoning ordinances, easements, deed restrictions, and other regulations affecting the use and planning of land. Zoning ordinances, for example, deal with the use of a piece of property, the density of buildings within a district and on a lot, the locations of buildings on a property, parking, and loading. Refer to Ch. 2 for a more detailed discussion of zoning and other land-use regulations. Refer to Ch. 30 for a discussion of regulations dealing with barrier-free design and accessibility.

HISTORY OF BUILDING CODES

The history of building codes dates to as early as 2000 B.C. The Babylonian Law of Hammurabi required a death sentence for any builder who constructed a house that later collapsed and killed the owner. The Greeks and Romans had various types of laws governing construction and the supervision of building. The Twelve Tales of Roman law even included setback requirements to allow for repairs and to prevent the spread of fire.

In London in the year 1189, England's first building code was published as the "Henry Fitz-Elwyne Assize of Buildings." Thatched roofs were forbidden, and the construction of party walls was specified. After the Great Fire of 1666 in London, an Act of Parliament set forth requirements for the rebuilding of the city. It set up different classes of buildings, described the types of materials that should be used, and established fees to cover the cost of inspection. Nearly 200 years later, Parliament revised the law as the Metropolitan Building Act of 1844. This act further extended building laws to set building areas and heights, types of buildings, and occupancies, and even established the idea of a building official.

The development of building regulations in the United States was prompted by fires and the spread of diseases as urban areas, especially New York, grew rapidly. The first recorded code in the United States was written in 1625 for the settlement of New Amsterdam (later New York). It regulated the types of roof coverings to protect buildings from chimney sparks.

As cities were expanding during the latter half of the nineteenth century, tenements in New York and elsewhere were overcrowded, poorly ventilated, combustible, and lacked

29-1

basic sanitary facilities. Insurance companies recognized that better fire protection was necessary, especially after the Chicago fire of 1871. By 1905, the National Board of Fire Underwriters wrote a model building code to decrease fire risk. This was the National Building Code, which was the beginning of the development of the three model building codes. In 1915, a group formed the Building Officials Conference of America and wrote what is now the BOCA National Building Code. The Uniform Building Code followed in 1927, and the Standard Building Code appeared in 1945. These three groups worked together in the 1990s and published a single code, the International Building Code, in 2000.

BUILDING REGULATIONS

Building codes are only one type of regulation affecting the design and construction of buildings. Additional requirements that may be applicable include legal and administrative regulations at the federal, state, and local levels. For example, a state may enforce environmental protection rules, while the building codes used in that state may not regulate environmental impact at all. As part of the predesign phase of a project, the architect must verify exactly which local, state, and federal regulations apply.

State and Federal Regulations

Most states have agencies that regulate building in some way. In addition to a state building code, a state government may enforce energy codes, environmental regulations, fabric flammability standards, and specific rules relating to state government buildings, institutions, and other facilities.

At the national level, several federal agencies may regulate a construction project, ranging from military construction to the building of federal prisons. Certain federal agencies may also regulate or issue rules covering a specific aspect of construction, such as the safety-glazing requirement issued by the Consumer Product Safety Commission (CPSC).

For architects, one of the most notable federal-level laws is the Americans with Disabilities Act (ADA), which regulates, among other things, removal of barriers for the physically disabled. The ADA requirements are based on the American National Standard Institute's (ANSI) ICC/ANSI A117.1, *Accessible and Usable Buildings and Facilities*. However, additional provisions are provided in the ADA regulations. Although very similar to the ICC/ANSI A117.1 standard, the ADA is not a code or standard, but is civil rights legislation. However, architects must adhere to its provisions when designing the facilities covered by the law. Chapter 30 covers requirements for barrier-free design.

Local Regulations

Local codes may include amendments to the model building code in use. These amendments usually pertain to specific concerns or needs of a geographical region or are provisions designed to alleviate local problems that are not addressed in the model codes. For example, a local amendment in a mountainous area might require a higher snowload factor for roof design based on the local climate.

Local regulations may also include requirements of agencies that govern hospitals, nursing homes, restaurants, schools, and similar institutions, as well as rules of local fire departments.

BUILDING CODES

Legal Basis of Codes

In the United States, the authority for adopting and enforcing building codes is one of the police powers given to the states by the Tenth Amendment to the United States Constitution. Each state, in turn, may retain those powers or delegate some of them to lower levels of government, such as counties or cities. Because of this division of power, the authority for adopting and enforcing building codes varies among the states.

Building codes are usually adopted and enforced by local governments, either by a municipality or, in the case of sparsely populated areas, a county or district. A few states write their own codes or adopt a model code statewide.

In Canada, the regulation of building rests with the provincial and territorial governments under the terms of the Constitution Act. The National Building Code of Canada (NBC) is a model code that is widely adopted by municipal bylaws or as the basis for a provincial building code. The Canadian National Fire Code and other complementary codes (such as the Canadian Plumbing Code and Canadian Housing Code) may also be adopted by local governments.

Codes are enacted as laws, just as any other local regulation would be. Before construction, a building code is enforced through the permit process, which requires that builders submit plans and specifications to the authority having jurisdiction (AHJ) for checking and approval before a building permit is issued. During construction, the AHJ conducts inspections to verify that building is proceeding according to the approved plans.

Even though code enforcement is the responsibility of the local building department or the AHJ, the architect is responsible for designing a building in conformance with all applicable codes and regulations. This is because an architect is required by registration laws to practice lawfully in order to protect the health, safety, and welfare of the public.

Model Building Codes

Local jurisdictions (including states) may write their own building codes, but in most cases a model code is adopted into law by reference. A model code is one that has been written by a group comprised of experts knowledgeable in the field, without reference to any particular geographical area. Adopting a model code allows a city, county, or district to have a complete, workable building code without the difficulty and expense of writing its own. If certain provisions need to be added or changed to suit the particular requirements of a municipality, the model code is enacted with modification. Even when a city or state writes its own code, that code is usually based on a model code. Exceptions include some large cities, such as New York and Chicago, and a few states that have adopted the Life Safety Code.

The primary model code is the International Building Code (IBC), first published in 2000 by the International Code Council (ICC). The IBC is an amalgam of the work of the three code-writing groups that previously published the three model codes in the United States. The IBC combines provisions of all three of the previous model codes and is organized in the same format that the three code-writing groups used in the most recent editions of their codes. At the time of this writing, many jurisdictions had adopted the IBC, and others were in the process or had set a date for adoption. Some jurisdictions were still using the most recent edition of one of the three previous model codes. The intent is for the IBC to bring uniformity to code practices across the country and in other countries, and eventually replace the other three model codes.

The three model codes previously published and still used by some jurisdictions in the United States include the following.

- the Uniform Building Code (UBC), used in the western and central portions of the United States and published by the International Conference of Building Officials (ICBO)

- the BOCA National Building Code, used in the northeastern part of the country and published by the Building Officials and Code Administrators Inter-national (BOCA)

- the Standard Building Code (SBC), used in much of the southeastern United States and published by the Southern Building Code Congress International (SBCCI)

The Life Safety Code, published by the National Fire Protection Association, is also used by some jurisdictions.

The primary code for Canadian provinces is the National Building Code of Canada (NBC), published by the National Research Council of Canada. Other Canadian codes regulate plumbing, housing, fire safety, and other specific areas of construction.

The eventual use of one model code throughout the United States will bring consistency and make it easier for designers and architects to work across the country. However, to complicate matters, the National Fire Protection Association (NFPA) has written its own code. First publication of the NFPA 5000 Building Code was in 2002. Some states may adopt the NFPA 5000 Building Code, so the designer may have to be familiar with its provisions as well.

The material in this chapter and in this book is based on the IBC, which will most likely become the most commonly used model code in the United States. Of course, building design and construction must conform to whatever code is in force in the locale where the structure is erected. Questions on the ARE are written to test the examinee's knowledge of universal code concepts rather than to specifically address one code.

The IBC and each of the three previously published model codes are prescriptive as opposed to performance based. This means that the code describes specific materials and methods of construction, or how a building component or design must be designed as opposed to how it is supposed to function. In most cases, the codes refer to nationally recognized standards of materials and testing so that, if a building component meets the test standard, it can be used. New or untested materials and construction methods can be used if they can pass the performance-based testing or if they can otherwise be shown to meet the requirements of the code. In the future, codes may be performance based.

Building codes are written to protect the health, safety, and welfare of the public. As such, all three model codes are written based on the idea of the "least acceptable risk." This is the minimum level required for building and occupant safety (even though just "meeting the code" is not always the best construction for a given circumstance).

Adjuncts to Building Codes

In addition to building codes, there are companion codes that govern other aspects of construction. The same groups that publish the model building codes publish these companion codes. For example, the ICC also publishes the International Residential Code, the International Fire Code, the International Mechanical Code, the International Plumbing Code, and the International Zoning Code, among others.

The electrical code used by all jurisdictions is the National Electrical Code (NEC), published by the National Fire

Protection Association (NFPA). In order to maintain greater uniformity in building regulations, the ICC does not publish an electrical code, but relies on the NEC.

Model codes also make extensive use of industry standards that are developed by trade associations, such as the Gypsum Association; government agencies; standards-writing organizations, such as the American Society for Testing and Materials (ASTM) and the National Fire Protection Association (NFPA); and standards-approving groups, such as the American National Standards Institute (ANSI). Standards are adopted into a building code by reference name, number, and date of latest revision. For example, most codes adopt by reference the American National Standard ICC/ANSI A117.1-1998, *Accessible and Usable Buildings and Facilities*. This standard was developed by the ICC based on previous ANSI accessibility standards and is approved by ANSI.

TESTING AND MATERIAL STANDARDS

All approved materials and construction assemblies referred to in building codes are required to be manufactured according to accepted methods or tested by approved agencies according to standardized testing procedures, or both. There are hundreds of standardized tests and product standards for building materials and constructions. Some of the more common ones are listed in this section.

As previously stated, standards are developed by trade associations, standards-writing organizations, and government agencies. By themselves, standards have no legal standing. Only when they are referred to in a building code and that code is adopted by a governmental jurisdiction do standards become enforceable.

Standards-Writing Organizations

The American Society for Testing and Materials (ASTM) is one organization that publishes thousands of Standards and test procedures that prescribe, in detail, such things as how the test apparatus must be set up, how materials must be prepared for the test, the length of the test, and other requirements. If a product manufacturer has one of its materials successfully tested, it will indicate in its product literature what tests the material has passed. Standards are developed through the work of committees of experts in a particular field. Although ASTM does not actually perform tests, its procedures and standards are used by testing agencies.

The National Fire Protection Association (NFPA) is another private, voluntary organization that develops standards related to the causes and prevention of destructive fires. NFPA publishes hundreds of codes and standards in a multivolume set that covers the entire scope of fire prevention including sprinkler systems, fire extinguishers, hazardous materials, fire fighting, and much more. As mentioned earlier in this chapter, NFPA has published its own building code, NFPA 5000™.

Other standards-writing organizations are typically industry trade groups that have an interest in a particular material, product, or field of expertise. Examples of such trade groups include the American Society of Heating, Refrigerating, and Air-Conditioning Engineers (ASHRAE), the Illuminating Engineering Society (IES), the Gypsum Association (GA), the American Concrete Institute (ACI), the American Iron and Steel Institute (AISI), and the American Institute of Timber Construction (AITC), among others. There are hundreds of these construction trade organizations.

The American National Standards Institute (ANSI) is a well-know organization in the field, but unlike the other standards groups ANSI does not develop or write standards. Instead, it approves standards developed by other organizations and works to avoid duplications between different standards. The ANSI approval process ensures industry consensus for a standard and avoids duplication of standards. For example, ANSI 108, *Specifications for Installation of Ceramic Tile*, was developed by the Tile Council of America and reviewed by a large committee of widely varying industry representatives. Although the ANSI approval processes does not necessarily represent unanimity among committee members, it requires much more than a simple majority and requires that all views and objections be considered, and that a concerted effort be made toward their resolution.

Testing Laboratories

When a standard describes a test procedure or requires one or more tests in its description of a material or product, a testing laboratory must perform the test. A standards-writing organization may also provide testing, but in most cases a Nationally Recognized Testing Laboratory (NRTL) must perform the test. An NRTL is an independent laboratory recognized by the Occupational Safety and Health Administration (OSHA) to test products to the specifications of applicable product safety standards.

One of the most well known NTRLs is Underwriters Laboratories (UL). Among other activities, UL develops standards and tests products for safety. When a product successfully passes the prescribed test, it is give a UL label. There are several types of UL labels, and each means something different.

When a complete and total product is successfully tested, it is *listed*. This means that the product passed the safety test and is manufactured under the UL follow-up services program. Such a product receives a *listed label*.

Another type of label is the *classified label*. This means that samples of the product were tested for certain types of uses only. In addition to the classified label, the product must also carry a statement specifying the conditions that were tested for. This allows field inspectors and others to determine if the product is being used correctly.

One of the most common uses of UL testing procedures is for doors and other opening protections. For example, fire doors are required to be tested in accordance with UL 10B, *Fire Tests of Door Assemblies*, and to carry a UL label. The results of UL tests and products that are listed are published in UL's *Building Materials Directory*.

Types of Tests and Standards

There are hundreds of types of tests and standards for building materials and assemblies that examine a wide range of properties from fire resistance to structural integrity to durability to stain resistance. Building codes indicate what tests or standards a particular type of material must satisfy in order to be considered acceptable for use. For example, gypsum wallboard must meet the standards of ASTM C36, *Standard Specification for Gypsum Wallboard*.

The most important types of tests for building components are those that rate the ability of a construction assembly to prevent the passage of fire and smoke from one space to another, and tests that rate the degree of flammability of a finish material. The following summaries include fire testing for building products and finishes. Flammability standards for carpet are described in Ch. 20.

Three tests are commonly used for fire-resistive assembly ratings. These include ASTM E-119, NFPA 252, and NFPA 257.

ASTM E-119

One of the most commonly used tests for fire resistance of construction assemblies is ASTM E-119, *Standard Methods of Fire Tests of Building Construction and Materials*. This test involves building a sample of the wall or floor/ceiling assembly in the laboratory and applying a standard fire on one side of it using controlled gas burners. Monitoring devices measure temperature and other aspects of the test as it proceeds.

There are two parts to the E-119 test, the first of which measures heat transfer through the assembly. The goal of this test is to determine the temperature at which the surface or adjacent materials on the side of the assembly not exposed to the heat source will combust. The second is the "hose stream" test, which uses a high-pressure hose stream to simulate how well the assembly stands up to impacts from falling debris and the cooling and eroding effects of water. Overall, the test evaluates an assembly's ability to prevent the passage of fire, heat, and hot gases for a given amount of time. A similar test for doors is NFPA 252, *Fire Tests of Door Assemblies*.

Construction assemblies tested according to ASTM E-119 are given a rating according to time. In general terms, this rating indicates the amount of time an assembly can resist a standard test fire without failing. The ratings are 1-hour, 2-hour, 3-hour, or 4-hour. Doors and other opening assemblies can also be given 20-minute, 30-minute, and 45-minute ratings.

NFPA 252

NFPA 252, *Fire Tests of Door Assemblies*, evaluates the ability of a door assembly to resist the passage of flame, heat, and gases. It establishes a time-based fire-endurance rating for the door assembly, and the hose stream part of the test determines if the door will stay within its frame when subjected to a standard blast from a fire hose after the door has been subjected to the fire-endurance part of the test. Similar tests include UL10B and UL10C.

NFPA 257

NFPA 257, *Standard on Fire Test for Window and Glass Block Assemblies*, prescribes specific fire and hose stream test procedures to establish a degree of fire protection in units of time for window openings in fire-resistive walls. It determines the degree of protection to the spread of fire, including flame, heat, and hot gasses.

Flammability tests for building and finish materials determine the following.

- whether or not a material is flammable, and if so, whether it simply burns with applied heat or supports combustion (adds fuel to the fire)

- the degree of flammability (how fast fire spreads across it)

- how much smoke and toxic gas it produces when ignited

Three tests are typically used for finish materials in building construction, although not all three may be in any one building code. These include ASTM E-84, NFPA 265, and NFPA 286. Refer to the section on furniture and flammability later in this chapter for tests related to fabrics and furniture.

ASTM E-84

ASTM E-84, *Standard Test Method for Surface Burning Characteristics of Building Materials*, is one of the most common fire testing standards. It is also known as the *Steiner tunnel test* and rates the surface burning characteristics of interior finishes and other building materials by testing a sample piece in a narrow test chamber that has a controlled flame at one end. The primary result is a material's flame-spread rating compared to glass-reinforced cement board (with a rating of 0) and red oak flooring (with an arbitrary rating of 100). ASTM E-84 can also be used to generate a "smoke-developed" index.

With this test, materials are classified into one of three groups based on their flame-spread characteristics. These groups and their flame-spread indexes are given in Table 29.1.

Table 29.1
Flame-Spread Ratings

class	flame-spread index
A (I)	0–25
B (II)	26–75
C (III)	76–200

Class A is the most fire resistant. Product literature generally indicates the flame spread of the material, either by class (letter or Roman numeral) or by numerical value. Building codes then specify the minimum flame-spread requirement for various occupancies in specific areas of the building. These are discussed in the next section under Finishes.

NFPA 265

The *room corner test*, NFPA 265, is sometimes required in addition to an ASTM E-84 rating for interior finishes or instead of it. This test determines the contribution of interior wall and ceiling coverings to room fire growth. It attempts to simulate real-world conditions by testing the material in the corner of a full-sized test room. It was developed as an alternate to the E-84 Steiner tunnel test. For the test, the textile wall covering is applied to three sides of an 8 ft by 12 ft by 8 ft high room (2440 by 3660 by 2440). An ignition source is placed in the room and provides a heat output of 40 kW for five minutes and then 150 kW for ten minutes. The textile receives either a pass or fail rating. It passes if (1) flame does not spread to the ceiling during the 40 kW exposure and (2) other conditions are met during the 150 kW exposure, including no flashover and no spread of flame to the outer extremity of the 8 ft by 12 ft wall.

NFPA 286

NFPA 286 is the *Standard Methods of Fire Tests for Evaluating Contribution of Wall and Ceiling Interior Finish to Room Fire Growth*. This standard, which evaluates materials other than textiles, was developed to address concerns with interior finishes that do not remain in place during testing according to the E-84 tunnel test. It is similar to NFPA 265 in that materials are mounted on the walls or ceilings inside a room, but with NFPA 286 more of the test room wall surfaces are covered, and ceiling materials can be tested. This test evaluates the extent to which finishes contribute to fire growth in a room by assessing factors such as heat and smoke released, combustion products released, and the potential for fire spread beyond the room.

FIRE-RESISTIVE STANDARDS

Building codes recognize that there is no such thing as a fireproof building; there are only degrees of fire resistance. Because of this, building codes specify requirements for two broad classifications of fire resistance as mentioned in the previous section: resistance of materials and assemblies, and surface burning characteristics of finish materials.

Construction Materials and Assemblies

In the first type of classification, the amount of fire resistance that a material or construction assembly must have is specified in terms of an hourly rating as determined by ASTM E-119 for walls, ceiling/floor assemblies, columns, beam enclosures, and similar building elements. Codes also specify what time rating doors and glazing must have as determined by NFPA 252 or NFPA 257, respectively. For example, exit-access corridors are often required to have at least a 1-hour rating, and the door assemblies in such a corridor may be required to have a 20-minute rating.

Building codes typically include tables indicating what kinds of construction meet various hourly ratings. Other sources of information for acceptable construction assemblies include Underwriters Laboratories' *Building Materials Directory*, manufacturers' proprietary product literature, and other reference sources.

Various building elements must be protected with the types of construction specified in IBC Table 601 (see Table 29.2) and elsewhere in the code. When a fire-resistive barrier is built, any penetrations in the barrier must also be fire rated. This includes doors, windows, and ducts. Duct penetrations are protected with fire dampers placed in line with the wall. If a fire occurs, a fusible link in the damper closes a louver that maintains the rating of the wall. The fire-resistive ratings of existing building components are important in determining the construction type of the building. This is discussed in more detail in a later section on classification based on construction type.

It is important to note that many materials by themselves do not create a fire-rated barrier. It is the construction assembly of which they are a part that is fire resistant. A 1-hour-rated suspended ceiling, for example, must use rated ceiling tile, but it is the assembly of tile, the suspension system, and the structural floor above that carries the 1-hour rating. In a similar way, a 1-hour-rated partition may consist of a layer of ⅝ in (15.9) Type X gypsum board attached to both sides of a wood or metal stud according to certain conditions. A

Table 29.2

Fire-Resistive Rating Requirements for Building Elements (hours)

BUILDING ELEMENT	TYPE I		TYPE II		TYPE III		TYPE IV	TYPE V	
	A	B	A[d]	B	A[d]	B	HT	A[d]	B
Structural frame[a]									
Including column, girders, trusses	3[b]	2[b]	1	0	1	0	HT	1	0
Bearing walls									
Exterior[f]	3	2	1	0	2	2	2	1	0
Interior	3[b]	2[b]	1	0	1	0	1/HT	1	0
Nonbearing walls and partitions									
Exterior				See Table 602					
Nonbearing walls and partitions									
Interior[e]	0	0	0	0	0	0	See Section 602.4.6	0	0
Floor construction									
Including supporting beams and joists	2	2	1	0	1	0	HT	1	0
Roof construction									
Including supporting beams and joists	$1^1/_2{}^c$	1[c]	1[c]	0	1[c]	0	HT	1[c]	0

For SI: 1 foot = 304.8 mm.

a. The structural frame shall be considered to be the columns and the girders, beams, trusses and spandrels having direct connections to the columns and bracing members designed to carry gravity loads. The members of floor or roof panels which have no connection to the columns shall be considered secondary members and not a part of the structural frame.

b. Roof supports: Fire-resistance ratings of structural frame and bearing walls are permitted to be reduced by 1 hour where supporting a roof only.

c. 1. Except in Factory-Industrial (F-I), Hazardous (H), Mercantile (M) and Moderate Hazard Storage (S-1) occupancies, fire protection of structural members shall not be required, including protection of roof framing and decking where every part of the roof construction is 20 feet or more above any floor immediately below. Fire-retardant-treated wood members shall be allowed to be used for such unprotected members.

   2. In all occupancies, heavy timber shall be allowed where a 1-hour or less fire-resistance rating is required.

   3. In Type I and Type II construction, fire-retardant-treated wood shall be allowed in buildings including girders and trusses as part of the roof construction when the building is:

     i. Two stories or less in height;

     ii. Type II construction over two stories; or

     iii. Type I construction over two stories and the vertical distance from the upper floor to the roof is 20 feet or more.

d. An approved automatic sprinkler system in accordance with Section 903.3.1.1 shall be allowed to be substituted for 1-hour fire-resistance-rated construction, provided such a system is not otherwise required by other provisions of the code or used for an allowable area increase in accordance with Section 506.3 or an allowable height increase in accordance with Section 504.2. The 1-hour substitution for the fire resistance of exterior walls shall not be permitted.

e. Not less than the fire-resistance rating required by other sections of this code.

f. Not less than the fire-resistance rating based on fire separation distance (see Table 602).

single piece of gypsum board cannot have a fire-resistance rating by itself, except under special circumstances defined by the new IBC.

Types of Fire-Resistance-Rated Walls and Partitions

One of the most common types of construction assemblies is the partition. The new IBC makes important distinctions between various types of fire-resistance-rated walls and partitions. These include fire partitions, fire barriers, fire walls, and smoke barriers. Fire partitions are one of the most common fire-resistance-rated partitions used.

A *fire partition* is a wall assembly with a 1-hour fire-resistance rating used in the following designated locations.

- walls separating dwelling units such as rooms in apartments, dormitories, and assisted living facilities

- walls separating guestrooms in Group R-1 occupancies, such as hotels

- walls separating tenant spaces in covered mall buildings

- corridor walls

The exceptions include (1) corridor walls permitted to be nonrated by Table 1016.1 (see Table 29.11) and (2) dwelling and guestroom separations in Types IIB, IIIB, and VB buildings equipped with automatic sprinkler systems. In these construction types, separation walls may be 1/2-hour rated.

In most cases, fire partitions must provide a continuous barrier. This means that they must extend from the floor to the underside of the floor or roof slab above or to the ceiling of a fire-resistance-rated floor/ceiling or roof/ceiling assembly. They must be securely attached top and bottom and extend continuously through concealed spaces, except where permitted to terminate below a fire-resistance-rated floor/ceiling or roof/ceiling assembly. There are several exceptions. Some of the more commonly used fire partitions are shown in Fig. 29.1. Refer to Sec. 708 of the IBC for complete information.

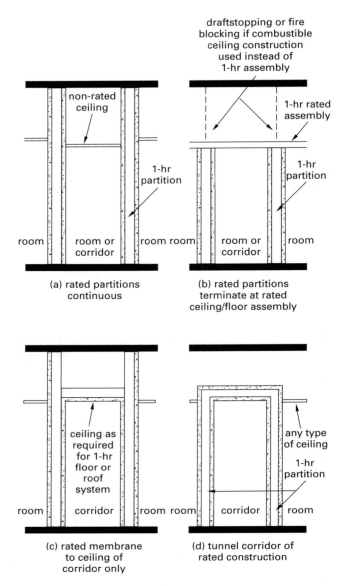

Figure 29.1 Options for Fire Partition Construction

Openings in fire partitions must have a minimum rating of ³/₄ hour, except for corridors, which must be protected by 20-minute fire-protection assemblies.

Although two options are available to separate rooms with fire partitions (as shown in Figs. 29.1(a) and 29.1(b)) and four options are available for corridor separation, for most commercial construction, using continuous slab-to-slab partitions is usually the best option. It provides the best passive control of smoke and fire without relying on the integrity of a ceiling assembly. It is also often the easiest and least costly for contractors to construct, although there could be instances where other methods may be preferred.

A *fire barrier* is a vertical or horizontal assembly that is fire-resistance rated and is designed to restrict the spread of fire, confine it to limited areas, and/or afford safe passage for protected egress. In general terms, a fire barrier offers more protection than a fire partition. Fire barriers are used for the following purposes.

- to enclose vertical exit enclosures (stairways), exit passageways, horizontal exits, and incidental use areas

- to separate different occupancies in a mixed-occupancy situation

- to separate single occupancies into different fire areas

- to otherwise provide a fire barrier where specifically required by a code provision in the IBC as well as the other international codes

Unlike fire partitions, fire barriers must always be continuous from the floor slab to the underside of the floor or roof slab above. There are only a few exceptions. Fire barriers may also be required to have a fire-resistance rating greater than 1 hour.

Openings in fire barriers are required to have a degree of protection that varies depending on the rating of the fire barrier and may range from 20 minutes to 3 hours according to IBC Table 715.3 (see Table 19.4 in Ch. 19). In any case, openings are limited to a maximum aggregate width of 25% of the length of the wall. Any single opening cannot exceed 120 ft² (11 m²) in area. Exceptions to these requirements include the following.

- Openings can be greater than 120 ft² if adjoining fire areas are equipped throughout with an automatic sprinkler system.

- Fire doors serving an exit enclosure can exceed the previous limitation.

- Openings are not limited to 120 ft² or 25% of the length of the wall if the opening protective assembly has been tested according to ASTM E-119 and has a fire-resistance rating equal to or greater than that of the wall. This allows the use of special fire-rated glazing.

In addition to openings, penetrations (as for pipes and conduit), joints (between the partition and other construction), ducts, and air transfer openings must also be protected as specified in the code.

A *fire wall* is a fire-resistance-rated wall that is used to separate a single structure into separate construction types or to provide for allowable area increases by creating what amounts to separate buildings even though they are attached. The unique thing about fire walls is that, in addition to providing 2- to 4-hour fire-resistance ratings, they must extend continuously from the foundation to or through the roof, and they must be designed and constructed such that, under fire conditions, the structure on one side can collapse without affecting the structural stability of the adjacent building.

A *smoke barrier* is a continuous vertical or horizontal membrane with a minimum fire-resistance rating of 1 hour that is designed and constructed to restrict the movement of smoke. It is a passive form of smoke control. Openings in smoke barriers must have at least a 20-minute rating.

Finishes

In the second type of fire-resistive classification, single layers of finish material are rated according to ASTM E-84, as discussed in the previous section, and their use is restricted to certain areas of buildings based on their rating and whether or not the building is sprinklered. See Table 29.3. The purposes of this type of regulation are to control the flame-spread rate along the surface of a material and to limit the amount of combustible material in a building.

The materials tested and rated according to surface burning characteristics include finishes such as wainscoting, paneling, heavy wall covering, or other finishes applied structurally or for decoration, acoustical correction, surface insulation, or similar purposes. In most cases, the restrictions do not apply to trim, such as chair rails, baseboards, and handrails, or to doors, windows, or their frames, or to materials that are less than $1/28$ in (0.9) thick cemented to the surface of noncombustible walls or ceilings.

Traditionally, the E-84 test was used exclusively for interior finishes, but the IBC provides an exception and also allows the use of finish materials, with the exception of textiles, if they meet requirements set forth in the IBC when tested in accordance with NFPA 286, the *Standard Methods of Fire Tests for Evaluating Room Fire Growth Contribution of Wall and Ceiling Interior Finish* (described in the previous section on types of tests and standards).

Refer to Ch. 20 for a discussion of carpet flammability and tests specifically related to carpet.

The UBC has a table similar to Table 29.3 except it uses the Roman numerals I, II, and III instead of letters and includes the different requirements for sprinklered and unsprinklered buildings in the text instead of as columns in the table. It still sets requirements for three areas of a building, but the most restrictive is enclosed vertical exitways, the next most restrictive includes other exitways, and the least restrictive includes rooms or areas.

If textile wall coverings are used, they must either be rated as Class A according to ASTM E-84 and be protected by an automatic sprinkler system or they must meet the requirements of NFPA 265, which is the room corner test described in an earlier section. In the older UBC only ASTM E-84 was referenced.

The IBC now regulates the ratings of some floor coverings, including textile coverings or those comprised of fibers—in other words, carpet. It specifically excludes traditional flooring types such as wood, vinyl, linoleum, and terrazzo.

The IBC requires textile or fiber floor coverings to be of one of two classes as defined by NFPA 253, the *flooring radiant panel test*. In this test the amount of radiant energy needed to sustain flame is measured and defined as the critical radiant flux.

Two classes are defined by the flooring radiant panel test: Class I and Class II. Class I materials have a critical radiant flux of not less than 0.45 W per square centimeter, and Class II materials have a critical radiant flux of not less than 0.22 W per square centimeter. Class I materials are more resistant to flame spread than are Class II materials. Class I finishes are typically required in vertical exits, exit passageways, and exit access corridors in Group I-2 and I-3 occupancies (hospitals, nursing homes, and detention facilities). Class II flooring is typically required in the same areas of Groups A, B, E, H, I-4, M, R-1, R-2, and S occupancies. In other areas carpet must conform to DOC FF-1 (ASTM D-2859), the pill test. Refer to Ch. 20 for more information on the pill test.

The exception to this is that if the building is equipped with an automatic sprinkler system, Class II materials are permitted in any area where Class I materials would otherwise be required. In addition, materials complying with DOC FF-1 may be used in other areas.

The 1997 UBC did not establish criteria for limiting the critical radiant flux of flooring materials.

Decorations and Trim

Curtains, draperies, hangings, and other decorative materials suspended from walls or ceilings in occupancies of Groups A, E, I, or R-1 and dormitories in Group R-2 must be flame resistant and pass the NFPA 701, vertical ignition test, or must be noncombustible. In Group I-1 and I-2 occupancies, combustible decoration must be flame retardant unless quantities are so limited as to present no hazard. The amount of noncombustible decorative materials is not limited, but the amount of flame-resistant materials is limited to 10% of the aggregate area of walls and ceilings, except in A occupancies, where it is limited to 50% if the building is fully sprinklered.

Material used as interior trim must have a minimum Class C flame-spread index and smoke-developed index. Combustible trim (such as wood trim), excluding handrails and

Table 29.3
Maximum Flame-Spread Classes for Occupancy Groups[k]

	SPRINKLERED[l]			NONSPRINKLERED		
GROUP	Vertical exits and exit passageways[a,b]	Exit access corridors and other exitways	Rooms and enclosed spaces[c]	Vertical exits and exit passageways[a,b]	Exit access corridors and other exitways	Rooms and enclosed spaces[c]
A-1 & A-2	B	B	C	A	A[d]	B[e]
A-3[f], A-4, A-5	B	B	C	A	A[d]	C
B, E, M, R-1, R-4	B	C	C	A	B	C
F	C	C	C	B	C	C
H	B	B	C[g]	A	A	B
I-1	B	C	C	A	B	B
I-2	B	B	B[h,i]	A	A	B
I-3	A	A[j]	C	A	A	B
I-4	B	B	B[h,i]	A	A	B
R-2	C	C	C	B	B	C
R-3	C	C	C	C	C	C
S	C	C	C	B	B	C
U	No restrictions			No restrictions		

For SI: 1 inch = 25.4 mm, 1 square foot = 0.0929 m².

a. Class C interior finish materials shall be permitted for wainscotting or paneling of not more than 1,000 square feet of applied surface area in the grade lobby where applied directly to a noncombustible base or over furring strips applied to a noncombustible base and fireblocked as required by Section 803.4.1.

b. In vertical exits of buildings less than three stories in height of other than Group I-3, Class B interior finish for unsprinklered buildings and Class C interior finish for sprinklered buildings shall be permitted.

c. Requirements for rooms and enclosed spaces shall be based upon spaces enclosed by partitions. Where a fire-resistance rating is required for structural elements, the enclosing partitions shall extend from the floor to the ceiling. Partitions that do not comply with this shall be considered enclosing spaces and the rooms or spaces on both sides shall be considered one. In determining the applicable requirements for rooms and enclosed spaces, the specific occupancy thereof shall be the governing factor regardless of the group classification of the building or structure.

d. Lobby areas in A-1, A-2 and A-3 occupancies shall not be less than Class B materials.

e. Class C interior finish materials shall be permitted in places of assembly with an occupant load of 300 persons or less.

f. For churches and places of worship, wood used for ornamental purposes, trusses, paneling or chancel furnishing shall be permitted.

g. Class B material required where building exceeds two stories.

h. Class C interior finish materials shall be permitted in administrative spaces.

i. Class C interior finish materials shall be permitted in rooms with a capacity of four persons or less.

j. Class B materials shall be permitted as wainscotting extending not more than 48 inches above the finished floor in exit access corridors.

k. Finish materials as provided for in other sections of this code.

l. Applies when the vertical exits, exit passageways, exit access corridors or exitways, or rooms and spaces are protected by a sprinkler system installed in accordance with Section 903.3.1.1 or Section 903.3.1.2.

International Building Code 2003. Copyright 2003. Falls Church, Virginia: International Code Council, Inc. Reproduced with permission. All rights reserved.

guardrails, cannot exceed 10% of the aggregate wall or ceiling area in which it is located.

Refer to the definitions at the end of this chapter for an explanation of the terms used in this section.

ADMINISTRATIVE REQUIREMENTS OF BUILDING CODES

All building codes include a chapter dealing with the administration of the code itself. Provisions that are normally part of the administrative chapter include what codes apply, the duties and powers of the building official, the permit process, what information is required on construction documents, fees for services, how inspections are handled, and what kinds of inspections are required. Also included are the requirements for issuing a certificate of occupancy, instruction on how violations are handled, and the provisions for appealing the decisions of the building official concerning the application and interpretation of the code. The architect may need to coordinate with the local

building official during several stages of the project from pre-design to completion of construction.

Refer to Chs. 2 and 3 for information on the architect's role in building code issues during pre-design. Refer to Ch. 23 for a discussion of the architect's responsibilities for providing required building code information on the construction documents.

REQUIREMENTS BASED ON OCCUPANCY

Occupancy refers to the type of use of a building or interior space, such as an office, a restaurant, a private residence, or a school. Uses are grouped by occupancy based on similar life-safety characteristics, fire hazards, and combustible contents.

The idea behind occupancy classification is that some uses are more hazardous than others. For example, a building where flammable liquids are used is more dangerous than a single-family residence. Also, residents of a nursing home will have more trouble exiting than will young school children who have participated in fire drills. In order to achieve equivalent safety in building design, each occupancy group varies by fire protection requirements, area and height limitations, type of construction restrictions (as described in the next section), and means of egress.

There are additional requirements for special occupancy types that include covered mall buildings, high-rise buildings, atriums, underground buildings, motor-vehicle-related occupancies, hazardous occupancies, and institutional occupancies, among others.

Occupancy Groups

Every building or portion of a building is classified according to its use and is assigned an occupancy group. This is true of the IBC as well as Canadian model codes and the three former U.S. model codes still used in some jurisdictions. The IBC classifies occupancies into ten major groups.

A	assembly
B	business
E	educational
F	factory and industrial
H	hazardous
I	institutional
M	mercantile
R	residential
S	storage
U	utility

Six of these groups are further divided into categories to distinguish subgroups that define the relative hazard of the occupancy. For example, in the assembly group, an A-1 occupancy includes assembly places, usually with fixed seats, used to view performing arts or motion pictures, while an A-2 occupancy includes places designed for food and/or drink consumption. Table 29.4 shows a brief summary of the occupancy groups and subgroups and gives some examples of each. This table is not complete, and the IBC should be consulted for specific requirements.

Further, because there are some significant differences between the 1997 UBC and the IBC, the designer must be clear about which code is being used in any particular jurisdiction. For example, the number of people in Group A occupancies in the IBC is no longer a driving factor in determining the subgroup. In Group R, apartments, dormitories, and condominiums have been taken out of the R-1 subgroup of the UBC and placed in a new R-2 subgroup. A new R-4 subgroup has been created for residential care or assisted living where the number of residents is between 5 and 16. There have been other changes to occupancy groups, but the concept is the same as with the other model codes: different uses in a building require different responses to maintain fire and life safety.

If a particular project does not seem to fit any of the categories, the architect should consult with the local building official for a determination of the occupancy classification of that project.

Knowing the occupancy classification is important in determining other building requirements, such as the maximum area, the number of floors allowed, and how the building must be separated from other structures. The occupancy classification also affects the following.

- calculation of occupant load
- egress design
- interior finish requirements
- use of fire partitions and fire barriers
- fire detection and suppression systems
- ventilation and sanitation requirements
- other special restrictions particular to any given classification

Mixed Occupancy and Occupancy Separation

When a building or area of a building contains two or more occupancies, it is considered to be of mixed occupancy. This is quite common. For instance, the design of a large office space can include office occupancy (a B occupancy) adjacent to an auditorium used for training, which would be an assembly occupancy (A occupancy). Each occupancy must be separated from other occupancies with a fire barrier of the hourly rating as defined by the particular code that applies. The idea is to increase the fire protection between occupancies as the relative hazard increases.

The required hourly rating determines the specific design and detailing of the partition separating the two spaces. The IBC shows required occupancy separations in a matrix table with hourly separations ranging from 1 to 4 hours. When the building is equipped with an automated sprinkler system, the required hourly ratings may be reduced by 1 hour. The other model codes have similar tables.

Accessory and Incidental Uses

In the IBC, there are two variations of the concept of mixed occupancies that have their own particular requirements. The first is the accessory use area, and the second is the incidental use area.

An accessory use area is a space or room that is used in conjunction with the main occupancy but that does not exceed 10% of the floor area of the main use. Accessory use areas

Table 29.4

Occupancy Groups Summary

occupancy	description	examples
A-1	assembly with fixed seats for viewing of performances or movies	movie theaters, live performance theaters
A-2	assembly for food and drink consumption	bars, restaurants, clubs
A-3	assembly for worship, recreation, etc. not classified elsewhere	libraries, art museums, conference rooms > 50
A-4	assembly for viewing of indoor sports	arenas
A-5	assembly for outdoor sports	stadiums
B	business for office or service transactions	offices, banks, educational above the 12th grade, post office
E	educational by > 5 people through 12th grade	grade schools, high schools, day care if > 5 children and > 2.5 years old
F-1	factory moderate hazard	see code
F-2	factory low hazard	see code
	hazardous—see code	see code
I-1	> 16 ambulatory people on 24-hour basis	assisted living, group home, convalescent facilities
I-2	medical care on 24-hour basis	hospitals, skilled care nursing
I-3	> 5 people restrained	jails, prisons, reformatories
I-4	daycare for > 5 adults or infants (<2.5 yrs.)	daycare for infants
M	mercantile	department stores, markets, retail stores, drug stores, sales rooms
R-1	residential for transient lodging	hotels and motels
R-2	residential with 3 or more units	apartments, dormitories, condominiums, convents
R-3	1 or 2 dwelling units with attached uses or child care < 6, less than 24-hour care	bed and breakfast, small child care
R-4	residential assisted living where number of occupants > 5 but < 16	small assisted living
dwellings	must use International Residential Code	
S	storage—see code	see code
U	utility—see code	see code

Note: This is just a brief summary of the groups and examples of occupancy groups. Refer to the IBC for a complete list or check with local building officials when a use is not clearly stated or described in the code.

do not need to be separated from the main occupancy with a fire barrier. For example, a small gift shop in a hospital would be considered an accessory use area and therefore not require the 2-hour occupancy separation normally required between an M occupancy and an I-2 occupancy. The two exceptions to this provision are for Group H occupancies or where the area must be separated as an incidental use area.

An *incidental use area* is an area that is incidental to the major occupancy and classified the same as the major occupancy of the portion of the building in which the incidental use area is located, but which, by code, must be separated from the main occupancy with a fire barrier. The incidental rooms or areas and the separations required are given in Table 302.1.1 of the IBC. See Table 29.5.

When the table allows a sprinkler system to substitute for a fire barrier, the incidental use area must be separated by a smoke barrier and the sprinklers only have to be in the incidental use area. Doors must be self-closing or automatic-closing.

CLASSIFICATION BASED ON CONSTRUCTION TYPE

Every building is classified into one of five major types of construction based on the fire-resistance rating (protection) of its major construction components. The purpose of this is to protect the structural elements of a building from fire and collapse, and to divide the building into compartments so that a fire in one area will be contained long enough to allow people to evacuate the building and firefighters to arrive.

These components, under the IBC, include the structural frame, bearing walls, nonbearing walls, exterior walls, floor construction, and roof construction. The five types of construction are Type I, II, III, IV, and V. Type I buildings are the most fire resistive, while Type V are the least fire resistive. Type I and II buildings are noncombustible, while Types III, IV, and V are considered combustible. The building type categories and fire-resistance rating requirements for each building element are shown in Table 29.2. The fire-resistance requirements for exterior, nonbearing walls are based on the distance from the building to the property line, the type of construction, and the occupancy group as shown in Table 29.6. Detailed requirements for the various construction types are contained in Chapter 6 of the IBC. It is advisable to read through this chapter and become familiar with their provisions.

In combination with occupancy groups, building type limits the area and height of buildings. For example, Type I buildings of any occupancy (except certain hazardous occupancies) can be of unlimited area and height, while Type V buildings are limited to only a few thousand square feet in area and one to three stories in height, depending on their occupancy. Limiting height and area based on construction type *and* occupancy recognizes that it becomes more difficult to fight fires, provide time for egress, and rescue people as buildings get larger and higher. It also recognizes that the type and amount of combustibles due to the building's use and construction affect its safety. Allowable height and area are discussed in the next section.

The fire zone is another consideration that is often encountered in urban areas. A municipality may, by action of the local government, divide a city into fire zones representing the degree of fire hazard. The fire hazard is usually based on factors such as density, access for fire fighting equipment, existing building heights, and so forth. The dense, central business district of a city is typically classed as fire zone 1. The local code may then restrict the types of construction that are allowed in the various fire zones.

For renovation or remodeling work, knowing the construction type is important if major changes are being made. For example, if the occupancy of a building or portion of a

Table 29.5
Incidental Use Areas

room or area	separation[a]
furnace room where any piece of equipment is over 400,000 Btu per hour input	1 hour or provide automatic fire-extinguishing system
rooms with any boiler over 15 psi and 10 horsepower	1 hour or provide automatic fire-extinguishing system
refrigerant machinery rooms	1 hour or provide automatic sprinkler system
parking garage (Section 406.2)	2 hours; or 1 hour and provide automatic fire-extinguishing system
hydrogen cut-off rooms	1-hour fire barriers and floor/ceiling assemblies in Group B, F, H, M, S and U occupancies, 2-hour fire barriers and floor/ceiling assemblies in Group A, E, I and R occupancies
incinerator rooms	2 hours and automatic sprinkler system
paint shops, not classified as Group H, located in occupancies other than Group F	2 hours; or 1 hour and provide automatic fire-extinguishing system
laboratories and vocational shops, not classified as Group H, located in Group E or I-2 occupancies	1 hour or provide automatic fire-extinguishing system
laundry rooms over 100 square feet	1 hour or provide automatic fire-extinguishing system
storage rooms over 100 square feet	1 hour or provide automatic fire-extinguishing system
Group I-3 cells equipped with padded surfaces	1 hour
Group I-2 waste and linen collection rooms	1 hour
waste and linen collection rooms over 100 square feet	1 hour or provide automatic fire-extinguishing system
stationary lead-acid battery systems having a liquid capacity of more than 100 gallons used for facility standby power, emergency power or uninterrupted power supplies	1-hour fire barriers and floor/ceiling assemblies in Group B, F, H, M, S and U occupancies. 2-hour fire barriers and floor/ceiling assemblies in Group A, E, I and R occupancies

For SI: 1 square foot = 0.0929 m², 1 pound per square inch = 6.9 kPa, 1 British thermal unit = 0.293 watts, 1 horsepower = 746 watts, 1 gallon = 3.785 L.

a. Where an automatic fire-extinguishing system is provided, it need only be provided in the incidental use room or area.

Table 29.6
Fire-Resistance Requirements for Exterior Walls[a]

FIRE SEPARATION DISTANCE (feet)	TYPE OF CONSTRUCTION	GROUP H	GROUP F-1, M, S-1	GROUP A, B, E, F-2, I, R[b], S-2, U
< 5[c]	All	3	2	1
≥ 5 < 10	I-A	3	2	1
	Others	2	1	1
≥ 10 < 30	I-A, I-B	2	1	1
	II-B, V-B	1	0	0
	Others	1	1	1
≥ 30	All	0	0	0

For SI: 1 foot = 304.8 mm.

a. Load-bearing exterior walls shall also comply with the fire-resistance rating requirements of Table 601.

b. Group R-3 and Group U when used as accessory to Group R-3, as applicable in Section 101.2 shall not be required to have a fire-resistance rating where fire separation distance is 3 feet or more.

c. See Section 503.2 for party walls.

building is being changed from a B (business) to an A (assembly) occupancy, the architect must know the construction type to verify that the maximum area is not exceeded. If it is, a fire wall may need to be constructed or sprinklers may need to be added. In addition, construction type can affect the required fire ratings of coverings of structural elements, floor/ceiling assemblies, and openings in rated walls. For example, during a remodeling a protected beam may be damaged or changed to accommodate new construction, degrading its required fire rating. The architect would have to detail or specify repairs or new construction to return the assembly to its original rating.

Allowable Floor Area and Heights of Buildings

Chapter 5 of the IBC sets forth the requirements for determining maximum height (in stories as well as feet or meters) and area of a building based on construction type. It also gives the allowed occupancy, and then presents conditions under which the height and area may be increased. The concept is that the more hazardous a building is the smaller it should be, making it easier to fight a fire and easier for occupants to exit in an emergency.

Table 503 of the IBC and similar tables in the other model codes give the maximum allowable area, per floor, of a building. A portion of IBC Table 503 is reproduced here in Table 29.7. This basic area can be multiplied by the number of stories up to a maximum of three stories under the IBC and up to two stories under the UBC.

If the building is equipped throughout with an approved automatic sprinkler system, the area and height can be increased. For one-story buildings, the area can be tripled, and for multistory buildings, the area can be doubled. The maximum height can be increased by 20 ft (6096), and the number of stories can be increased by one. Both area and height increases are allowed in combination.

If more than 25% of the building's perimeter is located on a public way or open space, the basic allowable area may be increased according to various formulas. Except for Group H, Divisions 1, 2, and 5 (hazardous occupancies), a Type I building may be of unlimited floor area and unlimited height, while other construction types are limited.

The basic allowable height and building area table (Table 29.7) can be used in one of two ways. If the occupancy and construction type are known, simply find the intersection of the row designating "occupancy" and the column designating "type," read the permitted area or height, and then increase the areas according to the percentages allowed for sprinklers and perimeter open space. More often, the occupancy and required floor area are known from the building program and a determination must be made on the required construction type that will allow construction of a building that meets the client's size needs. This is typically part of the pre-design work of a project.

Occasionally, an architect may be asked to design for an occupancy different than the original occupancy of the building as part of a remodeling project. If the existing building is not large enough to accommodate the new occupancy, the project may be infeasible, or other significant steps may need to be taken to make the project work. These steps include adding a sprinkler system or adding a fire wall.

For example, consider a 12,000 ft² (1125 m²), Type V building formerly used as a low-hazard factory (F-2 occupancy) proposed to be remodeled into a nightclub (A-2 occupancy). The IBC states the basic maximum allowable floor area for the F-2 occupancy as 13,000 ft² (1208 m²) and for the A-2 occupancy as 6000 ft² (557 m²) (Table 503 of the IBC, see Table 29.7). While the building would work as a factory, the entire area could not be used as a nightclub unless other steps were taken. If the client's program called for a 10,000 ft² nightclub, only 6000 ft² of the building could be used unless other changes were made, such as adding fire walls to separate the building into two areas.

Sometimes the required floor space of a project exceeds that allowed by the code and for the construction type the architect wants to use. In such cases, the architect can subdivide the building into smaller portions with fire walls (area separation walls in the previous UBC). The portions thus separated are then considered separate buildings, as long as all requirements for fire walls are met. A 4-hour fire-resistive wall is required in H-1 and H-2 occupancies. A 2-hour fire wall is required in F-2, S-2, R-3, and R-4 occupancies. A

Table 29.7

Allowable Height and Building Areas
(Height limitations shown as stories and feet above grading plane.
Area limitations as determined by the definition of "area, building" per floor.)

		type of construction								
		type I		type II		type III		type IV	type V	
		A	B	A	B	A	B	HT	A	B
group	hgt (ft)/ hgt (S)	UL	160	65	55	65	55	65	50	40
A-1	S	UL	5	3	2	3	2	3	2	1
	A	UL	UL	15,500	8,500	14,000	8,500	15,000	11,500	5,500
A-2	S	UL	11	3	2	3	2	3	2	1
	A	UL	UL	15,500	9,500	14,000	9,500	15,000	11,500	6,000
A-3	S	UL	11	3	2	3	2	3	2	1
	A	UL	UL	15,500	9,500	14,000	9,500	15,000	11,500	6,000
A-4	S	UL	11	3	2	3	2	3	2	1
	A	UL	UL	15,500	9,500	14,000	9,500	15,000	11,500	6,000
A-5	S	UL	UL	UL	UL	UL	UL	UL	UL	UL
	A	UL	UL	UL	UL	UL	UL	UL	UL	UL
B	S	UL	11	5	4	5	4	5	3	2
	A	UL	UL	37,500	23,000	28,500	19,000	36,000	18,000	9,000
E	S	UL	5	3	2	3	2	3	1	1
	A	UL	UL	26,500	14,500	23,500	14,500	25,500	18,500	9,500
F-1	S	UL	11	4	2	3	2	4	2	1
	A	UL	UL	25,000	15,500	19,000	12,000	33,500	14,000	8,500
F-2	S	UL	11	5	3	4	3	5	3	2
	A	UL	UL	37,500	23,000	28,500	18,000	50,500	21,000	13,000
H-1	S	1	1	1	1	1	1	1	1	NP
	A	21,000	16,500	11,000	7,000	9,500	7,000	10,500	7,500	NP
H-2	S	UL	3	2	1	2	1	2	1	1
	A	21,000	16,500	11,000	7,000	9,500	7,000	10,500	7,500	3,000
H-3	S	UL	6	4	2	4	2	4	2	1
	A	UL	60,000	26,500	14,000	17,500	13,000	25,500	10,000	5,000
H-4	S	UL	7	5	3	5	3	5	3	2
	A	UL	UL	37,500	17,500	28,500	17,500	36,000	18,000	6,500
H-5	S	3	3	3	3	3	3	3	3	2
	A	UL	UL	37,500	23,000	28,500	19,000	36,000	18,000	9,000
I-1	S	UL	9	4	3	4	3	4	3	2
	A	UL	55,000	19,000	10,000	16,500	10,000	18,000	10,500	4,500
I-2	S	UL	4	2	1	1	NP	1	1	NP
	A	UL	UL	15,000	11,000	12,000	NP	12,000	9,500	NP
I-3	S	UL	4	2	1	2	1	2	2	1
	A	UL	UL	15,000	11,000	10,500	7,500	12,000	7,500	5,000
I-4	S	UL	5	3	2	3	2	3	1	1
	A	UL	60,500	26,500	13,000	23,500	13,000	25,500	18,500	9,000
M	S	UL	11	4	4	4	4	4	3	1
	A	UL	UL	21,500	12,500	18,500	12,500	20,500	14,000	9,000
R-1	S	UL	11	4	4	4	4	4	3	2
	A	UL	UL	24,000	16,000	24,000	16,000	20,500	12,000	7,000
R-2[a]	S	UL	11	4	4	4	4	4	3	2
	A	UL	UL	24,000	16,000	24,000	16,000	20,500	12,000	7,000
R-3[a]	S	UL	11	4	4	4	4	4	3	3
	A	UL	UL	UL	UL	UL	UL	UL	UL	UL
R-4	S	UL	11	4	4	4	4	4	3	2
	A	UL	UL	24,000	16,000	24,000	16,000	20,500	12,000	7,000
S-1	S	UL	11	4	3	3	3	4	3	1
	A	UL	48,000	26,000	17,500	26,000	17,500	25,500	14,000	9,000
S-2[b,c]	S	UL	11	5	4	4	4	5	4	2
	A	UL	79,000	39,000	26,000	39,000	26,000	38,500	21,000	13,500
U[c]	S	UL	5	4	2	3	2	4	2	1
	A	UL	35,500	19,000	8,500	14,000	8,500	18,000	9,000	5,500

For SI: 1 foot = 304.8 mm, 1 square foot = 0.0929 m².
UL = Unlimited, NP = Not permitted.
a. As applicable in Section 101.2.
b. For open parking structures, see Section 406.3.
c. For private garages, see Section 406.1.

3-hour fire wall is required in other occupancies. Other codes may base the hourly ratings of fire walls (or area separation walls) on other requirements, such as the construction type, but the idea is the same—to separate one structure into two or more areas for the purpose of calculating maximum area.

Location on Property

One section of Ch. 6 of the IBC contains requirements for the siting of buildings relative to adjacent property lines based on occupancy group and construction type. It does this by specifying the fire resistance of exterior, nonbearing walls based on distance from property lines. The idea behind these regulations is to prevent the spread of fire from one building to another. If the exterior wall has openings, such as windows, provisions in Ch. 7 of the IBC regulate the maximum allowable area of openings based on distance from the property lines.

As with maximum allowable area, requirements for the location of a building on a site can be approached two ways during pre-design and site planning. If the building must be placed a certain distance from the property line, then the code specifies the minimum fire-protection rating and limitations on openings. On the other hand, if for cost or other reasons the architect wants to minimize the required fire ratings or increase the allowable opening area, or both, then the minimum allowable setback can be calculated.

MEANS OF EGRESS

Means of egress, or exiting, is one of the most important provisions of any building code and one with which the architect must be intimately familiar. Several parts of the written portion of the exam will contain questions related to exiting (as well as other code issues). In addition, the Block Diagram, Interior Layout, and Schematic Design vignettes in the ARE require that the examinee understand how to apply exiting requirements in an actual design. Except for minor mistakes, an error in planning for exiting on these vignettes is usually enough to result in a failing score. The following sections summarize some of the more important aspects of exiting.

At the time of this writing, many jurisdictions were in the process of adopting the International Building Code (IBC), but many jurisdictions were still using one of the three model codes or their own state or city code. However, even these older codes are based on the same principles discussed in this section. Refer to the definitions at the end of this chapter for specific terminology used in the following sections.

The Egress System

The IBC, UBC, and other codes define *means of egress* as a continuous and unobstructed path of vertical and horizontal egress travel from any point in a building or structure to a public way. The means of egress consists of three parts: the exit access, the exit, and the exit discharge. These must lead to a public way. A public way is any street, alley, or similar parcel of land essentially unobstructed from the ground to the sky that is permanently appropriated to the public for public use and has a clear width of not less than 10 ft. See Fig. 29.2.

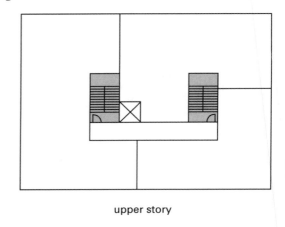

upper story

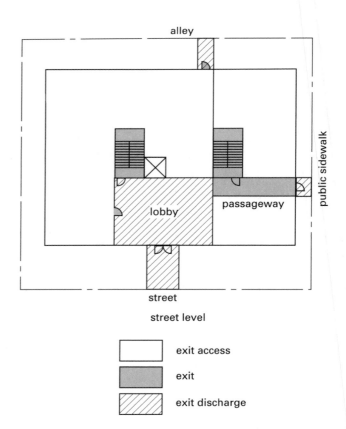

street level

exit access

exit

exit discharge

Figure 29.2 The Egress System

The *exit access* is that portion of the means of egress that leads to the entrance to an exit. Exit access areas may or may not be protected depending on the specific requirements of the code, based on occupancy and construction type. They may include components such as rooms, spaces, aisles, intervening rooms, hallways, corridors, ramps, and doorways. The exit access does not provide a protected path of travel. In the IBC, even fire-protection rated corridors are considered exit access. The exit access is the portion of the building where travel distance is measured and regulated (see the section on maximum travel distance in this chapter).

The *exit* is the portion of the egress system that provides a protected path of egress between the exit access and the exit discharge. Exits are fully enclosed and protected from all other interior spaces by fire-resistance-rated construction with protected openings (doors, glass, etc.). Exits may be as simple as an exterior exit door at ground level or may include exit enclosures for stairs, exit passageways, and horizontal exits. In the IBC, exits may also include exterior exit stairways and ramps. Depending on building height, construction type, and passageway length, exits must have either a 1- or 2-hour rating. Travel distance is not an issue once the exit has been reached.

The *exit discharge* is the portion of the egress system between the termination of an exit and a public way. Exit discharge areas typically include portions outside the exterior walls such as exterior exit balconies, exterior exit stairways, and exit courts. Exit discharge may also include building lobbies of multistory buildings if one of the exit stairways opens onto the lobby and certain conditions are met. These conditions require that the exit door in the lobby is clearly visible, that the level of discharge is sprinklered, and that the entire area of the area of discharge is separated from areas below by the same fire-resistance rating as for the exit enclosure that opens onto it. In the IBC, exterior exit stairways and ramps are considered exits, not exit discharge areas as they are in the UBC.

Occupant Load

The *occupant load* is the number of people that a building code assumes will occupy a given building or portion of a building. It is based on the occupancy classification as discussed earlier in this chapter, including assembly, business, educational, and the other categories. Occupant load assumes that certain types of use will be more densely packed with people than other types, and that exiting provisions should respond accordingly. For example, an auditorium needs more exit capacity to allow safe evacuation than does an office space with the same floor area.

The IBC requires that the occupant load be established by taking the largest number determined by one of three methods: by actual number, by table, or by combination.

In the first method, the actual number of people the building or space is designed to accommodate becomes the occupant load. For example, an auditorium with fixed seating can be calculated by counting the number of seats. However, because of the ease with which uses can change over time or how one space can be used for multiple purposes, this method is seldom used.

In the second method, the occupant load is determined by taking the area in square feet (or square meters) assigned to a particular use and dividing by an occupant load factor as given in the code. In the IBC, the occupant load factor (or floor area in square feet per occupant) is given in Table 1004.1.2, reproduced here as Table 29.8. This is the most common method of calculating occupant load. Other model codes have similar tables and use the same technique to calculate occupant load.

The *occupant load factor* is the amount of floor area presumed to be occupied by one person. It is based on the generic uses of building spaces and is *not* the same as the occupancy groups discussed earlier. The occupant load factors, over time, have been found to consistently represent the densities found in various uses. Table 29.8 also shows whether the occupant load must be calculated based on net or gross area. The gross floor area includes stairs, corridors, toilet rooms, mechanical rooms, closets, and interior partition thickness. Net floor area includes only the space actually used. Most common uses are included in the table, but the IBC gives the local building official the power to establish occupant load factors in cases where a use is not specifically listed.

The previous codes have tables similar to Table 29.8, although the exact factors may vary slightly. In previous editions of the UBC, the occupant load factor table also included a column describing the occupant load when two exits became necessary. In the IBC, this provision is now located in another part of the code and is based on occupancy as well as occupant load; it is discussed in the next section.

In the third method, when an occupant load from an accessory space exits through a primary space, the egress facilities from the primary space occupant load must include the occupant load of the primary space plus the occupant load of the accessory space. This provision simply requires that the occupant loads should be cumulative as occupants exit through intervening spaces to an ultimate exit.

Table 29.8
Maximum Floor Area Allowances per Occupant

occupancy	floor area in sq. ft. per occupant
agricultural building	300 gross
aircraft hangars	500 gross
airport terminal	
baggage claim	20 gross
baggage handling	300 gross
concourse	100 gross
waiting areas	15 gross
assembly	
gaming floors (keno, slots, etc.)	11 gross
assembly with fixed seats	see sec. 1003.2.2.9
assembly without fixed seats	
concentrated (chair only—not fixed)	7 net
standing space	5 net
unconcentrated (tables and chairs)	15 net
bowling centers, allow 5 persons for each lane including 15 feet of runway, and for additional areas	7 net
business areas	100 gross
courtrooms—other than fixed seating areas	40 net
dormitories	50 gross
educational	
classroom area	20 net
shops and other vocational room areas	50 net
exercise rooms	50 gross
H-5 fabrication and manufacturing areas	200 gross
industrial areas	100 gross
institutional areas	
inpatient treatment areas	240 gross
outpatient areas	100 gross
sleeping areas	120 gross
kitchens, commercial	200 gross
library	
reading rooms	50 net
stack area	100 gross
locker rooms	50 gross
mercantile	
areas on other floors	60 gross
basement and grade floor areas	30 gross
storage, stock, shipping areas	300 gross
parking garages	200 gross
residential	200 gross
skating rinks, swimming pools	
rink and pool	50 gross
decks	15 gross
stages and platforms	15 net
accessory storage areas, mechanical	
equipment room	300 gross
warehouses	500 gross

For SI: 1 square foot = 0.0929 m².

In determining the occupant load, all portions of the building are presumed to be occupied at the same time. However, the local building official may reduce the occupant load if the official determines that one area of a building would not normally be occupied while another area is occupied.

If there are mixed occupancies or uses, each area is calculated with its respective occupant load factor and then all loads are added together.

Example 29.1

What is the occupant load for a restaurant dining room that is 2500 ft² (232.5 m²) in area?

In Table 29.8, dining rooms are included under the use "Assembly without fixed seats, unconcentrated," with an occupant load factor of 15 ft². Dividing 15 into 2500 gives an occupant load of 167 persons (166.67 rounded up to 167).

Example 29.2

What is the occupant load for an office with a gross area of 3700 ft² that also has two training classrooms of 1200 ft² each?

An office, as a business area, has an occupant load factor of 100 gross, so 3700 divided by 100 gives an occupant load of 37 persons. Classrooms have an occupant load factor of 20. Two classrooms of 1200 give a total of 2400 ft². 2400 divided by 20 gives an occupant load for the classrooms of 120. The total occupant load of all the spaces, therefore, is 37 plus 120, or 157 persons.

Required Number of Exits

The number of exits or exit access doorways from a space, a group of spaces, or an entire building is determined based on several factors. These include the occupant load and occupancy of a space, the limitations on the "common path of egress travel," which is described in the next section, and specific requirements when large occupant loads are encountered.

All buildings or portions of a building must, of course, have at least one exit. When the number of occupants exceeds the number given in the code, then at least two exits must be provided. The idea is to have an alternate way out of a room, group of rooms, or building if one exit is blocked. The IBC requires two exits when the occupant load of a space exceeds the numbers given in Table 1014.1, reproduced here as Table 29.9.

Table 29.9
Maximum Occupant Load Spaces with One Exit

occupancy	maximum occupant load
A, B, E, F, M, U	50
H-1, H-2, H-3	3
H-4, H-5, I-1, I-3, I-4, R	10
S	30

There are several exceptions where the life-safety risk is so minimal that only one exit is acceptable. Two of these exceptions include the second story of an apartment with only four units and a maximum travel distance of 50 ft, and a business occupancy in a one-story building with a maximum occupant load of 50 and a maximum travel distance of 75 ft. Other exceptions are given in IBC Table 1018.2.

For large occupant loads, three exits are required when the occupant load is between 501 and 1000, and at least four exits are required when the occupant load exceeds 1000.

In the previous UBC, only the number of occupants determined if two exits were required. The provision of common path of egress travel was not used.

Common Path of Egress Travel

Even if the occupant load of a building space is less than that shown in Table 29.9, two exits are still required if the common path of egress travel exceeds limits given in the code. The *common path of egress travel* is that portion of an exit access that the occupants are required to traverse before two separate and distinct paths of egress travel to two exits are available. See Fig. 29.3. Even if two exits are not required based on occupant load, if the common path of travel exceeds 75 ft (32 m) for all except H-1, H-2, and H-3 occupancies, then two exits from a space are required. The distance is increased to 100 ft (30.5 m) in some occupancies if certain conditions are met. For example, in B, F, and S occupancies, if the building is fully sprinklered, the maximum length of common path of egress travel is increased to 100 ft.

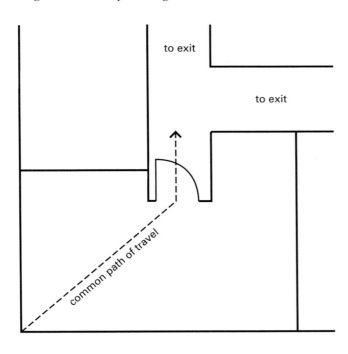

Figure 29.3 Common Path of Egress Travel

Maximum Travel Distance

Exit access travel distance is the distance that an occupant must travel from the most remote point in the occupied portions of the exit access to the entrance to the nearest exit. Because exit access areas are not protected, the code limits how far someone must travel to safety. Once a person is safely in an exit, travel distance is not an issue. Maximum travel distances are based on the occupancy of the building and whether or not the building is sprinklered. There are special requirements in the IBC as well as the older model codes that decrease the allowable travel distances in some occupancies and situations such as malls, atria, hazardous locations, educational uses, and assembly seating.

The maximum exit access travel distances are given in Table 1015.1 of the IBC. See Table 29.10. The footnotes to this table refer to other sections of the code for specific occupancy requirements.

Table 29.10

Exit Access Travel Distances[a]

occupancy	without sprinkler system (feet)	with sprinkler system (feet)
A, E, F-1, I-1, M, R, S-1	200	250[b]
B	200	300[c]
F-2, S-2, U	300	400[b]
H-1	Not Permitted	75[c]
H-2	Not Permitted	100[c]
H-3	Not Permitted	150[c]
H-4	Not Permitted	175[c]
H-5	Not Permitted	200[c]
I-2, I-3, I-4	150	200[c]

For SI: 1 foot = 304.8 mm.

a. See the following sections for modifications to exit access travel distance requirements:
   Section 402: For the distance limitation in malls.
   Section 404: For the distance limitation through an atrium space.
   Section 1015.2: For increased limitation in Groups F-1 and S-1.
   Section 1024.7: For increased limitation in assembly seating.
   Section 1024.7: For increased limitation for assembly open-air seating.
   Section 1018.2: For buildings with one exit.
   Chapter 31: For the limitation in temporary structures.
b. Buildings equipped throughout with an automatic sprinkler system in accordance with Section 903.3.1.1 or 903.3.1.2. See Section 903 for occupancies where sprinkler systems according to Section 903.3.1.2 are permitted.
c. Buildings equipped throughout with an automatic sprinkler system in accordance with Section 903.3.1.1.

In the previous UBC, the maximum travel distances were 200 ft in an unsprinklered building and 250 ft in a sprinklered building. These distances could be increased a maximum of 100 ft when the increased travel distance was the last portion of the travel distance and was entirely within a 1-hour-rated exit corridor. Although the IBC eliminated the 100 ft extension provision for rated corridors, the new table for sprinklered and unsprinklered buildings gives about the same limitations for most occupancies. For example, in the IBC, the maximum travel distance in a B occupancy in a sprinklered building is 300 ft. This is the same distance that was allowed in a sprinklered building with a 1-hour rated corridor under the 1997 UBC.

Separation of Exits

Once the number of exits or exit access doorways required for each room, space, or group of rooms is known, the arrangement of those exits can be determined. When two exits are required, they must be placed a distance apart equal to not less than one-half the length of the maximum overall diagonal dimension of the building or area to be served, as measured in a straight line between the exits or exit access doorways. This rule is shown diagrammatically in Figs. 29.4(a) and 29.4(b). This requirement is intended to prevent a fire or other emergency from blocking both exits because they have been positioned too close together.

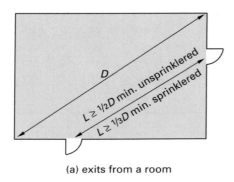

(a) exits from a room

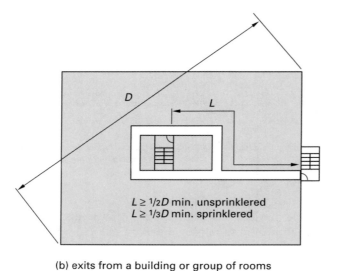

(b) exits from a building or group of rooms

Figure 29.4 Arrangement of Exits

If three or more exits are required, two must conform to the one-half diagonal distance rule, and the third and additional exits must be arranged a reasonable distance apart so that if one becomes blocked, the others will be available.

In the IBC, there is a new provision that reduces the minimum separation distance to one-third the maximum diagonal dimension of the room or area to be served if the building is fully sprinklered.

Exits or exit access doorways must also be located so that their availability is obvious.

Width of Exits

The required minimum width of exits is determined by multiplying the occupant load by the appropriate factor given in Table 1005.1 of the IBC. The resulting number is the minimum total width in inches (or mm). Other codes have similar methods of calculating total exit width. In other than H-1, H-2, H-3, H-4, and I-2 occupancies, the factor is 0.3 for stairways and 0.2 for egress components other than stairways in unsprinklered buildings. In sprinklered buildings, the factors are 0.2 for stairways and 0.15 for other egress components. The factors are higher for the H and I occupancies because of the increased risk these occupancies present. If a greater width is specified elsewhere in the code, the larger number must be used.

For example, consider the calculated office occupant load of 157 determined in the previous example. To determine the minimum width of a corridor in this office in an unsprinklered building, multiply 157 by 0.2 to get a required width of 31.4 in (798). However, elsewhere in the code the minimum width of a corridor serving an occupant load greater than 50 is given as 44 in (1118). Because 44 in is the larger of the two, it must be used as the minimum width.

If two or more exits are required, the total width must be divided such that the loss of any one means of egress does not reduce the available capacity to less than 50% of the required capacity.

The IBC also requires that if doors are part of the required egress width, their clear width must be used, not the width of the door. For example, a 36 in door actually provides about 33 in of clear width when the thickness of the door in the 90° open position and the width of the stop are subtracted from the full width.

Exiting Through Intervening Spaces

Normally, building codes intend to have means of egress from a room or space lead directly to a corridor, exit enclosure, exterior door, or some other type of exit element. However, egress can pass through an adjoining room provided that the room is accessory to the area served and the adjoining room is not an H occupancy. Additionally, there must be a discernible path of egress travel to an exit. For example, the door to a private office could lead into a larger general office area, which then leads into a corridor.

The code specifically states than egress cannot pass through kitchens, storerooms, closets, or spaces used for similar purposes. Exit access also cannot pass through a room that can be locked to prevent egress.

CORRIDORS

A *corridor* is a fully enclosed portion of an exit access that defines and provides a path of egress travel to an exit. The purpose of a corridor is to provide a space where occupants have limited choices as to paths or directions of travel. When two exits are required, corridors must be laid out so that it is possible to travel in two directions to an exit. If one path is blocked, occupants always have an alternate way out.

As part of the exit access portion of the egress system, corridors may or may not be constructed of fire-resistive construction depending on the occupancy, the occupant load, and whether or not the building is fully sprinklered. This is discussed in the next section.

As outlined in a previous section on exit width, corridors must be sized using the method of multiplying the occupant load by the appropriate factor. However, the width of an exit must not be less than 44 in (1118), with the following exceptions.

- 24 in (610): access to electrical, mechanical, and plumbing equipment

- 36 in (914): all occupancies where occupant load is 50 or less

- 36 in (914): within a dwelling unit

- 72 in (1829): Group E occupancies serving occupant load of 100 or more

- 72 in (1829): Group I occupancy corridors serving health-care centers for ambulatory patients incapable of self-preservation

- 96 in (2438): Group I-2 occupancies where bed movement is required

However, the minimum width of a corridor as determined by a building code should be verified with the minimum width required by the ADA, as discussed in Ch. 30.

The width of a corridor cannot be encroached upon, with the following exceptions. See Fig. 29.5.

- Doors opening into the path of egress travel can reduce the required width up to one-half during the course of the swing, but when fully open the door

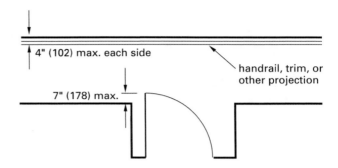

Figure 29.5   Allowable Projections into Exit Corridors

cannot project more than 7 in (178) into the required width.

- Horizontal projections such as handrails, trim, fixtures, and lights can project horizontally from either side up to a maximum of 4 in (102).

Corridor Construction

Corridors must be fire-resistance rated according to IBC Table 1016.1, shown here as Table 29.11, and they must be constructed as fire partitions, as described in Sec. 708 of the IBC. This means that the corridor walls must extend from the floor to the underside of the structural slab above or to the underside of a fire-resistive-rated ceiling. Some of the options are shown diagrammatically in Fig. 29.1.

There are four exceptions when corridors do not have to be fire-resistance rated. These include the following.

- Group E occupancies where classrooms and assembly rooms have half of their required egress leading directly to the exterior at ground level

- Corridors in a dwelling unit or a guestroom in a Group R occupancy

- Corridors in open parking garages

- Group B occupancies that only require one exit by other provisions in the code

One of the major differences between the IBC and the previous UBC is that corridors in buildings with a sprinkler system in occupancy Groups A, B, E, F, M, S, and U do not have to have a fire-resistive rating of 1 hour.

Openings in Corridors

Openings in corridors include doors, glazing, and fire shutters. These are required to have a minimum opening protection assembly rating of 20 minutes as prescribed in Sec. 715 of the IBC. (Normally, glazing in fire partitions is required to be 45-minute rated.) When interior windows are used between rooms and corridors, the total area of fire-protection-rated glazing (tested in accordance with NFPA

Table 29.11

Corridor Fire-Resistance Ratings

occupancy	occupant load served by corridor	required fire-resistance rating (hours)	
		without sprinkler system	with sprinkler system[c]
H-1, H-2, H-3	all	not permitted	1
H-4, H-5	greater than 30	not permitted	1
A, B, E, F, M, S, U	greater than 30	1	0
R	greater than 10	1	0.5
I-2[a], I-4	all	not permitted	0
I-1, I-3	all	not permitted	1[b]

a. For requirements for occupancies in Group I-2, see Section 407.3.
b. For a reduction in the fire-resistance rating for occupancies in Group I-3, see Section 408.7.
c. Buildings equipped throughout with an automatic sprinkler system in accordance with Section 903.3.1.1 or 903.3.1.2 where allowed.

International Building Code 2003. Copyright 2003. Falls Church, Virginia: International Code Council, Inc. Reproduced with permission. All rights reserved.

257) cannot exceed 25% of the area of the common wall between the corridor and the room. However, if fire-resistance-rated glazing (tested in accordance with ASTM E-119) is used, the 25% area limitation does not apply. Glazing in fire partitions is discussed in more detail in Ch. 19. Doors are discussed in a following section.

Corridor Continuity

When a corridor is required to be fire-resistance rated, it must be continuous to an exit and must not pass through intervening rooms. The concept is based on the idea that once an occupant reaches a certain level of safety in the egress path, that level should not be reduced as the occupant progresses through the remainder of the egress system. As with most requirements of the code, there are a few exceptions.

First, corridors may pass through foyers, lobbies, and reception rooms as long as these spaces are constructed as required for the corridors. In essence, these spaces become enlarged portions of the corridor.

The second exception allows corridors in fully sprinklered Group B buildings to pass through enclosed elevator lobbies if all areas of the building have access to at least one required exit without passing through the lobby.

Dead Ends

A *dead end* is a condition where the occupant of a building has only one choice of direction leading to an exit access doorway or an exit. When corridors are required to lead to two or more exits, the occupant should always have at least two choices of direction. The code does allow dead ends in corridors if they do not exceed 20 ft (6096) in length. There are three exceptions in the IBC where longer dead-end corridors are allowed.

- Dead ends are not limited in length where the length is less than 2.5 times the least width of the dead-end corridor.

- B and F occupancies may have 50 ft (15 240) dead-end corridors if the entire building is equipped with an automatic sprinkler system.

- Dead-end corridors may be 50 ft long in Group I-3 occupancies (detention) under certain conditions.

DOORS

Because doors present a potential obstruction to egress throughout the egress system, they are highly regulated by the IBC and other model codes. Means of egress doors must meet the following design criteria.

- They must be readily distinguishable from the adjacent construction.

- They must be readily recognizable as a means-of-egress door.

- They cannot be covered with mirrors or other reflective materials.

- They cannot be concealed with curtains, drapes, decorations, or similar materials.

Doors provided in excess of the minimum required number of doors must meet the same criteria as the required doors.

Size of Doors

The minimum width of egress door openings must be sufficient for the occupant load served, but the clear width must be at least 32 in (813). The clear opening width must be measured between the face of the door and the doorstop when the door is open 90°. In practical terms, this means that 36 in doors must be used as exit doors. The maximum width of swinging egress doors is 48 in (1219). The minimum height of egress doors is 80 in (2032).

There are several exceptions to the size requirements, including doors in residential occupancies, sleeping rooms in I-3 occupancies, and others. Refer to Sec. 1008.1.1 of the IBC for details on these exceptions.

Door Swing

Egress doors must be pivoted or side-hinged. This is to ensure the egress door is familiar to the user and easy to operate. There are some exceptions to the requirement for side-swinging doors, including private garages; office areas; factory and storage areas with an occupant load of 10 or less; individual dwelling units of R-2, R-3, and R-4 occupancies; power-operated doors; and a few others. Refer to Sec. 1008.1.2 in the IBC for all of the exceptions allowed.

In most cases, special doors (such as revolving, sliding, and overhead doors) are not considered to be required exits. Power-operated doors and revolving doors are sometimes allowed if they meet certain requirements. Revolving doors, for example, must have leaves that collapse under opposing pressure and must have a diameter such that at least 36 in (914) of exit width is provided when the leaves are collapsed. There must also be at least one conforming egress door in close proximity. For additional requirements for special doors, refer to Sec. 1008.1.3 in the IBC.

Further, egress doors must swing in the direction of travel when the area served has an occupant load of 50 or more. This is to prevent a door from being blocked when people are trying to get out in a panic. Candidates frequently make the mistake of not showing required doors—all building exit doors, stairway doors, and doors from spaces with a high occupant load—swinging in the direction of travel. See Fig. 29.6(a). Doors must also not swing into a required travel path such as a corridor. In many instances, exit doors must be recessed as shown in Fig. 29.6(b) to meet this requirement. Remember that recessed doors must be compensated for by providing at least 18 in (455), and preferably 24 in (610), on the pull side of the door next to the latch jamb for accessibility.

Doors without closers must have a maximum opening force of 5 lbf (22 N), and doors with closers must have a maximum opening force of 15 lbf (67 N). The maximum allowable force to set the door in motion is 30 lbf (133 N). The door must swing to a full-open position when subjected to 15 lbf (67 N). All of these required maximum forces are measured on the latch side of the door.

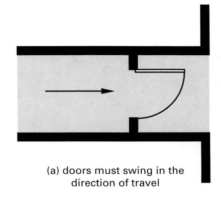

(a) doors must swing in the direction of travel

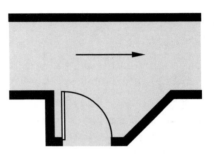

(b) doors must not swing into the required exit path more than 7 in (178)

Figure 29.6 Exit Door Swing

Fire-Resistive Rating Requirements

Egress doors in fire-resistance-rated partitions are required to have a fire rating. The specific fire rating varies depending on the rating of the partition. These ratings are shown in Table 19.4 in Ch. 19. For most applications, four door-assembly ratings are commonly encountered. These are summarized in Table 29.12. Remember that if a building is fully sprinklered under the IBC, corridors in A, B, E, F, M, S, and U occupancies (and in some other situations) do not have to have a fire rating, so fire-protection-rated doors are not required.

In addition to having a 20-minute fire rating, doors in corridors and smoke barriers must meet the requirements for positive-pressure fire testing (NFPA 252 or UL 10C, but without the hose stream test) as discussed in Ch. 19. These doors must also meet the requirements for smoke and draft control tested in accordance with UL 1784, *Standard for Safety for Air Leakage Tests for Door Assemblies*, with an artificial bottom seal installed across the full width of the bottom of the door during the test. These may need to carry an "S" label if required by the local authority having jurisdiction. Smoke barriers are commonly used to split health care

Table 29.12

Required Ratings of Doors Based on Partition Type

use of partition	rating of partition	required door assembly rating
corridors, smoke barriers	1 hour or less	20 minutes
fire partitions, exit passageways	1 hour	3/4 hour
exit stairs, occupancy separations, vertical shafts	1 hour	1 hour
exit stairs, fire separations	2 hours	1 1/2 hour

and detention facilities into separate zones. They are also required in vertical shafts, vestibules to stairways, and areas of refuge.

Additional requirements for power-operated doors, horizontal sliding doors, and revolving and access-control doors, as well as for delayed-egress locks, gates, thresholds, floor elevation, and door arrangement, are given in Sec. 1008.1.3 of the IBC.

Refer to Ch. 19 for more information on building code requirements for doors, hardware, and glazing in fire-rated doors.

STAIRWAYS

A *stair* is defined by the IBC as a change in elevation accomplished by one or more risers. A *stairway* is one or more flights of stairs with the necessary landings and platforms connecting them to form a continuous passage from one level to another.

Exit Stairways

Because vertical shafts provide the most readily available path for fire and smoke spreading upward from floor to floor, interior exit stairways must be completely enclosed. In buildings four or more stories in height, they must be enclosed with 2-hour-rated walls; in buildings less than four stories, 1-hour-rated construction is required. The stories include basements but exclude mezzanines. Doors into 2-hour stairways must be rated as 1½-hour doors, and doors in 1-hour stairways must have a 1-hour rating.

There are nine exceptions to the hourly rating requirements found in Sec. 1019.1 of the IBC. Three are commonly encountered. The first states that in other than Groups H and I occupancies, a stairway serving an occupant load less than 10 not more than one story above the level of exit discharge does not have to be enclosed. The second states that stairways serving and contained within a single residential dwelling unit in Group R-2 and R-3 occupancies and guestrooms in R-1 occupancies are not required to be enclosed. The third states that in other than Group H and I occupancies, up to 50% of the number of egress stairways serving only one adjacent floor do not have to be enclosed.

Requirements for All Stairways

Stairways serving an occupant load of more than 50 must be at least 44 in (1118) wide or as wide as determined by multiplying the occupant load by 0.3, 0.2, or another factor as discussed previously, whichever is greater. Stairways serving an occupant load of 50 or fewer must not be less than 36 in (914) wide. Handrails may project into the required width 4½ in (114). In the UBC, the allowed projection was limited to 3½ in (89).

If the stairway is also the accessible means of egress, the minimum clear width is 48 in (1219) between handrails. Because the ARE Schematic Design vignette may include an accessible stairway with an area of refuge, this stair should be made about 54 in (1372) wide. Any monumental stairs in the Schematic Design vignette, however, should be wider, as suggested by the programmed space given in the problem statement.

Stair risers cannot measure less than 4 in (102) or more than 7 in (178), and the tread must not be less than 11 in (279). Risers for barrier-free stairs cannot exceed 7 in; treads must have an acceptable nosing design as shown in Fig. 29.7. For residential occupancies and private stairways in R-2 occupancies, the maximum riser may be 7¾ in (197) and the minimum tread may be 10 in (254). In the UBC, the limits on residential stairs were 8 in (203) risers and 9 in (229) treads.

There are other requirements for circular stairways, winders, spiral stairways, and stairs serving as aisles in assembly seating areas. Winding, circular, and spiral stairways may be used as exits in R-3 occupancies and in private stairways of R-1 occupancies only if they meet the requirements shown in Fig. 21.6.

Landings must be provided at the top and bottom of every stairway, and the minimum dimension in the direction of travel must not be less than the width of the stair, but need not be more than 48 in (1219) if the stair is a straight run. The maximum distance between landings is 12 ft (3658), measured vertically.

Handrails must be provided on both sides of stairs. Intermediate handrails are required so that all portions of the stairway width required for egress capacity are within 30 in

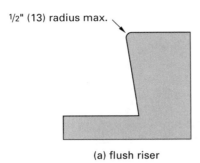

(a) flush riser

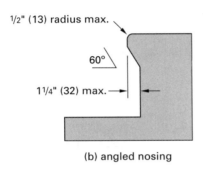

(b) angled nosing

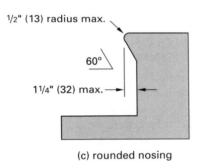

(c) rounded nosing

Figure 29.7 Acceptable Nosing Shapes for Safety and Accessibility

(762) of a handrail. Another way of stating this is that stairways wider than 5 ft (1524) must have intermediate handrails.

The exceptions to the requirement that handrails be provided on both sides include the following.

- aisle stairs with a center handrail

- stairs within dwelling units, spiral stairways, and aisle stairs serving seating only on one side

- decks, patios, and walkways that have a single change in elevation where the landing depth on each side is greater than what is required for landings

- single risers in Group R-3 occupancies at an entrance or egress door

- single risers within dwelling units of R-2 and R-3 occupancies

The top of a handrail must be between 34 in and 38 in (864 and 962) above the nosing of the treads and must extend not less than one tread depth beyond the top riser and not less than the depth of one tread beyond the bottom riser. Refer to Fig. 29.8. The ends must be returned or terminate in a newel post. The IBC requires handrails to be sized from 1 1/4 in to 2 in (32 to 51) in cross-sectional dimension and have a shape that is easily gripped. There must be a space at least 1 1/2 in (38) wide between the wall and the handrail.

Refer to Ch. 21 for additional discussion of building code requirements for stairway layout, as well as diagrams for the code requirements described in this section. Refer to Ch. 30 for accessibility requirements.

OTHER CODE REQUIREMENTS

High-Rise Buildings

High-rise buildings (those with occupied floors more than 75 ft (22 860) above fire department vehicle access) pose a unique problem for fire and life safety. Fire department apparatus cannot reach above this height, so special precautions need to be taken. Part of Ch. 4 of the IBC specifies the particular requirements for these buildings, which include office buildings, hotels, apartments, and other occupancies (with a few exceptions). The code requires that high-rise buildings be provided with an automatic sprinkler system, smoke detectors and alarms, communication systems, a central control station for fire department use, smoke control for exit stair enclosures, and standby power systems.

Glazing

Building codes regulate the use of glass in exterior windows (limiting the area and type based on wind loading, energy conservation, and other factors), in fire-rated assemblies, in hazardous locations subject to human impact, and in sloped glazing and skylights. Refer to Ch. 19 for more information on code requirements.

Guards (Guardrails)

A *guard* is a component whose function is to prevent falls from an elevated area. For example, an opening on the second floor that overlooks the first floor must be protected with a guard. In the UBC, guards were called guardrails. Guards are required along open-sided walking surfaces, mezzanines, industrial equipment platforms, stairways, ramps, and landings that are more than 30 in (762) above

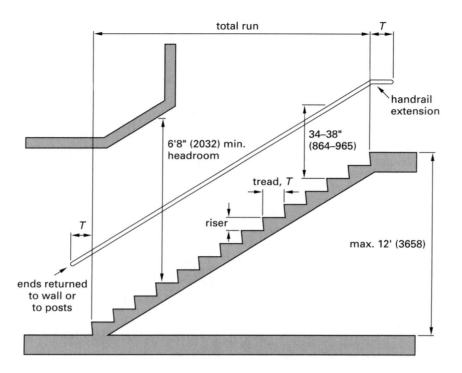

Figure 29.8   Code Requirements for Stairways

the floor below. There are several exceptions, including stages and raised platforms.

Guards must be a minimum of 42 in (1067) high and designed such that a 4 in diameter sphere (102) cannot pass through any opening up to a height of 34 in (864). Guards must be designed to resist a load of 50 lbf/ft (0.73 kN/m) applied in any direction at the top of the guard. There are other design requirements and exceptions, which are detailed in Sec. 1012 of the IBC.

Fire Detection and Suppression

Fire detection, alarm, and suppression systems have become important parts of a building's overall life safety and fire protection strategies. Almost all new buildings are now required to have some type of detection device, even if it is a single smoke detector in a residence. Other occupancies, such as high-rise buildings and hotels, must have elaborate detection and alarm systems, including communication devices on each floor to allow firefighters to talk with each other and occupants in the event of an emergency. Both audio and visual alarms are often required for people with hearing or visual impairments. Refer to Ch. 9 for more information on fire suppression systems and to Ch. 10 for more information on detection and alarm systems.

Mechanical Systems

The majority of code requirements related to mechanical systems are contained in companion volumes to the primary codes. The companion volume for the IBC is the International Mechanical Code, which details the requirements for materials and design of systems for heating, ventilating, and air-conditioning systems. This code includes the minimum ventilation rates and other aspects of health and safety. Refer to Chs. 5 and 6 for information on mechanical systems.

Plumbing Systems

The International Plumbing Code (IPC) is the companion volume to the IBC that regulates plumbing design and construction. Other codes have similar volumes. The IPC gives the minimum number of toilets, lavatories, drinking fountains, and other sanitary fixtures required in a building. The number required is based on occupancy and the number of people served. For convenience, these provisions are also given in Ch. 29 of the IBC. These should be considered minimum numbers, not necessarily optimum numbers. The IPC also outlines detailed requirements for plumbing system design, individual materials, and methods of installation. Refer to Ch. 9 for more information on plumbing systems.

Electrical Systems

The IBC and the other three former model codes reference the National Electrical Code (NEC), published by the National Fire Protection Association. As with other companion codes, the NEC details the requirements for materials and the design of the power supply and lighting systems of buildings. Refer to Ch. 10 for more information on electrical systems.

Sound Ratings

The IBC requires that wall and floor/ceiling assemblies in residential occupancies separating dwelling units or guestrooms from each other and from public spaces be designed and constructed to provide for sound-transmission control. The code specifies a minimum sound-transmission class (STC) of 50 (45 if field tested) for walls. This provision does not apply to dwelling unit entrance doors. However, these doors must be tight fitting to the frame and sill. The minimum impact insulation class (IIC) for floors must be 50 (45 if field tested). Construction details that satisfy these requirements must be selected. For example, penetrations in sound walls must be sealed or otherwise treated to maintain the required rating. Refer to Ch. 11 for more information on acoustics.

DEFINITIONS

The following terms are frequently used by building codes to precisely communicate meaning. Additional terms are defined in the main text of this chapter. Although the differences between terms are sometimes subtle, it is advisable to become familiar with them.

Area of refuge: an area where people unable to use stairways can remain temporarily while waiting for assistance

Automatic closing: as applied to a door, a door that is normally held in the open position but is released to close upon activation by a smoke detector or other type of fire alarm system. Automatic closing doors must be self-closing.

Combustible: material that will ignite and burn, either as a flame or glow, and that undergoes this process in air at pressures and temperatures that might occur during a fire in a building

Common path of egress travel: the portion of exit access that occupants must travel before two separate and distinct paths of egress travel to two exits become available

Corridor: an enclosed exit access component that defines and provides a path of egress travel to an exit. A corridor may or may not be protected depending on the particular requirements of the code.

Exit court: a court or yard (considered part of an exit discharge) that provides access to a public way for one or more required exits. (In the IBC this is now called an egress court.)

Exit enclosure: a fully enclosed portion of an exit that is only used as a means of egress and that provides for a protected path of egress either in a vertical or horizontal direction. Depending on construction type, height, and building occupancy, an exit enclosure must have either a 1- or 2-hour rating, and all openings must be protected. An exit enclosure must lead to an exit discharge or the public way.

Exit passageway: a horizontal, fully enclosed portion of an exit that is only used as a means of egress. An exit passageway leads from an exit doorway to an exit discharge or a public way. A common example of an exit passageway is an exit from the door at the ground level of an interior stairway that leads through the building to an outside door.

Fire assembly: an assembly of a fire door, fire window, or fire damper, including all required anchorage, frames, sills, and hardware

Fire barrier: a fire-resistance-rated vertical or horizontal assembly of materials designed to restrict the spread of fire, in which openings are protected. (This is a new term in the 2003 IBC.)

Fire door assembly: any combination of a fire door, frame, hardware, and other accessories that provides a specific degree of fire protection to an opening

Fire exit hardware: panic hardware that is listed for use on fire-door assemblies

Fire partition: a fire-resistive component used to separate dwelling units in R-2 construction, to separate guestrooms in Group R-1 construction, to separate tenant spaces in covered mall buildings, and as a corridor wall. (This is a new term in the 2003 IBC.) Fire partitions are generally required to have a minimum 1-hour-rated construction except in certain circumstances. They are similar to fire barriers, but the requirements for support are not as strict.

Fire-protection rating: the period of time in which an opening assembly, such as a door or window, maintains the ability to confine a fire or maintains its integrity, or both, when tested in accordance with NFPA 252, UL 10B, or UL 10C for doors, and NFPA 257 for windows. An assembly that requires a fire-protection rating must withstand fire exposure and thermal shock as with a fire-resistance rating, but not heat transmission as walls, columns, and floors do.

Fire-rated: See *Fire-protection rating*

Fire resistance: the property of a material or assembly to withstand or resist the spread of fire or give protection from it

Fire-resistance rating: the period of time a building component such as a wall, floor, roof, beam, or column is able to confine a fire or maintain its structural integrity, or both, when tested in accordance with ASTM E 119, *Standard Methods for Fire Tests of Building Construction and Materials*. This is different from "fire-protection rating," which involves protected opening assemblies.

Fire-resistive construction: See *Fire resistance*

Flame resistance: the ability to withstand flame impingement or give protection from it. This applies to individual materials as well as combinations of components when tested in accordance with NFPA 701, *Standard Methods of Fire Tests for Flame-Resistant Textiles and Films*.

Flame spread: the propagation of flame over a surface

Flame-spread index: the numerical value assigned to a material tested in accordance with ASTM E 84, *Standard Test Method for Surface Burning Characteristics of Building Materials*

Flammable: capable of burning with a flame and subject to easy ignition and rapid flaming combustion

Horizontal exit: an exit through a minimum 2-hour-rated wall that divides a building into two or more separate exit access areas to afford safety from fire and smoke

Noncombustible: material that will not ignite and burn when subjected to a fire. The IBC and UBC qualify a material as noncombustible only if it is tested in accordance with ASTM E 136, *Noncombustible Material—Tests*, or if it has a structural base of noncombustible material with a surfacing not more than $1/8$ in (3.18) thick that has a flame-spread index no greater than 50.

Occupant load: the number of people for which the means of egress of a building or part of a building is designed

Panic hardware: a door latching assembly that includes a device that releases the latch when a force is applied in the direction of egress travel

Self-closing: as applied to a door, a door that is equipped with a device (most commonly a door closer) that will ensure closing after the door has been opened

Stair: a change in elevation, consisting of one or more risers

Stairway: one or more flights of stairs, either exterior or interior, with the necessary landings and platforms connecting them to form a continuous and uninterrupted passage from one level to another

Travel distance: the measurement of the distance between the most remote occupied point of an area or room to the entrance of the nearest exit that serves it. It is part of the exit access and it is measured along the natural and unobstructed path of egress travel.

Trim: picture molds, chair rails, baseboards, handrails, door and window frames, and similar decorative or protective materials used in fixed applications

SAMPLE QUESTIONS

1. Exits may pass through which of the following areas?

I.   office reception areas
II.   building lobbies
III. unoccupied storage areas
IV.   apartment entries
V.   kitchens

    A.   I, II, and IV
    B.   I, III, and IV
    C.   II, III, and IV
    D.   III, IV, and V

2. The abbreviated table shown includes requirements for occupancy loads. A restaurant on the ground floor contains 3500 ft² of dining area, a 1000 ft² kitchen, and a 1200 ft² bar area.

use	occupant load factor
assembly areas, concentrated use (without fixed seats) auditoriums dance floors lodge rooms	7
assembly areas, less-concentrated use conference rooms dining rooms drinking establishments exhibit rooms lounges stages	15
hotels and apartments	200
kitchens—commercial	200
offices	100
stores, ground floor	30

What is the total occupant load?

    A.   202
    B.   318
    C.   380
    D.   409

3.   Which of the following exit door combinations would minimally satisfy the exit width required in an office with an occupant load of 290, assuming the building is not sprinklered?

    A.   a pair of 30 in entry doors and a 36 in door remotely located

    B.   two 36 in doors on opposite sides of the building

    C.   three 32 in doors remotely located

    D.   three 36 in doors remotely located from each other

4.   Under the IBC, what is the maximum allowable floor area of a sprinklered, two-story, Type III B, Group B occupancy building that has access on 20% of its perimeter?

    A.   38,000 ft^2

    B.   57,000 ft^2

    C.   76,000 ft^2

    D.   114,000 ft^2

5.   What does it mean when a building material is non-combustible?

    A.   It will not ignite and burn when subjected to fire.

    B.   It will withstand flame impingement.

    C.   It will not readily spread fire once ignited.

    D.   It has a minimum 1-hour fire rating.

6.   Restrictions on surface finishes in all model codes are based primarily on

    A.   occupancy and construction type

    B.   occupant load and location in the building

    C.   location in the building and occupancy

    D.   occupancy group and sprinklering

7.   Under the IBC, which of the following are correct statements?

I.   Fire zone 3 is the most restrictive.

II.   Fire resistance of exterior, nonbearing walls is determined by type of construction, occupancy, and distance from property lines.

III.   Exit doors must swing in the direction of travel.

IV.   The legal basis for building codes in the United States is the U.S. Constitution.

V.   Occupant load is independent of occupancy group.

    A.   I, III, and IV

    B.   II, III, and V

    C.   II, IV, and V

    D.   I, II, IV, and V

8.   Which of the following areas of a building are considered parts of the means of egress?

I.   storeroom

II.   corridor

III.   enclosed stairway

IV.   exterior courtyard

V.   public sidewalk

    A.   I, II, and III

    B.   II, III, and IV

    C.   I, II, III, and IV

    D.   I, II, III, IV, and V

9.   Which of the following statements about standards and testing is FALSE?

    A.   Trade association standards must be followed if they are adopted by a building code.

    B.   The American National Standards Institute does not write standards.

    C.   The American Society for Testing and Materials does not perform tests.

    D.   Building codes prescribe which laboratories must perform required tests.

10.   Construction type refers to the

    A.   major materials used to construct a building

    B.   fire-resistance ratings of various building components

    C.   maximum area and height of a building

    D.   use of a building and fire-protection methods used

BARRIER-FREE DESIGN

Barrier-free design is an important part of the ARE, especially since the Americans with Disabilities Act (ADA) became law in 1992. Although building codes and many federal and state agencies require accessibility, the overriding regulation today is the ADA. This federal law requires, among other things, that all commercial and public accommodations be accessible to people with disabilities. Although the ADA is not a national building code and does not depend on inspection for its enforcement, building owners must comply with its requirements or be liable for civil suits. Architects are likewise responsible for designing buildings that conform to the ADA requirements as well as local building code regulations.

The ADA does not cover single- or multi-family housing, but such housing is regulated by local building codes and by other federal and local codes, so multi-family housing must also be accessible. ADA regulations follow most of the standards set forth in ICC/ANSI A117.1, *Accessible and Usable Buildings and Facilities*. In addition, the ADA adds provisions regarding things such as the minimum numbers of facilities and accommodations. In some cases, the *Uniform Federal Accessibility Standards* may govern, but these are almost identical to ADA and ICC/ANSI A117.1 standards.

The standards discussed in this chapter include some of the basic requirements for accessibility inside a building as defined in the Americans with Disabilities Act and with ICC/ANSI A117.1. Additional accessibility provisions for site work are discussed in Ch. 4.

ACCESSIBLE ROUTES

An *accessible route* is a continuous unobstructed path connecting all accessible elements and spaces in a building or facility. It includes corridors, doorways, floors, ramps, elevators, lifts, and clear floor space at fixtures. The standards for accessible routes are designed to accommodate a person

with a severe disability who uses a wheelchair, and are also intended to provide ease of use for people with other disabilities.

Accessible routes and other clearances are based on basic dimensional requirements of wheelchairs. The minimum clear floor space required to accommodate one stationary wheelchair is 30 in by 48 in (760 by 1220). For maneuverability, a minimum 60 in (1525) diameter circle is required for a wheelchair to make a 180° turn. In place of this, a T-shaped space may be provided as shown in Fig. 30.1.

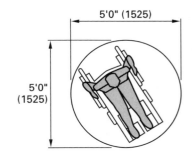

(a) turning diameter

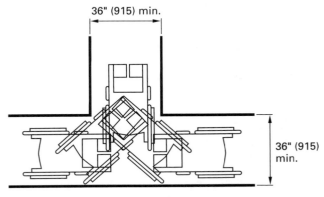

(b) T-shaped space for 180° turns

Figure 30.1 Maneuvering Clearances

The minimum clear width for an accessible route is 36 in (915) continuously and 32 in (815) clear at a passage point such as a doorway. The passage point cannot be more than 24 in (610) long. The minimum passage width for two wheelchairs is 60 in (1525). If an accessible route is less than 60 in wide, passing spaces at least 60 in by 60 in (1525 by 1525) must be provided at intervals not to exceed 200 ft (61 m). These requirements are shown in Fig. 30.2.

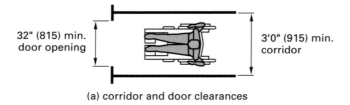

(a) corridor and door clearances

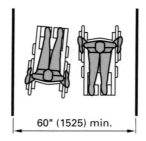

(b) minimum clear width for two wheelchairs

Figure 30.2 Wheelchair Clearances

In toilet rooms the turning space may overlap with the required clear floor space at fixtures and controls and with the accessible route. If turns in corridors or around obstructions must be made, the minimum dimensions are as shown in Fig. 30.3.

An accessible route may have a slope up to 1:20 (a 1 in rise for every 20 in distance). Slopes any greater than this are classified as a ramp and must meet the requirements given in the section later in this chapter.

DOORWAYS

Width and Arrangement

Doors must have a minimum clear opening width of 32 in (815) when the door is opened at 90°. The maximum depth of a doorway 32 in wide is 24 in (610). If the area is deeper than this, the width must be increased to 36 in (915). See Fig. 30.4.

Maneuvering clearances are required at standard swinging doors to allow easy operation of the latch and provide for a clear swing. For single doors the clearances are shown in Fig. 30.5. For two doors in a series the minimum space is

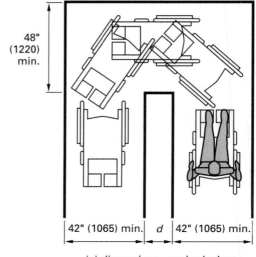

(a) dimensions required when
d is less than 48" (1220)

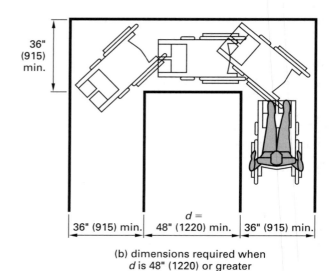

(b) dimensions required when
d is 48" (1220) or greater

Figure 30.3 Turn in Corridors or Around Obstructions

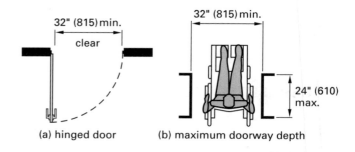

(a) hinged door   (b) maximum doorway depth

Figure 30.4 Doorway Clearances

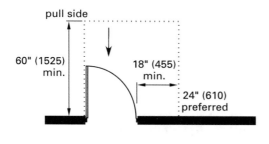

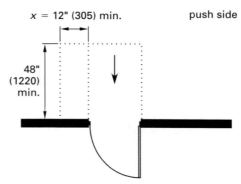

Note: $x = 12"$ (305) if door has both closer and latch.

(a) front approaches—swinging doors

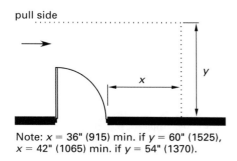

Note: $x = 36"$ (915) min. if $y = 60"$ (1525), $x = 42"$ (1065) min. if $y = 54"$ (1370).

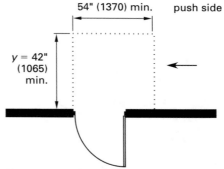

Note: $y = 48"$ (1220) min. if door has both latch and closer.

(b) hinge side approaches—swinging doors

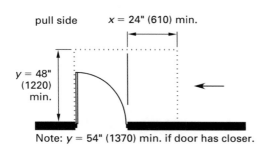

Note: $y = 54"$ (1370) min. if door has closer.

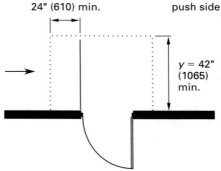

Note: $y = 48"$ (1220) min. if door has closer.

(c) latch side approaches—swinging doors

Figure 30.5 Maneuvering Clearances at Doors

shown in Fig. 30.6. Note the 48 in (1220) space requirement. If sufficient clearance is not provided, the doors must have power-assisted mechanisms or be automatic opening.

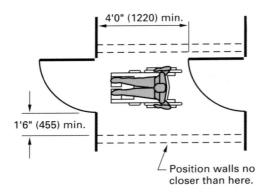

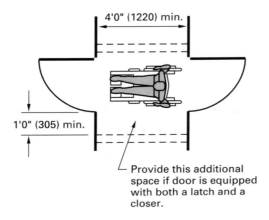

Figure 30.6 Double Door Clearances

Opening Force

The maximum opening force required to push or pull open interior hinged doors cannot be more than 5 lbf-ft (22.2 N). This force does not include the force required to retract the latch bolts or disengage other devices that may hold the door closed. Maximum opening forces may be greater if the door is a fire door and regulated by the local code jurisdiction. Automatic doors and power-assisted doors may also be used if they comply with ANSI/BHMA standard A156.10 (automatic doors) or ANSI/BHMA 156.19 (low-powered, automatic doors).

When closers are used, the sweep period of the door must be adjusted so that from an open position of 70°, the door will take at least 3 sec to move to a point 3 in (75) from the latch as measured to the leading edge of the door.

Hardware

Thresholds at doorways cannot exceed $^{1}/_{2}$ in (13) in height and must be beveled so no slope of the threshold is greater

than 1:2. Operating devices must have a shape that is easy to grasp. This includes lever handles, push-type mechanisms, and U-shaped handles. Round-shaped doorknobs are not allowed. If door closers are provided, they must be adjusted to slow the closing time. Hardware for accessible doors cannot be mounted more than 48 in (1220) above the finished floor.

PLUMBING FIXTURES AND TOILET ROOMS

ICC/ANSI A117.1 and the ADA govern the design of the components of toilet rooms as well as individual elements such as drinking fountains, bathtubs, and showers. As mentioned in a previous section, toilet rooms must have a minimum clear turning space of a 5 ft (1525) diameter circle in addition to the minimum access areas required at each type of fixture. The 5 ft circle can overlap with required access at controls and fixtures and with the accessible route.

Toilet Stalls

There are several acceptable layouts for toilet stalls. Minimum clearances for two standard stall layouts are shown in Fig. 30.7. When toilet rooms are being remodeled and it is technically infeasible to put in a standard stall, alternate layouts may be acceptable as shown in Fig. 30.8.

In all cases the clearance depth varies depending on whether a wall-hung or floor-mounted water closet is used. If the depth is increased by 3 in (76), a floor-mounted water closet can be used. In most cases, the door must provide a minimum clear opening of 32 in (815) and must swing out, away from the stall enclosure. Grab bars must also be provided as shown in the illustrations, mounted from 33 in to 36 in (840 to 915) above the floor. When ambulatory stalls are used they must be 36 in (915) wide and a minimum of 60 in (1525) deep.

If toilet stalls are not used, the centerline of the toilet must still be 16 in to 18 in (405 to 455) from a wall with grab bars at both the back and side of the water closet. A clear space in front of and beside open water closets should be provided as shown in Fig. 30.9. Toilet paper dispensers must be 7 in (180) minimum and 9 in (230) maximum in front of the water closet. The outlet of the dispenser must be between 15 in (380) and 48 in (1220) above the floor. It may be mounted either above or below the grab bar. If mounted above the grab bar there must be a minimum of 12 in (305) between the top of the bar and the outlet. If mounted below the grab bar, there must be a minimum clearance of $1^{1}/_{2}$ in (38) between the bottom of the bar and the top of the dispenser. Dispensers must not be of a type that controls delivery or that does not allow continuous paper flow.

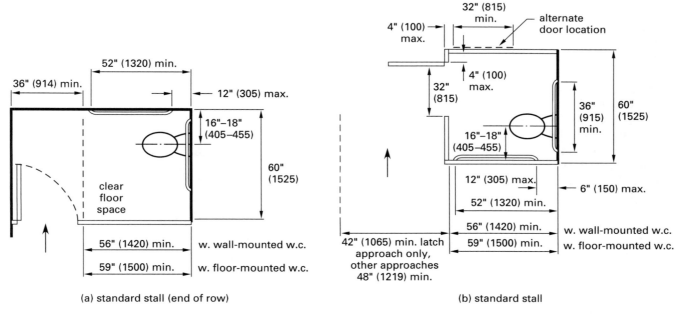

Figure 30.7 Toilet Stall Dimensions

(a) standard stall (end of row)

(b) standard stall

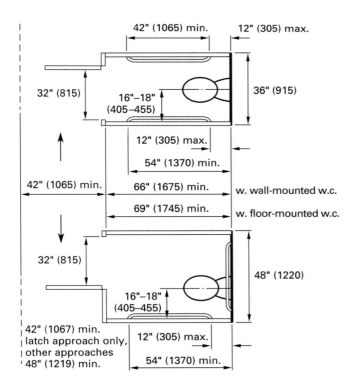

Figure 30.8 Alternate Toilet Stall Dimensions

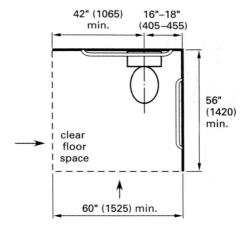

Figure 30.9 Clear Floor Space at Water Closets

Urinals

Urinals must be stall-type or wall-hung with an elongated rim at a maximum height of 17 in (430) above the floor. A clear floor space of 30 in by 48 in (760 by 1220) must be provided in front of the urinal, which may adjoin or overlap an accessible route. Urinal shields that do not extend beyond the front edge of the rim may be provided with 30 in (760) clearance between them.

Lavatories and Sinks

Lavatories must allow someone in a wheelchair to move under the sink and easily use the basin and water controls. The required dimensions are shown in Fig. 30.10. Notice that because of these clearances, wall-hung lavatories are the best type to use when accessibility is a concern. If pipes are exposed below the lavatory, they must be insulated or otherwise protected, and there must not be any sharp or abrasive surfaces under lavatories or sinks. Faucets must be operable with one hand and cannot require tight grasping, pinching, or twisting of the wrist. Lever-operated, push-type, and automatically controlled mechanisms are acceptable types.

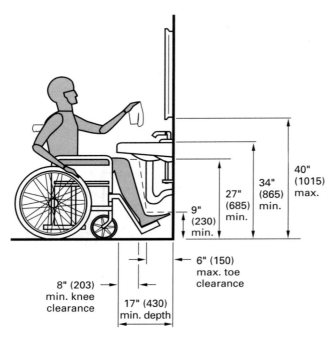

(a) lavatory clearances

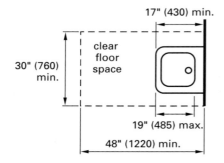

(b) clear floor space at lavatories

Figure 30.10   Clear Floor Space at Lavatories

Mirrors must be mounted with the bottom edge of the reflecting surface no higher than 40 in (1015) from the floor.

Requirements for sinks are the same as those for lavatories. The maximum depth of the sink bowl is 6$\frac{1}{2}$ in (165). The clear floor space requirement is the same as it is for lavatories.

Drinking Fountains

Requirements for drinking fountains with a front approach are shown in Fig. 30.11. A drinking fountain that is free-standing or built-in without clear space below must have a clear floor space in front of it at least 30 in by 48 in wide (760 by 1220) with the long dimension parallel to the fountain, which allows a person in a wheelchair to make a parallel approach. The spout must be a maximum of 5 in (125) from the front edge of the unit, for users making a forward approach.

Bathtubs

Bathtubs must be configured as shown in Fig. 30.12. An in-tub seat or a seat at the head of the tub must be provided as shown in the drawing. Grab bars must be provided as illustrated in Fig. 30.13. If an enclosure is provided, it cannot obstruct the controls or transfer from wheelchairs onto seats or into the tub. Enclosure tracks cannot be mounted on the rim of the tub.

Showers

Shower stalls may be one of two basic types as shown in Fig. 30.14. When facilities with accessible sleeping rooms or suites are provided, a minimum number of rooms are required that have roll-in showers as specified in the ADA requirements. A seat is required in the smaller shower stall configuration, while a folding seat is required in the larger configuration if a permanent seat is provided. Grab bars must be provided and mounted from 33 in to 36 in (840 to 915) above the floor.

FLOOR SURFACES

Floor surfaces must be stable, firm, and slip-resistant. If there is a change in level, the transition must meet the following requirements. If the change is less than $\frac{1}{4}$ in (6), it may be vertical and without edge treatment. If the change is between $\frac{1}{4}$ in and $\frac{1}{2}$ in (6 to 13), it must be beveled with a slope no greater than 1:2 ($\frac{1}{2}$ in of rise requires 1 in of length, for example). Changes greater than $\frac{1}{2}$ in (13) must be accomplished with a ramp meeting the requirements in the next section.

If carpet is used, it must have a firm cushion or backing, or it must have no cushion and a level loop, textured loop,

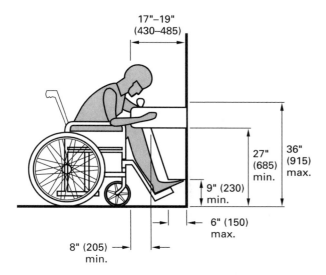

(a) spout height and knee clearance

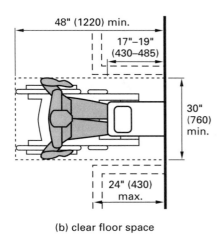

(b) clear floor space

Figure 30.11 Water Fountain Access

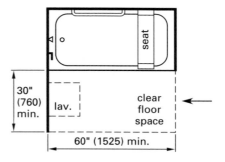

(a) with seat in tub, side approach

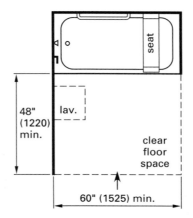

(b) with seat in tub, front approach

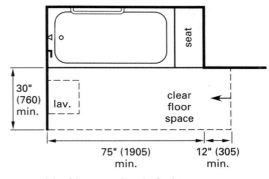

(c) with seat at head of tub

o drain
◁ shower head
⅂ shower controls

Figure 30.12 Clear Floor Space at Bathtubs

level cut pile, or level cut/uncut pile texture with a maximum pile height of ¹/₂ in (13). It must be securely attached to the floor and have trim along all lengths of exposed edges.

RAMPS AND STAIRS

Ramps are required to provide a smooth transition between changes in elevation for both wheelchair-bound persons as well as those whose mobility is otherwise restricted. In general, the least possible slope should be used, but in no case can a ramp have a slope greater than 1:12 (1 in rise for every 12 in of run [25 for 300]). The maximum rise for any ramp is limited to 30 in (760). Changes in elevation greater than this require a level landing before the next run of ramp is encountered. In some cases where existing conditions

prevent the 1:12 slope, a 1:10 slope is permitted if the maximum rise does not exceed 6 in (150), and a 1:8 slope is permitted if the maximum rise does not exceed 3 in (75).

The minimum clear width of a ramp is 36 in (915) with landings at least as wide as the widest ramp leading to them.

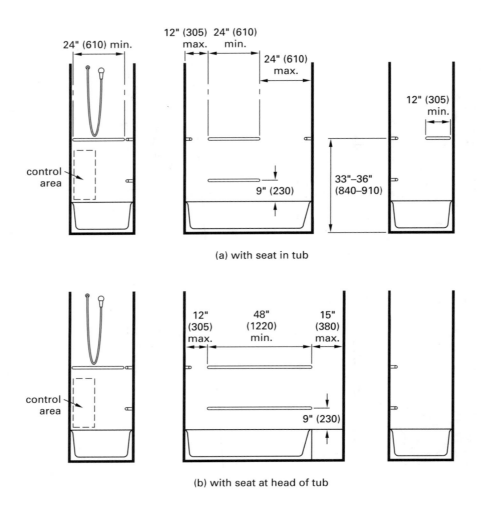

(a) with seat in tub

(b) with seat at head of tub

Figure 30.13 Grab Bars at Bathtubs

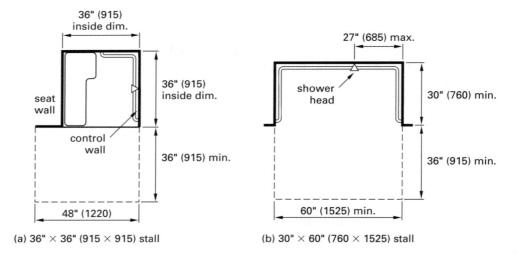

(a) 36" × 36" (915 × 915) stall

(b) 30" × 60" (760 × 1525) stall

Figure 30.14 Accessible Shower Stalls

Landing lengths must be a minimum of 60 in (1525). If ramps change direction at a landing, the landing must be at least 60 in square.

Ramps with rises greater than 6 in (150) or lengths greater than 72 in (1830) must have handrails on both sides, with the top of the handrail from 34 in to 38 in (865 to 965) above the ramp surface. They must extend at least 12 in (305) beyond the top and bottom of the ramp segment and have a diameter or width of gripping surface from $1^{1}/_{4}$ in to $1^{1}/_{2}$ in (32 m to 38 m). Handrails are not required for ramps adjacent to seating in assembly areas.

Stairs that are required as a means of egress and stairs between floors not connected by an elevator must be designed according to certain standards specifying the configuration of treads, risers, nosings, and handrails. The maximum riser height is 7 in (180), and the treads must be a minimum of 11 in (280) as measured from riser to riser as shown in Fig. 29.8. Open risers are not permitted. The undersides of the nosings must not be abrupt and must conform to one of the styles shown in Fig. 29.7. There should be contrasting strips at the top and bottom tread nosings.

Stairway handrails must be continuous on both sides of the stairs. The inside handrail on switchback or dogleg stairs must always be continuous as it changes direction. Other handrails must extend beyond the top and bottom risers as shown in Fig. 29.8. The top of the gripping surface must be between 34 in and 38 in (865 and 965) above stair nosings. The handrail must have a diameter or width of gripping surface from $1^{1}/_{4}$ in to 2 in (32 to 51). There must be a clear space between the handrail and the wall of at least $1^{1}/_{2}$ in (38).

When an exit stairway is part of an accessible route in an unsprinklered building (not including houses), there must be a clear width of 48 in (1220) between handrails.

PROTRUDING OBJECTS

Because objects and building elements that project into corridors and other walkways present a hazard for visually impaired people, there are restrictions on their size and configuration. These are shown in Fig. 30.15 and are based on the use of a cane by people with severe vision impairments. Protruding objects with their lower edge less than 27 in (685) above the floor can be detected so they may project any amount (as long as the minimum passage width is maintained).

Regardless of the situation, protruding objects cannot reduce the clear width required for an accessible route or maneuvering space. In addition, if vertical clearance of an area adjacent to an accessible route is reduced to less than 80 in (2030), a guardrail or other barrier must be provided.

DETECTABLE WARNINGS

Detectable warning surfaces consist of truncated domes 0.2 in (5.1) in height spaced between 1.6 in and 2.4 in (41 to 61) on center in a square grid pattern.

Detectable warning surfaces are generally required at passenger transit platform edges where there is no guard or other protection. Other locations where detectable warning surfaces are required depend on the locally adopted regulation. Both the ADA and the IBC require detectable warning surfaces at platform boarding edges, but the IBC does not require them at bus stops. ANSI A117.1 makes reference to detectable warning surfaces in both exterior and exterior locations but provides no scoping provisions stating precisely where they are required. Local codes should be verified to determine which rules might apply to a particular design project.

SIGNAGE AND ALARMS

Signage that gives emergency information and general circulation directions for visually impaired people must be provided. Signage is also required for elevators.

Emergency warning systems that provide both a visual and an audible alarm are required. Audible alarms must produce a sound that exceeds the prevailing sound level in the room or space by at least 15 dB. Visual alarms must be flashing lights that have a flashing frequency of about 1 Hz (1 cycle per second).

The Americans with Disabilities Act requires that certain accessible rooms and features be clearly identified with the symbol for accessibility and that identification, directional, and information signs meet certain specifications.

Permanent rooms and spaces must be identified with signs having lettering from $^{5}/_{8}$ in to 2 in (16 to 50) high, raised $^{1}/_{32}$ in (0.8) above the surface of the sign. Lettering must be all uppercase, in sans serif or simple serif type accompanied with Grade 2 Braille. If pictograms are used, they must be at least 6 in (152) high and must be accompanied with the equivalent verbal description placed directly below the pictogram. Signs must be eggshell matte or use some other nonglare finish with characters and symbols contrasting with their background. Permanent identification signs must be mounted on the wall adjacent to the latch side of the door such that a person can approach to within 3 in (76) of the signage without encountering protruding objects or standing within the door swing. Mounting height from the floor to the baseline of the characters must be 48 in (1220) minimum and 60 in (1525) maximum. When there is no

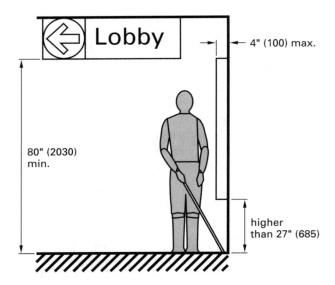

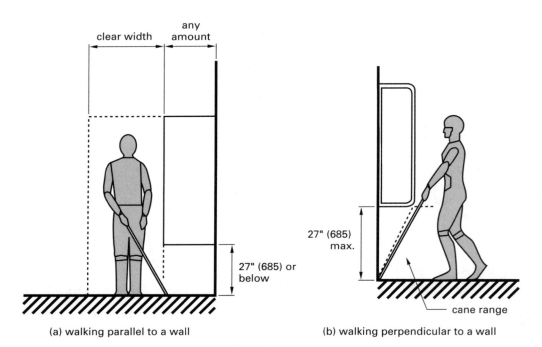

Figure 30.15   Requirements for Protruding Objects

wall space to the latch side of the door, including double leaf doors, the sign must be placed on the nearest adjacent wall.

Individual characters that are both tactile and visual must have a stroke thickness that is at least 10% and not more than 15% of the height of the character, based on an upper-case letter "I." For visual characters, only the maximum stroke thickness is 30% maximum.

The international symbol for accessibility is required on accessible parking spaces, passenger loading zones, entrances, and toilet and bathing facilities when not all are accessible. Building directories and signs that are temporary do not have to comply with the requirements.

TELEPHONES

If public telephones are provided, there must be at least one telephone per floor conforming to the requirements as shown in Fig. 30.16 and as specified in the ADA requirements. If there are two or more banks of telephones, there must be at least one conforming telephone per bank. When four or more public pay telephones are provided, then at least one interior public text telephone is required.

Accessible telephones may be designed for either front or side access. The dimensions required for both of these types are shown in Fig. 30.16. In either case, a clear floor space of at least 30 in by 48 in (760 by 1220) must be provided. The telephones should have pushbutton controls and telephone directories within reach of a person in a wheelchair.

The international TDD (text telephone) is required to identify the location of those phones, and volume control telephones must have a sign depicting a telephone handset with radiating sound waves. In assembly areas, permanently installed assistive listening systems must display the international symbol of access for hearing loss. See Fig. 30.17.

Refer to the ADA requirements and local codes for detailed rules on telephone types and installation requirements.

SEATING

If fixed or built-in seating or tables are provided in accessible public- or common-use areas, then at least 5%, but not less than one of the seating areas must be accessible. This includes facilities such as restaurants, nightclubs, churches, and similar spaces. In new construction and when possible in remodeling, the number of tables should be dispersed throughout the facility. If smoking and nonsmoking areas are provided, the required number of seating spaces must be proportioned among the smoking and nonsmoking

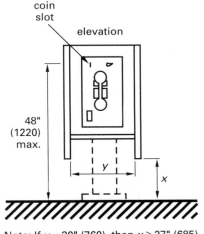

Note: If $y < 30$" (760), then $x \geq 27$" (685).

(a) forward reach possible

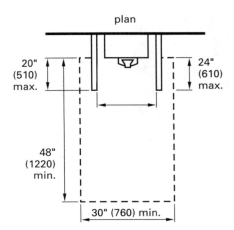

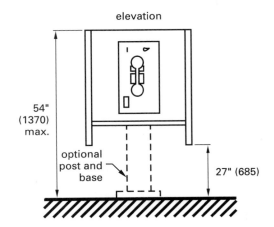

(b) side reach possible

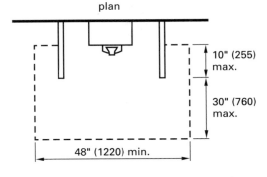

Figure 30.16   Telephone Access

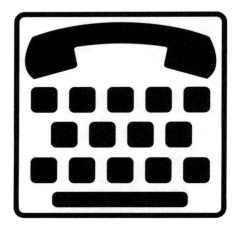

(a) TDD symbol

(b) access for hearing loss symbol

Figure 30.17 International TDD and Hearing Loss Symbols

areas. The area for this type of seating must comply with the dimensions shown in Fig. 30.18.

In places of assembly with fixed seating, the minimum number of wheelchair locations is given in Table 30.1. At least 1%, but not less than one of all fixed seats must be aisle seats with no armrests on the aisle side, or must have removable or folding armrests on the aisle side. Signs notifying people of the availability of these seats must be posted at the ticket office. The wheelchair areas must be an integral part of the overall seating plan and must be provided so people have a choice of admission prices and lines of sight comparable to those available for members of the general public. At least one companion seat must be provided next to each wheelchair area. Wheelchair areas must adjoin an accessible route that also serves as a means of emergency egress.

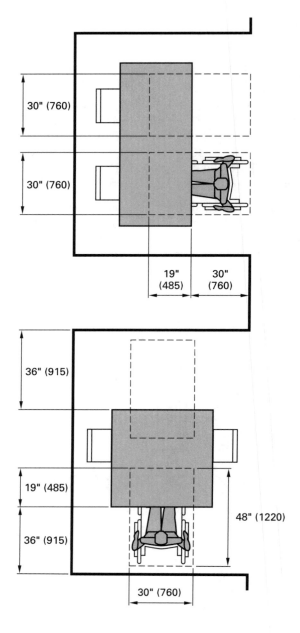

Figure 30.18 Minimum Clearances for Seating and Tables

When assembly areas are part of a remodeling and it is not feasible to disperse the seating areas throughout, the accessible seating areas may be clustered. These clustered areas must have provisions for companion seating and must be located on an accessible route that also serves as a means of emergency egress.

Refer to the complete text of the ADA for requirements for audio-amplification systems, assisted listening devices, and signage required for assembly areas.

Table 30.1

Minimum Number of Wheelchair Spaces for
Assembly Areas

capacity of seating in assembly areas	number of required wheelchair locations
4 to 25	1
26 to 50	2
51 to 300	4
301 to 500	6
over 500	6, plus 1 additional space for each total capacity increase of 100

SAMPLE QUESTIONS

1. An accessible route must serve

    A. all accessible spaces and parts of a building
    B. the corridors, stairs, elevators, and toilet rooms of a building
    C. entrances, parking, toilet rooms, corridors, and drinking fountains
    D. those areas where physically disabled people are likely to need access

2. What is the minimum clear width for an accessible door?

    A. 30 in (760)
    B. 32 in (815)
    C. 34 in (865)
    D. 36 in (915)

3. As measured vertically from the nosing, how high must a handrail be for barrier-free design?

    A. 28 in to 32 in (711 to 815)
    B. 30 in to 34 in (760 to 865)
    C. 32 in to 36 in (815 to 915)
    D. 34 in to 38 in (865 to 965)

4. During the design process to remodel toilet rooms to make them accessible, it is found to be impossible to provide adequate clearance on one side of a door. What is the best course of action?

    A. Apply to the building department for a hardship exemption because compliance is not "readily achievable."
    B. Tell the client that walls should be demolished and the toilet rooms replanned to provide the necessary clearances.
    C. Specify a power-assisted door opener that meets accessibility standards, and use this in the design.
    D. Plan for accessible toilet rooms in another location in the building where all requirements can be adequately met.

5. Which of the following ramp configurations meets barrier-free design requirements?

    A. 1:14 slope with maximum rise of 24 in (610)
    B. 1:12 slope with maximum rise of 34 in (865)
    C. 1:10 slope with maximum rise of 8 in (203)
    D. 1:8 slope with maximum rise of 4 in (100)

6. What type of sink is best for barrier-free design?

    A. wall-hung
    B. built-in
    C. vanity
    D. pedestal

7. Standard accessible toilet stalls must have a clear width of at least

    A. 54 in (1370)
    B. 56 in (1420)
    C. 60 in (1525)
    D. 66 in (1675)

8. In addition to providing the correct access to all fixtures in a toilet room, which of the following would most affect the size and configuration of the room?

    A. a 5 ft (1525) clear circular turnaround space
    B. maneuvering space on the outside of the entry door to the room
    C. clear space at towel dispensers and full-height mirrors
    D. a minimum 36 in (915) access route into and through the room

9.   In the diagram shown, what is the minimum distance, x, between two entry doors forming a vestibule when one opens out of the vestibule and one opens into the vestibule?

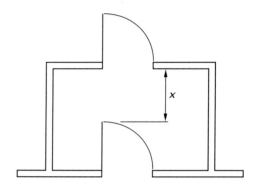

A.   36 in (915)
B.   42 in (1065)
C.   48 in (1220)
D.   60 in (1525)

10. In surveying an existing corridor to see if it met accessibility guidelines, an architect discovers the following two items that are questionable.

(a) a small fire-hose cabinet extending 5 in (127) from the wall

(b) a $1/4$ in (6) high threshold below a pair of normally open doors

Which items must be modified to make the corridor barrier-free?

A.   neither (a) nor (b)
B.   (a) but not (b)
C.   (b) but not (a)
D.   both (a) and (b)

SOLUTIONS

This chapter contains solutions and explanations for the sample questions in this book. The solutions to sample questions in Ch. 2 through Ch. 11 are listed first. Chapter 22 contains sample questions for the subjects of materials and methods that are covered in Chs. 12 through 21. The solutions for Chs. 23 through 30 are included here.

Ch. 2: PRE-DESIGN—ENVIRONMENTAL ANALYSIS AND PROJECT PLANNING

1.   B is correct.

Point 1 has a good view, but at the top of a hill it would be very windy. In addition, access to the lake is difficult due to the steep slope from this site to the lake. Point 3 is in a drainage pattern. This alone makes it unsuitable for development, but the location would also be cool due to its position at the bottom of two slopes and in the path of wind coming through the valley. Point 4 has a good view, has easy access to the lake, and could be used for development, but the slightly steeper slope might complicate grading and site work. Point 2 has level ground and a good view of and access to the lake, and its location on a south-facing slope would capture the sun and minimize the detrimental effects of the wind.

2.   C is correct.

If the floor area ratio is 2, the maximum amount of floor area that can be built is 120,000 ft². The available ground area that can be covered within the setbacks is 270 ft times 130 ft, or 35,100 ft². Dividing this figure into 120,000 gives 3.42 stories, which indicates that three full stories and a partial fourth story should be built.

3.   C is correct.

The Columbian Exposition revived interest in city planning and showed that desirable results could be achieved through organized efforts. It also prompted many cities to plan civic centers and parkways. The Ordinance of 1785 started the rectangular survey system, which reinforced grid planning begun with the plan for Philadelphia. Garnier's plan was one of the responses to the Industrial Revolution and the first to use the idea of zoning. The Industrial Revolution prompted a reform movement that led to many ideas about planning, many of which influenced urban design in Europe and the United States.

Although L'Enfant's plan was widely praised and publicized as a major planning effort, its Baroque planning approach was never widely adopted.

4.   A is correct.

A freeway can be considered a path, an edge, or both. It is a path to the person traveling on it. It is an edge if it divides a district or encloses an area. A popular neighborhood gathering spot would probably be considered a node because it can be entered and because it is a center of interest. It would most likely be the center of a neighborhood district as well. An area with many hospitals would be viewed as the hospital district. This image would be reinforced because of the likely support services, such as doctors' offices and pharmacies, that would also be nearby. A group of houses by themselves would have little image unless they formed an edge or surrounded a park or similar node.

5.   D is correct.

A variety of informal spaces would promote social contact. Choice A is incorrect because forcing too many people within close, personal space would be counterproductive. People would become uncomfortable and defensive. Choice B is incorrect because the orientation of the benches would be sociofugal, requiring that people face away from each other. Choice C is incorrect because the cooking and serving area would be one of the most popular gathering spaces and a destination for people. Here, people could watch food being prepared, serve themselves, and informally meet other people.

6.   B is correct.

Using the scale on the drawing, the distance between the two points is about 15 ft. Using formula 2.1, the slope is

$$G = \left(\frac{8 \text{ ft}}{15 \text{ ft}}\right) \times 100\% = 53\%$$

7.   C is correct.

Choice B is incorrect because either a relatively thin layer of clay only 6 ft thick could be removed and replaced with better soil, or the foundations could be placed on the good underlying layer of sandy soil. Both A and D would pose minor problems, but these would probably not affect the final decision to build. A speculative office building depends on a wide catchment area, and a lack of arterial roads in some portions of it would most likely not affect the marketability of the project. If there was strong objection to parking lots, the visual impact could be minimized through landscaping, or parking could be placed underground or in a well-designed parking structure. The vacancy rate is the one factor that would most affect the financial success of the project and the decision to build.

8.   D is correct.

All of the conditions listed would create unusual excavation and foundation problems.

9.   C is correct.

Statement II, the size of utility easements, would be found on the site survey. If a site survey had not been performed, the information would come from the utility company. Statement III, minimum lot size, is usually a part of a subdivision regulation. Statement V, roof coverings, would be prescribed either in restrictive covenants for the property or as part of a building code. Covenants would dictate the type and appearance of the material for aesthetic reasons, whereas the building code would specify types of roofing based primarily on fire-resistance needs.

10. B is correct.

Point A is too close to another intersecting street. Point C intersects the street at an angle that is unsafe. Point D intersects an arterial street. Although sometimes possible, this situation should be avoided, especially if it is as close to an intersection as is this one.

Ch. 3: PRE-DESIGN— BUILDING PROGRAMMING

1.   D is correct.

A multilevel system of pedestrian circulation implies a definite type of physical solution. This should not be confused with a programming statement. A statement that might precede the design concept would be something like "separate incompatible circulation functions."

2.   A is correct.

None of the enclosed mall would be rentable, so subtract the 6% (5100 ft²) right off the top.

$$85,000 \text{ ft}^2 - 5100 \text{ ft}^2 = 79,900 \text{ ft}^2$$

Then take 75% of the remainder, which gives about 60,000 ft² (59,925 ft² exactly).

3.   C is correct.

There are a number of ways of arriving at the same answer for this question. City B has a higher cost index, so divide the lower into the higher.

$$\frac{1517}{1440} = 1.053$$

Multiply this factor by the cost in city A ($1,500,000) to get $1,580,208. Then increase this by the 5% inflation factor.

$$(\$1,580,208)(1.05) = \$1,659,218 \quad (\$1,659,000)$$

Alternately, increase for inflation first, then use the cost index factor.

4.   D is correct.

Contractor's overhead and profit are typically 15% to 40% of the construction cost.

5.   B is correct.

Grouping waiting areas to encourage interaction would probably be the least desirable option for two reasons. People are usually a little nervous while waiting with strangers and prefer the option to avoid contact in sociofugal space. In addition, because there are different departments in a medium-sized facility, having everyone in one space would be inefficient as well as uncomfortable. One large waiting area would make people less at ease and therefore would be counterproductive to the client's goals.

6. D is correct.

Because the facility is expected to grow and because there are several distinct departments, a radial organization would work for the first phase and allow for easy growth. Because the site is ample and flat, terrain would probably not restrict this type of organizational pattern. An axial pattern might work, but because everyone enters in one place for directions and orientation, the central focus of a radial pattern would probably be preferable.

7. C is correct.

For the first phase of this type of building, most functions would probably be fixed, requiring little need for convertibility in the future or multiple use initially. The primary need of expansibility would guide the structural framing system so that the building could be added onto easily.

8. A is correct.

Reducing the total time by 3 months means about a 15% reduction. Fast-track construction would probably take this amount of time off the process. CPM scheduling would not help much, and negotiation rather than bidding would reduce the time a little, but certainly not by 3 months. In addition, negotiation would most likely result in a higher cost to the client, so choice B is not correct. Adding more people to the design process would only help a little, and overtime is generally not efficient, so C is incorrect. Streamlining the decision-making process would not reduce the time required and would probably not be acceptable to the client.

9. D is correct.

The architect can, of course, control his or her own fees and, to a certain extent, can negotiate with consultants, so C is incorrect. Because the architect can control building costs and site work through design, B is not correct. Although the rate of escalation cannot be controlled, the amount depends on the base cost of construction, which can be controlled through design, so A is not correct, even though it is a tempting answer.

10. B is correct.

Because the amount is only 8%, this could probably be made up through a slight reduction in area (statement III) and modifying some levels of quality (statement IV). Because it is only the programming phase, value engineering is not possible, so statement II is not correct. Statements I and V are not appropriate because school districts cannot borrow money from other accounts and usually need to have schools completed as originally scheduled.

Ch. 4: PRE-DESIGN AND SITE PLANNING—SITE ANALYSIS AND DESIGN

1. B is correct.

All roads should have a crown, or high point, in the center to ensure positive drainage to either side.

2. C is correct.

A township contains 36 sections. A check is 24 mi^2 and consists of 16 townships.

3. D is correct.

The difference in elevation between the bottom of a sewer line at two points causes the water flow. The term *invert* is also used to call out the bottom elevation of drains, catch basins, and manholes.

4. B is correct.

Without knowing other conditions of the site, the best placement of the building and road is based on road grading and building construction on the existing topography. Roads should cut across slopes gradually to minimize steep grades, so this eliminates choice D where the road runs perpendicular to the slope. The road is well placed in C, but the length of the building runs perpendicular to the slope, which would make construction more difficult and expensive. Choice A works fairly well, with a gradual slope for the road and the building on level ground, but the road is in a valley and on the north side of the building. Choice B places the building parallel to the contour lines, is on a south-facing slope, and has a road gently rising across the grade with curves following the direction of the contours, so this is the best choice.

5. D is correct.

Most roads should be kept at a grade less than 10% except those of very short distances; parking garage ramps are also an exception. In northern climates, where snow and ice are a problem, it is even more important to maintain gentle slopes. A 12% grade would not be safe and could make driving difficult. Refer to Table 2.1 for recommended site work slopes.

6. B is correct.

Statement II is incorrect because automobile and pedestrian traffic should always be kept separate. Statement IV may be considered partially correct due to the idea of separating parking from walks, but a single entrance may create conflicts with vehicles pulling into and out of parking spaces and entering and leaving by the same drive. The other three statements are generally good guidelines for planning site circulation.

7.   D is correct.

All three of these methods are used to describe property, although the metes and bounds method is not used as much as the other two methods.

8.   C is correct.

Choice A is incorrect because overhangs are not effective on the west and east sides of a building due to the low sun angle. Vertical louvers, or fins, are more effective in these locations. Choice B is incorrect because the south side actually receives less solar radiation than the east or west sides because the sun is high during the middle of the day. It would be more effective to minimize the roof area to cut down on solar radiation.

9.   D is correct.

This pattern is characteristic of roads with a crown in the middle sloping toward curbs on either side. As with any contour map, contour lines representing a ridge (which is what a crown of a road is in miniature) point in the direction of the downslope, so this road slopes down from east to west (or up from west to east as the answer choice states). The contours pointing in the other direction represent a ditch. Just as with any valley on a contour map, the lines point in the direction of the upslope.

10. A is correct.

90° parking layouts are always the most efficient if space is limited, so choices B and C are incorrect. Choice D is incorrect because a single-loaded circulation drive providing access to parking is not as efficient as two rows of parking sharing one drive.

Ch. 5: HUMAN COMFORT AND MECHANICAL SYSTEM FUNDAMENTALS

1.   C is correct.

Although motors, people, and lighting may be less critical in residences and some other types of occupancies, all of the items listed produce heat except humidity.

2.   A is correct.

The sling psychrometer measures wet-bulb temperature. As shown in the abbreviated psychrometric chart in Fig. 5.3, wet-bulb temperature is one of the ordinates on the chart. A sling psychrometer may have a dry-bulb thermometer on it, but its primary purpose is to measure wet-bulb temperatures.

Likewise, relative humidity can be determined from the difference between dry- and wet-bulb levels, but this is not what the device measures directly.

3.   A is correct.

Although heat loss and gain through glazing is complex and results from a combination of conduction, convection, and radiation, insulating glass is separated by an air space. Therefore, most heat loss is through convection, and not conduction, because the air circulates within the glass, picking up heat on the warm side and transferring it on the cold side where it is lost to the outside through the glass by conduction. Even if the air space is evacuated, there is still some air present.

4.   B is correct.

Equivalent temperature difference is incorrect because that value is used to calculate the heat gain through the building envelope, such as walls and roofs.

5.   D is correct.

Because resistance is the number of hours it takes for one Btu (watt) to be transferred through 1 ft^2 (m^2) of material when the temperature differential is 1°, the higher value is better.

6.   D is correct.

Weatherstripping serves to seal joints and cracks around doors and windows. Because infiltration is a major factor in heat loss, weatherstripping is always a good strategy.

7.   A is correct.

Although relative humidity affects human comfort, by itself it is not the only measure of comfort. For example, even at a high humidity of 75%, if the temperature is cool enough or there is enough of a breeze, most people will feel comfortable. Effective temperature (ET) is a better indicator of comfort because it takes all the variables into account.

8.   D is correct.

The design equivalent temperature difference has no bearing on the solution to this problem. First, calculate the U-value. Because the R-value is given as 38, the U-value is just the reciprocal, or

$$U = \frac{1}{38}$$
$$= 0.026 \text{ Btu/hr-ft}^2\text{-°F}$$

The temperature difference, Δt, is 75°.

The roof area is 40 ft by 80 ft, or 3200 ft². Using formula 9.3, the total heat loss can be calculated as follows.

$$q = UA\Delta t$$

$$= \left(0.026 \ \frac{\frac{\text{Btu}}{\text{hr}}}{\text{ft}^2\text{-}^\circ\text{F}} \right) (3200 \ \text{ft}^2)(75^\circ\text{F})$$

$$= 6240 \ \text{Btu/hr}$$

9.   D is correct.

Latent heat is the heat required to produce a change in state of a material. Simply introducing sensible heat to raise the temperature from 32° to 33° would not melt ice. Additional heat is required, which is the latent heat.

10. C is correct.

When the temperature is above about 85°F (29°C), the body loses more heat through evaporation than through convection or radiation. In a humid climate this process is retarded, so encouraging air movement would be the best strategy, although overhangs and light-colored surfaces would help minimize heat buildup in the structure itself.

Ch. 6: HVAC SYSTEMS

1.   D is correct.

Water-loop heat pumps use a continuous flow of temperate water to extract heat from those areas that need to be cooled and add heat to other areas requiring very little, if any, additional energy input.

Energy recovery ventilators work best in climates where the difference between indoor and outdoor air temperature is high. Heat pipes are not appropriate because they would simply pre-warm cool outdoor air. A recuperative fuel economizer is another type of system that simply uses hot exhaust gas to preheat incoming air or water. While saving energy, this type of equipment would only increase the efficiency of the heating plant.

2.   D is correct.

Generally, all of the parties listed are present, except the civil engineer, because that consultant does not have direct involvement in the operation of the building systems.

3.   C is correct.

The shopping mall would be planned for relatively fixed sizes of rental spaces. Although flexibility might be a concern, it would not be most important. Statement I is not correct. Because the tenant mix would probably not be completely known at the time of design, the tenant's preference could not be solicited even if it was appropriate. In most cases, the tenants would not care what the HVAC system was as long as it worked, so statement IV is not correct.

4.   D is correct.

For most mid-sized buildings, an all-air or air-water system needs about 3% to 9% of the gross area for HVAC system mechanical space. Office buildings fall somewhere near the midpoint of the range, so use 6% for this question. 6% of the estimated 126,000 ft² gross area is 7560 ft². This is rounded up to 7600, so D is correct as a minimum estimated area.

5.   C is correct.

Propane has a heating value of 2500 Btu/ft³, whereas natural gas has a heating value of 1050 Btu/ft³.

6.   D is correct.

A round duct is the most efficient choice and offers the most area for the least perimeter area, which causes friction and pressure loss. A square duct is the next most efficient shape, being the closest to a circle. A square shape would use the available space most efficiently, but it is not as efficient as a round duct. As ducts become more rectangular, they become less efficient and have increased friction loss. A rectangular duct with the long dimension horizontal would only be used if space was a problem.

7.   B is correct.

A standard gas furnace does not have a damper. Only a special energy-saving furnace would sometimes have a damper that automatically closes when the furnace is off.

8.   A is correct.

A ton of air conditioning is equivalent to 12,000 Btu/hr. Dividing 108,000 by 12,000 gives 9 tons.

9.   B is correct.

An economizer cycle uses outdoor air when its temperature is low enough to assist in cooling.

10. C is correct.

Cooking produces a change in state of water and other substances, so latent heat is required and must therefore be off-set with air conditioning. Sensible heat is also present, so both types are present.

Ch. 7: ENERGY EFFICIENCY AND ALTERNATE ENERGY SOURCES

1. C is correct.

The Taos Pueblo adapts the cubic form to get as much volume for the least amount of surface area, thus minimizing heat gain in the summer.

There is little sun shading, but the pueblos do utilize very small windows. Skin-dominant loading does describe residential building, but it is not a design principle. Wind effect is not correct because this would require long, narrow buildings with many openings.

2. D is correct.

Vapor pressure does not cause air infiltration or exfiltration; rather, vapor pressure is a movement of moisture.

3. D is correct.

There is no such thing as a transparent photovoltaic cell, although thin-film cells can be placed on transparent materials, such as glass.

4. B is correct.

Choice A is not correct because air locks only protect door openings. Earth sheltering would protect a larger portion of the building. Green roofs are primarily used to protect against solar radiation and to reduce runoff. Landscaping can reduce the negative effects of wind, but not as well as does solid earth.

5. C is correct.

The solar heat-gain coefficient is the ratio of solar heat gain through a window to the total solar radiation striking the window. Because it includes the frame and the glass spacer, the solar heat-gain coefficient is a better indicator of heat gain than is the shading coefficient, which is a similar measure but does not include the effects of the frame. The daylight factor and the window-to-wall ratio are not measures of heat gain.

6. A is correct.

Because ground-source heat pumps require an extensive network of buried piping, vertically or horizontally, a rocky site would make the installation prohibitively expensive.

7. D is correct.

A Trombe wall is a type of thermal storage wall that is placed directly behind glass on the south side of a building to store solar energy during the day for release at night.

Option A is incorrect because a direct gain system uses various types of massive materials (even gypsum wallboard) in various locations inside a building to store heat. Option B is incorrect because a greenhouse uses a south-facing room enclosed with extensive glass, not masonry. Option C is incorrect because active assist includes mechanical devices in addition to thermal mass.

8. A is correct.

The apparent angle of the sun above the horizon is the altitude.

9. B is correct.

For a window with no light shelf, daylighting is effective for a distance of about 1.5 times the head height of the window. With a light shelf, the effective distance increase to about 2.0 to 2.5 times the head height.

10. C is correct.

Glass that changes darkness in response to a change in the level of daylight is photochromic.

Ch. 8: SUSTAINABLE DESIGN

1. B is correct.

Option A is incorrect because post-consumer materials are those that have served their intended use. Option C is incorrect because recycled products are finished materials or products that have been either reused as they are or converted into another material. Option D is incorrect because renewable materials refer to something that can be grown or naturally replenished faster than humans can deplete it.

2. B is correct.

Bagasse (the residue from the processing of sugar cane) and rice straw are both alternative agricultural products that are made into panel products. Wheat straw is a little more common and is also used for straw particleboard.

3. C is correct.

Although ventilation rates vary depending on the use of the space, 15 cfm/person (8 L/s/person) is the lowest rate recommended by ASHRAE 62-2001.

4. A is correct.

Graywater systems, when allowed by local building and health departments, are most appropriately used where the ratio of nonpotable to potable water needs is relatively high. Of the choices given, a laundry would best meet this need.

Restaurants also have a high ratio, but health concerns would suggest that graywater not be used in this building type.

5. B is correct.

A life-cycle assessment evaluates the environmental impact of using a particular material over its entire useful life, including disposal. It could be used to compare the impacts of two or more materials so the architect could select the most sustainable one.

Option A is incorrect because an environmental impact study, or EIS, is used to evaluate the impact of a development on the environment. Option C is incorrect because an impact assessment is one phase of a life-cycle assessment. Option D is incorrect because there is no sustainability evaluation method by the name "matrix comparison chart."

6. A is correct.

A building can receive a LEED credit for using a carpet system that meets or exceeds the requirements of the Carpet and Rug Institute's IAQ Carpet Testing Program. Such carpet may be on the Greenguard Registry or have a Green Seal label, but neither is sufficient for LEED credit. The SCAQMD sets standards for VOCs, but meeting their requirements is not sufficient for receiving LEED credit.

7. C is correct.

The Environmental Protection Agency (EPA) banned the spray application of asbestos-containing fireproofing and insulation materials in 1973.

8. D is correct.

Although radon detection and remediation can be done by a specialty contractor, detection and remediation can be done by anyone.

9. D is correct.

Options A and B are incorrect because Greenguard and Green Seal are both product rating systems. Greenguard certifies for acceptable emission levels while Green Seal certifies products that meet certain environmental standards. Option C is incorrect because ISO 14000 refers to the International Standards Organization's collection of standards and guidelines that relate to a variety of environmental standards, including labeling, life-cycle assessment, and others. ISO standards are used as a measure for performance of other organizations that certify products and make other environmental claims. Only LEED certifies the entire building as it meets sustainability standards.

10. B is correct.

Pervious paving allows rainwater to soak into the ground while providing support for parking or other outdoor activities.

Option A is incorrect because cisterns are designed for holding rainwater for further use, not to minimize the runoff. Option C is incorrect because rip-rap is stone reinforcement for the banks of rivers or lakes. Option D is incorrect because silt fences are used to prevent erosion and sediment runoff during construction.

Ch. 9: PLUMBING SYSTEMS

1. A is correct.

The size of a leaching field is determined by the quantity of effluent that must be accommodated and the ability of the soil to let the effluent soak in. This permeability of the soil is measured by the percolation test, and because there is no answer related to quantity, this is the correct response.

2. B is correct.

Although there are many concerns in a private water supply related to both water quality and the method of pumping the water, of the answers provided, hardness is the most important.

3. C is correct.

The static head is the part of water supply design affected by building height.

4. C is correct.

Statement I is incorrect because the type of sprinkler system has nothing to do with its efficiency. Statement III is incorrect because sprinkler spacing is dependent on which hazard classification exists.

5. C is correct.

In order to find the maximum height, first take the pressure in the water main and subtract other known pressure losses and the pressure required for the fixture to operate properly.

$$57 \frac{\text{lbm}}{\text{in}^2} - 23 \frac{\text{lbm}}{\text{in}^2} - 12 \frac{\text{lbm}}{\text{in}^2} = 22 \text{ psi}$$

Because 1 psi is required to lift water 2.3 ft, the maximum height is

$$\left(22 \frac{\text{lbm}}{\text{in}^2}\right)\left(2.3 \frac{\text{ft}}{\frac{\text{lbm}}{\text{in}^2}}\right) = 50.6 \text{ ft}$$

6.   A is correct.

Even though the nearest water line is 300 ft away, the best recommendation would be to use city water, where the quality and quantity are known and a long-term supply is assured. Although nearby property owners might or might not be willing to share the cost, the owner would still be best advised to extend the line.

Drilling a test bore could help determine the depth, potential yield, and water quality, but would cost almost as much as a complete well.

Petitioning the city to extend the line would be time-consuming and probably not successful if they had already decided against it.

Asking nearby property owners who use wells about their experience would yield useful information, but even if the cost and water quality were acceptable, extending the municipal line would still be the preferred course of action.

7.   D is correct.

Statement I is incorrect because the minimum slope of drains depends on the size of the pipe. Statement II is incorrect because the vent stack may sometimes extend through the roof but does not always have to. In many cases, the vent stack connects with the stack vent above the highest fixture served by the stack.

8.   B is correct.

Water hammer occurs when a valve is suddenly turned off and causes the water to stop, forcing the pipes to shake.

9.   A is correct.

A stack vent extends a soil or waste stack to vent through the roof, and every stack must have one of these. A vent stack is a separate vent connected to a waste or soil stack in multistory buildings, so not every building has this. A house trap is not mandatory in many codes, and a backflow preventer is not required in many plumbing installations.

10. C is correct.

Type M copper pipe is only used for low-pressure piping. Type L is the one most commonly used in plumbing installations.

Ch. 10: ELECTRICAL SYSTEMS

1.   D is correct.

Choice A is correct because lamps with a higher efficacy could be selected, although this would have to be balanced against the change in color temperature. Choice B is correct

because lumen output decreases as lamps age and as dirt accumulates on them. Changing lamps often would help maintain the initial footcandle level. Choice C is correct because room finishes have a significant effect on the total light level in a room.

2.   B is correct.

In this problem, the footcandle level must first be determined. Because the source is perpendicular to the wall, the inverse square law is used.

$$E = \frac{I}{d^2}$$
$$= \frac{3500 \text{ cd}}{(15 \text{ ft})^2}$$
$$= 15.56 \text{ fc}$$

Once the footcandle level is determined, it is multiplied by the reflectance to find the brightness.

$$(15.56 \text{ fc})(0.75) = 11.7 \text{ ftL}$$

3.   C is correct.

Because of the potential for oxidation, the leads of aluminum conductors must be cleaned prior to installation, so statement I is correct. Statement III is correct because all the special requirements of aluminum conductors and the danger of incorrect installation require that a licensed electrician do the work. Statement V is correct because larger conductors are required to carry the same amperage as that of copper conductors.

4.   B is correct.

Although all of the choices listed should be considered and are potentially important, the question asks which ones are most important. For office space where video display tubes (VDTs) and standard office tasks are present, the architect should be concerned with two results of glare. Veiling reflection would be of concern for standard office tasks such as writing and reading, whereas reflected glare would be critical in using the VDTs. Therefore, statements III and IV are correct. Likewise, the brightness ratios between the tasks and their surroundings are important, especially with VDTs, so statement V is correct. The color rendering index is less important. Although visual comfort probability deals with sources of direct glare, this answer is not given in conjunction with the others.

5. A is correct.

As voltages increase, current decreases to provide the same amount of power. Lower currents require smaller conductors. For large commercial buildings, smaller conductors translate to less expense in conductors and conduit, as well as easier installation of smaller wires.

6. B is correct.

A large school building would require high voltage service from the utility and step-down transformers provided by the owner. This rules out choice A. A transformer vault near the exterior wall would be the best choice for protection, ventilation, and ease of installation and removal. Although the transformer could be placed on a pad outside the building, this would leave it exposed to possible vandalism and might present a danger to the students.

7. B is correct.

A temperature rise detector would not give early warning to the occupants. If properly located, either an ionization or photoelectric detector would work.

8. C is correct.

Footcandle is the unit of measure of the light incident on a transmitting or reflecting surface. *Footlambert* is the unit of measure of the brightness (or luminance) of a surface and takes into account the transmittance properties of the glass. *Candela* is the SI unit for *candlepower*, which is the unit of luminous intensity.

9. B is correct.

Choice B offers the best balance between appropriate color rendering, accent lighting, and energy efficiency. Daylighting would provide natural light for viewing clothes, and warm white deluxe lamps would be efficient and provide a pleasant, overall light.

Choice A would not be appropriate because of the cooler colors of mercury lamps and metal halide lighting. Choice C is not good because of the potentially damaging effects of too much daylighting on fabrics. Choice D would not be energy efficient and would also present the problem of daylight damaging the fabrics.

10. D is correct.

Low-pressure sodium lamps produce a monochromatic yellow light that would not be appropriate in a storage warehouse where people may have to discriminate between colors.

Ch. 11: ACOUSTICS

1. A is correct.

Sensitivity to sound is not dependent on gender, so statement I is not true. Although the lower end of sensitivity to sound is somewhere between 20 Hz and 30 Hz, 15 Hz is too low. The generally accepted upper limit is about 20,000 Hz, so statement III is also incorrect.

2. B is correct.

The assembly shown would not be the best for controlling impact noise or mechanical vibration, so these two answers are incorrect. Because the sound-absorbing panel is in room B, this would help control excessive reverberation, so statement II is correct. The decision to be made is between III and IV. Because noise reduction between two spaces is dependent on the transmission loss of the wall, the area of the wall, and the absorption of the surfaces in the receiving room, statement III is more correct. It is true that adding absorption to a space will result in a noise reduction within that space.

3. A is correct.

The rule of thumb when the difference between two sound sources is 4 dB to 8 dB is to add 1 dB to the higher value, which in this case is 69 dB.

4. D is correct.

STC, or sound transmission class, gives the designer a quick way to evaluate tested partitions in the common frequency ranges.

5. B is correct.

Noise criteria curves are used to specify the allowable sound pressure levels at octave band center frequencies.

6. C is correct.

Even though reverberation is dependent on total room absorption and room volume, room volume is the only variable listed.

7. C is correct.

Although placing absorptive materials on both sides of the wall would not hurt and would decrease the noise level in the "noisier" room, the three most important variables are the transmission loss of the wall, the wall's stiffness (damping qualities), and minimizing the area of the separating barrier.

8.   D is correct.

To find the total absorption when calculation at specific frequencies is not required, the NRC, or noise reduction coefficient, is used. The total absorption is the summation of all the individual absorptions according to the formula $A = \Sigma Sa$.

floor:	(15 ft)(20 ft)(0.10 sabins/ft²) =	30 sabins
walls:	(((15 ft + 15 ft + 20 ft + 20 ft)	
	× (8.5 ft)) - ((3.5 ft)(8 ft)))	
	× (0.05 sabins/ft²) =	28 sabins
window:	(3.5 ft)(8 ft)(0.15 sabins/ft²) =	4 sabins
ceiling:	(15 ft)(20 ft)(0.60 sabins/ft²) =	180 sabins
total		242 sabins

9.   B is correct.

Because a change in intensity level of 3 dB is considered "just perceptible," it would probably be better not to use the material regardless of how low the added cost was. Trying to modify the material to 6 dB would also probably not be worth the trouble. For an STC rating 6 dB higher, it would be better to look at another construction assembly instead of trying to make do with a modified material. Choice D could be correct if the material was such that simply doubling it rather than modifying it would result in a 6 dB increase.

10. A is correct.

In this question, the phrase "If cost is a consideration" affects the order of priority of the suggestions. Although adding an extra layer of gypsum board might be one of the best suggestions from an acoustical point of view, it would cost money. The simplest, least expensive suggestion during design development would be to reorient the operable windows so sound from one classroom did not reflect off an open window and onto the window in the adjacent classroom. Also, during design development, it is an easy matter to coordinate routing of mechanical and electrical work to minimize acoustical problems.

The third priority would be to add the extra layer of gypsum board to improve the transmission loss of the partition. For the small additional cost of materials and labor, sound transmission would be greatly reduced. Next, substituting carpeting for tile would reduce the noise in each room, but not so much the loss through the wall. The cost would probably be more than that of the gypsum board but still reasonable for the benefits obtained.

Statement IV would be the next-to-least-valid suggestion. Even though it would greatly limit sound transmission between the two rooms and would be easy to do during the early planning stages, it does not make sense to place a storage room along the windows when the potential acoustical problem can be solved by other means.

Least desirable is hiring an acoustical consultant for this situation only. The anticipated noise sources are not so unusual that the preceding steps would not sufficiently solve the problem.

Ch. 22: MATERIALS AND METHODS

1.   D is correct.

Monel is a trade name for a metal alloy of copper and nickel. Muntz metal is a common alloy of 60% copper and 40% tin. Nickel silver is a name given to an alloy of 65% copper, 25% zinc, and 10% nickel.

2.   B is correct.

All of the answer choices listed would need to be addressed, but because the question asks which is *most* important, a judgment call is required. Choice D is unlikely because a large building would probably utilize piers or caissons for the foundation, so the load-carrying capacity of the soil would not be as critical. Foundation insulation could be easily selected to avoid deterioration problems, so choice C is an unlikely answer. Of the two remaining answers, hydrostatic pressure could cause the most problems, so this is the primary problem to be solved.

.   B is correct.

Vapor barriers should always be located on the warm side of insulation to prevent moisture from condensing when it cools and reaches the dew point. Moisture penetrating the insulation can reduce the insulation's effectiveness and damage other materials.

3.   A is correct.

If the block shown is not used, the carriages must be toe nailed to the floor, which is a weaker construction detail than that shown.

4.   B is correct.

The member supporting the treads is the carriage, and the tread member overhanging is the nosing.

.   D is correct.

Safety glazing is required in all areas subject to human impact. This includes, of course, glass doors, and any glass within 1 ft of doors. Glass farther than 1 ft from doors and with a sill over 18 in above the floor does not have to be safety glazed.

6 D is correct.

Choice A describes organic material, choice B describes gravels, and choice C describes clays.

8. B is correct.

Annealed glass is the standard glass used in most noncritical glazing situations. All of the other types of glass listed have greater strengths and could be used in a tall building with large panels of glass subject to high wind loads and thermal cycling.

9. D is correct.

Fire-rated partitions must be constructed according to tested and approved methods that include using Type X gypsum board, the method of attachment to the framing, how the joints are finished, the type and size of studs, and other details. In addition, the fire separation must extend from the slab to the rated slab above, not just to a suspended, finish ceiling.

10. A is correct.

Type M masonry has a compressive strength of 2500 psi. Types S and N have strengths of 1800 psi and 750 psi, respectively, and Type O is the lowest with a compressive strength of 350 psi.

11. D is correct.

SW stands for severe weathering and would be the type that should be specified for the northeastern United States. NW is normal weathering, and MW is moderate weathering. FBX refers to the finish appearance.

12. C is correct.

Plain slicing produces a figured pattern with the characteristic "cathedral" appearance. Rotary slicing produces the most varied grain pattern, and half-round slicing yields a moderate amount of pattern. Because quarter slicing cuts perpendicular to the growth rings, this gives the straightest pattern of the choices listed. Rift slicing would also give a very uniform grain pattern.

13. B is correct.

Although asphalt-impregnated paper can act as a vapor barrier, the fact that it is placed on the outside of the sheathing precludes choice C (and also choice D) from being correct. It does add a little to the thermal resistance, but its primary purpose is to prevent any water that seeps behind the siding from getting into the structure. It also serves to prevent air infiltration.

14. A is correct.

A raked joint like that shown in the masonry wall above the ledge is not a good one to use because water running down the wall can seep into the joint by capillary action. The details at points B and C are correctly executed. The flashing and sealant at B would keep water out, and the drip at point C would prevent water from running under the ledge and into the masonry joint at D.

15. C is correct.

Control joints placed where separate sections of concrete are poured and in walks are placed 5 ft (1500) apart. Expansion joints with a joint filler are placed a maximum of 20 ft (6100) apart.

16. B is correct.

Stainless steel can be welded and is stronger than bronze, so statements I and V are incorrect. It is primarily an alloy of steel and chromium, but sometimes nickel is added.

17. A is correct.

Breast boards are horizontal boards between soldier beams, and rakers are diagonal braces that support walers.

18. B is correct.

The height of the dump bucket is important because dropping concrete too far causes segregation, which should not be allowed. The location of rebar is important because of the minimum coverages required to protect the steel from moisture. The method of form support is important because unstable forms can affect the final appearance and size of the concrete. They can also be a safety hazard, but this is the contractor's responsibility.

19. C is correct.

Any piece of lumber from 2 in to 5 in (51 to 127) nominal thickness is considered dimension lumber. Timber is lumber 5 in (127) and over, whereas boards are 2 in (51) or less.

20. C is correct.

Shear plates, not split ring connectors, are used for structures that must be disassembled. The face of the shear plate is flush with the face of the lumber, and the two pieces are connected with a bolt.

21. C is correct.

Type III cement is high-early-strength—the type needed for rapid slip form construction. Type I is normal cement. Type II is low heat and sulfate resistant, and Type IV is slow setting and low heat for massive structures.

22. A is correct.

A split extends completely through the wood, so this would affect both horizontal shear resistance and bending strength. The other defects listed extend only partially into the wood.

23. D is correct.

Conductivity is the unit of conductance for 1 in of material. Conductance is the amount of heat loss through a material other than 1 in thick. Resistance is the amount of time it takes a certain amount of heat to pass through a material. The coefficient of heat transmission is the overall rate of heat flow.

24. B is correct.

Rock wool is a loose insulation poured or blown into cavities. It is usually not used in commercial construction and can settle when installed in any type of cavity wall. The other types of insulation listed would be more appropriate, although fiberglass batts would be difficult because the usual method of attaching them is stapling the flanges of the insulation to wood studs. However, fiberglass batts could be fit in steel stud cavities by friction.

25. B is correct.

A *bull stretcher* is a brick laid on its face so that the width of the brick is visible. With a width of 3⅝ in (90) and a mortar joint of ⅜ in (10), three courses would be 12 in (300). Three *standard stretcher* courses equal 8 in (200).

26. A is correct.

Choice B is a full mortise hinge, choice C is a half mortise, and choice D is a full surface hinge.

27. B is correct.

Closers are always required for fire-rated doors. The other statements are correct.

28. D is correct.

Silicone coatings would provide the best coverage for rough walls because they can be sprayed, painted, or rolled on. If the wall was below grade, the correct choice would be a cementitious coating or a bituminous coating.

29. C is correct.

The depth should be at least 1½ times the depth of the car, but no less than 10 ft (3000). Because the question does not give any information about car depth, assume that the minimum depth is the correct answer.

30. C is correct.

The advantages of copper roofs include their workability and corrosion resistance, so statements I and IV are correct. Because copper roofs are relatively soft and expensive, statements II and III are reasons for not using them.

31. A is correct.

Vertical cracking is usually an indication that the brick wall is not able to move laterally, which is a condition caused by lack of vertical expansion joints.

32. B is correct.

Base flashing extends from the roof over the cant strip and up the wall, so choice A is incorrect. Counter flashing covers the base flashing to extend from the wall over the base flashing and to cover any expansion joint that may occur at this point. Coping protects the top of the parapet, so choice D is incorrect. Sealants by themselves are not adequate to cover a major expansion joint as would occur at the roof and wall intersection, so choice C is incorrect.

33. C is correct.

The vehicle consists of two parts: the nonvolatile part called the *binder*, which forms the final coating, and the volatile part called the *solvent*, which evaporates or dries. Pigments, if added, are part of the vehicle and form the color of the coating.

34. D is correct.

Forming corners in concrete always adds to the cost, so making the wall a uniform thickness would be most economical even though more concrete would be required. Making the column square would decrease the amount of concrete but would still require the same amount of forming. Separating the pilaster from the wall would actually increase the cost of form work. Forming the pilaster with a diagonal would not be appropriate because of the structural problems caused by decreasing the column area and placing reinforcement.

35. C is correct.

Steel with over 2.0% carbon is classified as cast iron. The other choices are all used, but choice C is considered medium-carbon steel and is most common.

36. A is correct.

A *chamfer strip* is a small, triangular piece of material placed in the corners for forms to prevent sharp 90° corners, which are difficult to cast and have a tendency to break off during use or when the forms are removed.

37. A is correct.

The lockset of a panel door is mounted in the stile.

38. C is correct.

A coordinator prevents the door leaf with the astragal from closing before the other leaf, so the pair of doors seals properly.

39. D is correct.

Concrete masonry partitions are usually hollow, so the actual thickness of the solid material, not the actual overall width, is used to rate the fire resistance of the unit.

40. A is correct.

A bond beam is a masonry unit made to accommodate reinforcing and grout to span openings in masonry walls. These are often used in place of steel lintels.

41. A is correct.

Dissimilar metals should be physically separated by nonconducting materials in order to prevent galvanic action. Increasing the thickness of the materials may postpone the complete deterioration of the materials but not prevent it, so choice B is incorrect. Reducing direct contact with water will minimize galvanic action, but moisture in the air is sufficient to cause galvanic action, so choice C is incorrect.

42. C is correct.

Geared traction elevators can be designed to serve a wide variety of slower speeds and high capacities, so they are ideal for low-rise buildings with heavy loads, such as department stores. A geared traction elevator could be used for a small medical office building, but a higher speed would offer better service. A 16-story office building would need a high-speed, moderate-capacity elevator, so a geared traction type would be inappropriate. An apartment building would require a low capacity but higher speeds.

43. C is correct.

The thickness of the gypsum board is not critical because there is little difference in the weights of $^3/_8$, $^1/_2$, and $^5/_8$ in boards. The number of layers, on the other hand, can affect the total weight significantly.

44. C is correct.

Welding is joining two metals by heating them above their melting points. *Soldering* is joining two metals using lead-based or tin-based alloys as filler metals that melt below 500°F (260°C).

45. A is correct.

The gravel provides open spaces for any water under hydrostatic pressure to lose its pressure and drip to drains near the footing. Although it does this by preventing direct contact of the soil with the wall, this is not the sole purpose.

46. B is correct.

Only noncorrosive metals, such as stainless steel, should be used to anchor stone. Both copper and steel would deteriorate over time.

47. D is correct.

All of the choices listed are considerations in detailing wood floors, so select the *most* important. Moisture is one of the biggest problems with wood floors, so keeping moisture out in the first place would minimize other problems such as expansion at the perimeter. Therefore, D is the best choice.

48. B is correct.

Statement III is not as important because the characteristics of defects are implied in the grading of the lumber. Statement V is not of prime importance.

49. A is correct.

Mullions are members that separate large sections of glass, whereas *muntins* are framing that separates individual panes of glass. *Stiles* are vertical members of doors, and rails are horizontal members of doors.

50. C is correct.

A mortise lock offers the most flexibility in the number of operating functions available and is a very durable type of lockset. The next best choice would be a cylindrical lock.

51. C is correct.

Statement I is partially correct because built-up roofs can be applied to flat roofs. However, they should not be; there should be a minimum of $^1/_4$ in/ft (6/305) of slope. Even if statement I is selected as correct, there is no answer choice containing statement I and the other correct statements. Statement II is incorrect because built-up roofs can be applied over nailable and non-nailable decks.

52. B is correct.

A full bed of portland cement mortar offers the best durability and water resistance for high-use, wet areas.

53. B is correct.

The structural slab is a consideration, but only as part of the entire floor/ceiling assembly, so statement II is an incorrect choice. Statement III is incorrect because thermal insulation is not a consideration in a ceiling's fire resistance. Statement V is incorrect because the style is not as important as whether or not the grid is rated.

54. B is correct.

As with any beam, the deeper the member, the more efficient the beam. Using a cored slab rather than a solid slab allows the depth to be increased without increasing the weight in the center of the beam where it is not needed. Choices A and D are partially correct, but choice B is the best choice.

55. A is correct.

Choice A shows a strong keyed joint with a waterstop to prevent water penetration. The other selections show joints that are weak structurally or that do not provide for adequate waterproofing.

56. B is correct.

2000 lbm (1000 kg) elevators are only used for small apartments, and 6000 lbm (3000 kg) elevators are used for freight. A 4000 lbm (2000 kg) capacity is often used for large office buildings and retail stores, but 3000 lbm (1500 kg) is more common for small and medium-sized buildings.

57. A is correct.

Statement I is incorrect because ratings up to 3 hours are possible. Statement V is incorrect because the standard thickness is $1^3/_4$ in (44).

58. D is correct.

The allowable stress ratings for lumber in the building codes are based primarily on size groups, species, and types of defects.

59. B is correct.

The southwestern portion of the United States is the driest, so moisture content should approximate the conditions in which the lumber will be used. However, it is difficult to reduce the moisture content much below 5%, so A is an unrealistic answer.

60. A is correct.

A membrane is part of a total assembly that also includes reinforcing and a thick bed of mortar on which the granite is laid or that is part of the terrazzo. The membrane allows the structural slab to move independently of the finish flooring so that any deflection does not crack the floor.

Ch. 23: CONSTRUCTION DRAWINGS AND DETAILS

1. B is correct.

A subcontractor would be most interested in the number of times equipment must be brought to a job site, what kinds of workers will be required to complete the work, and possible interference with other trades, because all of these have cost and time implications. The types of tools needed may, under some circumstances, have some bearing on cost if they must be purchased or rented, but normally tools are available and do not represent a significant portion of the total cost.

To a certain extent, the architect can control these variables and therefore exercise some control over cost by designing and detailing so that construction proceeds in the most straightforward manner.

2. D is correct.

Of the four detailing considerations implied by the choices (structural integrity, safety from contact, fire safety, and maintainability), fire safety is the most important, so A is eliminated. The choice is then between III and V. Either the actual flame spread or the code requirements could be investigated first, but generally it is more important to know the performance requirements before designing or determining whether a building assembly conforms to them. Choice D is therefore the better answer.

3. B is correct.

The most significant problem with this detail in a cold climate like that of Boston is the lack of insulating glazing. The detail only indicates a single pane of glass. Although the question does not address this issue, notice also that there is no insulation between the ceiling and the floor above.

4. B is correct.

Although flashing is shown and noted below the sill of the second-floor framing, extending it under the framing to the edge of the carpet is questionable. In addition, there is no sealant called out for the joint between the sill and the flashing. Water dripping down the window could be drawn into the framing by capillary action. Choice D might be considered the correct answer, except the ceiling-to-floor dimension is small enough and the structure rigid enough that cracking would probably not occur.

5.   B is correct.

Statement I is incorrect because there is not enough information given to determine if tolerances smaller than industry standard are called out. Simply increasing tolerances greater than normal will not decrease the cost because contractors will price standard tolerances unless there is reason to do otherwise.

Statement II would be correct if life-cycle costs were a concern. Although this is implied because it is a corporate office presumably owner occupied and maintained, the question clearly states that "estimated construction costs" should be reduced, which means initial costs. Statements III, IV, and V would all help reduce costs.

6.   A is correct.

The architect (or the architect's representative, such as the project manager on the job) is responsible for the overall coordination of all the contract documents.

7.   A is correct.

Holding direct meetings with the people responsible for the programming, design, and execution of the project is the best way to facilitate communication. Having another architect look at the drawings may be a good way to do a technical check, but that person could not know what the client's design goals were. It is common to request from the client necessary information to design and complete the working drawings, but isolating the client in reviewing them (unless specifically requested) does not allow the architect to participate in the process. In addition, this is not a normal duty of the client. Making a checklist for the drafting staff is a good tool and one that is often used, but in the context of the question, choice A is the method most likely to ensure the results desired.

Ch. 24: THE PROJECT MANUAL AND SPECIFICATIONS

1.   A is correct.

A bid log is used by the architect to record the bids as they are opened and to help the owner evaluate them. It is never included in the project manual. A subsurface soil conditions report, although not a part of the contract documents, may be included in the project manual for information only. A site work specification, as one of the technical sections, is also included in the manual, as is a bid bond. The bid bond, however, is also not a part of the contract documents because it is a bidding document.

2.   C is correct.

The specification simply states how the hangar anchorage devices must perform; that is, they must support a certain amount of weight. As long as they do this, they can be any type, size, or style that the contractor selects. The requirements for the fasteners are simply those selected as appropriate by the manufacturer. The hangar wire specification is a reference type because it refers to a particular industry-standard specification. The ceiling suspension main runner is a descriptive specification because it describes various qualities (size, material, and method of fabrication) of the ceiling runner.

3.   D is correct.

All of the responses are correct. A performance specification lets the contractor, material supplier, and fabricator decide how best to supply the required building component. Although performance specifications are detailed, there are still many ways to satisfy them. They are more difficult to research, write, and review, so there is more work for the architect. For ordinary materials, there is usually no need to write performance specifications because the requirements are so well established in the construction industry.

4.   D is correct.

Statement I is incorrect because the specifications take precedence over the drawings, so the more expensive material in the specifications would be the one used. In general, any time there are conflicts in the project documents, the best that can happen is no change to the cost, but usually an increase results.

Statement II is incorrect because litigation would be a last result and other remedies would be sought and implemented before a lawsuit occurred. Any conflicts in the documents can be corrected with an addendum prior to bidding or negotiation, by change order, or by modification after the construction contract is signed.

5.   B is correct.

An "or equal" type of specification for asphalt roofing is not preferable because, in general, strict "or equal" specifications leave too much to the discretion of the contractor with no review by the architect. This would be especially true with shingles, where there are many inferior products available for such an important part of the building. A better specification would be the base bid with alternate manufacturer.

6.   C is correct.

Statement II is incorrect because the specifications take precedence over the drawings. This fact is usually stated in the instructions to bidders and in the technical sections in Division 1, General Requirements of the Project Manual. Also, courts have held that the specifications override the drawings in case of conflicts.

10.   D is correct.

Testing of materials and equipment is in part 3 of each technical section if appropriate to the section. Refer to Fig. 24.2 for an outline of the three-part format.

7.   B is correct.

Division 11, Equipment, is the CSI specification division for larger, specialty items. Division 10 is for smaller specialties, Division 12 is for Furnishings, and Division 13 is for special construction.

8.   B is correct.

Light-gage metal framing for interior partitions is specified in Division 09, Finishes.

9.   A is correct.

Procedures for submittals are in Division 01, General Requirements. The requirements in individual technical sections refer back to Division 01. The only thing that would be in the individual technical sections would be specific samples required.

Ch. 25: THE PRIMARY CONTRACTUAL DOCUMENTS

1.   D is correct.

The owner is obligated to furnish the contractor with reasonable evidence that financial arrangements have been made to fulfill the owner's obligations under the contract. This is contained in the AIA General Conditions of the Contract. Therefore, the owner cannot refuse to do this, even with good cause.

2.   B is correct.

The Design and Contract Administration portion of AIA B141 clearly states what constitutes evaluations of the work: periodic site visits, but not exhaustive or continuous on-site inspections. In the Schedule of Services article there is a list of services that the architect will furnish only if specifically designated. One of these is on-site project representation.

3.   B is correct.

The Owner-Architect Agreement states that nothing in that agreement will create a contractual relationship with a third

party against either the architect or the owner. This reinforces the idea of privity—two parties to a contract are not liable to a third party.

4.   C is correct.

Withholding money gives the owner leverage to make the contractor finish the job and provides a reserve in case liens must be satisfied. Surety bond is not the correct answer because this involves a third party (the surety) who ensures completion of the project if the contractor fails to meet his or her obligations.

5.   B is correct.

It is very likely that clients undertaking their first construction project without a program would spend a great deal of their time and the architect's time determining needs and making decisions. A cost-plus-fee method such as multiple of direct personnel expense would ensure that no matter the time spent on the project, the architect would still meet expenses and make a profit. This is the best answer because the question asked what the architect would prefer. The client, of course, might prefer a fixed sum.

6.   D is correct.

The first step is to officially notify the contractor that the work is incorrect. Although the architect may have done this during the site visits, it must be done in writing. As part of the architect's normal duties, the incorrect work should be rejected, and the contractor should be told to promptly correct it in accordance with the General Conditions of the Contract. If the contractor does not correct the work, the owner should be aware of the alternative courses of action available up to and including terminating the contract. However, it is a better course of action for the owner to correct the work (if the contractor refuses) than to first terminate the contract.

Choice A is not the best course because stopping the work always has a detrimental effect on the entire project, and it does not provide for the normal notice to the contractor of nonconforming work.

Choice B is incorrect because quick termination of the contract without trying other remedies is not in accordance with the General Conditions of the Contract.

Choice C is not the best choice because the contractor, again, should be notified in writing of the problem and requested to correct the situation. Only then should the owner consider accepting nonconforming work. This is also not the best course of action because there is almost always a disagreement about what amount should be deducted from the contract sum for accepting nonconforming work.

7. D is correct.

An agent acts on behalf of another and assumes certain specified authority and duties, but does not take on responsibilities another person normally would have. Choice B is incorrect because agency does not involve mediation or vendors. Choice C is incorrect because the architect is the agent, not the principal.

8. B is correct.

The fast-track method would help keep costs down and be appropriate for a client who must move to a new facility as soon as possible. In this situation, it is likely that the owner is familiar with the process, knows what is needed, and would be comfortable with letting early construction proceed before the final design was worked out. With a flexible line of credit, knowing a fixed price would not be as important as with some other types of clients.

9. B is correct.

The contractor's bid, like other bidding documents, is not part of the contract documents unless specifically stated in the agreement. The General Conditions of the Contract outlines what is and is not included in the contract documents.

10. A is correct.

The architect has a duty and ethical responsibility to keep the contractor informed of any nonconforming work and to cooperate in getting the job done, but may not be held legally responsible. The General Conditions of the Contract states that the contractor will not be relieved of obligations to perform the work in accordance with the contract documents by activities or duties of the architect. It also states that if the contractor performs any construction activity knowing it involves an error, the contractor will assume responsibility.

Ch. 26: BIDDING PROCEDURES AND DOCUMENTS

1. B is correct.

Addenda are used to make changes to the contract documents after they are issued for bidding but before the contract is awarded. Change orders and construction change directives also modify the original contract documents, but they are used after the contract is awarded. An alternate listing is simply the list of alternates that the contractor must include in the bid.

2. D is correct.

Although not all of the items listed are included in every set of bidding documents, they can all be used in bidding. Of the five, a list of subcontractors is used least frequently.

3. B is correct.

The most reasonable approach, in light of the fact that none of the bids has been opened and the contractor was only 3 minutes late, would be to ask the other bidders if there is an objection. If not, accept the bid. If one of the bids had been opened, it would certainly not be advisable to accept any other late submittals, nor should a bid that is 3 minutes late be prejudiced if it is accepted, simply because it was late.

4. A is correct.

Bidding procedures should always be clearly stated, but not because there are so many variables. In fact, bidding procedures are fairly well established in the construction industry, regardless of whether there is open bidding or private bid openings.

Open bidding does usually present more problems because nearly anyone can bid, regardless of experience. Evaluating qualified bidders can be a problem. The extra advertising required can also add complexity to the process.

5. D is correct.

A performance bond is issued by a surety company that obligates itself to finish a project should the contractor default. A labor and material payment bond is designed to pay liens if they occur. Other provisions of the Owner-Contractor Agreement, such as liquidated damages, are designed to encourage the contractor to finish on time. The general contractor is responsible for the performance of the subcontractors under provisions of the Owner-Contractor Agreement.

6. C is correct.

Choice A is incorrect because it is unlikely that the client could afford to increase the budget, or would want to. Choice B is incorrect because rebidding, even with new contractors, would probably not result in much, if any, cost savings. All the deduct alternates might not be a desirable course of action and may not even be enough to compensate for the cost overrun, so choice D is not the best.

7. C is correct.

The answer to this question is deceptively simple. Labor and materials are by far the biggest influence on the cost of a job because they represent about 80% of the cost. Sub-contract bids could be considered the correct answer, especially on jobs where most of the work of the general contractor is subcontracted, but labor and materials still account for subcontract bids.

8.   C is correct.

For bidding, the procedure a contractor must follow to propose a substitution is in the instructions to bidders. After the contract is awarded, there are requirements in the General Requirements of the specifications. The advertisement to bid simply states that bidding is being accepted for a particular project and gives information about how to submit a bid. There is no such document as "bidding procedures."

9.   A is correct.

When the owner wants to make sure some amount of money is included in the bid before the exact amount of the item is known, the architect should use an allowance.

Option B is incorrect because alternates are used to require the contractor to provide an alternate price for something that varies from the base bid. Option C is incorrect because a material bond is a way to guarantee payment for materials by a bonding company. Option D is incorrect because a unit price is a way to obtain a price commitment from a contractor on a portion of work before the total quantity of the work is known.

10. C is correct.

The owner is ultimately responsible for deciding which contractor to award the contract to. The architect is generally involved but only *assists* with the process and gives advice.

Ch. 27: CONSTRUCTION ADMINISTRATION SERVICES

1.   B is correct.

Although the contractor must notify the architect when the project is ready for the punch list inspection, notification for final inspection comes after the punch list. It is during this final inspection that the architect verifies that the project has been completed according to the contract documents and the contractor is entitled to final payment. The issuance of a certificate of substantial completion comes only after the final inspection, and if followed by the consent of surety, the payment certificate can be prepared.

2.   A is correct.

All of the answers given are possible, but only choice A includes the technical definition of substantial completion. Choice D is incorrect because choice B is not entirely correct. The job can be substantially complete and there can still be a few items left on the punch list that the contractor must correct.

3.   D is correct.

Choice D is the best answer because the architect has a duty to cooperate with the contractor and should at least mention the potential problem during the site visit. The contractor may then check on the equipment while the architect is following up with the mechanical engineer. The observation should be noted on the architect's field report to keep the client informed of the progress of the work. If, in fact, the equipment being installed is incorrect, corrective action may be taken. When the contractor is notified immediately, he or she can decide whether or not to suspend work on the installation of the equipment until the situation is resolved.

Choice B is incorrect because the architect never stops the work. Choice C is incorrect because notifying the owner first is a premature step. Choice A is incorrect because by the time the mechanical engineer is notified and visits the site, the installation of the equipment may have proceeded to a point where it is difficult to remedy.

4.   C is correct.

Because the additional exit signs would necessitate an increase in construction cost and possibly in contract time, an order for minor change would not be appropriate. An addendum is used before the contract is signed, so this is not the correct answer. It is possible that the contractor and owner might disagree with the cost of the additional exit signs and a construction change directive would be used initially, but it is more likely that everyone would realize the need for the extra signs and agree on a price. In any event, a change order would ultimately be needed.

5.   A is correct.

Statement I is incorrect because field reports are the responsibility of the architect. Statement IV is incorrect because the architect is responsible for reviewing claims. A subcontractor may make a claim directly to the contractor, but the contractor, in turn, would have to make a claim to the owner. Statement V is incorrect because both the contractor and the architect are responsible for reviewing shop drawings, although only the contractor is responsible for the accuracy of the shop drawings.

Because scaffolding is part of the means of construction, the contractor is solely responsible for this. The General Conditions of the Contract specifically states that the contractor is responsible for arranging and coordinating field tests.

6. A is correct.

The contractor must review submittals prior to giving them to the architect.

7. C is correct.

The General Conditions of the Contract specifically states that the architect must respond within 10 days of notification of the claim by the contractor. One of the architect's responses may be to ask for supporting data.

8. A is correct.

A mock-up is a full-sized sample of a portion of the construction, commonly built on the job site, either separate from the building or made part of the building. A mock-up is called for in individual sections of the specifications. The specification may state that if approved, the mock-up may become part of the final construction.

9. B is correct.

The contract name is not necessary because the submittal log itself will be identified with the project name and number. Individual entries do not need to include the contract name.

10. C is correct.

A construction change directive requires the signatures of the architect and owner. A minor change in the work only requires the architect's signature. A change order requires the signatures of all three parties. No document requires just the architect's and contractor's signatures.

Ch. 28: PROJECT AND PRACTICE MANAGEMENT

1. B is correct.

There is no absolute need for duty to be established by a written agreement, although this is most often the case. Duty can arise based on the actions of the architect.

2. C is correct.

The business organization best suited to minimize the individual liability of the owners is the limited liability company.

Option A is incorrect because the general partners have responsibility for the actions of the other partners and their personal assets are vulnerable. Option B is incorrect because a joint venture simply refers to how two or more offices temporarily organize to complete a project. The individual offices may be organized in any form, including a sole proprietorship. Option D is incorrect because the general partners (owners) are still financially responsible, as with the general partnership. The limited partners only have liability to the extent of their investment, but they do not take part in the management of the company.

3. A is correct.

Determining the cause of the problem should be the first step in solving this type of problem. There could be a simple solution that could be implemented immediately, or it could be something more complex. In any event, this course of action would be a first step before the firm's owners would be notified because they would want to know the cause of the problem. The remainder of the schedule may have to be modified, but only after the root cause of the original problem was determined. If the problem was caused by the architectural firm, the client should not be asked for more money.

4. C is correct.

A tort is a civil wrong, resulting from negligence as opposed to a criminal act. The other three choices represent criminal acts.

5. B is correct.

A sole proprietor can have unlimited liability for negligence or other claims against the company, including claims on personal property and other assets.

6. A is correct.

In an agency relationship, the architect is the agent, the owner is the principal, and the contractor is the third party. Any legal advisor is not the agent in the relationship established by standard architectural documents, but is the owner's agent in regard to legal matters.

7. B is correct.

The full wall schedule technique requires everyone on the project to work on developing the project schedule. In this way discussion about work tasks, responsibilities, and project deadlines is encouraged and everyone has a vested interest in the final schedule.

8. C is correct.

The architect cannot and should not give insurance advise other than to tell the owner that a situation is the owner's responsibility and that the owner's insurance or legal advisors should be involved.

9. B is correct.

Most projects, large or small, are monitored on a weekly basis. This provides the ability to catch problems early enough to take corrective action and fits into the normal weekly cycle of other office management. Daily management would require too much time and would not give a broad enough view of the project as it progresses. Biweekly monitoring could be done for very large and lengthy jobs, but it might not allow corrections of problems to be made in time. Monitoring on a monthly basis would definitely allow problems to grow before being discovered.

10. D is correct.

The studio format of office organization gives individual employees the most job satisfaction.

Option A is incorrect because employees get stuck with doing only one type of job or task. While some employees like this, most architects and intern architects like to do different types of jobs. Option B is incorrect because there is no specific organization called pyramidal, but it could refer to a top-down type of organization where the principal makes decisions and hands off the work to subordinates who do not have the opportunity to get involved in all aspects of a business. Option C is incorrect for similar reasons, although most sole proprietorships are small businesses where individual employees often get to do a variety of work.

Ch. 29: BUILDING CODES AND REGULATIONS

1. A is correct.

The code specifically states that exits cannot pass through kitchens, storerooms, closets, or spaces used for similar purposes or through rooms that can be locked to prevent egress.

2. B is correct.

From the table, assembly areas, including restaurants and bars, have an occupant load of 15. Commercial kitchens have an occupant load of 200. Therefore,

$$\frac{3500 \text{ ft}^2}{15 \frac{\text{ft}^2}{\text{occupant}}} = 233 \text{ occupants}$$

$$\frac{1000 \text{ ft}^2}{200 \frac{\text{ft}^2}{\text{occupant}}} = 5 \text{ occupants}$$

$$\frac{1200 \text{ ft}^2}{15 \frac{\text{ft}^2}{\text{occupant}}} = 80 \text{ occupants}$$

$$\text{total} = 318 \text{ occupants}$$

3. B is correct.

To find the total exit width required, multiply the occupant load, 290, by 0.2.

$$(290)(0.2 \text{ in}) = 58 \text{ in}$$

Because the minimum width of any exit door must provide at least a clear width of 32 in, choices A and C cannot be correct because their clear width would be less than 32 in. Three 36 in doors would be acceptable, but the question asks for the minimally acceptable solution, which is two 36 in doors; this would provide approximately 66 in of width (considering the clear width of the door to be from the doorstop to the face of the door when open).

4. C is correct.

From Table 29.7 (IBC Table 503), the basic allowable floor area for a one-story building of B occupancy, type III-B construction is 19,000 ft². If the building is fully sprinklered, the allowable area per floor can be doubled for multi-storied buildings, so the maximum allowable floor area is 38,000 ft². The basic area can be multiplied by the number of stories up to three, so the maximum total allowable area is 76,000 ft².

5. A is correct.

A noncombustible building material will not ignite and burn when subjected to fire.

6. C is correct.

The primary determinants as shown in Table 29.3 (IBC Table 803.5) are the occupancy group and the location in the building according to exiting requirements. Having a building with a sprinkler system only modifies the basic requirements and allows the required flame-spread rating to be dropped one class in some instances.

7.   C is correct.

Option I is an incorrect statement because fire zone 1 is the most restrictive. Option III is incorrect because doors must only swing in the direction of travel when the occupant load is greater than 50. Option V is a correct statement because occupant load is dependent on the uses given in IBC Table 1004.1.2 (Table 29.8) and the various factors based on net or gross floor area.

8.   C is correct.

Option V is not part of the means of egress because it is an example of the public way. All of the other building areas listed are part of the exit access, the exit, or the exit discharge.

9.   D is correct.

Building codes only prescribe what tests a material or construction element must meet in order to be acceptable. Any qualified Nationally Recognized Testing Laboratory (NRTL) may perform a test, as long as the lab follows the procedures described in the test.

10.   B is correct.

The hourly ratings of major building components, such as the structural frame, bearing walls, exterior walls, floor structure, and roof structure, together determine the construction type according to Tables 601 (Table 29.2) and 602 in the IBC.

Ch. 30: BARRIER-FREE DESIGN

1.   A is correct.

By definition, any part of a building that is required to be accessible must be accessible from the entrance of the building.

2.   B is correct.

The minimum clear width for an accessible door is 32 in (815). Refer to Figure 30.4.

3.   D is correct.

For barrier-free design, a handrail must be 34 in to 38 in (865 to 965) high, measured vertically from the nosing.

4.   C is correct.

Although choices B, C, and D would all solve the problem, providing a power-assisted door would be the least expensive option and require the least amount of construction time.

5.   A is correct.

Choice B includes an acceptable slope, but the maximum total rise between landings is limited to 30 in (760). A 1:10 slope is allowed, but only if the maximum rise is held to 6 in (150) or less. A 1:8 slope is also allowed, but only if the maximum rise is 3 in (75) or less.

6.   A is correct.

All the sink installations listed as possible answers can work if they meet the measurement requirements shown in Fig. 30.10, but a wall-hung lavatory gives the most open access, usually exceeding the minimum requirements.

7.   C is correct.

Although alternate designs for toilet stalls can be 36 in (915) or 48 in (1220) as shown in Fig. 30.8, a standard stall must be 60 in (1525) as shown in Fig. 30.7.

8.   A is correct.

Providing for a 5 ft (1525) turning circle requires the most space of the four choices listed. In addition, B is incorrect because it concerns the outside of the room. If the turning circle is provided, it is very likely that a 36 in (915) access space and clear space at the towel dispensers will also be available.

9.   C is correct.

The minimum distance between two entry doors forming a vestibule when one opens out and one opens in is 48 in (1220). Refer to Fig. 30.6.

10.   B is correct.

No objects greater than 4 in (100) can protrude into an accessible route if the lower edge of the object is greater than 27 in (685) above the floor. It is reasonable to assume that a small fire-hose cabinet would have its lower edge higher than this distance, so it would be limited to a maximum 4 in protrusion. Therefore, choice A would have to be modified. Any change in level of $1/4$ in (6) or less does not require any edge treatment, so option B would not have to be modified.

RECOMMENDED READING

General Reference

Ballast, David Kent. *Architecture Exam Review, Solved Problems: Multiple-Choice Divisions*. Belmont, CA: Professional Publications, Inc.

Guthrie, Pat. *Architect's Portable Handbook*. New York: McGraw-Hill.

Harris, Cyril M., ed. *Dictionary of Architecture and Construction*. New York: McGraw-Hill.

Hoke, John Ray. *Architectural Graphic Standards*. New York: John Wiley & Sons.

Mendler, Sandra F., and William Odell. *The HOK Guidebook to Sustainable Design*. New York: John Wiley & Sons.

Pre-Design

Ambrose, James. *Subsurface Conditions*. Washington, DC: National Council of Architectural Registration Boards.

Ambrose, James, and Peter Brandow. *Simplified Site Design*. New York: John Wiley & Sons.

Beall, Christine, and Deborah Slaton. *Guide to Preparing Design and Construction Documents for Historic Projects* (TD-2-8). Alexandria, VA: Construction Specifications Institute and Association for Preservation Technology International.

Brown, G. Z., and Mark DeKay. *Sun, Wind, and Light*. New York: John Wiley & Sons.

Givoni, Baruch. *Climate Considerations in Building and Urban Design*. New York: John Wiley & Sons.

Katz, Peter. *The New Urbanism: Toward an Architecture of Community*. New York: McGraw-Hill.

Kostof, Spiro. *A History of Architecture: Settings and Rituals*. New York: Oxford University Press.

Kostof, Spiro, and Richard Tobias. *The City Assembled: The Elements of Urban Form Through History*. Boston, MA: Bulfinch Press.

Lynch, Kevin. *The Image of the City*. Cambridge, MA: MIT Press.

Lynch, Kevin, and Gary Hack. *Site Planning*. Cambridge, MA: MIT Press.

McHarg, Ian L. *Design with Nature*. New York: John Wiley & Sons.

Newman, Oscar. *Creating Defensible Space*. Washington, DC: U.S. Department of Housing and Urban Development.

Olgyay, Victor. *Design with Climate*. New York: Van Nostrand Reinhold.

Parker, Harry, John W. MacGuire, and James Ambrose. *Simplified Site Engineering*. New York: John Wiley & Sons.

Peña, William, *and Steven A. Parshall. Problem Seeking: An Architectural Programming Primer*. New York: John Wiley & Sons.

U.S. Department of Energy and Public Technology, Inc. *Sustainable Building Technical Manual: Green Building Design, Construction, and Operations*. Washington, DC: Public Technology, Inc.

Mechanical and Electrical Systems

American Institute of Architects. *Environmental Resource Guide*. Washington, DC: American Institute of Architects.

Brown, G. Z., and Mark DeKay. *Sun, Wind, and Light: Architectural Design Strategies*. New York: John Wiley and Sons.

Cavanaugh, William J., and Joseph A. Wilkes, eds. *Architectural Acoustics: Principles and Practice*. New York: John Wiley & Sons.

Cowan, James. *Architectural Acoustics Design Guide*. New York: McGraw-Hill.

Egan, M. David, and Victor Olgyay. *Architectural Lighting*. New York: McGraw-Hill.

Guzowski, Mary. *Daylighting for Sustainable Design*. New York: McGraw-Hill Professional Publishing.

Kristensen, Poul, and Roman Jacobiak, eds. *Daylight in Buildings*. New York: John Wiley & Sons.

Lechner, Norbert. *Heating, Cooling, Lighting: Design Methods for Architects*. New York: John Wiley & Sons.

Patterson, James. *Simplified Design for Building Fire Safety*. New York: John Wiley & Sons.

Rush, Richard. *The Buildings Systems Integration Handbook*. Woburn, MA: Butterworth-Heinemann.

Steffy, Gary. *Architectural Lighting Design*. New York: John Wiley & Sons.

Stein, Benjamin. *Building Technology: Mechanical and Electrical Systems*. New York: John Wiley & Sons.

Stein, Benjamin, and John S. Reynolds. *Mechanical and Electrical Equipment for Buildings*. New York: John Wiley & Sons.

Building Design, Materials and Methods

Allen, Edward. *Architectural Detailing: Function, Constructability, Aesthetics*. New York: John Wiley & Sons.

_____. *Fundamentals of Building Construction: Materials and Methods*. New York: John Wiley & Sons.

ARCOM and American Institute of Architects. *The Graphic Standards Guide to Architectural Finishes: Using Masterspec® to Evaluate, Select, and Specify Materials*. New York: John Wiley & Sons.

Ching, Francis, and Cassandra Adams. *Building Construction Illustrated*. New York: John Wiley & Sons.

McGowan, Maryrose, and Kelsey Kruse. *Interior Graphic Standards*. New York: John Wiley & Sons.

Mendler, Sandra F., and William Odell. *The HOK Guidebook to Sustainable Design*. New York: John Wiley & Sons.

Simmons, H. Leslie, and Harold B. Olin. *Construction: Principles, Materials, and Methods*. New York: John Wiley & Sons.

Spiegel, Ross, and Dru Meadows. *Green Building Materials: A Guide to Product Selection and Specification*. New York: John Wiley & Sons.

Tuluca, Adrian. *Energy Efficient Design and Construction for Commercial Buildings*. New York: McGraw-Hill.

Wakita, Osamu A., and Richard M. Linde. *The Professional Practice of Architectural Detailing*. New York: John Wiley & Sons.

Construction Documents and Services

American Institute of Architects. *The Architect's Handbook of Professional Practice*. Washington, DC: The American Institute of Architects. (Includes AIA standard documents.)

Committee of Canadian Architectural Councils and The Royal Architectural Institute of Canada. *Canadian Handbook of Practice for Architects*. Royal Architectural Institute of Canada.

Construction Specifications Institute. *CSI Manual of Practice*. Alexandria, VA: The Construction Specifications Institute.

_____. *MasterFormat™*. Alexandria, VA: The Construction Specifications Institute.

_____. *The Uniform Drawing System*. Alexandria, VA: The Construction Specifications Institute.

Liebing, Ralph. *Architectural Working Drawings*. New York: John Wiley & Sons.

National Council of Architectural Registration Boards. *Rules of Conduct*. Washington, DC: National Council of Architectural Registration Boards.

Rosen, Harold J. *Construction Specifications Writing: Principles and Procedures*. New York: John Wiley & Sons.

Sweet, Justin. *Legal Aspects of Architecture, Engineering, and the Construction Process*. Pacific Grove, CA: Brooks Cole.

Building Regulations

Access Board. *ADAAG Manual: A Guide to the Americans with Disabilities Accessibility Guidelines*. East Providence, RI: BNI Building News.

Canadian Commission on Building and Fire Codes. *National Building Code of Canada*. Ottawa, ON: National Research Council of Canada.

Ching, Francis D. K., and Steven R. Winkel. *Building Codes Illustrated: A Guide to Understanding the International Building Code®*. New York: John Wiley & Sons.

International Code Council. *Standard on Accessible and Usable Buildings and Facilities* (ICC/ANSI A117.1-1998). Falls Church, VA: International Code Council.

_____. *International Building Code*. Falls Church, VA: International Code Council.

Patterson, Terry L. *Illustrated 2003 Building Code Handbook*. New York: McGraw-Hill.

INDEX

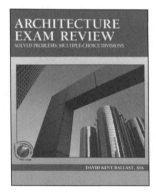
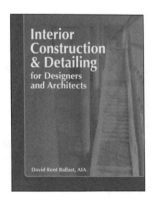